Scientific Programming and Computer Architecture

Scientific and Engineering Computation

William Gropp and Ewing Lusk, editors; Janusz Kowalik, founding editor

A complete list of books published in the Scientific and Engineering Computation series appears at the back of this book.

Scientific Programming and Computer Architecture

Divakar Viswanath

The MIT Press
Cambridge, Massachusetts
London, England

This book was set in LyX by the author. Printed and bound in the United States of America.

Library of Congress Cataloging-in-Publication Data

Names: Viswanath, Divakar, author.
Title: Scientific programming and computer architecture / Divakar Viswanath.
Description: Cambridge, MA : The MIT Press, [2017] | Series: Scientific and
    engineering computation | Includes bibliographical references and index.
Identifiers: LCCN 2016043792 | ISBN 9780262036290 (hardcover : alk. paper)
Subjects: LCSH: Computer programming. | Computer architecture. | Software
    engineering. | C (Computer program language)
Classification: LCC QA76.6 .V573 2017 | DDC 005.1–dc23 LC record
    available at https://lccn.loc.gov/2016043792

10 9 8 7 6 5 4 3 2 1

To all my teachers, with thanks.

Contents

> The website `https://github.com/divakarvi/Book-SPCA` has all the programs discussed in this book.

Preface

It is a common experience that minor changes to C/C++ programs can make a big difference to their speed. Although all programmers who opt for C/C++ do so at least partly, and much of the time mainly, because programs in these languages can be fast, writing fast programs in these languages is not so straightforward. Well-optimized programs in C/C++ can be even 10 or more times faster than programs that are not well optimized.

At the heart of this book is the following question: what makes computer programs fast or slow? Programming languages provide a level of abstraction that makes computers look simpler than they are. As soon as we ask this question about program speed, we have to get behind the abstractions and understand how a computer really works and how programming constructs map to different parts of the computer's architecture. Although there is much that can be understood, the modern computer is such a complicated device that this basic question cannot be answered perfectly.

Writing fast programs is the major theme of this book, but it is not the only theme. The other theme is modularity of programs. Structuring programs so that their structure explains what they do is a valuable principle. Computer programs are organized into a series of functions to serve the purpose of that principle. Yet when computer programs become large, merely dividing a program into functions becomes highly inadequate. It becomes necessary to organize the computer program into distinct sources and the sources into a source tree. The entire source tree can be made available as a library. We pay heed to program structure throughout this book.

Most books on computer programming are written at the same level of abstraction as the programming language they utilize or explain. If we want to understand program speed, we have to understand the different parts of a computer, and such an approach is not feasible. It is inevitable that choices have to be made regarding the type of computer system that is studied.

The big choices in this book are to opt for the x86 line of computers backed by Intel and AMD corporations, and for the Linux operating system. Nearly 100% of the computers in use today as servers, desktops, or laptops are x86 based, and the x86 line has been dominant for more than 30 years. So a great deal is not lost. The choice of the operating system does not have such a great impact on program speed. We pick Linux because it is the preferred platform for scientific computing and because it is open source. Because it is open source, we can peer into its inner workings when necessary to understand program speed.

A computer program is mathematical logic in action. The picture of the computer that emerges from this book shows how layered, and therefore complex, that logic can be. There is of course the design of the program that we ourselves write. But that is only a small part of the overall design. There are other computer programs, the biggest of which is the operating system kernel (the Linux kernel for our purposes), which handle the program we write and make it run on the computer. These systems programs make the computer a more tractable device, hiding the complexity of many of its parts, such as the hard disk or the network interface. The hardware, which includes the processor architecture and memory system, is itself designed using complex logic similar in kind to the computer programs we ourselves write but vastly different in degree of complexity.

The conventional approach to high-performance computing revolves around general principles, such as Amdahl's laws, weak and strong scaling, data and functional parallelism, SIMD/MIMD programming, load balancing, and blocking. The approach taken in this book is diametrically opposite. Our focus really is on understanding the computer as a whole, especially as viewed through programs. We dig into linkers, compilers, operating systems, and computer architecture to understand how the different parts of the computer interact with programs. The general principles are useful in getting a sense of the average program. However, in writing any particular program, the general principles are never so straightforward to apply. Understanding the parts of a computer can be far more nettlesome and also fascinating. Once that is done, the general principles, insofar as they are useful in actual programming, become self-evident.

The main principles of design that will concern us and that have an impact on program speed have not changed for decades. The approach we adopt is to begin with specific programs that are generally quite simple in what they do. We move up to general principles gradually using these specific programs as a vehicle. There are two advantages to this approach. First, it makes the discussion vivid, more organized, and far less reliant on rules of thumb that may appear arbitrary. Second, it lends useful context to the principles that inform the writing of well-optimized computer programs.

The context is essential. There are no general principles of the range, precision, and completeness of Schrödinger's equation in this area. Such principles as there are do not go far beyond common sense. Take, for example, the idea of load balancing. It says that if a task is to be divided between equally capable workers, we are better off dividing the task equally, rather than burdening a single worker with an excessive share of the work. There can be absolutely no doubt that this principle has been known for millennia. Without the appropriate context, the principle is quite sterile. Indeed, to call it a principle seems an exaggeration.

Overview of chapters

Chapter 1 begins with a rapid review of C/C++. The reader is assumed to have an undergraduate knowledge of C/C++ programming. Our review emphasizes a few parts of these languages that students typically don't learn in introductory classes. The C programming language is the most fundamental of all languages, to the extent that one can no longer speak of a computer without C. The C language is close to the machine and provides only a basic, although highly valuable, layer of abstraction. The C++ language is a colossal extension of C that includes many mechanisms for representing abstract concepts to bring the program closer to the problem domain. The idiom of C++ we use is close to C. However, we discuss more C++ than we actually need to dispel myths about C++ being slow.

Libraries and makefiles are the basis of modular programming in C/C++. In chapter 2, we explain how libraries and linkers work. Although we do not recommend Fortran, it is not uncommon to have to use old Fortran 77 programs in scientific programming. This chapter explains how to call Fortran programs from C/C++. Knowledge of the GNU `make` utility explained in this chapter is far more valuable than complex C++ syntax. There is no modular programming in C/C++ without `make`. Yet it is a neglected topic.

A significant part of the answer to what makes programs fast or slow is contained in chapter 3. Compilers convert C/C++ programs into a stream of machine instructions, native to the processor. A small subset of x86 assembly language is introduced and used to understand how structuring loops in different ways leads to different instruction streams.

Although part of chapter 3 is about optimizing for the processor pipeline, which has to be programmed in assembly language, in general we do not recommend programming in assembly. The small part of x86 assembly language introduced in that chapter is mainly used to understand how loop-nests map to machine instructions. There can be no rational account of program speed without a discussion of machine instructions. The discussion of assembly language is like a ladder that helps us understand how to structure loops and loop-nests, one of the most important tasks in optimizing a program. As in Wittgenstein's famous metaphor, the ladder can be thrown away once the understanding is gained.

Even skilled programmers are often unaware of registers. In chapter 3, we not only talk about registers but also introduce techniques for optimizing for the instruction pipeline. This type of optimization can improve program speeds considerably—by as much as a factor of 3 to 15 in the example discussed in chapter 3. However, the reader may wonder whether these techniques may become obsolete quickly because of rapid changes in hardware. The answer is an emphatic no. Although hardware changes rapidly, the design principles do not change so fast. In addition, the value of optimizing for the instruction pipeline has increased rapidly over time. Such optimization implied a speedup by a factor of 3 in 2010, whereas the speedup is much greater and nearly a factor of 15 in 2015. Yet the programming methodology is unchanged.

Although optimizing for the instruction pipeline is a very difficult skill, it can be a valuable one. It can speed up C/C++ programs by a factor of 10, or even a factor of 100 if the C/C++ coding is naive to begin with. As an argument for the value of instruction pipeline optimizations, we mention that although discussion of new algorithms overwhelmingly dominates the scientific literature, algorithms that speed up any nontrivial computation by a factor of 10 or even a factor of 2 are rare.

Chapters 4 and 5 have wider applicability than chapter 3. The sort of loop optimizations discussed in chapter 3 apply mainly when data is regular, as in image processing or the solution of differential equations. However, memory optimizations, discussed in chapter 4, are useful in all kinds of programming. For simplicity, our examples use regular data, but the same principles apply even when dynamic data structures such as linked lists or graphs are used.

Much of program optimization is optimization of memory access, and many of the principles are the same for single- and multithreaded programs. Memory usually refers to Dynamic Random Access Memory (DRAM), which can be 10s, or even 100s, of gigabytes in extent. Faster and smaller caches are maintained to speed access to DRAM by nearly a factor of 100. In addition, memory is organized into pages to give an independent view of memory to disparate processes. Memory accesses may be optimized for both caching and the paging system.

Perhaps an even more important point that arises in chapter 4, as a natural consequence of the discussion of instruction level parallelism in chapter 3, is the role of parallelism in the memory system. Programs that allow the processor to parallelize multiple memory accesses will be much faster. Thus, for example, there can be a huge difference in speed between a program that uses linked lists, which disrupt parallelism, and another program that accomplishes the same task by accessing an array in sequence.

The clock speed of processors stopped improving around 2005. Much of the growth in processing power since then is from putting more and more processor cores inside the same computer. All these processor cores share the same memory. Programming with threads, the topic of chapter 5, derives its importance from this well-established trend. Many threaded programs can be written quite easily. Yet there are always subtleties under the surface whenever different threads or processes share memory.

Many of the subtleties of threaded programming are related to the memory system. Threaded programming is impossible without coherent caches, and any programmer who writes threaded programs in C/C++ without understanding as much will be befuddled sooner rather than later. Even the simplest threaded programs for adding a sequence of numbers, using OpenMP or Pthreads, rely on the memory model in ways that are often not appreciated.

In addition to the memory system, threaded programs interact with the operating system. The simple act of creating threads can involve an overhead that swamps the benefits of parallelizing. When is it advantageous to invoke multiple threads? Why is it not a good idea to change the number of threads between OpenMP parallel regions? Why should threaded programs avoid abusing the stack? These questions are answered in a rational manner once the role of the operating system is understood.

Much of a C/C++ programmer's time is spent dealing with segmentation faults. The precise manner in which segmentation faults and other memory errors arise from inside the operating system is explained in chapter 5. Chapter 5 concludes what may be seen as the core of this book. Topics covered up to this point are relevant to many kinds of programming, well beyond the scientific world.

The Top 500 list (see `http://www.top500.org/`), which uses a linear algebra problem to benchmark and then rank the fastest computers in the world, has provided powerful impetus to scientific computing. For more than two decades, the most powerful computers in the world have been clusters where many computers are tightly connected using a high-performance network. In such clusters, concurrent processes communicate over the network by sending and receiving messages. Message passing is the topic of chapter 6.

An example of the outcome of our choice to focus on computer architecture instead of general principles may be found in this chapter. The general principle is to overlap processor and network activity. Few can contest the utility of such a principle or argue that there is anything in it beyond ordinary common sense. However, our discussion of the matrix transpose in chapter 6 shows that it requires deep knowledge of network architecture to in fact overlap processor and network activity, although the general principle is quite obvious. It is precisely that type of knowledge that gets lost when we do not look past general abstractions and examine details of systems software and computer architecture.

When a large group of computers is tightly coupled, message passing is the preferred paradigm. Because there is no truly credible challenge to message passing in the context of supercomputing, the largest physics computations are likely to continue to rely on message passing. However, a single computer today can tackle complex 3D problems with more than a billion grid points. The vast majority of scientific projects can be effectively implemented on a single node. When a single computer is so powerful, the additional difficulty of resorting to message passing between multiple computers, which can be considerable, becomes less attractive.

Market forces that are propelling the Internet are powerful, indeed amazingly powerful, and should not be ignored by the scientific programmer. The pertinence of the Internet is more obvious in newer areas such as genomics and data science than in classical physics. Chapter 6 includes a section about the Internet. As in other parts of the book, here too we look behind the abstractions to understand the plumbing of the Internet.

The final two chapters, chapters 7 and 8, are about coprocessors. In 2007, the NVIDIA corporation showed how its graphics processors can be used to speed up a range of scientific problems. The excitement that resulted was undoubtedly justified. The graphics coprocessors hint at the possibilities for architectural design that may be available beyond the x86 line. Intel, which could not afford to ignore this competition, has introduced its own coprocessor. It must be said that excitement about coprocessors has not been matched by utilization. When the coprocessor competes with the processor to execute the same tasks, there is a major disruption of modularity at the hardware level. The resulting heterogeneity makes it difficult to break tasks into subtasks in a uniform manner. Heterogeneity overly complicates programming models, which are already quite complicated.

The brief appendix may be the right place to begin reading this book. The appendix begins with a table of machines used to time programs. The rest of the book makes frequent references to that table.

Although interpreted languages such as Python or Matlab are easier to use, the resulting programs will be much slower. How much slower does not seem to be widely understood, and the appendix dispels a few myths. This author has heard estimates of the slow-down factor ranging from a few percent to a factor of 2 to a better informed guess of a factor of 10. In fact the interpreted languages can be several hundred times for even fairly simple programs that run on a single core. As the complexity of the program and the hardware platform increases, the slow-down penalty can get much worse. Even for moderately complex programs, the slow-down can be by a factor of 10^4, as we note in the appendix. If the effort for mastering C/C++ is much greater, so is the reward.

The entire source code corresponding to this book, which runs to more than 15,000 lines of C/C++, is available at `https://github.com/divakarvi/Book-SPCA`. The appendix briefly introduces two tools—GIT and the `cscope` utility—essential for downloading and working with the code. Both GIT and `cscope` are of great value in programming in general. Even in the era of Internet search, `cscope`, which has been around since the 1970s, is an excellent option for browsing and searching source trees.

The examples in this book rely on Intel's `icc/icpc` compiler. However, except for chapter 7, the widely used, easily available, and open source `gcc/g++` compiler may be substituted with little trouble. The few nuances that arise are described in the appendix.

Acknowledgments

Most of all, I thank my undergraduate teachers at the Indian Institute of Technology, Bombay. From them I began to learn much of what is found in this book.

I taught a graduate class based on this book on four occasions at the University of Michigan. The class typically covered about a third or more of the material in the book, with greater emphasis on the beginning sections in each chapter. I thank all the hundred or so students who took that class. Thanks in particular to Zhongming Qu, who penetrated the material quite deeply. I am especially grateful to Zhongming for helping me understand Makefiles much better.

I was privileged to have access to superbly maintained systems at the University of Michigan. I thank Bennet Fauber, Brock Palin, Andy Caird, Neil Tweedy, Charles Antonelli, Reed Hoyer, and Rusty Dekema for their help. I am especially grateful to Seth Meyer for showing me how to build and load the Linux operating system. All who work with computers are aware of the peculiar difficulty of getting started. In the memorable words of Kernighan and Ritchie, it is a big hurdle, and once crossed "everything else is comparatively easy." In addition to showing me how to get started with Linux, Seth also freely shared his deep knowledge of the Internet with me.

The last three chapters of this book were written using systems deployed at the Texas Advanced Computing Center (TACC), with access obtained through XSEDE. I am thankful to XSEDE as well as TACC for the wonderful support they offered. At TACC, I am especially grateful to Chris Hempel for being so accommodating. The technical help desk at TACC answered numerous questions with unfailing promptness and helped me in many ways. At the risk of omission, I thank Doug James, Lars Koesterke, Hang Liu, Si Liu, Robert McLay, Cyrus Proctor, and Frank Willmore.

I thank Paul Besl, Tim Prince, and Mike Tucker of Intel Corporation for being gracious and helpful when difficulties arose with the Westmere microarchitecture. I also thank Intel's Russian team for resolving these technical difficulties and Tim Prince for his expert comments.

I thank my colleagues Danny Forger and Hans Johnston for offering advice and much needed support.

I wrote this book using LyX, relying on Inkscape to produce figures. The html version of the book was produced using eLyXer. I thank all the people responsible for these wonderful open source tools. Technical information accessed via the Internet was invaluable, and I have acknowledged this help wherever possible.

Finally, I am grateful to Dr. John Sarno for curing my chronic back pain through his books and to Dr. Howard Schubiner for a helpful consultation.

Chapter 1

C/C++: Review

A computer program is a sequence of instructions to a machine. In this chapter and the next, we emphasize that it is a sequence of instructions that *builds on* other computer programs and that in turn can be *built on*. Codes that exist in isolation are often limited to quite trivial tasks and can hardly be considered computer programs.

This chapter is a review of C/C++. The C programming language is the most fundamental of all programming languages. Computing machines come in great variety and are put together using many parts. The computer's parts, consisting of the processor at the center, and with memory, hard disk, network interfaces, graphics devices, and other peripherals connected to it, are very different from each other. It would be an almost impossible task for any single programmer to deliver instructions to such a complicated machine. The C programming language is a major part of the setup to give the programmer a uniform view of computing machines. No modern computing device can exist and be useful without C.

Much of the time when programs are written, the programmer is not at all aware of the many parts of the computer. Indeed, the programmer may not even be aware that there is a processor. It is more natural to think in terms of the abstractions of the programming language. This is in general a good thing because the purpose of programming languages is to set up abstractions that hide the complicated parts of the computer. In addition, programs written in this way can be moved from computer to computer easily.

In this book, our goal is to understand what makes programs fast or slow. As soon as we set ourselves this goal, we have no choice but to peer behind the abstractions of programming and understand how those abstractions are realized through the many parts that constitute a computer. The C programming language is the most natural vehicle in moving toward this goal. In fact, it is the only vehicle that is really appropriate.

The C programming language is close to the machine. There are high-level languages, a notable and outstanding example being Python, which bring programming much closer to the problem domain. Concepts and ideas intrinsic to the problem domain are expressed far more easily in these programming languages. Programs that would take days to write in C can be written in hours, or even minutes, in Python.

Although these high-level languages are much easier on the programmer, programs in these languages run slowly. As shown in the appendix, these high-level programs can be more than 100 times slower, or even worse. In fact, even C programs written without a knowledge of computer architecture can be several times slower than C programs written with that knowledge. The C++ language is a compromise. It strives to combine the speed of C with the abstraction facilities of higher level languages. It can be quite useful, although it lacks the simplicity and elegance of C. The C++ idiom we use is close to C. Some of the facilities of C++, mainly the facility of defining classes, are adopted to make C a little easier and a little more presentable.

The review of C/C++ in this chapter attempts to bring out certain features that people often do not learn from a single course or two. Beginning programmers often tend to think of a C/C++ program as a single `.c` or `.cpp` source file. Modular organization of sources is far superior. Modular organization is essential for writing programs whose structure reflects and explains how they work as well as the underlying concepts.

Section 1.1 sets up an example to exhibit the modular organization of sources in C/C++. The example is a technique called the Aitken iteration, which can transform certain sequences to hasten their convergence. In sections 1.2 and 1.3, we review some features of C and C++ using this example. The concluding section 1.4 introduces a little Fortran. For reasons explained at length later, we do not recommend programming in Fortran. However, a lot of scientific programs are written in Fortran, mainly Fortran 77. A scientific programmer needs to know just enough Fortran to be able to use these old Fortran codes.

1.1   An example: The Aitken transformation

The Aitken transformation maps a sequence of numbers to another sequence of numbers. It serves as the vehicle to introduce aspects of C, C++, and Fortran in this chapter. It is also interesting in its own right.

The Aitken transformation is given by the following formula:

$$t_{n-1} = s_{n-1} - \frac{(s_n - s_{n-1})^2}{s_{n+1} - 2s_n + s_{n-1}}. \tag{1.1}$$

It transforms a sequence $s_0, s_1, \ldots, s_N$ into a new sequence $t_0, t_1, \ldots, t_{N-2}$, which has two fewer terms.[1] The idea behind the Aitken transformation is as follows. If the s_n sequence is of the form $s_n = S + a\lambda^n$, all terms in the t_n sequence are equal to S. It is useful for speeding up the convergence of a number of sequences, even those that do not directly fit the $S + a\lambda^n$ pattern. Section 1.1.1 illustrates the dramatic power of the Aitken iteration on a couple of examples—the Leibniz series and the logarithmic series. To be sure, these examples are chosen carefully.

This section begins to make the point that it is generally advantageous to split a program into multiple sources. We could use a single source file to code the Aitken iteration and apply it to the Leibniz series as well as the logarithmic series. Such a program would work just as well to begin with. A few days later, we may want to apply the Aitken iteration to another example. If we also throw that example into the same source file, the source file will become a little more unwieldy. A few months later, we may want to use the Aitken iteration as part of a large project. If we insist on using a single source file, there are two equally unpleasant alternatives: copy the whole Aitken program into the large project or copy the large project into the Aitken program. There is a heavy price to pay for avoiding modular organization of programs. Section 1.1.2 gives a preliminary discussion of the modular organization of program sources using the Aitken iteration as an example. Later sections build on this preliminary discussion.

---

[1] Sequence extrapolation and Aitken iteration are treated in Baker and Graves-Morris (1996); Brezinski and Zaglia (1991).

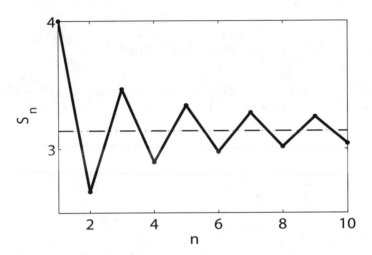

Figure 1.1: Convergence of the Leibniz series to π (dashed line).

1.1.1   Leibniz series and the logarithmic series

The Leibniz series[2] is given by

$$\pi = 4 - \frac{4}{3} + \frac{4}{5} - \frac{4}{7} + \frac{4}{9} - \frac{4}{11} + \cdots$$

This series, whose terms alternate in sign and diminish in magnitude monotonically, will be a recurring example. So we will begin by looking at it carefully. Let S_n be the sum of the first n terms. As shown in figure 1.1, the partial sums S_n are alternately above and below π. Further, the convergence is slow. In fact, $\left|\pi - S_n\right| > 2/(2n + 1)$, which implies that the first million terms of the Leibniz series can give only slightly more than six digits of π after the decimal point.

If we look at figure 1.1, we may notice that although the convergence to the limit is slow, the partial sums seem to follow a certain trend as they approach π. The partial

---

[2]The Leibniz series was discovered by Madhava (c. 1350-c. 1410), well before Leibniz (1646-1716). Madhava reported it in the following passage: "Multiply the diameter by 4. Subtract from it and add alternately the quotients obtained by dividing four times the diameter by the odd integers 3, 5, etc." (Sarma (1992)).

4.0000000000	3.1666666667	$\cdots$	3.1415926540	3.1415926536
2.6666666667	3.1333333333		3.1415926535	
3.4666666667	3.1452380952		3.1415926536	
2.8952380952	3.1396825397			
3.3396825397	3.1427128427			
2.9760461760	3.1408813409			
3.2837384837	3.1420718171			
3.0170718171	3.1412548236			
3.2523659347	3.1418396189			
3.0418396189	3.1414067185			
3.2323158094	3.1417360993			
3.0584027659				
3.2184027659				

Table 1.1: The first column lists the first 13 partial sums of the Leibniz series. Every other column is gotten by applying the Aitken transformation (1.1) to the previous column. The number at the upper right corner is π correct to 10 digits.

sums are alternately above and below, and it seems as if we can fit a smooth curve through the iterates. The Aitken iteration guesses this trend quite well and speeds up the convergence of the Leibniz series.

Table 1.1 shows Aitken's transformation (1.1) applied repeatedly to the first 13 partial sums of the Leibniz series. After each application, we have a sequence with two fewer numbers, and at the end of the sixth application of the Aitken transformation, we have just one number that equals π to 10 digits of accuracy. Because none of the 13 partial sums gives even the first digit after the decimal point, it seems astonishing that an answer with 10 digits of accuracy can be produced from those numbers.

Computing the digits of π is a mathematical sport of unending interest. Even Isaac Newton had a weakness for it.[3] The Aitken iteration, although impressive, is far from being the best method for computing π.[4]

The logarithmic series[5] $\log(1 + x) = x - x^2/2 + x^3/3 - x^4/4 + \cdots$ diverges for $|x| > 1$. However, as shown in table 1.2, the Aitken transformations of the first 13

---

[3]See Westfall (1980) (p. 112).

[4]For the mathematics of approximating π, see Borwein and Borwein (1998).

[5]The logarithmic series was discovered by Nicholas Mercator (c. 1620-1687). See Kline (1990).

x	Partial Sum	Extrapolate
0.00	0.0000000000	0.0000000000
0.20	0.1823215568	0.1823215568
0.40	0.3364723763	0.3364722366
0.60	0.4700395318	0.4700036292
0.80	0.5895867562	0.5877866649
1.00	0.7301337551	0.6931471806
1.25	1.5615505069	0.8109302162

Table 1.2: The partial sum column is the sum of the first 13 terms of the Taylor series of $\log(1+x)$. Each number in the last column is produced by applying the Aitken transformation 6 times to the first 13 partial sums, which leaves us with just one number. The last column shows that number, which gives $\log(1+x)$, with all the digits shown being correct.

partial sums recover the value of $\log(1+x)$ for $x = 1.25$. If x were larger, just the first 13 partial sums would not be enough to produce 10 digits of accuracy after the decimal point.

Here we have our first programming problem. There is a simple iteration (1.1) to begin with. The problem is to code it in C/C++ and apply it to the Leibniz series and the logarithmic series.

1.1.2   Modular organization of sources

Before we delve into the syntax of C/C++, let us look at how to structure a program for the Aitken iteration. In particular, we look at how to split the program between source files.

It is not uncommon to introduce computer programming using programs that reside in a single source file.[6] A computer program as a single source file is a bad idea to allow into one's head. It is a bad idea that can grow and grow. This author has heard of Fortran programs longer than 100,000 lines in a single file. Even the simple Aitken example shows why a single monolithic source is a bad idea.

---

[6]Even programs limited to a single source file rely on the runtime library. Strictly speaking, there is no such thing as a program that entirely resides in a single source file.

The Aitken iteration, as we have discussed it so far, consists of the iteration (1.1) and its application to the Leibniz and Mercator series. One way to write this program is to code a function for the Aitken iteration, another function to set up and apply it to the Leibniz series, and likewise yet another function to apply it to the logarithmic series.

Breaking up programs into functions is the first step. However, throwing all the three functions into the same source file would not be a good idea. There is a simple conceptual reason for this. The Aitken iteration is a general technique, and its applications to the Leibniz and logarithmic series are two specific examples. Coding all the functions in the same source file limits the usefulness of the Aitken iteration.

In later sections, we will implement the Aitken iteration and the two examples in three separate source files. The first source file `aitken.c` codes the Aitken iteration in a form that would apply to any sequence. The specific applications are in the source files `leibniz.c` and `logseries.c`.

If the program is separated into three sources in this manner, the question of how they may interface with each other and work together arises. The first part of the interfacing is a header file that we will call `aitken.h`. This header file gives a basic summary of what is found inside `aitken.c` but does not have the implementation of any function. The source files `leibniz.c` and `logseries.c` include this interface within their code. Thus, the sources will look as follows:

```
aitken.h
aitken.c
leibniz.c
logseries.c
```

with the header file `aitken.h` included in all the three `.c` source files.

This manner of breaking up a program into multiple source files is deeply integrated into C/C++. A C/C++ compiler converts a source file into a sequence of machine instructions independently of all other sources. For this reason, a source file is sometimes called a compilation unit. In our Aitken example, three object files `aitken.o`, `leibniz.o`, and `logseries.o`, holding machine instructions corresponding to the respective source files, result from compilation.

The source `leibniz.c` will include calls to functions defined in `aitken.c`. The header `aitken.h`, which is included in `leibniz.c`, includes just enough information to partially set up this function call when the machine instructions of `leibniz.o` are

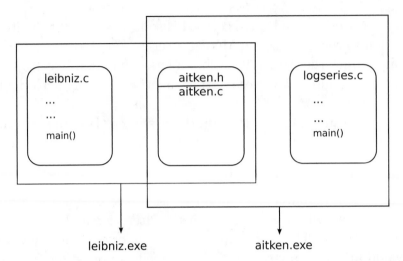

Figure 1.2: The three program sources are `aitken.c`, `leibniz.c`, and `logseries.c`. They are combined to produce two different executables, for extrapolating the partial sums of the Leibniz series and the Taylor series of $\log(1 + x)$, respectively. The `.o` object files are omitted from this figure.

being compiled. The crucial information that is missing is the address and definition of the function in `aitken.c` that is invoked in `leibniz.c`. That information is supplied only when the object files `aitken.o` and `leibniz.o` are combined into an executable, which we will call `leibniz.exe`,[7] by the linker. It is the linker's job to eliminate unresolved references in the object files and put together an executable without any unresolved references. The executable is the program that ultimately runs on the computer.

We will make the discussion of compilation and linking far more concrete in later sections. The overall picture is as follows: the program is separated into multiple source files, the source files are compiled separately into object files holding machine instructions, and the linker merges the object files and eliminates unresolved references to produce an executable. The overall picture for the Aitken program is shown in figure 1.2.

Exercise 1.1.1. Substitute $s_n = S + a\lambda^n$ into the Aitken formula (1.1) and verify that

---

[7]Although we assume the GNU/Linux operating system, the executable files will use the `.exe` extension as in Windows for greater clarity.

each new term t_n is equal to S.

Exercise 1.1.2. In (1.1), $S = s_{n-1}$ if $s_{n-1} = s_{n-2}$ and there is a divide by zero if $s_{n+1} - 2s_n + s_{n-1} = 0$. Interpret both conditions.

Exercise 1.1.3. Prove that

$$\frac{1}{1+x^2} = 1 - x^2 + x^4 - \cdots + (-1)^{n-1}x^{2n-2} + R_n,$$

where $R_n = (-1)^n x^{2n}/(1+x^2)$. Integrate from 0 to 1, while noting that

$$\int_0^1 \frac{x^{2n}}{1+x^2}\, dx < \frac{1}{2n+1},$$

to deduce the Leibniz series.

Exercise 1.1.4. If S_n is the partial sum of the first n terms of the Liebniz series for π (not $\pi/4$), prove that $|\pi - S_n| > 2/(2n+1)$, showing that the Leibniz series converges slowly.

Exercise 1.1.5. To understand the Aitken iteration, it is helpful to look at singularities. Prove that the function $\arctan z$ has singularities at $z = \pm i$ in the complex plane. Determine the type of the singularities.

1.2   C review

The C programming language is concise. In this review, we go over a few features of C, emphasizing points that introductory classes often miss. Thus, we discuss header files, arrays, and pointers, with emphasis on the distinction between lvalues and rvalues, as well as the distinction between declarations and definitions. We go over the compilation and linking process while adding more detail to the picture in figure 1.2. Although C is concise, it demands precision in thinking. The emphasis in this review is toward greater precision. Table 1.3 shows two of the best books to learn C and C++.[8]

---

[8]Kernighan and Ritchie (1988) is quite possibly the most influential book in computer science. There is no better place to begin to learn the art of programming.

C programming	B.W. Kernighan and D.M. Ritchie, The C programming language, 2nd ed.
C++ programming	B. Stroustrup, The C++ programming language, 3rd ed.

Table 1.3: Books on C and C++ written by their inventors.

1.2.1   Header files

A header file in C is an interface to one or more source files, with each source file a collection of function definitions. As an example of a simple header file, we look at `aitken.h`. This header file is an interface to the functions defined in `aitken.c`.

```
1 #ifndef aitkenJuly09DVsfe
2 #define aitkenJuly09DVsfe
3 void aitken(double *seq1, double *seq2, int len);
4 double aitkenExtrapolate(double *seq1, double* seq2,
5                 int len);
6 #endif
```

The two symbolic names `aitken` and `aitkenExtrapolate` are introduced in this header file. These are the names of two functions that are defined in `aitken.c`. For the two functions, the declarations in the header file specify the type of the arguments as well as the type of the value that is returned. Thus, this header file is saying that `aitken()` is a function that takes three arguments—the first two of type pointer to `double` and the last of type `int`—and returns nothing (`void`). The function `aitkenExtrapolate()` is stated to take three arguments of the same types, but it returns a `double`.

Both of these are examples of function declarations. The declarations specify the arguments the functions take in as well as the types of what they return. When a declaration is made, the function is stated to exist somewhere. However, a sequence of statements defining the functions is lacking.

The source files `aitken.c`, `leibniz.c`, and `logseries.c` include `aitken.h` within their text using the line `#include "aitken.h"`. The `#include` statement has the effect of splicing all of `aitken.h` into those source files. The source `aitken.c` includes the header `aitken.h` and goes on to define the functions declared in the header. The arguments and return type of a function at the point of definition must exactly match the declaration in the header. The sources `leibniz.c` and `logseries.c` include the header `aitken.h` with a different intent. Their intent is to obtain license to make calls to the functions `aitken()` and `aitkenExtrapolate()`.

The header file acts as an interface, and it is natural, as well as typical, to include comments in it about the arguments to functions declared in it and about what those functions do. In this book, there are few comments in the code listings. The comments are instead found in the text.

The function `aitken()` (line 3) applies one step of the Aitken transformation (1.1) to the array `seq1[0..len-1]` and leaves the result in the array `seq2[0..len-3]`. The function `aitkenExtrapolate()` (line 4) applies the Aitken transformation repeatedly to the array `seq1[0..len-1]` while using `seq2[]` as scratch space, until only one or two numbers are left. One of the remaining numbers is returned as the extrapolated value.

At the beginning of `aitken.h` and at the end, three lines (1, 2, and 6) begin with the special character `#`. These lines are directives to the macro preprocessor, one of the initial phases of compilation. Sources are manipulated textually by the macro preprocessor.

The source file `leibniz.c` includes `aitken.h` using a `#include` directive. When the compiler is applied to `leibniz.c`, the initial preprocessing stage handles the `#include` directive. When processing that directive, the file `aitken.h` is opened by the preprocessor. The first directive in that file (`#ifndef` on line 1) asks the preprocessor to check whether a name called `aitkenJuly09DVsfe` is already defined. If the name `aitkenJuly09DVsfe` is not defined, the second line of `aitken.h` (`#define` directive) asks the preprocessor to define such a name, which it does. The preprocessor splices in all the text between the second and last lines of `aitken.h` (lines 3 to 5) into the source file that issued the `include "aitken.h"` directive. The splicing into `leibniz.c` is done at the point where the `#include` directive was issued.

However, if such a name is already defined (because the header file was included by an earlier directive), it skips over everything until it sees a `#endif` directive (line 6); in this case, it would be skipping the entire `aitken.h` file.

Using `#ifndef`, `#define`, and `#endif` directives ensures that if a directive to include the same header file is issued twice by the same source file, the second directive has no effect. That may not sound useful at first. However, in practice, a source file may include a header file that includes some other header file and so on. So two directives to include different header files may end up including the same header file twice. Such a thing is prevented by the combination of preprocessor directives we just discussed.

The macro variable `aitkenJuly09DVsfe` is chosen to be complicated to avoid accidentally using the same name in two different header files. Such accidental reuse will mean that the two header files can never be simultaneously included in the same source. Such errors at the macro preprocessing stage can be a little bothersome.

1.2.2 Arrays and pointers

Arrays and pointers are the heart of the C language. An array is a sequence of locations in memory. A pointer-type variable is a variable that holds the address of a memory location. The word pointer can be used for either such a variable or an expression that evaluates to an address. The two concepts may appear different, but the C language blurs the distinction between them. In C, arrays and pointers are almost interchangeable.

There is a very good reason for blurring the distinction between arrays and pointers. Suppose we want to pass a long sequence, occupying a great deal of memory, as an argument to a function. It would be wasteful to allocate new memory and copy the sequence entry by entry at every function call. In C, arrays are passed as pointers.

The key idea in almost identifying arrays with pointers is as follows. A sequence of data items in memory can be specified using three pieces of information: the address of the first item, the size in bytes of each item, and the number of entries in the sequence. In C, a pointer holding an address is specified as a pointer of a certain type. The size of each item is inferred from type information. For example, in an array of `doubles`, the size of each item is 8 bytes and in an array of `ints` the size of each item is 4 bytes (on GNU/Linux). Thus, from merely knowing a pointer, we can infer the first two pieces of information: the address of the first item in memory and the size of each item in bytes. The last piece of information, namely, the length of the array, is often tagged along separately. Thus, arrays and pointers may be identified, and arrays may be passed to functions efficiently as pointers with the length of the array tagged along as an extra parameter.

How this idea plays out in practice, we will examine presently.

A(0..3)	A(4..11)	A(12..15)	A(16..19)	A(20..23)
37	A			
x	a	list[0]	list[1]	list[2]

Figure 1.3: A schematic and simplified view of computer memory. The symbol x is of integer type, whereas the symbol a is a pointer. Addresses are shown on top.

Arrays, pointers, lvalues, and rvalues

The C language takes a certain view of computer memory, and arrays and pointers are both best understood in terms of computer memory. Figure 1.3 is a schematic view of a portion of the computer memory (in hardware, this would be DRAM in most circumstances). Names that we introduce into our code—whether they correspond to variables of basic types such as `char` or `int` or `double`, or to arrays, or to pointers—will all ultimately correspond to locations in computer memory.[9] To introduce a name of a variable of basic type, we may use a definition such as `int x;` to introduce a name of an array, we may use a definition such as `int list[3];` to introduce a name of a pointer, we may use a definition such as `int *a`.

In C semantics, an expression may evaluate to a value that is the name of a memory location. Such a value is called an *lvalue*. The "l" refers to the fact that such values may occur on the left-hand side of an assignment. In contrast, an expression may evaluate to a value that may be used to fill a memory location but is not necessarily the name of any location in memory. Such a value is called an *rvalue*. The "r" here refers to the possible occurrence of such a value on the right-hand side of an assignment statement. The concept of rvalues and lvalues is useful for understanding arrays and pointers.

The distinction between lvalues and rvalues arises fundamentally because of the assignment statement. In an assignment, what occurs on the left is the name of a memory location or an lvalue. What occurs on the right is a value that is used to fill a memory location or an rvalue. The distinction is important in the context of pointers and arrays because, although a pointer is naturally thought of as an address and an address is nothing but a number naming a memory location, pointers themselves may be stored in pointer-type variables.

---

[9]In practice, as opposed to C semantics, program variables may be allocated using registers or DRAM. They may even be eliminated during compiler optimizations.

If the variable x is introduced using the definition int x, it is an lvalue because it is the name of a memory location as shown in figure 1.3. If the assignment statement x=37 executes, the location is filled with 37 as shown in the figure. The variable x can be both an lvalue and an rvalue. In the statement x=x+7, the occurrence on the left is an lvalue and the occurrence on the right is an rvalue.

Addresses are shown in figure 1.3 in a slightly nonstandard way. At the top of the figure, the address of the memory location named by x is shown as A(0..3). On a typical computer system today, A may be understood as a 64-bit (8-byte) address. An int occupies four bytes in GNU/Linux, and the addresses of the four bytes named by the variable x are $A + 0, A + 1, A + 2, A + 3$. This is shown in the figure as A(0..3).

The C language allows us to take the address of a variable (in general, the address of any lvalue). To get the address of the variable x of type int, we may use the syntax &x. Although the int location is 4 bytes with addresses $A, A + 0, A + 1, A + 2$, the value of &x is A, which is the address of the first byte in the memory location named by x. Here &x is an rvalue (its value being A) but not an lvalue because it is not the name of any location in memory. In the same expression &x, x is an lvalue.

We may define a pointer using the syntax int *a. As shown in figure 1.3, a is the name of 8 bytes of memory and not just 4, as in the case of x. This is because the pointer-type variables are meant to hold addresses, and as we have already said, an address is 8 bytes on most computers today.

If we now say a=&x, the memory location named a gets filled with the address of x, which is A in figure 1.3. If we were to say a=&x+1, the location a would get filled with $A + 4$ and not $A + 1$. That is because both &x and a are of type pointer to int, and the C compiler knows that an int is 4 bytes and not just 1 byte. In the assignment a=&x, a is an lvalue and &x is an rvalue. Less obviously, x is an lvalue in the same expression. The distinction between names of memory locations (lvalues) and values that may be used to fill memory locations (rvalues) is valuable to keep in mind.

The operator & allows us to extract the address of an lvalue. Conversely, the operator * converts an address to the name of a memory location (an lvalue). So if we say a=&x and then say *a=7, the effect is as follows. First, the location named a is filled with the address of x. Next, when we say *a=7, *a is the name of the location whose address is the value held in a. The lvalue in this assignment is *a, not a. Of course, the location named by *a is the same as the location named by x. So the effect of *a=7 is to change the value of x to 7.

It is worth noting that the word pointer may refer to an lvalue or an rvalue. A variable, or any lvalue, that holds addresses may be called pointer. In addition, the address itself (an rvalue) may be called a pointer. The picture behind either usage is of an address pointing to a location.

If `e` is an expression that evaluates to a pointer to a `double` (rvalue), the numerical value of `e+1` is 8 more than the value of `e`. That is because a `double` is 8 bytes. If `e` is a pointer to a more complex type such as a `struct`, the C compiler calculates the size of the `struct` in bytes and increments `e` by that amount when evaluating `e+1`. Thus, `e+1` advances the pointer by one item and `e+27` advances the pointer by 27 items, taking into account the data type that `e` points to. If `p` is a pointer-type variable, the assignment `p=p+17` advances the pointer by 17 items. Likewise, the assignment `p=p-17` moves the pointer backward by 17 items.

An array may be introduced using a definition such as `int list[3]`. After this definition `list` is an rvalue but not an lvalue (it is not the name of any memory location). The (r)value of `list` is the address of the first of three consecutive memory locations of type `int` set aside by the definition. In figure 1.3, it is $A + 12$. If we use syntax such as `list[1]=8`, `list[1]` is an lvalue as shown in the figure. It is nothing but an abbreviation of `*(list+1)`. Similarly, `list[0]` and `list[2]` are also valid lvalues as shown in the figure. In fact, `list[100]` is also a syntactically valid lvalue. The only problem is that an assignment such as `list[100]=2` will most likely lead to a runtime error because only three `int` locations have been legally claimed. Such runtime errors are triggered by the operating system in a manner that is explained in a later chapter.

We began by noting that a sequence may be specified using three pieces of information: a pointer to the first location, the size of each item, and the number of items. The definition `int list[3]` supplies all three pieces of information. The address of the first location is the value of `list`. The size of each item is 4 bytes (on GNU/Linux) because an `int` is four bytes. Finally, the number of items in the array is 3 as shown in figure 1.3. The first two pieces of information are contained in the type and value of `list`. If `list` is passed as an argument to a function, the length of the array, which is the third piece of information, must be supplied separately.

Machine or assembly languages too access data items in a sequence using an address, the size of each item, and the index of the item, much as in C.

A C source with arrays and pointers

So far our discussion of arrays and pointers has been with reference to figure 1.3. We will now write a simple C program illustrating the discussion.

Before looking at C source, a few comments about indentation are in order. For program source not meant for display in a book, we use eight-space indentation.[10] Tab stops are separated by eight characters and terminal screens are conventionally 80 character wide. When the program code is lined up according to tab stops, the code is much easier to browse. The nesting level of loops becomes readily evident. The nesting level is an indication of the level of complexity of the code. Therefore, it is useful to be able to recognize the nesting level immediately. Too many levels of nesting often imply that the code is poorly structured.

Let us look at the following code, which uses five-space indentation. The suggestion of eight-space indentation assumes 80-character-wide lines. Here the lines are about 50 characters, and the indentation has been scaled down proportionally.

```
1  #include <stdio.h>
2  int main()
3  {
4        int x;
5        int list[3];
6        int *a;
7        a = &x;
8        list[1]=2;
9        *a = 35+list[1];
10       printf("%p %p %d\n", &x, list, x);
11 }
```

We are allowed to say `list[1] = 2;` (line 8), but `list = &x;` would have been illegal. The reason is that `list` has a value but is not the name of any location. On one run, this code had the following output (line 10).

```
0x7fff3cb8e414 0x7fff3cb8e400 37
```

___
[10]The Linux kernel programming guidelines require eight-space indentation. See `www.kernel.org/doc/Documentation/CodingStyle`. While noting that style is a matter of personal choice, Linus Torvalds, the creator of the Linux operating system, adds that using four-space indentation "is akin to trying to define the value of PI to be 3."

The value of x is printed as 37, as we may have expected. The address of x and the value of list are printed in hexadecimal as indicated by the 0x at front. Thus, each address is 48 bits long. Figure 1.3 may give the impression that each address is the address of a location in physical memory. In fact, the addresses that are printed out are virtual addresses, a concept we will discuss in later chapters.

The printf() function used on line 10 is part of the standard C library. Its declaration will be in the standard header file stdio.h, which is included on line 1. The C compiler knows where to look for this header file.

1.2.3   The Aitken iteration using arrays and pointers

As already noted, arrays and pointers are almost equivalent in C. The principal advantage of thinking of arrays in this way arises in passing arrays as arguments to functions. Here we use the Aitken example to illustrate how arrays may be passed as pointers.

The file aitken.c begins with two directives:

```
#include <assert.h>
#include "aitken.h"
```

the second of which includes the header file aitken.h. Including aitken.h allows the compiler to ensure that the definitions in aitken.c are consistent with the declarations in the header file. The first line includes the standard header assert.h. The job of finding that header file is left to the compiler. Including that header file allows us to use the assert statement to check a condition in the body of the code (see line 4 below).

The function aitken() operates on arrays that are passed to it as pointers.

```
1  void aitken(double* seq1, double* seq2, int len){
2        int i;
3        double a, b, c;
4        assert(len > 2);
5        for(i=0; i < len-2; i++){
6              a = seq1[i];
7              b = seq1[i+1];
8              c = seq1[i+2];
9              seq2[i] =  a - (b-a)*(b-a)/(a-2*b+c);
```

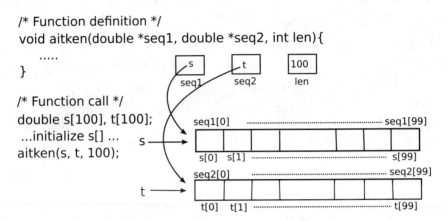

Figure 1.4: Passing arrays as pointers. In this picture, s and t are values but not names of any locations.

10   }
11 }

In a function that calls `aitken()` from some other source file, we may have declared two arrays using `double s[100]`, `t[100]`. Those two arrays will correspond to two segments of memory each equal to 100 `doubles` (see figure 1.4). As we have noted, `s[0]`...`s[99]` and `t[0]`...`t[99]` are names of `double` locations, which make up those segments of memory. In contrast, s and t have values of type `double *` but are not names of any locations in memory. If a call is made as

```
aitken(s, t, 100);
```

it has the following effect. The function parameters `seq1` and `seq2` are names of locations in memory that can hold `double *`. The values of s and t are copied to the locations in memory whose names are `seq1` and `seq2`, respectively (see figure 1.4). The value of `seq1+17` is the same as the value of `s+17`. Thus, `seq1[17]`, which is exactly the same as `*(seq1+17)`, is another name for the memory location `s[17]`. Thus, we see that by indexing into `seq1` and `seq2` as `seq1[0]`...`seq1[99]` and `seq2[0]`...`seq2[99]`, we may refer to any entry in the arrays s and t defined by the caller (see figure 1.4).

There is a little catch here, however. What happens if we say `seq1[100]` or `seq1[200]`? We would be generating a name for a location in memory that was not legally claimed by the caller. That is likely to result in a run-time error. By just using the pointers seq1 and seq2, there is no way we can tell how long the array is. Therefore, the length of the array is the third parameter, which is named len, in the function definition. The caller has to explicitly give the length of the array, as it does here by passing 100 as the third argument.

Line 9 of the listing corresponds directly to the Aitken transformation formula (1.1).

The assert(len>2) statement on line 4 works as follows. If the code is compiled with the option -DNDEBUG, it is as if that line were not there and no extra overhead is incurred. If that option is not used during compilation, the condition len>2 is checked during run-time. If it is violated, the program will abort and print a message indicating the name of the file and the line number of the assertion that turned out to be false. The assert statements are valuable aids to debugging and indirectly useful as comments.

The definition of aitkenExtrapolate(), which is also in aitken.c, is shown below to give a complete account of the source aitken.c.

```
1  double aitkenExtrapolate(double *seq1, double* seq2,
2                               int len){
3      int n, i, j;
4      n = len/2;
5      if(len%2==0)
6          n--;
7      for(i=0; i < n; i++){
8          aitken(seq1, seq2, len-2*i);
9          for(j=0; j < len-2*(i+1); j++)
10             seq1[j] = seq2[j];
11     }
12     return (len%2==0)?seq1[1]:seq1[0];
13 }
```

We assume familiarity with the level of C that occurs in this function, although reading programs such as this can be harder than writing them. Writing good for-loops is the heart of C programming, and there are two nested for-loops in this program. Line 12 uses a conditional expression that may be less familiar. The conditional expression (a<b)?c:d tests the condition a<b. If the condition is true, it evaluates to c but to d otherwise.

1.2.4   Declarations and definitions

Names introduced into a C program are for the most part names of either functions
or variables. The names can be introduced as either declarations or definitions.

Suppose a variable name is introduced using `int x`. When the compiler encounters that statement, it sets aside a location in memory for an `int` and makes `x` the
name of that memory location. This statement is a variable definition, not merely a
declaration, because it sets aside memory for `x`.

A declaration gives type information about a variable that is expected to be
defined elsewhere. An example of a variable declaration is a statement such as `extern`
`int x`. When the compiler encounters such a statement, it notes that `x` is a variable
of type `int` that is expected to be defined in some other source file. It does not set
aside any location in memory. If it later encounters a statement such as `x=x+2`, it
does not complain. However, it cannot generate complete machine instructions to
carry out that statement because it has no idea where `x` is defined and what address
it corresponds to. That information has to be supplied by the linker later.

Both the lines in the header file `aitken.h` are function declarations not definitions. When the compiler encounters a declaration such as

```
    void aitken(double *seq1, double *seq2, int len);
```

it notes that `aitken()` is the name of a function that takes three arguments, the
first two of which are of type `double *` and the last of which is an `int`, and returns
nothing (`void`). We can omit `seq1`, `seq2`, and `len` from the declaration. Such an
omission would make the declaration difficult to read and understand for us, but it
makes no difference as far as the compiler is concerned. The compiler does nothing
more than note the types of the arguments (or parameters).

When the compiler later encounters a function call such as `aitken(s, t, n)`, it
first checks that `s` and `t` are of type `double *` and `n` is of type `int`. If the check
succeeds, the compiler will generate instructions to set up the arguments and pass
control to the function `aitken()`. If the function `aitken()` is defined in some other
source file, which it may well be, the compiler has no idea where in memory the
code for `aitken()` is located. So it cannot generate complete machine instructions
for passing control. That job is the linker's responsibility.

A function definition such as

```
    void aitken(double *seq1, double *seq2, int len){
```

```
        . . .
    }
```

has a totally different effect. When the compiler encounters a function definition, it generates machine instructions for the body of the function (which is omitted here) and figures out where to place these instructions in memory. After that, `aitken` corresponds to the chunk of memory that contains machine instructions that implement the body of the function. Just as with variables, defining a function amounts to setting aside memory for it during compilation.

1.2.5   Function calls and the compilation process

Here we take a look at the mechanism of function calls and the compilation process. Much of the discussion is centered around the file `leibniz.c`, which uses the functions defined by `aitken.c` to extrapolate the partial sums of the Leibniz series and produces data corresponding to table 1.1.

The source file `leibniz.c` begins with two directives:

```
#include "aitken.h"
#include <stdio.h>
```

The first directive includes `aitken.h` to interface to functions defined in `aitken.c`. The second directive includes `stdio.h` to interface to printing functions defined in the `stdio` (standard input/output) library.

The `leibniz()` function, which generates partial sums of the Leibniz series, is defined below without comment.

```
//partial sums of 4(1-1/3+1/5-1/7+1/9-...)
void leibniz(double* seq, int len){
    int i;
    for(i=0; i < len; i++)
      if(i==0)
            seq[i] = 4.0;
      else if(i%2==1)
            seq[i] = seq[i-1] - 4.0/(2.0*i+1);
      else
            seq[i] = seq[i-1] + 4.0/(2.0*i+1);
}
```

The `printseq()` function prints a sequence using the `printf()` function defined in the `stdio` library.

```
void printseq(double* seq, int len){
    int i;
    printf("\n \n");
    for(i=0; i < len; i++)
        printf("%-.10f\n",seq[i]);
}
```

The logic used by the `main()` function for generating the data shown in table 1.1 is similar to that of `aitkenExtrapolate()`. In a C or C++ program, the function named `main()` is the first to gain control when a program is run.

```
1  int main(){
2      const int len = 13;
3      double seq1[len];
4      double seq2[len];
5      int n, i, j;
6      leibniz(seq1, len);
7      n = len/2;
8      if(len%2==0)
9          n--;
10     for(i=0; i < n; i++){
11         printseq(seq1,len-2*i);
12         aitken(seq1, seq2, len-2*i);
13         for(j=0; j < len-2*(i+1); j++)
14             seq1[j] = seq2[j];
15     }
16     if(len%2==0)
17         printseq(seq1, 2);
18     else
19         printseq(seq1, 1);
20 }
```

The `main()` function calls other functions on lines 6, 11, 12, 17, and 19. All calls except the one to `aitken()` on line 12 are to functions defined in the same source file. We have looked at the call to `aitken()` from the point of view of the callee in section 1.2.3. Let us look at the function call `leibniz(seq1, len)` on line 6 from the point of view of the caller.

Within `main()`, `seq1` is the name of an array of length 13 and `len` is an `int` (because it is declared `const`, it must be treated as something that is merely an rvalue). When the function call `leibniz(seq1, len)` is executed, the value of `seq1` is copied to the location whose name is `seq` within `leibniz()` (see the definition of `leibniz()` given above). In addition, the content of the location whose name is `len` inside `main()` is copied to the location whose name is `len` inside `leibniz()`. This is the call-by-value semantics of C.

The function call `aitken(seq1, seq2, len)` on line 12 invokes a function that is not defined in the `leibniz.c` compilation unit. To see what difference that makes, let us see what happens when we issue the command

```
icc -c leibniz.c
```

The `-c` option tells the `icc` C compiler that it should only produce the object file and not the executable. The object file it produces will be called `leibniz.o` (on Unix systems). To produce the object file, the compiler runs through the code and converts the `leibniz()` function definition into a sequence of machine instructions. Next it converts `printseq()` into a sequence of machine instructions before turning to `main()`. When it hits the function call `leibniz(seq1, len)` on line 6 of the `main()` function, it copies the arguments `seq1` and `len` into a place where the `leibniz()` function can retrieve them. After that it simply generates a machine instruction to make the function call. That machine instruction will pass control to the `leibniz()` function, which the compiler has already converted into a set of machine instructions.

When the compiler sees the `aitken(seq1, seq2, len)` call on line 12 of the `main()` function, the process is initially similar. Thanks to the included header `aitken.h`, the compiler will have already seen the declaration of `aitken()` to be `void aitken(double *seq1, double *seq2, int len)`. So the compiler generates machine instructions to copy `seq1`, `seq2`, and `len` into a place where the definition of `aitken()` can find them. At this point, there is a problem: the compiler cannot generate machine instructions to pass control to `aitken()`. The compiler has no idea where the machine instructions for `aitken()` are. The name `aitken()` remains an unresolved reference in the object file `leibniz.o`.

Thus, the object file `leibniz.o` by itself cannot be turned into an executable. To turn it into an executable, we must first compile `aitken.c` as follows:

```
icc -c aitken.c
```

The `-c` option tells the `icc` command to compile only. Without that option, the command will try to compile and then link and produce an executable with the default name `a.out`. With the compile only option, the command will generate an object file called `aitken.o` with machine instructions for the two functions defined in `aitken.c`. To generate the executable, we run the following command:

```
icc -o leibniz.exe leibniz.o aitken.o
```

The `-o` option tells the `icc` command to leave its output in the file `leibniz.exe` instead of the default `a.out`. The C linker uses the definition of `aitken()` in `aitken.o` to eliminate the unresolved reference to `aitken()` in `leibniz.o`. The executable file `leibniz.exe` it generates is a sequence of machine instructions with no unresolved names. It is ready to be loaded and run.

The extensions `.cpp`, `.c`, and `.o` correspond to C++ source files, C source files, and object files, respectively. In the command `icc -c aitken.c`, the file extension of `aitken.c` indicates to the `icc` command that it is operating on a C source file. So the command will invoke the C compiler. In the linking command, the filename extension `.o` indicates that `leibniz.o` and `aitken.o` are both object files. Therefore, `icc` invokes the C linker.

We have used the `icc` compiler/linker from Intel . But the syntax is almost identical if we used GNU's `gcc` or the Portland Group's `pgcc`. Commands such as `icc`, `pgcc`, and `gcc` look at the file name extension to determine the type of the file.

We use Intel's C/C++ compilers in this book because it is easier to link certain libraries that we will discuss later. In addition, the Intel compilers were the default standard on some supercomputing systems used in later chapters. GNU's `gcc/g++` compiler is widely used, open source, and reputed to be of excellent quality.[11] For work unrelated to this book, this author normally uses the GNU compilers.

---

[11]The Intel compiler appears to carry some loop optimizations better, but this is not a major point.

Conventionally, the executable files in Linux do not use the file name extension `.exe`. The `.exe` filename extension for executables is a Windows convention. We have adopted the Windows convention throughout this book as it makes for greater clarity.

Going back to `leibniz.exe`, we may wonder how the name `printf()` in `leibniz.o` gets resolved. It is used in the definition of `printseq()`, and we understood that `printf()` is defined in the `stdio` library. However, the linking command gave no explicit instructions to fetch that library. It did not need to because the linker fetches and links a number of standard libraries by default and `stdio` is one of them.

Exercise 1.2.1. Look up the meaning of the options `-c -o -I -L -lm -lmath` in the C compiler's user's guide.

Exercise 1.2.2. Use a short C program and the `sizeof()` facility to print the size in bytes of variables of `char`, `int`, `long int`, `double`, `char *`, `int *`, and `double *` types. Notice that all pointer are the same size (8 bytes).

Exercise 1.2.3. If p and q are pointers of type `char *` and `double *`, p=p+1 moves p by one byte while q=q+1 moves q up by eight bytes, so that p or q point to the next `char` or `double`, respectively. Write a short C program to demonstrate this aspect of pointer arithmetic.

Exercise 1.2.4. In C, a pointer can be an lvalue or an rvalue. Give an example of a pointer that is an rvalue but not an lvalue.

Exercise 1.2.5. The list of numbers $1, 2, \ldots, n$ can be rearranged in $n!$ different orders. Write a function that takes an argument n of the type `int` and prints the $n!$ different permutations.

Exercise 1.2.6. Suppose a[] is an array of type `double` and size n. Write a function that takes a and n as arguments and sorts the entries of the array. The basic sorting algorithms are bubble sort, quick sort, and heap sort.[12]

Exercise 1.2.7. Rewrite `aitken()` to confirm to the declaration

```
void aitken(double *seq, int len);
```

so that it takes a single sequence and transforms it in place.

---

[12]Many different sorting algorithms are derived and discussed in Knuth (1998). Most sorting problems are typically handled using library functions.

Exercise 1.2.8. What is special about the following C program?[13]

```
char *s="char *s=%c%s%c;%cmain(){printf(s,34,s,34,10,10)};%c";
main(){printf(s,34,s,34,10,10);}
```

The program does not #include the header file stdio.h, which contains the declaration of printf(). Modify the program to #include that header file while serving the same purpose.

Exercise 1.2.9. The following C function copies one array to another array, if the two arrays do not overlap.

```
void arr_copy(int* in, int* out, int len)
{
  int i;
  for(i=0; i < len; i++)
    out[i] = in[i];
}
```

If $1, 2, 3, 4$ is rotated left, it becomes $2, 3, 4, 1$. Write a C function for rotating an array left (in-place rotation) that does not use a loop but is allowed to make one call to arr_copy(). Can you write a similar function to rotate right?

Exercise 1.2.10. Suppose that double **x points to an array of pointers of length n and that each entry of the array points to an array of doubles, whose length is also n.

- Interpret x as a square matrix and write a function

  ```
  void transpose(double **x, int n);
  ```

  which transposes the matrix.

- Write a function that rotates the matrix columnwise and another function that rotates it rowwise.

- Write a function that rotates each diagonal forward by one step. More precisely, an entry in position (i, j) with $0 \le i, j < n$ must end up in the position $(i + 1 \bmod n, j + 1 \bmod n)$.

---

[13]Kozen (1997) (p. 288) states that, "once you understand this program you have understood the main idea" behind Gödel's proof of his incompleteness theorem.

1.3   C++ review

The C language has a simple philosophy. Its aim is to offer a uniform view of the computer, especially computer memory, to the programmer. C has been so successful that nearly every object that can be called a computer, ranging from supercomputers to routers to embedded and mobile devices, is equipped with a C compiler or a cross-compiler. C is the best vehicle for highly optimized programs.

Because C seeks to be close to the machine, it is a low-level language. There is often a considerable distance between concepts that are native to a problem domain and their expression as C programs. High-level languages provide constructs and syntax that bring the program much closer to ideas and concepts that are native to the problem domain.

The C++ language is something of a compromise to provide the facilities of high-level languages without sacrificing the speed of C. Despite its name, it is not an incremental extension of C. It is a colossal expansion of C syntax. It does not have the seamless nature of truly high-level languages such as Python. Classes in Python use very little syntax and fit cleanly within the highly modular architecture of Python programs. However, languages such as Python are much slower than C++.

Although the C++ language is a compromise, or perhaps because of being a compromise, it has found a great range of uses. On the one hand, C++ has all of C inside it. On the other hand, it provides many mechanisms for capturing concepts and ideas more precisely. Its downside is its complexity. Although clear and careful thinking are essential to all programming, a failure in this respect has particularly acute consequences in C++.

Because our focus is on program speed, the part of C++ we use is quite small. Narrowly defined and flat (as opposed to hierarchical) classes, references, occasional function name overloading, and the ability to define variables in the middle of programs is an almost complete list of the C++ features we use. The classes we define are no more than C `struct`s endowed with functions. C features such as `enum`, `struct`, `typedef`, and `static` can be quite powerful for representing concepts and ideas when used judiciously.

Classes in C++ are a mechanism for representing concepts and endowing them with functionality that makes them easy to use. Classes can be general or narrow. The `Vector` class studied in this section is an example of a general class. It can be made even more general. The `Vector` class assumes that each entry of a vector is a `double`. Using templates, one may define a class that allows each entry to be a `double` or a `float` or an `int` or even some user defined type or class.

The `Vector` class is the only example in this book of a class that attempts to capture a general concept (in this instance, the concept of vectors in linear algebra). Every other class discussed in this book is narrowly defined. We begin our discussion of C++ with the `Vector` class for two reasons. It is a good vehicle for reviewing some of the features of C++. Indeed, we introduce more features of C++ than we need, but that too serves a purpose. C++ is sometimes believed to lead to slow programs. This example helps us explain thoroughly how that may come about. In later chapters, we illustrate the overhead of the `Vector` class and the related `Matrix` class, when used in inner-loops or for disk input/output.

1.3.1   The `Vector` class

The C++ language can be used in many different ways. Using general classes, one may make C++ look like easy to use languages such as Python or Matlab without incurring the enormous cost of such interpreted languages. Our interest is in fast programs and, even more so, in understanding what makes programs fast or slow. The C++ style we adopt is quite close to C.

Nevertheless, we begin with a general type of class, namely, the `Vector` class. This class helps us review a few of the features of C++ and is used to implement the Aitken iteration later. In a later chapter, we criticize the use of this class and show it to be slow.

Header file with class definition

The `Vector` class is defined in the header file `Vector.hh`. The C++ class consists of data members and member functions. With respect to computer memory, a class object is a collection of data items. The data items could be of basic types such as `double` or `char`, or pointers. The data items may also be other class objects or C structures. The member functions provide various means to manipulate the class object or, equivalently, the package of data items that constitutes the class object.

It is typical for header files to give only part of the definition of the class. Many of the member functions are typically defined in a separate source. Here the entire class definition is in the header file `Vector.hh`, which makes the header file a bit long. We present the contents of the header file in stages, gradually unveiling features of C++. The skeleton of the header file is listed below.

```
 1  #ifndef MYVECTOR
 2  #define MYVECTOR
 3  #include <cassert>
 4  #include <cmath>
 5  #include <cstdlib>
 6  #include <cstring>
 7  #include <iostream>
 8  #include <fstream>
 9
10  using namespace std;
11
12  class Vector{
13  private:
14        ...
15  public:
16        ...
17  };
18
19  #endif
```

Lines 1, 2, and 19 ensure that the header file expands to the source code in between if and only if the macro variable MYVECTOR is defined. Here MYVECTOR is not good nomenclature, as it may be inadvertently reused by some other header, subverting our attempt to ensure conditional inclusion of header files.

It is typical for C/C++ sources to begin by including a number of header files to interface to other source files or libraries. C programs include the header assert.h to use the assert() macro (see section 1.2.3). C++ programs may include either assert.h or cassert, as on line 3, to emphasize that a C facility is being employed.

The Vector class uses other C facilities as well. It uses the fabs() function from cmath (line 4) in one of its member functions to compute the norm of the vector. C facilities to allocate and release memory are defined in stdlib (line 5).

C++ facilities for input/output from terminals and files are in iostream (line 7) and fstream (line 8), respectively. Member functions that input/output vectors to/from files use these facilities.

To output a variable x to standard output (typically the terminal), we may say

```
cout<<x<<endl;
```

Here cout is the name of standard output declared in iostream. The end of line character endl is also declared in iostream. In C, input/output syntax is sensitive to the type of data items being handled. The abstraction features of C++ are used by the iostream library to provide a uniform interface for input/output regardless of the type of the variable. Even class objects may be input/output in this manner if the operators << (for output) and >> (for input) are overloaded suitably.

To output to a file, the syntax looks as follows:

```
ofstream ofile("tmp.txt");
ofile<<x<<endl;
```

Here ofile is defined as an ofstream object. At the point of definition, it is tied to the file tmp.txt.

To input x from standard input, we may say

```
cin>>x;
```

To input from a file, we may say

```
ifstream ifile("tmp.txt")
ifile>>x;
```

This will work regardless of whether x is a double or an int or a long or a char.

The class names ofstream and ifstream as well as class object names cout and cin are defined in the namespace std. In general, we should say std::cout and std::ofstream because these names do not exist outside the namespace. However, the using namespace declaration on line 10 brings in all the names in std into scope. It allows us to say cout instead of std::cout.

It is often not a good idea to bring in the entire std namespace, especially within header files. The C++ standard library is vast. Bringing in the entire std namespace, as we do on line 10, pollutes the namespace considerably. For example, a programmer may define a function called copy() to copy double arrays in a program-specific manner and conflict with the std namespace. There are functions with common names such as copy() and sort() in the standard library.

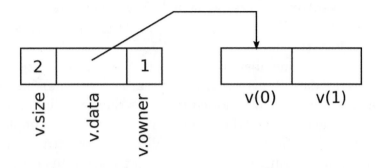

Figure 1.5: Schematic picture of a `Vector` of length 2, which "owns" its data.

The listing shows the outline of the definition of the class `Vector` (lines 12 through 17). There is a private section (line 13) in the class definition and a public section (line 15). The class definition must end with a semicolon as on line 17. Omitting the semicolon at the end of class definitions is a common novice error.

Private section of the `Vector` class

A class is a collection of data members and member functions. In the `Vector` class all the data members are in the private section.

```
class Vector{
private:
     long int size;
     double *data;
     int owner;
public:

     . . .
};
```

The class member `size` is the length of the vector and `data` is a pointer to the contents of the vector; so `data[i]` is in effect a name for the `i`th entry of the vector. The `owner` field will be either 0 or 1—its meaning is explained later.

If `v` is a variable of type `Vector`, then it is a name for a segment of memory that includes a location of type `int`, a location of type `double *`, and a location of type `int`. A schematic view of a `Vector` of length 2 is shown in figure 1.5. If `v` is the name of an object of class `Vector`, `v.size`, `v.data`, and `v.owner` are names for members of `v` as shown in the figure. One may say that the class object `v` is a package of the data items `v.size`, `v.data`, and `v.owner`.

If a data member or a member function is in the private section, its access is restricted. Because the data items `v.size`, `v.data`, and `v.owner` are in the private section, only member functions are allowed to access them.[14] Whatever functionality we want must be defined through the member functions. For example, suppose we want to input a vector from a file. We are not allowed to directly set the size of the `Vector` object during input using syntax such as `v.size=100`. Instead, we may define a member function `input()`, which takes care of reading data and setting `v.size` appropriately.

Member functions of the `Vector` class

All the member functions of the `Vector` class are in the public section.

```
1  class Vector{
2  private:
3      ...
4  public:
5       Vector(){...}
6       Vector(long int  n){...}
7       Vector(const Vector& v){...}
8       ~Vector(){...}
9       void shadow(double *dataptr, long int len)
10      {...}
11      void shadow(const Vector& v){...}
12      void shadow(const Vector& v,  long int i,
13             long int len){...}
14      long int getSize() const{...}
15      double * getRawData() const{...}
16      double& operator()(long int i){...}
17      const double& operator()(long int i) const{.}
```

---

[14]This statement is not exactly true. C++ has a notion of `friends`, which too get access to the private section of a class.

```
18        Vector& operator=(const Vector& v){...}
19        void add(const Vector& v){...}
20        void sub(const Vector& v){...}
21        void mul(const Vector& v){...}
22        void div(const Vector& v){...}
23        void scale(const double x){...}
24        void add_constant(const double x){...}
25        double norm() const{...}
26        void output(const char* fname)const{...}
27        void input(const char* fname){...}
28  };
```

There is a basic difference between data members and member functions. Suppose v is a `Vector` class object. Then `v.size`, `v.data`, and `v.owner` refer to the data items packaged inside v. In contrast, `v.norm()` applies the member function `norm()` (line 25) with the class object v as its target.

The member functions exist within the namespace defined by the class. Each class defines a namespace. The `Vector` class defines the eponymous namespace `Vector::`. If we want to refer to a member function such as `norm()` outside the scope of the class (the scope here is from lines 1 through 28), the name must be given as `Vector::norm()`.

For example, we may define the member function `norm()` in a compilation unit and outside the scope of the class `Vector` as

```
double Vector::norm() const{
      ...
}
```

We have chosen to define all the member functions in `Vector.hh` and within the scope of the `Vector` class.

Before delving into the member functions, we give an example of how `Vector` objects are used.

```
#include "Vector.hh"

int main(){
     Vector v(20);
```

```
        for(int i=0; i < 20; i++)
            v(i) = i;
        Vector w1, w2;
        w1.shadow(v, 0, 10);
        w2.shadow(v, 10, 10);
        w1.add(w2);
        w1.output("w1.txt");
}
```

The definition `Vector v(20)` invokes the class constructor on line 6. This constructor will make `v.data` point to 20 `doubles`, set `v.size to` 20, and set `v.owner=1`, making `v` the owner of its data.

The body of the for-loop has `v(i)=i`. When we say `f(x)` in C/C++, `f()` is a function being applied to `x`. Here we say `v(i)`, but `v` is a class object not a function being applied to `i`. However, thanks to operator overloading, the compiler interprets `v(i)` as `v.operator()(i)`—in words, the member function `operator()` is applied to the target `v` with `i` as the sole argument. The member function defined on line 16 is called. This member function will look at `v.data`, access the ith entry, and return a reference to it. Thus, when we say `v(i)=i`, the ith entry of the `Vector` object `v` gets set to i. At the end of the for-loop, the entries of v are $0, ..., 19$.

At the definition `Vector w1, w2;`, the `Vector` objects `w1` and `w2` are created using the empty constructor (line 5). This empty constructor sets `w1.size` to 0, `w1.data` to `NULL`, and `w1.owner` to 0, and likewise for `w2`. Neither `w1` nor `w2` owns any data. To begin with, they are vectors of size 0.

When we say `w1.shadow(v, 0, 10)`, the member function `shadow()` defined on line 12 gets invoked. Its effect is to set `w1.data` to `v.data` and `w1.size` to 10. However, `w1.owner` remains 0 because the data is owned by `v`. The `Vector` object `w1` is a shadow of the first 10 entries of `v`. Likewise, after `w2.shadow(v, 10, 10)`, `w2.data` is set to `v.data+10`, and `w2` becomes a shadow of entries 10 through 19 of `v`.

When we say `w1.add(w2)`, the member function `add()` (line 19) is invoked with `w1` as the target and `w2` as its argument. This member function verifies that its target and its argument are vectors of the same size and adds `w2` to `w1`, entry by entry.

The final line `w1.output("w1.txt")` outputs `w1` to the file `w1.txt` via the member function `output()` (line 26). Thus, the numbers $10, 12, ..., 28$ will be output to `w1.txt`.

The program is not done yet, however. When the class objects `v`, `w1`, and `w2` go out of scope at the end of `main()`, the compiler inserts calls to the destructor (line 8). The destructor is called thrice. When destroying `v`, the destructor notes that `v` is the owner of its data and releases the memory that `data` points to. There is nothing to be done to destroy `w1` and `w2` because they do not own their data. The destructor returns as soon as it notes that they are not owners.

References

We will step through a few C++ concepts using the public member functions of the class `Vector` as illustrations. The first of these is references.

A reference in C++ is another name for an object that is already in existence. For example, we may say

```
double &x = y;
```

and `x` becomes another name for `y`, which is assumed to be of type `double`. If we say `x=2` and then print `y`, its value will be `2`.

The `&` character is used to take the address of locations. It is also used for references as illustrated. Overloading the `&` operator in this way may create some confusion initially, but in fact references are really just a shorthand for the use of pointers.

We may use references in passing arguments to a function. For example, if we define a function as

```
double f(double &x){
    . . .
}
```

we may call it as `f(z)`, assuming `z` is a variable of type `double` and `x` will become a reference to `z`. The call `f(2.0)` is not legal, however, because 2.0 is a value and not the name of a `double` location.

References are commonly used to pass class objects as arguments to functions. The `Vector` class holds just three data items (`size`, `data`, and `owner`), but in general a lot of data can be packaged into a single class. When a class object is passed as an argument to a function, do we really want a fresh copy to be made of all the data inside that object? Typically, the answer is no. First, the expense of having to copy all that data may be undesirable. Second, even if there is only a small amount of data, the semantics could be incorrect. For `Vector` objects, item-by-item copying results in multiple objects incorrectly owning the same data.

A declaration of a member function can specify that some of the arguments are references. The declaration void add(const Vector& v) (line 19) specifies that the argument named v is passed by reference (the const qualifier is discussed later). The crucial symbol here is the &, which precedes v in the declaration. If arguments are passed as references, we do not have to worry about the correct semantics for copying.

Functions may also return a reference as does the member function operator() (line 16) . This function is defined as

```
double& operator()(long int i){
    assert(i < size);
      return(data[i]);
}
```

in Vector.hh within the scope of the class Vector. Here size and data are data members of the target. So if v is a Vector object and we say v(6)=17, this member function is called with v as the target and with argument i equal to 6. Assuming the vector is of size 6 or greater, the member function returns data[i], which is the same as v.data[i] by reference. Whatever is returned is another name for the 6th entry of the Vector object v. Thus, saying v(6)=17 has the effect of setting that entry to 17.

Operator and function name overloading

We have already seen how the function call operator is overloaded. Below is another example. In this example, the assignment operator is overloaded.

```
Vector& operator=(const Vector& v){
     assert(size==v.size);
     memcpy((char *)data, (char *)v.data,
             size*sizeof(double));
     return(*this);
}
```

The assignment operator uses memcpy() to copy the data in v to its target.[15] If we say w=v, with both v and w being Vector objects, the member function operator=()

---

[15]Strictly speaking, the overloaded = operator should check that data and v.data do not overlap.

is invoked with `w` as the target and `v` as its argument. As before, `size` and `data` refer to the corresponding items of the target.

A new bit of syntax here is the keyword `this`. Within a member function, `this` is a pointer to the target. Therefore, `*this` is the target. The overloaded assignment operator returns a reference to the target.

If `u`, `v`, and `w` are `Vector` objects, and we say `u=v=w`, the compiler interprets that as `u=(v=w)`. In C/C++, the assignment operator is right associative. The result of `v=w` is a reference to `v`, which is the argument in the next call to the overloaded assignment operator that assigns to `u`.

C++ also allows function name overloading. For instance, we can define a function as

```
void add(double *v, const double *w,
         const int len){...}
```

which adds the array `w` to the array `v`. We can define another function

```
void add(const double *u, const double *w, double *v,
         const int len){...}
```

which leaves the sum of `u` and `w` in `v`. In C, the two definitions would conflict because they are both trying to bind a definition to the same name `add`. However, in C++, the compiler allows both the definitions because they can be disambiguated using the number and types of the arguments. The compiler internally generates mangled names to keep the definitions separate in the object file, so as not to confuse the linker.

Function call inlining

The member functions of the class `Vector` are defined in the header file `Vector.hh` within the scope of the class definition. If we wanted to define the overloaded function call operator elsewhere, we can give its definition as

```
double& Vector::operator()(long int i){
    assert(i < size);
    return(data[i]);
}
```

In fact, it is better to define the overloaded function call operator within the scope of the class as we did. Every source that uses the `Vector` class will include the header `Vector.hh`. Thus, every compilation unit will see the complete definition of the function call operator. If we say `v(i) = 7.0`, with `v` being a `Vector` object, the compiler does not actually generate a function call for `v(i)`. Instead it scans the definition of the overloaded function call operator and splices in the body of the function at the point of call. The overhead of making a function call is eliminated. This is called function call inlining.

The function call overhead in modern processors is quite small and is typically less than 10 cycles.[16] Much of the time it is nothing to worry about. However, if a member function compiles to only a few machine instructions and is called frequently, one must ensure that the member function is inlined.

In C++, one can explicitly ask the compiler to inline functions that are not member functions. For instance, if a function with the declaration `void add(Vector u, Vector v)` is instead declared `inline void add(Vector u, Vector v)` and defined within the header file, the compiler will try to and almost certainly succeed in inlining that function call. The compiler may refuse or fail to inline functions that are long and complicated without warning.

If several source files are compiled and linked simultaneously with interprocedural optimization turned on (`-ipo` option in `icc` and `icpc`), the compiler will again try to inline certain function calls. Normally, we will avoid interprocedural optimization, preferring to build object files for each source file or compilation unit separately.

Inlining is not quite the panacea it is sometimes believed to be. Suppose we need to replace each entry of an array by the cumulative sum of the preceding entries. We can write the loop in C using pointers and pointer arithmetic or we can use a class such as the `Vector` class. A well-written C-style loop will lead to faster and more compact assembly code for reasons explained in a later chapter (see section 3.2.6). Inlining occasionally leads to worse code as we illustrate later in this chapter.

Constructors and destructors

Constructors and destructors are central to the class mechanism in C++. The three constructors of the `Vector` class are defined below.

---

[16]The function call overhead depends on the number of arguments, types of the arguments, number of registers used by the caller, context of the function call, and other factors.

```
//empty constructor
Vector(){
    size = 0;
    data = NULL;
    owner = 0;
}


//only constructor to allocate space for data
Vector(long int  n){
    size = n;
    data = (double *)malloc(sizeof(double)*n);
    owner = 1;
}



//*this becomes shadow of Vector v
//(copy constructor)
Vector(const Vector& v){
    size = v.size;
    data = v.data;
    owner = 0;
}
```

The empty constructor and the copy constructor do not allocate space. The constructor in the middle allocates space using `malloc()`, which is in `cstdlib`. These member functions are understood to be constructors because they have the same name as the class. Constructors are not allowed to return anything.

Constructors are called implicitly at the point of definition of class objects. It is essential to understand when constructors are called. Suppose we define a vector object as

```
Vector v;
```

the empty constructor is called to initialize the object v. If we define an array of vectors

```
Vector v[100];
```

the empty constructor is called for each object in the array. It is illegal to define an array of objects if the class is not equipped with an empty constructor.

If we define a vector object as

```
Vector v(27)
```

the constructor in the middle is called. The compiler notes that the object v is being built with the single argument 27, which is a constant of type int. The constructor that calls malloc() takes long int as an argument. In C/C++, an int is automatically promoted to a long int if necessary.

The constructor uses malloc() to claim space for this Vector object. If we make the call

```
malloc(1000*1000)
```

the function returns a pointer to 10^6 bytes of memory. The pointer is of type void *.

In the usage

```
data = (double *)malloc(sizeof(double)*n);
```

void * is *cast* to double *. Type casts are used to convert values of one type to another type. For example, we may say (int)1.4142 to convert the double value 1.4142 to an int (it will be truncated). The cast is needed here because data is of type double * while malloc() returns void *.

What happens during malloc()? The short answer, which will be elaborated later, is that the function call first goes to the C library. The C library may in turn call the operating system if it is not able to come up with the memory by itself. The operating system typically allocates an area in virtual memory to the calling process. No region in physical memory is set aside. Physical memory is set aside only when the process first tries to access the memory it has claimed for itself. There is a page fault during first access, and the page fault handler sets aside physical memory.

Suppose we need an array of Vector objects of length 100 with each vector of size 1000. The definition

```
Vector v[100]
```

will not do. The 100 Vector objects it creates all use the empty constructor and therefore have length 0 and do not own any data. We need the following code:

```
Vector *v[100];
```

```
for(int i=0; i < 100; i++)
    v[i] = new Vector(1000);
```

What we get here is an array of pointers to `Vector` objects and not an array of `Vector` objects. The for-loop initializes each pointer in the array to point to a `Vector` object of size 1000. In C++, the usage

```
new Vector(1000)
```

calls a constructor explicitly and returns a pointer to the object that was created.

The `new` operator may also be used to allocate arrays. For example, we can say

```
data = new double[size]
```

to make `data` point to an array of `doubles` of length `size`. Thus, `new` can be an alternative to `malloc()`. But `malloc()` cannot create class objects, although `new` can.

We come at last to the copy constructor. The copy constructor makes its target a shadow of its argument. If we define `v` as

```
Vector v(w)
```

where `w` is an object of type `Vector`, the copy constructor is invoked with `w` as its argument. A standard situation where the copy constructor is invoked is as follows. Suppose we define a function

```
void add(Vector v1, Vector v2)
```

and call it `add(v, w)`. By default, arguments are passed by copying (pass by value) in C/C++. At the point of call, `v` is copied to `v1` and `w` is copied to `v2`. In C++, copying class objects means calling the copy constructor. Here, class objects `v1` and `v2` are created using copy constructors.

For the sake of completeness, we give the definition of one of the member functions named `shadow()`.

```
//makes *this shadow v(i:i+len-1)
void shadow(const Vector& v,  long int i,
            long int len){
    assert(!owner);
    assert(i+len<=v.size);
    size = len;
```

```
        data = v.data + i;
        owner = 0;
    }
```

The target becomes a shadow of v of length len beginning at the ith entry of v.

The sole destructor of the class is defined as follows:

```
~Vector(){
    if(owner!=0)
        free(data);
}
```

This member function is understood to be a destructor because its name is the class name prefixed with a tilde. Destructors are not allowed to return anything nor can they take any arguments. Destructors are called automatically when the class object goes out of scope. The destructor of the Vector class frees its data if it is an owner.

The function free() is defined in the C library, like malloc(). The space allocated by malloc() was stored in data. It is released by free().

If a class object is allocated using new, as in

```
Vector *vptr = new Vector(1000);
```

where vptr is a pointer to Vector, it must be released using the delete operator:

```
delete vptr;
```

The class destructor is called when vptr is deleted. If an array is allocated using new[], as in

```
double *data = new double[size];
```

it must be released using delete[]:

```
delete[] data;
```

The const qualifier

The following definition is contained in the first few lines of Vector.hh (but omitted from earlier listings):

```
const double PI = 3.1415926535897932384e+00;
```

Because the definition of `PI` is qualified using `const`, any attempt to change the value of `PI` is illegal. If a user attempts to change the value of `PI`, the compiler will catch the error.

The `Vector` class is equipped with member functions `output()` and `input()` to facilitate output to files and input from files. Definition of the member function `input()` begins as follows:

```
void input(const char* fname){...}
```

Here the argument `fname` (file name) is a pointer to a `char` (character). In C and C++, a `char` is a single byte with ascii encoding. Strings are arrays of characters terminated by '\0' or equivalently the byte of value 0. If a string is passed as a pointer to a `char`, its length need not be passed explicitly. The convention for terminating strings determines its length.

A pointer holds an address which points to some data. Prefixing the `const` qualifier to the declaration or definition of a pointer implies that the data does not change, but the pointer may change. So it is illegal to say `fname[0]='M'` within the body of the function, but it is legal to say `char c; fname = &c;`.

Suppose we want to initialize a vector of length 20 using data stored in a file named `init.dat` in the current directory. The data in the file must be a sequence of 20 (or more—the extra values are ignored) values separated by whitespace. The following code does that:

```
1  char fname[9]={'i','n','i','t','.','d','a','t','\0'};
2  Vector v(20);
3  v.input(fname);
```

In line 1, the number 9, which gives the length of the array, can be omitted because the compiler can use the initializing sequence to determine the length. The usage below is much more convenient.

```
Vector v(20);
v.input("init.dat");
```

We are allowed to pass `"init.dat"` as an argument explicitly because the first argument of the member function `input()` is of the type `const char *` and not just `char *`.

Use of `const` qualified references is illustrated by the member function `add()`.

```
void add(const Vector& v){...}
```

Here the `const` qualifier indicates that `add()` will read entries of `v` but not change them. The target will be changed when `v` is added to it. The usage of the `const` qualifier in the member function `norm()` is different.

```
double norm()const{...}
```

This function returns the ∞-norm of its target vector (largest magnitude of an entry of the vector). Therefore, if it is called `v.norm()`, the returned value is the ∞-norm of v. The `const` qualifier specifies that the member function will not change its target. Any attempt to change the entries of `v` inside the definition of `norm()` is illegal.

The `const` protections can be easily broken using shadows. For example, inside the definition of the member function `add()`, we can say

```
Vector w(v);
```

and go on to modify the entries of `v`.

Default arguments

Unlike C, C++ allows default arguments. Suppose the function

```
double f(double x, int flag){
       ...
}
```

is defined in the source file `xyz.cpp`. In the header file `xyz.hh`, we may declare it as

```
double f(double x, int flag = 0);
```

Then we are allowed to call the function as

```
f(1.4142, 1);
```

or

```
f(1.4144);
```

In the latter case, the compiler supplies the second argument (`flag`) as 0. Only trailing arguments can be assigned default values.

The -> operator

Suppose we define an array of pointers to `Vector` objects as

```
Vector *v[100];
```

Each entry may be made to point to a `Vector` object as explained already. Suppose all those `Vector` objects are initialized in some way and we want to print the norm of each `Vector` object. The following syntax will not do:

```
for(int i=0; i < 100; i++)
    cout<<v[i].norm()<<endl;
```

The problem here is that `v[i]` is a pointer to a `Vector` and not a `Vector`. The correct syntax is as follows:

```
for(int i=0; i < 100; i++)
    cout<<(*v[i]).norm()<<endl;
```

The parentheses in `(*v[i]).norm()` are needed. The `*` dereferencing operator has lower precedence than the `.` selection operator. This usage occurs often enough that there is a special operator `->` that combines dereferencing and selection. It may be used as follows:

```
for(int i=0; i < 100; i++)
    cout<<v[i]->norm()<<endl;
```

We will look at another example of the element selection through pointer operator `->`. Consider the C `struct`

```
struct node{
    double val;
    struct node *next;
};
```

A `struct` is a package of data items. Here the two data items of `struct node` are `val` and a pointer to the next node. The pointer `next` is a link from one node to the next. A series of nodes may be chained together to form a linked list.

Figure 1.6 shows a linked list with each node pointing to the next. The variable `llist` points to the beginning of the list. The `next` pointer of the last node is set to `NULL`.

The following function finds the length of a linked list:

llist

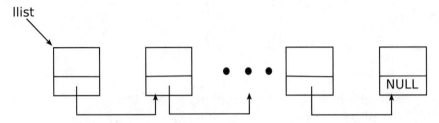

Figure 1.6: Schematic view of a linked list.

```
int llen(struct node *llist){
    int len = 0;
    while(llist != NULL){
        llist = llist ->next;
        len ++;
    }
    return len;
}
```

The element selection through pointer operator `->` occurs frequently in the context of linked lists, trees, and graphs.

Abstraction features of C++

The C++ language has a number of powerful features to bring programming closer to ideas and concepts intrinsic to the problem domain. Classes that arise later are all narrowly defined, provide a single service, and do not use these features. The `Vector` class defined above attempts to capture the abstract notion of vectors. C++ has a number of abstraction features beyond the basic class mechanism we have studied.

C++ supports object-oriented programming through inheritance of classes, multiple inheritance, and virtual and pure virtual functions. On many occasions, a single problem morphs into multiple instances, each of which has its own distinctive features while sharing a great deal in common with other instances. Object-oriented programming is the best way to tackle such problems.

An example of a problem well suited to object-oriented programming is the implementation of file systems. A file system creates the concept of file, which may be read, written, opened, and closed in standard ways. File systems vary in the way they cache data, store meta information, and other respects. Yet they have a great deal in common. In addition, each file system is ultimately realized on disparate storage devices.

Mapping of file systems to devices too can be organized using object-oriented techniques. Another example is the implementation of a graphics library for plotting that supports a variety of backends.

Object-oriented programming can be done in plain C as well as using function pointers. However, it becomes far more laborious. Object-oriented techniques do not really come up in this book, although we do use templates on one occasion in chapter 8. Therefore, we include the following basic example of a templated function:

```
1  template<class Num> Num sum(Num *arr, int len){
2       Num ans;
3       ans = 0;
4       for(int i=0; i < len; i++)
5           ans += arr[i];
6       return ans;
7  }
```

In this function, `Num` is a generic class or type. It can stand for `int` or `double` or some user-defined class that overloads the operator `+=` (line 5) and therefore supports addition. If the template is instantiated by setting `Num` to a user-defined class, it must also support the empty constructor (line 2) as well as assignment to zero (line 3).

A templated function may be invoked as shown below.

```
1       int x[5] = {1, 2, 3, 4, 5};
2       cout<<"1 + ... + 5 = "<<sum(x, 5)<<endl;
3       double y[5] = {6, 7, 8, 9, 10};
4       cout<<"6 + ... + 10 = "<<sum(y, 5)<<endl;
```

A templated function is called just like an ordinary function as evident from the invocations of `sum()` on lines 2 and 4. Because `x[]` is an array of `int`s, the C++ compiler replaces the generic type `Num` by `int` to generate code for a new function. On line 2, `sum(x,5)` invokes that function. However, `sum(y,5)` on line 4 invokes a quite different function generated by replacing `Num` by `double`.

1.3.2   Aitken transformation in C++

The source files `Aitken.cpp`, `Leibniz.cpp`, and `Logseries.cpp` contain the C++
implementation of the Aitken transformation and its application to the Leibniz and
log series. The listing below is of the C++ header file `Aitken.hh`.

```
1 #ifndef AitkenAugust09DVjli
2 #define AitkenAugust09DVjli
3 #include "Vector.hh"
4 void Aitken(const Vector& seq1, Vector& seq2);
5 void Aitken(Vector& seq);
6 double AitkenE(const Vector& seq, int printflag=0);
7 #endif
```

This header file declares three functions, two of which have the same name. The
function name `Aitken` is overloaded (lines 4 and 5). We can make the function call
`Aitken(v,w)`, where v and w are both `Vectors`. After the call, the `const` in the
first declaration guarantees that v is not changed. The use of `const` simplifies the
documentation of this function. The other way to make the function call takes the
form `Aitken(v)`. In this later usage, the transformed sequence overwrites the original
data, and the last two entries are set to 0. We can get away with using the same
name for two different functions because the compiler can tell them apart by looking
at the list of arguments.

Although there is just one declaration for `AitkenE()` (line 6), it can be called with
one or two arguments. If we call it in the form `AitkenE(v)`, the compiler interprets
the call as `Aitken(v, 0)`. The declaration of `AitkenE()` (line 13) gives its second
parameter as `int printflag=0`, thus indicating to the compiler that the second argument assumes the default value of 0 if it is omitted. We can also call it in the
form `AitkenE(v,1)`, where the value of the second argument is given explicitly as 1.
Usually it is best to use the default argument facility only for the last argument.

The function `AitkenE()` transforms the sequence repeatedly until the sequence
has only one or two numbers. The function `Aitken()` listed below performs a single
transformation of the sequence.

```
1 void Aitken(Vector& seq1){
2     int len = seq1.getSize();
3     for(int i=0; i < len-2; i++){
```

```
 4            double a = seq1(i);
 5            double b = seq1(i+1);
 6            double c = seq1(i+2);
 7            seq1(i) = a - (b-a)*(b-a)/(a-2*b+c);
 8        }
 9        seq1(len-2) = 0;//invalid entries
10        seq1(len-1) = 0;
11  }
```

Entries of the `Vector` object `seq1` are accessed on lines 4, 5, 6, 9, and 10. Each one of these accesses is resolved using the overloaded function call operator and is not a simple array look-up.

The function `AitkenE()` listed below is defined in the source file `Aitken.cpp`. It uses the shadowing capability of the `Vector` class. It repeatedly transforms the sequence, and each transformation is effected using a call to `Aitken()` on line 13.

```
 1  double AitkenE(const Vector& seq, int printflag){
 2      int len = seq.getSize();
 3      Vector myseq(len);
 4      myseq = seq;
 5      Vector v;
 6      v.shadow(seq);
 7      int n = len/2;
 8      if(len%2==0)
 9          n--;
10      if(printflag==1)
11          printseq(v);//defined in Aitken.cpp
12      for(int i=0; i < n; i++){
13          Aitken(v);//defined in Aitken.cpp
14          v.shadow(v, 0, v.getSize()-2);
15          if(printflag==1)
16              printseq(v);
17      }
18      int indx = v.getSize()-1; //can be 0 or 1
19      return v(indx);
20  }
```

The function `AitkenE()` uses shadows instead of creating new `Vector`s of different lengths repeatedly. After each invocation of `Aitken(v)` on line 13, `v` is made a shadow of itself, with the last two entries dropped, on line 14.

Object files are produced from `Aitken.cpp`, `Leibniz.cpp`, and `Logseries.cpp` using the `icpc` compiler with the `-c` option. The linking command builds the executable.

```
icpc -c Aitken.o
icpc -c Leibniz.o
icpc -o Leibniz.exe Leibniz.o Aitken.o
```

The executable `Logseries.exe` is built similarly. Instead of `icpc`, we may use `g++` or `pgCC`, and the compilation and linking syntax shown here does not change.

Exercise 1.3.1. Use the `sizeof()` facility to determine the size of a `Vector` object. Does the reported size agree with your expectation?

Exercise 1.3.2. Copy the file Vector.hh to VectorEX.hh and modify it as follows. Insert a line right at the beginning of the first three constructors that makes them print "empty constructor" or "constructor to acquire space" or "copy constructor" in a single line. Similarly, add a line right at the top of the destructor that prints "destructor." When the following code is run

```
#include "VectorEX.hh"
void donthg(Vector v1, Vector& v2){
}
int main(){
        Vector u(20), v(10), w(v), ww;
        donthg(v, w);
        donthg(u, v);
}
```

it produces exactly 12 lines of output. Explain each line carefully. Exactly which object and place in the code does each line correspond to?

Exercise 1.3.3. Explain why the default copy constructor, which copies `size`, `data`, and `owner` fields, is semantically incorrect for the `Vector` class.

Exercise 1.3.4. Consider the following C++ program.

```
#include <iostream>
using namespace std;

int main(){
   cout<<"Hello World!"<<endl;
}
```

It prints "Hello World!" as you may expect. Modify the program so that it prints

```
Big Bang
Hello World!
Apocalypse
```

You are not allowed to modify main().[17]

Exercise 1.3.5. Consider the 100 numbers $\sqrt{1}, \sqrt{2}, \ldots, \sqrt{100}$. Write a C/C++ program that partitions the numbers into two sets such that the difference of the sums of the two sets is as small in magnitude as possible. Does your program work for 1000 numbers or for 10^6 numbers?[18]

Exercise 1.3.6. Write a C/C++ program that will open a file and print the last n lines of the file. The name of the file and n are inputs to the program.

Exercise 1.3.7. Let $p(z)$ be a polynomial of nth degree with complex coefficients. The fundamental theorem of algebra states that $p(z) = 0$ has n complex roots. The Newton iteration for finding the roots is $z_{n+1} = z_n - p(z_n)/p'(z_n)$. The iteration converges to different roots depending on the initial iterate z_0. Write a C/C++ program that takes a polynomial $p(z)$ and z_0 as inputs and determines which root the Newton iteration converges to. Color the complex plane depending on which root the Newton iteration converges to.

Exercise 1.3.8. In sexagesimal, a non-negative integer is written in the form $\sum_{i=0}^{n-1} a_i \times 60^i$, where

$$a_i \in \{0, 1, \ldots, 59\}.$$

There are exactly 144 sexagesimal numbers with leading digit $a_{n-1} = 1$, $n \leq 6$, and a terminating sexagesimal expansion for their reciprocals. Determine all 144 such numbers

---

[17]This problem is based on Stroustrup (1997).
[18]This is the Floyd partitioning problem. See Knuth (1996). The Karmarkar-Karp algorithm for partitioning gives an interesting approach to this problem.

and their sexagesimal reciprocals. For $n = 6, 7, \ldots, 20$, determine the number of sexagesimal numbers with $a_{n-1} \neq 0$ and a terminating reciprocal.[19]

Exercise 1.3.9. C `structs` are like C++ classes with public data members but no function members. In the following `struct`

```
struct node{
    double x;
    struct node *next;
}
```

each node points to the next to form a linked list (see figure 1.6). The `next` field of the last node is assumed to be `NULL`. Write a function that takes a pointer to the first node in a linked list and reverses the linked list.

Exercise 1.3.10. The definition of `Aitken()` given here overwrites the input sequence. Give an implementation that does not overwrite the input sequence and that corresponds to the declaration on line 6 of `Aitken.hh` listed on page 48.

Exercise 1.3.11. Time C++ (page 48) and C (page 17) implementations of the Aitken transformation and compare.

1.4   A little Fortran

In this section, we show a bit of Fortran syntax. The syntax is deliberately Fortran 77 and not the newer varieties. When the need to use old Fortran codes arises, it is often Fortran of this variety. We do not recommend programming in Fortran.[20] The language is rigid and does not allow for dynamic data structures such as linked lists, trees, and graphs in its 77 version. Such data structures are increasingly used in scientific computing and are indispensable to computer science.

---

[19]See chapter 11 of Knuth (1996); originally published as Ancient Babylonian Algorithms in Communications of the ACM, vol. 15 (1972), with errata in vol. 19 (1976). Inakibit-Anu, priest of Anu and Antub in Uruk around 300 BC, determined 105 of the 144 sexagesimal numbers with terminating reciprocals. Inakibit-Anu's table gave the reciprocal of $60^2 + 45$ as $59 \times 60^{-3} + 15 \times 60^{-4} + 33 \times 60^{-5} + 20 \times 60^{-6}$.

[20]Ritchie (1996) has noted that the inadequacy of Fortran for systems programming became apparent as soon as Ken Thompson attempted to write Unix in Fortran in 1969. Fortran was an amazing advance in compiler theory and technology for its time but has been forgotten in the world of systems programming for more than four decades.

The core data structure in Fortran is the array. In our opinion, Fortran does not do a good job here. In Fortran, the array is thought of as a variable name, the length of the sequence, and the type of each item, which determines the size of each item in bytes. The variable name is actually a pointer (an address), but only covertly and not explicitly as in C. Fortran does not allow pointers in any generality. The Fortran array is an abstraction that strives to be close to what happens on the machine. However, it is an awkward abstraction because the notion of pointers is not thrown away but adopted covertly in a highly restricted form.

Unlike C/C++, the Fortran language does not provide access to machine capabilities. For some of the more sophisticated optimizations, the Fortran language is inadequate.

There is a belief that Fortran is faster than C/C++. This belief is a complete myth, being no more than an indication of the proficiency of those who believe in it, and will be completely dispelled later.

Part of the Fortran code for applying the Aitken iteration to the logarithmic series follow. The listing of the function `partialsum(x,n)` follows.[21] It returns the partial sum of the first n terms of the Taylor series of $\log(1 + x)$.

```
double precision function partialSum(x, n)
double precision x
integer n
double precision prod
integer i
partialSum = 0
prod = 1.0D0
do 10 i=1,n,1
    prod = prod*x
    if(mod(i,2).eq.0) then
        partialSum = partialSum - prod/i
    else
        partialSum = partialSum + prod/i
    endif
10    continue
```

---

[21] Seasoned Fortran programmers would use `implicit none` in the function definitions to preclude the compiler from assuming undeclared function parameters to be of type `integer`.

```
        return
        end
```

The `main` program listed below prints the nth partial sum, the extrapolated value using the first n partial sums, and the true value of $\log(1 + x)$ for a few values of x. It corresponds to the data shown in table 1.2. It calls the function `extrapolateSum()` in addition to `partialSum()`, but the definition of the former is not listed.

```
        program main
        double precision xlist(11), seq1(13), seq2(11)
        double precision val1, val2, val3
        double precision partialSum, extrapolateSum
        integer n, i
        xlist(11) = 1.25D0
        do 30 i=0,9,1
            xlist(i+1) = i*1.0D0/9
30      continue

        n = 13
        do 40 i=1,11,1
            val1 = partialSum(xlist(i),n)
            val2 = extrapolateSum(xlist(i),n, seq1, seq2)
            val3 = log(1+xlist(i))
            write (6, 100) val1, val2, val3
100         format(F14.10, F14.10, F14.10)
40      continue
        stop
        end
```

There are huge differences between C and Fortran in the way function calls work. Let us look at the first function call that occurs here:

```
val1 = partialSum(xlist(i),n)
```

Here `xlist` is a name for an array of `doubles` and `xlist(i)` is a name for the `i`th location in that array. Similarly, `n` and `val1` are names for locations that are big enough to hold an `int` and a `double`, respectively.

So far, nothing is really different from C. The difference is in the way the arguments of `partialSum()` are set up. The function `partialSum()` has two arguments that are

called x and n. If we were in the C world, new locations would be created, and x
and n would become names for those two new locations. In Fortran, nothing of that
sort happens. Instead, x and n merely become names for the locations named by
xlist(i) and n in the main program. So if we change x inside partialSum(), that
will change xlist(i) inside the main program. This awkward semantics is a result
of using pointers implicitly to represent arrays efficiently but not allowing pointers
into the language.[22] To reconcile these opposing tendencies, Fortran passes even int
and double arguments by reference.

1.5   References

G.A. Baker and P. Graves-Morris. *Padé Approximants*. Cambridge University Press,
   Cambridge, 2nd edition, 1996.

J.M. Borwein and P.B. Borwein. *Pi and the AGM: A Study in Analytic Number
   Theory and Computational Complexity*. Wiley-Interscience, New York, 1998.

C. Brezinski and M. Redivo Zaglia. *Extrapolation Methods: Theory and Practice*.
   North Holland, Amsterdam, 1991.

B. Kernighan and D. Ritchie. *The C Programming Language*. Prentice-Hall, Upper
   Saddle River, 2nd edition, 1988.

Morris Kline. *Mathematical Thought from Ancient to Modern Times*, volume 1. Oxford University Press, Oxford, 1990.

D.E. Knuth. *Selected Papers on Computer Science*. Cambridge University Press,
   Cambridge, 1996.

---

[22]Languages such as Python and Java also use pointers implicitly. However, both languages have
a more abstract as well as more consistent view of objects, and the awkwardness associated with
Fortran does not arise. In Python, every variable is really a pointer to an object, and not to a
memory location as in Fortran. So if we say $x = 7$, the variable x points to the object 7. If x is
passed as an argument to a function $f(y)$, y begins to point to the object 7. The crucial difference
from Fortran is as follows: suppose we say $y = 5$ in the body of the function then y begins to point
to the object 5, and at the point of call, x *continues* to point to the object 7. Analogously to Fortran,
if x is a pointer to a large object such as a Numpy array, one may change its entries using syntax
such as $y[0] = -1$.

D.E. Knuth. *The Art of Computer Programming*, volume 3, Sorting and Searching. Addison-Wesley, Upper Saddle River, 2nd edition, 1998.

D. Kozen. *Automata and Computability*. Springer-Verlag, New York, 1997.

D. Ritchie. The development of the C language. In T.J. Bergin and R.G. Gibson, editors, *History of Programming Languages II*. Addison-Wesley, Upper Saddle River, 1996.

K.V. Sarma. *A History of the Kerala School of Hindu Astronomy*. Vishveshvaranand Institute, Hoshiarpur, 1992.

B. Stroustrup. *The C++ Programming Language*. Addison-Wesley, Reading, Massachusetts, 3rd edition, 1997.

R.S. Westfall. *Never at Rest: A Biography of Isaac Newton*. Cambridge University Press, Cambridge, 1980.

Chapter 2

C/C++: Libraries and Makefiles

Splitting a program into several source and header files, as in the previous chapter, is essential but not sufficiently powerful in itself to capture the conceptual relationships of many programs. When the interdependence between the modules is complex, it is no longer adequate to put all the source files in a single directory. The source files must be organized into directories and subdirectories to bring greater order and clarity.

There are two powerful ideas for bringing greater modularity into C/C++ programs, and both of them will be introduced in this chapter. The first idea is to combine object files into libraries, and the second idea is to organize program sources into a source tree.

In outline, a C/C++ program is built as follows. There are program sources to begin with. These are turned into object files, which mainly consist of machine instructions, by the compiler. The linker eliminates unresolved external references and merges the object files to produce an executable. The two ideas for bringing greater modularity occur at different points in this process.

The organization of sources into a tree precedes both compilation and linking. The solution to most problems naturally breaks up into several components. For example, an image-processing program may be broken up into modules for handling different image formats, modules for displaying images, modules for image transformations, modules for image enhancements, modules for combining images, and so on. If the sources for each of these functions is put in separate directories, the directories become modules, and the sources are now submodules within these directories. Although an overly deep hierarchy can cause complications and must be used only for truly complex programs, one can easily imagine directories within directories so that the source files are grouped into modules, and these modules are grouped into higher level modules, and so on in a tree-like hierarchy.

In contrast, libraries follow compilation and precede linking. The linking model is always flat. It does not matter how or if the sources are arranged in a tree. The linker takes in a flat list of object files and smashes them together to form an executable, regardless of where the object files or their sources are located. A library is simply a group of object files that may be fed to a linker as a single unit.

It is easy to see why libraries are so useful. An image-processing program may use linear algebra, Fourier analysis, and yet other tools. Although linear algebra and Fourier analysis are used, those functions are extraneous to image processing, and it is not right to include them within an image-processing source tree. Programs for optimization, solving differential equations, clustering, and other tasks have an equal right to use linear algebra and Fourier analysis. Thus, the most natural thing to do here is to combine all the linear algebra object files into a linear algebra library and all the Fourier analysis object files into a Fourier analysis library. Commercial vendors may sell libraries of object files without the sources to safeguard their profitability.

Section 2.1 exhibits an important feature of the translation of C/C++/Fortran sources to object files. In the previous chapter, we have looked at C/C++/Fortran sources. Several names appear within these sources. There are names of variables used to hold data and then there are names of functions. If a function or a variable defined in one source may be used by another, the name of that function or variable is retained in the object file, although in a transmuted form. An object file uses the same machine language (we will look at machine instructions only in the next chapter) and has nearly the same format, syntax, and semantics regardless of whether it is from a C, C++, or Fortran source. However, the transmutation of names from source to object file is different in C, C++, and Fortran. Once the convention for transmuting names is understood, it is easy to call Fortran programs from C/C++. The convention is the simplest and the most natural in C. In addition, C uses a relatively simple runtime library. It is typical to have to use C in the middle if one wants interoperability between other languages such as Java or Python.

Section 2.2 is a brief introduction to the BLAS/LAPACK linear algebra libraries. There is no area of mathematics that is as ubiquitous in applications as linear algebra, and there are no scientific libraries as widely used as BLAS/LAPACK. Every scientific programmer needs some familiarity with these libraries. Optimizing or even implementing the BLAS/LAPACK libraries would be an impossible task for almost any programmer or team. There is much to be gained from using good libraries whenever they are available. Like their bricks and mortar counterparts, libraries are a powerful means to propagate knowledge.

When a program is split into several source files and the source files are grouped into modules, compiling source files into object files and then generating executables become tedious, repetitive, and error-prone. Makefiles and the `make` utility bring organization and coherence to compilation and linking. Section 2.3 gives an account of GNU `make`. The importance of understanding `make` cannot be overstated. There is no such thing as modular programming in C/C++ without it. Although there are other ways to manage sources, the `make` utility is the oldest and most widely used.

The final section of this chapter, section 2.4, makes a transition to the rest of the book. In addition, it demonstrates the importance of well-optimized libraries. An implementation of the Fast Fourier Transform (FFT), one of the most important algorithms in science, which is coded expertly but without regard to computer architecture, is compared with libraries that are cognizant of computer architecture. The optimized libraries are found to be nearly an order of magnitude faster. Section 2.4 also shows how unpredictable compilers can be. A slight change degrades performance of one of the optimized libraries by nearly a factor of two.

2.1 Mixed-language programming

Compilers translate `.c` (C), `.cpp` (C++), and `.f` (Fortran) sources into `.o` object files. The `.o` object files are mainly a sequence of machine instructions. If the source file calls functions defined externally, which is the typical scenario, there will be unresolved names in the corresponding object file. In section 2.1.1, we look at the map from sources to object files as a precursor to mixed-language programming.

The manner in which for-loops and other constructs map to machine instructions is the topic of the next chapter. In this section, we only look at the map from globally

visible names in the sources to names in the object file. The `aitken.c` source looks
as follows:

```
#include <assert.h>
#include "aitken.h"
void aitken(const double* seq1, double* seq2,
            int len){
...
}


double aitkenExtrapolate(double *seq1, double* seq2,
                int len){
...
}
```

In this source, only the function names `aitken` and `aitkenExtrapolate` are globally
visible. Names of arguments are local to the function body. Other variables defined
inside the function body have only local scope as well. Names with local scope are
not mapped to object files.

   The CPP and Fortran sources for the Aitken iteration define functions with similar
names. The main point of section 2.1.1 is that the same name maps to a different
name in the object file depending on whether the source is C, C++, or Fortran. Once
this point is understood, making C, C++, and Fortran work together becomes much
simpler. The mapping is the most straightforward in C, where names are unchanged
from sources to object files. In Fortran, the map is a little more complicated. In C++,
the mapping is a great deal more complicated.

   In section 2.1.2, we explain how to call Fortran from C or C++. Beyond the
transmutation of names, which differs between the three languages, the additional
issue of runtime libraries has to be dealt with.

2.1.1   Transmutation of names from source to object files

A `.o` object file is mostly a collection of machine instructions that translate the
corresponding source into machine-intelligible language. If the source has a statement
such as `a=b+c`, for example, the names `a`, `b`, `c` typically disappear from the object
file. The compiler decides the memory locations or registers that these variable names

map to. What is found in the object file is simply an add instruction of some type with operands being either memory locations or registers.

Not all names present in the source disappear, however. Those names present in the source that survive in the object file are some of the most important. These are, typically, names of functions that may be called from other object files or names of functions defined in external object files that are called from this one. Variable names also may have global scope.

The names present in the object file are needed to resolve undefined references during linking of object files. The names may not be exactly the same as in the original source. Compilers may alter names before mapping them from source to object files. In C, the names are not altered at all. In C++, the names must necessarily be altered to support the overloading facility that allows the same name for multiple functions. In Fortran, too, the names are altered, although the only reason here seems to be to maintain compatibility with earlier conventions.

The GNU/Linux command nm[1] lists the names present in an object file. To examine the object file `aitken.o`, we use the command `nm aitken.o`. A part of the output of that command follows.

```
1                        U _intel_fast_memcpy
2  0000000000000000  T aitken
3  0000000000000070  T aitkenExtrapolate
```

The second and third lines verify that names are unchanged when a C source is transformed to an object file. This object file was produced using Intel's `icc`. The first line refers to a function call inserted by the compiler that was not present in our source. That name is undefined, but the linker will supply the appropriate definition. Any compiler may insert function names during optimization.

The function names are preceded by an address that is 16 hexadecimal digits long and by the letter `T`. The letter is `T` because both functions reside in the text area of the object code. The letter would be `C` for the name of a Fortran common block or a C global variable defined outside the scope of any function. The hexadecimal addresses indicate that code for `aitken()` begins at 0 and for `aitkenExtrapolate()` at 70 (hexadecimal). These addresses will be shifted by the linker when it merges several object files into a single executable.

---

[1]The nm utility is part of GNU's binutils package.

A partial listing of the output of `nm leibniz.o` is included to make one more point about the transmutation of names from C sources to object files.

```
                    U  __intel_new_proc_init_H
                    U  _intel_fast_memcpy
                    U  aitken
00000000000002e0    T  leibniz
0000000000000000    T  main
                    U  printf
0000000000000280    T  printseq
```

This object file two includes a couple of names introduced by `icc`. These appear at the top and are undefined. There are two more undefined names—`aitken` and `printf`. The `leibniz.c` source calls the function `aitken()`, which is externally defined. Within the object file `leibniz.o`, that name is undefined.

At this point, we have a clear picture of what the linker does. The linking command

```
   icc -o leibniz.exe aitken.o leibniz.o
```

concatenates the object files while resolving the undefined symbols. The symbol `aitken`, which is unresolved in `leibniz.o`, is resolved using the definition in the object file `aitken.o`. The linker uses a runtime library to resolve the undefined symbol `printf`. Likewise, the undefined symbols inserted by the compiler are resolved using internal libraries.

The C function names survive intact in the object code. The Fortran names change only slightly. The command `nm logseriesf.o` produces the following output (partial listing):

```
 1   0000000000000000   T  MAIN__
 2                       U  __intel_new_proc_init_H
 3                       U  aitkenextrapolate_
 4   0000000000000280   T  extrapolatesum_
 5                       U  for_set_reentrancy
 6                       U  for_stop_core
 7                       U  for_write_seq_fmt
 8                       U  for_write_seq_fmt_xmit
 9                       U  log
10   0000000000000230   T  partialsum_
```

The names `extrapolatesum` and `partialsum` have changed to `extrapolatesum_` (line 8) and `partialsum_` (line 15) in the object files. Fortran names are typically changed by appending an underscore at the end. The name `aitkenextrapolate_` (line 7) is undefined and has to be resolved using another object file. All the other undefined names are introduced by the Intel Fortran compiler and are resolved using standard libraries by the Fortran linker.

Unlike in C or Fortran, the transmutation of names in C++ is quite extensive. The command `nm Aitken.o` produces output that is much more complicated. We show only part of the output.

```
0000000000000090  T  _Z6AitkenR6Vector
0000000000000350  T  _Z6AitkenRK6VectorRS_
0000000000000110  T  _Z7AitkenERK6Vectori
0000000000000000  r  _Z7AitkenERK6Vectori$$LSDA
0000000000000030  T  _Z8printseqRK6Vector
0000000000000000  W  _ZN6VectorD1Ev
                  U  _ZNSt8ios_base4InitC1Ev
                  U  _ZNSt8ios_base4InitD1Ev
                  U  _intel_fast_memcpy
                  U  printf
```

None of the names in Aitken.cpp can be easily recognized here. The transmutation of names in C++ follows involved rules and is called name mangling. We can issue the command `nm --demangle Aitken.o` to get names in a form that is easily recognizable.

```
1   0000000000000090  T  Aitken(Vector&)
2   0000000000000350  T  Aitken(Vector const&, Vector&)
3   0000000000000110  T  AitkenE(Vector const&, int)
4   0000000000000000  r  _Z7AitkenERK6Vectori$$LSDA
5   0000000000000030  T  printseq(Vector const&)
6   0000000000000000  W  Vector::~Vector()
7                     U  std::ios_base::Init::Init()
8                     U  std::ios_base::Init::~Init()
9                     U  _intel_fast_memcpy
10                    U  printf
```

In the demangled listing, we can recognize not only the function names but also the types of the arguments.

Because of the overloading mechanism, several different C++ functions can have the same name. The names have to be mangled in the object code to distinguish between different functions with the same name. The C++ standard strongly recommends that each compiler use its own conventions for name mangling. If that suggestion is heeded, object code produced by one C++ compiler cannot be linked with the object code produced by another C++ compiler. However, the Intel C++ compiler uses the same name mangling as the defacto g++ standard on Linux (and the same as Microsoft vc++ on Windows). Therefore, in principle at least, C++ object files compiled using icpc and g++ can be linked together. Linking g++ object files using the icpc linker appears reasonably safe but not the other way around.

2.1.2   Linking Fortran programs with C and C++

In scientific computing, C and C++ functions may need to call Fortran routines. Scientific software from earlier generations tends to be in Fortran 77.

To use Fortran functions within C or C++ programs, the naming used for the Fortran functions in C or C++ has to be cognizant of the way the names in the source files are altered in the object file. We want the names to agree in the object files because it is the object files and not the source files that get linked against each other. If the naming is right, the linker takes care of resolving the function calls.

Let us implement the repeated application of Aitken transformations to partial sums of the Leibniz series by mixing Fortran and C programs. Part of the output of nm aitkenf.o is given below.

```
                       U _intel_fast_memcpy
  0000000000000000 T aitken_
  0000000000000220 T aitkenextrapolate_
                       U for_write_seq_fmt
                       U for_write_seq_lis
  0000000000000150 T printseq_
```

We will write a C program that calls the functions defined in aitkenf.o to extrapolate the Leibniz series to illustrate the nature of mixed-language programming.

The C code includes the following declarations near its beginning.

```
extern void aitken_(double *seq1, double *seq2,
            int *len);
extern void printseq_(double *seq, int *len);
extern double aitkenextrapolate_(double *seq1,
                 double* seq2, int * len);
```

The **extern** keyword indicates that the three function names that are declared must be found in some other object file. The underscore is appended to the names to follow the convention of the Fortran compiler. This convention is common among Fortran compilers but not universal. The three arguments to **aitken_** have types **double ***, **double ***, and **int ***. The first few lines of the definition of **aitken()** in the Fortran source are as follows.

```
subroutine aitken(seq1, seq2, len)
    double precision seq1(*), seq2(*)
    integer len
```

The first argument of **aitken()** must be an array of double-precision numbers; once the function is called, **seq1** becomes another name for that array. The first argument is nothing other than a pointer to a double, although in Fortran we simply think about it as an array not as a pointer. When calling the function from C, we have to drop that pretension and say explicitly that the first argument will be a pointer to **double**. The last argument to **aitken()** is an integer type in Fortran. Once the function is called, **len** becomes another name for that argument. When calling the function from C, we have to be explicit and specifically state that the last argument is of pointer to **int** type (and not of type **int**). Every use of **len** inside the Fortran code of **aitken()** will in effect dereference that pointer.

The C function below calls the Fortran routines. The **leibniz()** function used to generate partial sums of the Leibniz series (see line 6 below) is in C. Its definition was given earlier (see page 21).

```
1  int main(){
2      const int len = 13;
3      double seq1[len];
4      double seq2[len];
5      int n, i, j; int farg;
6      leibniz(seq1, len);
```

```
 7         n = len/2;
 8         if(len%2==0)
 9                 n--;
10         for(i=0;  i < n;  i++){
11                 farg = len-2*i;  printseq_(seq1,&farg);
12                 aitken_(seq1,  seq2,  &farg);
13                 for(j=0;  j < len-2*(i+1);  j++)
14                         seq1[j] = seq2[j];
15         }
16         if(len%2==0)
17                 {farg = 2;  printseq_(seq1,  &farg);}
18         else
19                 {farg = 1;  printseq_(seq1,  &farg);}
20 }
```

Line by line, this is almost the same as the C program for extrapolating the Leibniz
series using functions defined in C (see page 22). There are only a few differences.
Using function names with the underscore appended is the most obvious one. Another
difference is that we invoke `printseq_` as `printseq_(seq1, &farg)` after taking care
to store `len-2*i` in `farg` on line 11. Similarly, the call to `aitken_()` on line 12
gives the third argument as `&farg`. A value such as `len-2*i` cannot be passed as an
argument to a Fortran function. The value must be stored in a memory location, and
the address of that memory location must be passed as a pointer. On lines 17 and
18, the second argument of `printseq_` is `&farg` for the same reason.

To build the executable, we save the C source (comprised of the **extern** declarations, the definition of `main()` given above, and the definition of `leibniz()` on
page 21) in the file `leibnizFinC.c`. The following three commands are issued using
a makefile.

```
icc -c leibnizFinC.c
ifort -c  aitkenf.f
icc -o leibnizFinC.exe leibnizFinC.o aitkenf.o
```

The first two commands create the object files. The -c option tells `icc` to compile
only. The third command attempts to build the executable using the object files. This
command uses the `icc` linker and not the Fortran linker, which leads to a problem.
We have seen already that the object code for `aitkenf.o` contains some undefined

names that have to do with the workings of the `ifort` compiler. An `ifort` linker would automatically take care of resolving those names, but the `icc` linker does not. So we have to do something explicit to resolve the undefined names created by the `ifort` compiler.

To figure out what to do, we will build an executable using Fortran object files and the following command.

```
ifort -v -o leibnizf.exe leibnizf.o aitkenf.o
```

The `-v` option to the `ifort` linker asks the linker to be verbose and point out every step of what it does. The linker produces quite an eyeful. From that output, it appears that the Fortran runtime library is fetched by `-lifcore`.

We are now in a position to tackle the linking of `aitkenf.o` produced from Fortran source with `leibnizFinC.o` produced from a C source. We issue the command

```
icc -o leibnizFinC.exe leibnizFinC.o aitkenf.o \
        -lifcore
```

Fortunately, the `-lifcore` option resolves all the undefined names and an executable is generated. With the GNU compilers, the `-lgfortran` option ensures that the Fortran runtime libraries are linked.

Linking object files generated from Fortran with C++ object files presents a new issue. Suppose we copied the C source file `leibnizFinC.c` as follows:

```
cp leibnizFinC.c leibnizFinCPP.cpp
```

We can try to build the executable as follows.

```
icpc -c leibnizFinCPP.cpp
ifort  -c  aitkenf.f
icpc -o leibnizFinCPP.exe leibnizFinCPP.o \
        aitkenf.o -lifcore
```

The linking will fail because of C++ name mangling. In `leibnizFinCPP.cpp`, we have the extern declaration

```
extern void aitken_(double * seq1, double * seq2,
                        int * len);
```

When it generates object code for that source file, the `icpc` compiler assumes that `aitken_` is externally defined and the name of a *C++* function. So it mangles the name. Issuing the `nm leibnizFinCPP.o` command shows the mangled name to be as follows:

```
U _Z7aitken_PdS_Pi
```

Of course there is no such mangled name in the `aitkenf.o` file, and the linking has to fail. To get around this problem, we have to change all the three `extern` declarations in `leibnizFinCPP.cpp` slightly. For instance, the declaration of `aitken_` should be as follows:

```
extern "C" void aitken_(double * seq1, double * seq2,
                        int * len);
```

Here we are specifically telling the compiler that the name `aitken_` has C linkage. So the C++ compiler will not mangle that name.

The C++ language is an extension of the C language. Every C program should be a valid C++ program. But name mangling becomes an issue if we want to call C programs from C++ programs. For instance, if `aitken.h` is the header file for `aitken.c`, any C source can include the header, and the linker will find the definitions of the names declared in the header in `aitken.o`. However, if a C++ source includes the header, the names in the header will get mangled by the C++ compiler. The linker will not be able to find the mangled names in `aitken.o`.

There is a simple workaround that makes a C header file good for inclusion in both C and C++ sources. The workaround encloses the body of the header file within a few lines.

```
#ifdef __cplusplus
extern "C" {
#endif
...(declarations)...
#ifdef __cplusplus
}
#endif
```

As required by the standard, `__cplusplus` is defined in all C++ source files but not in C source files. If the header file is included in a C++ source file, all the declarations are enclosed in an `extern "C"{}` block and have C linkage. The C++ compiler will not mangle their names. If the header file is included in a C source file, the declarations are not enclosed in an `extern "C"{}` block.

Exercise 2.1.1. The object file of the program source

```
char *s="char *s=%c%s%c;%cmain(){printf(s,34,s,34,10,10)};%c";
main(){printf(s,34,s,34,10,10);}
```

has a name that is undefined, a name in the data segment, and a name in the text segment. Which are these? Verify using nm.

Exercise 2.1.2. Look up the nm man page and figure out the meaning of W and r designations attached to some symbols in object files compiled from C++.

Exercise 2.1.3. Use the verbose option for the linking command and make a list of all the object files and libraries that are used to build the executables `leibniz.exe` and `Leibniz.exe`, respectively.

Exercise 2.1.4. Following gcc and the GNU compiler collection, icc and icpc report all the header files that get included during compilation when invoked with the -M option. Make a list of all the header files that get included in `leibniz.c` and `Leibniz.cpp`, respectively.

Exercise 2.1.5. The `aitken.h` header file (defined on page 10) is not suitable for inclusion in a C++ source. Modify it so that it may be used in either C or C++ source files.

Suppose you are not allowed to modify it. Explain how you can still include it in a C++ source.

2.2 Using BLAS and LAPACK libraries

The basic concepts of linear algebra are matrices and vectors. Many problems in science, such as the numerical solution of partial differential equations and numerical optimization, reduce to problems in numerical linear algebra. BLAS and LAPACK are widely used numerical linear algebra libraries.[2]

The BLAS library is split into three levels. Functions for vector operations such as dot products are included in the first level, for matrix-vector operations in the second level, and for matrix-matrix operations such as matrix multiplication in the third level. The split into three levels is conceptual and reflects the historical order in which the interfaces for the BLAS functions were specified. Implementations of

---

[2]The original papers on BLAS are Lawson et al. (1979); Dongarra et al. (1988, 1990). The basic reference for LAPACK is Anderson et al. (1999). The Intel MKL manuals include documentation for BLAS and LAPACK.

BLAS and LAPACK such as MKL and ACML, which are supported by Intel and AMD, respectively, bundle all three levels of BLAS as well as LAPACK into the same library.

The specifications of the BLAS functions have been frozen for nearly three decades. However, LAPACK evolves from time to time to include new algorithms. LAPACK is built on top of BLAS. Functions for solving systems of matrices, solving linear least squares problems, finding eigenvalues, and finding singular values are found in LAPACK.

Although the BLAS specifications have been frozen for decades, implementations of BLAS have to constantly respond to the rapid changes in computer architecture. A good implementation of matrix multiplication in 1990 looks nothing like a good implementation of matrix multiplication in 2015. In the intervening decades, computer architecture has advanced to include instruction pipelines, instruction-level parallelism, multiple levels of cache memory, expanded register sets, out-of-order execution, and multiple processing cores. Good implementations optimize BLAS for all these features of modern computers.

The early specifications of BLAS were given in Fortran. However, Fortran does not provide adequate access to features of computer architecture. One cannot see the source code of commercial BLAS implementations in libraries such as MKL and ACML are coded. However, it is almost certain that BLAS functions are coded in C and in assembly language native to the computer architecture that is targeted. C functions can easily mimic the interfaces and calling conventions of Fortran subroutines.

Many LAPACK functions were coded in Fortran using BLAS years ago. The hope was that architecture-specific optimizations would be confined to BLAS as computers evolved. However, modern implementations of LAPACK functions such as LU and Cholesky factorizations use specialized algorithms that are a great deal more complicated than using the BLAS routines in a direct manner.[3]

In this chapter, our discussion is limited to programs that run on a single processor core, although the basic algorithms of dense linear algebra can be effectively adapted to many processor cores and large networks. We will discuss some of the aspects of

---

[3]For a general discussion of BLAS and LAPACK, see Demmel (1997). Toledo (1997) gives a taste of optimizing LAPACK functions such as LU factorization. For a survey of blocking algorithms in matrix computations, see Elmroth et al. (2004).

concurrent programs as they relate to numerical linear algebra in later chapters.

Our introduction to BLAS/LAPACK in this section begins with a discussion of
the representation of matrices using arrays (section 2.2.1). One may think that the
natural way to represent matrices is to use two-dimensional arrays. In fact, matrices
are represented using one-dimensional arrays, as we explain. A brief introduction to
BLAS/LAPACK functionality in section 2.2.2 is followed by the discussion of a C++
class interface in section 2.2.3. This class is unlike the general `Vector` class of the
previous chapter and more typical of the way we use C++. The class is specific, is
narrowly defined, and does just one thing, which is to provide an easy interface to
LAPACK's linear solver.

2.2.1 Arrays, matrices, and leading dimensions

We look at multidimensional arrays in C/C++ briefly, although it is nearly always
better to work with one-dimensional arrays. A two-dimensional array in C can be
defined as follows:

```
double two_d[20][40];
```

Here `two_d[][]` can be thought of as a two-dimensional array with 20 rows and 40
columns. One-dimensional arrays are almost equivalent to pointers. However, two-
dimensional arrays are not.

The array subscripting operator `[]` has left to right associativity. Therefore, the
compiler parses our definition as

```
double (two_d[20])[40];
```

In words, `two_d` is an array of size 20, each entry of which is an array of 40 doubles. In
memory, the 800 `double` locations are next to each other same as for a one-dimensional
array of size 800. However, it is illegal to say

```
double *p = two_d;
```

The value `two_d` is of type pointer to an array of 40 `doubles` and not `double *`. The
following usage would be legal.

```
double (*p)[40];
p = two_d;
```

Here `p`, like `two_d`, is a pointer to an array of 40 `doubles`. The connection of multidimensional arrays in C to pointers is not straightforward, which is the principal reason to avoid multidimensional arrays in C/C++. Legitimate uses of multidimensional arrays are rare but do exist.

Suppose we want a matrix of dimension 20×40. We can simply say

```
double a[800];
```

It is a bad idea to allocate large data structures statically.[4] More generally, we can make room for an $m \times n$ matrix as follows:

```
double *a = (double *)malloc(m*n*sizeof(double));
```

We must remember to say `free(a)` when the memory is no longer needed.

Here we come to the distinction between column-major and row-major storage. In column-major storage, the (i,j)th entry of `a[]` is accessed as

```
a[i+j*m]
```

Here $0 \le i < m$ and $0 \le j < n$. The column-major format is used by Fortran, BLAS, and LAPACK. In row-major storage, the (i,j)th entry of `a[]` is accessed as

```
a[i*n+j]
```

There is a natural way to approach the distinction between column-major format and row-major format. To access the entries of `a[]` in the order of storage, we may code as follows assuming column-major format.

```
for(int j=0; j < n; j++)
     for(int i=0; i < m; i++)
          a[i + j*m] = ...
```

Here the inner-loop is accessing the entries of column j. So columns are "innermost" in column-major format. Likewise rows are innermost in row-major storage. When a matrix (or a higher dimensional tensor) is stored in a one-dimensional array, we need two items of information to access entries of the array. First, we need the bounds of the index variables. Here the bounds are $0 \le i < m$ and $0 \le j < n$. Second, we

---

[4]Statically defined variables are allocated on the stack and the stack size is limited to the order of several MB in threaded programming. That is one half of the reason it is a bad idea to allocate large data structures on the stack. The other half is that memory allocated on the stack is not released until program termination.

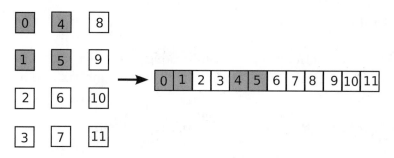

Figure 2.1: Column-major storage of a matrix in a one-dimensional array. The shaded submatrix can be extracted by setting the leading dimension to 4.

need the ordering of matrix (or tensor) indices from inner to outer. In column-major format, the row index is innermost (which corresponds to columns being innermost).

The crux of the matter is to think of row and column indices as loop variables in a loop-nest. Figure 2.1 shows a matrix with the row index i in the range $0 \leq i < 4$ and the column index j in the range $0 \leq j < 3$ laid out in a one-dimensional array with columns innermost.

If we think of i and j as loop variables in a loop-nest, a way to extract submatrices suggests itself. Suppose we want to extract the top-left 2×2 matrix shaded in figure 2.1. We can take $0 \leq i < 2$ and $0 \leq j < 2$. Assuming a is a pointer to the entry 0, we may access the (i, j)th entry of the submatrix as

```
a[i+j*4]
```

The leading dimension is 4 here and not 2 because the 2×2 matrix is embedded in a matrix whose columns have 4 entries. A submatrix is accessed using its dimensions, the pointer to its first entry, and the leading dimension.

The leading dimension is the number of entries in the innermost dimension of the array. It is probably more appropriate to call it the inner dimension, implying a connection to the innermost loop, but the current usage is well established. Suppose we want to extract the 2×2 submatrix of the matrix shown in figure 2.1 whose top-left corner is 5. We may do so by taking b=a+5 to point to the first entry, which is 5, and setting the leading dimension to 4. The leading dimension is once again the number of entries in the innermost dimension of the enclosing matrix. In this example, the gap between two columns of the submatrix straddles both columns.

2.2.2   BLAS and LAPACK

BLAS and LAPACK functions typically have long argument lists. For example, the Fortran interface to the BLAS function for multiplying a matrix and a vector has the following declaration in C:

```
extern "C" void dgemv_(char *,int *,int *,double *,double *,
                       int *,double *,int *,double *,double *,
                       int *, int );
```

This function, which has 12 arguments in total, implements the operation $y \leftarrow \alpha Ax + \beta y$ or $y \leftarrow \alpha A^T y + \beta y$. The first argument, which is a character string, allows us to specify whether the matrix A must be transposed or not. The next 10 arguments allow us to specify the entries and dimensions of the matrix A and of the vectors x and y, as well as the scalars α and β.

The last argument to `dgemv_()` is the only one that is not a pointer. Because all arguments to Fortran subroutines are passed by reference, we may expect all arguments in the C declaration of a Fortran subroutine to be pointers. Why then is the last argument not a pointer? The answer lies in the differing conventions for character strings in C and in Fortran. In C, a character string may be passed as a pointer of type `char *`. Its length is determined by the convention that the terminating character is '\0'. There is no such convention in Fortran, and the lengths of character strings must be supplied explicitly. The last argument of type `int` must be the length of the first argument, which is a character string. This last argument is invisible in Fortran as the Fortran compiler takes care to supply it surreptitiously.[5]

The naming convention used by BLAS/LAPACK is described by table 2.1. According to that convention, `DGETRF` is the name of the LAPACK function for triangular factorization of general matrices with double-precision entries. As we already mentioned, many LAPACK functions were written in Fortran long ago. If we want to call an LAPACK Fortran routine named `DGETRF` from C, we have to be aware of the convention for altering names when Fortran source files are converted to object code. However, to save us the trouble, the header file `mkl_lapack.h,` which is included by the header file `mkl.h`, allows many possible names for the same function.

---

[5]It is typical for Fortran compilers to use an additional argument at the end to indicate the length of a character string, but this practice is not mandated by the Fortran standard.

S	single precision	GE	general	TRF	triangular factorization
D	double precision	GT	general triangular	TRS	triangular solve
C	complex single precision	PB	positive definite banded	LSS	least squares solver
Z	complex double precision	SP	symmetric packed storage	SVD	singular values
		TB	triangular banded	EV	eigenvalues

Table 2.1: Convention for naming functions in BLAS and LAPACK. Function names are formed by adjoining codes in columns 1, 3, and 5. For instance, DGETRF() implements triangular factorization of general matrices with double-precision entries. Columns 3 and 5 list only a small subset of the possible codes.

```
void DGETRF( MKL_INT *m, MKL_INT *n, double *a, MKL_INT
    *lda, MKL_INT *ipiv, MKL_INT *info );
void DGETRF_( MKL_INT *m, MKL_INT *n, double *a,
    MKL_INT *lda, MKL_INT *ipiv, MKL_INT *info );
void dgetrf( MKL_INT *m, MKL_INT *n, double *a, MKL_INT
    *lda, MKL_INT *ipiv, MKL_INT *info );
void dgetrf_( MKL_INT *m, MKL_INT *n, double *a,
    MKL_INT *lda, MKL_INT *ipiv, MKL_INT *info );
```

These four names are all bound to the same function in the object code of the library. So we may call the function by any one of the four names. MKL_INT is used as a synonym for int to facilitate porting the library to systems with different conventions for int and long int. The parameters m and n of dgetrf_ are the number of rows and columns of the matrix whose (i, j)th entry is a[i+j*lda].

Triangular factorizations are useful for solving matrix systems. The following is a

2×2 example:

$$\begin{pmatrix} 0 & 1 \\ 1 & 0 \end{pmatrix} \begin{pmatrix} 5 & -3 \\ 10 & 1 \end{pmatrix} = \begin{pmatrix} 1 & 0 \\ 1/2 & 1 \end{pmatrix} \begin{pmatrix} 10 & 1 \\ 0 & -3.5 \end{pmatrix}.$$

The left-most matrix flips the rows to ensure that the subdiagonal entries of the lower triangular factor are at most 1 in magnitude. Such row pivoting promotes numerical stability.

DGETRF carries out the triangular factorization in place, and when the function returns, the lower and upper triangular factors will be stored using the same array a. The unit diagonal of the lower triangular matrix is not stored. The row that ends up as the ith row after pivoting is ipiv[i] (ipiv must be allocated as an integer array of length m before the function is called). The last parameter info returns information about possible errors: if *info=0, the execution was successful; if *info=-i, the ith argument had an illegal value; and if *info=i with $i = 1, \ldots, m$, the input matrix is singular and the $(i - 1, i - 1)$ entry of the upper triangular factor is zero.

After triangular factorization, matrix systems are solved using DGETRS. Here TRS is the code for triangular solve. Within MKL, there are four possible names for the same function as shown by declarations in mkl_lapack.h. One of these is dgetrs_():

```
void dgetrs_( char *trans , MKL_INT *n,
              MKL_INT *nrhs , double *a,
              MKL_INT *lda , MKL_INT *ipiv ,
              double *b, MKL_INT *ldb ,
              MKL_INT *info );
```

Before this function is called, the matrix stored in the array a must have undergone triangular factorization. The first argument to this function is a character string named trans. This string allows us to ask for the solution of the transposed system. The system is not transposed if trans='N' but is transposed if trans='T'. When the Fortran function is called from C, we must ordinarily pass the length of the string explicitly as the last argument. However, MKL takes advantage of the way strings are handled by LAPACK's Fortran routines and does not require us to pass that last argument.

Once A has been factorized as $PA = LU$, where P is the pivoting matrix and L and U are lower and upper triangular factors, respectively, the solution of $Ax = b$ is calculated by solving $Ly = P^{-1}b$ for y and then $Ux = y$ for x. In a triangular system such as

$$
\begin{aligned}
l_{11}x_1 &= b_1 \\
l_{21}x_1 + l_{22}x_2 &= b_2 \\
&\vdots \\
l_{n1}x_1 + \cdots + l_{nn}x_n &= b_n
\end{aligned}
$$

the first equation is solved for x_1, the second equation for x_2, and so on. The numerical stability of this obvious back substitution algorithm is quite subtle.[6]

2.2.3   C++ class interface to BLAS/LAPACK

The `Vector` class of section 1.3.1 is an attempt to capture the general concept of vectors. The `LU_Solve` class of this section is narrowly defined. It does just one thing, which is to provide an easy interface to LAPACK's LU solver functions `dgetrf()` and `dgetrs()`.

The class is defined (in the header file `lusolve.hh`) as follows:

```
class LU_Solve{
private:
      int dim;
      double *A;
      int *ipiv;
public:
      LU_Solve(double *a, int dimi);
      ~LU_Solve();
      void factorize();
      void solve(double *v);
};
```

In the `Vector` class, the member functions were defined within the class definition itself. In the `LU_Solve` class, the member functions are declared as part of the class definition, but they are defined separately. The class constructor `LU_Solve()` takes the matrix to be solved as well as its dimension as arguments. The member function `factorize()` factorizes the matrix. Linear systems are solved using the member

---

[6]See Higham (2002).

function `solve()`. The argument `v` is the right-hand side at entry to the member function. It is overwritten by the solution at exit. The `factorize()` function must be invoked immediately after a class object is defined, and it must be invoked just once. Once the matrix is factorized, any number of linear systems may be solved using `LU_Solve::solve()`.

The BLAS/LAPACK functions for LU factorization are cumbersome to call directly. The `LU_Solve` class is a hassle-free interface. To solve two linear systems of dimension 1000, we may code as follows:

```
double *A = (double *)malloc(81*1000*1000);
... initialize A ...
double *v = (double *)malloc(11*2*1000);
double *w = v + 1000;
... initialize v and w ...

LU_Solve lu(A, 1000);
lu.factorize();
lu.solve(v);
lu.solve(w);

... report/graph v and w ...

free(v);
free(A);
```

Here `lu.solve(v)` overwrites `v` with the solution and likewise for `w`.

The class constructor is defined (in `lusolve.cpp`) as follows:

```
1 LU_Solve::LU_Solve(double *a, int dimi)
2        :dim(dimi)
3 {
4        A = new double[dim*dim];
5        ipiv = new int[dim];
6        for(int i=0; i < dim*dim; i++)
7              A[i] = a[i];
8 }
```

There is a bit of new syntax here. On line 2, the colon introduces the member initializer list. The only entry of that list is `dim(dimi)`, where `dim` is a data item in the class object being constructed and `dimi` is an argument to the constructor. Saying `dim(dimi)` is equivalent to calling the constructor of the class that `dim` belongs to with `dimi` as the argument. Because `dim` is an `int`, which is a basic type, it is equivalent to saying `dim=dimi` at the beginning of the function. On lines 4 and 5, `A` and `ipiv` are allocated using the `new` operator (instead of `malloc()`). The for-loop copies the input matrix to `A[]`.

The member functions of the class `LU_Solve` are declared within the namespace `LU_Solve` introduced by the class definition. When the member functions are defined externally, their names must be qualified using `LU_Solve::` as for the constructor above. The names of the other three member functions are similarly qualified in `lusolve.cpp`.

```cpp
LU_Solve::~LU_Solve(){
    delete[] A;
    delete[] ipiv;
}

void LU_Solve::factorize(){
    int m = dim;
    int n = dim;
    int lda = dim;
    int info;
    dgetrf_(&m, &n, A, &lda, ipiv, &info);
}

void LU_Solve::solve(double *v){
    char trans[3] = "N ";
    int nrhs = 1;
    int lda = dim;
    int ldv  = dim;
    int info;
    dgetrs_(trans, &dim, &nrhs, A, &lda, ipiv, v,
```

```
                        &ldv, &info);
    }
```

The simplicity of the `LU_Solve` interface to LAPACK's LU solver comes at the cost of lesser generality. The member function `factorize()` assumes the matrix to be square, with its leading dimension exactly equal to the size of its columns. Similarly, `solve()` assumes that the number of right-hand sides is `nrhs=1` to offer a simpler interface.

Some LAPACK routines, including triangular solve, are optimized for multiple right-hand sides in the MKL library. Making repeated calls instead of a single call with a suitable `nrhs` may degrade program speed considerably.

Narrow classes such as `LU_Solve` are simple to code but can still be quite useful. All C++ classes defined in this book from here onward are of the same type.

If the Intel compilers and the MKL library are used, one may include the header file `mkl.h`, which includes declarations of BLAS/LAPACK functions. One simply needs to pass the `-mkl` option to the compiler and it will look for the header file in the right place. Linking is equally easy. One needs to pass the `-mkl=sequential` option to the linker to link the sequential version of the MKL library.

If the GNU compilers are used, compiling and linking open source BLAS and LAPACK libraries can be equally easy. If the header file is put in a standard location such as `/usr/include`, there is no need to do anything special when the CBLAS header file `cblas.h` is included. One may need to explicitly declare the LAPACK functions with extern C linkage. Likewise, if BLAS functions are used, instead of CBLAS, they too may need to be declared explicitly. If the libraries are put in a standard place such as `/usr/lib`, it suffices to pass options `-lblas` and `-llapack` to link the BLAS and LAPACK libraries. The online MKL link advisor may be consulted to link MKL libraries with `gcc/g++`.

Exercise 2.2.1. Assume that a square matrix of dimension `dim` is stored in the array `a[]` with leading dimension equal to `lda`. Assume that `dim` is divisible by 4. Write a function

```
    print_center(double *a, int dim)
```

which prints the square matrix of dimension `dim/2` at the center of the matrix store in `a[]`.

Exercise 2.2.2. Assume that `a[]` is an array of dimension $n_1 n_2 n_3$, which stores three-dimensional data indexed by $0 \leq i < n_1$, $0 \leq j < n_2$, and $0 \leq k < n_3$. The three indices can be ordered from innermost to outermost in six different ways. For each ordering, calculate the location in `a[]` of the entry with index (i, j, k).

Exercise 2.2.3. Assume that the array `a[]` of dimension $n_1 n_2 n_3$ stores three-dimensional data indexed using i, j, k as in the previous exercise. Assume that i is innermost and k is outermost. Explain how to extract the submatrix with $i_0 \leq i < i_1$, $j_0 \leq j < j_1$, and $k = k_0$.

Exercise 2.2.4. If the array `a[]` is as in the previous exercise, explain how to extract a submatrix with $i_0 \leq i < i_1$, $j = j_0$, and $k_0 \leq k < k_1$.

Exercise 2.2.5. The `LU_Solve` class relies on its user to remember to factorize exactly once before attempting to solve linear systems. Add a data member `state` in addition to `dim`, `A`, and `ipiv` to the private section of the class and use it verify that the matrix is factorized exactly once before any call to `solve()`.

Exercise 2.2.6. The BLAS function `dgemv()` multiplies a matrix into a vector. Define a function

```
void mult_mv(const double *A, int m, int n, double *x)
```

which multiplies the $m \times n$ matrix `A` into the vector `x`. There is no need for even a narrowly defined class to build a usable interface to `dgemv()`.

Exercise 2.2.7. Program and test a narrowly defined class that interfaces to LAPACK's least squares solver.

Exercise 2.2.8. Program and test a narrowly defined class that interfaces to LAPACK's tridiagonal solver. For multiple right-hand sides, calling the tridiagonal solver just once can be far more efficient than making multiple calls. Therefore, endow your class with the ability to solve multiple right-hand sides in a single function call.

2.3 Building programs using GNU Make

The organization of source files into directories and subdirectories is the heart of modular programming. Typically, several source files cooperate to do a task, and yet more source files are involved in bigger tasks. A directory holds source files that are related or perform similar tasks. Directories may be organized further into subdirectories in a source tree to reflect the structure of the program.

The `make` utility provides a method for building a program from its source tree. Each source file must be turned into an object file, and the object files must be linked together to form executables. Compiling and linking become quite repetitive

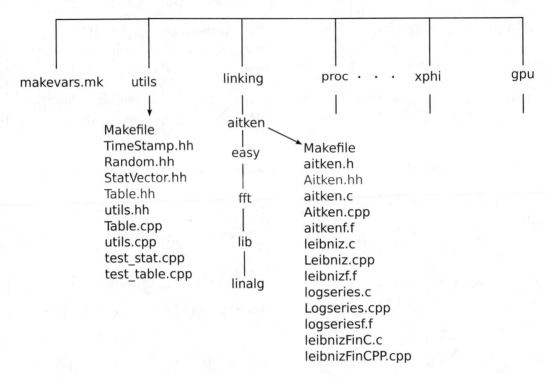

Figure 2.2: Directories and files in the source tree for this book. The entire source tree is found at `https://github.com/divakarvi/Book-SPCA`.

and error-prone if done from the command line. Makefiles offer a more systematic approach to building programs.

A build system such as `make` is essential to C/C++ programming. The Makefiles hold valuable information about the structure of the program as a whole, which is absent from the source files. In Python, the correspondence between modules and the directory hierarchy is wired into the language, but there is no such facility in C/C++. Modular programming aims to organize and conquer. There can be no modular programming without organization of program sources into a directory hierarchy. Well-thought-out source trees aid programming as much as structured definitions of functions and classes.

We begin our discussion of GNU `make` by looking at the source tree shown in figure 2.2. The `makevars.mk` file at the root of the source tree defines `make` variables that are used in modules such as `utils` and `linking`. These modules correspond to directories. Some modules have several submodules. For example, the `linking` module has submodules `aitken`, `easy`, `fft`, `lib`, and `linalg`.

Much of the discussion in this chapter pertains to these submodules of `linking`. All the Aitken iteration programs are in the `aitken` submodule. The programs we used to illustrate use of the BLAS and LAPACK libraries are in `linalg`. We will discuss the use of shared and static libraries as well as the Fast Fourier Transform (FFT) later in this chapter. The programs and makefiles that will aid that discussion are in `lib` and `fft`.

The source tree shown in figure 2.2 is partial. The module `proc`, which is at the root, corresponds to the next chapter. The next chapter deals with the x86 processor core, its instruction set, registers, and pipeline. The modules corresponding to the last two chapters about the Xeon Phi and GPU programming are show in the figure, but many others are omitted.

The source files are the leaves of the source tree. The source tree as a whole includes 173 `.cpp` files, 65 `.hh` headers, 12 `.c` files, 6 `.h` files, 6 `.cu` (CUDA/GPU) files, and 14 `.py` (Python) files. Most of these are omitted in figure 2.2. The only source files shown belong to the module `utils`, which is at the root of the source tree and the submodule `aitken` of the module `linking`. The modules `utils` and `linking/aitken` will be the basis of our discussion of makefiles.

In section 2.3.1, we begin by looking at part of the `utils/` directory and part of the `linking/linalg` directory shown in the source tree of figure 2.2. A testing program in `linking/linalg` uses some utilities defined in `utils/`, thus providing an example of a program that depends on sources in distinct directories in the source tree. This example will be used to exhibit how the `make` utility may be used to build programs with sources scattered across the source tree.

The introduction to GNU `make` in sections 2.3.2 through 2.3.6 emphasizes the two-pass structure of `make`, the use of pattern rules, and recursive `make`. Recursive `make` is the simplest method for handling a source tree with multiple directories. Although it has certain disadvantages, it is adequate for small projects, and even some large projects use recursive `make`. In section 2.3.7, we discuss some of the disadvantages of recursive `make` and how to overcome them.

Finally, section 2.3.8 has an importance that is far beyond its length. Here we discuss how static and shared libraries work, and how to find out exactly which library has been linked. Linking and loading problems that every C/C++ programmer will encounter are discussed along with suggestions of how to tackle them.

2.3.1   The `utils/` folder

A testing program in the source `linking/linalg/test_lusolve.cpp`, which uses functions defined in sources in a different folder in the source tree `utils/` (see the source tree in figure 2.2), will be described here. Later in section 2.3.7, this program is used to illustrate how GNU's `make` utility builds an executable from sources scattered in different parts of the source tree.

The modules in `utils/` facilitate timing, generation of random numbers, gathering statistics, making tables, and manipulation of `double` arrays. All the modules in `utils/` are used extensively. The modules are used for testing, timing, and laying out data elsewhere in the source tree. The corresponding code is almost always omitted from the text. We avoid mentioning the modules in `utils` for the most part, but a brief discussion is given here.

In more complicated settings, there will be many dependencies between the directories and subdirectories of the source tree. In the source tree for this book, the directories are mostly self-contained. Most of the dependencies are on utilities in `utils/` and on modules for plotting and displaying data that are not shown in the source tree in figure 2.2.

The header file `utils.hh` defines a macro called `assrt()`. This macro, which is used frequently, is similar to `assert()`, which is defined in the C standard header file `assert.h`. The only difference is that `assrt()` always checks its assertion, and not only if the preprocessor macro `DEBUG` is defined. We find little use for debuggers. The debugger is a blunt tool that works without an idea of the logical structure of the program. When programs are compiled in debug mode, the memory layout of their data can change. Memory errors may not be reproduced faithfully in debug mode.

In addition to `assrt()`, `utils.hh` declares the following functions:

```
void array_abs(double *v, int n);
double array_max(double *v, int n);
void array_show(double *v, int n, const char* mesg);
void array_diff(double *restrict v,
          double *restrict w, int n);
void array_copy(double *restrict v,
          double *restrict w, int n);
void array_out(double *v, int m, int n,
          const char *fname);
```

```
void array_in(double *v, int size,  const char* fname);
```

These functions are defined in `utils.cpp`. Most of the declarations are self-explanatory. The function `array_max()` takes the absolute values of n entries of v and returns the maximum. The function `array_out()` interprets v as an $m \times n$ matrix in column-major order and outputs it to a file. These functions are used for testing and timing.

Another function declared in `utils.hh` and defined in `utils.cpp` is the following:

```
void verify_dir(const char *dir);
```

This function uses Linux system calls to verify whether `dir` is already present, and if it is not, it creates such a directory. Linux system calls are declared in the header file `unistd.h`. A basic familiarity with system calls is of much value in programming.[7]

Programs must be tested as extensively as possible. Although details of testing are normally omitted, we give a single example here, partly to illustrate how some of the modules in `utils/` are used and partly to set up later discussion of recursive `make`.

The `LU_Solve` class of section 2.2 is tested using the function `testlu()`. It is defined in a source file in `linking/linalg`.

```
1  void testlu(int n){
2      assrt(n > 0);
3      double *A = new double[n*n];
4      double *v = new double[n];
5      for(int i = 0; i < n; i++){
6          v[i] = rand()*1.0/RAND_MAX-0.5;
7          for(int j = 0; j < n; j++)
8              A[i+j*n] = rand()*1.0/RAND_MAX-0.5;
9      }
10     verify_dir("DBG/");
11     array_out(A, n, n, "DBG/A.dat");
12
13     LU_Solve lu(A, n);
14     lu.factorize();
15     array_out(v, n, 1, "DBG/b.dat");
```

---

[7]For a detailed, systematic, thorough, and readable account of Linux system calls, see Kerrisk (2010).

```
16          lu.solve(v);
17          array_out(v, n, 1, "DBG/x.dat");
18
19          system("test_lusolve.py DBG/A.dat"
20                  " DBG/b.dat DBG/x.dat");
21
22          delete[] v;
23          delete[] A;
24  }
```

The first block of `testlu()` (lines 2 through 11) initializes the arrays `A[]` and `v[]` with a square matrix and a vector of dimension n. Notice the use of `assrt()` on line 2. Line 10 creates the `DBG/` directory if it does not already exist. The matrix `A[]` is saved in `DBG/A.txt` using `array_out()` (line 11). On lines 10, 11, 15, and 17, `testlu()` calls functions that are defined in source file in an external module (`utils/utils.cpp`). This testing program is later used to illustrate how we may handle programs with sources scattered in multiple directories.

The middle block (lines 13 through 17) solves the linear system $Ax = b$ and saves x as well as b.

Lines 19 and 20 invoke `system()`, which is a C library function.[8] This function forks a shell process and runs its argument as a shell command. The argument is a single string of type `const char *`, but it is broken across two lines. In C/C++, a string such as `"one two"` can be written as `"one" "two"`. Long strings can be conveniently split across lines.

The shell command

```
test_lusolve.py DBG/A.dat DBG/b.dat DBG/x.dat
```

calls a Python script that looks at the output data and verifies that Ax is indeed nearly equal to b. It prints the relative error $||b - Ax||/||b||$.

Of course, we could have called the Python script from the command line. But then `testlu()` is incomplete by itself, and we have to remember to do something more to complete the test. It is usually good practice to make dependencies explicit

---

[8]The C library function `system()` must never be invoked from a privileged process: `http://linux.die.net/man/3/system` explains that strange values for environment variables may be used to break the system.

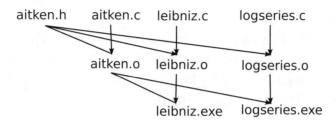

Figure 2.3: Makefile dependency graph.

in the source and not rely on memory. The testing program calls `testlu()` multiple times.

```
int main(){
    testlu(10);
    testlu(100);
    testlu(1000);
}
```

Like `testlu()`, this `main()` function is also defined in `test_lusolve.cpp`.

2.3.2   Targets, prerequisites, and dependency graphs

Dependencies are fundamental to `make`. Figure 2.3 shows that each object file depends on a single source and a header. Typically, the dependency is on multiple header files, unlike the simple situation shown in the figure. Each executable in turn depends on multiple object files.

The first purpose of a Makefile is to capture the dependency graph between headers, sources, object files, and executables. Each object in the dependency graph is typically a file as in figure 2.3. All files that have incoming edges in the dependency graph are targets. The incoming edges indicate that a target file must be built using a set of some other files. Those other files are the prerequisites. The targets may reappear as prerequisites, as is the case for all the object files in figure 2.3.

Typically, `make` assumes that a target file may not exist. The target file is considered out of date if its time stamp (accessed using `stat` on GNU/Linux) is older than that of any of its prerequisites. If a target either does not exist or is out of date, `make` takes it upon itself to create a file corresponding to the target.

The question arises of how `make` can create a new file corresponding to a target. To answer that question is the second purpose of a Makefile. The Makefile associates each target with a recipe, and the recipe is a shell command invoked by the `make` utility to build the target if the target is either absent or out of date.

The executables `leibniz.exe` and `logseries.exe` are built using the following Makefile:

```
 1  leibniz.exe: leibniz.o aitken.o
 2      icc -o leibniz.exe leibniz.o aitken.o
 3
 4  logseries.exe: logseries.o aitken.o
 5      icc  -o logseries.exe logseries.o aitken.o -lm
 6
 7  aitken.o: aitken.c aitken.h
 8      icc -fPIC -c aitken.c
 9
10  leibniz.o: leibniz.c aitken.h
11      icc -c leibniz.c
12
13  logseries.o: logseries.c aitken.h
14      icc -c logseries.c
```

This listing is a fraction of the Makefile in the `linking/aitken` directory in the source tree. Other parts of the Makefile are used to build executables from Fortran and C++ sources.

This simple Makefile consists of two types of information. Lines 1, 4, 7, 10, and 13 are dependencies. In each dependency, the item before the colon is the target. Thus, the targets in lines 1, 4, 7, 10, and 13 are `leibniz.exe`, `logseries.exe`, `aitken.o`, `leibniz.o`, and `logseries.o`, respectively. The prerequisites follow the colon. In the rule on line 1, the prerequisites are `leibniz.o` and `aitken.o`.

Together the five rules specify the dependency graph shown in figure 2.3. For each executable, the dependency graph shows all the object files on which it depends. For each object file, the graph shows the source file and one of the header files on which the object file depends. When an executable is built, the flow of information is from source files to objects files and from object files to executables as shown in the figure.

The other type of information in the Makefile are the recipes. Lines 2, 5, 8, and 11 are recipes. Each recipe begins with a tab and corresponds to the target in the dependency above it. Beginning each recipe with a tab is a *major* aspect of `make` syntax. Thus, line 2 corresponds to the target `leibniz.exe`. Together the dependency and the recipe form a rule. For example, lines 1 and 2 form a rule.

The `make` utility makes two passes. In the first pass, it consumes all the dependency rules and builds a dependency tree such as the one shown in figure 2.3. In addition, targets are associated with recipes. In our example, there are five targets: `leibniz.exe`, `logseries.exe`, `aitken.exe`, `leibniz.o`, and `logseries.o`. These targets appear on lines 1, 4, 7, 10, and 13, respectively. The recipes that are bound to these targets in the first pass occur on the following lines.

In the second pass, the `make` utility brings the target list given at its invocation up to date. For each target, it first makes sure that its prerequisites are up to date before bringing the target up to date. In general, this leads to a depth first traversal of part of the dependency graph.

Once the prerequisites are up to date, the `make` utility checks whether the target is older. If every target and prerequisite is assumed to be a file, `make` finds the date of each file using a GNU/Linux command called `stat` (or a system call of the same name) and takes that to be the date of the target or the prerequisite. A target is out of date or older if any of its prerequisites is newer. If the target is out of date or older, the corresponding recipe is invoked to bring it up to date (`make` does not check the date of the target after executing the recipe). This two-pass operation is the heart of how `make` works.

Suppose we change to the `linking/aitken` directory and invoke the `make` utility at a shell prompt as follows:

```
make logseries.exe
```

During the first pass, the `make` utility notes that the target `logseries.exe` depends on `logseries.o` and `aitken.o`. These object files in turn depend on the corresponding sources and the header file `aitken.h`. If the object file `logseries.o` is *older* than either `logseries.c` or `aitken.c`, the target `logseries.o` is considered to be out of date during the second pass. Each file is stored with a time stamp that indicates the time at which it was last modified or changed (you can use the GNU/Linux utility `stat` to look at the time stamp of a file). If the target does not exist as a file, it is considered to be out of date.

If the target `logseries.o` is out of date, the `make` utility will execute the corresponding recipe during the second pass. More specifically, the command

```
icc  -c  logseries.c
```

is issued to bring the target up to date. Here the `-c` option to the C compiler tells it to compile only. The target `aitken.o` is brought up to date in a similar manner by executing the recipe corresponding to it if it is out of date with respect to either of its prerequisites.

Once the two object files `logseries.o` and `aitken.o` are ensured to be up to date, the second pass of the `make` utility checks whether the executable `logseries.exe` is out of date with respect to either of its prerequisites. The check is carried out by looking at the time stamps of the files as before. As noted already, a target such as `logseries.exe` is considered out of date if no file by that name exists. If the executable is out of date, the `make` utility issues the linking command

```
icc -o logseries.exe logseries.o aitken.o -lm
```

during the second pass. Here the `-o` option tells the `icc` linker to leave the output in `logseries.exe`. The `-lm` option at the end tells the `icc` linker to link the library `libm.so`. The shared library `libm.so` defines math function such as log, exp, and the trigonometric functions.

The reader may notice the `-fPIC` option in the recipe for `aitken.o` (line 8). This object file will be included in a shared library later in this section. The `fPIC` option is needed for that purpose.

The Makefile we have examined so far is quite simple. Yet it brings out the two passes in `make`'s operation, targets, prerequisites, recipes, and dependency graphs. We emphasize that nothing is done if a target is already up to date. For example, if we build `leibniz.exe` and then make a small change to `aitken.c`, the invocation `make leibniz.exe` will recognize that the prerequisite `aitken.o` is out of date and recompile `aitken.c`. However, `leibniz.o` is not out of date and the source file `leibniz.c` is not recompiled. The `make` utility uses the dependency graph to eliminate needless compilations. In a large source tree, the resulting saving can be considerable.

In our listing, there is a single rule for each target that specifies all the prerequisites for that target. The prerequisites can be given separately, but for each target, there can be only one effective recipe. For example, we can delete lines 1 and 2 of the listing and replace them by the following:

```
leibniz.exe: leibniz.o
leibniz.exe: aitken.o
leibniz.exe:
     icc -o leibniz.exe leibniz.o aitken.o
```

Here the two prerequisites are given in separate rules, and the recipe for the target `leibniz.exe` is given as part of a rule with no prerequisites. The three rules here can be given in any order. Because of the two-pass nature of `make`'s operation, the effect is the same.

We are also allowed to specify a dependency with multiple targets. The entire Makefile may be rewritten as follows:

```
aitken.o: aitken.c
     icc -c aitken.c
leibniz.o: leibniz.c
     icc -c leibniz.c
logseries.o: logseries.c
     icc -c logseries.c
leibniz.exe: leibniz.o
logseries.exe: logseries.o
leibniz.exe logseries.exe: aitken.o
     icc -o $@ $^ -lm
```

The last rule in this Makefile has two targets. The recipe for the last rule uses two automatic variables: `$@`, which expands to the target, and `$^`, which expands to the list of all prerequisites of the target. We will study automatic variables soon, but this is a little hint of what is to come. Thanks to automatic variables, we can use the same recipe for both the targets `leibniz.exe` and `logseries.exe`.

Many of the operations in building an executable are repetitive. In particular, executables are nearly always built by linking together all the object files in their prerequisite list along with libraries. The Makefile here fails to recognize that each `.o` object file is built from a `.c` source following the same pattern, which is to invoke `icc` with the `-c` compile only option. If pattern rules are defined appropriately, the entire Makefile can be reduced to two lines.

```
leibniz.exe: leibniz.o aitken.o
logseries.exe: logseries.o aitken.o
```

With suitable pattern rules, make will automatically generate the dependency of .o object files on .c prerequisites, invoke the right compilation command to update object files, and invoke the right linking command to build the executable targets. Automatic variables, make variables, and pattern rules enable us to simplify repetitive tasks as we will now learn.

2.3.3   Make variables in makevars.mk

Almost all Makefiles have make variables. We use makevars.mk at the root of the source tree to show how make variables are used (see figure 2.2).

The makevars.mk file will serve us throughout this book. If has three sections. The first section defines variables.

```
 1  #########
 2  CPP     := icpc
 3  CFLAGS    := -xHost -O3 -prec-div -no-ftz -restrict \
 4   -Wshadow -MMD -MP
 5  FFTWINC   := $(FFTW_INC)
 6  MKLINC := -mkl
 7  #########
 8  MKLLIBS := -mkl=sequential
 9  MKLTHRD := -mkl=parallel
10  FFTWLIBS   :=  $(FFTW_LINK)
```

In C/C++, a variable is a name for a location in memory. In make, a variable is a string.

The variable definitions from CPP to FFTWLIBS use := and not = following the variable. The use of := implies that the variables are evaluated immediately during the first pass. We do not discuss the other type of variable evaluation, which is called deferred evaluation.

All characters in a line following the # character, including that character, are ignored. Lines 1 and 7 begin with the # character and are therefore comment lines.

The variable CPP is set to icpc (line 2). It is the name of the C++ compiler used later in makevars.mk.

The CFLAGS variable (lines 3 and 4) stands for the options passed to the C++ compiler. The definition of CFLAGS is split across two lines using the continuation character \. It merits careful scrutiny. The optimization level is -xHost -O3. The -xHost flag ensures that the compiler generates instructions corresponding to the highest capability of the machine. This flag is essential for our purposes.

We do not bother with debug levels such as -g or -O0. The recommended optimization option in icpc is -fast. We do not use that option. It turns on -ipo or interprocedural optimization, which we do not want. Other dubious flags are also turned on by -fast.

By default the icpc compiler may use a less precise but faster division for IEEE double-precision numbers, according to the compiler's manual. It is unclear whether the faster division is ever really faster or whether the flag ever really has any effect. The -prec-div flag (line 3) forces conformance to IEEE arithmetic. The compiler manual states that the flush-to-zero optimization is used for really small numbers that almost underflow. This is another "optimization" of dubious value and uncertain meaning. It is turned off using -no-ftz (line 3).

The -restrict option (line 3) enables restrict qualified pointers, a C99 feature we find to be quite valuable in the next chapter and later.

C++ member functions may accidentally redefine a class variable, leading to runtime errors. For example, state could be a data member that keeps track of the state of the class object, and a member function, which wants to set it to 1, may say int state=1 instead of state=1. The -Wshadow option (line 4) tells the compiler to issue a warning when variables defined in an outer scope are redefined in an inner scope.

The -MMD and -MP options (line 4) to the icpc compiler tell it to generate a .d file listing all dependencies of the source on header files. The way dependencies of C/C++ sources on header files is handled is discussed in section 2.3.6.

A few of our programs make use of the FFTW library. On line 5, the make variable FFTWINC is set to $(FFTW_INC). The understanding is that FFTW_INC is defined in the shell environment before calling make. It can be set to whatever is needed to find the FFTW header files. If the installation is along standard lines, the header file will be in a standard place such as /usr/local/include/, where the compiler always looks. So the shell variable FFTW_INC can be even blank or undefined. If the header is not in a standard place, the shell variable (assuming the bash shell)[9] must be set as in

```
export FFTW_INC=-I <dir-with-fftw-header>
```

---

[9]We always assume the shell to be bash.

The $-$I option tells the compiler to look for headers at the directory that follows the option, in addition to the standard places. The directory is typically given as a full path.

If FFTW_INC is defined as a shell variable, it may be evaluated using $(FFTW_INC) as if it were just another make variable. If it is in fact not defined in the shell, it evaluates to the empty string.

Similarly, on line 10, the make variable FFTW_LIB is set by evaluating FFTW_LINK, which is presumed to be set in the shell. The shell variable FFTW_LINK can be as simple as $-$lfftw3 if the installation is along standard lines, which leaves the libraries in standard places such as /usr/local/lib/ or /usr/local/lib64. If the installation is not standard, the shell variable must be set as follows:

```
export FFTW_LINK=  -L <dir-with-fftw-lib> -lfftw3
```

The $-$L option tells the linker to look for libraries in an additional place, and $-$lfftw3 tells it to look for the fftw3 library.

Handling the MKL library is easy if the Intel compilers are used. The option $-$mkl (line 6) to the compiler tells it to look for the MKL header files in the right places. Linking is equally easy. We may use $-$mkl=sequential or $-$mkl=parallel (lines 8 and 9).

2.3.4   Pattern rules in makevars.mk

Makefile rules are made up of dependencies and recipes. The variables defined in the first section of makevars.mk, which we just discussed, are used to construct recipes. The recipes have a formulaic character. For example, if the target is an object file to be built from a C++ source, the recipe generally invokes the C++ compiler specified by CPP using the options listed in CFLAGS. Pattern rules take advantage of the repetitive nature of recipes to simplify their specification.

Automatic variables, partially listed and explained in table 2.2, are the basis of pattern rules. Automatic variables enable a recipe to parse and extract tokens from the dependency that precedes it (in the same rule). For example, in the rule

```
leibniz.exe: leibniz.o aitken.o
        icc -o $@ $^
```

the automatic variable $@ evaluates to the target, which is leibniz.exe for this rule, and the automatic variable $^ evaluates to leibniz.o aitken.o, which is the

$@	Target
$<	The first prerequisite
$?	Prerequisites newer than the target
$^	All prerequisites with duplicates eliminated
$+	All prerequisites including duplicates

Table 2.2: Automatic variables recognized by the `make` utility.

list of *all* prerequisites of the target. If a dependency `leibniz.exe: xyz.o` is given elsewhere in the Makefile, `xyz.o` will be in `$^` as well. The three most important automatic variables are `$@`, `$^`, and `$<`.

Pattern rules form the second section of the `makevars.mk` file at the root of the source tree (see figure 2.2 for the source tree).

```
11  .SUFFIXES:
12  .SUFFIXES: .cpp .o .exe .s .d
13  %.o: %.cpp
14        $(CPP)  $(CFLAGS)  -c $<
15  %.s: %.cpp
16        $(CPP) $(CFLAGS) -fno-verbose-asm  -S $<
17  %.o: %.s
18        $(CPP) $(CFLAGS) -c $<
19  %.exe: %.o
20        $(CPP) -o $@ $(filter %.o,$^) $(LIBS)
```

Line 11 is a rule with `.SUFFIXES` as the target and an empty list of prerequisites. If has the effect of deleting many suffixes and pattern rules stored by GNU `make` by default. The rule on line 16 specifies the suffixes we want to use in pattern rules that are explicitly given later.

The rule on lines 13 and 14 is the pattern rule for generating an object file from a C++ source with the file name extension `.cpp`. The pattern in the dependency is as follows:

```
%.o: %.cpp
```

It matches a dependency such as

```
Aitken.o: Aitken.cpp Aitken.hh
```

The % in the target matches with `Aitken`. The `make` utility substitutes `Aitken` for %
in `%.cpp`. It looks for `Aitken.cpp` in the prerequisite list to complete a match to the
pattern rule. Because the prerequisite list has `Aitken.cpp` the match is complete.

Even if the dependency of `Aitken.o` on `Aitken.cpp` is not explicitly given, there
is still a pattern match if the current directory contains a file named `Aitken.cpp`.
The `make` utility generates the dependency automatically.

If a rule with target `Aitken.o` has a recipe, that recipe is used to update `Aitken.o`.
If no recipe is explicitly specified for a target, the recipe of the pattern rule that
matches the target is used for updating it. In this instance, that rule would be

```
$(CPP) $(CFLAGS) -c $<
```

We have gone over the definition of variables such as `CPP` (line 2) and `CFLAGS` (lines
3 and 4). When a variable is evaluated, the evaluation is specified as in `$(CPP)`. The
difference in syntax between the point of definition of a variable and its point of use
is one of the oddities of `make`.

The recipes are evaluated and applied only during the second pass; the variables
are evaluated during the first pass. Therefore, some of the variables may be defined
after the pattern rules. Here `CPP` and `CFLAGS` are defined before the recipe. However,
a later makefile that includes `makevars.mk` may append additional options to `CFLAGS`,
and those will be used by the recipe during the second pass. The `-c` option tells `icpc`
to compile only (and not attempt to link against any libraries). The `-c` option could
have been folded into `CFLAGS`, but it is perhaps a little clearer to make it explicit in
the recipe. The recipe uses the automatic variable `$<` to find the name of the source. It
assumes that the source for generating the object file is given as the first prerequisite.

The recipe expands to

```
icpc -O3 -prec-div -no-ftz -restrict -Wshadow -c $<
```

after substituting for `CPP` and `CFLAGS`. A makefile that includes `makevars.mk` may
extend `CFLAGS` as

```
CFLAGS := $(CFLAGS) $(MKLINC) $(FFTWINC) -openmp
```

The recipe will then include options for finding MKL and FFTW headers, as well as
`-openmp`. OpenMP is the topic of a later chapter. We can influence the compilation
command by appending to `CFLAGS` because assignments to variables are evaluated
during the first pass, whereas recipes are evaluated during the second pass.

Suppose there is no rule in the Makefile with `Aitken.o` as the target and we say `make Aitken.o` at the prompt. GNU `make` then notes that `Aitken.o` matches the target pattern `%.o` in a target rule. If the directory contains a file named `Aitken.cpp`, the pattern rule on lines 13 and 14 is considered a match. Its recipe will be used to build `Aitken.o`. Thus, pattern rules are capable of generating dependencies automatically.

The pattern rule for generating `%.s` from `%.cpp` (lines 15 and 16) is used in chapter 3 to look at assembly code. The `-fno-verbose-asm` option leads to less cluttered assembly output. The `-S` option to the compiler tells it to generate the assembly code instead of the object code.

Lines 19 and 20 define a pattern rule for building `%.exe` executables from `%.o` object files. The recipe for that rule uses a `make` construct that is new to us:

```
$(filter %.o,$^)
```

GNU `make` has several built-in functions, and `filter` is one of them. As used here, it goes through the list of all prerequisites `$^` and selects only those that match the pattern `%.o`. Therefore, the recipe on line 20 has the effect of building the executable using all the object files, and only the object files, in the list of prerequisites. In general, the dependency list of a `.exe` target will contain all the object files needed to build it in addition to a few phony targets (see below), which are eliminated.

The recipe on line 20 is

```
$(CPP) -o $@ $(filter %.o,$^) $(LIBS)
```

The list of libraries is passed to the linker using the variable `LIBS`. The evaluation of recipes is always deferred to the second pass, but variables such as `LIBS` are evaluated in the first pass, as explained already. Therefore, this variable does not need to be defined when the pattern rule is consumed during the first pass. If `LIBS` is defined as

```
LIBS := $(FFTWLIBS) $(MKLLIBS) -openmp
```

during the first pass, the recipe for building a `%.exe` target that depends on the corresponding `%.o` object file will automatically link the MKL, FFTW, and OpenMP libraries (in that order). The order in which libraries are linked can be significant.

2.3.5 Phony targets in `makevars.mk`

We will discuss recursive make, useful for building programs with object files in several subdirectories, shortly. Recursive make relies on phony targets. Our first encounter with phony targets is in a simpler context. The third and last section of `makevars.mk` is listed below.

```
21  .PHONY: clean cleanxx
22  clean:
23         rm *.o; rm *.exe; rm a.out;
24  cleanxx:
25         rm *.o; rm *.a; rm *.so;  rm *.exe;  rm *.d
```

The rule with target .PHONY has clean and cleanxx as prerequisites (line 22). These are treated as phony targets. Ordinarily, make expects to find a file with the same name as a target and checks the latest modification time of that file to determine whether the target is out of date. For phony targets, make does not look for a file of the same name. Phony targets are always assumed to be out of date.

In this example, saying make clean will remove all object files and executables in the current directory (the directory from which make is invoked). Making the target cleanxx removes certain other files in addition. The .d files (see below) used to capture dependencies of a C++ source on header files get removed with cleanxx.

2.3.6 Recursive make and .d files

The make utility, as we have discussed it so far, applies to programs all of whose source files are in a single directory. That assumption fails for even moderately large programs. When the source and object files required to build a single executable reside in several subdirectories, recursive make may be used to complete the build.

Recursive make is a straightforward concept. It consists of calling make within a recipe for a phony target. The linking/linalg/ module defines interfaces to LA-PACK's LU factorization routines as discussed in a previous section. These interfaces reside in the source file lusolve.cpp. The source test_lusolve.cpp tests the interface. It uses a few utilities such as verify_dir() defined in utils/utils.cpp. Building the executable test_lusolve.exe offers a simple example of recursive make.

```
1  include ../../makevars.mk
2  CFLAGS := $(CFLAGS) $(MKLINC)
3  LIBS := $(LIBS) $(MKLLIBS)
4  ######
5  .PHONY: ../../utils objl
```

```
 6  ../../utils:
 7        make --directory=$@ objl
 8  ######
 9  objl: lusolve.o
10  lusolve.o: lusolve.cpp
11  -include lusolve.d
12  test_lusolve.o: test_lusolve.cpp
13  -include test_lusolve.d
14  ######
15  test_lusolve.exe: test_lusolve.o lusolve.o \
16              ../../utils ../../utils/utils.o
```

This Makefile is used as the basis for three somewhat distinct discussions.

The first discussion is of recursive make. There are two targets declared as phony on line 5. The first of these, which is ../../utils, enables recursive build using the Makefile in ../../utils. The other phony target objl is the target in the present Makefile that builds all object files and libraries that may be useful externally. Indeed, we use objl generally in Makefiles as the name of the phony target that builds all object files and libraries in the same directory as the Makefile that may be useful externally.

Thus, the recipe for the phony target ../../utils (lines 6 and 7) is

```
        make --directory=$@ objl
```

The --directory option implies that a new shell process is forked with

```
    ../../utils
```

as the current directory and make objl is invoked within that directory (see table 2.2 for the meaning of $@). The Makefile in ../../utils defines objl as a phony target. Its recipe updates all the object files and libraries that may be used externally, including utils.o, which will be used in this Makefile.

The rule with the phony target objl (line 9) updates lusolve.o, which is the one object file in the linking/linalg/ folder that may be linked externally. Therefore, when other modules recursively call the Makefile in linking/linalg with objl as the target, the only object file that will be built is lusolve.o.

Recursive invocation of make is a consequence of the dependency on lines 15 and 16. The executable test_lusolve.exe is built using three object files (lines 15 and 16). Two of these object files, `test_lusolve.o` and `lusolve.o`, are built in the current directory. The object file `utils.o`, however, resides in `../../utils`. To build that object file correctly, the phony target `../../utils` is listed as a prerequisite. Updating `../../utils` will lead to a recursive invocation of `make`, which builds `utils.o` in `../utils.o` (lines 6 and 7). The linking recipe defined in `makevars.mk` filters out the phony target.

The second discussion is of `.d` files and the way dependencies on header files are handled.

Line 10 gives the dependency of `lusolve.o` on the source `lusolve.cpp`. It is typical for each object file to depend primarily on one source file. However, the source file typically includes several header files that in turn include other header files. The source `lusolve.cpp` includes the following header files:

```
#include <cmath>
#include <iostream>
#include <mkl.h>
#include "../utils/utils.hh"
#include "lusolve.hh"
```

These header files include yet others, and the command

```
icpc -O3 -restrict -M -mkl -c lusolve.cpp
```

shows all the included files, which are 123 in number. This command uses the `-mkl` option supported by the `icpc` compiler to find the MKL header files. The `-M` option tells the compiler to give a list of all the included header files. If any of these header files is altered, the object file `lusolve.o` must be rebuilt, although `lusolve.cpp` is unchanged.

Lines 11 and 13 are responsible for tracking the dependence of `lusolve.o` and `test_lusolve.o`, respectively, on header files. To understand how these lines work, we should go back to line 4 of `makevars.mk`, which included the `-MMD` and `-MP` options in `CFLAGS`. When `icpc` is invoked with `-MMD -MP`, it creates a `.d` file along with the object file. The `.d` file contains dependencies on the header files. For example, the generated `lusolve.d` contains the following lines:

```
lusolve.o: lusolve.cpp ../utils/utils.hh lusolve.hh \
  /opt/caen/intel-12.1/mkl/include/mkl.h \
  [... mkl header files omitted ...]          \
```

```
/opt/apps/intel -12.1/mkl/include/mkl_vsl_types.h
```

```
../utils/utils.hh:
```

```
lusolve.hh:
```

The first rule here, with `lusolve.o` as target, has generated the dependencies on all the MKL header files as well as `lusolve.hh` and `../utils/utils.hh`. The dependencies on system header files such as `iostream` are omitted if the flag is `-MMD` but included with `-MD`.[10]

Line 11 of the Makefile reads

```
-include lusolve.d
```

The directive here is `-include` and not `include`. When the directive is `include` (as on line 1), GNU `make` signals an error if the file to be included is not found (or cannot be built using `make` rules). In contrast, `-include` moves forward silently if the file to be included is not found. If `lusolve.o` has been built, `make` will definitely find `lusolve.d` during its first pass because the compiler outputs the `.d` file along with the `.o` file. If the `.d` file is missing, the `.o` file must also be missing, and there is no need to track dependencies on the header files.

There can be a subtle problem with generating the `.d` files that list dependencies on header files during every compilation. Suppose `lusolve.o` is built correctly by the compiler, which also outputs a `.d` file as above, and then the implementation is changed. Suppose the header file `../utils/utils.hh` is deleted during the new implementation. If we try to rebuild `lusolve.o`, GNU `make` looks at the old `.d` file and tries to resolve a dependency of `lusolve.o` on `../utils/utils.hh`. There will be an error as the header file has since been removed. To handle this problem, the compiler generated `.d` files include `make` rules such as

```
../utils/utils.hh:
```

If the header file is not found, it is assumed to be built correctly by doing nothing.

Although the `-M` and related options supported by `icpc` and `gcc/g++` make it relatively painless to handle dependencies of C/C++ sources on header files, it must

---

[10]I thank Zhongming Qu for showing me how to use the `-MMD` and `-MP` options to handle dependencies on header files.

be said that the use of .d files is far from a perfect solution. The .d files replicate information that is already present in the C/C++ sources and header files. Such replication of information or logic is usually not a good idea. Every time information or logic is replicated, it creates room for inconsistencies.

The third and final discussion reiterates points that have already arisen in a concrete way.

The include directive on line 1 splices in all of makevars.mk at this point. This Makefile resides in linking/linalg, while makevars.mk is at the root of the source tree (see figure 2.2). Therefore, line 1 refers to the file to be included as ../../makevars.mk. Once this file is included, all the variables and pattern rules defined in it become available.

We want the compilation command to look for MKL header files at the right places. The CFLAGS variable is modified to do that on line 2. It will be evaluated during the first pass and used when the recipe for generating %.o targets that depend on %.cpp sources is invoked during the second pass. That recipe of course is in makevars.mk, which is above the definition of CFLAGS. Similarly, line 3 sets the value of LIBS so that the MKL libraries are linked when the %.exe target that depends on %.o object file is built using the recipe in makevars.mk.

The dependencies on lines 10 and 12 may be omitted. GNU make will use the pattern rule for %.o targets depending on %.cpp sources to generate those rules automatically—if the corresponding source files lusolve.cpp and test_lusolve.cpp are in the directory.

Makefiles capture the dependence of object files on source files and headers perfectly. Such a perfect capture is possible because typically an object file depends only on the source file (of the same name but with a different extension) and the header files included from inside the source file. In contrast, no attempt is made to capture the dependencies between object files. Each object file is a collection of functions. Because functions may call one another, the dependency graph between the object files is typically more complicated. Circular dependencies between object files are common. Resolving these dependencies is left to the linker.

If suitable pattern rules have been defined, the dependencies of object files on sources is deduced automatically by make. In contrast, we almost always need to indicate which object files are used to build an executable explicitly. We usually include rules such as lines 10 and 12, which indicate the dependence of object files on sources, to make the structure of the program more explicit within the Makefiles.

Makefiles bring order into the translation of sources to object files and the building of executables from the object files. They reflect the hierarchy of the source tree. Makefiles can get quite complicated when executables must be built on multiple platforms. If the source tree of figure 2.2 must be built for Linux machines using GNU, Intel, or PGI compilers, or if they must be built for both Linux and Windows, the Makefiles get much more complicated. In such situations, it is common to write configure scripts that generate the Makefiles. Configure scripts are typically written as shell scripts, although Python is equally effective and far more pleasant to use.

2.3.7 Beyond recursive `make`

Modularity and simplicity are two virtues of recursive make. However, there are several problems with it.[11] It can be slow for large projects because a new shell process is created every time `make` is called recursively. It does not gel too well with parallel `make` using the `-j` option. It leads to needless compilation because all object files and libraries that may be externally needed are built during recursive `make` and not just those that are actually needed. It must be said that these deficiencies are not fatal. Recursive `make` is still used.

There appears to be a fundamental tension between the two-pass structure of the `make` utility and recursive invocation of `make`. The first pass is supposed to build a dependency graph, for example, of object files on sources and executables on object files. The second pass is supposed to invoke recipes to update targets that are out of date with respect to their prerequisites. The recursive invocation of `make` happens during the second pass. The dependency graph of object files and sources in the external module is built only when its Makefile is invoked recursively. The result is to splinter the dependency graph, leading to multiple first and second passes.

It is possible to avoid recursive `make` entirely by building a single dependency graph for all the sources, object files, and executables in the project.[12] One way to do

---

[11]See Peter Miller (Recursive Make considered harmful, 1997, `http://aegis.sourceforge.net/auug97.pdf`).

[12]One way to avoid recursive `make` was suggested by Peter Miller (Recursive Make considered harmful, 1997, `http://aegis.sourceforge.net/auug97.pdf`) and developed further by Emile van Bergen (`http://evbergen.home.xs4all.nl/nonrecursive-make.html`). This method relies on stack manipulation using `make` variables. Another method developed by Zhongming Qu is briefly described in the text. The heart of Qu's idea is to use pattern rules specific to each subdirectory or submodule.

this is to include a `rules.mk` file in each subdirectory or submodule. The `rules.mk` file contains pattern rules specific to the subdirectory as well as dependencies of object files on sources present in the subdirectory.

In each `rules.mk`, it is assumed that a variable R, which expands to the full absolute path of the root of the project, is defined. A `rules.mk` file in `linking/lingalg` may look as follows:

```
 1  saved  :=  $(D)
 2  D  :=  $(R)/linking/linalg  #R  defined  externally
 3  $(D)CFLAGS  :=  $(CFLAGS)  -mkl
 4
 5  $(D)/%.o:  $(D)/%.cpp
 6          $(CPP)  $($(@D)CFLAGS)  -o  $@  -c  $<
 7
 8  $(D)/lusolve.o:  $(D)/lusolve.cpp
 9  $(D)/test_lusolve.o:  $(D)/test_lusolve.cpp
10  D  :=  $(saved)
```

This `rules.mk` file defines the variable D (line 2) to be the absolute path to the directory that contains itself as well as the source files that it manages. The variable R is assumed to point to the root of the source tree.

On line 3, we define the variable `$(D)CFLAGS`. Here `$(D)` evaluates to the absolute path of the directory, and the variable name is in fact that absolute path name with `CFLAGS` appended to it. This variable holds compilation flags specific to the directory. In this example, the only change is to append the `-mkl` flag.

On lines 5 and 6, the pattern rule for generating a `.o` object file from a `.cpp` source is made specific to the directory. In GNU make, `@D` is a variable that evaluates to the current directory. Therefore, the syntax

```
    $($(@D)CFLAGS)
```

which occurs on line 6, evaluates the variable defined on line 3. GNU `make` always chooses the most specific pattern rule. On lines 5 and 6, the pattern rule is made specific to the object files to be generated in the current module.

The use of `$(D)` to evaluate the `make` variable D on lines 8 and 9 implies that the object and source files are given in full as absolute paths. Giving object and source file names in full as absolute paths is essential to the technique being described.

A `rules.mk` file for the module `utils/` written along the same lines looks as follows:

```
saved := $(D)
D := $(R)/utils
$(D)CFLAGS := $(CFLAGS) -fPIC

$(D)/%.o: $(D)/%.cpp
        $(CPP) $($(@D)CFLAGS)   -o $@ -c $<

$(D)/utils.o: $(D)/utils.cpp
$(D)/Table.o: $(D)/Table.cpp

D := $(saved)
```

A Makefile in `linking/linalg` that builds the executable to test the LU solver looks as follows.

```
1  include ../../root.mk #define R, CPP, CFLAGS
2  D := $(R)/linking/linalg
3  LIBS := -mkl=sequential
4
5  %.exe:
6          $(CPP) -o $@ $(filter %.o,$^) $(LIBS)
7
8  include rules.mk
9  include $(R)/utils/rules.mk
10
11 test_lusolve.exe: $(D)/test_lusolve.o $(D)/lusolve.o
12         $(R)/utils/utils.o $(R)/utils/Table.o
```

The `root.mk` file included on line 1 defines the variables `R`, `CPP`, and `CFLAGS`. It is similar to the `makevars.mk` file described earlier.

The `rules.mk` file included on line 8 brings in the pattern rules and dependencies that govern object files and sources in the present `linking/linalg` module. The pattern rules for the `utils/` module are brought in using an `include` directive on line 9. The latter `include` directive uses an absolute path name.

In the dependency rule with target `test_lusolve.exe` on lines 11 and 12, all object file names are given in full as absolute path names. The object files in the local module are prefixed with `$(D)/`. In contrast, the object files that are external to the module are given relative to the root with prefix `$(R)/`. By using absolute path names and pattern rules specific to each module, we avoid recursive make entirely and instead build a single dependency graph.

One disadvantage of the technique just described is that when **make** runs and echoes the commands that it passes to the shell, the messages that appear have absolute path names that are almost unreadable. This deficiency can be remedied by resorting to complicated **make** syntax.

2.3.8   Building your own library

Our discussion of GNU **make** is uncommonly detailed and for a reason. Much of the time spent on C/C++ syntax is wasted without a fairly good knowledge of **make**. There is no modular programming in C/C++ without the **make** utility or an equivalent build system. The programmer is limited to single source files or awkward collections of source files in a single directory.

We end our discussion of **make** by showing how to build and link static and shared libraries. Libraries provide a level of modularity beyond what is possible within a source tree. Any program that is linked against a library in effect treats the external library as a module.

The `utils/` subdirectory in the source tree (see figure 2.2) has `utils.cpp`, which provides basic facilities such as `verify_dir()`. The `linking/aitken/` subdirectory implements the Aitken iteration in the C source `aitken.c`. The source `fft_mkl.cpp` in `linking/fft/` provides an interface to part of MKL's Fast Fourier Transform (FFT) facilities. The FFT is the topic of the next section. The Makefile below is in `linking/lib/`. It shows how to combine `utils.o`, `aitken.o`, and `fft_mkl.o` and build a shared or static library.

```
1  include ../../makevars.mk
2  CFLAGS := $(CFLAGS) $(MKLINC)
3  ######
4  MODS := ../../utils ../aitken ../fft
5  .PHONY: $(MODS)
6  $(MODS):
```

```
 7        @echo
 8        make --directory=$@ objl
 9        @echo
10 ######
11 test_lib.o: test_lib.cpp
12 -include test_lib.d
13 ######
14 libxmath.so: $(MODS)
15        icpc -shared -o $@ ../../utils/utils.o  \
16                      ../aitken/aitken.o     \
17                      ../fft/fft_mkl.o
18 libxmath.a: $(MODS)
19        ar rcs $@ ../../utils/utils.o       \
20                      ../aitken/aitken.o       \
21                  ../fft/fft_mkl.o
22 ######
23 #link against shared lib
24 #to link against static, rm .so file
25 test_lib.exe: test_lib.o
26        icpc -o $@ $^ $(MKLLIBS) -L$(PWD) -lxmath
```

Line 1 includes makevars.mk, so that the pattern rules we have discussed become effective in this Makefile. The three modules being combined are listed on line 4. Each module is a phony target (line 5). The phony target triggers recursive make in the appropriate subdirectory with the target objl (line 8) (lines 6 and 7 print empty lines to make the recursive invocation of make more visible as make runs). It is assumed that the Makefile in each directory will build the requisite object files when invoked on the phony target objl.

The rule for building the shared library is on lines 14 through 17. The target libxmath.so is the name of the shared library. Its prerequisites are the phony names for the three modules. The recipe here is almost the same as the recipe for linking. The only difference is the -shared option (line 15). The three object files referenced in the recipe are built using recursive make. The object files must be compiled with the -fPIC option. We explicitly showed the -fPIC option for aitken.o earlier in this section. The -fPIC options for the other two compilations are given through the

Makefiles in the respective directories.

The rule for building the static library `libxmath.a` is on lines 18 through 21. The recipe uses the archive command `ar` with the options `rcs`.

The source `test_lib.cpp` has a simple program to test the functions in the `xmath` library. The target for building the corresponding executable is on line 25. This recipe will override the recipe in the pattern rule for `%.exe` targets with `%.o` prerequisites. The recipe (line 26) links the MKL libraries as it should. The `icpc` linker is told to look for libraries in the current directory (in addition to standard places) using the `-L$(PWD)` option (line 26). This is needed because both the static and share versions of `xmath` are built in the current directory. The `-lxmath` option to the `icpc` linker (line 17) makes the linker look for `libxmath.so` or `libxmath.a`. Shared libraries are linked preferentially.

Static libraries are conceptually simpler than shared libraries. A static library is simply an archive of object files. However, linking a static library is not the same as listing all the object files that are archived in it. If we list the object files explicitly, the executable will certainly include all the object files. In contrast, when a static library is linked, only those object files archived in the library that resolve undefined names in object files and libraries listed before it, as well as those undefined names that arise when object files archived in the same library are linked, are included. Thus, the order in which libraries are linked can be quite important.[13]

When we invoke

```
test_lib.exe
```

at the command line, the executable initially does not have the definitions of the functions defined in `xmath`—if the linking is against the shared version of the library. It looks for the shared library at runtime. The search for shared libraries at runtime goes through a number of directories, but the directory containing `libxmath.so` is not one of them. We must add that directory to the shell variable `LD_LIBRARY_PATH` explicitly.

---

[13]A bug related to the order in which libraries are linked persisted in the source code for this book for nearly 5 years. A program to compare the speed of FFTW and MKL was linked against both libraries, with MKL *first* and FFTW *later*. MKL implements many of the FFTW functions, and in fact, what we thought was FFTW was really again MKL. So the program was comparing MKL against MKL's implementation of the FFTW interface.

One advantage of shared libraries is that the system needs to load only one copy of the library if many processes are linked against the same shared library. Another advantage is that programs benefit automatically from updates and bug-fixes to shared libraries (at least in theory). The memory map and page tables of a process change when a shared library is loaded. Shared libraries must be supported by the operating system kernel.

The list of shared libraries available on a system may be obtained using the `ldconfig -v` command. The list can be long, and the only purpose it serves may be to overwhelm.

The GNU/Linux `ldd` command can be used to find which shared libraries are being linked with the executable. There can be several versions of MKL or FFTW on a system, for example, making it uncertain which version of a library has been linked. If we say `ldd test_lib.exe` at the command prompt in GNU/Linux, we get the following sort of information:

```
libmkl_sequential.so => /opt/intel/.../mkl/lib/...
libxmath.so => not found
```

Of the list of 10 libraries, we have shown only two. For the MKL library, the command outputs the full path to the shared library that will be linked dynamically at run time. For our `libxmath.so`, it says "not found" because the shell variable `LD_LIBRARY_PATH` has not been set to include the current directory. If this program is run, there will be an error at runtime because the `xmath` library cannot be found.

Another useful command is `ld` with `-verbose` option. With that option, we may find out how the system looks for libraries . For example, if we say `ld -verbose -lfftw3`, we get a sense of what happens if the `-lfftw3` option is used to link `fftw3`.

```
  ...
attempt to open //usr/local/lib64/libfftw3.so failed
attempt to open //usr/local/lib64/libfftw3.a failed
  ...
attempt to open //lib64/libfftw3.so failed
attempt to open //lib64/libfftw3.a failed
attempt to open //usr/lib/x86_64-linux-gnu/libfftw3.so
succeeded
-lfftw3 (//usr/lib/x86_64-linux-gnu/libfftw3.so)
libm.so.6 needed by ...
```

```
//usr/lib/x86_64-linux-gnu/libfftw3.so
found libm.so.6 at //lib/x86_64-linux-gnu/libm.so.6
...
```

We see the order in which the loader goes through a number of directories looking for FFTW3. In every directory, it first looks for the shared and then the static version of FFTW3. When FFTW3 is found, it begins to look for shared libraries needed by FFTW3, and so on.

The loader looks for shared libraries in the following order.[14] First, it looks at directories that may be explicitly embedded in the executable file using options such as -rpath. Second, it looks at directories in LD_LIBRARY_PATH. Third, it looks in the cache file /etc/ld.so.conf. The entries of this library cache file may be manipulated using the ldconfig command. Fourth, it looks at /usr/lib.

Understanding the manner in which programs using shared libraries are loaded and set up requires knowledge of the paging system, reviewed later in section 4.4, and the concept of system calls, which are functions defined by the operating system kernel and which may be invoked by user programs (see section 5.4.1). To complete our discussion of shared libraries, we anticipate later discussion of those topics and explain how shared libraries are set up.

There are three parts to understanding how shared libraries work at the level of machine instructions. The first of these is the manner in which shared libraries are loaded into memory. Suppose a program abc.exe, which calls functions in shared libraries that in turn may call functions in other shared libraries, is invoked from the command line or in some other way. The Linux system call execve() is invoked with the file abc.exe as one of its arguments. Linux creates a process descriptor that holds administrative information about the program or process for its own use. It maps the contents of abc.exe to the virtual address space of the process with the intention of passing control to the process. However, before passing control it notices that the executable relies on shared libraries. Consequently, it loads the dynamic linker ld-linux.so or ld.so into the *same* virtual address space and passes control to the dynamic linker. The dynamic linker looks for the library in the file system in the order given above. Once the library is found, it issues the mmap() system call to load the library into the virtual address space of the process. If the library is already

---

[14]For a far more detailed discussion, see Levine (1999) and Kerrisk (2010).

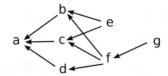

Figure 2.4: Dependencies between make targets.

in physical memory, perhaps because it was loaded by some other process, mmap() will only update the page tables and not load the library again into physical memory.

The handling of global variables defined by shared libraries is the second part to be understood. References to global variables involve additional levels of indirection and go through the Global Offset Table (GOT). The GOT is set up by the dynamic linker.

The final part to be understood is the handling of calls of functions defined in shared libraries. Here, too, additional levels of indirection are employed, and all function calls are routed through the Procedure Linkage Table (PLT). Unlike the GOT, PLT entries are not fully resolved by the dynamic linker to begin with. When a shared library function is called by the program, the program calls a PLT function. The first time a PLT function is called, the function sends the call to ld.so, which is still sitting in virtual memory, and it is only then that the reference to that shared library function is fully resolved. All later calls of the shared library function jump to the PLT entry and then directly to the library function.

Exercise 2.3.1. The dependencies between targets a through g are shown in figure 2.4. Assume that the recipe to update the targets is as given below:

```
a b c d e f g:
      echo $@
```

- Give exactly four dependency rules that capture all the dependencies shown in the figure.

- If you say make a at the command line, explain why either g or e is the first to be printed.

- Give the dependency rules in two ways, such that either e or g is the first to print.

- Explain why there is no way to present the dependencies such that g prints first and e prints immediately afterward.

Exercise 2.3.2. Suppose you have the following Makefile:

```
X  := hello
Y  := world
mesg:
        echo $(X) $(Y)
Y  := universe
```

If you say `make mesg`, will it print "hello world" or "hello universe"?

Exercise 2.3.3. Add a pattern rule to `makevars.mk` to generate .o files from .c files. Your pattern rule should be such that the entire Makefile to build `leibniz.exe` and `logseries.exe` in the directory `linking-aitken` can be reduced to the following three lines:

```
include ../makevars.mk
leibniz.exe: leibniz.o aitken.o
logseries.exe: logseries.o aitken.o
```

Exercise 2.3.4. The `icpc` compiler/linker provides the options `-mkl=sequential` and `-mkl=threaded` to fetch header files and link against the MKL library. Modify `makevars.mk` to use these options.

Exercise 2.3.5. Consider the Makefile to build `test_lusolve.exe` discussed in section 2.3.6. Suppose the phony target `../utils` is removed from the list of prerequisites of the target `test_lusolve.exe`. The object file `utils.o` will still be built correctly, but it will end up in the directory `linking-linalg/` instead of `utils/`, and the linking will fail. Explain why.

Exercise 2.3.6. Record the size of the executable `test_lib.exe` when both `libxmath` and MKL are linked dynamically, when `libxmath` is linked statically, and when the `-static` option is used to link both `libxmath` and MKL statically. Explain why the size of the executable increases only slightly from the first linking to the second and by a lot more from the second linking to the third.

Exercise 2.3.7. Use the `ldd` command to find all the shared libraries that

```
test_lusolve.exe
```

is linked against. Use the `nm` command (also part of GNU's binutils) to find the shared library in which `dgetrf()` is defined. Verify that `dgetrf`, `dgetrf_`, `DGETRF`, and `DGETRF_` are all bound to the same address in the text area, so that they are really different names for the same function.

2.4 The Fast Fourier Transform

So far in this book, modular programming in C/C++ has been the focus. Organization of sources into a source tree, Makefiles, and libraries is the basis of modular programming. The `make` utility, or an equivalent build system, is indispensable to modular programming in C/C++.

Among programming languages, the C/C++ framework is the best—and often by far—for writing fast programs. C/C++ programs can be several hundred or even several thousand times faster than programs written in interpreted languages. In this last section, we look at the speed of a few implementations of the Fast Fourier Transform (FFT). Program speed is a major theme of the rest of this book.

Program speed is influenced by many factors, including programming skill, compilers, the processor hardware, and the memory system. Each layer of software and hardware is heavily designed. Program speed is a discontinuous function of the design parameters. A small change in a program, or in the environment in which it runs, can result in unpredictable changes in program speed. In this section, we look at a few FFT implementations to gain an understanding of some of the factors that influence program speed. What does it mean to say that an implementation is optimal? To what extent does programming skill affect program speed? These are some of the questions we ask. We find already that programming skill has a great influence on program speed. Later chapters set forth many of the concepts that must be understood to produce efficient implementations of scientific programs.

A program's speed depends on the hardware configuration. In this chapter, we stick to a single processor core. In later chapters, we will see that even if a program is multithreaded or networked, understanding what happens on a single core is a big part of the game.

About 100% of the computers in use for scientific programming use the x86 architecture. Thus, this book too adopts the x86 architecture. The x86 architecture evolves constantly. There are only a few particulars of the x86 architecture that will be of concern to us. These are discussed in the next chapter.

For the most part, all that concerns us is the level of the instruction set, in particular, whether the instruction set is SSE2, AVX, AVX2, or AVX-512 (see table 3.1 of the next chapter). Thus, the machines we use will be designated as 2.6 GHz SSE2 or 2.2 GHz AVX. The full names of the machines may be looked up from table A.1 of the appendix. The SSE2 machines support 128-bit XMM registers, and the AVX/AVX2 machines support 256-bit YMM registers.

The clock signal that is fed into each processor core is the heart beat of the computer. The activities of the processor are synchronized with the clock signal. The memory system and other parts of the computer must accommodate themselves to the processor. If we measure program speed in cycles, we get a better sense of how well the program is exploiting the hardware.

In this book, program speeds are reported using cycles. We use measures such as flops (floating point operations) per cycle for program speed and bytes per cycle for memory bandwidth. For some programs, we report the number of cycles consumed directly. Measuring program speed in terms of cycles is somewhat unconventional. It is more typical to see GFlops (Gigaflops per second) for arithmetic speed and GB/s (Gigabytes per second) for memory bandwidth. The second is a standard unit of time and its use is most appropriate when different hardware configurations are being compared. Our concern, which is to write efficient programs on a given hardware configuration, is quite different. Although we report timing measurements in cycles, they can be easily converted to seconds using the frequency in GHz of the processor clock.

The FFT is one of the most widely used algorithms in scientific computing and is fundamental to many areas of science. It is an appropriate starting point for the discussion of the speed of scientific programs. In section 2.4.1, we introduce the FFT algorithm in outline. The purpose of this outline is to help understand the speed of FFT implementations. The two major FFT implementations in the MKL and FFTW libraries are introduced in sections 2.4.2 and 2.4.3, respectively.

Programs run in a complex environment and the complexity of the environment influences program speed in ways we cannot fully grasp. The manner in which a program is timed can make a big difference. In addition, a program may behave quite differently from when it is used as part of a larger program to when it is timed by itself. The purpose of section 2.4.4 is to give a sense of how the complexity of the environment influences program speed.

Section 2.4.5 compares MKL, FFTW, and another expertly coded FFT. The last of these is the type of program a good C/C++ programmer without knowledge of computer architecture may write. The optimized MKL and FFTW libraries can be even 10 times faster, illustrating both the value of optimized libraries and programming with a knowledge of computer architecture.[15]

2.4.1 The FFT algorithm in outline

The discrete Fourier transform of $f_0, \ldots, f_{N-1}$ is defined as

$$\hat{f}_k = \frac{1}{N} \sum_{j=0}^{N-1} \omega^{-jk} f_j, \quad \text{for} \quad k = 0, \ldots, N-1. \tag{2.1}$$

Here $\omega = \exp\left(2\pi\sqrt{-1}/N\right)$ is a primitive Nth root of unity. The $\hat{f}_k$ are linear functions of f_j. The discrete Fourier transform from $f = (f_0, \ldots, f_{N-1})$ to $\hat{f} = \left(\hat{f}_0, \ldots, \hat{f}_{N-1}\right)$ can be written as $\hat{f} = Mf$, where M is the $N \times N$ matrix whose (j, k)th entry is ω^{-jk}/N.

The inverse discrete Fourier transform is given by

$$f_j = \sum_{k=0}^{N-1} \omega^{jk} \hat{f}_k. \tag{2.2}$$

It too can be thought of as a matrix-vector product.

The discrete Fourier transform and its inverse have an intimate connection to Fourier series. Suppose $f(x)$ is a function with period 2π. Its Fourier coefficients are defined by

$$c_n = \frac{1}{2\pi} \int_0^{2\pi} f(x) \exp\left(-\sqrt{-1}nx\right) \, dx \quad \text{for} \quad n = 0, \pm 1, \pm 2, \ldots$$

If $f_j = f(2\pi j/N)$, then $\hat{f}_k \approx c_k$ for $0 \leq k < N/2$ and $\hat{f}_k \approx c_{k-N}$ for $N/2 < k \leq N-1$. If N is even, $\hat{f}_{N/2} \approx \left(c_{N/2} + c_{-N/2}\right)/2$. Here $f(x)$ is assumed to be a function that is integrable and sufficiently smooth.

---

[15]Our discussion assumes that the FFTW library has been built correctly using `--enable-avx` (for machines with YMM registers) or `--enable-sse` (for machines with XMM registers). Without a proper build, FFTW can be too slow by a factor of 2 or even 4.

The FFT is a method to effect the discrete transform (2.1) or its inverse (2.2) using $\mathcal{O}\left(N \log_2 N\right)$ arithmetic operations, which is a considerable improvement over the $\mathcal{O}\left(N^2\right)$ arithmetic operations required by direct matrix-vector multiplication.[16] The improvement in operation count is vital to making the FFT fast but is not the full story. The implementation can make a difference of more than a factor of 10 to the program speed. We present the structure of the power of 2 FFT but omit mathematical details.

Suppose $N = 2^n$. We assume the data to be N complex numbers. The first step in the power of 2 FFT is to separate the data into even and odd parts as follows:

$$f_0, f_2, \ldots, f_{N-2} \quad \text{and} \quad f_1, f_3, \ldots, f_{N-1}.$$

An $N/2$ FFT is applied separately to the even and odd parts. The odd part is multiplied by the twiddle factors $1, \omega, \ldots, \omega^{N/2-1}$. The FFT of size N is generated by adding and subtracting corresponding points in the even and odd parts.

Because $N/2$ is also a power of 2, the FFTs of size $N/2$ are effected using the same strategy. Thus, the even part and odd part are once again separated into even and odd parts to obtain four lists of numbers. Repeated separation into even and odd parts leads to the bit-reversed permutation, which is perhaps the most important element in an efficient implementation of the FFT.

The N data items are indexed using binary numbers with n bits. The bit-reversed permutation is obtained by reversing indices in binary and reordering the data using the reversed binary numbers. The last bit moves to the first position, and it is immediately evident that the bit reversal separates the data into even and odd parts. If $N = 8$, the bit-reversed permutation is given by

$$f_0, f_4, f_2, f_6, f_1, f_5, f_3, f_7.$$

Once the data is bit-reversed, the FFT begins by operating on successive pairs of numbers.

Figure 2.5 illustrates the power of 2 FFT assuming the data to be in bit-reversed order. The innermost (lowermost in the figure) step operates on consecutive pairs. The next levels operate on quartets, octets, and so on. At each level, the data items in solid squares are first multiplied by twiddle factors. At each level, the data item in

---

[16]The modern discovery of the FFT is due to Cooley and Tukey (1965).

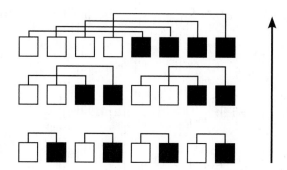

Figure 2.5: Structure of the power of 2 FFT assuming bit reversal. At each level, the solid positions are multiplied by twiddle factors and either added to or subtracted from the corresponding unfilled positions.

a solid square is paired with another data item in an empty square (see figure). The iteration at a level is complete, when each pair of data items is replaced by their sum and difference. Bit reversal improves the locality of memory references.

Figure 2.5 assumes that each level is complete before we move to the next level. In fact, there is a lot more freedom in the way the operations are ordered. For example, we may complete operations on the first half of the bit reversed data before operating on any of the pairs, quartets, and so on in the second half. Judicious orderings of the operations result in better usage of the memory system and better performance.

The power of 2 FFT moves through $\log_2 N$ levels. The number of arithmetic operations in each level consists of $N/2$ twiddle factor multiplications, $N/2$ additions, and $N/2$ subtractions. Additions and subtractions have the same cost and may both be counted as additions. A complex addition is equal to two floating point double precision additions and a complex multiplication is equal to 4 floating point multiplications and two additions. Therefore, a power of 2 FFT of size N costs $3N \log_2 N$ floating point additions and $2N \log_2 N$ floating point multiplications. The total cost is $5N \log_2 N$. There are other variants, such as the power of 4 FFT, which have slightly lower operation counts.

2.4.2 FFT using MKL

The header file `mkl_dfti.h` declares the FFT functions implemented in the MKL library. The following class simplifies application of the FFT and its inverse to complex data:

```
class fft_mkl{
private:
    int n;
    DFTI_DESCRIPTOR_HANDLE handle;
public:
    fft_mkl(int nin);
    ~fft_mkl();
    void fwd(double *f){
        DftiComputeForward(handle, f);
    }
    void bwd(double *f){
        DftiComputeBackward(handle, f);
    }
};
```

Unlike the `Vector` and `Matrix` classes from before, `fft_mkl` is a narrowly defined class. It does just one thing, which is to provide an interface to MKL's FFT for complex one-dimensional data. It is typical of the way we use C++.

The class may be used as shown below to apply the FFT to a complex data of size n. It is assumed that v is of type `double` * pointing to $2n$ or more `double` locations.

```
for(int i=0; i < n; i++){
    v[2*i] = rand()*1.0/RAND_MAX - 0.5;
    v[2*i+1] = rand()*1.0/RAND_MAX - 0.5;
}
fft_mkl fft(n);
fft.fwd(v);
```

Here the array v[] is initialized with uniformly distributed random numbers and its FFT is taken. All the details of the MKL library are cleanly hidden away.

The member functions `fft_mkl::fwd()` and `fft_mkl::bwd()` are defined completely within the class definition. These member functions correspond to (2.1) and (2.2), respectively.

The two private data members of the class `fft_mkl` are n, for saving the dimension of the transform, and `handle`. The `handle` is initialized by the constructor and used for effecting the transform. The constructor is defined as follows:

```
1  fft_mkl::fft_mkl(int nin)
2     :n(nin)
3  {
4        DftiCreateDescriptor(&handle,
5                        DFTI_DOUBLE,DFTI_COMPLEX, 1,n);
6        DftiSetValue(handle, DFTI_FORWARD_SCALE, 1.0/n);
7        DftiSetValue(handle, DFTI_PLACEMENT, DFTI_INPLACE);
8        DftiCommitDescriptor(handle);
9  }
```

The colon initialization on line 2 shows C++ syntax we have not encountered so far. Its effect is to call the constructor for the class object n with nin as the argument. It is essential for initializing class members, which are themselves class objects. But n is an int, which is a basic type. Here the effect is the same as saying n=nin just after line 3.

The MKL call on lines 4 and 5 sets up handle. The function call tells MKL that the data is complex double precision, one-dimensional, and of size n. The handle is a pointer to a data structure called a descriptor. Within that data structure, MKL can store a variety of information. For example, it can precompute and store twiddle factors.

The forward transform computed by default is unnormalized. The division by N in (2.1) is omitted. Line 6 tells MKL to normalize the forward transform. Line 7 tells MKL to compute in-place transforms. In-place transforms modify the array in place. The forward transform is effected by the MKL call

```
    DftiComputeForward(handle, f);
```

in the class fft_mkl because the transform is in place. If the transform were out-of-place, we would need a call such as

```
    DftiComputeForward(handle, f, fout);
```

In this call, the data in f will be unchanged, and the result of the transform will be left in fout. The FFT is naturally implemented in place. The out-of-place FFT is slower because it touches more data.

The descriptor that handle points to becomes usable only after the commit on line 8. It is here that MKL actually computes and saves the twiddle factors, and so on. The order in which the FFT operations are applied may also be determined and saved here.

The class destructor is defined as follows:

```
fft_mkl::~fft_mkl(){
        DftiFreeDescriptor(&handle);
}
```

The definition of the `fft_mkl` class is now complete.

The C language has a facility for defining functions with a variable number of arguments. An example of such a function is `printf()`. The first argument to `printf()` is a format string, and the types and number of the subsequent arguments depend on the format string. Like `printf`, the MKL function `DftiComputeForward()` uses the `varargs` facility to handle both in-place and out-of-place transforms.

2.4.3   FFT using FFTW

The FFTW library[17] has a much cleaner interface than MKL, although that may not be clear from the one-dimensional complex-to-complex case we deal with. The header file is `fftw3.h`. The following tightly defined class offers a means to use FFTW functions for the FFT:

```
class fft_fftw{
private:
      int n;
      fftw_plan pf;
      fftw_plan pb;
public:
      fft_fftw(int nin);
      ~fft_fftw();
      void fwd(double *f){
            assrt((long)f%16 == 0);
            fftw_execute_dft(pf, (fftw_complex *)f,
                                 (fftw_complex *)f);
            for(int i=0; i < 2*n; i++)
```

---

[17]See www.fftw.org as well as Frigo (1999) and Johnson and Frigo (2005).

```
                    f[i] /= n;
    }
    void bwd(double *f){
        assrt((long)f%16 == 0);
        fftw_execute_dft(pb, (fftw_complex *)f,
                             (fftw_complex *)f);
    }
};
```

The sole task of the `fft_fftw` class is to offer an easy interface to FFTW transforms for one-dimensional complex data. FFTW stores `fftw_plans` instead of a `handle` as with MKL. There are different plans for forward and backward transforms. The `fwd()` and `bwd()` member functions are implemented within the class definition.

Both the member functions use `assrt()` (defined in `utils/utils.hh`) to verify that the pointer `f` is 16-byte aligned. A pointer is 16-byte aligned if it is divisible by 16 or, equivalently, if the last 4 bits are zero. Because of the way the FFTW plans are set up, the pointers must be 16-byte aligned for correctness. FFTW recognizes that the transforms are in place because the same pointer `f` is used as the input and output argument to `fftw_execute_dft()`.

FFTW does not offer a facility for normalizing the forward transform. Therefore, the member function `fwd()` normalizes explicitly using a for-loop. As we will see, this seemingly innocuous bit of code nearly halves the program speed.

The constructor and destructor for `fft_fftw` are defined below.

```
fft_fftw::fft_fftw(int nin)
    :n(nin)
{
    double *f = (double *)
                _mm_malloc(2*n*sizeof(double), 16);
    fftw_complex *ff  = (fftw_complex *)f;
    pf = fftw_plan_dft_1d(n, ff, ff, -1,
                            FFTW_MEASURE);
    pb = fftw_plan_dft_1d(n, ff, ff, 1,
                            FFTW_MEASURE);
    _mm_free(f);
}
```

```
fft_fftw::~fft_fftw(){
     fftw_destroy_plan(pf);
     fftw_destroy_plan(pb);
}
```

The constructor aligns the pointer `f` with 16-byte boundaries by using `_mm_malloc()` instead of `malloc()`. The forward plan `pf` uses the flag -1, while the backward plan uses the flag 1. These refer to the sign of the exponents in (2.1) and (2.2), respectively. Both the forward and backward plans use the `FFTW_MEASURE` flag. The FFTW library uses the planning stage to measure different implementations of the FFT in an attempt to pick a good one.

2.4.4   Cycles and histograms

How many cycles does a one-dimensional complex FFT of dimension $2^{10} = 1024$ take? Program performance is influenced by so many factors that the question is too simple to be answered. First, we have to say how the measurement is taken and which implementation of the FFT is used. Here we assume the implementation to be from the MKL library.

The issue of measurement is more complicated. Suppose a single measurement is made. The cycle count is likely to be atypically large. Suppose a great number of measurements are made but while applying the FFT to the same data. This time the average or median cycle count is likely to be an underestimate. A great part of the expense of the FFT is in reading data from memory. If the same data is repeatedly transformed, the data locations will be cached near the processor core in cache memory. Caching reduces the expense of reading data.

We measure FFTs of dimension $N = 2^{10}$ in a way that mimics what we consider to be a realistic scenario. We line up 10^6 problem instances in one long array of $2 \times 2^{10} \times 10^6$ double-precision numbers (the factor 2 at the front accounts for complex data). This array is 16 GB. We successively apply the inverse FFT to each problem instance and record 10^6 cycle counts. The median (or average) cycle count obtained is likely to be a fair estimate of the cost of an FFT of dimension 1024 in a large computation.

The statistics of the 10^6 measurements does not follow the normal law or any such well-known probability distribution. The histograms in figure 2.6 show the peculiar

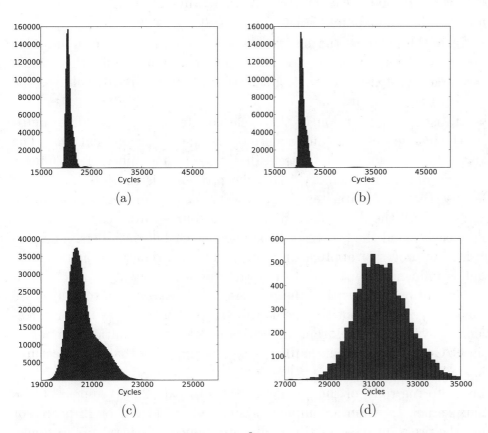

Figure 2.6: Histograms of cycles of 10^6 trials of 1D FFT of size 1024 on 2.66 GHz SSE2 machines.

nature of cycle statistics. Parts (a) and (b) of the figure show histograms of measurements taken on two distinct computers (2.66 GHz SSE2 machines)[18] of identical specifications. Both measurements have medians of around $20,000$ cycles. However, the histograms are noticeably different. On both computers, the histograms have a big bump near the median and a much tinier bump to the right of the median. The tinier bump is beyond $25,000$ cycles and barely visible in figure 2.6(b). The tinier bump is much closer to the median in (a).

Part (c) of figure 2.6 enlarges the histogram of part (b) near its median. This histogram looks more like a smooth distribution, but it is quite unlike the normal law. There is a marked protrusion to the right of the median. Part (d) enlarges the histogram of part (b) near the tiny bump.

Why is the statistical distribution of the cycle counts so peculiar? The multi-bump nature of the histograms is a consequence of the multiple factors at play. The FFT fetches data from memory and subjects that data to a number of arithmetic operations. Fetching data from memory on to the processor is the job of memory controllers. Because the same data item is accessed multiple times during a single transform (see figure 2.5), the data locations are often sourced from caches. Moving data between the caches and the processor is handled by cache controllers. The execution units inside the processor apply arithmetic operations to data in the registers. The cycle count is influenced by the design of the memory controllers, cache controllers, and the execution units within the processor. It is reasonable to conjecture that the protrusion to the right of the median in figure 2.6(c) is due to some feature of the memory system. There are a large number of discontinuities (similar to if-statements in C/C++ programs) in hardware design, implying that some features are only occasionally excited.

The tiny bump to the right of the median shown in figure 2.6(d) appears to be due to the Linux kernel. Even on a computer system where 11 out of 12 processor cores are idling, the program receives timer interrupts once in several milliseconds. The kernel uses timer interrupts to ensure fairness in scheduling, gather statistics for its own use, and other purposes. It is conjectured that the tiny bump is due to timer interrupts or some other activity of the Linux kernel. If the program runs for a long time, the kernel will change the way it issues timer interrupts. To even speak of the distribution function of the number of cycles consumed by an FFT of size $n = 1024$

---

[18]For more information about the machine, see table A.1.

may not be correct.

2.4.5   Optimality of FFT implementations

What is the fastest possible speed of an FFT implementation? The many system features that intrude into the histograms hint that this question may not have a straightforward answer. However, a discussion is worthwhile. It helps us understand what makes an FFT implementation efficient. The discussion is based on a 2.2 GHz AVX machine.[19]

The power of 2 FFT performs $5N \log_2 N$ double-precision floating point operations. Additions and multiplications are in the ratio 3 : 2. Thanks to instruction-level parallelism and 256-bit YMM registers, a single AVX processor core can complete four additions and four multiplications every cycle. If we consider arithmetic operations alone, a theoretical lower bound is $.75N \log_2 N$ cycles.

We would be justified in ignoring memory accesses if the number of arithmetic operation for each memory access were large. The total number of bytes that must be accessed is $16N$ (16 bytes for each complex number). For large N, we indeed have $0.75 \log_2 N > 16$. However, the structure of the FFT does not allow the outer iterations (upper levels in figure 2.5) to be cached if N is large. The inner iterations (lower in the figure) operate on small packets of data, such as pairs or quartets. Caching can be effective for the inner iterations. As the size of the data packets in the outer iterations becomes comparable to cache size, caching becomes less and less effective. The FFT is caught between two opposing currents. On the one hand, large N means more arithmetic operations per item of data. On the other hand, the data items accessed in the outer iterations cannot be cached as effectively.

Table 2.3 shows the cycle counts for MKL, FFTW, and Numerical Recipes[20] for a variety of N. Problem instances sufficiently numerous to occupy 8 GB of memory were used for each N. The inverse FFT was successively applied to the problem instances. The reported figures are medians. The Numerical Recipes implementation applies only to $N = 2^n$.

Numerical Recipes is 5 to 10 times worse than the optimized libraries. The sheer volume of effort needed to produce optimized implementations such as MKL and FFTW will become clear in later chapters. There is no doubt that the scientific

---

[19]For more information about the machine, see table A.1.

[20]Press et al. (2007) is a handy and wide-ranging, if brisk, work on numerical methods..

N	MKL	FFTW	Numerical Recipes
32	0.86	1.6	8.12
64	1.14	1.62	6.71
80	1.72	1.58	*
$8 \times 3 \times 7$	1.76	1.96	*
192	1.82	1.84	*
1024	1.83	1.51	5.69
1024×128	2.05	1.66	14.33
1024×1024	1.89	2.96	17.62

Table 2.3: Number of cycles consumed by the FFT divided by $N \log_2 N$ on a 2.2 GHz AVX machine.

N	MKL	FFTW
32	0.81	1.62
64	0.67	1.16
192	0.90	1.04
1024	0.88	0.89
1024×128	1.16	1.48
1024×1024	1.50	2.51

Table 2.4: Number of cycles consumed by in-cache FFT divided by $N \log_2 N$ on a 2.2 GHz AVX machine.

programmer must seek out optimized libraries as far as possible. MKL is faster than FFTW for $N = 32$ and $N = 64$. Overall, the two libraries are comparable.

None of the operation counts match the theoretical lower bound of $0.75 N \log_2 N$ cycles, although MKL gets quite close for $N = 32$. For large N, the deviation from the theoretical bound is greater. We may be tempted to conclude that this is because of the memory references at the outer iterations of the FFT. In fact, there is so much cache on the 2.2 GHz AVX machine that all the data for even the problem instance with $N = 1024 \times 1024$ can comfortably fit in L3 cache. It is unclear whether optimizations to hide the cost of streaming data items from L3 cache are possible or whether they have been attempted.

N	MKL	FFTW
32	0.975	4.86
64	1.61	4.04
1024	2.00	3.16

Table 2.5: Number of cycles consumed by forward FFT divided by $N \log_2 N$ on a 2.2 GHz AVX machine.

In table 2.4, the cycle counts are much closer to the $0.75 N \log_2 N$ lower bound. These in-cache cycle counts were obtained by applying the inverse FFT to the same array of $2N$ double-precision numbers initialized to 0. In fact, MKL goes below the theoretical bound for $N = 4^3 = 64$.

The power of 4 FFT is applicable to $N = 4^3$ and has a lower operation count than $5 N \log_2 N$.[21] MKL may be using an algorithm with an operation count lower than $5 N \log_2 N$. The 2.2 GHz AVX machine (see table A.1) has an in-core frequency that can exceed 2.2 GHz. The in-core acceleration may as well be the reason for the observed speed of MKL's $N = 64$ FFT being greater than the theoretical bound.

The in-cache numbers for MKL are better than for FFTW and sometimes significantly better. The fraction of scientific programs that remain in cache appears to be fairly large, and the in-cache advantage of MKL over FFTW is not insignificant. In the next chapter, we will discuss the type of instruction pipeline optimizations needed to achieve MKL speeds. MKL is certainly optimizing better for the instruction pipeline than FFTW.

So far, we have only been applying the inverse FFT. The inverse discrete transform (2.2) is unnormalized, and there is no need to divide by N at the end. In table 2.5, we turn to the forward FFT, which must be normalized by dividing by N, and get a nasty surprise. The performance of FFTW has deteriorated by more than a factor of 4 in one instance and by about a factor of 2 in the other two instances.

How can as simple an operation as dividing by N cause such sharp deterioration? The answer will become clearer in the next chapter. The loop for dividing by N in the member function `fwd()` of the class `fft_fftw` looks innocuous:

```
for(int i=0; i < 2*n; i++)
        f[i] /= n;
```

---

[21]See van Loan (1992).

The member function `fwd()` is defined within the class and therefore gets inlined. As we have already indicated in passing, `icpc` does not seem to optimize loops of inlined functions adequately.[22] The loop for dividing by N can be optimized by turning the division into multiplication by $1.0/N$. Multiplications are much faster than divisions. However, `icpc` does not do this optimization nor does it attempt to exploit loop-level parallelism—facts that can be ascertained by inspecting the assembly code.

The next chapter shows how to inspect assembly code and what to expect from the compiler. Optimizations that may appear obvious to the programmer are sometimes not effected by compilers, as we just saw.

Exercise 2.4.1. If $\omega = \exp(2\pi\sqrt{-1}/N)$, prove that $\omega^k \neq 1$ and $\omega^{kN} = 1$ for $k = 1, 2, \ldots, N-1$. Prove that

$$\sum_{j=0}^{N-1} \omega^{kj} = 0$$

for $k = 1, 2, \ldots, N-1$.

Exercise 2.4.2. Use the previous exercise to argue that the matrix with (j, k)th entry equal to $\omega^{jk}/\sqrt{N}$ has orthonormal columns. Conclude that the transforms (2.1) and (2.2) are inverses of each other.

Exercise 2.4.3. The inverse discrete Fourier transform is defined by

$$f_j = \sum_{k=0}^{N-1} \omega^{jk} \hat{f}_k,$$

where $\omega = \exp(2\pi\sqrt{-1}/N)$. Suppose N is even and $N = 2n$. We may write $k = 2\ell + p$, with $p = 0$ or $p = 1$, and decompose the sum as

$$f_j = \sum_{\ell=0}^{n-1} \sum_{p=0}^{1} \omega^{2j\ell} \omega^{jp} \hat{f}_{2\ell+p}$$

$$= \sum_{\ell=0}^{n-1} \omega^{2j\ell} \hat{f}_{2\ell} + \omega^j \sum_{\ell=0}^{n-1} \omega^{2k\ell} \hat{f}_{2\ell+1}.$$

Notice that $\omega^2 = \exp(2\pi\sqrt{-1}/n)$ and interpret the two summations above as inverse discrete Fourier transforms of dimension n. Explain how to reduce a transform of dimension $N = 2n$ to two transforms of dimension n.

---

[22]This statement about `icpc` has been verified for versions 10 through 15.

Exercise 2.4.4. Suppose $N = 2^n$. The array `a[]` of dimension N may be indexed using bit sequences of length n with the index ranging from $0 = 00...0$ to $N - 1 = 11...1$. In the bit-reversed permutation, `a[j]` and `a[k]` are interchanged if the bit sequence of length n corresponding to k is the reversal of the one corresponding to j.

- Write a program to effect the bit-reversed permutation of an array of `doubles` in place.

- Assume that `a[]` is an array of complex numbers, with each complex number represented using two adjacent `doubles`. Write a program to effect the bit-reversed permutation of `a[]` in place.

Exercise 2.4.5. Let $f(x) = |\sin(x)|$, $x_j = 2\pi j/N$, and $f_j = f(x_j)$. Graph the discrete Fourier transform of f_j with $N = 10^4$. Repeat with $f(x) = \sin(\sin(x))$. What do you observe?

Exercise 2.4.6. Let $N = 1024$ and initialize a complex array of size N to 0. Apply MKL's inverse FFT to the same array 10^6 times. Histogram the 10^6 cycle counts (you will need the `TimeStamp` class described in the next chapter). If your machine has L1 data cache of at least 16 KB, you will observe something closer to the normal distribution than the plots in figure 2.6. Why? Fit the normal law and calculate the mean and variance of the fit.

Exercise 2.4.7. Tables 2.3 and 2.4 report the number of cycles consumed by an in-place, complex one-dimensional FFT of dimension N, the latter with data in cache and the former with data out of cache. For each value of N in the tables, find the bandwidth to memory realized in bytes/cycles as well as GB/s, under the assumption that all the extra cycles for out-of-cache FFT are due to data access. Investigate the possibility that the in-cache numbers are artificially low because the FFT operates on an array that is always zero.

Exercise 2.4.8. Assuming versions 11 or 12 of the `icpc` compiler, the member function `fwd()` of the class `fft_fftw` may be sped up as follows. Remove the for-loop for dividing the array `f[]` by n. Instead, call a function `scale_fwd(double *f, int n)`. The function first calculates `double x = 1.0/n` and then multiplies each of the $2n$ `double` entries of `f[]` by `x`. Compile using `-fno-inline-functions`. Recalculate table 2.5 and show that the forward transform with FFTW is now much faster.

2.5   References

E. Anderson, Z. Bai, C. Bischof, S. Blackford, J. Demmel, J. Dongarra, J. Du Croz, A. Greenbaum, S. Hammarling, A. McKenney, and D. Sorensen. *LAPACK User's Guide*. SIAM, Philadelphia, 3rd edition, 1999. 1st ed. 1987.

J.W. Cooley and J.W. Tukey. An algorithm for the machine calculation of complex Fourier series. *Mathematics of Computation*, 19:297–301, 1965.

J.W. Demmel. *Applied Numerical Linear Algebra*. SIAM, Philadelphia, 1997.

J.J. Dongarra, J. Du Croz, S. Hammarling, and R.J. Hanson. An extended set of Fortran basic linear algebra subprograms. *ACM TOMS*, 14:1–17, 1988.

J.J. Dongarra, J. Du Croz, S. Hammarling, and I. Duff. A set of level 3 basic linear algebra subprograms. *ACM TOMS*, 16:1–17, 1990.

E. Elmroth, F. Gustavson, I. Jonsson, and B. Kågström. Recursive blocked algorithms and hybrid data structures for dense matrix library software. *SIAM Review*, 47: 3–45, 2004.

M. Frigo. A fast Fourier transform compiler. *Proc. 1999 ACM SIGPLAN conference*, 35:169–180, 1999.

N.J. Higham. *Accuracy and Stability of Numerical Algorithms*. SIAM, Philadelphia, 2nd edition, 2002.

S.G. Johnson and M. Frigo. The design and implementation of FFTW3. *Proc. of the IEEE special issue on Program Generation, Optimization, and Platform Adaptation*, 93:216–233, 2005.

M. Kerrisk. *The Linux Programming Interface*. No Starch Press, San Francisco, 2010.

C.L. Lawson, R.J. Hanson, D.R. Kincaid, and F.T. Krogh. Basic linear algebra subprograms for Fortran usage. *ACM TOMS*, 5:308–323, 1979.

J.R. Levine. *Linkers and Loaders*. Morgan Kaufmann, San Francisco, 1999.

W.H. Press, S.A. Teukolsky, W.T. Vetterling, and B.P. Flannery. *Numerical Recipes 3rd edition: The Art of Scientific Computating*. Cambridge University Press, Cambridge, 2007.

S. Toledo. Locality of reference in lu decomposition with partial pivoting. *SIAM J. Matrix Anal. Appl,* 18:1065–1081, 1997.

C. van Loan. *Computational Frameworks for the Fast Fourier Transform*. SIAM, Philadelphia, 1992.

Chapter 3

The Processor

The 80286 processor of 1982 had a mere 134,000 transistors. The Pentium 4 of 2001 had 4.2 million transistors. Processor packages in the x86 line for sale in 2015 have several billion transistors packed into less than $0.25\,\mathrm{cm}^2$.[1] These advances in processor technology are correlated with the rise of computer technology as a whole.

Early x86 computers, such as the 80286 or the Pentium 4, featured a single central processor. Modern processor packages may have a dozen or so processors, and this number is constantly increasing. As a result of the explosion in the number of transistors, the design of each processor has changed considerably. A great deal of parallelism is built into modern processors, and this parallelism is active even when the thread of execution is serial.

In contrast to this rapid progress in hardware, the software environment of the scientific programmer is nearly the same as what it was 15 years ago. In recent years, innovation in software has been driven by the Internet and mobile gadgetry and largely sidesteps the great difficulties in programming modern hardware optimally. If a compiler of 20 years ago was likely to generate excellent code for the processor of its day, that was less so in the case of a compiler of 10 years ago. Even for many simple

---

[1] This data is for Intel Xeon E5 v3 (Haswell) family.

programs, the compilers of today do not generate optimal code or anything like it.

Good, or nearly optimal, programs for modern platforms can be written only with a knowledge of the nuances of the computer's hardware. With that in mind, this chapter, indeed the rest of this book, will introduce programming models in close concert with computer architecture.

This chapter is organized into three sections. Section 3.1 is an overview of x86 architecture and assembly programming. The x86 line has held sway for more than three decades to the extent that nearly 100% of the computers in use outside of the mobile world in 2015 belong to this line. The x86 architecture is vast,[2] and our interest is limited to a tiny part of it.

To understand program speed and to determine whether compilers are doing a good job, it is essential to know a little about the register set and about the instruction mix. Our interest in sections 3.1.1 and 3.1.2 is limited to this part of the x86 architecture and no more. Although we introduce assembly programming, we do so only to the extent necessary to identify assembly code generated by compilers for inner loops and to make sense of function calls. There is no suggestion in those sections that the reader should program in assembly. The need to program in assembly is only for the rare expert. However, inasmuch as our intention is to gain understanding of programming and program speed on a rational basis, it is essential to understand the assembly code generated by compilers for inner loops.

Section 3.2 is one of the more important parts of this book. Sections 3.2.2 through 3.2.7 have a single focus, which is to expose some of the inner workings of the compiler. In these sections, we inspect the assembly code generated by compilers to gain an understanding of the quality of assembly code generated for inner loops. Only a limited understanding of assembly programming is needed. It suffices to identify the type of registers and instructions that are being used in the innermost loop for the most part. In section 3.2.1, we explain how to gather statistics and make tables and plots easily in C/C++. Such preliminaries simplify programming.

Sections 3.2.2 through 3.2.7 put to rest a popular belief that Fortran programs are faster than C/C++. If the `restrict` qualifier is used appropriately, compilers can effect every loop optimization applicable in Fortran in C/C++. Section 3.2.6

---

[2]The x86 instruction set architecture is documented in Intel 64 and IA-32 Architectures' Software Developer's Manual, Volumes 1, 2A, 2B, 3A, 3B, and AMD64 Architecture Programmer's Manual, Volumes 1, 2, 3, 4, 5. The entire documentation runs to more than 5,000 pages.

directly takes on the false belief that C++ programs are condemned to be slower than Fortran. In that section, we write a naive C++ program for multiplying matrices using general classes for vectors and matrices and show that it is more than an order of magnitude slower. The culprit here is the naivety of the programmer and not the C++ language. A C++ program written with an idea of how compilers work, and the kind of instruction stream they may generate, will be faster than a Fortran program written without that knowledge. The C/C++ programming languages provide every available means for writing optimized programs, and there is no other programming language or paradigm, including Fortran, that is remotely comparable to them in this respect.

The skill of writing loops explained in section 3.2 is about 40% of what the typical scientific programmer needs to know to produce well-optimized programs. Another 40% is about optimizing memory accesses in a single-core program, a closely related topic discussed in the next chapter. Many subtle concepts and techniques come up when we study threads and networks. However, in optimizing scientific programs, much of the game is in structuring loops carefully, as explained in this chapter, and in organizing memory accesses, as explained in the next chapter. For example, when we optimize a program to effect a matrix transpose in chapter 6, much of the optimization boils down to structuring loops and organizing accesses to memory, even though the program makes sophisticated use of networking and threading.

The brief summary, in the preceding paragraph, of the relative worth of various techniques of optimization is for scientific programs, which generally tend to work with known amounts of data that are laid out in regular patterns. In computer science, data tends to be dynamic and highly unpredictable in extent. Dynamic data structures such as linked lists, trees, and graphs are commonly employed. When such data structures are used, the relative worth of various optimization techniques changes considerably. Optimizing for memory, which is the topic of the next chapter, is considerably more important. Loop optimizations discussed in this chapter are not as important. However, more and more scientific programs are taking on qualities of systems programming, and, conversely, some newer areas of computer science such as data analysis and image processing give rise to programs that are similar to traditional scientific programs.

In section 2.4, we found that optimized libraries such as MKL and FFTW can be nearly an order of magnitude faster than Numerical Recipes. Why are optimized libraries nearly an order of magnitude faster? A big part of the answer has to do with optimization for the instruction pipeline and the register set.

Optimizing for the processor's register set and instruction pipeline is a difficult skill, and section 3.3 explains how to do it. Although sections 3.3.1 and 3.3.2 are not overly technical, the following two sections, 3.3.3 and 3.3.4, are not for the faint of heart. This is the only part of the book where assembly programming is essential.

The value of optimizing for the instruction pipeline and the register set is well known in dense numerical linear algebra and, as already pointed out, in computational Fourier analysis. However, even in these areas, the technical knowledge essential for effecting such optimizations is known only to a small number of cognoscenti. There can be little doubt that wider knowledge of such techniques will uncover more opportunities for such optimizations. Even for the Fast Fourier Transform (FFT), theoretical lower bounds are well below actual out-of-cache performance, and there could be room for additional investigations in this gap. Knowledge of computer architecture creates more possibilities for the programmer and opens a whole new point of view.

To conclude this introduction, we turn to a question that may be on the reader's mind. If we are delving as deeply into processor architecture as we do in this chapter, won't much of this chapter become irrelevant as the hardware changes? The answer is no, and emphatically no as long as the x86 dominance persists.

A look at table 3.1, to which we will return many times, will help explain why that is so. It shows the gradual evolution in instruction set architectures from 1999 to 2016/2017 and beyond. Section 3.2 connects the workings of the compiler to XMM (SSE2) and YMM (AVX/AVX2) registers. This section will hardly change when the ZMM registers and their successors come along, except that the kind of concepts discussed in it will increase in importance. None of the C/C++ programs discussed in that section needs to be changed. Indeed, many of the same points could have been made in 2001.

Table 3.1 shows the gradual evolution in instruction set architectures from Streaming SIMD Extensions (SSE) to SSE2 to Advanced Vector Extensions (AVX) to AVX2. The expansion in register width from 128-bit XMM registers to 256-bit YMM registers to 512-bit ZMM registers is one part of the evolution. Another part of the evolution is the addition of new instructions. In the instruction vaddpd, v stands for vector, as may be expected, and pd for packed double. The packed double instructions operate on all the double-precision numbers stored in a vector register simultaneously. Thus, a single vaddpd instruction applied to YMM registers results in four additions. The AVX2 instruction set architecture introduced fused-multiply-add instructions,

ISA	Year	Family	Registers	Instructions
SSE	1999	Pentium	XMM (128 bit)	ADDPS, MULPS
SSE2	2001	Pentium 4, Nehalem, Westmere, Opteron, Athlon	XMM (128 bit)	ADDPD, MULPD
AVX	2011	Sandy Bridge, Ivy Bridge, Bulldozer, Jaguar	YMM (256 bit)	VADDPD, VMULPD,
AVX2	2013	Haswell, Broadwell	YMM (256 bit)	VADDPD, VMULPD, VFM*ADDPD
AVX-512	2015	Skylake	ZMM (512 bit)	VADDPD, VMULPD, VFM*ADDPD

Table 3.1: Generations of x86 instruction set architectures (ISAs) and machines implementing them. The machine families typically include several machines. For example, Xeon-5650 and Xeon-5670 are machines in the Westmere family (or microarchitecture). This table was prepared by consulting several Wikipedia pages. For a list of machines used in this book, see table A.1 in the appendix. Not all versions of Skylake support AVX-512.

namely, `fmadd132pd`, `fmadd213pd`, and `fmadd231pd`. These instructions implement operations of the form $c = c + ab$ or $a = c + ab$ while operating on three vector registers. Thus, a `fmadd*pd` instruction applied to three YMM registers results in four additions and four multiplications.

We will refer to machines as 2.6 GHz SSE2 or 3.6 GHz AVX2. The full information about the machine may be found by looking up table A.1 in the appendix. The instruction set is the part of the computer's architecture most pertinent to program speed, which explains the nomenclature we adopt.

The type of processor design we see today is a product of research that happened as early as the 1960s, with important additions in the 1970s and 1980s.[3] These design

---

[3]See Hennessy and Patterson (1990-2011). The 1960s reference is to Tomasulo's algorithm, which

principles were incorporated into the x86 line in the 1990s, and the underlying design principles have not changed greatly since then. The x86 instruction set has evolved gradually and methodically. Therefore, not only do the fundamental concepts of optimization for processor architectures remain the same, the particular form they take within C/C++ programs does not change much either.

In addition, there has been a great deal of convergence in processor technology since 2000 so that nearly 100% of desktop processors are now x86 based. The pertinence of the particular examples, as well as that of general principles of program optimization described in this chapter, is unlikely to diminish anytime soon. In fact, the pertinence of computer architecture to program optimization appears to be growing.

Section 3.3 shows how to optimize for the instruction pipeline for SSE2 machines. The instruction pipeline depends on the instruction set architecture and to a far lesser extent on its microarchitectural realization (family in table 3.1). Because the programs in this section are in assembly, they will need to be updated for machines with YMM and ZMM registers (AVX, AVX2, AVX-512). The updating for the YMM registers is the topic of several exercises. ZMM registers are discussed in chapter 7 on the Xeon Phi. Using XMM registers has the advantage that the programs we discuss will run on almost any computer, including AVX and AVX2 machines.

The payoff from this type of optimization is increasing rapidly. A matrix multiplication program written in 2010 in C/C++ approached nearly a third of the speed of a program optimized for the SSE2 processor pipeline. Five years later, the C/C++ program does not even come within a tenth of the speed of a program optimized for the AVX2 processor pipeline.

In section 3.2.5, we explain why the same C/C++ program has become so much worse, when compared to a fully optimized program, over a span of five years. There are two related reasons. After clock speeds flat-lined around 2003, and even before, processors have used greater and greater numbers of transistors for greater and greater parallelism. At one level, that translates to more and more processor cores in a single processor package. Inside a processor, the same trend translates to vector registers and instruction pipelines that can simultaneously execute multiple instructions. Even as there is a greater pay-off in optimizing for such pipelines, it becomes harder for the compilers to do so.

---

is mentioned later in this chapter.

In 2015, nearly 100% of non-mobile computers and laptops run on x86 processors. It would take a cataclysmic event (cataclysmic for Intel Corporation), such as Apple Computers switching its MacBooks and desktops from the x86 line to ARM, for the x86 line to be truly challenged.[4] Intel is not as invulnerable to market forces as it used to be one or two decades ago, but it still dominates the processor benchmarks overwhelmingly. Such a cataclysmic event is not on the horizon as of 2015.

3.1 Overview of the x86 architecture

This section is a basic introduction to the x86 instruction architecture, which has dominated since its introduction in 1978. We look at registers and a little bit of assembly programming. Our intention is to lay the foundation for the next section, where we look at compilation and show how to tell whether a compiler has generated good code or not. All that is required is a familiarity with the names of some of the registers and a few instructions. The instruction names are often self-explanatory.

Accordingly, the assembly programming we exhibit is basic. Yet one of the programs we look at is quite useful. This program implements a C++ class `TimeStamp` for accessing the Time Stamp Counter, which is one of the best methods to measure time on a computer. This C++ class is used throughout the book.

The x86 assembly language is known for its huge complexity. Understanding assembly programming is a mammoth task meant for compiler writers and computer architects, not for the average scientist. Our intention here is to gain a basic understanding only—in other words, our aim is to splash a little water, not to become expert swimmers. Without some understanding of assembly programming, many aspects of computer architecture as well as the workings of compilers and linkers take on a remote quality. In addition, it is impossible to gain an appreciation of the value of optimized scientific codes.

3.1.1 64-bit x86 architecture

Perhaps a good way to begin is by looking at a processor package. Figure 3.1 shows what a processor package looks like from the outside.[5] There are pins to transfer

---

[4]I thank Hans Johnston for this point.

[5]The land coordinates in the figure are from Quad-core Intel Xeon Processor 5400 Series: Datasheet.

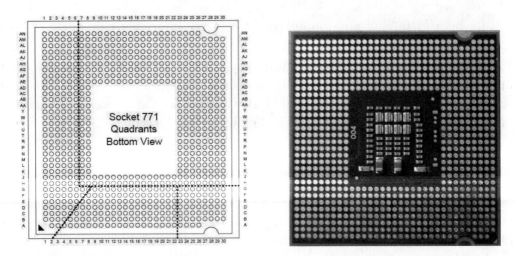

Figure 3.1: Land coordinates of Intel's Xeon 5400 processor and a photograph of the same processor. The land coordinates are used to identify pins, which are shown in the photo.

addresses and data to and from memory, pins to interrupt the processors, and so on. The processor package shown has only four processor cores. More recent packages have many more cores, and it takes multiple pages to describe their land coordinates.

When we write programs, we do so with an awareness of memory. Every variable name is ultimately the name for a segment of memory. However, in most programming, we have no awareness of the registers at all. Registers are locations that reside on the chip that are capable of holding data or addresses. They are very special locations because they are wired into the circuits for carrying out arithmetic and logical operations. When arithmetic operations are executed by the processor, all the operands may be registers. To add two numbers in memory, for instance, typically we have to first move one or both of them to registers, add the two registers, and move the result from a register to a memory location. The addresses of the memory locations can also be held in the registers.

Registers

The x86 64-bit architecture is first of all a specification of registers (see figure 3.2). The architecture was first introduced by AMD and later adopted by Intel. Some

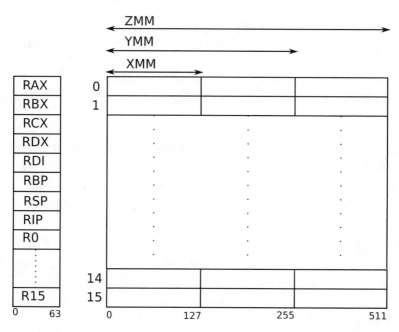

Figure 3.2: Partial register diagram of an x86 processor. The general-purpose registers (RAX to R15) are all 64-bit wide. The XMM, YMM, and ZMM registers are 128, 256, and 512 bit wide, respectively.

variable names may only correspond to specific registers. The following are some of the registers in the 64-bit x86 architecture:

- Eight 64-bit registers, including %rax, %rbx, %rcx, %rdx, %rdi, %rbp, %rsp.

- If the r in the above names is replaced by e, we get names for 32-bit registers. These are the lower halves of the 64-bit registers.

- Eight more 64-bit general-purpose registers %r8 through %r15.

- To access only the lower 32 bits, we can use %r8d through %r15d. Here d stands for double word.

- Floating point register stack with eight 80-bit registers called %st(0) through %st(7). Eight 64-bit MMX registers %mm0 through %mm7. We will never use these registers.

- Sixteen 128-bit registers `%xmm0` through `%xmm15`. Each register can hold two double-precision numbers. These are the so-called SSE registers.

- Each XMM register is extended to a 256-bit YMM register in AVX (see table 3.1). The YMM registers are `%ymm0` through `%ymm15`. The YMM registers have in turn been extended in AVX-512 (see table 3.1).

The AMD/Intel manuals use slightly different names for the registers. For instance, `%rax` becomes `RAX`. The naming in our list anticipates our use of GAS (the GNU assembler). The partial list omits a number of registers. From some of the registers we have listed, we can get 16-bit or word-length registers and 8-bit or byte-length integers by changing the names appropriately.

This list of registers may appear long and a bit intimidating. To master it all can indeed be quite a task. For our purposes, it suffices to know that there are 16 general-purpose registers and 16 XMM/YMM registers. The different uses that these registers are put to will emerge as this chapter progresses. The XMM/YMM registers are the basis of fast scientific programs.

There is a 64-bit register called `%rip` that users normally do not access. That register is the instruction pointer. It is the offset of the address of the next instruction to be executed relative to some base. But that interpretation can be problematic because of instruction pipelining and out-of-order execution.

Backward binary compatibility

The 64-bit x86 architecture carries within it ghosts from decades past. Some of these ghosts are easily seen in the naming of the register set, which is the most basic feature of all processor architectures. At first there seems to be no good reason to call a register `rax` or `rbx`. However, when the first 8086 16-bit processor was introduced back in 1978, large numbers of registers must have seemed a distant dream. So it was natural to use the first few letters of the alphabet for the registers. When the 32-bit 80386 was introduced in 1985, names such as `ax` were changed to `eax`, signaling the enhancements to the size of the registers. The register names in the 64-bit x86 architecture reflect this evolution.

Binary compatibility is the reason for this peculiar evolution. It may make no sense to expect a 64-bit x86 processor of today to run a 16-bit binary from 1978, but it makes sense to expect it to run the 32-bit binaries of a few years ago. All the 64-bit x86 processors have a 32-bit mode that can be turned on by the operating system. If they did not have such a mode, nearly every one of the many 32-bit software systems available would have failed when the 64-bit architecture was first introduced. Backward binary compatibility gives software developers, especially developers of operating systems, time to catch up. Backward compatibility means that an instruction such as MOVL EAX EBX that made sense in the 32-bit architecture must also make sense in the 64-bit x86 architecture. Not only that, its encoding using bits must be exactly the same (its encoding is 89 C3 in hexadecimal—the first byte is the opcode for MOVL and the second byte, which encodes the source and destination registers, is the so-called ModR/M byte).

The disadvantage of backward binary compatibility is that it constrains the design of the instruction set and the microarchitecture used to implement it in hardware. Every time the instruction set is extended, the binary encoding of the earlier instruction set as well as its semantics must be preserved intact. This burden can be considerable. For instance, programs written in 1990 could rely on the register %eip to point to the address of the next instruction to be executed and manipulate that register to jump to some other point in the program. Not only must today's x86 architecture include that register, it should also give the same effect when the %eip is altered to jump to some other location in the program. Having to bear this considerable burden has meant that the x86 architecture is infamous for its extremely complicated binary encodings of instructions.

History has shown that the disadvantages of backward binary compatibility are outweighed by the advantage of being readily usable. The x86 architecture always seeks to be usable. A new design that is brought out today must run yesterday's binaries. This emphasis on usability has meant that the vast majority of today's computers (excluding mobile devices) use x86 processors.[6]

Yet one must not exaggerate the benefits of backward binary compatibility in relation to the x86 architecture. Intel, the foremost champion of the x86 line, is no longer the invincible behemoth it once was. Intel is tied to the PC business, which is in gradual decline, and has no control over hardware or software platforms in the rapidly

---

[6]The ARM architecture has a much simpler instruction set and has achieved wide use on mobile gadgets. The number of ARM devices is greater than the number of x86 computers. Thus, the ARM architecture does not suffer from a lack of widespread adoption and the consequent lack of economy of scale, which has been a bane of previous challengers to x86. However, the terms of commercial licensing of ARM are such that the benefits of its wide adoption are shared by many companies.

growing mobile computing and networking sectors. Despite the enormous investment in design accumulated over many years, the volume of profit being generated in the computer business is now so great that a legitimate challenger to the x86 line is not inconceivable. In a business that is growing exponentially, what happens in the next five years can be of more consequence than what happened in the past four decades.

3.1.2   64-bit x86 assembly programming

Each processor core fetches instructions from memory and executes them. These instructions are stored in memory as a sequence of bytes. In assembly language, the bytes that encode machine instructions are replaced by mnemonics. For example, an instruction to move a quad word, which is eight bytes in size, from register r8 to register rax is coded as the following hex sequence 4C 89 C0. The first byte 4C is the so-called REX byte, the second byte 89 is the opcode, and the third byte C0 encodes the fact that the source register is r8 and the destination is rax.[7] In the 64-bit x86 architecture, opcodes can be one, two, or three bytes. A single instruction can be as many as 17 bytes.

Unlike processors, we can't just look at bits and make sense of them, which is why the assembly languages provide mnemonics. In the GNU assembler, which is called GAS, the mnemonic for the instruction to move a quad word from r8 to rax is movq %r8, %rax. To move a double word, which is four bytes stored in the lower halves of the 64-bit registers, the mnemonic is movl %r8d, %eax. These mnemonics vary with the assembler. In the MASM assembler, the mnemonic for moving a quad word from r8 to rax would be MOVQ RAX R8—notice that the registers are given in reverse order.

There is no standardization in the world of x86 assembly languages. The documentation for the instruction set, which include the mnemonics for various instructions, is published by AMD and Intel. However, the mnemonics can change in a predictable fashion depending on the assembly language. For instance, a register referred to as R8 in the AMD/Intel documentation becomes %r8 in GAS. One point is important to keep in mind. In the AMD/Intel manuals, the destination precedes the source. In GAS, the destination follows the source. We will always use the GAS convention. On Linux computers, even the Intel compilers use the GNU assembler.

---

[7]The third byte is given by the AMD manuals.

The reader may find it a little puzzling that "double" (or "long") is used for 32-bit operands and "quad" for 64-bit operands. A word in the original 8086 machine of 1978 was 16 bits. Thus, double words are 32 bits and quad words are 64 bits, as a result of a choice made long ago.

Getting started

For our first assembly program, we begin with the following simple C code:

```
#include <stdio.h>
int main(){
  int x, y, z;
  x = 1;
  y = 2;
  z = 3;
  printf("The sum of %d and %d is %d \n", x, y, z);
}
```

It is compiled using

```
gcc -S -O3 add.c
```

The -S flag tells the compiler to generate assembly only and leave it in the file add.s. Optimization is turned on with the -O3 flag so that the compiler generates cleaner code.

Below is a listing of the addtwo.s assembly code. The listing is a cleaned up version of the code generated by the compiler. In particular, we removed some code at the bottom related to an error handler.

```
1  .file      "addtwo.s"
2        .section   .mydata,"aMS",@progbits,1
3  .LC0:
4        .string    "The sum of %d and %d is %d\n"
5        .text
6  .globl main
7        .type      main, @function
8  main:
9        movl $3, %ecx
```

```
10        movl $2, %edx
11        movl $1, %esi
12        movl $.LC0, %edi
13        xorl %eax, %eax
14        call printf
15        ret
```

The instructions are specified using mnemonics in the **main** block, which begins at line 9. The earlier lines are assembler directives. The syntax for the directives can vary considerably between different assemblers.

The first line, which gives the name of the file, is a directive. The second line asks the compiler to begin a section called .mydata. One has to dig through the GAS documentation to decipher the portion that follows. The second line states that the section is meant to hold data, that each character is one byte, and that the strings will be terminated by 0. The strings are terminated by 0, anticipating the need to pass them to the **printf** function in the C library. In C, strings are always NULL or 0 terminated.

.LC0 is the name of the string specified in line 4. It corresponds to a location in memory. Here the assembler takes on the responsibility of storing the specified string in the data section and gives the location the name .LC0.

The text section, which is not named, begins on line 5. The text section will contain instructions. The name **main** is specified to be a global, and the name of a function in lines 6 and 7—**main** will be visible outside the file and is the name for an address in the text segment, which corresponds to line 8.

In the following code, the 32-bit registers %esi, %edx, and %ecx are filled with 1, 2, and 3, respectively. These are the second, third, and fourth arguments in the call to printf. Because .LC0 is the address of a location in the data segment, it can only be 32 bits. Thus, the **movl** instruction is used to move it into the register %edi. The **xorl** instruction zeros the **eax** register as a precaution.

The 64-bit x86 architecture requires the first four arguments to be placed in %edi, %esi, %edx, and %ecx. The call to **printf** is made with those arguments. Here **printf** is an externally defined name and has to be resolved during linking.

To assemble,[8] we may use

---

[8]The **icc** compiler uses the GNU Assembler (GAS). For its documentation, see (Using as, D. Elsner and J. Fenlason).

```
icc -c addtwo.s
```

to produce the object file `addtwo.o` (we are back to using `icc`). The object file can be linked to produce an executable using

```
icc -o addtwo.exe addtwo.o
```

The `icc` linker takes care of resolving the reference to `printf` in `addtwo.o`. When the executable `addtwo.exe` is run, we are told that

```
The sum of 1 and 2 is 3
```

More about function calls

The output of the next listing, which is

```
The sum of 1 2 3 4 5 6 7 8 is 36
```

is hardly more exciting. However, it illustrates function calls made after placing some arguments on the stack.

```
 1   .file       "addmany.s"
 2       .section   .mydata,"aMS",@progbits,1
 3   .LC0:
 4       .string    "The sum of %d %d %d %d %d %d %d %d  is %d \n"
 5       .text
 6   .globl main
 7       .type      main, @function
 8   main:
 9       subq $32, %rsp
10       movl $36, 24(%rsp)
11       movl $8, 16(%rsp)
12       movl $7, 8(%rsp)
13       movl $6, (%rsp)
14       movl $5, %r9d
15       movl $4, %r8d
16       movl $3, %ecx
17       movl $2, %edx
18       movl $1, %esi
```

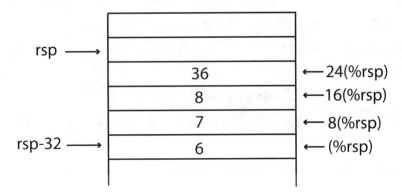

Figure 3.3: The stack pointer is moved downward by 32 and the numbers 6, 7, 8, and 36 are placed on the stack before a call to `printf`. The labeling on the right assumes that the stack pointer has been moved downward.

```
19        movl  $.LC0 , %edi
20        xorl  %eax , %eax
21        call  printf
22        addq  $32 , %rsp
23        ret
```

The `addmany.s` program calls `printf()` (on line 21) with a total of 10 arguments. These are first the format string, next the numbers 1 through 8, and finally their sum, which is 36. The last four of these arguments are pushed onto the program stack (see figure 3.3) and the first six are placed in registers as before. It helps to think of the registers as an extension of the stack.

Each argument pushed onto the stack is an `int` and therefore 4 bytes. Thus, we would need 16 bytes on the stack. However, in 64-bit x86 architecture, each entry on the stack must be a multiple of 8 bytes. Therefore, we need 32 bytes on the stack.

By convention, `%rsp` is the pointer to the top entry of the stack. On line 9, the stack pointer `%rsp` is decremented by 32 bytes to make room for four more entries. In x86, the stack grows downward from a high address as shown in figure 3.3. The arguments are pushed onto the stack in reverse order. Thus, the final argument 36 is pushed first onto the stack (line 10). That is followed by the preceding three arguments 8, 7, and 6 (lines 11, 12, and 13, respectively). For addressing modes of the type `(%rsp)` and `8(%rsp)`, see figure 3.3. They are explained in greater detail below. The stack pointer

%rsp points to the top, which is 6 (see the right part of figure 3.3).

We may think of the registers used to pass arguments as an extension of the stack. These are %r9, %r8, %rcx (or %ecx), %rdx (or %edx), %rsi (or %esi), and %rdi (or %edi), in bottom to top order (lines 14 through 19). Thus, the top six entries of the call stack are in registers, with %rdi at the top by convention. If a function call has six or fewer arguments, the entire call stack is stored in registers.

When the call to printf is made, the function has to retrieve some arguments from the registers and some from the stack. Line 22 moves the stack pointer back to its original location: the caller cleans up the stack after the function that is called returns.

Addressing modes

Let us go back to the listing and look at usages such as (%rsp) and 8(%rsp) once again. The first usage (%rsp) is a memory reference using a base register. Here the base register is %rsp and it stores a 64-bit address. When memory is referenced in this way using a base register, it is as if the base register is a pointer that is dereferenced.

The memory reference 8(%rsp) uses a base register and a displacement. The displacement is 8 and the base register is %rsp. The memory location referred to is the one whose address is the content of the base register with the displacement added to it.

Memory references in machine language are similar to the way pointers are handled in C. If rsp is thought of as a pointer-type variable in C, the meaning of (%rsp) is the same as *rsp. In other words, an address is dereferenced and an rvalue converted to an lvalue. Likewise, 8(%rsp) has the same meaning as rsp[8] or *(rsp+8) in C, but we must be a little careful here. In C, +8 would be +64 if rsp pointed to double (8 bytes) and +32 if rsp pointed to int (4 bytes). In assembly, there is no notion of types, and +8 is always +8.

Although +8 is always +8 in assembly, the analogy to C goes further. A reference such as 8(%rax,%rdx) that fits the format

```
displacement(base register, index register)
```

evaluates to the memory location whose address is the sum of the base, index, and the displacement. Thus, (%rax, %rdx) is equivalent to rax[rdx] in C syntax, with the caveat about +8 being +8. In x86 assembly, a memory location can be either a destination (lvalue) or a source (rvalue).

Yet another memory addressing mode is as follows:

```
displacement(base register, index register, scale)
```

Its meaning is almost self-explanatory. Thus, 8(%rax, %rbx, 16) is equivalent to rax[16*rbx+8] in C syntax, with the caveat stated above. The scale is allowed to take only certain values such as $1, 2, 4, 8, 16$.

3.1.3   The Time Stamp Counter

To do anything useful with assembly code, it helps to have a method to make it part of a C or C++ program. The asm directive allows us to embed assembly code in a C or C++ program. The implementation of the asm directive varies with the compiler. AMD's PGI compiler manual describes inline assembly in detail. The implementations of inline assembly by Intel and GNU compilers seem to correspond to the PGI documentation.

RDTSC or rdtsc is an x86 machine instruction for reading the Time Stamp Counter. The behavior of the Time Stamp Counter varies. Its basic function is to record the clock cycles. After the instruction is executed, the number of clock cycles is saved as a 64-bit number using two 32-bit registers, namely, eax and edx, with the higher bits in edx.

Why are 64 bits needed? A 2 GHz clock would tick 5×10^9 times in two and a half seconds, whereas the maximum unsigned integer that we can represent using 32 bits is $2^{32} - 1 \approx 4.3 \times 10^9$. A 2 GHz clock would wrap around in less than 10 seconds if the counter were to use only 32 bits. With 64 bits, the Time Stamp Counter is guaranteed not to wrap around for 10 years. However, the counter is reset every time the machine is booted.

The following inline assembly can be embedded into a C or C++ program:

```
asm volatile("rdtsc" : "=a" (a1), "=d" (d1));
```

Before this statement, a1 and d1 must be defined to be of type unsigned int. After the rdtsc instruction is completed, the registers eax and edx are copied to the variables a1 and d1, respectively. The segment that follows the colon is the output part of the inline assembly statement. In this case, the output part is

```
="a"(a1),="d"(d1)
```

The =a and =d are saying that the %eax and %edx registers must be output, using a as the code for eax and d as the code for edx, as may be verified by checking the documentation. The destinations for the output are given as (a1) and (d1), where a1 and d1 are variables of type unsigned int defined in the C or C++ program. In this way, we are able to execute a machine instruction and bring in information into variables that can be accessed within the C or C++ program.

The volatile qualifier asks the compiler not to change the assembly code as part of an optimization. In addition, if two inline assembly statements have the volatile qualifier, the compiler will not move the two statements past each other.

In some processors, such as those of the Pentium M family, the Time Stamp Counter is incremented every clock cycle. However, the frequency of clock ticks can vary. To decrease energy consumption, computers vary the frequency of clock ticks and the operating voltage. In other processors, such as the Intel Atom, the Time Stamp Counter is incremented at a constant rate regardless of the operating voltage and the actual frequency of the clock. The architectural behavior "moving forward" has been stated to be of the latter type.

Between two calls to rdtsc made on the same processor core, the second call is guaranteed to return a higher count.[9] However, rdtsc is not a serializing instruction. In the presence of multiple pipelines and out-of-order scheduling, some instructions that occur after rdtsc may complete sooner, although some instructions that occur before may complete later. However, one does not need to worry too much about such possibilities. With careful use, the Time Stamp Counter can be used to time events that take only a few nanoseconds.

It is of course a nuisance if we have to think about machine instructions every time we want to read the Time Stamp Counter in a C++ program. A simple C++ class greatly simplifies the use of the Time Stamp Counter. The interface of the TimeStamp class is given below.

```
class TimeStamp{
public:
   TimeStamp(){};
```

---

[9]Processes may be moved from core to core by the operating system. When that happens, the second reading of the Time Stamp Counter may be lesser than the first. See http://en.wikipedia.org/wiki/Time_Stamp_Counter.

```
    void tic();
    double toc();
};
```

The entire `TimeStamp` class is defined in the header file `TimeStamp.hh` to avoid function call overhead using function inlining. The constructor does nothing. A call to the member function `tic()` will issue the `rdtsc` instruction and record the counter in two variables of type `unsigned int`. A call to the member function `toc()` will read the Time Stamp Counter in the same way and will return the number of cycles elapsed since the last call to `tic()` as a `double`. The calculation to turn the information from the two readings of the Time Stamp Counter into a `double` is not shown.

The `TimeStamp` class can be used as follows:

```
TimeStamp ts;
ts.tic();
//... code to be timed ...
double cycles = ts.toc();
```

The `cycles` variable will hold the number cycles between `tic()` and `toc()`.

3.1.4   Cache parameters and the CPUID instruction

The registers on a processor are few in number. Large arrays and other large data structures cannot be stored in their entirety using registers. They are typically stored in memory (DRAM). However, memory is outside the processor chip. Although it takes only a few cycles to operate on registers, it takes a few hundred cycles to fetch a word from memory. To hide the cost of the large number of cycles required to access a word from memory, some memory words are *cached* on the chip itself. Cache memory is organized into several levels.

We will take a closer look at cache memory in the next chapter. Here we will use the `cpuid` instruction to ask the processor to report information about its cache and thus give us a preliminary idea of cache memory. As we look at assembly code and explore certain facets of the processor, it will help to have some idea of cache memory. Caches influence the performance of nearly every program.

The `cpuid` instruction can be used to extract a variety of information about the processor. If you type `cat /proc/cpuinfo` on a Linux computer, the command returns information about the processor's instruction set, power consumption, caches, support for specific technologies, and clock speed. Much of that information is obtained by the operating system using cpuid. The cpuid instruction has a manual of its own. The AMD and Intel processors use different conventions for cpuid.

The inline assembly statement for extracting information about caches using the cpuid instruction is given below. eax, ebx, and ecx must be defined as variables of type unsigned int, and i must be an integer value.

```
asm volatile("cpuid"                     //instruction
    :"=a"(eax), "=b"(ebx), "=c"(ecx)//output list
    :"a"(0x04), "c"(i)               //input list
    :"edx");                         //clobber list
```

This inline assembly statement has more complicated syntax than the one we used to read the Time Stamp Counter. The instruction, which is given as cpuid, is followed by three colons and not just one. We do not need to pass any parameters to the rdtsc instruction and all the data items created by the instruction are output to program variables. In the case of the cpuid instruction, we need to leave some data in the registers to tell the cpuid instruction what to do. In addition, not all the data items returned by the cpuid instruction are output to program variables. The syntax of this inline assembly statement is more complicated for these reasons.

The three colons in this inline assembly statement divide the part inside the parentheses into four segments. The first segment, which is before the first colon, gives the instruction to be executed. The second, third, and fourth segments give the output list, the input list, and the so-called clobber list, respectively. In this case, the output list specifies that the contents of the registers %eax, %ebx, and %ecx, which are indicated by =a, =b, and =c, respectively, must be output to the program variables eax, ebx, and ecx, respectively.

The input list specifies that the register %eax must be loaded with the hexadecimal number 04. This hexadecimal code tells cpuid to get information about cache. By loading other codes into %eax, cpuid can be asked to return information about performance counters, power managment, processor name, and other features of the processor. The input list loads the integer value i into the %ecx register. A processor typically has multiple levels of cache, and an integer value is loaded into %ecx to tell cpuid which cache it must get information about.

CPUID returns information in four registers: %eax, %ebx, %ecx, and %edx. Of these, only three are output to program variables. We have elected not to output the %edx register. Therefore, the clobber list, which is the segment following the third and last colon, includes %edx to tell the compiler that the instruction will write over that register. That way the compiler knows it must not save information in %edx with plans of using it later. The registers %eax, %ebx, and %ecx are also clobbered by the cpuid instruction. However, these should not be in the clobber list because the compiler can figure out that they are being clobbered from the input and output segments.

A program that uses the cpuid instruction to extract information about cache memory follows:

```
1    cout<<"CPUID with code 04h"<<endl;
2    unsigned int eax, ebx, ecx;
3    for(int i=0;;i++){
4      asm volatile("cpuid"
5              :"=a"(eax), "=b"(ebx), "=c"(ecx)
6              :"a"(0x04), "c"(i)
7              :"edx");
8      if((eax&0xF)==0)
9        break;
10     printf("cache type = %x\n",eax&0xF);
11     printf("cache level = %x\n", (eax>>5)&(0x7));
12     printf("ways of associativity = %u\n",
13         ((ebx>>22)&0xFFF)+1);
14     printf("physical line partitions = %x\n",
15         ((ebx>>12)&0x3FF)+1);
16     printf("cache line size = %u\n",(ebx&0xFFF)+1);
17     printf("number of sets = %u\n",ecx+1);
18     printf("cache size in bytes = %u\n\n",
19         (((ebx>>22)&0xFFF)+1)* //ways of associativity
20         (((ebx>>12)&0x3FF)+1)* //physical line partns
21         ((ebx&0xFFF)+1)* //cache line size
22         (ecx+1)); //number of sets
23   }
```

Lines 4 to 7 issue the cpuid instruction with $i = 0, 1, \ldots$ For each value of i, cpuid returns information about a different cache. It signals that there are no more caches by putting zeros in the last four bits of %eax. On line 8, (eax&0xF) extracts the last four bits of eax using a bitwise and operation with the hexadecimal number 0xF. If cpuid has signaled that there are no more caches, line 9 uses break to exit from the loop. Lines 10 to 22 extract information about the cache.

When the cpuid instruction was used to query a 2.6 GHz SSE2 machine (see table A.1 for the full names of the machines), it reported 32 KB of L1 instruction cache, 32 KB of L1 data cache, .26 MB of L2 cache, and 12.6 MB of L3 cache. On a 2.2 GHz AVX machine, the L3 cache is 20 MB. On a 3.6 GHz AVX2 machine, the L3 cache is 4 MB. These are some of the machines we use for timing programs.

Exercise 3.1.1. Find the hex codes for the following instructions:

- movq %rax, %rcx

- movq %rax, %r15

- movq %r9, %r10

In MOVQ, Q stands for quad word, which is equal to 64 bits. In the Intel convention used by AMD/Intel manuals, the destination register comes first. In the ATT convention used by Unix machines, which we follow, the source comes first and the destination register comes last. You may consult the AMD and Intel manuals to answer this question. Alternatively, you may use the objdump utility. How many bytes is each instruction? Are all three instructions of the same length?

Exercise 3.1.2. Explain why the arguments in a function call are pushed onto the stack in reverse order.

Exercise 3.1.3. Write a function in assembly code that works as follows. The first argument is an integer n. It is assumed that the next n arguments are also integers, and the function should return the sum of these arguments if $n > 0$.

Exercise 3.1.4. Look up the hexadecimal opcodes of rdtsc, cpuid, and CALL. Which of these are serializing instructions?

Exercise 3.1.5. In a file called dummy.cpp, define a function void dummy(), which returns after doing nothing. In another file write a for-loop that makes n calls to dummy(). Compile the files separately and then link them together to ensure that the compiler does not eliminate the function call. Verify that the function call is present by inspecting the assembly.

Time the for-loop using the Time Stamp Counter and with n varying from 1 to 10^9. To get a good reading for each n, you can do several timings and then take the median. Graph the number of cycles as a function of n.

Fit the graph to the line $An + B$. How good is the fit? Assuming that all the cycles are consumed by function calls and the overhead of timing, interpret A and B. Is B positive or negative? The assumption is not perfectly valid, however. Some of the cycles will be consumed by instructions that increment and test the loop counter, and the branch prediction introduces some overhead as well.

Exercise 3.1.6. Use the command `cat /proc/cpuinfo` to see some cpu parameters. Be aware that this command doubles the number of cores on certain Intel machines if hyper-threading is turned on. Hyper-threading is not good for some scientific applications. How much of the output can you verify using `cpuid`?

3.2   Compiler optimizations

Anyone who seeks to write fast programs must begin by grasping what compilers do. C/C++ programs are turned into machine instructions by the compiler. The speed of the program can vary by a factor of 10, or even more, depending on the instruction stream the compiler generates. While generating machine instructions, compilers can alter the structure of the program considerably.

In sections 3.2.2 through 3.2.5, we go over a number of compiler optimizations of loops and loop nests. The two big lessons are to use the `restrict` qualifier, where appropriate, and to present loops to the compiler in as simple a form as possible. What is meant by simple is a little vague and will become clear during the discussion.

Compilers can be highly unpredictable. The only way to get a sense of whether the compiler has done as well as expected is to look at the assembly code. Although writing assembly programs can be difficult, scanning the assembly code to find inner loops and checking the instruction mix is much easier to do. Thus, our discussion of compiler optimization is not so much about the optimizations themselves as it is about what to look for in the assembly code. There can be no rational discussion of program speed without an idea of what the assembly code looks like.

A dramatic example of the unpredictability of compilers occurs in section 3.2.5. In that section, we look at a few simple programs for multiplying matrices. The programs are nearly identical, but their speeds can be quite different. That is not the dramatic part, however. The same programs are run on an SSE2 machine, an AVX machine, and an AVX2 machine that is theoretically more than 4 times faster than the SSE2 machine (see table A.1 for the full names of the machines). Surprisingly, our simple matrix multiplication programs are faster on the SSE2 machine, which leaves us wondering whatever happened to the speedup of a factor of 4. The SSE2 instruction set stabilized over a period of 10 years before it was superseded. The AVX2 instruction set is only a couple of years old as of this writing. Although AVX2 programs can be 4 times faster, compiler technology has not yet caught up.

In section 3.2.6, we look at a C++ program for multiplying matrices, in which matrices and vectors are represented using classes. This program is slow because C++ constructs are used without an understanding of how they map to machine instructions. C++ programs can be as fast as programs in any other language, or they can be slow, depending on the skill and intention of the programmer.

Compilation is a difficult task because compilers have to look at a program character by character, token by token, and statement by statement until they have an internal representation of the whole program. The programmer's view of a computer program is from the reverse direction. The programmer often starts with a problem to be solved and with a global view of a solution to it. The global view, which is so easy for a human programmer, is very hard to attain for the compiler. In the final section, 3.2.7, we explain a little theory to show how compilers go about building a global view.

Before getting into the meat of this section, we begin by discussing a few preliminaries.

3.2.1   Preliminaries

Cache effects in simple trials can give unrealistically good figures for program speed. Cache flush, which we describe here, is one way to eliminate cache effects. We also review compiler options.

The C++ classes `PyPlot` for plotting, `StatVector` for gathering simple statistics, and `Table` for making tables are used extensively in the source code for this book. However, they appear only rarely in the text. All three classes are described in the appendix.

Cache flush

When programs are timed, one may inadvertently ignore the effects of caching and come up with unrealistically good numbers. Suppose we initialize three matrices to time algorithms for matrix-matrix multiplication.

```
for(int i=0; i < dim; i++) //intialize a, b and c
  for(int j=0; j < dim; j++){
    a[i+j*dim] = (1.0*rand()/RAND_MAX-0.5)*2;
    b[i+j*dim] = (1.0*rand()/RAND_MAX-0.5)*2;
    c[i+j*dim] = (1.0*rand()/RAND_MAX-0.5)*2;
}
```

The C library function rand() generates a pseudorandom integer between zero and RAND_MAX. It is handy for timing and testing but may not be a well-tested random number generator.[10] When pseudorandom numbers with specific properties, such as uniformity and independence, are needed, a good library of statistical functions must be used instead. For our purposes here, rand() is adequate, but the manner in which the matrices a, b, and c are initialized means that they will all be in cache if dim is small. If dim=100, for example, the matrices will remain in the L2 cache of any of the processors of table A.1, which is more than 0.2 MB. In a realistic program, even small matrices are unlikely to be in cache when they are needed because the program may touch a lot of data before it starts operating on the small matrices. Thus, timing immediately after initialization can give unrealistically good numbers.

The matrices can be evicted from cache as follows:

```
//clear a, b, c from cache
  for(int i=0; i < dim; i++)
    for(int j=0; j < dim; j++){
      _mm_clflush(a+i+j*dim);
      _mm_clflush(b+i+j*dim);
      _mm_clflush(c+i+j*dim);
}
```

The function _mm_clflush() is an *intrinsic*. It corresponds directly to the instruction CLFLUSH. The effect of cache flush is to evict the entire cache line that corresponds to

---

[10]The general opinion that rand() is of poor quality appears to be from decades before. Whether that really applies to modern gcc and icpc runtime libraries is uncertain and possibly untrue.

its argument. Its argument must be a pointer. All transfers to and out of cache occur in blocks or lines. A cache line is typically 64 bytes. The declaration of `_mm_clflush()` is made visible through the header file `ia64intrin.h` by the `icpc` compiler. After `CLFLUSH`, the cache line is found in DRAM memory but not in any of the caches.

The use of `CLFLUSH` can introduce artifacts and give pessimistic timing figures. There is no such thing as a perfect timing protocol. A better way is to arrange inputs to the program in a long array, which is larger than the size of the cache, and apply the program to the inputs in succession. For some programs, such as matrix multiplication, such a precaution is not really necessary, and the use of `CLFLUSH` may be much more convenient.

Compiler options

The other preliminary topic is the use of compiler options. We have recommended the options

```
-xHost -O3 -prec-div -no-ftz -restrict
```

for the `icpc` compiler. Here we add a few more comments. The `icpc` compiler has a default `-fast` option, which includes `-xHost` and `-O3`. The `-xHost` option ensures that the compiler generates instructions assuming the highest capability of the machine. The `-O3` option sets the optimization level. However, the `-fast` option is not suitable for our use. For one thing, it uses `-no-prec-div`, which we decided to abjure earlier. It turns on `-ipo` for interprocedural optimization, which interferes with many of the points we seek to make throughout this book. It is uncertain whether interprocedural optimization yields a measurable improvement for well-written programs.

An important compiler option shown above is `-restrict`. It is discussed in greater depth later. It enables the `restrict` qualifier, which is essential for making programs fast.

Typically, we turn off function inlining using the `-fno-inline-functions` option (not shown above). Function inlining changes the structure of the code in ways that make discussion of the corresponding assembly code difficult. On many occasions, we have noticed that loops are not well optimized when functions are inlined. However, function inlining should probably be enabled in some programs. It is too important a part of C++ design to be simply turned off without thought.

	Cycles
Unoptimized code	32
With -xHost -O3 optimization	14
With -xHost -O3 optimization and loop unrolling	7

Table 3.2: Number of cycles per term of the Leibniz series on a 3.6 GHz machine with AVX2 instructions (see table A.1 for the full name of the machine).

3.2.2 Loop unrolling

A program to compute the nth partial sum of the Leibniz series follows:

```
1  //sum of first n terms of 4(1-1/3+1/5-1/7+1/9-...)
2  double leibniz(long int n){
3       long int i;
4       double ans;
5       for(i=0; i < n; i++)
6            if(i==0)
7                 ans = 4.0;
8            else if(i%2==1)
9                 ans -=  4.0/(2.0*i+1);
10           else
11                ans +=  4.0/(2.0*i+1);
12       return ans;
13 }
```

This function will be run for large values of n, such as $n = 10^9$ or 10^{10}. With $n = 10^9$, the partial sum is generated in a few seconds.

Normally, if a program is compiled with optimizations turned on, the resulting code can be two to three times faster. This speedup is not only because the compilers are clever, which they sometimes are, but also because the unoptimized code can be long and roundabout. Table 3.2 shows that turning on compiler optimization doubles the speed of the code. Rewriting leibniz() to enable loop unrolling, which is one

of the most important optimizations, doubles the speed once again. We will use the
leibniz() function and its variants to explain how loop unrolling works.

First, we will understand why unoptimized code is nearly always quite slow. The
first few lines of the unoptimized assembly of leibniz() are as follows:

```
pushq       %rbp
movq        %rsp, %rbp
subq        $32, %rsp
movq        %rdi, -32(%rbp)
movq        $0, -24(%rbp)
movq        -24(%rbp), %rax
movq        -32(%rbp), %rdx
cmpq        %rdx, %rax
jl          ..B1.4
jmp         ..B1.9
```

The function leibniz() receives its argument n in the register %rdi. This code
fragment is checking whether 0 is less than n. If $n > 0$, the program jumps to the
address ..B1.4. If not, it jumps to the address ..B1.9, where it terminates quickly
by returning 0 as the answer. Deciphering this code fragment is left to the reader. It
is a roundabout way to check whether $n > 0$ or not.

The optimized code performs the same action as follows:

```
testq       %rdi, %rdi
jle         ..B2.9
```

The testq instruction ands the %rdi register, which contains the argument n, with
itself and sets certain flags. The instruction discards the result of anding and does
not alter the contents of %rdi. If n is negative, the result will be negative as well,
and the sign flag is set. If n is zero, the result is zero as well, and the zero flag is
set. The next instruction jle jumps to a location where the program terminates with
a ret statement if either the sign or zero flag is set, in other words, if $n \leq 0$. The
optimized code is checking whether $n \leq 0$ or $n > 0$ using a single instruction, while
the unoptimized code takes more than half a dozen to do the same check.

We get a sense here of why unoptimized assembly is nearly always slow. Unoptimized assembly code is characterized by a certain listlessness. The compiler takes a
local view of the program.

Thus, if an expression such as $(j+1)(j+2)$ occurs in multiple statements, the nonoptimizing compiler may fail to recognize that each instance evaluates to the same value. If the same variable is used repeatedly in a loop, the nonoptimizing compiler may fail to assign the variable to a register. Poor use of registers is typical of unoptimized code. Even when more than a dozen registers are available, unoptimized code often uses only a few.

With the -xHost -03 options, the icpc compiler generates code, which is more than twice as fast. As shown in table 3.2, the number cycles per term of the Leibniz series decreases from 32 for the unoptimized code to 14 for the optimized code. The listing below displays the assembly of the for-loop of the leibniz() partial sum function on page 160. We shall not examine the listing line by line. Our intention is to figure out whether the the compiler has done a good job. For that purpose, it suffices to scan the assembly of the inner loop. After the listing, we explain how to generate the assembly and locate the inner loop in it.

```
..B3.4:
        vxorpd      %xmm3, %xmm3, %xmm3
        lea         1(%rax), %rsi
        movq        %rsi, %rdx
        vcvtsi2sdq  %rsi, %xmm3, %xmm3
        shrq        $63, %rdx
        vfmadd213sd .L[omit]pkt.4(%rip), %xmm1, %xmm3
        lea         1(%rax,%rdx), %rcx
        andq        $-2, %rcx
        cmpq        %rax, %rcx
        je          ..B3.6
..B3.5:
        vdivsd      %xmm3, %xmm2, %xmm3
        vaddsd      %xmm3, %xmm0, %xmm0
        jmp         ..B3.7
..B3.6:
        vdivsd      %xmm3, %xmm2, %xmm3
        vsubsd      %xmm3, %xmm0, %xmm0
..B3.7:
        movq        %rsi, %rax
```

```
        cmpq            %rdi, %rsi
        jb              ..B3.4
```

To generate the assembly, the compiler is invoked with the

```
    -S -fno-verbose-asm
```

options, in addition to the compilation options, as in the pattern rule in section 2.3.4. The assembly of the entire `leibniz.cpp` program, which contains the `leibniz()` function of page 160, is more than 1,300 lines. Locating the inner loop within that assembly is an easy skill. One has to search for "leibniz" or its mangled name "_Z7leibnizl" (which may be found as explained in section 2.1), and the beginning of the function definition will be obvious.

Within the function definition, paying a little attention to the jump statements helps identify the inner loop. In our listing, the final line is a `jb` (jump if below) instruction, and it is jumping back to the instruction labeled `..B3.4`, which is the top of the loop. In between, we have two more jump instructions. The `je` (jump if equal) instruction jumps to the case where the term of the Leibniz series is negative and must be subtracted. The `jmp` (unconditional jump) instruction follows the addition of a positive term of the Leibniz series. It jumps to `..B3.7`, where the loop termination condition is verified before possibly jumping back to the top of the loop.

Even in this short snippet of assembly code, there are many unfamiliar instructions. Because our purpose is only to understand the quality of the code generated by the compiler, we do not need to understand many of these. The crucial part for us is first the snippet

```
    ..B3.5:
        vdivsd          %xmm3, %xmm2, %xmm3
        vaddsd          %xmm3, %xmm0, %xmm0
```

In this assembly snippet, the first instruction divides the `%xmm2` register by the `%xmm3` register and stores the result in the register `%xmm3`. The source registers are `%xmm3` and `%xmm2`, and the destination register is `%xmm3`. The `%xmm2` has 4.0 and `%xmm3` has $2i + 1$ (as a `double`). So the effect is to compute the $4/(2i + 1)$ term of the Leibniz series. In this case, i is even. Therefore, the second instruction is adding the computed answer to `%xmm0`. The answer is being accumulated in `%xmm0`, and the approximation to π will be found in this register at the end of the loop. The second snippet tackles the case where i is even.

```
..B3.6:
        vdivsd      %xmm3 , %xmm2 , %xmm3
        vsubsd      %xmm3 , %xmm0 , %xmm0
```

The second instruction here is vsubsd and not vaddsd. Therefore, the $4/(2i+1)$ term is being subtracted and not added.

How do we tell whether the compiled assembly is satisfactory? First, we may notice that the assembled code is using XMM registers even though wider YMM registers are available on this AVX2 machine. In fact, it is worse than that. Even the 128-bit XMM registers (see table 3.1) are not being used fully. Each XMM register is wide enough to hold two doubles. Yet the trailing sd in the vdivsd, vaddsd, and vsubsd instructions, which stands for "single double," is indicating that only one half of the XMM registers is being used. The leading v in these instructions indicates that these are vector instructions that operate on the vector XMM/YMM/ZMM registers (see table 3.1).

To use the vector registers effectively, the compiler has to find parallelism in the loop. In this case, it has found no parallelism. The $4/(2i + 1)$ terms are being alternately added and subtracted in sequential order, just as in our program.

The other deficiency in this assembly are the two branch statements (je and jmp instructions) in the loop body. Branches are undesirable because they interfere with instruction-level parallelism. The first two instructions in our assembly listing are as follows:

```
        vxorpd      %xmm3 , %xmm3 , %xmm3
        lea         1(%rax) , %rsi
```

These two instructions operate on entirely different registers and may be executed in parallel. Very probably, that is just what the x86 processor does. The processor decodes multiple instructions simultaneously in a single cycle. In addition, it has multiple units to execute instructions. The processor constantly looks ahead in the instruction stream. Wherever it finds opportunities for parallelism, it schedules instructions for parallel execution. Thus, even a sequential program is executed in parallel. Much of the improvement in single-processor speeds over the last 15 years may be attributed to greater and greater instruction-level parallelism.

Branches (or jump statements) interfere with instruction-level parallelism because it is impossible to tell in advance whether a conditional branch will be taken or not. This uncertainty may mean the processor cannot look ahead and execute instructions in parallel. In fact, branches are so common inside loops (in particular, there is always a branch at the end of the loop body) that instruction-level parallelism would be almost completely ineffective without branch prediction. Fortunately, much of the branching is highly predictable. In our assembly snippet, the `je` branch is alternately taken or not taken, and the `jb` branch at the end is always taken except at loop termination. Processors can predict such branches quite easily. If there is a misprediction, so that the wrong sequence of instructions have been executed, there are mechanisms to recover and resume with a correct instruction stream.[11]

If branches are likely to be predicted with nearly 100% accuracy in our assembled code, why are branches a problem here? There is a misprediction overhead that should be negligible for our program. To answer this question more fully, we have to go back to the C++ code of the `leibniz()` partial summation function on page 160. The loop body of that function splits into three cases: $i = 0$, i odd, and i even. The compiler in fact has moved the $i = 0$ case out of the loop. Only two cases occur within the loop body in the assembled code, so that the overhead of checking whether i is zero does not occur in every iteration. The problem with the branching in the loop body is that it prevents the compiler from finding parallelism in the loop body. This is the reason the code is stuck with XMM registers and single double instructions. In general, it is a good idea to move `if` statements out of loop bodies in C/C++.

In the following C++ definition, we have manually removed the even/odd branch from the loop body to illustrate how the compiler exploits parallelism in the loop body.

```
double leibnizX(long int n){
    long int i;
    double ans0=4.0;
    double ans1=0;
    for(i=2; i < n; i=i+2)
        ans0 += 4.0/(2.0*i+1);
    for(i=1; i < n; i=i+2)
        ans1 += 4.0/(2.0*i+1);
    return ans0-ans1;
}
```

---

[11] For a great deal more about instruction-level parallelism and branch prediction, see Hennessy and Patterson (1990-2011).

The assembly code of this function is more than 300 lines and almost impossible to understand. The compiler goes to feast on this function and optimizes it very well. We show only three instructions in the body of the first loop to verify that the compiler has done a good job.

```
vfmadd132pd .L_2il0floatpacket.8(%rip), %ymm0, %ymm6
vdivpd      %ymm6, %ymm2, %ymm3
vaddpd      %ymm7, %ymm3, %ymm9
```

In vfmadd132pd, vdivpd, and vaddpd, the v stands for vector as before, and pd stands for "packed double." This means that the instructions are operating on all four doubles that fit into a 256-bit YMM register. Not only are YMM registers being used now, but they are being used in full. That is the main reason that this program takes only seven cycles per term and is twice as fast as the earlier program (see table 3.2).

We have explained the vdivpd and vaddpd instructions above. In vfmadd132pd, the fmadd stands for fused multiply add (FMA). The code "132" indicates that the first and third operands are multiplied and added to the second source operand. The result is stored in the first operand (the destination). In our code snippet, the operands must be read in reverse (because of the difference between Intel and GNU/Linux conventions in assembly code). The first (or destination) operand is %ymm6, the second operand is %ymm0, and the third operand is a float packet (stored constant in text area). The effect of this instruction is $i \rightarrow 2i + 1$.[12] The FMA instruction is not found in SSE or AVX (see table 3.1).

The compiler has "unrolled" the loop partially. Because the assembly code of the unrolled loop is rather opaque, we give a listing of a C++ definition that unrolls the loop manually.

```
double leibnizXX(long int n){
    long int i;
```

---

[12] To decipher this assembly snippet, one needs its complete context, which is omitted from the text. Deciphering the meaning of the float packet is crucial. To decipher the float packet, one may search for it in the assembly code and find its definition to be "4000000000000000" in hexadecimal. A web service such as http://babbage.cs.qc.cuny.edu/IEEE-754.old/64bit.html may be used to convert from the binary IEEE 754 format to decimal and discover that the float packet is 2.0. Similarly, one may uncover that %ymm0 is storing 1.0, at which point it is almost obvious that %ymm2 must be storing 4.0.

```
double ans[10]={0};
for(i=0; i < n; i+=10){
        ans[0] += 4.0/(2.0*i+1);
        ans[1] += 4.0/(2.0*i+3);
        ans[2] += 4.0/(2.0*i+5);
        ans[3] += 4.0/(2.0*i+7);
        ans[4] += 4.0/(2.0*i+9);
        ans[5] += 4.0/(2.0*i+11);
        ans[6] += 4.0/(2.0*i+13);
        ans[7] += 4.0/(2.0*i+15);
        ans[8] += 4.0/(2.0*i+17);
        ans[9] += 4.0/(2.0*i+19);
}
return ans[0]+ans[2]+ans[4]+ans[6]+ans[8]
        -ans[1]-ans[3]-ans[5]-ans[7]-ans[9];
}
```

In this program, the terms of the Leibniz series are grouped into 10 sets, and each iteration of the loop updates the sum over each set. The statements inside the loop body are independent of each other and may be executed in parallel using the packed double instructions. Loop unrolling is one of the most popular and effective loop transformations.

In the assembly of the loop bodies of leibnizX(), in fact four sets of packed double instructions operate on YMM registers. Because each YMM register is wide enough for four doubles, each loop has been unrolled by a factor of 16. It is as if the i=i+2 increment of the loop counter in each for-loop has been replaced by i=i+32 and the loop body expanded to treat 16 terms in parallel.[13]

As shown in table 3.2, the program with unrolled loops (with the unrolling done either manually or by the optimizing compiler) takes seven cycles per term, which is half that of the leibniz() function, which branched inside the loop body. It must be said that seven cycles per term is probably far from the optimum. Optimizing the

---

[13]It may occur to the reader that incrementing the loop counter i by 32 instead of 2 may cause a problem if the number of loop iterations is not a multiple of 16. Indeed, it does, and the compiler has to generate code at either the beginning or end to handle the case where the number of iterations is not a multiple of 16.

program for the instruction pipeline, which is the topic of section 3.3, may even cut that number in half.

3.2.3   Loop fusion

Because the speed of modern x86 computers relies on instruction-level parallelism and vector registers, it is often a good idea to have a lot of parallelism in the innermost loops. If sets of instructions in the body of the innermost loop are independent of each other, the processor is likely to execute them in parallel.

Loop fusion addresses the situation where we have two distinct loops. It is assumed that the iterations of each loop have dependencies that make loop unrolling ineffective. In such a scenario, merging the bodies of the two loops may be the best way to produce a loop body that is amenable to instruction-level parallelism. The transformation where distinct loop bodies are merged is called loop fusion.

For a simple example, we consider the power series for sine and cosine.[14]

$$\sin x = \frac{x}{1!} - \frac{x^3}{3!} + \frac{x^5}{5!} - \cdots$$
$$\cos x = 1 - \frac{x^2}{2!} + \frac{x^4}{4!} - \cdots$$

The following program computes the sine and cosine of x and returns them in the reference variables c and s. The number of terms of the series to be used is input to the function as n.

```
void sincos(double x, int n, double& c, double& s){
    c = s = 0;
    double ci = 1;
    for(int i=0; i<n; i++){
        c += ci;
        ci *= -x*x/(2.0*i+2)/(2.0*i+1);
    }
    double si = x;
    for(int i=0; i<n; i++){
        s += si;
```

---

[14]These series were discovered by Madhava around 1400 AD according to Sarma (1992).

```
        si  *=  -x*x/(2.0*i+3)/(2.0*i+2);
    }
}
```

The cosine loop accumulates the answer in c and stores the current term in ci. Each iteration updates the current term ci. When we look at the terms of the series for $\cos x$, we see a lot of parallelism because the terms can be grouped and summed in many different ways. However, when the loop presented to the compiler generates each term by updating the previous term, it is quite difficult for a compilation algorithm to automatically detect such parallelism. Similar comments apply to the sine loop.

Thus, simply unrolling the loops will not introduce much parallelism into the instruction stream and will not enable the compiler to generate packed double instructions.

A better idea may be to fuse the two loops. To a human observer, it is obvious that the two loop bodies can be merged, assuming ci and si are appropriately initialized. However, even if the loops are fused, it will be hard for the compiler to generate packed double instructions. It is true that c and s, as well as ci and si, can be packed into the two halves of an XMM register. However, when the terms are updated, we will need an XMM register that saves $-x^2$ in both its halves and, perhaps more problematically, another XMM register that stores $(2i + 2)(2i + 1)$ and $(2i + 2)(2i + 3)$ in its two halves. A human programmer can easily see how to get around the problem. One XMM register can hold $2i + 2$ in both its halves, and a second XMM register can hold $2i + 1$ and $2i + 3$ in its two halves. The two XMM registers can be multiplied to get $(2i + 2)(2i + 1)$ and $(2i + 2)(2i + 3)$ and updated by adding $(2, 2)$ saved in either an XMM register or a cached location.

All this proves to be too much for the icpc compiler, however. Here are some of the instructions in the body of the cosine inner loop on an SSE2-capable machine (see table 3.1):

```
addsd        %xmm6,  %xmm5
subsd        %xmm1,  %xmm8
addsd        %xmm6,  %xmm7
addsd        %xmm6,  %xmm5
addsd        %xmm6,  %xmm7
divsd        %xmm5,  %xmm8
divsd        %xmm7,  %xmm8
```

```
mulsd        %xmm8, %xmm2
```

There is no need to decipher the assembly code. All that matters is that the cosine
and sine loops are not fused, and both loops use single double instructions in the loop
body (notice the **sd** in instruction mnemonics). On an AVX2 machine, the compiler
does generate fused-multiply-add instructions, but the instructions are still single
double, and loops are not fused.

3.2.4   Unroll and jam

In this section, we will study a compiler optimization that applies to nested loops.
So far we have considered loop unrolling and loop fusion. In loop nests, it may be
desirable to unroll the outer loop and fuse several copies of the inner loop that result.
That is the unroll and jam transformation.

The following C++ program computes a sine table:

```
//sine table for x = (pi/(2*n))*i
//with i=0,...,n.
//therefore stab must be of size n+1.
void sinetable(int n, double *restrict stab){
        double dx = 3.14159265358979323846/(2*n);
        for(int i=0; i <= n; i++){
                double x =  i*dx;
                stab[i] = 0;
                double si = x;
                for(int j=0; j < 20; j++){
                        stab[i] += si;
                        si *= -x*x/((2*j+3)*(2*j+2));
                }
        }
}
```

This program computes $\sin x$ for $x = 0, \pi/(2n), \ldots, (n-1)\pi/(2n), \pi/2$ and leaves the
$n + 1$ computed values in the array **stab**. If we choose $n = 360$, the resulting table
corresponds to the chord table presented by Ptolemy in his treatise on mathematical

astronomy, which became known as the *Almagest*.[15] Ptolemy did not use power series, however. One of his key tools was a generalization of the Pythagoras theorem to cyclic quadrilaterals.

This program gives the type of `stab` as `double *restrict`. The `restrict` qualifier tells the compiler that any location addressed using the pointer will not be addressed using some other pointer. Its use is not significant here because only one pointer is in sight. However, in general, judicious use of the `restrict` qualifier can help the compiler generate good code. We will discuss the `restrict` qualifier in greater detail later.

In this program, the outer loop variable i generates different values for x in the range $[0, \pi/2]$. The inner loop variable j generates terms of the power series of $\sin x$. We have fixed the number of terms at 20. So the numerical bounds of the inner loop variable j are known to the compiler.

If the compiler chooses to, it can unroll the inner loop completely. However, not much can be gained by unrolling the inner loop. The new value of `si`, which holds a term of the power series, is obtained using its previous value. If the loop is unrolled, this chain, in which each iteration of the inner loop depends on the previous iteration, remains intact, making it quite hard for the compiler to generate packed double instructions.

The assembly generated by the compiler does not unroll the inner loop nor does it unroll the outer loop on an SSE2-capable machine. Some of the instructions in the body of the inner loop are shown below.

```
pxor        %xmm5 , %xmm5
subsd       %xmm1 , %xmm5
addsd       %xmm2 , %xmm3
cvtsi2sd    %r8d , %xmm4
divsd       %xmm4 , %xmm5
mulsd       %xmm5 , %xmm2
```

---

[15]Chord tables are equivalent to sine tables, and one of the earliest chord tables was computed by Hipparchus around 150 BC. The first book of the *Almagest*, a textbook of mathematical astronomy written by Claudius Ptolemy of Alexandria around 150 AD, has a table of chords in sexagesimal. See Toomre (1998).

On an AVX2-capable machine, the compiler does unroll the inner loop, but the instructions are all single double, as they are here. So there is no real gain from the
compiler's code transformation.

Our experience with unroll and jam, so far, is similar to that with loop fusion.
We wrote a program expecting the compiler to make a certain loop transformation,
and it did not. This time we will persist and alter the program to get the compiler
to generate better code.

```
void sinetable(int n, double *restrict xlist,
               double *restrict stab){
    for(int i=0; i <= n; i++){
        stab[i] = 0;
        double si = xlist[i];
        for(int j=0; j < 20; j++){
          stab[i] += si;
          si *= -xlist[i]*xlist[i]/((2*j+3)*(2*j+2));
        }
    }
}
```

This program takes in the list of values at which the sine function must be computed
in the array xlist[0...n], which is of length $n+1$. The use of the restrict qualifier
is crucial here. It tells the compiler that the arrays xlist and stab do not overlap in
memory. Without that qualifier, the compiler has to allow for the case in which xlist
and stab are indexed to address the same location in memory. Having to preserve
the semantics of the program when the two arrays are aliased would preclude loop
transformations. The assembly of the inner most loop follows.

```
..B3.4:
            pxor        %xmm3, %xmm3
            lea         2(%rdi,%rdi), %r8d
            pxor        %xmm4, %xmm4
            lea         3(%rdi,%rdi), %r9d
            subpd       %xmm0, %xmm4
            addpd       %xmm1, %xmm2
            imull       %r8d, %r9d
            mulpd       %xmm0, %xmm4
```

```
cvtsi2sd    %r9d, %xmm3
incl        %edi
unpcklpd    %xmm3, %xmm3
cmpl        $20, %edi
divpd       %xmm3, %xmm4
mulpd       %xmm4, %xmm1
jb          ..B3.4
```

We do see packed double instructions here, indicating that the unroll-and-jam optimization has been carried out. On AVX/AVX2-capable machines, however, packed double instructions are not generated.

3.2.5   Loop interchange

Loop interchange is the next compiler optimization for discussion, and matrix multiplication is the example we use to bring it out. In our discussion of matrix multiplication and loop interchanging, the following points will emerge:

- One should use **restrict** pointers as far as possible. The use of **restrict**-qualified pointers can speed up a program by more than a factor of 2.

- It is best to present loops to compilers in a simple and transparent form.

- Although AVX2-capable machines are faster than SSE2-capable machines, generating AVX2 code is a bigger struggle for a compiler. Therefore, much of the advertised advantage of an AVX2 machine over an SSE2 machine may not be realized.

- Compilers are capricious, and no assumptions about the generated assembly code can be made without inspecting it.

- Optimizing for the instruction pipeline can yield far greater speedups on more recent processors than on earlier ones.

Some of these points have come up already. Many of these points are much broader in scope than any particular compiler optimization.

Before we begin, we make some remarks about the peak capabilities of SSE2- and AVX2-capable machines. As shown in table 3.1, SSE2 provides XMM registers wide

	dim=1000 (SSE2)	dim=2000 (SSE2)	dim=1000 (AVX2)	dim=2000 (AVX2)
multijk()	0.37	0.22	0.62	0.46
multijkx()	0.40	0.33	0.76	0.53
multIJK()	1.72	1.62	1.30	1.21
multIJKX()	1.72	1.62	1.31	1.21
MKL BLAS	3.81	3.84	14.0	14.6

Table 3.3: Floating point operations per cycle in the multiplication of square matrices. The SSE2 and AVX2 processors used here had clocks of 2.6 and 3.6 GHz, respectively (see table A.1 for the full names of the machines used).

enough to hold two `doubles`. The `mulpd` (or `vmulpd`) instruction applied to XMM registers carries out two multiplications in a single instruction. Similarly, the `addpd` (or `vaddpd`) instruction carries out two additions in a single cycle. Typical SSE2 processors can simultaneously issue an `addpd` and a `mulpd` to separate execution units in the same cycle. Therefore, the peak capability of a single SSE2 processor core is 4 flops (floating points operations) per cycle.

The AVX2 processor has YMM registers, which are twice as wide as XMM. In addition, it has the `fmadd*pd` instruction, which does a fused multiply add of the type $c = c + ab$ on the entire width of the YMM registers. A single `fmadd*pd` instruction is equal to 8 flops. The AVX2 processor can issue two of these instructions to separate execution units in the same cycle. Therefore, the peak capability of a single AVX2 processor is 16 flops per cycle.

Some Intel processors accelerate the clock in-core. For such machines, the actual theoretical limit can be slightly greater than the bounds derived above. Neither the 2.6 GHz SSE2 machine nor the 3.6 GHz AVX2 machine of table A.1 features in-core acceleration of the clock.

All the points we wish to make in this section emerge from table 3.3. One of the points is so glaring that we will begin by commenting on it. The point is that matrix multiplication is much faster using Intel's MKL library. On SSE2, MKL is more than twice as fast as functions such as `multijk()` and `multIJK()` that we write in C/C++. The programs that we write are the type one can write in C/C++ and are not optimized for the instruction pipeline. MKL's optimization for the instruction pipeline, which must be coded in assembly, yields a far greater speedup of more than a factor of 10 on AVX2 machines. In both cases, MKL comes close to the peak floating point throughput, while the C/C++ programs fall short. In fact, the C/C++ programs do better in SSE2 than in AVX2, although the peak capability of the more recent AVX2 architecture is four times as high.

We step through four simple implementations of matrix multiplications. These are the sort of C/C++ programs one may be expected to write. For each implementation, we explain how the compiler views the program and what it does with it. The sort of optimizations that yield the amazing speed of MKL BLAS are discussed in section 3.3.

The (i,j)th entry of the square matrix a of dimension dim is a[i+j*dim] (we assume that the leading dimension is equal to dim). Here a is of type double * and points to the first location of the contiguous segment of memory where the dim*dim entries of the matrix are stored. As always, we assume that matrices are stored columnwise.

The function multijk() defined below multiplies matrices a and b and adds their product to the matrix c.

```
void multijk(double *a, double *b, double *c, int dim){
    for(int i=0; i < dim; i++)
        for(int j=0; j < dim; j++)
            for(int k=0; k < dim; k++)
                c[i+j*dim] += a[i+k*dim]*b[k+j*dim];
}
```

None of the pointers is qualified as restrict. Thus, the arrays a, b, and c could be indexed to point to the same location, and the compiler has to preserve program semantics even in the event of such aliasing. There is no room for the compiler to apply loop transformations.

On both SSE2 and AVX2, the compiler-generated assembly code (not shown) closely follows the C code of multijk(). There is no dramatic code transformation. From table 3.3, we see that AVX2 is nearly twice as fast for multijk(). That speedup is easily explained. On both SSE2 and AVX2, the compiler generates only single double instructions, and nothing more can be expected. On SSE2, the single double instructions are vaddsd and vmulsd. On AVX2, they are fmadd*pd. The speedup of

two results because the fused-multiply-add combines addition and multiplication into
a single instruction.

Next we make a slight change to the matrix multiplication program.

```
void multijkx(double *a,double *b,double *c,int dim){
     for(int i=0; i < dim; i++)
          for(int j=0; j < dim; j++){
               double x = c[i+j*dim];
               for(int k=0; k < dim; k++)
                    x += a[i+k*dim]*b[k+j*dim];
               c[i+j*dim] = x;
          }
}
```

This program does not use **restrict** pointers either. However, it alters the innermost
loop and makes it accumulate its computation in the scalar variable x. Even if the
arrays are aliased, the addition operations in the innermost loop can be done or
grouped in any order, addition being commutative and associative (modulo rounding
errors).[16] The **icpc** compiler exploits that room to unroll the innermost loop and
generate packed double instructions on both SSE2 and AVX2. From table 3.3, we see
that this optimization results in better performance for both matrices of dimension
1000 and 2000, although the improvement is minor. AVX2 is again about twice as
fast and for the same reason as before.

The programs below are exactly the same except all the pointers are qualified
with **restrict**.

```
void multIJK(double *restrict a, double *restrict b,
          double *restrict c, int dim){
     for(int i=0; i < dim; i++)
          for(int j=0; j < dim; j++)
               for(int k=0; k < dim; k++)
                    c[i+j*dim] += a[i+k*dim]*b[k+j*dim];
}
```

---

[16]On very rare occasions, code transformations effected by compilers under the assumption that
machine arithmetic is commutative and associative may become problematic.

```
void multIJKX(double *restrict a, double *restrict b,
          double *restrict c, int dim){
    for(int i=0; i < dim; i++)
        for(int j=0; j < dim; j++){
            double x = c[i+j*dim];
            for(int k=0; k < dim; k++)
                x += a[i+k*dim]*b[k+j*dim];
            c[i+j*dim] = x;
        }
}
```

These programs are nearly four times faster on SSE2 and twice as fast on AVX2 (see table 3.3). We may wonder why they are four times faster on SSE2 and only twice as fast on AVX2. Inspection of the assembly code will bring out the explanations. In fact, overall, the program is faster on SSE2 than AVX2, although the peak capability of the latter is four times as high (the peak capability factor is more than 4 if we allow for the clock speeds reported in table 3.3).

The crucial point here is that because a[], b[], and c[] are all restrict qualified, the compiler knows that the arrays are not supposed to alias. The compiler may assume that the arrays are nonoverlapping and distinct areas of memory.

On SSE2, the compiler takes full advantage of those assumptions and changes the order of nesting of the loops so that the i-loop becomes innermost and the j-loop becomes outermost. The innermost loop is unrolled, and packed double instructions are generated.

Why does the compiler make the i-loop the innermost (on SSE2) and why does that lead to a faster program? In our discussion of compiler optimization so far, we have focused on arithmetic operations. We have seen that parallelism and packed double instructions in the innermost loops are likely to lead to faster programs. In addition to instruction-level parallelism and the judicious ordering of arithmetic, an optimizing compiler will do well to consider the pattern of memory access.

For matrix multiplication, the pattern of memory access has a big impact on program performance. When the k-loop is innermost, each successive location of the a[] array accessed in the innermost loop is separated from the previous location by a stride of length dim. Similarly, if the j-loop is the innermost, the accesses of the b[] in the innermost loop have a stride equal to dim. Striding has the disadvantage that

multijk()	dim=1000 (SSE2)	dim=2000 (SSE2)	dim=1000 (AVX2)	dim=2000 (AVX2)
Using Matrix objects	.10	.07	0.18	0.15

Table 3.4: Floating point operations per cycle. Compare with table 3.3.

when a `double` word is brought into memory, we do not immediately use the other `double` words in the same cache line.

When the i-loop is innermost, successive iterations of the innermost loop touch the same location in the `c[]` array but move through the `a[]` and `b[]` arrays with a stride equal to 1. That leads to better utilization of the cache line. The cache line is typically 64 bytes (large enough for 8 `doubles`).

Unfortunately, on AVX2, the compiler does not interchange the loops. It simply unrolls the inner loop and generates packed double instructions. Cache line utilization is therefore poor. The failure to unroll loops on AVX2 could be because the `icpc` compiler is not as mature for AVX2 as it is for the earlier SSE2 architecture. The size of the assembly code for SSE2 is nearly a 1,000 lines. For AVX2, it is fewer than 200 lines, showing that compilers fare worse with more modern architectures.

However, it may not be simply a case of compiler maturity. As computer architecture advances, for example, with vector registers getting wider, compilation becomes harder, and the compiled assembly code is more likely to fall short of being optimal. This point may be illustrated by comparing against the AVX case, which was omitted from table 3.3. On a 2.2 GHz AVX machine, the compiler generates assembly code for `multIJK()` that is very similar to the assembly code for SSE2, except with YMM registers in place of XMM registers. Nevertheless, the speed of the compiled code is less than 15% of MKL, whereas on the SSE2 machine of table 3.3, the compiled code runs at more than 40% of MKL's speed.

3.2.6   C++ overhead

Table 3.4 shows performance data for two implementations of matrix multiplication in C++. The implementations of section 3.2.5 are also in C++, but the syntax and style properly belong to C. They are C++ functions mainly because C++ is an extension of C. The functions were coded using arrays and pointer arithmetic. In contrast, the

C++ function timed in table 3.4 uses `Matrix` class objects (see chapter 1 for the definition of the `Vector` class, the `Matrix` class is similar).[17]

If matrices are multiplied using objects of the class `Matrix`, the C++ syntax mimics mathematical syntax quite closely as shown below.

```
void multijk(Matrix& A, Matrix& B, Matrix& C){
    int l = A.getm();
    int m = A.getn();
    assrt(B.getm()==m);
    int n = B.getn();
    assrt(C.getm()==l);
    assrt(C.getn()==n);
    for(int i=0; i < l; i++)
        for(int j=0; j < m; j++)
            for(int k=0; k < n; k++)
                C(i,k) += A(i,j)*B(j,k);
}
```

The price paid for staying close to mathematical syntax is very poor performance. Comparing tables 3.3 and 3.4, we find that on AVX2, the C++ is slower than MKL BLAS by a whopping factor that is nearly 100!

The matrix multiplication program here may look nice to a human reader. But it looks far more complex than a function such as `multIJK()` defined earlier to the compiler. A usage such as `C(i,j)` is in fact an overloaded function call. It is more difficult for the compiler to figure out the pattern in which the indices are mapping to locations in the array. If we want the compiler to do a good job, we have to make the loops easy to read and optimize for the compiler.

Of course, the fault here is not that of C++. C++ provides a gigantic vocabulary and numerous modes of expression. It is for the programmer to decide how to use it.

To end this discussion, we turn to the persistent belief in some quarters that Fortran programs are faster than C or C++ programs. The basis of this belief is that arrays do not alias in Fortran the way pointers can alias in C/C++. As we have seen in this chapter, the assurance of no aliasing allows the compiler to generate better code. Given that the `restrict` qualifier was introduced only around 2000 and was

---

[17]The timing information was collected with function inlining enabled.

implemented by compilers only several years after that, one has to acknowledge that there is some basis to that belief. Modern C++ compilers such as `icpc` and `g++` support `restrict` pointers. So the point about aliasing is no longer valid.

Once C and C++ are well understood, their advantages are considerable. The C language often encourages and seldom impedes thinking of how program variables and objects are laid out in memory. A variety of data structures ranging from linked lists to trees to graphs to hash tables can be implemented with a suppleness that is not approached by languages such as Fortran. While C and C++ are routinely used to implement device drivers, operating systems, compilers, and network protocols, the limitations of Fortran's idiom would become immediately apparent if anyone attempted to use it for such complicated programming tasks. Even when the programming task is not so complicated, C/C++ have much to offer if the idiom native to these languages is understood.

3.2.7   A little compiler theory

The compiler's view of a program is quite different from that of a human programmer. A human programmer has a problem to be solved and an idea to solve that problem that is expressed as a computer program. What the compiler sees is a sequence of statements that obey the syntactic rules of the programming language. The global view of what the program does is lost.

To generate good assembly, the compiler has to grasp which variables are being used heavily and other global aspects of the program. Uncovering global information from a program, which is presented to the compiler as a sequence of statements, is quite hard. In this section, we will consider some of the ideas on which optimizing compilers rely.[18]

In a sequential program, the statements depend on one another. We assume that `x`, `y`, and `z` are program variables. The following is an example:

```
y = x ;
 . . .
z = x ;
```

---

[18]Our main reference is Allen and Kennedy (2002). In it may be found bibliographic discussions of the work of Kuck, Bannerjee, Kennedy, and other researchers. Our earlier discussion of compiler optimizations drew heavily from this reference.

Here the second statement has an input dependence on the first because both of them read the same variable x. The input dependence is also called Read After Read (RAR).[19] RAR is the mildest form of dependence and poses virtually no obstacle to the code transformations the compilation algorithm may want to attempt. If we have a sequence of statements and the only dependencies between them are RAR, the statements can be permuted in any manner without changing the semantics of the program.

The Read After Write (RAW) dependence is also called a true dependence.

```
x=y;
 . . .
z=x;
```

Here the variable x is read by the second statement, which assigns it to z, after the first statement writes into x by assigning y to it. For a compiler, RAW is the most problematic dependence. When a statement consumes the output produced by a previous statement, the ordering of the statements cannot be changed. The notion of what it means for a program to be sequential is closely tied to the RAW dependence.

There are two more kinds of dependencies. In Write After Read (WAR), a location is read and then overwritten as in the example below.

```
y=x;
 . . .
x=z;
```

Here the variable x is read by the first statement and then overwritten by the second statement. WAR is also called an antidependence. Write After Write (WAW) is just what the reader may expect it to be, as shown by the example below.

```
x=y;
 . . .
x=z;
```

In this example, the two statements have a WAW dependence because both write over WAW. The WAW dependence is also called an output dependence. If we interchange two statements with a WAR or WAW dependence, the semantics of the

---

[19]The RAR, RAW, WAR, and WAW terminology for dependencies is from Hennessy and Patterson (1990-2011).

program may be affected because of a statement in the passage in between that has a RAW dependence on the first statement. Once again, we see how important RAW dependencies are for program correctness. A sequential program is sequential because of RAW dependencies.

Programs spend little time executing straight line code. Much of the time is spent inside loops. Therefore, the compiler has to pay special attention to dependencies carried by loops.

```
s = 0;
for(int i=0; i < n; i++)
    s = s + a[i];
```

This loop computes the sum of an array. To find the loop-carried dependencies, it is helpful to think of the loop in its fully unrolled form.

```
s = s + a[0];
s = s + a[1];
s = s + a[2];
...
s = s + a[n-1];
```

In this sequence of statements, each statement reads and writes into the program variable s. Because the dependencies emerge after the loop is unrolled, we say that the statement within the for-loop has loop-carried RAR, RAW, WAR, and WAW dependencies on itself.

The following loop computes the cumulative sum of the entries of an array:

```
for(int i=1; i < n; i++)
    a[i] = a[i]+a[i-1];
```

The only statement in this for-loop has loop-carried RAR and RAW dependencies on itself.

Such dependence analysis is used by compilers to figure out whether statements can be reordered and whether loop transformations of the type we studied in earlier sections may be applicable. For example, if there are no loop-carried dependencies at all, the iterations of the loop can be executed in any order. A for-loop that doubles every entry of an array has no loop-carried dependencies.

If there are no cyclic dependencies within the body of a loop, the loop can be split into independent loops. In the loop below, we assume that there is no aliasing between the a, b, and c arrays.

```
for(int i=0; i < n-1; i++){
    a[i+1] = b[i] + c[i];
    b[i] = a[i];
};
```

This loop carries a RAW dependence. However, there is no cycle of dependencies between the two statements in the body of the loop. Therefore, it is legal to rewrite the code as follows:

```
for(int i=0; i < n-1; i++)
    a[i+1] = b[i] + c[i];
for(int i=0; i < n-1; i++)
    b[i] = a[i];
```

The theory of dependence analysis is used by compilers to ascertain the validity of loop transformations.

Exercise 3.2.1. We may write a function `double leibniz(int n)` that returns the partial sum of the first n terms of the Leibniz series. We may alter the definition of `leibniz()` and make n a `const` variable whose value is 20 instead of passing it as an argument. Examine the assembly code generated by `icpc` assuming such a modification and comment.

Exercise 3.2.2. Suppose that n is a `const` whose value is 10^9 and not 20 as in the previous exercise. Time `leibnizX()`. How many cycles per term does it take? Discuss the observed cycle count by relating to the assembly code generated by the compiler.

Exercise 3.2.3. Compile the programs for summing the Leibniz series using `-fast`, thus replacing `-prec-div` we normally use by `-no-prec-div`. Is there any improvement in speed?

Exercise 3.2.4. Write a function in C that takes a double-precision array `a[0..n-1]` as input, determines the sums $\sum_{i=0}^{i<(n-r)/4} a_{4i+r}$ for $r = 0, 1, 2, 3$, and return the value of r for which the sum is maximum. Make sure that the loops are unrolled and that packed double instructions are being issued.

Exercise 3.2.5. Write a function in C that takes a double-precision array `a[0..n-1]` as input and replaces a_i by the sum $\sum_{j=0}^{j=i} a_j$ for $i = 0, \ldots, n-1$. Can you get the compiler to unroll the loop and issue packed double instructions in this example?

Exercise 3.2.6. Look up the `icpc` compiler documentation and figure out what `-fast` does. Suppose both `-fast` and `-prec-div` are given as compiler options. Which will take precedence? Suppose both `-fast` and `-O2` are given as compiler options. Which will take precedence?

Exercise 3.2.7. Change the program for computing the sine and cosine at the value x to a program that computes the cosine at two input values x and y. Present two separate loops to the compiler as in the program above. Does the compiler fuse the loops and generate packed double instructions?

Exercise 3.2.8. Fuse the two loops in the program that computes sine and cosine of x manually. Try to write the body of the loop in such a way that the compiler generates packed double instructions.

Exercise 3.2.9. Utilize the parallelism within the power series expansions of $\sin x$ and $\cos x$ to write loops that are partially unrolled and for which the compiler can easily generate packed double instructions. Compare the execution times of programs that compile to packed double instructions with those that compile to single double instructions. It is useful to try large values of n when timing the loops even though the series converge rapidly, making any value of n above 20 or so superfluous.

Exercise 3.2.10. Change the first definition of `sinetable()` so that the loops are interchanged. Does the compiler now generate packed double instructions?

Exercise 3.2.11. In the second definition of `sinetable()`, can the computation of $-x^2$ from x be moved out of the inner loop in the generated assembly code?

Exercise 3.2.12. Write a program that replaces the columns of a square matrix with the cumulative column sum. In other words, the kth column must be replaced by the sum of columns 0 through k. Assuming the program uses a loop over rows and a loop over columns, what is the better way to order the loops? If the loops are not ordered the better way, does the compiler switch the order of loops?

Exercise 3.2.13. Write a program that computes the cumulative row sums of a square matrix and answer the same questions as above.

Exercise 3.2.14. Alter the implementation of the `Vector` and `Matrix` classes so that member functions that overload the function call operator `()` cannot be inlined. How does the matrix multiplication function of section 3.2.6 perform after the alterations?

Exercise 3.2.15. Explain why the for-loop

```
for(int i=0; i < n-1; i++){
    a[i+1] = b[i] + c[i];
    b[i] = a[i];
};
```

carries the RAW dependence.

Exercise 3.2.16. Give examples of for-loops whose bodies have just a single statement and that exhibit loop-carried dependence of exactly one of the types RAR, RAW, WAR, and WAW.

Exercise 3.2.17. Explain why the following loop

```
for(int i=1; i < n; i++){
    a[i] = b[i]+c[i];
    d[i] = a[i-1];
}
```

carries the RAW dependence. Rewrite the loop so that there is no loop-carried dependence.

Exercise 3.2.18. Assume that the array a stores a square matrix of size dim. In the loop nest

```
for(int i=1; i < n; i++)
    for(int j=1; j < n; j++)
        a[i+j*dim] = a[i-1+j*dim]+a[i+(j-1)*dim];
```

explain why both the inner and outer loops carry dependencies. Visualize the computation graphically and show how to transform the loop nest so that the inner loop carries no dependence.

Exercise 3.2.19. In the multIJK() program of the previous section, a single statement comprises the body of a loop nest of depth 3. List and explain the dependencies carried by the i, j, and k loops.

Exercise 3.2.20. Write a C++ program for Aitken extrapolation with transparent loops that enable the compiler to generate good assembly code. The loop bodies should not have any if statements. Compare the generated assembly code with that of the C++ programs of chapter 1. By what factor is the program with transparent loops faster?

3.3   Optimizing for the instruction pipeline

Earlier, we found that MKL's fast Fourier transform and matrix multiplication can be 10 times faster than ordinary C/C++ programs. If the C++ program is written without care, the speedup can even be a factor of 100. What does Intel's MKL do to be so much faster than ordinary C/C++ programs?

The biggest part of the answer to that question is optimizing for the instruction pipeline, which is the topic of the present section. The compiler converts a C/C++ program into a stream of machine instructions. When the program runs, this instruction stream is consumed by the processor. From a programmer's point of view, the instructions are executed one by one, but that is not the way processors consume instructions. The x86 processors consumed instructions in that manner before 1990. If processors still worked that way, they would be slower by at least a factor of 10.

All modern processors consume instructions using a pipeline, although semantically it is as if the instructions were executed one after another. The pipeline has different stages for fetching, decoding, execution, and accessing memory. Each of these stages has considerable parallelism built into it. Modern x86 processors fetch and decode multiple instructions in a single cycle. For example, an AVX2 processor of the Haswell family (see table 3.1) has seven execution ports. Therefore, seven instructions can be dispatched to execution units simultaneously on that processor.

The point of optimizing for the instruction pipeline is to keep the execution units working in parallel as far as possible.[20] Like register sets, the instruction pipeline is invisible within the confines of C/C++. Unlike the registers, the instruction pipeline is invisible even within assembly code. It appears impossible to get compilers to generate instruction streams that are optimized for the instruction pipeline. The difficulties here are of a fundamental kind, and it is unlikely that compilers can ever do this type of optimization satisfactorily. Optimizing for the instruction pipeline involves accounting for instruction size and alignment, usage of register ports, and many other factors that are completely invisible in a C/C++ program. The disparity between architectural design and the abstract view of the computer in C/C++ appears too great to be bridged automatically and perfectly by a compiler. The disparity is growing rapidly, increasing the importance of optimizing for the instruction

---

[20]The chief source for technical details of the x86 pipeline is *Intel® 64 and IA-32 Architectures Optimization Reference Manual*, 2013.

pipeline. That is true even though one of the aims of architectural design is to be an easy target for compilation.

In sections 3.3.1 and 3.3.2, we give a general overview of the processor pipeline and related matters. This overview is specialized to x86. A distinction must be made between instruction set architectures such as SSE2 and AVX2 (see table 3.1) and microarchitectures. The microarchitecture specifies the type of pipeline implemented in hardware to consume instructions. Even when the instruction set architecture is the same, microarchitectures can differ. The differences in microarchitecture can be of importance in optimizing for the instruction pipeline. Therefore, we pay attention to the microarchitecture in addition to the instruction set.

Sections 3.3.3 and 3.3.4 get into the gritty details, which can be hair-rising but also exciting. The thrill of making nontrivial programs faster by factors of 2 or 10 by understanding how machine instructions map to the microarchitecture is undeniable. However, the thrill is not easily attained. Part of the difficulty is that some details of the microarchitecture need to be discovered through reverse-engineering.

The chief example in sections 3.3.3 and 3.3.4 is matrix multiplication. We have already seen that MKL can be more than twice (on SSE2) or more than 10 times (on AVX2) faster than ordinary C/C++ programs (see table 3.3). Our aim is to understand how that speedup comes about.

The number of arithmetic operations in $C = C + AB$, if all matrices are square of dimension n, is $2n^3$ with equally many additions and multiplications. Because each `double` is 8 bytes, the total amount of memory used by the three matrices is $24n^2$ bytes. As n increases, the number of arithmetic operations increases superlinearly, as the 1.5th power, against the size of data in memory. This is better than with the FFT, where the superlinear factor is only logarithmic.

There are two stages in writing a good matrix multiplication. The first stage is to produce a microkernel that multiplies small matrices while using instruction pipeline resources optimally. The second stage is to use the microkernel to code multiplication of larger matrices while hiding the cost of memory access. The cost of memory accesses can be almost completely hidden because the number of arithmetic operations grows superlinearly in data size. Thus, coding a good microkernel is decisive. The second stage, like most memory optimizations, can be implemented in C/C++ and is deferred to the next chapter. In this chapter, we focus on the microkernel.

The exposition assumes the SSE2 instruction set (see table 3.1). Although the SSE2 instruction set has been superseded by AVX and AVX2, all the main principles of optimizing for the instruction pipeline are brought out in our exposition. An advantage of using SSE2 is that our programs will run on almost any computer. In addition, the exposition is simplified because SSE2 instructions are less complex. Because our aim is to bring out the principles of optimizing for the instruction pipeline, the programs we discuss come close to MKL speeds (on SSE2 machines) but stay away from additional details and clutter necessary to actually reach such speeds. Optimizing for the AVX2 pipeline is covered in the exercises.

Computer architecture, systems software, program compilation, and program optimization are all full of minute details. Among these, computer architecture changes at the most rapid pace. Yet the understanding gained using one particular microarchitecture applies across past and future generations. That is so because the fundamental principles of instruction pipeline design have not changed for decades. Thus, the concepts and techniques that we learn using an SSE2 pipeline in section 3.3.4 carry over to more modern AVX2 pipelines, as illustrated in our discussion and as evident from the exercises, as well as to AVX-512 pipelines of the future.

3.3.1   Instruction pipelines

General remarks

The automobile assembly line offers a useful point of comparison to clarify concepts. An automobile assembly line may take 48 hours to assemble a single car. However, thanks to pipelining and multiple assembly lines, the factory may produce a car every minute. For such a factory, the latency would be 48 hours and the bandwidth 1 car per minute.

The assembly of the car is broken down into a number of steps that are executed sequentially in the assembly line. Crucially, these steps or pipeline stages are independent of each other. Therefore, car B can be pushed onto the first stage as soon as car A completes the first stage and moves to the second. When car A moves to the third stage and car B to the second, car C is pushed to the first stage. Ideally, the various stages of the assembly line should take nearly the same time. The bandwidth of the assembly line is constrained by the slowest stage. If the number of stages in the assembly line is increased, the bandwidth increases (assuming that the stages take the same amount of time), even though the latency is unchanged.

The analogy to car manufacturing omits many complications that arise in processor pipelines. Instructions are not as independent as cars. If there is a RAW dependence between two instructions, the second instruction cannot begin to execute until the first completes. Even ignoring dependencies, it takes a lot of design to make the stages of the instruction pipeline relatively independent. For example, the instruction cache should be separate from data cache if the instruction fetch stage is to be kept relatively independent of the stage where operands are read from memory. Another source of complication comes from interrupts or exceptions raised by an external device or the operating system. If the interrupt is of high enough priority, the entire pipeline must be abandoned to service the interrupt and restored after the interrupt is serviced.

Although RAW dependencies cannot be eliminated, modern processors eliminate WAW and WAR dependencies on the fly. Those dependencies are eliminated using register renaming.[21] Suppose we have two instructions as follows:

```
movq %r8 %rax
 . . .
movq %r9 %rax
```

Evidently, the second instruction has WAW dependence on the first because both instructions write into the %rax register. It would be illegal for the processor to execute the second instruction before the first because there may be some other instruction in the middle that reads from %rax and therefore has RAW dependence on the first instruction. But suppose the processor dynamically renames the second %rax to some other internal register. Suppose as well that the processor renames %rax to the same internal register in all later instructions that read what the second instruction writes into %rax. If the processor does such renaming of registers, it can go ahead and execute the second instruction before the first.

Using register renaming, the processor can eliminate WAR and WAW dependencies and greatly increase available parallelism in the instruction stream. Instructions can be scheduled out of order and even executed in parallel.

Because of the sophistication of the algorithms used by processors to execute instructions, it is a misconception to think that processor performance is somehow proportional to clock speed. The 3.2 GHz Pentium 4 from 2004 used between 1.19

---

[21]For a detailed account of Tomasulo's algorithm for register renaming, see Hennessy and Patterson (1990-2011).

and 5.85 cycles per instruction for 10 programs in the SPEC CPU benchmark.[22] The 2.66 GHz AMD Opteron of that time used fewer cycles per instruction by a factor of 1.27. As a result, the 2.66 GHz Opteron performed slightly better than the 3.2 GHz Pentium. The use of deep pipelines by the 3.2 GHz Pentium to accommodate a higher clock rate resulted in more pipeline stalls and more cycles per instruction, thus outweighing the advantage of greater clock speed.

For the SPEC CPU benchmark programs, the Pentium 4 did not do better than 1.19 cycles per instruction, although its peak bandwidth is 1/3 of a cycle per instruction. Unsurprisingly, typical performance is well short of the peak bandwidth. Apart from making simplifying assumptions about the instruction stream, the definition of the peak bandwidth entirely ignores the cost of memory accesses. Yet processor bandwidth is a useful metric. From 1982 to 2001, the processor bandwidth increased by a factor of 2,250. The processor performance increased by a factor close to 2,250 (an annual rate of about 50%) in the 19 years from 1982 to 2001, as measured by the SPECint benchmarks.

AVX2 and SSE2 pipelines

Figures 3.4 and 3.5 show instruction pipelines for the SSE2-capable Nehalem/Westmere microarchitecture and the AVX2-capable Haswell microarchitecture. If we want to write programs that approach MKL speeds for matrix multiplication and other tasks, such microarchitectures must be understood in some detail.

The pipelines shown have four parts. The first part, called the front-end, fetches and decodes instructions. Certain instructions, mainly instructions that store in memory, may be broken up into micro-ops. The front-end can fetch and decode multiple instructions in a single cycle.

The second part, called the reorder engine, is responsible for renaming registers as well as scheduling instructions. Instructions may be scheduled for execution out of order. Predicting branches and recovering from mispredictions is also the responsibility of this part. The reorder engine includes reorder buffers. The reorder buffer holds partially complete instructions or "instructions in flight." It corresponds roughly to renamed registers.

---

[22]See sections 2.10 and 1.8 of Hennessy and Patterson (1990-2011) (4th ed.).

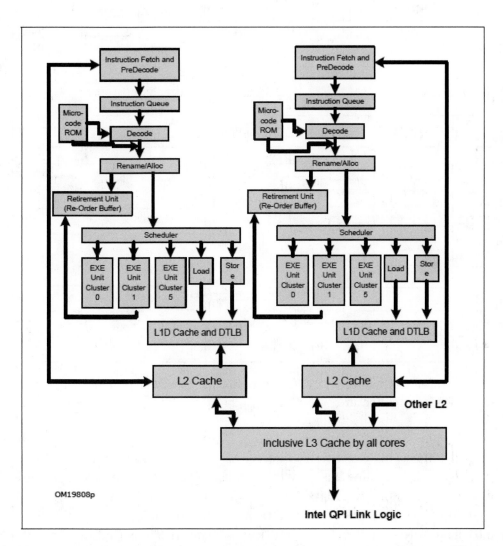

Figure 3.4: Instruction pipeline (two copies for two processor cores) on an SSE2-capable machine. The pipeline here corresponds to the Nehalem/Westmere microarchitecture.

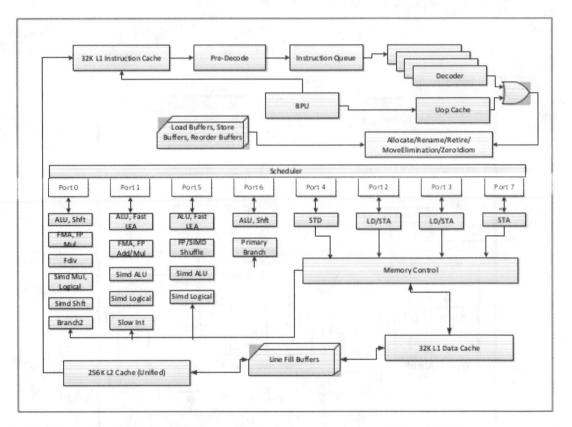

Figure 3.5: Instruction pipeline on an AVX2-capable machine. The pipeline here corresponds to the Haswell microarchitecture.

The third part is for execution. The AVX2 pipeline has seven execution units, while the older SSE2 pipeline has only five. Of the seven execution units in the AVX2 pipeline, two can execute `fmadd*pd` instructions (port 0 and port 1 in figure 3.5). If peak capability of 16 flops per cycle is to be approached during matrix multiplication, we have to make sure that two fused-multiply-add instructions that operate on YMM registers are dispatched to execution ports 0 and 1 almost every cycle. That will involve finding sufficient parallelism in the instruction stream as well as understanding how the front-end and the reorder engine work.

The final part in the instruction pipeline is for memory access. Each part is broken up into multiple stages, and there is considerable parallelism at every level of the pipeline. As evident from figures 3.4 and 3.5, the stages within a pipeline are not linearly laid out, contrary to the image conjured by the word "pipeline," but have more complicated interconnections with each other.

The SSE2 pipeline shown in figure 3.4 is for the Nehalem/Westmere architecture. The AVX2 pipeline shown in figure 3.5 is for the Haswell microarchitecture. The front-end, the reorder engine, and the execution units can differ even when the instruction set is the same. However, such differences in microarchitecture are not always of the greatest significance for program optimization, although they could be on occasion.

3.3.2 Chipsets

So far we have mainly been looking at the processor core. We are about to go even more deeply into the processor. So let us pause for a moment and look at the rest of the computer.

The processors are central to the computer but are only one among the many components that make up a computer or compute node. Some of the other components are DRAM memory, graphics processor, hard disk, solid state storage, network adapter, keyboard, and monitor. To understand how the processor is connected to all the components, we have to look at chipsets. Chipsets are chips used to assemble computers from many components.

Figure 3.6 shows the block diagram of the Intel 5500P chipset and gives a good idea of the layout of a computer. We pick a particular chipset, but many others would do just as well at the level of generality of our discussion. The basic problem in assembling a computer is that the various components operate at very different speeds. The processors are very fast, DRAM memory is not so fast, peripherals such as keyboards are very slow, and the network is capricious. The task of reconciling components that operate at very different speeds falls partly on the chipset.

Two processor packages are shown in figure 3.6 as P1 and P2. Each processor package fits into a socket on the motherboard. Each processor package may have four or six cores in this instance. On more recent machines using other chipsets, each processor package may even have 16 cores.

From figure 3.6, we see that DDR3 memory is connected directly to the sockets housing the processor chips. The processor packages contain multiple levels of cache and memory controllers to handle transfer of data to and from the DRAM channels. It is obvious from visual inspection that some DRAM memory channels are closer to

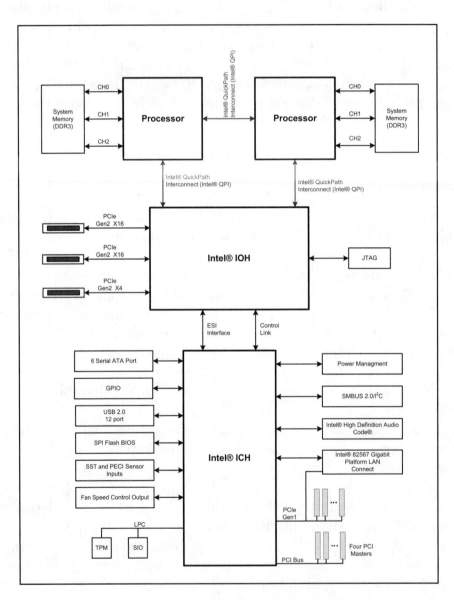

Figure 3.6: Block diagram of the Intel 5000P chipset used to build computers of the Xeon 5500 or 5600 series.

certain processor cores. In particular, DRAM memory that is connected to the other socket will be slower to access from a processor core than DRAM memory that is connected to the same socket. If the DRAM memory is on the other socket, it has to come through the memory controller on the other chip. The two processors are connected to each other (with QPI or Quick Path Interconnect), as shown in the figure.

This sort of organization of memory makes memory access nonuniform. Non-uniform memory access (NUMA) architecture was introduced by AMD into its x86 product line in 2003. Intel followed suit in 2008.

The graphics processor is connected to I/O handler (IOH) via a PCI express link. Although certain graphics processors can deliver processing and memory bandwidths that can rival the processor cores, the graphics processor is no more than just another peripheral device as far as the organization of the computer is concerned.

Like the graphics processors, the adapters for the Infiniband network are connected using PCI express links. The Infiniband network is used to build high-performance clusters from compute nodes. Ethernet cards and adapters used for Internet connectivity may also use PCI express links.

Hard disks, audio, keyboard, and other I/O devices are connected to I/O controller handler (ICH). The way in which the chipset allows the processing cores to talk to I/O devices and yet work at something like their normal speed involves substantial involvement of the operating system. Device drivers and interrupt handlers are the operating system components that mediate between the processor and the I/O devices.

Direct memory access is one of the major functions of the chipset. Suppose a processor wants to transfer 10 GB from hard disk to memory. Because the hard disk is very slow, the transfer would slow down the processor greatly. So the processor delegates the transfer to the chipset and starts executing some other instruction stream, while the chipset is working on direct memory transfer. During direct memory transfer, data is transferred directly between the hard disk and DRAM memory without processor intervention.

Direct memory access is used for transfers between the processor's memory and graphics coprocessor memory or Xeon Phi coprocessor memory. It is used by Infiniband adapters to directly transfer data between memory and the network. The use of direct memory access in such situations must respect the operating system's role in memory management, as we will explain later. Direct memory access enables parallelism between network activity and processor activity (chapter 6) or between coprocessor activity and processor activity (chapters 7 and 8).

3.3.3   Peak floating point performance

The SSE2 instruction set architecture (see table 3.1) provides for 16 XMM registers on each processor. Each XMM register is 128 bits wide and capable of holding two `doubles`. A single instruction that uses an XMM register as source and another XMM register as destination can carry out two additions, if the instruction is `addpd`, or two subtractions, if it is `subpd`, or two multiplications, if it is `mulpd`. The addition and multiplication instructions are dispatched using separate ports, which means that an addition and a multiplication instruction can be issued as well as completed in the same cycle. Thus, the peak rate at which double-precision floating point operations (flops) are executed by a single SSE2 processor is 4 flops per cycle.

Table 3.3 on page 174 showed us that the matrix multiplication routines of the MKL library achieve more than 3.8 flops per cycle. However, to write such a program is no simple matter. It requires intimate knowledge of the processor pipeline, which is shown in figure 3.4.

Our objective is to understand matrix multiplication routines of the sort implemented by MKL. We will not aim to match MKL's performance. Such a thing would require us to write more assembly code than is pedagogically desirable or appropriate. Knowledge of the processor pipeline is one aspect of optimizing matrix multiplication. Memory hierarchy is equally important. Memory is the topic of the next chapter.

In this section, we write a few programs that do nothing meaningful but that get close to the peak performance of 4 flops per cycle, with the 4 flops comprised of two additions and two multiplications of double-precision floating point numbers. Although the programs are not required to be meaningful, getting close to peak performance is not easy. This exercise requires us to understand many aspects of how instructions are decoded and then dispatched to execution units using several ports. Instruction latencies and throughputs, register read stalls, and register renaming are other aspects of instruction-level parallelism we encounter during the exercise. Where appropriate, we shall look back to figure 3.4 to make the discussion concrete, even though the SSE2/Nehalem pipeline is too complicated for a schematic sketch of the type given in that figure to be either complete or totally accurate.

This section is a prelude to the discussion of matrix multiplication, which begins in the next section. We understand matrix multiplication on modern processors in two steps. In the next section, we take the first step by writing programs or microkernels[23] to multiply $4 \times n$ matrices with an $n \times 4$ matrices for values of n such as $n = 1, 4, 200$. The microkernels with $n = 50, 100, 200$ approach peak performance if the matrices are assumed to be in cache. The final stage, which is to use a microkernel as the building block of a program for multiplying large matrices in DRAM memory, is one of the examples discussed in the next chapter.

Understanding matrix multiplication on modern processors will take us more deeply into computer hardware than is customary in textbooks on scientific computing or indeed even computer architecture. The programs are run on a 2.6 GHz SSE2 processor and a 3.6 GHz AVX2 processor (see table A.1 for their full names; neither processor has in-core acceleration of the clock). Although the programs are not optimized for the AVX2 pipeline, they are still more than three times faster than compiled code.

Optimization for the more recent AVX2 instruction set is dealt with in the exercises. The AVX-512 instruction set, which is yet to be introduced in the main x86 line, is dealt with in chapter 7. An advantage of using SSE2 is that our programs will run on almost all x86 computers. Because the SSE2 instructions are simpler than AVX2 instructions, there is considerable simplification in the discussion. Most of the points that we make about latencies and throughputs of instructions, such as `addpd` and `mulpd`, remain valid on AVX and AVX2 machines, sometimes with minor modifications. It is a little surprising that the SSE2 programs we discuss have not become dated even with the advent of AVX and AVX2. Of course, these programs no longer approach peak performance. Yet the concepts they bring out related to instruction-level parallelism remain valid in the context of the specific programs found in our discussion, and the programs will continue to run.

XMM registers and packed double instructions

We have examined compiler-generated assembly code on a number of occasions earlier in this chapter. It appears impossible to write C/C++ programs in such a way that the compiled code achieves peak floating point performance. C and C++ give us a

---

[23]The microkernel nomenclature was introduced by R.A. van de Geijn. The concept may be found in Goto and van de Geijn (2008). I thank Robert van de Geijn for this information.

uniform view of memory. One can write cache-aware programs in C/C++, as we will in the next chapter. As we saw in earlier sections, we can write C/C++ programs with an eye on the kind of instruction stream the compiler will generate and the processor executes. However, to achieve peak floating point performance, we must pay attention to instruction-level parallelism and the instruction pipeline as well as the cache hierarchy. The design of the instruction pipeline is quite intricate and constrains the instruction stream needed to approach peak performance in many ways. Within the confines of the abstract view of the computer provided by C/C++, it appears impossible to heed such constraints on the instruction stream.

We use macros and the inline assembly facility to embed instructions that manipulate XMM registers into C/C++ programs. The first of these macros is as follows:

```
/* R must be "%xmmi" 0<=i<=15 */
#define zeroxmm(R)                        \
    asm volatile("xorps %" R ", %" R "\n\t":::R);
```

The 16 XMM registers are %xmm0 through %xmm15 in GNU assembly (GAS). To zero one of them, say %xmm7, we say zeroxmm("%xmm7") inside a C/C++ program. Macro expansion and inline assembly produce the machine instruction

```
xorps %xmm7, %xmm7
```

followed by a newline and a tab for better formatting. The mnemonic xorps may be read as XOR packed single. Its two operands must both be 128 bits wide. It treats each operand as four packed single-precision floating point numbers. Its effect is to exclusive or (xor) the two operands bit by bit. The xor of two bits is 1 when exactly one of the two bits is 1, the other being 0. Because we are xor-ing %xmm7 with itself, we get 0 for each of the 128 bits.

There are other ways to set a register to zero. For example, we can move the constant value 0 into each part of the 128-bit XMM register, or we can store 0 in memory and load it to the XMM register. The use of xorps is preferred because the instruction is three bytes, if the register is one of %xmm0 through %xmm7, or four bytes, if the register is one of %xmm8 through %xmm15. Other options may lead to longer instructions. For example, the xorpd instruction is a byte longer. In addition, the xorps instruction takes only a single cycle to execute.

Four more macros that expand to inline assembly statements follow.

```
//R1 and R2 must be "%xmmi" 0<=i<=15
```

```
#define addxmm(R1, R2)                                          \
  asm volatile("addpd %" R1 ", %" R2 "\n\t":::R1, R2);

//R1 and R2 must be "%xmmi" 0<=i<=15
#define mulxmm(R1, R2)                                          \
  asm volatile("mulpd %" R1 ", %" R2 "\n\t":::R1, R2);

//R = "%xmmi" 0<=i<=15
//a = double * (16 byte aligned)
#define loadxmm(a, R)                                           \
  asm volatile("movaps %0, %" R "\n\t"::"m"(*(a)):R);

//R = "%xmmi" 0<=i<=15xmm
//a = double * (16 byte aligned)
#define storexmm(R, a)                                          \
  asm volatile("movaps %" R ", %0 \n\t":"=m"(*(a))::R);
```

The macros generate `addpd`, `mulpd`, and `movaps` instructions. PD stands for packed double. APS in `movaps` stands for aligned packed single. The `movaps` instruction is one byte shorter than the `movapd` instruction. The `movaps` instruction can be used to move an XMM register to another XMM register, store an XMM register to memory, or load an XMM register from memory. The memory address must be 16-byte aligned.

The macros help us write easily readable assembly code. For example, if we write

```
__declspec(align(16)) double a[2]={1,2};
__declspec(align(16)) double b[2]={-1,-2};
loadxmm(a, "%xmm0");
loadxmm(b, "%xmm1");
addxmm("%xmm1", "%xmm0");
storexmm("%xmm0", a);
printf("%f %f \n", a[0], a[1]);
```

it is evident that the `printf()` statement will print two zeros. The four macros expand to the following assembly statements:

```
movaps      (%rsp), %xmm0
movaps      16(%rsp), %xmm1
```

```
addpd       %xmm1 , %xmm0
movaps      %xmm0 , (%rsp)
```

This assembly code was extracted after compiling the C++ program with the -S option. It is evident that the arrays a and b begin at the locations (%rsp) and 16(%rsp). The value of a equals the content of the %rsp register and the value of b equals %rsp+16. Both pointers are 16-byte aligned, but that information is not found in the extract.

Another way to recover the assembly instructions corresponding to the four macros is to disassemble the object file. The command objdump -d file.o disassembles the object file file.o. The machine instructions are written in binary format in the object file. Disassembly converts it to more familiar assembly language mnemonics. An extract from the output of objdump -d peakflops.o, where peakflops.o is the object file compiled from the C++ program that adds two entries of b to two entries of a, follows:

```
69:  0f 28 04 24                movaps  (%rsp),%xmm0
6d:  0f 28 4c 24 10             movaps  0x10(%rsp),%xmm1
72:  66 0f 58 c1                addpd   %xmm1,%xmm0
76:  0f 29 04 24                movaps  %xmm0,(%rsp)
```

Here we see the address at which each instruction begins on the left (the addresses are given in hexadecimal), followed by the hexadecimal code for the instruction followed by the assembly statement.

The load and store macros assume the memory address to be 16-byte aligned. The last hexadecimal digit of the address must be zero. We can generate 16-byte-aligned arrays by prefixing __declspec(align(16)) if the array is statically defined as shown above. For memory that is allocated dynamically, versions of malloc() such as _mm_malloc() allow alignment to be specified.

The macros such as zeroxmm() are certainly convenient. However, their use exposes us to a *dangerous error*. If we have two lines such as

```
addxmm("%xmm1", "%xmm0");
storexmm("%xmm0", a);
```

the compiler is allowed to use %xmm0 for its own purposes in between the two lines. The inline assembly statements are guaranteed to appear in order, but the compiler may use %xmm0 for some temporary computation in between the two lines. This danger is especially great when inline assembly statements written in this style appear within the loop body.

We use macros given here to generate inline assembly statements for expository convenience. In a real program, it is better to write functions entirely in assembly or to use a single `asm volatile` statement for entire blocks of assembly instructions. Where macros are used for expository convenience, we assume that the assembly code is examined to ensure that dangerous side effects are not present.

Instruction latencies and throughputs

Instruction latency (according to Intel manuals) is the number of cycles spent by the instruction in an execution unit of the instruction pipeline. Instruction throughput is the maximum rate at which an instruction can be dispatched to the execution units.

The definition of the C++ function `addreg()` follows.

```
void addreg(double *a, double *b, long int nitns){
    long int i;
    loadxmm(a, "%xmm0");
    loadxmm(b, "%xmm1");
    for(i=0; i < nitns; i++)
        addxmm("%xmm0","%xmm1");
    storexmm("%xmm1", a);
}
```

This function replaces `a[0]` and `a[1]` by `b[0]+nitns*a[0]` and `b[1]+nitns*a[1]`, respectively.

What the function does is irrelevant to the point we want to make. When such functions arise later, only the relevant part of the code is given. For `addreg()`, the relevant part of the code is as follows:

```
for(i=0; i < nitns; i++)
    addxmm("%xmm0","%xmm1");
```

For simplicity, when code fragments such as this one arise, we may assume that all XMM registers are initialized to zero. The number of iterations is assumed to be large.

If this code fragment is timed, we find that it takes slightly more than 3 cycles per iteration. Why 3 cycles? The answer is that the latency of `addpd` is 3 cycles. Like every instruction, the `addpd` instruction probably begins its life in the instruction pipeline at the instruction fetch stage of the pipeline (see figure 3.4), which is the first stage in the pipeline. The instruction fetch stage fetches instruction from memory. If the instruction is inside a loop, as in this instance, almost all the fetches are from L1 cache.[24] Once the operands are available, the scheduler dispatches the instruction to the execution unit. The latency is the number of cycles spent by the instruction in the execution unit.

For `i>0`, every `addpd` instruction receives one of its operands from the previous `addpd` instruction. Thus, each `addpd` instruction can be scheduled only after the previous iteration is complete. Thus, the observed speed of 3 cycles per iteration is the best possible.

Although each `addpd` instruction spends 3 cycles in the execution unit, it is possible to dispatch an `addpd` to the execution unit every cycle. This assumes of course that the instruction dispatched does not need to wait for some other instruction that is currently executing to complete. Thus, there should be a sufficient level of parallelism in the instruction stream for the maximum throughput of one `addpd` instruction per cycle to be realized. The following program takes 3 cycles per iteration.

```
for(i=0; i < nitns; i++){
   addxmm("%xmm0","%xmm1");
   addxmm("%xmm2","%xmm3");
   addxmm("%xmm4","%xmm5");
}
```

The three `addpd` instructions in the loop body are completely independent of each other. Each instruction in a given iteration of the loop body can be scheduled only after the same instruction has completed in the previous iteration. However, the maximum throughput is realized because three independent instruction streams can be executed in parallel.

On both SSE2/Nehalem (see figure 3.4) and AVX2/Haswell (see figure 3.5), the latencies of `addpd` and `mulpd` are 3 cycles and 5 cycles, respectively. The maximum throughput of `addpd` is 1 cycle per instruction, meaning that at most one `addpd` can be issued in a single cycle on both platforms. The throughput of `mulpd` is 1 cycle per

---

[24]The Nehalem/Westmere pipeline has a loop stream detector that skips instruction fetch for loops with a small body.

instruction on SSE2/Nehalem but 0.5 cycles per instruction (meaning that 2 `mulpds` can be issued in a single cycle) on AVX2/Haswell.

Multiple dispatch ports and register read stalls

The `mulpd` instructions are dispatched for execution on port 0 and the `addpd` instructions are dispatched on port 1 (see figure 3.4, where the units are numbered). Because the dispatch ports are separate, it is possible to dispatch a `mulpd` and an `addpd` in the same cycle. In fact, even on the more recent AVX/AVX2 architectures, at most one `mulpd` can be simultaneously dispatched with an `addpd`. So much of the discussion remains valid.

Our first attempt to observe this type of parallelism is the following program:

```
for(i=0; i < nitns; i++){
   addxmm("%xmm8", "%xmm0");
   addxmm("%xmm9", "%xmm1");
   addxmm("%xmm10", "%xmm2");
   mulxmm("%xmm11", "%xmm3");
   mulxmm("%xmm12", "%xmm4");
   mulxmm("%xmm13", "%xmm5");
   mulxmm("%xmm14", "%xmm6");
   mulxmm("%xmm15", "%xmm7");
}
```

In each block of five cycles, we may expect the five `mulpd` instructions and three `addpd` instructions in the loop body to be scheduled. There is certainly enough parallelism in the loop body to permit such a schedule. Thus, we may expect 5 cycles per iteration.

The observed number is 8 cycles per iteration and is greater than our expectation. The initial observation is in fact slightly more than 9 cycles per iteration. By unrolling the loop, we get close to 8 cycles per iteration.

It is as if the `addpd` and `mulpd` instructions cannot be dispatched in the same cycle even though they have separate execution ports. Why is that happening? Because of register read stalls.[25]

---

[25]The five-part optimization manual, made available by Agner Fog on his web page (see `http://www.agner.org/optimize/`.), is a valuable source on x86 processors. Fog's discussion of register read stalls was essential input for writing this section.

During every cycle, it is possible to read only three registers from the register file in the SSE2/Nehalem microarchitecture. Here the `addpd` would need to read two registers and the `mulpd` would need to read two other registers. The initial answer is to point out that one of the two instructions cannot be dispatched because four registers cannot be read in the same cycle.

That is not a complete answer, however. After an instruction completes, it spends some time in the reorder buffer (ROB) (see figure 3.4) before it is retired. If an operand needed to dispatch an instruction can be captured directly as the *output* of an instruction that is waiting in ROB, there is no need to use a register port. In fact, in the earlier Core 2 or Merom microarchitecture, the program takes only 5 cycles per iteration as expected, although the Core 2 microarchitecture provides only two ports to read from the register file. It appears that each `addpd` and `mulpd` instruction in the loop body captures the result of the previous iteration directly from ROB on Core 2. The reason that SSE2/Nehalem does not read from ROB as well as Core 2 is unknown.

Another confirmation that register read stalls are responsible for slowing the program down to 8 cycles per iterations, instead of the expected 5, may be found by running the same program on an AVX/AVX2 machine. On those more modern machines, there are more register read ports, and therefore register read stalls are not an issue. The same program realizes 5 cycles per iteration.

Our second attempt is the following program:

```
for(i=0;  i < nitns;  i++){
   addxmm("%xmm8",  "%xmm0");
   addxmm("%xmm8",  "%xmm1");
   addxmm("%xmm8",  "%xmm2");
   mulxmm("%xmm8",  "%xmm3");
   mulxmm("%xmm8",  "%xmm4");
   mulxmm("%xmm8",  "%xmm5");
   mulxmm("%xmm8",  "%xmm6");
   mulxmm("%xmm8",  "%xmm7");
}
```

In this program, each `addpd` and `mulpd` instruction uses `%xmm8` as its source register. Only three registers need to be read from the register file to dispatch an `addpd` and

mulpd in the same cycle. There is no register read stall, and after suitable unrolling, the number of cycles per iteration is only slightly greater than 5.

Peak performance without loads or stores

The loop body of the following program issues five **addpd** instructions and five **mulpd** instructions.

```
for(long int i=0;  i < nitns;  i++){
   addxmm("%xmm0",  "%xmm1");
   mulxmm("%xmm1",  "%xmm2");
   addxmm("%xmm3",  "%xmm4");
   mulxmm("%xmm4",  "%xmm5");
   addxmm("%xmm6",  "%xmm7");
   mulxmm("%xmm7",  "%xmm8");
   addxmm("%xmm9",  "%xmm10");
   mulxmm("%xmm10",  "%xmm11");
   addxmm("%xmm12",  "%xmm13");
   mulxmm("%xmm13",  "%xmm14");
}
```

The source operand of each **mulpd** is the destination operand of the **addpd** above it. The hope is that this source operand is read directly from ROB, thus relieving pressure on the register ports. If that hope bears out, we should observe 5 cycles per iteration.

If the loop is unrolled 10 times, we observe 5.13 cycles per iteration in line with expectation. Some operands are indeed being read from ROB instead of from the register file.

If the loop is not unrolled, it takes 7 cycles per iteration. Why does unrolling help? The assembly code for the loop includes an instruction to increment the loop counter **i**, which is stored in a register such as **%rax**. It includes another instruction to compare the loop counter with **nitns**. The variable **nitns** is stored in a register. These instructions create additional pressure on the register ports. An overhead of 2 cycles is not unreasonable. With unrolling, the overhead is amortized.

On a more modern AVX2/Haswell machine, the same program takes 5.8 cycles per iteration, even with unrolling. Evidently this program interacts with the

AVX2/Haswell pipeline in a different manner. Although the AVX2/Haswell pipeline is newer, it does not seem to recapture operands from ROB as effectively.

A total of 20 flops are carried out in the loop body. Therefore, 5.13 cycles per iteration corresponds to 3.89 flops per cycle. One can approach the theoretical bound of 4 flops per cycle much more closely with a shortfall that is less than .01. The program which does that uses a more complicated staggered pattern of instructions with more parallelism in the loop body and more reuse of registers that have been recently modified. Because the program is long and makes no fundamentally new point, it is not given here.

Peak performance with loads

The load instructions are dispatched on port 2. A SSE2/Nehalem program is capable of dispatching a `mulpd` on port 0, an `addpd` on port 1, and a load instruction on port 2 in the same cycle (the statement so far is true on AVX2/Haswell as well, as shown by figure 3.5), assuming the number of reads from the register file is not more than three. The following program demonstrates the capability:

```
for(long int i=0; i < nitns; i++){
  loadxmm(a, "%xmm0");
  mulxmm("%xmm1", "%xmm0");
  addxmm("%xmm0", "%xmm2");

  loadxmm(a+12, "%xmm0");
  mulxmm("%xmm1", "%xmm0");
  addxmm("%xmm0", "%xmm3");

  loadxmm(a+24, "%xmm0");
  mulxmm("%xmm1", "%xmm0");
  addxmm("%xmm0", "%xmm4");

  loadxmm(a+36, "%xmm0");
  mulxmm("%xmm1", "%xmm0");
  addxmm("%xmm0", "%xmm5");

  loadxmm(a+48, "%xmm0");
```

```
        mulxmm("%xmm1", "%xmm0");
        addxmm("%xmm0", "%xmm6");
    }
```

After unrolling by a factor of four, this program takes 5.01 cycles per iteration. On AVX2/Haswell, it reaches 5.0 cycles per iteration with or without unrolling.

Each load instruction uses %xmm0 as the destination. It may seem that each triplet of load, multiply, and add has to wait for the previous triplet to complete. But such WAW dependencies are eliminated using register renaming. The processor may, for example, dynamically rename the %xmm0 in loadxmm(a+12,"%xmm0") to something else, possibly an internally maintained reservation station.[26] In that case, the processor will automatically rename the references to %xmm0 in the next two instructions to the same thing. Register renaming is a stage in the instruction pipeline (see figure 3.4). Each triplet of load, multiply, and add is completely independent of other triplets in the same iteration. Register renaming allows the processor to exploit this high degree of parallelism in the instruction stream.

It is interesting to think of how the instructions may get scheduled across cycles. Many different schedules are admissible. At the beginning, the scheduler cannot exploit the parallelism in the instruction stream completely. The locations that are loaded may not be in L1 cache at the beginning. There must be a kind of dynamics to the way the scheduling changes as the iteration count increases. In a case such as this, one may expect the instruction schedule to reach a single "steady state." However, one wonders whether there could be periodic, quasi-periodic, or chaotic oscillations in the instruction schedule as the iteration count increases.

Peak performance with loads and stores

We have seen that the instruction pipeline can schedule two or three instructions in the same cycle. For such a capability to be effective, every stage in the pipeline must be capable of pushing several instructions per cycle to the next stage. If instructions are fetched at a slow rate, for example, instruction fetch will be the bottleneck, and the capability of executing several instructions in the same cycle may not be fully utilized.

---

[26]See Hennessy and Patterson (1990-2011).

Instruction fetch and decode are early stages of the pipeline (see figure 3.4). The SSE2/Nehalem microarchitecture fetches instructions in 16-byte blocks. The blocks are aligned in memory. If an instruction crosses a 16-byte boundary, it will take two cycles to fetch the instruction. The maximum throughput of these early stages of the pipeline is six instructions per cycle.

Occasionally, the instruction fetch and decode may limit the throughput. Below is an example.

```
for(long int i=0; i < nitns; i++){
  loadxmm(a, "%xmm0");
  mulxmm("%xmm1", "%xmm0");
  addxmm("%xmm0", "%xmm2");
  storexmm("%xmm2", a+100);

  loadxmm(a+12, "%xmm0");
  mulxmm("%xmm1", "%xmm0");
  addxmm("%xmm0", "%xmm3");
  storexmm("%xmm3", a+200);

  loadxmm(a+24, "%xmm0");
  mulxmm("%xmm1", "%xmm0");
  addxmm("%xmm0", "%xmm4");
  storexmm("%xmm4", a+300);

  loadxmm(a+36, "%xmm0");
  mulxmm("%xmm1", "%xmm0");
  addxmm("%xmm0", "%xmm5");
  storexmm("%xmm5", a+400);

  loadxmm(a+48, "%xmm0");
  mulxmm("%xmm1", "%xmm0");
  addxmm("%xmm0", "%xmm6");
  storexmm("%xmm6", a+500);
}
```

Each block of load, multiply, add, and store is independent of all others. Each store instruction is sent to ports 3 and 4. If we reason as before, expecting register renaming to help exploit the high degree of parallelism, we may conclude that this program will take 5 cycles per iteration.

The observed throughput (after unrolling) was 6.6 cycles per iteration. Even in theory, this program cannot attain 5.0 cycles per iteration. For a single block of load, multiply, add, and store, `objdump -d` gives the following information:

```
ef5:       0f 28 47 60                movaps  0x60(%rdi),%xmm0
ef9:       66 0f 59 c1                mulpd   %xmm1,%xmm0
efd:       66 0f 58 d8                addpd   %xmm0,%xmm3
f01:       0f 29 9f 40 06 00 00 movaps  %xmm3,0x640(%rdi)
```

The load, multiply, and add instructions are 4 bytes long. The store instruction is 7 bytes long. There is no way that four of these instructions can be fetched and decoded in a single cycle on SSE2/Nehalem. On AVX2/Haswell, the observed throughput was 5.75 cycles per iteration.

3.3.4 Microkernel for matrix multiplication

Let A be an $l \times m$ matrix and B an $m \times n$ matrix. The operation $C := C + AB$, where C is a $l \times n$ matrix, requires $2lmn$ flops, half of which are additions and half of which are multiplications.[27] A single `addpd` instruction performs two additions and a single `mulpd` performs two multiplications. If `addpd` and `mulpd` instructions are issued nearly every cycle, the matrix multiplication can be completed in slightly more than $lmn/2$ cycles.

We will abuse terminology slightly and refer to the operation $C := C + AB$ as matrix multiplication. In the special case where C is initialized to zero, this operation coincides with matrix multiplication.

In this section, we write programs that multiply matrices of dimensions $4 \times n$ and $n \times 4$ using slightly more than $8n$ cycles. The microkernel with $n = 200$ is the basis of matrix multiplication routines given in the next chapter. For $n = 200$, the desired cycle count is 1,600. Our gets to 1,840. With better optimization, microkernels that get closer to the ideal cycle count can be written.

---

[27]Algorithms such as Strassen's matrix multiplication achieve a lower operation count. See Cormen et al. (2001).

The one we present has a particularly simple design and uses only a few instructions. Yet it brings out many of the essential features of this type of programming. One of these is the tension between two constraints that must be simultaneously satisfied by such s. On the one hand, to utilize multiple dispatch ports and execute instructions in parallel, it is favorable to interleave segments of the instruction stream that are independent of each other. On the other hand, too much independence would mean that instructions dispatched during the same cycle are more likely to have unrelated operands. Register read stalls would result from too much independence in the instruction stream. We need the instructions to be independent so that they can be dispatched in parallel, and, at the same time, we want each instruction to be reading an operand that was written to recently by another instruction or we want two instructions scheduled during the same cycle to have common operands.

Working with such constraints on the instruction stream will require us to get into many aspects of the microarchitecture. We limit ourselves to a relatively simple microkernel, partly to keep the exposition tractable and partly because many details of the microarchitecture are unknown to us. Figuring out the microarchitecture calls for laborious and time-consuming experimentation. For the most part, we stick to those aspects of the microarchitecture that have already been uncovered in the previous section. We have seen the `movaps` instruction, used for storing, loading, and moving one register to another, as well as `addpd` and `mulpd`. Our microkernel uses these three instructions and `shufpd` but no others. The instruction

```
shufpd $1, %xmm0, %xmm0
```

flips the upper and lower halves of `%xmm0`, or of whichever XMM register that appears in place of `%xmm0`, and that is all we need about `shufpd`.

Product of 4×1 and 1×4 matrices

If A is 4×1 and B is 1×4, then $C = C + AB$ updates C with an outer product. This instance of matrix multiplication takes 32 flops, and we will try to do it using slightly more than 8 cycles. The microkernel is built upon this outer product.

The assignment of the entries of A, B, and C to registers is hinted at by the following diagram:

$$\begin{pmatrix} c_0 \nearrow & c_2 \nearrow \\ c_1 \searrow & c_3 \searrow \\ c_4 \nearrow & c_6 \nearrow \\ c_5 \searrow & c_7 \searrow \end{pmatrix} + = \begin{pmatrix} \boxed{\begin{matrix} a_0 \\ * \end{matrix}} \\ \boxed{\begin{matrix} a_1 \\ * \end{matrix}} \end{pmatrix} \begin{pmatrix} \boxed{b_0 \quad *} & \boxed{b_1 \quad *} \end{pmatrix}$$

Eight XMM registers are used to store C, which is 4×4. The c_0 register holds c_0 and the entry that is immediately southeast, the c_1 register holds c_1 and the entry that is immediately northeast, and so on. Loading the C matrix into registers and then storing the registers in the matrix becomes particularly convenient if the matrix is stored in "skew" order in memory. If the 2×2 matrix

$$\begin{pmatrix} a & b \\ c & d \end{pmatrix}$$

is skewed, it becomes

$$\begin{pmatrix} a & c \\ d & b \end{pmatrix}.$$

A matrix of dimension $2m \times 2n$ is said to be skewed if each of the $m \times n$ blocks of size 2×2 is skewed. Notice that if a skewed matrix is skewed twice, we get back the original matrix.

As far as matrix multiplication is concerned, assuming C to be stored in skew order is a minor point in terms of performance but simplifies the exposition. We shall assume C to be stored in skew order.

The diagram indicates that the register a_0 holds a_0 and the entry immediately below it. The contents of the registers a_1, b_0, and b_1 follow from the diagram in the same way.

We assume C to be stored in a contiguous array of size 16 in column-major order but after skewing. We assume A and B to be stored in contiguous arrays of size 4.

If the XMM register holding b_0 is multiplied into a_0 using `mulpd` and the result is added to c_0 using `addpd,` we have completed updating c_0. If a_0 is flipped, using `shufpd` to interchange its lower and upper half, and then multiplied by b_0 and added to c_1, we have updated c_1. The c registers with an even subscript do not require flipping. The ones with an odd subscript require flipping.

Using the notation introduced so far, we give the method for implementing $C :=$ $C + AB$ in a kind of pseudocode. The assembly code given later corresponds closely to this pseudocode. There is some vagueness in the way the a_i are assigned to registers, which is cleared up by the assembly code (see figure 3.7).

1. Load $c_0, \ldots, c_7$ from memory.
2. Load a_0 from memory.
3. Load b_0 from memory.
4. Use `mulpd` to replace a_0 by $b_0 * a_0$ (entrywise product of two XMM registers).
5. Load a_1.
6. Move a_1 to aa_1, which is another XMM register.
7. Replace a_1 by $b_0 * a_1$ using `mulpd`.
8. Add a_0 to c_0 using `addpd`.
9. Add a_1 to c_4 using `addpd`.
10. Load b_1.
11. Replace aa_1 by $b_1 * aa_1$.
12. Load a_0.
13. Replace a_0 by $b_1 * a_0$.
14. Add a_0 to c_2.
15. Add aa_1 to c_6.
16. Load a_0.
17. Flip a_0.
18. Move a_0 to aa_0.
19. Replace aa_0 by $b_1 * aa_0$.
20. Replace a_0 by $b_0 * a_0$.
21. Add aa_0 to c_3.
22. Add a_0 to c_1.
23. Load a_1.
24. Flip a_1.
25. Move a_1 to aa_1.
26. Replace a_1 by $b_0 * a_1$.
27. Replace aa_1 by $b_1 * aa_1$.
28. Add a_1 to c_5.
29. Add aa_1 to c_7.
30. Store $c_0, \ldots, c_7$.

Each of the 28 items from 2 to 29 corresponds to exactly one instruction. Items 1 and

30 correspond to eight load and eight store instructions, respectively.

Each of the eight registers c_0 to c_7 used to store the 16 entries of C is updated using one `mulpd` and one `addpd` instruction. Thus, there are eight `addpd` and eight `mulpd` instructions.

The cost of loading and storing C is amortized when matrices of dimensions $4 \times n$ and $n \times 4$ are multiplied for large n. There are no store instructions except those used to write to C in item 30. If the instructions used to load C in item 1 are ignored, there are 7 load instructions. Two of these are used to load b_0 and b_1. The others are for loading A.

There are 3 move instructions (items 6, 18, and 25) and 2 `shufpd` instructions for flipping an XMM register (items 17 and 24).

Thus, the 28 instructions from items 2 to 29 are comprised of 16 arithmetic instructions, 7 loads, 3 moves, and 2 `shufpd`s. The matrix A can be loaded using just 2 instructions, and the number of loads can be reduced to 2. But then the number of moves increases to 8. The move instructions as well as the shuffle instructions are dispatched using port 5. Having a total of 10 move and shuffle instructions creates too much pressure on port 5. Another reason to favor the load instructions is that they seem to work better with respect to register renaming and the capture of modified registers from ROB.

Among the 28 instructions left after disregarding the first and last items, there are 8 `mulpd`s that are dispatched on port 0, 8 `addpd`s that are dispatched on port 1, 7 store instructions that are dispatched on port 2, and 5 move or shuffle instructions dispatched on port 5. Ports 3 and 4 are unused because there are no store instructions.

If the 28 instructions of items 2 to 29 are put inside a loop body, in effect we have a program that adds the product AB to C repeatedly. Given the way the instructions are distributed between ports, it is not unreasonable to expect each iteration to take 8 cycles.

But of course there are other constraints on the instruction stream to be considered. One of these is the availability of only 3 ports to read from the register file. The load instructions do not create any pressure on the register read ports. However, all the other instructions do. So if we are to get to 8 cycles per iteration, it is absolutely necessary to ensure that some of the operands are read from ROB.

Each of the `addpd` instructions is likely to capture one of its operands from the corresponding `mulpd`, which is placed not too far above it. The `mulpd` of item 7 is likely to capture one of its operands from item 5, which is a load instruction. Similarly, the `mulpds` of items 11 and 13 may capture an operand from item 10, which is a load instruction.

Instruction lengths impose yet another constraint. If the average instruction were 5 bytes long, it would take more than 8 cycles to fetch the instructions because each instruction fetch brings in an aligned block of 16 bytes. The majority of instructions are only 4 bytes, however. Instruction lengths and instruction alignment may have a significant effect when the program is unrolled to multiply matrices of size $4 \times n$ and $n \times 4$ for $n > 1$. We do not pay much attention to this constraint, preferring to keep the microkernel relatively simple. If items 2 through 29 are put in a loop, it takes 8.53 cycles per iteration if the top of the loop is aligned at a 16-byte boundary. That is not bad considering that the instructions to increment the loop counter and compare against the loop count create some pressure on the register read ports.

Product of $4 \times n$ and $n \times 4$ matrices

The complete assembly program for multiplying a 4×1 matrix with a 1×4 matrix is shown in figure 3.7. It corresponds closely to the pseudocode and is the building block for programs to multiply matrices of dimensions $4 \times n$ and $n \times 4$ with $n > 1$. The C/C++ declaration of this function is

```
extern "C"{
        void asm4x1x4(double *a, double *b, double *c);
}
```

Each instruction in the middle block labeled `#mult 4x1x4` (see figure 3.7) corresponds to exactly one of the items 2 to 29 in the pseudocode.

There are many conventions that govern assembly programming on GNU/Linux. These conventions specify which registers are used to pass arguments, which registers are used to return the function value, which registers are caller saved, which are callee saved, and the manner in which the stack must be used.[28] The three arguments to `asm4x1x4()` are pointers (to arrays that hold the matrices A, B, and C) and therefore 64 bits wide. They are passed using the registers `%rdi`, `%rsi`, and `%rdx`, respectively. Fortunately, we need to know very little of the calling conventions. The

---

[28]By far the best guide to the calling conventions of Linux or Windows is part 5 of Agner Fog's optimization document posted on his web page: `http://www.agner.org/optimize/`.

```
        .align  16, 0x90                              #storing c
        .globl      asm4x1x4                              movaps       %xmm4, (%rdx)
asm4x1x4:                                                 movaps %xmm5, 32(%rdx)
# parameter 1: %rdi (a)                                   movaps %xmm6, 64(%rdx)
# parameter 2: %rsi (b)                                   movaps %xmm7, 96(%rdx)
# parameter 3: %rdx (c)                                   movaps %xmm8, 16(%rdx)
        #loading c                                        movaps %xmm9, 48(%rdx)
        movaps      (%rdx), %xmm4                         movaps %xmm10, 80(%rdx)
            movaps 32(%rdx), %xmm5                        movaps %xmm11, 112(%rdx)
            movaps 64(%rdx), %xmm6                    ret
            movaps 96(%rdx), %xmm7                .align  16, 0x90
            movaps 16(%rdx), %xmm8                .type  asm4x1x4, @function
            movaps 48(%rdx), %xmm9
            movaps 80(%rdx), %xmm10
            movaps 112(%rdx), %xmm11


        #mult 4x1x4
            movaps (%rdi), %xmm2
            movaps (%rsi), %xmm0
            mulpd  %xmm0, %xmm2
            movaps 16(%rdi), %xmm3
            movaps %xmm3, %xmm12
            mulpd  %xmm0, %xmm3
            addpd  %xmm2, %xmm4
            addpd  %xmm3, %xmm8
            movaps 16(%rsi), %xmm1
            mulpd  %xmm1, %xmm12
            movaps (%rdi), %xmm2
            mulpd  %xmm1, %xmm2
            addpd  %xmm2, %xmm6
            addpd  %xmm12, %xmm10
            movaps (%rdi), %xmm3
            shufpd $1, %xmm3, %xmm3
            movaps %xmm3, %xmm2
            mulpd  %xmm1, %xmm3
            mulpd  %xmm0, %xmm2
            addpd  %xmm3, %xmm7
            addpd  %xmm2, %xmm5
            movaps 16(%rdi), %xmm2
            shufpd $1, %xmm2, %xmm2
            movaps      %xmm2, %xmm3
            mulpd  %xmm0, %xmm2
            mulpd  %xmm1, %xmm3
            addpd  %xmm2, %xmm9
            addpd  %xmm3, %xmm11
```

Figure 3.7: Assembly function `asm4x1x4()` for multiplying matrices of dimensions 4×1 and 1×4.

XMM registers are all caller saved, and `asm4x1x4()` is free to use them to perform its calculations.

The definition of `asm4x1x4()` as an assembly program has three blocks. The first block is for loading C, the second block multiplies A and B and adds the product to the registers that hold C, and the last block is for storing C. The code to multiply matrices of dimensions $4 \times n$ and $n \times 4$ is obtained essentially by replicating the middle block n times but with some modifications. This is possible because the product

$$
\begin{pmatrix}
a_{11} & a_{12} & \cdots & \cdots & \cdots & a_{1n} \\
a_{21} & a_{22} & \cdots & \cdots & \cdots & a_{2n} \\
a_{31} & a_{32} & \cdots & \cdots & \cdots & a_{3n} \\
a_{32} & a_{42} & \cdots & \cdots & \cdots & a_{4n}
\end{pmatrix}
\begin{pmatrix}
b_{11} & b_{12} & b_{13} & b_{14} \\
b_{21} & b_{22} & b_{23} & b_{24} \\
\vdots & \vdots & \vdots & \vdots \\
\vdots & \vdots & \vdots & \vdots \\
\vdots & \vdots & \vdots & \vdots \\
b_{n1} & b_{n2} & b_{n3} & b_{n3}
\end{pmatrix}
$$

is a sum of outer products:

$$
\begin{pmatrix} a_{11} \\ a_{21} \\ a_{31} \\ a_{41} \end{pmatrix}
\begin{pmatrix} b_{11} & b_{12} & b_{13} & b_{14} \end{pmatrix}
+ \cdots +
\begin{pmatrix} a_{1n} \\ a_{2n} \\ a_{3n} \\ a_{4n} \end{pmatrix}
\begin{pmatrix} b_{n1} & b_{n2} & b_{n3} & b_{n4} \end{pmatrix}
$$

The matrices A and B are assumed to be stored in arrays of size $4n$ double-precision numbers. The matrix A is assumed to be stored column after column. In contrast, the matrix B is assumed to be stored row after row, making it easier to access the columns and rows for each outer product. To form the kth outer product, where $0 \leq k < n$, we may add $4k$ to the pointers A and B to advance to the kth column of A and the kth row of B.

To multiply matrices of dimensions $4 \times n$ and $n \times 4$, we modify `asm4x1x4()`. The middle block is replicated n times. In the second block, the memory references

```
(%rdi), (%rsi), 16(%rdi), 16(%rsi), (%rdi), (%rdi), 16(%rdi)
```

are replaced by

```
32(%rdi), 32(%rsi), 48(%rdi), 48(%rsi), 32(%rdi), 32(%rdi), 48(%rdi)
```

n	Flops per cycle
20	3.19
40	3.33
100	3.43
200	3.48

Table 3.5: Floating point performance for routines that multiply a $4 \times n$ matrix into an $n \times 4$ matrix for various n on SSE2/Nehalem pipeline (the 2.6 GHz SSE2 processor of table A.1).

Adding 32 to the displacement corresponds to moving forward by 4 doubles because each double is 8 bytes. The third, fourth, and fifth replications are treated similarly by adding 64, 96, and 128 to the displacement fields. After the fifth replication, we add 160 to %rdi and %rsi using the instructions

```
addq        $160 , %rdi
addq        $160 , %rsi
```

and repeat the first five replications. Note that 160 bytes equals 20 doubles. This design tries to balance competing requirements for shorter instructions and fewer instructions.

The function asm4x200x4() defined in this manner achieves 3.48 flops per cycle (see table 3.5) on SSE2/Nehalem. It serves as the microkernel for programs that multiply larger matrices in the next chapter. One might ask, why stop at $n = 200$? Further unrolling does not improve the performance significantly, and we are close to the limit of the $4 \times 1 \times 4$ design used to build the microkernel. The code for ams4x200x4() occupies 24 KB and fills three quarters of the L1 instruction cache. In addition, the matrices multiplied by the microkernel are assumed to fit comfortably with room to spare in L1 data cache, which is 32 KB, when the microkernel is used to build efficient programs to multiply large matrices in the next chapter. The choice of n is limited by the data cache as well as the instruction cache.

Throughout the design of the asm4x200x4() microkernel, we have emphasized register read stalls. Verification that register read stalls are a key issue may be found by running the same program on AVX2/Haswell (the 3.6 GHz AVX2 processor of table A.1). On AVX2/Haswell the program realizes 3.98 flops per cycle, which is much closer to the best possible 4.0 flops per cycle for a program built using mulpd and `addpd` instructions than what we see in table 3.5. Evidently, the greater number of register ports available on AVX2/Haswell is helping.

This finding might suggest that writing an optimal microkernel is easier on AVX2 than SSE2. That hope is unfortunately unlikely to be true. An optimal microkernel on AVX2 must issue two `fmadd*pd` instructions operating on YMM registers every cycle to realize 16 flops per cycle (these are scheduled on ports 0 and 1; see figure 3.5). The `fmadd*pd` instructions operate on three registers, and not just two, as with `addpd` or `mulpd`, creating greater pressure on register ports.

A point that came up in our discussion of the `asm4x200x4()` microkernel for SSE2/Nehalem is that independence in the instruction stream is good because instructions can be scheduled in parallel. However, too much independence is bad because it leads to register read stalls. This tension persists in an optimal microkernel for AVX2/Haswell (and may be expected to persist in architectures yet to be released) and remains the key issue to be dealt with in optimizing for the instruction pipeline.

Exercise 3.3.1. Summing the Leibniz series with loop unrolling takes 7 cycles per term on an AVX2 machine, as we saw in section 3.2.2. Examine the assembly code and determine the realized bandwidth in terms of instructions consumed per cycle.

Exercise 3.3.2. Why does having a deep pipeline with many stages help accommodate a faster clock?

Exercise 3.3.3. Write macros `zeroymm()`, `addymm()`, `mulymm()`, `storeymm()`, and `loadymm()` to issue instructions to manipulate YMM registers. The respective instructions are `vxorps`, `vaddpd`, `vmulpd`, and `vmovaps`. You may consult *Intel® 64 and IA-32 Architectures Software Developer's Manual* for information about these instructions. Keep in mind that the order of sources and destinations is reversed between the Intel manuals and the GNU/Linux assembler. Write a simple program to test your macros.

Exercise 3.3.4. Use GNU's `objdump` utility to find out the size in bytes of a `vmovaps` instruction, with both source and destination being YMM registers, with the source an address in memory, and with the destination an address in memory.

Exercise 3.3.5. The AVX2 instruction set provides for three fused-multiply-add instructions `vfmadd231pd`, `vfmadd132pd`, and `fmadd213pd`. Write macros to issue these instructions. Why are there exactly three fused-multiply-add instructions?

Exercise 3.3.6. Look up the latency and throughput of `vmulpd` and `vaddpd` for your AVX2 microarchitecture in *Intel® 64 and IA-32 Architectures Optimization Reference Manual* or its AMD equivalent. Write programs that verify that information.

Exercise 3.3.7. On the Haswell/Broadwell microarchitectures implementing AVX2, the latency of any of the `fmadd*pd` instructions is 5 cycles. The throughput is 0.5 cycles, implying that 2 `vfmadd*pd` instructions can be simultaneously dispatched to execution units. Write programs verifying the latency and throughput of fused-multiply-add instructions. To complete this exercise, it is crucial to find out the number of register read ports available. Finding that out may require some reverse-engineering.

Exercise 3.3.8. Write a program using `vfmadd*pd` instructions that reaches peak floating point performance of 16 flops per cycle and loads into a YMM register once for each `vfmadd*pd` instruction issued.

Exercise 3.3.9. Code a program that issues `vfmadd*pd` instructions and that is impeded from reaching peak performance of 16 flops per cycle because instructions are too long and cannot be fetched fast enough.

Exercise 3.3.10. Investigate the `vperm` instructions for permuting the contents of a YMM register.

Exercise 3.3.11. Code a microkernel for multiplying $4 \times n$ and $n \times 4$ matrices that approaches peak performance on an AVX2 machine for a suitable value of n.

Exercise 3.3.12. Try another microkernel design, this time for multiplying $8 \times n$ and $n \times 8$ matrices. For a suitable n, does it get closer to AVX2 peak performance of 16 flops per cycle than the previous design?

3.4 References

R. Allen and K. Kennedy. *Optimizing Compilers for Modern Architectures*. Morgan Kaufmann, San Francisco, 2002.

T.H. Cormen, C.E. Lieserson, and R.L. Rivest. *Introduction to Algorithms*. MIT Press, Cambridge, Massachusetts, 2nd edition, 2001.

S. Goto and R. A. van de Geijn. Anatomy of high performance matrix multiplication. *ACM TOMS*, 34:art:12, 2008.

J.L. Hennessy and D.A. Patterson. *Computer Architecture: A Quantitative Approach.* Morgan Kaufmann, San Francisco, 1st-5th edition, 1990-2011.

M. Kerrisk. *The Linux Programming Interface.* No Starch Press, San Francisco, 2010.

K.V. Sarma. *A History of the Kerala School of Hindu Astronomy.* Vishveshvaranand Institute, Hoshiarpur, 1992.

G.I. Toomre. *Ptolemy's Almagest.* Princeton University Press, Princeton, 1998.

Chapter 4

Memory

The memory pyramid shown in figure 4.1 has hard disk at the bottom and registers at the top. Hard disk can have capacity well into the terabytes, while the registers are few in number. It can take milliseconds to access the hard disk, while the registers can be accessed in less than a nanosecond. As we ascend the memory pyramid, capacity decreases and speed increases. Registers have been dealt with in the previous chapter.

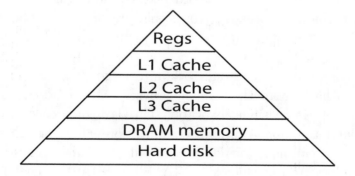

Figure 4.1: Memory hierarchy is a pyramid of decreasing capacity and increasing speed.

Here we discuss caches, Dynamic Random Access Memory (DRAM), and hard disk. Much of the time memory refers to DRAM memory.

The stored program concept is regarded as an early landmark in the development of computers. Instead of thinking of instructions and data as separate entities, the stored program slightly blurs the distinction between the two, with both programs and data stored in the same computer memory. In modern computers, including supercomputers, desktops, laptops, and all kinds of mobile devices, memory invariably refers to DRAM. Although file systems reside on hard disk or some other storage medium, when a program is running, much of the data that is handled is from DRAM. DRAM sits external to the processor as shown in section 3.3.2 (see figure 3.6). It is estimated that 40% of the instructions in a typical computer are loads and stores, and all these instructions address locations in DRAM. Thus, within a program, for most purposes, memory means DRAM memory. In DRAM memory, every bit is stored on a single microscopically small capacitor, which is accessed using a single transistor.

DRAM technology is cheap, ubiquitous, and relatively stable. In section 4.1, we take a look at how DRAM hardware and caches are configured. Accessing a word from DRAM can be more than 100 times slower than accessing a register. Although memory available through registers is only of the order of kilobytes (KB), a register can be accessed in a single cycle. In contrast, memory available through DRAM runs into tens, even hundreds, of gigabytes (GB), but it can take more than 100 cycles to access a word from DRAM. A great part of computer design is an attempt to mitigate this extreme gap in speed and capacity. The aim or hope is to approximate the speed of registers with the capacity of DRAM. A key idea is to store caches on the processor itself. The cache is a record of those words in DRAM that are most frequently accessed by the processor. Words that are cached may be accessed directly within the processor itself without exchanging signals with DRAM units external to the processor.

On modern computers, caches can be quite large. It is not unusual for a processor package to have more than 10 megabytes (MB) of cache. Both cache and DRAM capacities are increasing inexorably. The day when caches are large enough to comfortably hold a million grid point computation is firmly in the past. In a lot of scientific computing, computations do not go out of cache. Caches are implemented using Static Random Access Memory (SRAM). In SRAM, each bit is stored using multiple transistors with circuitry to switch the bit on or off rapidly. Caches are intermediate between DRAM and registers in expense, speed, and capacity.

Companies that make DRAM are about as profitable as low-end grocery stores, if they are lucky enough to make a profit. DRAM is as close to a commodity, mass-market technology as there exists in the world of computing. Its low cost has made it ubiquitous across the whole computing spectrum. Engineers have been able to meet market demand for increasing capacity at a low cost, and the potential for disruptive innovations in this area appears limited.

Section 4.1 gives an overview of DRAM and cache memory. The organization of DRAM into memory channels and of caches into multiple levels influences programming technique in several ways. For example, the organization of memory into channels is under the assumption that memory accesses from separate processor cores (of the same system) are relatively independent and far apart. If in fact the memory accesses are tightly correlated and reference nearby locations, there can be a severe penalty.

DRAM memory is shared by multiple programs running on the same computer. Virtual memory creates the illusion that every program has its own exclusive memory. Virtual memory, which is implemented by the operating system kernel with help from the processor hardware, influences programming speed in several ways too. In section 4.1, we give a basic introduction to virtual memory. In section 4.1, we describe a program to measure the latency to DRAM memory. This program exposes many aspects of the memory system, such as parallelism of memory access, cache line size, and virtual memory, which are vital to efficient programming. In addition, latency to memory is a figure of much importance, especially when dynamic data structures such as linked lists and trees are employed.

Section 4.2 presents many techniques to optimize memory access. These techniques have not changed greatly over the years. This section could have been written even 15 years ago in mostly the same form. Of course the parameters used for successive levels of blocking, which are related to the sizes of caches and other aspects of computer architecture, would have been different. But all the principles are the same with one important exception. Even that one principle (packing data in caches to reduce TLB misses) would have applied in an identical manner to machines of the past, but it was not known 15 years ago.

Sections 4.1 and 4.2 may well be the most important parts of this book. Optimizing memory access is just as relevant to your cell phone as it is to supercomputers. In addition, the principles are the same. Its importance only increases when programs are threaded or networked. The techniques of memory optimization described in section

4.2 are applicable to regular and structured data, as in images and grids for solving partial differential equations. When dynamic data structures such as linked lists and graphs are used, one needs to be more mindful of latency to memory.

Memory optimizations can be done in C, without resorting to assembly code, to a far greater extent than instruction pipeline optimizations. Like the previous chapter, this chapter too discusses optimizations in the context of SSE2, AVX, and AVX2 machines (see table 3.1), although the role of the instruction set is not as great. Much of the time the distinction between these instruction sets does not matter greatly. All programs are written in C. The compiled code may be suboptimal as before, but the penalty to pay for the suboptimality of the compiler is not as high. Although the penalty can exceed a factor of 10 for instruction pipeline optimizations, as shown in the previous chapter, the penalty with regard to memory optimizations seldom exceeds a factor of 1.5.

Section 4.3 explains how to write and read from hard disk. If DRAM memory can run into hundreds of GB, hard disk can run into tens of terabytes on even a small computer. However, hard disk can be very slow, with latencies of the order of milliseconds. The operating system kernel plays a great role in determining the observed speed of disk input/output.

In section 4.4, we return to virtual memory and look at its implementation inside the Linux kernel. All programs run at the mercy of the operating system kernel. The systems programming perspective and knowledge of the paging system, which implements virtual memory, help understand disk input/output, network programming, and multithreaded programming at an advanced level.

4.1 DRAM and cache memory

DRAM was invented by Intel in 1973. In DRAM, a single capacitor is used to store a single bit, and each capacitor is equipped with an access transistor. DRAM technology has evolved over the years to the point where it is the primary form of memory in almost all computing and mobile devices. For a schematic illustration of where DRAM memory fits into the computer as a whole, see figure 3.6, where it is labeled as system memory.

Section 4.1.1 is an overview of DRAM technology. At the finest level, DRAM is an array of bits. Arrays of bits are organized into banks, ranks, and channels. There is a memory controller on each processor package that drives the memory channels.

Most of the details of the memory controller are entirely hidden from the programmer (as well as the operating system). Fortunately, one does not need knowledge of the hardware at the level of the memory controllers or channels to write optimized programs. Thus, the principal purpose of the information in section 4.1.1 is to provide context. The information is not directly useful in writing actual programs. However, its indirect implications can be of considerable importance.

In section 4.1.2, we look at caches. Unlike DRAM, caches reside on the processor package. Accessing cached memory is much faster than accessing DRAM. Caching is done automatically by the hardware, and in principle, the programmer does not even need to know that caches exist. However, a basic knowledge of cache organization, including items such as the cache line size, is essential for writing optimized programs.

When the same data item is stored in DRAM memory as well as multiple caches, there is the problem of keeping caches coherent. In the next chapter, we will find that cache coherence is the basis of multithreaded programming. Inasmuch as multithreaded programming is a central paradigm from scientific computing to web servers and mobile apps, it is inadvisable to program with an ignorance of caches. Technically, multithreaded programs can be written without heeding caches. Doing so would imply inefficiencies as well as the danger of falling into error without realizing it.

DRAM memory is a shared resource. At any given point in time, dozens of programs on a computer could all be using DRAM memory. Each of these programs is written as if the program owns its own memory. The Linux kernel implements virtual memory, with the help of the processor hardware. Thanks to virtual memory, programs can be written assuming a tractable memory model. Section 4.1.3 is an introduction to virtual memory. The way virtual memory is set up can have major implications for program speed, especially in the multithreaded context, as we will see on several occasions later.

Sections 4.1.4 and 4.1.5 utilize knowledge of DRAM, cache lines, as well as virtual memory to measure latency to DRAM. Latency to DRAM is the number of cycles between issuing an instruction to load a word into a register from DRAM and the completion of that instruction. Finding the latency to DRAM might appear straightforward. It might appear that all we need to do is time a load or store instruction.

In fact, determining latency to memory is not so straightforward. Just as in register pipelines, there is a great deal of parallelism in the memory system. Although this parallelism is a great boon, it gets in the way of finding latency. Similarly, the virtual memory system can also get in the way. Thus, this simple exercise of finding latency to DRAM exposes several important elements of the memory system.

To access a register, the latency is 1 cycle. To access the L1 cache, the latency is 4 cycles. The latency to DRAM, however, can be hundreds of cycles. It is estimated that 40% of the instructions access DRAM, and therefore hiding this large latency to DRAM is a major part of computer architectural design. It is important for the programmer to understand when this latency to DRAM can be hidden and when it cannot be hidden, but that is a point we will turn to in the next section. Briefly, the latency to DRAM can be effectively hidden when the data access is sequential and predictable. It cannot be hidden in linked lists and other dynamic data structures because the location of the next item is determined by a link from the present item. However, even in such situations, programming techniques can mitigate the latency to DRAM.

4.1.1   DRAM memory

By opening the cover of a computer and peering inside, we can look at memory plugged into the mother board. The devices that are plugged in are called Dual Inline Memory Modules (DIMMs). DIMMs can be purchased to add more memory to the computer. Each DIMM is a package of several little chips. The little chips are DRAM devices.

Figure 4.2 shows two levels in the organization of DRAM memory: the finest and the outermost.[1] On the left, it shows a DRAM array of bits. The DRAM array is the finest level of organization. Each DRAM channel is composed of several DRAM arrays of size $16K \times 2K$. On the right, it depicts six channels. The memory controllers that reside on the two packages drive the six channels. There are several other levels of organization between the DRAM array and the channel to memory. The memory channels are driven by memory controllers that reside on the processor packages as shown in the figure.

Figure 4.2 assumes a typical array size, which can of course vary and vary a lot, and six channels. Some of the more recent AVX2 computers have eight channels to memory, with four on each processor package. The number of channels can also vary quite a bit.

---

[1] The treatise by Jacob et al. (2008) has much more information than we give here.

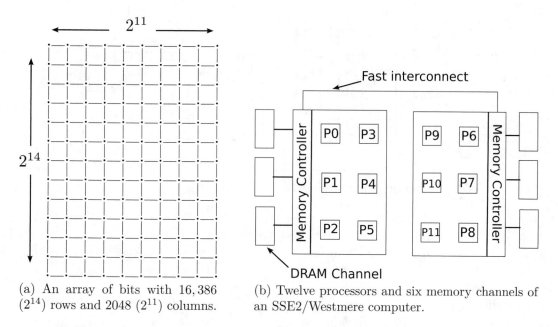

(a) An array of bits with $16,386$ (2^{14}) rows and 2048 (2^{11}) columns.

(b) Twelve processors and six memory channels of an SSE2/Westmere computer.

Figure 4.2: Organization of DRAM memory.

Banks, ranks, channels, and DRAM technology

To access a single bit in a $2^m \times 2^n$ DRAM array takes $m + n$ address bits. These are the lowest bits in the memory address. In figure 4.2, $m + n = 25$. The DRAM arrays are organized in banks so that 2^a arrays constitute a bank. In figure 4.3, $a = 6$ so that each bank consists of 64 arrays.

When $m + n$ address bits are used to pick a bit from an array, the same $m + n$ bits are applied to every one of the arrays in a bank. Thus, the output from applying $m + n$ address bits will be 2^b bits of data. In figure 4.3, the output would be 2^6 bits or 8 bytes.

There is one point related to banks of DRAM arrays that can have a significant impact on program speed. The way DRAM arrays work, it is easy to move from one bit in a given row to some other bit in the same row. Therefore, typically, consecutive addresses within a bank map to the same row. However, if a program generates memory addresses that require frequent switching between rows, there will be bank conflicts. Such bank conflicts slow down the program.

Although bank conflicts slow down programs, there is not much a programmer can

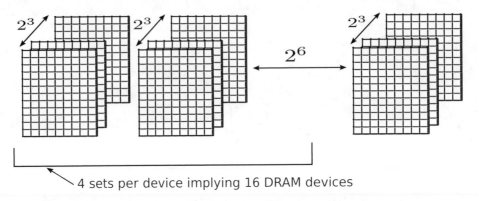

Figure 4.3: A single row of 2^6 arrays in this figure constitutes a bank. All arrays in the same bank operate in concert. In the figure, a rank is composed of 2^3 banks. The $2^3 \times 2^6$ arrays are split across 16 devices, with each bank spanning all 16 devices.

do to avoid them. The organization of memory varies quite a bit from computer to computer, and it can be difficult to find out the parameters of memory organization.[2] Even if the parameters of DRAM organization are known, the manner in which the memory controllers split memory accesses between channels can be almost impossible to determine.

As shown in figure 4.3, the next level of organization after the bank is the rank. If 2^b banks constitute a rank, then $b+m+n$ address bits are used to pick a bank within a rank and then extract a word from the arrays that constitute that bank. The b bits used to pick the bank are higher than the other $m+n$ bits. In figure 4.3, $b=3$.

The ranks are grouped further to obtain a memory channel, and the entire address space is split between the memory channels. Typically, the maximum amount of memory that may be installed will be much less than the maximum amount addressable. For example, a 48-bit-wide address bus can address 256 terabytes of memory, which is 1,000 times more than what even a high-end machine may provide for.

Given the speed at which modern computers operate, an error rate of one in a billion would imply several memory errors every second. DRAM almost always provides for error correction, a point we did not go into here.

---

[2]To determine the parameters of memory organization, such as the number of arrays in a bank, on a given computer, one may start with the GNU/Linux command `dmidecode` and then look up the corresponding JEDEC manuals.

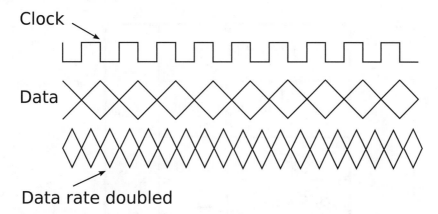

Figure 4.4: Each diamond in this figure stands for a bit. DDR technology doubles the data rate by transferring a bit at both the rising and falling edges of the clock signal.

Almost all DRAM in use today is double data rate (DDR), and it has been that way for a long time. DDR was a major advance in DRAM technology. In earlier technology, a single bit of data was pushed out to a single pin (connected to a single line of the data bus) during one period of the clock signal. DDR initiates a data transfer during the rising edge as well as the falling edge of the clock (see figure 4.4). Two bits of data are pushed out in a single period of the clock, doubling the bandwidth.

DDR memory is often advertised to be DDR3 or DDR5 and so on. The numerical suffixes 3 or 5 give the prefetch length. In DDR3, when $m + n$ address bits are sent to a bank of 2^a arrays, the DRAM outputs not just 2^a data bits, with 1 bit for each array, but 2^{a+3} bits. It outputs the 2^a bit word corresponding to the $m + n$ bit address as well as 2^3 words corresponding to 8 consecutive addresses, including the one that was sent to it. The assumption here is that when a program asks for a certain word, it will probably also ask for the next word. So when 2^3 words are sent to the memory controllers, the memory controllers may be able to service multiple load/store instructions while triggering a single DRAM access. This technique improves peak bandwidth assuming sequential, or nearly sequential, data access.

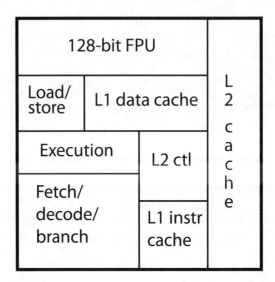

Figure 4.5: Layout of a single core of AMD Opteron (code named Barcelona) (layout based on Patterson and Hennessy).

4.1.2   Cache memory

An instruction such as `movq %rax, %rdx`, which moves one register to another, takes a single cycle. However, a load instruction such as `movq (%rsi), %rdx`, which moves a quad word from memory to a register, can take more than 100 cycles. An instruction that writes can take even longer. Computer processors cache frequently used parts of DRAM memory so that they can execute instructions at the speed of the registers, although nearly half the instructions are loads and stores from the much slower DRAM devices.[3]

Figure 4.5 shows the layout of a single processor core. About half the area of the chip is taken up by cache memory and the memory controller. The latency to L1 cache memory is a mere 4 cycles. It is much faster to access cache than to access DRAM memory.

The basic principle of cache organization is data locality. Once a word is accessed

---

[3]The classic by Hennessy and Patterson (1990-2011) has a thorough discussion of caches. There is a lot of information in the Intel manuals as well.

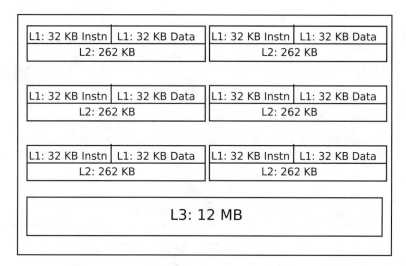

Figure 4.6: Schematic sketch of the cache hierarchy of typical SSE2/AVX/AVX2 processors. The L1 and L2 parameters do not vary much (e.g., these are the same for all the machines of table A.1), but the L3 size can vary a lot. The L3 cache as shown is 12 MB here but can be four times higher or only one quarter as much.

from DRAM memory, computer programs have a tendency to access the same word or nearby words repeatedly. Thus, it makes sense to keep the word in a fast cache after it is first accessed. Later accesses can be serviced quickly from the cache without contacting the slow DRAM devices.

All transfers between DRAM memory and the processors is in cache line multiples. A cache line is 64 bytes or 512 bits on most x86 computers today. Thus, a cache line is big enough to hold 8 `doubles` or 16 `ints`. The cache lines are aligned in memory to begin at addresses whose last 6 bits (notice that $2^6 = 64$) are zero.

Cache parameters

Figure 4.6 shows cache organization on typical x86 processors. Each processor core has its own L1 and L2 caches. The L1 cache is smaller than L2 but faster to access. All processor cores on the same package share L3 cache. The L3 cache is much bigger in size than the L2 cache.

Having multiple levels of cache implies that the penalty of a miss at a certain level is not too high if the cache line is found at the next level. Thus, the cost of a cache

	Number of Sets	Associativity	Size
L1 (instruction)	64	8 way	32 KB
L1 (data)	128	4 way	32 KB
L2	512	8 way	262 KB
L3	12,288	16 way	12 MB

Table 4.1: Cache parameters of typical SSE2/AVX/AVX2 processor packages. The L1 and L2 parameters are the same for all the machines of table A.1. The size of the L3 cache varies quite a bit, the other parameters less so.

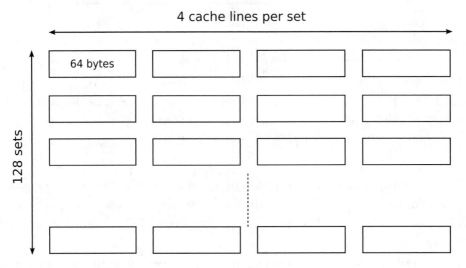

Figure 4.7: Depiction of the L1 data cache with 128 sets and 4-way associativity assuming a cache line to be 64 bytes or 512 bits (which is very typical).

miss worsens gradually.

The cache parameters of typical x86 computers are given in table 4.1. The parameters were found using the cpuid instruction. The size of the cache in bytes is equal to the product of the number of sets, associativity, and 64, which is the number bytes in a single cache line. Cache size and cache associativity influence program speed, with greater being better.

To understand what sets and associativity mean in the context of cache organization, we turn to figure 4.7. Suppose the processor wants to look for a byte whose physical address is α in L1 data cache. The address of its cache line will be

$$\frac{\alpha - \alpha \bmod 64}{64}$$

because a cache line begins every 64th byte. Cache lines are mapped to sets cyclically. The cache line containing the byte whose address is α maps to set number

$$\left(\frac{\alpha - \alpha \bmod 64}{64}\right) \bmod 128$$

if there are 128 sets in the L1 data cache. The cache line could be in any of the four slots in that set. The processor will check the four slots simultaneously for a match. If there is a match, the processor will extract the byte from the cache line in the matching slot.

If too many addresses map to the same set, there will be cache conflicts even if other sets of the cache are not heavily used. If the most frequently used addresses in a program segment map to only a few sets, the effectiveness of the cache is reduced, and cache conflicts become more likely. A fully associative cache, which has a single set and in which a cache line can be stored in any of the slots, is the best for reducing cache conflicts. However, such an ideal cache is too expensive to implement.

The effect of cache conflicts is not as easy to detect in modern computers as used to be the case. Multiple levels of caching, instruction-level parallelism, the large size of the caches, and the sheer complexity of the memory system can make the effect of cache conflicts on strided accesses difficult to detect.

Cache protocols

How do the cache controllers decide which cache lines to keep in cache and which ones to evict from cache? Suppose a certain cache line is accessed. If the cache line is already in cache, the access is serviced without altering the mapping of cache lines from DRAM to the cache. If the cache line is not in cache, it will be brought into cache. Some other cache line has to be evicted from the set the newly accessed cache line maps to. A popular strategy is to evict the least recently used cache line.

Reads from memory are handled differently from writes to memory. If a processor writes to a cache line that is in cache, usually the cache line is modified in cache but the write is not propagated to DRAM memory. A dirty bit is turned on to inform the cache controllers that the cache line must be written back to memory when it is evicted. This policy of handling writes is called *write back*. An alternative is *write through*. In this policy, the write is propagated to DRAM memory. Yet another alternative is to propagate writes that modify the L1 cache to L2 cache but not to DRAM memory.

An implication of the *write back* policy is that cache lines in DRAM memory may become invalid. The same cache line may be stored in the L1 or L2 caches of multiple processor cores. If one of them writes to its cache, the cache lines in other processor cores become invalid. The cache controller on each processor has to "snoop" on the traffic in the other processors to maintain a coherent cache.

As a consequence of the write back policy, a single write instruction can trigger two DRAM accesses. Consider a write instruction of the type `movq %rax, (%rdi)`. If the quad word (8 bytes) that `%rdi` points to is not in cache, the corresponding cache line must be brought in triggering the first DRAM access. Future instructions that read and write from the same cache line will be serviced without accessing DRAM. However, a second DRAM access is triggered when the cache line is evicted. In contrast, if all operations a cache line is subjected to are reads, there is no need for the second DRAM transfer.

4.1.3   Physical memory and virtual memory

Virtual memory is implemented by the operating system and the processor hardware working in concert. Its main purpose is to prevent processes from interfering with each other's memory. A single process will have only part of the DRAM memory for itself. The part of the DRAM memory that is available to a specific process is determined only when the process is loaded and can change as it runs.

Virtual memory is an illusion that simplifies programming, compilation, and linking in addition to keeping programs from interfering with each other. As the program runs, the memory addresses generated by a program are automatically mapped to physical addresses in the DRAM memory. So, for example, if a program issues an instruction such as `movq %rax, (%rdi)`, the address in `%rdi` is a virtual address. During instruction execution, the page tables are consulted by the hardware to map that address to a physical address. A separate map is maintained for each process to keep the processes from interfering with each other. The map is typically hierarchical and stored in multiple page tables. Page tables are the essence of virtual memory.

Virtual memory in action

Let us consider an instruction that generates the memory reference (%rax, %rsi, 2).
The reference is to the memory location whose address is rax+2*rsi. The registers
%rax and %rsi are 64-bit. Therefore, a 64-bit virtual address is formed. Strictly
speaking, the virtual address is the last 48 bits of the address. If we print a pointer
in a C program, the program prints 12 hex digits because a virtual address is 48 bits.
A 48-bit virtual address should get us past 2020 and can then be extended without
changes to the instruction set architecture.

How does the hardware look up an actual word in memory using a virtual address?
The answer is complicated. The first step on x86 computers is to form a 64-bit linear
address by adding a segment register. This step is trivial and we will ignore it.

The next and far more important step is to map virtual addresses to physical
addresses. Once a physical address is formed, it may be used to look up DRAM or
the caches.

To map addresses from virtual to physical memory, virtual memory is partitioned
into pages. A page is typically 4,096 bytes (the command getconf PAGESIZE may be
used to find out the page size). Thus, in a virtual address of 48 bits, the first 36 bits
constitute a page address, and the following 12 bits are the address within that page.
Correspondingly, DRAM memory is broken up into page frames, each of which is of
the same size as a page. Page tables map page addresses to page frame addresses.

The manner in which page tables are set up does not concern us here. They are set
up by the operating system kernel and left in a place where the processor hardware
can look them up.The translation look-aside buffer (TLB) is a cache of the page
tables. When an address such as (%rax, %rsi, 2) is formed, the next step is to look
up the TLB to convert it to a physical address. Each entry in the TLB maps exactly
one page to a page frame. If there is a TLB miss, the processor looks up the page
tables.

TLB organization is similar to cache organization. Table 4.2 shows TLB parameters for a few machines. When the processor switches from one process to another,
it is the operating system kernel's responsibility to furnish a new set of page tables
and flush the TLB.

Even a partial picture of what it takes to resolve a single memory reference such as
(%rax, %rsi, 2) is mind-bogglingly complex. As noted already, 40% of the instructions are estimated to be loads or stores. For every such instruction, the processor

	Number of Sets	Associativity	Size
Instruction TLB	32/16/32	4/8/4 way	128 entries
Data TLB	16	4 way	64 entries
Level 2 TLB (Shared)	128/128/_	4/8/_ way	512/1024/_ entries

Table 4.2: TLB parameters for three x86 processors: 2.6 GHz SSE2, 2.2 GHz AVX, and 3.6 GHz AVX2 (see table A.1 for the full names of the machines). The 3.6 GHz AVX2 machine does not have level 2 TLB.

first forms a virtual address. To map the virtual address to the physical address, it looks up the TLB; if there is TLB miss, it must look up the page tables. Looking up the page tables may trigger additional DRAM accesses if the page tables are not in cache.

The page table lookup may trigger a page fault if the virtual page is yet to be mapped to a page frame. If so, the page fault handler, which is an important component of the operating system kernel, is invoked. The page fault handler allocates an actual page frame so that a physical address may be formed. Once a physical address is formed, the processor can look by the caches and trigger a DRAM access if necessary.

We think of a simple instruction such as `movq (%rax, %rsi, 2), %rbx` as taking a few cycles. If there is a page fault, the actual cost can be in the millions of cycles. In fact, there can be two page faults from this single instruction if the quad word crosses page boundaries. Even if there is no page fault, there can be a TLB miss, which can consume of the order of 100 cycles.

Virtual memory and program speed

Given that the virtual memory setup is exceedingly complex and is invoked almost every other instruction, it follows that the mechanisms used to implement virtual memory may influence program speed in many ways.

When memory is dynamically allocated by a program using `malloc()`, `new[]`, or `_mm_malloc()`, the last of which is preferred if memory needs to be aligned, the allocation function returns an address in virtual memory, and pages may be allocated only in virtual memory. There is always a page fault the first time a page is accessed. The pages are mapped to page frames by the page fault handler. If there is enough

DRAM memory, page faults do not occur except when pages are accessed for the first time.

On most computers, the memory controllers predict memory accesses and prefetch words to cache. The prefetching normally does not cross page boundaries to prevent page faults from being triggered.

Another scenario where the paging system is in play is when large amounts of data are transferred from DRAM memory to the network card or to graphics processor memory. During the transfer, some of the pages may get moved out of DRAM memory into hard disk by the memory management unit of the operating system kernel, complicating the transfer. One way around is to copy the data to be transferred to kernel buffers and incur a substantial overhead. Another way is to request the operating system kernel to keep the pages "pinned" to DRAM memory.

There are many more ways in which virtual memory impacts program speed. The role of cache and TLB misses is explained later in this chapter. Other aspects related to multithreaded programming are found in the next chapter.

4.1.4 Latency to DRAM memory: First attempts

In this section, we make our first attempts at measuring the access time to DRAM memory. All our attempts fail, but we are led into certain aspects of the memory system that have a bearing on program performance.

The organization of memory is such that if we attempt to investigate one part of it, we need to be aware of the other parts as well. All the parts of the memory system are interrelated. Thus, to measure the access time to DRAM memory, we need to know about the size of the cache. We begin by giving a basic picture of the memory system as a whole. The measurement of latency brings to light some other parts of the memory system, and as we progress, we fill in some of the details in the picture.

A significant point is that all the traffic between DRAM and the processor packages is in multiples of the cache line size. The cache line is 64 bytes or 512 bits. If we attempt to read a single byte or a single word (2 bytes or 16 bits) or a double word or a quad word from memory, the memory system will bring the entire cache line into cache, anticipating that we will access other locations in the same cache line soon.

Latency to DRAM memory is defined as the time to issuing a load/store instruction that triggers a DRAM access and its completion. The latency of writing to memory can differ from the latency of reading for certain types of DRAM. We limit ourselves to read latency for simplicity.

Measuring the latency to DRAM memory is a more complicated matter than one may realize at first sight. Many techniques are used to hide the latency to DRAM memory. Among these, the two most important are instruction-level parallelism and caching. Instruction-level parallelism enables the processor to issue a sequence of load or store instructions to set up a pipeline of memory accesses. If the pipeline can hold 10 memory accesses in various stages, the effective latency of a long stream of DRAM accesses is cut to a tenth. For example, if the latency to DRAM is 200 cycles, the nth memory access may be initiated during cycle number $20n$ and completed during cycle number $20n + 199$. This sort of overlapping is possible only if the memory accesses are independent and there is sufficient parallelism in the instruction stream. Caching greatly reduces the effective latency of DRAM memory access as well. These techniques for hiding latency to memory are so effective that many programs do not realize how large the latency to DRAM memory can be.

Here is a first and not very careful attempt at measuring latency.

```
int unitstride(int *a){
        int sum=0;
        for(int i=0; i < 1000*1000*1000; i++)
             sum += a[i];
        return sum;
}
```

The function `unitstride()` loads 10^9 entries of `a[]` and computes their sum. The compiler unrolls the loop and introduces parallelism in the loop body. As a result, the running time of this function is determined by instructions that load entries of `a[]` and not by arithmetic.

The function `unitstride()` is timed as follows:

```
1  void time_unitstride(){
2         int a[1000*1000*1000];
3         for(int i=0; i < 1000*1000*1000; i++)
4              a[i] = 0;
5         TimeStamp clk;
6         clk.tic();
7         unitstride(a);
```

```
 8        double cycles = clk.toc();
 9        cout<<"cycles/access = "<<
10           cycles/(1000*1000*1000)<<endl;
11 }
```

The function `time_unitstride()` defines `a[]` statically, initializes every entry of `a[]` to 0, and makes a single call to `unitstride()` on line 7. The function call is timed, and the number of cycles it consumes is divided by 10^9 to derive the cycles consumed per access. Each array dereferencing `a[i]` in `unitstride()` is counted as a memory access.

The two functions `unitstride()` and `time_unitstride()` are defined in separate files and compiled separately. As usual, we do not use the `-ipo` option for interprocedural optimization during compilation, and we use `-fno-inline-functions` to eliminate function inlining. If the two functions are in the same file or if interprocedural optimization is turned on, the compiler will figure out that the call to `unitstride()` is doing nothing meaningful and simply eliminate the call.

Initializing the array to zero on line 4 ensures that page frames in physical memory have been allocated to the entire array before the function `unitstride()` is called.

The program reports 0.92 cycles per access. Cycle counts are quite similar on SSE2, AVX, and AVX2 machines. Therefore, we only report the numbers for a 2.6 GHz SSE2 machine (for the full name of the machine, see table A.1). The 0.92 cycles per access figure is a woeful underestimate of the latency to DRAM memory. The single for-loop in `unitstride()` has a loop-carried RAW dependency. The excellent `icpc` compiler has little difficulty recognizing that a list of numbers can be grouped before it is summed to introduce parallelism into the loop body. The generated code uses the XMM (or YMM) registers, each of which is large enough to pack four (or eight) `int`s, to decrease the number of instructions used to load entries of `a[]` into the registers. Why is the access time here so much smaller than the latency to DRAM? One reason is that a cache line is large enough to hold 16 `int`s, and only one of 16 accesses of the array is fetching data from outside the cache.

Any program that accesses data sequentially with unit stride will benefit from the size of the cache line. To avoid cache hits, the program below accesses only one of every 16 locations.

```
int stride16(int *a){
    int sum=0;
```

```
    for(int i=0; i < 1000*1000*1000; i+=16)
         sum += a[i];
    return sum;
}
```

In `stride16()`, the cost of accessing a single entry of the array is about 13 cycles, which is once again much smaller than the latency to DRAM. As many as 10 memory reads can be in flight at the same time. Strided accesses benefit from parallelism in the instruction pipeline and in the memory system. Strided accesses are particularly easy to predict. It is likely that the prefetch engines in the memory controller are able to prefetch many of the locations accessed in `stride16()` into cache ahead of time.

A more refined attempt follows.

```
 1  //List must be 64 byte aligned
 2  void accessList(long int *List, long int n, int count,
 3           double &x){
 4      long int  index = 0;
 5      for(int i=0; i < count; i++){
 6          x += List[index];
 7          index = List[index]%n;
 8          index = index - index%8;
 9      }
10  }
```

The loop defined in lines 5 through 9 works as follows. It reads the entry `List[index]` on lines 6 and 7, and the next entry that is read is determined by the earlier entry on lines 7 and 8. It is assumed that all entries of `List[]` are initialized to be non-negative. The next load instruction cannot be issued until the earlier load instruction is complete because the address of the next load instruction is determined by the result of the earlier load instruction. This way of accessing memory breaks instruction-level parallelism.

The function `accessList()` is called with $n = 10^9$ and `count` =6,000. The array `List` is initialized with pseudorandom numbers. We verified explicitly (verification not shown here) that the 6,000 entries accessed in the body of the loop were all distinct. Line 8 ensures that every `index` used to look up `List[]` is a multiple of 8.

All transfers between DRAM memory and cache are done in cache lines. A single cache line is 64 bytes. The array `List` is assumed to be 64 byte aligned (the last 6 bits of the address `List` are zero). Because every `index` used to look up `List[]` is a multiple of 8 and a `long int` is 8 bytes, every memory reference on line 6 brings in a new cache line. No cache line is accessed more than once. The total number of memory accesses is 6,000.

When the cycles consumed by the entire function was divided by 6,000, we got 270 cycles. So is the latency to DRAM memory about 270 cycles? Not really. We were careful to break instruction-level parallelism. We flushed the entire array out of cache (not shown here) before calling the function and respected cache line boundaries. However, we forgot to think about a third element. Memory management is done using pages, page frames, page directories, and page tables. Because the array is so large, every new memory reference is likely to hit a new page. The page table entry for that page is unlikely to be in TLB and may have to be brought in from DRAM memory. What we thought was one memory access is likely to be two or more.

This little example may give us a sense of the complex way in which parts of the memory system interact. Cache line size, parallelism in memory access, and the cost of TLB misses are all of much significance to program optimization.

4.1.5 Latency to DRAM

Our earlier attempts to measure latency to DRAM memory failed because we did not account for the overhead of creating and accessing page table entries. The more careful program in this section breaks instruction-level parallelism, ensures that none of the cache lines accessed is from L1, L2, or L3 cache, and accesses all of the 256 cache lines within four pages of memory (so that TLB misses are not a factor).

To begin with, we look at the function `randomp()`, which initializes the n entries of the array `List[]` to be a random permutation of the numbers $0, 1, \ldots, n-1$.

```
1 void randomp(int *List, int n){
2      for(int i=0; i < n; i++)
3          List[i] = i;
4      for(int i=0; i < n; i++){
5          int j = rand()%(n-i)+i;
6          int temp = List[j];
7          List[j] = List[i];
8          List[i] = temp;
9      }
```

```
10  }
```

On lines 2 and 3, the array `List[]` is initialized to be the identity permutation $0, 1, \ldots, n - 1$. The loop from lines 4 through 9 picks j to be a random number from the set $i, \ldots, n - 1$ and swaps `List[i]` and `List[j]` for each value of i from 0 to $n - 1$. The random number generator `rand()` used on line 5 is convenient, being part of the standard C libraries, and sufficient for our purposes here. However, faster and more rigorously tested random number generators are available.

The program for measuring latency uses two methods for clearing the array used for measurement from cache memory. If the preprocessor variable `MEMWALK` is undefined at the top of the file using

```
#undef MEMWALK
```

then it uses the `CLFLUSH` instruction issued using an intrinsic. However, if `MEMWALK` is defined at the top of the file, it uses the following function:

```
1  void dummy(double *a, int len){
2      for(int i=0; i < len; i++)
3          a[i] = (i%77)*(i*1001);
4  }
```

A large array `a[]` is passed to this function, which writes something into every entry on line 3. The array `a[]` is not used for measuring latency. Its sole purpose is to occupy the cache completely and evict the array used for measuring latency from the cache.[4] The function `dummy()` must be defined in a separate compilation unit to prevent the compiler from eliminating the function call.

The function `latency()`, whose listing follows, touches all the cache lines in four pages of memory and prints an estimate of the latency to DRAM memory.

```
1  void latency(){
2      int List[256];
3      randomp(List,256);
4      int LList[256];
5      for(int i=0; i < 256; i++)
6          LList[List[i]]=List[(i+1)%256];
```

---

[4]To be certain that the cache is occupied, one has to check the assembly and make sure that instructions such as `MOVNTPD`, which avoid cache pollution, are not generated.

```
 7          //int is 4 bytes
 8          __declspec(align(4096)) int FourPages[4096];
 9          for(int i=0; i < 256; i++)
10                  FourPages[16*i] = LList[i];
11 #ifdef MEMWALK
12          double a[1000*1000*100];
13          dummy(a, 1000*1000*100);
14 #else
15          for(int i=0; i < 4096; i++)
16                  _mm_clflush(FourPages+i);
17 #endif
18          int index = 17;
19          TimeStamp clk;
20          clk.tic();
21          for(int i=0; i < 256; i++){
22                  index = FourPages[16*index];
23          }
24          double cycles = clk.toc();
25          cout<<"index = "<<index<<endl;
26          cout<<"cycles per access = "<<cycles/256<<endl;
27 }
```

The key to this function are the three arrays List[], LList[], and FourPages[] defined on lines 2, 4, and 8, respectively. The array List[] is set to be a random permutation of the numbers $0, \ldots, 255$ on line 3. The array LList[] is initialized using List[], and FourPages[] is initialized using LList[].

The key idea for breaking instruction-level parallelism is to access the entries of the array List[] in the following order:

```
List[i], List[List[i]], List[List[List[i]]],...
```

If the entries are accessed in this manner, no access can be initiated before the earlier access is complete. However, there is the problem that one of the entries may cycle back to List[i]. For example, if List[i] is j and List[j] is i, the sequence above will repeat with a period of just 2.

We need a permutation that is one big cycle. Lines 5 and 6 create and initialize the array LList[] to be such a permutation. The sequence

LList[i], LList[LList[i]], LList[LList[LList[i]]],...

will have a period of 256 for any i, $0 \leq i < 256$. However, each int is 4 bytes, and 16 of the entries of LList[] will be in the same cache line. Although the sequence above breaks instruction-level parallelism and generates entries of LList[] in an order that is random enough to preempt cache prefetches, the same cache line is accessed 16 times.

Line 8 declares FourPages[] to be an array of 4,096 ints. Because each int is 4 bytes, the array is four pages long. The declaration qualifier on line 8 (which is valid only with the icpc compiler) ensures that FourPages is 4,096-byte aligned or page aligned. Every 16th entry of FourPages[] is set to an entry of List[] in line 10. The loop from lines 21 to 23 accesses only those entries of FourPages[] whose index is a multiple of 16. Every cache line is accessed only once.

Before the entries are accessed and the program is timed, the array FourPages[] must be evicted from cache. Lines 12 and 13 define a large array and write to each entry of the array and indirectly remove FourPages[] from cache. Lines 15 and 16 use the CLFLUSH instruction to explicitly flush the cache lines of FourPages[] from cache memory.

If the program is correct, line 25 should print index to be 17, same as the value it was assigned on line 18. Because the permutation has period 256, the last index generated by the for-loop on lines 17 to 19 must equal the first index. The print statement on line 25 forces the compiler to generate code for the entire program. Otherwise, the compiler can easily figure out that the program is doing nothing useful and ignore all the trouble we have taken to set up FourPages[] and then cycle through it.

Table 4.3 reports several measurements of latency. The program was modified to be able to handle $4n$ pages for $n \geq 1$. The numbers reported are medians obtained from a large number of measurements.

Table 4.3 shows that the measured latency depends on the number of pages accessed. On an AVX2 machine, the latency is of the order of 100 cycles when the number of pages accessed is 32 or less. When the number of pages used in our experiment is 40 or more, the latency jumps to around 250 cycles. We are not certain of the explanation. Our best guess is that the jump in latency may have something to do with the number of arrays in a bank of DRAM memory as well as the number of columns in each array. When the number of pages used is few, it is possible that all

# of pages	mwalk	clflush	# of pages	mwalk	clflush
4	122	94	60	247	254
8	126	93	1000	251	257
16	130	95	10000	257	256
32	148	100	100000	265	263
40	247	248			

Table 4.3: Latency to DRAM memory on a 3.6 GHz AVX2 machine (see table A.1 for the full name of the machine). Latencies on older SSE2 or AVX machines are similar. For example, on a 2.6 GHz SSE2 machine, the latency is around 100 cycles when the number of pages is 16 or fewer and increases to 180 thereafter. Data is cleared from cache by either accessing a long array (mwalk) or using the cache flush instruction (clflush).

the pages map to the same row in a bank of DRAM memory.

Table 4.3 reports measurements of latency using two different techniques. In "mwalk," the array FourPages[] is evicted from cache by writing to some other large array (line 13). In "clflush," the array is evicted using the CLFLUSH instruction (line 16). When the number of pages is 32 or less, the "mwalk" figure is noticeably higher. That appears to be because writing to some other array to evict FourPages[] from cache implies write-backs of that other array when FourPages[] is used to measure latency. The write-backs are likely to cause row switching within a bank.[5]

Exercise 4.1.1. What is the size of DRAM memory on your machine? Write a simple C program to find out the maximum amount of memory that can be allocated with malloc() or _mm_malloc() on your machine. Does that limit depend on how many other programs are running on your system and how much memory they are using?

Exercise 4.1.2. How many DRAM arrays constitute a bank in your machine's memory? Is your memory DDR3, DDR5, or DDR with some other prefetch parameter? How many bytes of data are transferred between DRAM and the memory controllers after a single load instruction?

Exercise 4.1.3. Use the CPUID instruction to determine the cache and TLB parameters on your machine.

---

[5]To test this hypothesis, we modified "mwalk" to read from a large array rather than write to a large array. Reading does not trigger write-backs. As expected, the "mwalk" figures after this modification are close to the "clflush" figures.

Exercise 4.1.4. Why do processors prefer to have separate L1 caches for instructions and data? Similarly, what may be desirable in having separate level 1 TLBs for instruction and data?

Exercise 4.1.5. Upon `malloc()`, virtual memory is allocated, but the pages of virtual memory are not mapped to page frames in physical memory. Therefore, the first access of every page triggers a page fault. Write a C program to demonstrate this phenomenon and determine the cost of invoking the page fault handler.

Exercise 4.1.6. In section 4.1.4, we determined the cost per access of an `int` assuming sequential access, strided access that reads just one `int` per cache line, and a more complex pattern that triggers TLB misses. Repeat these measurements on your machine. Determine the cost per access if each access is a write instead of a read.

Exercise 4.1.7. Measure the latency to L1, L2, and L3 caches.[6]

Exercise 4.1.8. Modify the program to measure latency given in section 4.1.5 so that the four pages are not contiguous in virtual memory. How does that affect the measurement?

Exercise 4.1.9. The function `latency()` prints the final value of index as well as the measured latency. Modify the program so that neither quantity is printed within the function itself. Does the change make a difference to the measured latency?

Exercise 4.1.10. Write a program that measures the latency of writes to memory and another program that measures the latency to memory when writes and reads are intermixed.

Exercise 4.1.11. Does the validity of the program to measure latency given in section 4.1.5 depend on whether the memory is DDR3 or DDR5? Does it depend on the number of arrays in a bank?

4.2   Optimizing memory access

In this section, we look at optimization of memory access using three examples. The first example, in section 4.2.1, is to simply access a long array of numbers to sum or to copy. With this simple example, we learn what may be the most important lesson related to memory access, which is to utilize each cache line as fully as possible.

---

[6]For latency and bandwidth to DRAM memory as well as caches, see Molka et al. (2009) and Bubka and Tuma (2009).

The examples in sections 4.2.2 and 4.2.3 are more involved. Although cache lines are the units of transfer of data between DRAM and the caches, cache organization involves multiple levels and sets. In every memory access, a virtual address must be translated to a physical address. This translation using the TLB and possibly the page tables can be a source of considerable overhead.

The chief technique in optimizing for multiple cache levels and the TLB is the same, namely, blocking. In section 4.2.2, we study blocking using matrix transposition as an example. Section 4.2.3 also illustrates blocking in addition to the technique of streaming data from cache to reduce cache and TLB misses.

Fortunately, much of the time we do not need to program in assembly when optimizing memory access. This is partly because the memory system is so complicated that overly refined optimizations do not make sense. Another reason is that the memory system is more amenable to optimization than the instruction pipeline. For the vast majority of nontrivial programs, speed is limited by memory access. Thus, the memory system's greater amenability to optimization is probably by design. Although it would be incorrect to assume that compilers generate optimal instruction streams, the penalty for suboptimality is not as great.

The design of the memory system consisting of DRAM, memory controllers, and caches is relatively stable across platforms. Therefore, the techniques of optimization may be expected to be the same on graphics devices, non-x86 platforms, and mobile devices.

Our discussion of the memory system in the previous section began with aspects of hardware design and virtual memory and concluded with a measurement of latency. In contrast, through much of this section, the emphasis is on bandwidth to memory. In all the examples discussed in this section, the large latency to memory can be hidden with little effort.

Examples in which latency to memory can be hidden completely are characterized by parallelism in the instruction stream. For example, if a program adds an array of numbers by accessing entries in sequence, the processor can issue multiple loads from memory in parallel. If the memory accesses can be overlapped, the effective latency to memory becomes manageable.

However, if memory accesses cannot be overlapped, the program is exposed to latency to DRAM memory. Our program to measure latency, given in the previous section, is an example where memory accesses cannot be overlapped. In general, memory accesses cannot be overlapped if the location of the next memory access depends on the result of the previous memory access.

Situations in which memory accesses cannot be overlapped are exceedingly common. Such scenarios arise whenever linked lists, trees, or graphs are used to handle dynamic data. Even in these situations, some of the techniques of memory optimization we discuss may still be relevant. For example, if successive items of a linked list are packed closely in memory, some advantage may be derived from caching. Techniques for dynamic data structures are deferred to the exercises. In general, when the use of dynamic data structures cannot be avoided, it is likely that exposure to DRAM latency also cannot be completely avoided.

4.2.1   Bandwidth to DRAM

The most predictable and common pattern of memory access is to access a long line of data in sequence. Every memory controller is likely to be optimized to handle that pattern efficiently. Thus, to determine bandwidth to memory, we will access a long array in sequence.

The following simple function returns the sum of an array of `doubles`:

```
double sum(double *restrict a, long int n){
    double s = 0;
    for(long int i=0; i < n; i++)
        s += a[i];
    return s;
}
```

The loop body uses XMM/YMM registers, as we may verify by inspecting the assembly code. The single statement in the loop has a loop-carried RAW dependency. Nevertheless, the simple structure of the loop helps the compiler unroll the loop and introduce parallelism in the loop body. The entries of the array `a[]` are read from memory in parallel. The additions do not introduce an overhead above the time it takes to read the array from memory.

The program was called with an array `a[]` that was 8 GB. The array was initialized in the same sequence it is summed. It is important to initialize the array before the function `sum()` is called. Pages of virtual memory are mapped to page frames of physical memory only at first access. If the array is not initialized at all, the mapping of virtual memory to physical memory takes place when `sum()` executes.

The cache is too small to hold 8 GB data. So none of the load instructions will hit the cache. Every byte accessed by `sum()` must be loaded from memory.

Because each `double` is 8 bytes, if the function `sum()` takes c cycles to execute, we may take the bandwidth to memory to be $8n/c$ bytes per cycle. The bandwidth to memory on a 2.66 GHz SSE2 machine (see table A.1 for the full names of the machines) was measured to be 4.36 bytes per cycle or, equivalently, 11.6 GB/s. On a more recent 2.20 GHz AVX machine, the bandwidth was 5.40 bytes per cycle or 11.9 GB/s. On a yet more recent 3.6 GHz AVX2 machine, the bandwidth was 4.85 bytes per cycle or 17.46 GB/s.

We use strided memory accesses to lead up to what is perhaps the single most important item a programmer should know about accessing memory. The following function sums entries of the array `a[]`, beginning with the zeroth entry and in steps of length `stride`:

```
double sumstride(double *restrict a, long int n,
        int stride){
    double s = 0;
    for(long int i=0; i < n; i+=stride)
        s += a[i];
    return s;
}
```

The bandwidth to memory realized in strided access is

$$\frac{8n}{c \times \text{stride}}$$

assuming the function takes c cycles.

Before we begin making measurements with non-unit strides, it is a good idea to try `stride=1`. It turns out that `sumstride()` realizes a bandwidth of only 2.4 bytes cycle on the SSE2 machine for unit stride, which is well short of the 4.36 bytes per cycle realized by `sum()`. Evidently, the compiler is not optimizing as well when stride is passed as a parameter.

We make the stride a `const int` to coax the compiler to optimize better. For unit stride, we use the definition

```
const int STR=1;
```

Stride	Read	Copy
1	4.36	3.53
2	2.25	1.83
4	1.21	0.92
8	0.80	0.60

Table 4.4: Bandwidth to memory in bytes per cycle on a 2.6 GHz SSE2 machine. The measured read and copy bandwidths are 5.3 bytes per cycle and 2.4 bytes per cycle on a 2.2 GHz AVX machine. The read and copy bandwidths are both 4.85 bytes per cycle on a 3.6 GHz AVX2 machine (see table A.1 for the full names of the machines).

To make the stride equal to 8, we modify the definition to

```
const int STR=8;
```

The function sumconststride() given below uses STR as its striding parameter.

```
double sumconststride(double *restrict a, long int n){
    double s = 0;
    for(long int i=0; i < n; i+=STR)
        s += a[i];
    return s;
}
```

Because the compiler knows the numerical value of the stride, it can optimize the loop much better.

Table 4.4 gives the measured bandwidth for strides equal to 1, 2, 4, and 8. The bandwidth is nearly halved every time the stride is doubled. This behavior is easily explained. A cache line is equal to 64 bytes or 8 doubles in size. All traffic between DRAM and the processor packages is cache line by cache line. When we stride by 2, 4, or 8, we utilize only a half, a quarter, or an eighth of every cache line that is brought in. The single most important memory optimization is to ensure that a cache line is utilized as fully as possible.

Bandwidth to memory depends on the type of access. Typically, reads are faster than writes to memory. The functions copy() and copyconststride() are used to measure bandwidth to memory when one array is copied into another array.

```
void copy(double *restrict a, double *restrict b,
```

```
        long int n){
    for(long int i=0; i < n; i++)
        b[i] = a[i];
}


void copyconststride(double *restrict a,
            double *restrict b, long int n){
    for(long int i=0; i < n; i+=STR)
        b[i] = a[i];
}
```

If `copyconststride()` takes c cycles, the bandwidth realized is

$$\frac{16n}{c \times \text{stride}}.$$

The factor 16 in the numerator accounts for copying an 8-byte-long `double` to another `double`. The bandwidth realized when one array is copied to another is listed in table 4.4.

Typically, bandwidths for copying and writing are lower than that of reading. In table 4.4, the copying bandwidth (with stride 1) is 80% of the read bandwidth. In simple situations, there are ways to approach the read bandwidth more closely, however. One may invoke special instructions to get around the write-back cache policy. In fact, on a 3.6 GHz AVX2 machine, the compiler invokes a runtime library function for copying, and the copy and read bandwidths are both 4.85 bytes per cycle.

4.2.2 Matrix transpose

The only cache parameter of significance for strided accesses studied in the last section was cache line size. The sizes of the caches, their organization into sets, as well as the size of the TLB influence the performance of the example studied in this section.

The example we study here is out-of-place matrix transpose. It is always best to access data sequentially with unit stride, but when a matrix is transposed to another matrix stored in the same column-major format, there is no way to access both matrices with unit stride. In many problems of this type, it is useful to break up the data into blocks.

When a single array is accessed with a constant stride, a cache line brought into cache is used in a single go. Once the array moves past a cache line, we do not return to it. In matrix transpose with blocking, we rely on a cache line remaining in cache as we return to it repeatedly after working on other columns of the matrix block. This type of cache usage is more delicate. We find that the performance of the matrix transpose depends in a nonmonotonic manner on the size of the blocks. The performance degrades abruptly if the leading dimension of the matrix is divisible by a high power of 2. Such effects, though disconcerting to the programmer, cannot be eliminated.

The cache and TLB parameters of SSE2/AVX/AVX2 machines we use are given in tables 4.1 and 4.2. On all the machines, the L1 data cache is big enough to hold 4,000 `doubles` and the L3 cache can hold more than a million double-precision numbers.

Blocking

The function `easytrans()` listed below uses a simple doubly nested loop to transpose the matrix `a[]` to the matrix `b[]`. The matrices are of dimension $m \times n$ and $n \times m$. Both of them are assumed to be stored in column-major order with leading dimension (see section 2.2.1) equal to the number of rows.

```
void easytrans(double *restrict a, double *restrict b,
          int m, int n){
    for(int i=0; i < m; i++)
        for(int j=0; j < n; j++)
            b[j+i*n]  =  a[i+j*m];
}
```

This function is easy to write and easy for the compiler to analyze. The array references use indices that are linear combinations of the loop variables, and the loop variables are incremented in steps of 1. The assembly code generated by the compiler is far more complicated than the code presented to it. The total number of double-precision numbers accessed by this program is $2mn$. Because each `double` is 8 bytes, the bandwidth to memory realized is

$$\frac{8mn}{\text{cycles for a single transpose}}$$

bytes per cycle. The compiler-optimized `easytrans()` realizes a bandwidth of 1.48 bytes per cycle when $m =$20,000 and $n =$30,000. The best bandwidth we could have hoped for is 3.53 bytes per cycle, which is the bandwidth realized when an array is copied to another array with unit stride (see table 4.4). Despite compiler optimization, the realized bandwidth falls well short of that mark.

The function `blocktransx()` listed below implements matrix transpose block by block. The block size is $B \times B$, and B is defined as a `const int` (definition is not shown). The matrix dimensions are assumed to be divisible by B. The function `blocktransx()` uses a nest of four loops.

```
1  void blocktransx(double *restrict a, double *restrict b,
2                    int m, int n){
3    assert((m%B==0)&&(n%B==0));
4    for(int i=0; i < m; i+=B)
5      for(int j=0; j < n; j+=B)
6        for(int ii=0; ii < B; ii++)
7          for(int jj=0; jj < B; jj++)
8            b[j+jj+(i+ii)*n] = a[i+ii+(j+jj)*m];
9  }
```

When writing functions such as `blocktransx()`, it helps to think directly in terms of the for-loop construct of C/C++.

The loop variable `i` defined on line 4 steps through the rows of the $m \times n$ matrix stored in the array `a[]` in steps equal to the block size B. The loop variable `ii` defined on line 6 steps through the B rows of a single block of rows. Thus, `i+ii` is the index—relative to the $m \times n$ matrix—of row `ii` within the block of B rows from `i` to `i+B-1`. Similarly, `j+jj` is the index—relative to the matrix `a[]` as a whole—of column `jj` within the block of B columns from `j` to `j+B-1`. The loop body of `blocktransx()`, which is comprised of the single statement

```
b[j+jj+(i+ii)*n] = a[i+ii+(j+jj)*m];
```

corresponds to the statement `b[j+i*n]=a[i+j*m];`, which comprises the loop body of `easytrans()`.

It is significant that the block size parameter B is a `const int`. Knowledge of the numerical value of B allows the compiler to optimize better.

The bandwidth to memory realized by `blocktransx()` is given in table 4.5 for block sizes from $B = 8$ to $B = 1000$. Once again, $m =$20,000 and $n =$30,000. From the columns headlined "nest," we may observe that the realized bandwidth is worse when $B \leq 25$ than it is for `easytrans()`. The highest bandwidth of 2.60 bytes per cycle is realized when $B = 125$. The bandwidth to memory begins to degrade as B is increased.

While the optimal block size from the table is $B = 125$, the degradation is more severe for small block sizes than for larger ones. Block sizes $B \leq 25$ realize lower bandwidth to memory than `easytrans()`. Small block sizes inhibit the compiler from optimizing the inner loops, lowering the realized bandwidth. When the block size is large, the compiler optimizes the inner loops and generates code that is considerably different from what is presented to it.

Why does blocking improve memory bandwidth? First, it helps with reuse of cache lines. Suppose the blocks are small enough to fit into cache. Then every cache line in a block is fetched from memory only once if we ignore cache conflicts and misalignment.

Second, blocking helps reduce TLB misses. A single page is 4,096 bytes. Therefore, if $m \geq 512$, each entry of a row will be in a different page. Thus, if the size of a row is greater than the number of TLB entries, row-by-row traversal of the entire matrix will trigger TLB misses for every entry. Blocking can eliminate TLB misses by limiting the number of entries in a row.

The function of `blocktransx()` uses only one level of blocking. Because the caches and the TLB are organized hierarchically in multiple levels, it is natural to wonder whether multiple levels of blocking may bring some advantage. In this setting, recursive blocking, which is described in the exercises and which uses multiple levels of blocking, appears to be no better (see table 4.5) and does not make it easier to find an optimal block size.

The best bandwidth for transposing in table 4.5 is 2.60 bytes per cycle. On the 2.6 GHz SSE2 machine, that is 60% of the peak read bandwidth. In contrast, on a 3.6 GHz AVX2 machine, the best bandwidth for transposing was 1.96 bytes per cycle, which is about the same as SSE2 in GB/s and which is only 40% of the read bandwidth.

The reason for poorer performance on the modern AVX2 machine is not entirely clear. Generating good code for the inner block is crucial in this example, and the compiler does not appear to do anything special beyond translating the code as it

B	Nest	Recurse	B	Nest	Recurse
8	0.90	0.80	80	2.37	2.44
10	0.96	0.98	100	2.37	2.46
20	1.33	1.56	125	2.60	2.51
25	1.47	1.55	200	2.12	2.13
40	1.86	1.97	500	2.02	2.02
50	2.06	1.93	1000	1.88	1.88

Table 4.5: Bandwidth to memory in bytes per cycle for matrix transpose using $B \times B$ blocks on a 2.6 GHz SSE2 machine (see table A.1 for the full name of the machine). One-level blocking using a loop nest is compared with recursive blocking (recursive blocking is described in the exercises). With no blocking, the bandwidth realized is 1.48 bytes per cycle. The matrix had $20,000$ rows and $30,000$ columns.

is written. If the compiler were doing a good job, one should see `movpd` instructions (`pd` stands for packed double), which use the entire capacity of the YMM registers, in the innermost loop. Instead, one sees `movsd` instructions (`sd` for single double), which use only a quarter of the YMM registers. Thus, the poorer performance could be a consequence of suboptimal compilation, a phenomenon we encountered several times in the previous chapter and whose probability increases on more recent hardware.

Leading dimension divisible by a high power of 2

If two locations in memory are separated by a high power of 2, they are likely to map to the same set in cache and TLB. Table 4.6 shows the bandwidth realized when a matrix of dimension $2^{14} \times 2^{14}$ is transposed. Successive entries in the same row of this matrix are separated by 2^{11} cache lines. All entries of a row map to the same set in L1 and L2 caches as well as level 1 and level 2 TLB.

For a matrix of dimension $2^{14} \times 2^{14}$, `easytrans()` realizes a bandwidth of 0.43 bytes per cycle, which is less than a third of the bandwidth it realizes for a matrix of dimension $20,000 \times 30,000$. With blocking, the best bandwidth observed is 1.34 bytes per cycle and the optimal block size is 16×16. TLB and cache misses occur more frequently for the matrix of table 4.6 because the leading dimension is divisible by a high power of 2. As a result, the observed bandwidth is 35% of the best possible

B	nest	recurse	recurse/loop
8	0.84	0.92	0.95
16	1.30	1.32	1.34
32	1.17	1.22	1.22
64	1.17	1.18	1.18
128	0.58	0.58	0.58

Table 4.6: Bandwidth in bytes per cycle (on a 2.6 GHz SSE2 machine). The transposed matrix was square and of dimension $2^{14} = 16,384$. One level of blocking using a loop nest is compared against recursive blocking implemented using explicit recursion or loops (recursive blocking is discussed in the exercises). Transpose with no blocking had a bandwidth of only 0.43 bytes per cycle. Compare with table 4.5.

instead of 60%, as in the case where the matrix dimensions are not divisible by high powers of 2.

4.2.3   Optimized matrix multiplication

Some of the most nettlesome issues in implementing matrix multiplication arise at the level of the processor pipeline. In section 3.3.4, we wrote an assembly program for $4 \times 200 \times 4$ matrix multiplication, which reached 3.5 flops per cycle, against the theoretical limit of 4.0 flops per cycle, assuming all the matrices to be in cache. Here we assume the matrices to be in DRAM memory and not in cache, and we show how to optimize matrix multiplication.

Suppose A, B, and C are matrices of dimensions $\ell \times m$, $m \times n$, and $\ell \times n$, respectively. The matrices are assumed to be in DRAM memory. The cost of the operation $C = C + AB$ is $2\ell mn$ arithmetic operations, half of which are additions and half of which are multiplications. If the cache were large enough, each of the matrices can be loaded into cache and kept there as the matrix multiplication is performed. Loading the matrices into cache would take $\ell m + mn + \ell n$ DRAM memory accesses. If ℓ, m, and n are large, the number of arithmetic operations is much greater than the number of memory accesses. We may expect the cost of the computation to be dominated by the arithmetic operations, allowing us to approach the peak bandwidth of 4 flops per cycle on a single core of an SSE2 machine (the figures are 8 flops per cycle and 16 flops per cycles for AVX and AVX2 machines, respectively).

Matrix Dimensions	b/w
$4 \times 200 \times 4$	3.48
$4 \times 200 \times 12$	3.32
$600 \times 200 \times 12$	3.22
$600 \times 200 \times 3000$	3.21
$3000 \times 200 \times 3000$	3.19
$9000 \times 9000 \times 9000$	3.19

Table 4.7: Bandwidth in flops per cycle on a 2.6 GHz SSE2 machine for the multiplication of an $\ell \times m$ matrix with an $m \times n$ matrix. Matrix dimensions are reported as $\ell \times m \times n$.

We want the matrices to be big so that the arithmetic operations are far more numerous than memory accesses, but the catch is that the matrices will not fit into cache when they are too big. One way to overcome this dilemma is to use block matrix multiplication. We can pick the block sizes to be small enough to fit into cache but large enough that the cost of loading from memory is outweighed by the cost of arithmetic operations. Careful blocking would indeed improve the simple programs of section 3.2.5 but not enough to get anywhere close to peak bandwidth. A much more powerful set of ideas[7] shows how a program for multiplying matrices can approach the peak bandwidth for floating point arithmetic.

In outline, the basic idea remains to multiply in blocks, but intermediate blocks are stored in scratch space and in convenient formats to minimize TLB and cache misses. As far as possible, data is stored in a format that enables sequential access with unit stride. The actual execution of this idea can make it look more complicated than it is, but the idea is elegant as well as possibly applicable to many other problems.

As shown in table 4.7, our implementation progresses systematically from the $4 \times 200 \times 4$ microkernel described in section 3.3.4 to the multiplication of square matrices of dimension 9,000. We code a hierarchy of matrix multiplication functions with a function corresponding to each row of the table. Square matrices of dimension 9,000, which occur in the last row, are too large to fit into cache memory. Limiting ourselves to matrices of specific dimensions keeps the exposition tractable.

The square matrices of dimension 9,000 at the bottom of table 4.7 are stored in column-major order. However, the storage format of the matrices in every other row

---

[7]Goto and van de Geijn (2008).

is different. The storage format for the $4 \times 200 \times 4$ microkernel was assumed to be such as to lead to a high throughput of arithmetic operations. For the following rows of the table, the storage formats are chosen to allow for convenient and efficient invocation of the function that corresponds to the preceding row of the table.

The matrices are denoted using capitalized letters when they are in column-major order with a leading dimension that may exceed the number of rows. Lowercase letters are used for other storage formats.

So, for example, the arrays that store the arguments to the $4 \times 200 \times 4$ microkernel are a[], b[], and c[]. The microkernel interprets $4 \times 200 \times 4$ matrix multiplication as the sum of 200 outer products of 4×1 and 1×4 matrices. Accordingly, the array a[] is assumed to store a 4×200 matrix in column-major order. The array b[] is assumed to store a 200×4 matrix in row-major order. In both cases, the leading dimension is equal to 4. The ith outer product accesses the entries

$$a[4i, \ldots, 4i + 3] \quad \text{and} \quad b[4i, \ldots, 4i + 3].$$

The array c[] is of length 16 and stores a 4×4 matrix. In section 3.3.4, we assumed that the storage format of c[] was column-major with "skewing." The skewing can be undone using a single step of unskewing, which introduces only an insignificant overhead at the end. Therefore, we ignore it, although skewing percolates down the rows of table 4.7, implying that the matrix C of dimension 9,000 corresponding to the last row of the table needs to be unskewed. Thus, the array c[] is assumed to store a 4×4 matrix in column-major format (with skewing, which we ignore here) with leading dimension equal to 4.

As we progress down the rows of table 4.7, the implementation of each row reuses the lower case letters a, b, c, assuming whatever format is most suitable for its purposes.

Closely related to storage formats is the use of work space. To allow for changes in storage format, the matrix multiplication functions use extra memory stored in an array called scratch[]. The size of this array in its original incarnation is

$$600 \times 12 + 600 \times 200 + 200 \times 3000$$

double-precision numbers. The three terms correspond to c[], a[], and b[], respectively. The multiplication of square matrices of dimension 9000 is partitioned repeatedly into multiplications of lower dimensional matrices. The array scratch[] changes at every level in this hierarchy.

As we step through the design, it is helpful to keep a few numbers in mind. The L1 cache is 32 KB and big enough to hold 4,000 double-precision numbers. The L3 cache is 12 MB and big enough to hold 1.5 million double-precision numbers. The second-level TLB has 512 entries (see tables 4.1 and 4.2). To keep the design simple, we ignore the L2 cache and the first level TLB.

In section 4.2.1, we found that it takes about two cycles to load a single double into memory at peak bandwidth. The changes in storage formats that occur, when we begin with the microkernel and increase the dimensions of the matrices that are multiplied, are too complicated to permit access to memory at peak bandwidth. It is perhaps reasonable to take the cost of accessing a double from DRAM memory as 10 cycles. At peak floating point bandwidth, the cost of a single arithmetic operation is 1/4 cycle on an SSE2 machine. To approach peak floating point bandwidth, we should perhaps expect to perform a few hundred arithmetic operations for every double loaded from DRAM memory.

$4 \times 200 \times 12$

The microkernel of section 3.3.4 performs a $4 \times 200 \times 4$ multiplication and reaches 3.48 flops per cycle, assuming all matrices to be in L1. The $4 \times 200 \times 12$ multiplication function that follows is written under the assumption that a[] will need to be loaded from L3 cache. To pay for the cost of loading a[] from L3, it reuses a[] three times.

```
void mult4x200x12(double *a, double *b, double *c){
    asm4x200x4(a, b, c);
    asm4x200x4(a,b+800,c+16);
    asm4x200x4(a,b+1600,c+32);
}
```

In the mult4x200x12() function, the arrays a[], b[], and c[] are of lengths 800, 2,400, and 48, respectively. The L1 cache is big enough to hold all three of them. In the next step, this function is called repeatedly with the same b[] but with a[] and c[], which change with iteration. Therefore, we assume that b[] is in L1 cache.

The function mult4x200x12() assumes a[] to be in column-major format with leading dimension equal to 4—the same as in the microkernel. But b[] has a pretty strange format. The first four columns of the 200×12 matrix are stored in b[0..799] in row-major order, the next four columns are similarly stored in b[800..1599], and the final four columns are in b[1600..2399]. The array c[] is in column-major format (except for skewing, which we are ignoring).

How much is lost when a[] and c[] are loaded from L2 or L3 cache? Table 4.7 shows that the floating point bandwidth drops from 3.48 to 3.32. The following function run4x200x12() was used to figure out that answer. A number of points about timing functions such as mult4x200x12() are made in the discussion after the listing.

```
1  void run4x200x12(){
2    __declspec(align(16)) double a[800*150];
3    __declspec(align(16)) double b[2400];
4    __declspec(align(16)) double c[48*150];
5    TimeStamp clk;
6    double cycles;
7    for(int i=0; i < 2400; i++)
8      b[i] = rand()*1.0/RAND_MAX;
9    for(int i=0; i < 48*150; i++)
10     c[i] = 0;
11   for(int i=0; i < 800*150; i++)
12     a[i] = rand()*1.0/RAND_MAX;
13   clk.tic();
14   for(int i=0; i < 1000*1000*10; i++)
15     mult4x200x12(a+800*(i%150), b, c+48*(i%150));
16   cycles = clk.toc();
17   cycles = cycles/1e7;
18   cout<<"flops per cycle = "<<2.0*16*200*3/cycles<<endl;
19 }
```

The arrays a[], b[], and c[] defined on lines 2, 3, and 4, respectively, are 16-byte aligned. The $4 \times 200 \times 4$ microkernel requires that its arguments be 16-byte aligned, and we must be careful to respect that requirement.

The array a[] is too large to fit into L1 or L2 cache but fits comfortably into L3 cache. It is big enough to hold 150 matrices of size 4×200. The array c[], which holds 150 matrices of size 4×4, fits into L2 cache but not L1.

On lines 8 and 12, the arrays b[] and a[] are initialized with random numbers. Initializing with simple numbers such as 0 or 1 gives timing numbers that are misleading and not reproducible.

The mult4x200x12() function is called 10^7 times on line 15. The function calls cycle through the 150 possibilities for the first argument so that the function has to load a[] and c[] from L2 or L3 cache after each call. This pattern of function calls imitates the manner in which the function is called in the next stage.

$600 \times 200 \times 12$

The mult600x200x12() function requires scratch space of 600×12 to store c[], which is then unpacked to the array C[] in column-major format with the right leading dimension.

```
void mult600x200x12(double *a, double *b,
              double *C, int ldC,
              double *scratch){
    double *c = scratch;
    for(int i=0; i < 7200; i++)
        c[i] = 0;
    for(int  i=0; i < 150; i++)
        mult4x200x12(a+i*800, b, c+i*48);
    unpackC(c, C, ldC);
}
```

The array a[] stores a 600×200 matrix. The 600×200 matrix is thought of as 150 matrices of dimension 4×200 one below the other. These 150 submatrices must be lined up in a[], with each submatrix stored in the column-major format required by mult4x200x12().

The array c[] stores a 600×12 matrix. The 600×12 matrix is thought of as 150 matrices of dimension 4×12 one below the other, and these submatrices are lined up in c[] with each submatrix in the format required by mult4x200x12().

The function mult600x200x12() makes 150 calls to mult4x200x12(). At the end it unpacks c[]. The function unpackC() listed below converts c[] to the column-major format of C[].

```
void unpackC(double *c, double *C, int ldC){
```

```
        for(int i=0; i < 600; i+= 4)
            for(int ii=0; ii < 12; ii++)
                for(int iii=0; iii<4; iii++)
                    C[i+iii+ii*ldC] += c[12*i+4*ii+iii];
    }
```

Deciphering this triply nested loop is an exercise we omit. The main point is that the cost of unpacking, whatever it may be, is far less than the savings obtained in calling mult4x200x12() 150 times with c[] in a format that permits sequential access.

$600 \times 200 \times 3000$

The earlier function for $600 \times 200 \times 12$ multiplication assumes a[] to be in packed format. The 600×200 entries of a[] store 150 submatrices of dimension 4×200. Each submatrix occupies 800 contiguous entries and is in column-major order. The function packA() packs A[], which is in column-major format, into this format.

```
    void packA(double *A, int ldA, double *a){
        for(int j=0; j < 200; j++)
            for(int i=0; i < 150; i++)
                for(int ii=0; ii < 4; ii++)
                    a[i*800+ii+j*4] = A[4*i+ii+j*ldA];
    }
```

Deciphering this triply nested loop is another exercise we omit.

The function mult600x200x3000() reuses a[] as soon as it is packed by making 250 calls to the function at the previous stage in our design, thus more than making up for the cost of packing. It claims 600×200 entries of scratch[] to store the packed array.

```
    void mult600x200x3000(double *A, int ldA,
                    double *b,
                    double *C, int ldC,
                    double *scratch){
        double *a = scratch;
        scratch += 600*200;
        packA(A, ldA, a);
```

```
        for(int i=0; i < 250; i++)
            mult600x200x12(a, b+i*2400, C+i*12*ldC, ldC,
                           scratch);
    }
```

For every **double** entry in the packed array `a[]` of size 600×200, the $600 \times 200 \times 3000$ multiplication function performs 6,000 arithmetic operations. We may expect the cost of the arithmetic to greatly outweigh the cost of packing `a[]`. The multiplication function has floating point performance of 3.21 flops per cycle (see table 4.7). As expected, the decline from 3.22 flops per cycle yielded by the previous stage is marginal.

$3000 \times 200 \times 3000$

The earlier function `mult600x200x3000()` assumes that the array `b[]` stores a 200×3000 matrix in packed format. The matrix is thought of as 250 matrices of dimension 200×12 next to each other. Each of these 200×12 matrices is stored in the packed format required by the $4 \times 200 \times 12$ multiplication function.

The function `packB()` packs a submatrix of `B[]`, which is in column-major format, into `b[]`.

```
    void packB(double *B, int ldB, double *b){
        for(int j=0; j < 750; j++)
            for(int i=0; i < 200; i++)
                for(int jj=0; jj < 4; jj++){
                    b[jj+i*4+j*800] = B[i+(4*j+jj)*ldB];
                }
    }
```

Deciphering this triply nested loop is yet another exercise we omit.

The function `mult3000x200x3000()` resues `b[]` five times as soon as it is packed, thus making up for the cost of packing. It claims 200×3000 entries from `scratch[]` for the packed array. The packed array fits comfortably in L3 cache.

```
    void mult3000x200x3000(double *A, int ldA,
                           double *B, int ldB,
                           double *C, int ldC,
                           double *scratch){
```

```
   double *b = scratch;
   scratch += 200*3000;
   packB(B, ldB, b);
   for(int i=0; i < 5; i++)
      mult600x200x3000(A+i*600, ldA, b, C+i*600, ldC,
                                             scratch);

}
```

For each of the entries in the packed array, this function performs 6,000 arithmetic operations. Its floating point performance is 3.19 flops per cycle, a marginal decrease from that of the previous stage (see table 4.7).

Block multiplication

The function blockmult() listed below carries out an $\ell \times m \times n$ multiplication if ℓ, m, and n are multiples of 3,000, 200, and 3,000, respectively.

```
void blockmult(double *A, double *B, double *C,
               int l, int m, int n,
               double *scratch){
   assert(l%3000==0);
   assert(m%200==0);
   assert(n%3000==0);
   int ldA = l;
   int ldB = m;
   int ldC = l;
   l = l/3000;
   m = m/200;
   n = n/3000;
   for(int i=0; i < l; i++)
      for(int j=0; j < m; j++)
         for(int k=0; k < n; k++){
            double *AA = A + (i*3000)+(j*200)*ldA;
            double *BB = B + (j*200)+(k*3000)*ldB;
            double *CC = C + (i*3000)+(k*3000)*ldC;
            mult3000x200x3000(AA, ldA, BB, ldB, CC, ldC,
```

$$\text{scratch);}$$
$$\text{\}}$$
$$\text{\}}$$

This function implicitly partitions A into $3{,}000 \times 200$ blocks, B into $200 \times 3{,}000$ blocks, and C into $3{,}000 \times 3{,}000$ blocks. The function `mult3000x200x3000()`, defined at the previous stage, is used to multiply a single block of A into a single block of B to get a single block of C.

The floating point bandwidth realized is 3.19 flops per cycle for the multiplication of square matrices of dimension 9,000 on a 2.6 GHz SSE2 machine. For the same problem, the MKL library realizes more than 3.8 flops per cycle. Why is our design worse? Much of the blame falls on the microkernel. To begin with, the microkernel yields only 3.48 flops per cycle, assuming all its arguments are in L1 cache. On a 3.6 GHz AVX2 machine, on which the microkernel yields 3.98 flops per cycle, the bandwidth realized for the multiplication of square matrices is 3.75 flops per cycle.

Exercise 4.2.1. The function `sum()` of section 4.2.1 adds an array of numbers in sequence. Assuming the array to be several gigabytes long, explain why the number of cycles consumed by the function depends solely on memory access, with the additions not introducing any extra overhead.

Exercise 4.2.2. Initialize a long array. Sum its entries with a stride that ensures only one entry is read from a page. What is the peak bandwidth to memory realized? That is the peak bandwidth to DRAM in the presence of TLB misses.

Exercise 4.2.3. Write a program to measure the bandwidth of writing to DRAM memory. Compare write bandwidth to read and copy bandwidths given in table 4.4.

Exercise 4.2.4. Explain why the copy bandwidth in table 4.4 is lower than the read bandwidth.

Exercise 4.2.5. Write a program that maps an $n \times n$ array of numbers to another $n \times n$ array, with each entry replaced by the average of north, south, east, and west entries. The arrays are assumed to be in column-major order. Compare the speed of a program that traverses the arrays columnwise with a program that traverses the arrays rowwise. Why do you expect columnwise traversal to be faster? Implement the same computation using blocking. Explain why blocking is likely to help make the program faster.

Exercise 4.2.6. In recursive transpose,[8] if a matrix A to be transposed to a matrix B has more rows than columns, the matrices are split as follows:

$$\begin{pmatrix} A_1 \\ A_2 \end{pmatrix} \quad \text{and} \quad \begin{pmatrix} B_1 & B_2 \end{pmatrix}.$$

Recursion is used to transpose A_i to B_i. The case with more columns than rows is handled similarly. Write a program that implements this algorithm.

Exercise 4.2.7. Rewrite the matrix multiplication programs of section 3.2.5 to use blocking. Compare program speeds with and without blocking.

Exercise 4.2.8. Rewrite matrix multiplication using one level of blocking as in the previous exercise. But this time use scratch space to copy matrix subblocks with the blocks stored in scratch space having leading dimension equal to block dimension. The storage format of the blocks must be row-major or column-major to permit sequential access of entries. Time the program and compare to matrix multiplication with more straightforward blocking.

Exercise 4.2.9. Write a program to transpose a square matrix in place. Compare program speeds with and without blocking.

Exercise 4.2.10. Write a program that stores a sequence of double-precision numbers in a linked list. Write a program to sum all the numbers. Find the number of cycles per entry assuming that the linked list has more than 10^9 entries. Compare program speed in the following two situations: the entries of the linked list are in random locations in memory, and the entries of the linked list are next to each other. Explain what you observe.

Exercise 4.2.11. A balanced binary tree can be represented in two ways. The first way is to use an array with the convention that the two children of item i are items $2i + 1$ and $2i + 2$, with $i = 0$ being the root. The second way is to use a `struct` with a pointer to the left child, the right child, and the parent. Write a program that replaces each entry of a node by the sum of all its descendants and itself. Compare program speed between the two implementations.

4.3   Reading from and writing to disk

The data in registers and DRAM memory disappears when the computer is powered off. In contrast, hard disk storage is permanent. The hard disk is a collection of

---

[8]Frigo et al. (1999).

platters. Bits stored on circular tracks on either side of the platters are turned on and off using a magnetic field. More than 100 billion bits can be packed into a single square inch of a platter.

File systems, implemented inside the operating system kernel, impose a logical structure on hard disk storage and facilitate its use. Files and directories are stored on the hard disk. In everyday usage, files are read from and written to with the understanding that the data is stored on a hard disk. Between the file as viewed inside a C/C++ program and the hard disk, there are several layers of software. These layers of software provide modularity, enabling the operating system kernel to handle several different file systems with a uniform interface and greatly improve speed of access.

The Linux kernel implements a number of optimizations to speed up access to the disk. The most important optimization is to store a page cache. The page cache is a list of page frames that corresponds to data in the disk. When a file is read, Linux will service the read using the page cache if possible. A read or write file operation has to fall through a number of software layers before it reaches the disk. It begins as a system call. The `read()` and `write()` system calls are issued by the C library functions `fread()` and `fwrite()`. The C library function may do some buffering of its own. The kernel will service the system calls using a page cache if possible. If not, it invokes the file system to which the file belongs. There are software layers for combining, queuing, and scheduling requests to read or write to the hard disk. The request is finally issued using a device driver.[9]

The Linux command `lspci -v` may be used to find out the type of hard disk as well as the device driver that is in use. Although it is useful to understand that every disk access falls through layers of the file system within the operating system kernel, knowing specific details about the type of hard disk and the device driver is of little use in actual programming. There can be considerable variation in capacity as well as bandwidth of different hard disk systems, but that does not affect programming technique.

The C versus C++ discussion in section 4.3.1 is on programming technique. The C++ language provides a convenient interface to file input/output using `ifstream`

---

[9]When the file access falls through to the driver, the driver issues a DMA request and puts the calling process to sleep. The process is woken up by an interrupt handler when the request is complete. The Linux kernel will page cache the data before returning control to the user program.

and `ofstream` objects. Although less convenient, the no-nonsense `fread()`, `fwrite()` interface in C can be much faster, by as much as a factor of 100. In section 4.3.1, we explain why there can be such a big difference in speed.

In sections 4.3.2 and 4.3.3, we investigate latency and bandwidth to DRAM memory. In both of these sections, the page cache maintained by the Linux kernel plays a big role. The page cache is a cache of the hard disk maintained in main memory. DRAM memory can be tens of GB in size, and the page cache can occupy a considerable portion of that memory. A lot of file input/output is serviced by the operating system kernel using the page cache. To get a real picture of latency and bandwidth to hard disk, one needs to get beyond the page cache, and that implies file sizes that are in the hundreds of GB.

Latency to hard disk is of the order of milliseconds and can therefore be 10^5 times the latency to DRAM memory. Bandwidth to hard disk is of the order of hundreds of MB/s, which is only a thousandth of the bandwidth to DRAM on typical computers. However, hard disk capacity can be 100 or even 1,000 times DRAM capacity on typical computers. With respect to hard disk capacity, many supercomputing systems (and high-end workstations) are not well balanced. The need to provide a common file system across many computers for many users often implies that the hard disk capacity is not as high as it should be.

4.3.1   C versus C++

With regard to the programming technique for reading and writing files, the simplest lesson is also the most valuable. The C interface can be much faster than the C++ interface as we show and for reasons we explain.

The following functions use C++ `ifstream` and `ofstream` objects to read and write a `double` array `v[]` from or to a file of name `fname`.

```
void write_easy(double *v, long len,
        const char *fname){
    ofstream ofile(fname);
    ofile<<scientific;
    ofile.precision(16);
    for(long i=0; i < len; i++)
        ofile<<v[i]<<endl;
    ofile.close();
```

```
        }

        void read_easy(double *v, long len, const char *fname){
            ifstream ifile(fname);
            for(long i=0; i < len; i++)
                ifile>>v[i];
        }
```

The C interface below can be more than 100 times faster.

```
1   #include <cstdio>
2   void write_direct(double *v, long len,
3                   const char *fname){
4       FILE *fptr;
5       fptr = fopen(fname, "w");
6       fwrite((void *)v, len, sizeof(double), fptr);
7       fclose(fptr);
8   }
9
10  void read_direct(double *v, long len,
11                  const char *fname){
12      FILE *fptr;
13      fptr = fopen(fname, "r");
14      fread((void *)v, len, sizeof(double), fptr);
15      fclose(fptr);
16  }
```

The FILE type as well as the functions fopen(), fwrite(), fread(), and fclose() are declared in the stdio.h header file included on line 1. On line 5, a file is opened for writing and on line 13 for reading.

The library function fwrite() (line 6) has a quite simple interface. Its first argument is a pointer to a location in memory. The second argument is the number of items to be written, and the third argument is the size of each item in bytes. The final argument is a pointer to a file.

The library function fread() (line 14) has an identical interface. It returns the number of items read, which may be less than the number requested if there is an error. Following our usual practice, we do not check for error conditions. Open files are closed using `fclose()` (lines 7 and 15).

Why is the C++ interface more than 100 times slower? There are three reasons.

First, while the C library functions `fread()` and `fwrite()` can read and write objects of any type or class, they do not waste a single byte of storage. Each `double` is 64 bits and gets stored as exactly 8 bytes. If file streams are used and each `double` is stored in ascii, as in the earlier program, each `double` uses 23 bytes (+1 if the number is negative).

Second, the C++ interface incurs an overhead in converting every `double` from binary to ascii.

Third, the C interface does the entire reading and writing using a single call to the C library. In contrast, the C++ interface reads or writes item by item, with the C++ `fstream` library being invoked for every item. The overhead of calling the library so frequently can build up. What is worse, the `fstream` library probably invokes the file system inside the operating system kernel quite frequently, although it presumably does some buffering. Every system call is like another function call, which can lead to many more function calls inside the file system. This overhead can build up.

4.3.2 Latency to disk

The measurement of latency to hard disk brings up issues not unlike the ones encountered in measuring the latency to DRAM memory. Hard disk is so slow relative to memory that the operating system kernel goes to great lengths to cache file data in DRAM memory. The hard disk maintains a cache and attempts to predict future accesses. The true latency to hard disk is not easily visible to simple computer programs.

The plan for measuring latency is to create a number of files and access several different positions in several different files to gather latency statistics. The plan does not work so easily. If 100 files each of 100 MB are used in the measurement, the latencies for a 1 TB hard disk come out quite low and of the order of microseconds, not milliseconds. That is because all of 10 GB can fit comfortably inside the page cache of a system with 16 GB of memory.

The size of page cache can run into several GB. The size of the page cache may be seen in `/proc/meminfo` against the item labeled "Cached." If we write to a file of size 1 GB on a computer with several GB of memory, the entire file ends up in the page cache. To clear the page cache, one may use the GNU/Linux command

```
echo 1 > /proc/sys/vm/drop_caches
```

One may look at /proc/meminfo after this command to verify that the page cache has indeed been cleared.

The latency2disk() function defined below reads a single double from a given position in a given file and returns it. The idea is to use 100 files each of 1 GB to make the total file size in play of the order of 100 GB, and then read a double-precision number at a random location in a random file.[10] As a result, the actual measurement of latency makes a large number of calls to latency2disk() and the code for which is now shown.

```
1  struct disk_latency{
2        double fopen_cycles;
3        double fseek_cycles;
4        double fread_cycles;
5        double fclose_cycles;
6  };
7  double latency2disk(const char *dir, int filenum,
8                  long posn,struct disk_latency& lat){
9        char fname[200];
10       sprintf(fname, "%s/file%d.dat", dir, filenum);
11       TimeStamp clk;
12       FILE *fptr;
13       clk.tic();
14       fptr = fopen(fname,"r");
15       lat.fopen_cycles = clk.toc();
16       clk.tic();
17       fseek(fptr,81*posn,SEEK_SET);
18       lat.fseek_cycles=clk.toc();
19       double x;
```

[10]On some computer systems, there is so much memory that even 100 GB may fit comfortably inside a page cache and be too small for latency measurement. Thus, the file count as well as the file size may need to be changed.

Computer	fsize	nfiles	open	seek	read	close
HP-Z220	1 GB	100	.007	6.84	2.68	.010
ThinkStation-P300	1GB	100	.001	9.29	.681	.002

Table 4.8: Latency to hard disk in milliseconds. The measurements are made using *nfiles* each of size *fsize*. The measurements in the first two rows are not valid.

```
20        clk.tic();
21        fread(&x,sizeof(double),1,fptr);
22        lat.fread_cycles=clk.toc();
23        clk.tic();
24        fclose(fptr);
25        lat.fclose_cycles = clk.toc();
26        return x;
27 }
```

The arguments to `latency2disk()` specify the directory and the file number (line 7). The file name is composed on line 10. The file is thought of as an array of `double`s, and `posn` (line 8) gives the position of the number to be retrieved in that array.

The function opens the file (line 14), seeks to the specified position (line 17), reads a `double` from the file (line 21), and closes the file (line 24).

Each of the four function calls is timed, and the number of cycles is saved in a `struct` (lines 1 to 6), which is passed by reference (line 8). The only new syntax here is `fseek()` for seeking to a new position in the file (line 17).

Table 4.8 was obtained on two different computers, differing by 3 to 4 years in age. On both computers, opening and closing a file is fast, taking only a few microseconds. On both computers, the total latency is of the order of 10 milliseconds. Latency changes very little from computer to computer or with time.

The total latency is limited by the seek time of the head assembly. Seek time of a hard disk refers to the time it takes for the head assembly to move between tracks of varying radii. This latency is of the order of milliseconds, and it takes of the order of 10 milliseconds for the hard disk platter to complete a rotation. Thus, it is clear that these are the parameters limiting latency to hard disk.

4.3.3   Bandwidth to disk

The functions `write_direct()` and `read_direct()` defined earlier in this section illustrated the use of `fwrite()` and `fread()`. These functions read or write a single array of `doubles`. A single array cannot exceed the available DRAM, although it is desirable to work with files much larger than the size of DRAM memory when estimating bandwidth to disk.

The function `write_direct()` is modified below to write to files that are much bigger than available memory.

```
void write_direct(double *v, long len,
          const char *fname){
    FILE *fptr;
    fptr = fopen(fname, "w");
    fwrite((void *)v, len, sizeof(double), fptr);
    for(int i=1; i < FLUSH_COUNT; i++)
        fwrite((void *)v, len, sizeof(double),
            fptr);
    fclose(fptr);
}
```

By setting `FLUSH_COUNT`, the array `v[]` is written to the same file multiple times. The purpose of using a large count is to flush the page cache. Linux provides the system call `fsync()` to flush the page cache, but we do not use it here.

As noted already, the page cache can run into several GB. If the system crashes before the dirty pages in the page cache are written back to disk, the file system will be left in an inconsistent state. Journaling file systems, such as ext4, record information about dirty pages on the disk. Journaling file systems can be restored to a consistent state much faster after a system crash.

Table 4.9 reports the read and write bandwidths for the same two computers as in table 4.8. The newer computer has nearly twice the bandwidth, although the latency is the same. Bandwidth to hard disk can be increased through greater storage density and parallelism. Bandwidth will increase with time in proportion to storage density and other parameters of the computer system.

Exercise 4.3.1. Write a program to determine the maximum size of the page cache on your system.

Device	fsize	Write	Read
HP-Z220	100GB	0.11	0.10
ThinkStation-P300	25 GB	0.19	0.19

Table 4.9: Bandwidth to hard disk in GB/s. The bandwidths are measured by writing to and then reading from a single file of size *fsize*.

Exercise 4.3.2. Write a program to demonstrate that the page cache that comes into existence when one program accesses a file speeds up reading of the same file by any other program.

4.4   Page tables and virtual memory

In this section, we make our first foray into the operating system kernel.[11] The cost of a single write to memory by an instruction such as `movq %rax, (%rsi)` brings in many layers of complexity. It could be a cache hit or a cache miss. If the DRAM memory is accessed, the cost of the access depends on preceding and following memory accesses. It depends on the manner in which the memory controllers operate the DRAM devices. It depends on the parallelism in the instruction stream. It depends on the pressure on dispatch ports in the instruction pipeline among other factors. On top of the layers of complexity engineered into hardware, the operating system introduces yet more complexity.

The operating system is a process manager and has the responsibility of laying down and enforcing the rules that govern nearly all activity on the computer. It creates the environment under which all processes run. It goes about its job so surreptitiously that its presence is ignored in most programming.

However, the activities of the operating system introduce a cost. The map from virtual memory addresses (generated by running programs) to physical DRAM memory is maintained by the operating system. A page is typically 4,096 bytes of virtual memory, as may be verified using the GNU/Linux command `getconf PAGESIZE`. The operating system creates page tables to map pages to page frames. A page frame is a 4,096-byte-long region of DRAM memory. As explained in section 4.1.3, before ac-

---

[11]Bovet and Cesati (2005) is a superb account of the workings of the Linux kernel and the chief source for this section.

cessing a word in DRAM memory, the processor uses page tables to convert a virtual address to a physical address. The operating system is invoked if there is a page fault or if the address is illegal.

Even ignoring page faults, having to look up the page tables every time a memory location is accessed introduces an overhead. At worst, as explained in section 4.1.3, each memory access can turn into two or more memory accesses. The processor cores use a Translation Lookaside Buffer (TLB) to eliminate this overhead. Programs that transpose and multiply matrices must be mindful of the TLB, as evident from earlier sections. Managing the TLB is one of the kernel's functions.

An account of program performance will be incomplete without discussion of the kernel's activities. The kernel plays a big role in managing memory, creating processes and threads, and scheduling threads. The kernel mediates between the processes and the network when processes running on remote computers take on a task in parallel.

A knowledge of the kernel's activities gives the programmer a better appreciation of the complex environment in which programs run. The occasional deterioration in performance will not seem so bizarre. The variation in performance from run to run will not seem inexplicable and erratic.

There is a self-referential quality to the operating system. The memory management unit is part of the kernel and resides in the memory that it manages. The kernel associates a memory descriptor with each process or thread to encapsulate its usage of memory. The memory descriptors are stored in memory accessible only to the kernel. The page tables map virtual memory to physical memory. The page tables themselves reside in memory. The virtual addresses of the region of memory holding the page tables are mapped to physical addresses by those very page tables.

Although it is a mere process manager, the operating system is far more complicated than almost any process or program. The operating system kernel is perhaps as complicated as any engineered system. Some of this complexity originates from the hardware environment the kernel manages. DRAM memory, network cards, hard disc, flash memory, graphics cards, monitors, and keyboards, along with many other parts of the computer, differ from each other as much as an airplane differs from a horse carriage. The kernel takes on the job of blending this cacophony of devices into a seamless computer system. Many of the parts, such as DRAM memory and the network, are quite complicated to operate. Some of the complexity arises from the need to guarantee a secure environment to processes and users. Some of the complexity is engineered. For example, the Linux kernel is monolithic. Every unit of the kernel and every device driver use the same virtual address space. Microkernel-based operating systems are more modular, but the coordination of and communication between microkernels incurs a penalty, which Linux is unwilling to pay.

Section 4.4.1 uses a simple program to show how a user program as well as the data it uses is laid out in virtual memory. This information can be useful, not least when interpreting error messages. Section 4.4.2 continues that discussion and shows how the kernel establishes itself in physical memory and then in virtual memory. Section 4.4.2 gives an overview of the paging system implemented jointly by the operating system and the hardware. Although that topic may appear a little advanced, its relevance to programming is beyond debate. Demand paging plays a big role in multithreaded programming and networking. TLB flushes, necessitated during some context switches, can be a source of considerable overhead. In addition, having a full overview of the virtual memory system helps understand the manner in which multiple threads coexist and communicate using shared memory—an important point, inasmuch as multithreaded programming appears set to be the major paradigm for the next few decades.

It has been stated that "memory management is by far the most complex activity" in the Linux kernel.[12] Our account of memory management will focus on the interaction between the hardware and operating system kernel.

4.4.1   Partitioning the virtual address space

Because a virtual address is 48 bits, a user process can in principle address 2^{48} or more than 64,000 GB of memory. The physical memory can be less than a thousandth of that figure. Much of virtual address space is an unclaimed wilderness. Figure 4.8 is an incomplete schematic view of the partitioning of the virtual address space of a typical user process. Much of the virtual address space is taken up by the unutilized regions shown as empty gaps.

The boundary shown as PAGE_OFFSET separates user code and data from the kernel. User code and data map to virtual addresses lower than PAGE_OFFSET. The kernel code and data are beyond it. Every process uses exactly the same value for PAGE_OFFSET, which is defined as a constant by the kernel. Therefore, the kernel oc-

---

[12]Bovet and Cesati (2005).

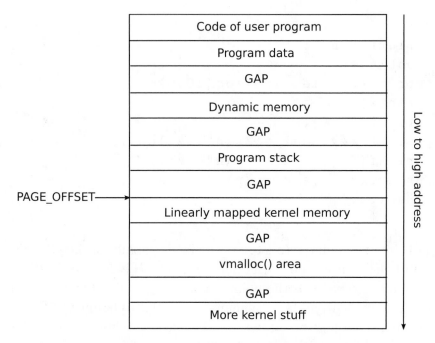

Figure 4.8: Schematic view of the virtual address space of a user process.

cupies exactly the same portion of virtual memory in every process. We will first look at the way the virtual memory addresses that precede `PAGE_OFFSET` are organized.

A simple C program can help us understand the way functions, local variables, global variables, and dynamically allocated memory are mapped to virtual address space. The complete listing of such a program follows.

```
1  #include <stdio.h>
2  #include <stdlib.h>
3  int global;
4  void f(){
5       double farray[512];
6       printf(" farray = %p\n", farray);
7  }
8  int main(){
9       double marray[512];
10      printf(" marray = %p\n", marray);
```

```
11          f();
12          printf("\n");
13          double *ptr;
14          ptr = (double *)malloc(1000);
15          printf("     ptr = %p\n", ptr);
16          printf("\n");
17          printf("&global = %p\n", &global);
18          printf("       f = %p\n", &f);
19          printf("    main = %p\n", &main);
20          free(ptr);
21  }
```

The program prints the pointer to global, defined globally on line 3, the pointer to the function f() defined on line 4, the pointer farray[] defined locally within f() on line 5, the pointer to main(), the pointer marray[] defined locally within main() on line 9, and ptr, which points to memory allocated dynamically on line 14. The printing is in order from highest address to the least. When compiling this function, one must remember to use the -fno-inline-functions option. If not, the compiler will likely eliminate the call to f() on line 11.

The following is output from a single run of this program.

```
marray = 0x7fffb6be1380
farray = 0x7fffb6be0370

   ptr = 0xc60010

&global = 0x604730
      f = 0x400ad0
   main = 0x400a00
```

Because marray[] is allocated on the stack, it has a high address as indicated in figure 4.8. The stack grows downward in virtual memory, and when a call is made to f(), the pointer farray has a lower value because of the downward growth of the stack. We will have more to say about stacks in the next chapter.

The lowest addresses belong to the locations that store the set of instructions compiled from main() and f(). The global variable defined on line 3 is allocated in the data region. As indicated in figure 4.8, the global data map to higher addresses than code.

The dynamically allocated memory is in between. The principle way to allocate memory dynamically is using `malloc()` in C. In C++, we may also use `new[]`. In some of our earlier examples, we used `_mm_malloc()` to force alignment of allocated memory at 16-byte boundaries, cache line boundaries, or page boundaries.

The sketch in figure 4.8 has omitted a few things, namely, shared libraries and variables local to threads. Like dynamically allocated memory, these are also mapped to virtual addresses higher than code and data regions and lower than the stack region.

Kernel code and data are mapped to addresses beyond `PAGE_OFFSET`. We will look at that mapping shortly.

4.4.2   Physical address space and page tables

Program speed is influenced by the paging system in several ways. Typically, 40% of the instructions are loads and stores, and each memory access involves the paging system. The TLB (translation look-aside buffer) is a shortcut past the huge overheads of the paging system. If a memory word is found in L1 cache and its virtual address is found in TLB, the latency of the memory access would be just 4 cycles. However, if there is a TLB miss, the latency can go up to several hundred cycles. If there is a page fault, the latency of a single memory access can go up to millions, even billions, of cycles. It is also true that the first access of a page in virtual memory always leads to a page fault, and the page fault handler is responsible for allocating a page frame in physical memory.

The paging system is responsible for protecting a program's memory from other programs and preventing programs from making illegal memory accesses. During a context switch, when the kernel evicts one process and schedules another, the kernel may need to flush the TLB (using a privileged instruction) to protect the address space of the processes. The TLB flush can be expensive. We will look at how the kernel and hardware work together to implement the paging system to get a sense of the overheads of the paging system.

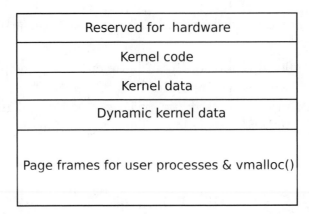

Figure 4.9: Simplified sketch of the kernel in physical memory.

Physical address space

Soon after the computer is powered on, the kernel starts running in real mode. In real mode, the kernel generates physical addresses directly. Its first job is to load itself completely into physical memory. The kernel can call the BIOS using the `int` (interrupt) instruction to find out about other devices in the system, read information from tables stored in specific areas of memory, or talk to the devices directly using special instructions. Any code that gets control of the computer in real mode can do almost anything it likes with the computer.

As shown in figure 4.9, the kernel is not allowed to use the lowest physical addresses for itself. That region of memory is used by BIOS and the hardware. The kernel loads itself in a low address region of physical memory. In addition to the physical memory used by initialized kernel data and code at startup, the kernel will need to dynamically allocate memory as more threads and processes are created. The memory claimed dynamically by the kernel is marked "dynamic kernel data" in figure 4.9.

The virtual memory region marked "linearly mapped kernel memory" in figure 4.8, just beyond `PAGE_OFFSET`, is mapped to the chunk of physical memory the kernel reserves for its own exclusive usage. This mapping is the same for all processes and does not change as long as the computer is powered on. Furthermore, this mapping is linear. The virtual address is converted to a physical address by subtracting a constant.

The areas marked "kernel code," "kernel data," and "dynamic kernel data" in the schematic sketch of figure 4.9 hold page frames that are linearly mapped. The linearly mapped page frames extend monotonically in physical address space (except for memory regions reserved for BIOS, hardware, and other purposes). When the kernel attempts to claim a page frame dynamically and extend the linearly mapped region of address space, it may come into conflict with a user process that has already claimed the page frame the kernel needs. Resolving this conflict will be expensive as the kernel has to map the user's page to some other page frame or swap it to disc before claiming the page frame for itself. The kernel keeps a few free page frames handy so that it can service urgent requests quickly.

After the kernel has established itself in memory and created some of the data structures, such as an initial set of page tables, it will enter "protected" mode by loading a specific value into the `cr0` register. The paging system is turned on in protected mode, and all references to memory are now interpreted as virtual addresses. The virtual addresses are converted to physical addresses by the paging system.

When the kernel needs more memory for its own use, it can get the memory in three different ways. The first method is to request more pages using `alloc_pages()` or another equivalent facility. The pages allocated in this way will be in the linearly mapped region just beyond `PAGE_OFFSET` in virtual memory. The kernel associates a kernel stack with each process that allows it to execute system calls and handle interrupts. The kernel stack is typically two pages or 8,096 bytes and it is allocated using `alloc_pages()`. The memory claimed by `alloc_pages()` is linearly mapped.

The second method the kernel uses for claiming memory is `kmalloc()`. The memory claimed using `kmalloc()` is also linearly mapped. Many a time, the kernel needs memory in much smaller units than a page, for example, when creating process descriptors, memory region descriptors, or page descriptors. The kernel uses `kmalloc()` in such circumstances.

A third method is used for loading modules and related activities. In Linux, device drivers are loaded as modules. The kernel programmer has no way of estimating in advance how many devices there could be on the system or how big the device drivers could be in size. Some of the network card and graphics card drivers can be quite complicated. The kernel claims space for such modules and their activities using `vmalloc()`. The page frames (physical memory) claimed by `vmalloc()` come from the general pool, and the virtual addresses are in the "vmalloc" area shown in figure 4.8. The map to page frames is not linear. The page tables must be changed after calling `vmalloc()`.

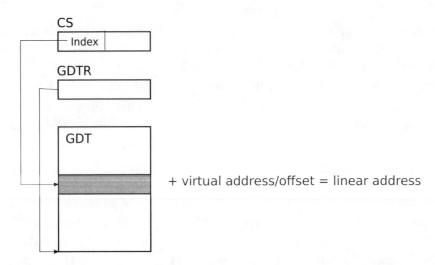

Figure 4.10: Conversion of a virtual address/offset to a linear address. Here cs (code segment) and gdtr are system registers, and GDT is the global descriptor table. The code segment register also has information about the privilege level of the process.

The monolithic Linux kernel uses the same map to physical memory for every virtual address beyond PAGE_OFFSET. Every kernel function and module uses the same virtual address space.

Page tables

Figure 4.10 shows how the linear addresses are generated. In Linux, linear and virtual addresses are practically identical, and the conversion of a virtual address to a linear address is heavily optimized so as to be essentially cost-free. We do not distinguish between the two.

The global descriptor table of figure 4.10 is set up by the operating system kernel. It comes into play whenever the processor switches from a user program to the operating system kernel. A process may issue a system call using either the int 0x80 or sysenter instructions. Any external device can cause an interrupt. Internal events such as page faults trigger exceptions. When any of these events happen, the processor uses the %tr task register (also set up by the kernel) to index into the global descriptor table and locate the address of the kernel stack. The hardware switches %rsp to the kernel stack before handing control to the kernel.

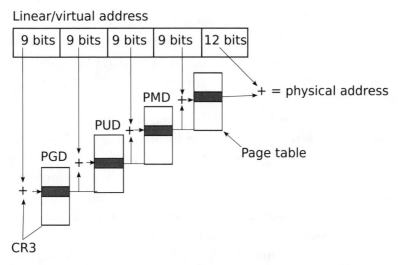

Figure 4.11: Page table look up using a virtual address. The `cr3` register holds a pointer to the base of the PGD table.

Figure 4.11 shows the way page tables are organized. It is the kernel's job to set up the PGD, PUD, PMD, and page table shown in that figure for each process. The sheer complexity of storing a multilevel table in memory shows why a TLB that bypasses page table lookup is essential.

Every process has its own page tables. When a process is created, the operating system has to set up page tables for it. The page tables of each process map valid virtual addresses below as well as above `PAGE_OFFSET` to physical memory. When the process makes a system call or if the kernel takes over to handle an interrupt or exception, it uses the page tables of the preempted process. It is illegal for a user process to generate a virtual address above `PAGE_OFFSET`. However, the kernel generates such addresses and uses the page tables of the user process to map them to physical memory.

The kernel has a reference set of page tables mapping virtual addresses above `PAGE_OFFSET`. When a process is created, that information is incorporated into the process's page tables.

If a process defines an array locally or if it claims memory dynamically, it is allocated a chunk of memory in the virtual address space. Thus, the extent of the virtual address space a process may legally address changes as it runs. The virtual addresses are not mapped to page frames in physical memory as soon as they are allocated. The kernel waits until the first memory reference, which results in page fault because no page frame has been assigned. The page fault handler finds a free page frame, assigns it to the page, and updates the page tables. This is known as demand paging.

Demand paging has its uses. For example, when several threads are using the same virtual address space, the kernel or, more specifically, the page fault handler can map a page to the memory channel that is as close as possible to the processor core that generates the first access. This "first touch policy" can be exploited in a program to improve bandwidth to memory, as we show in the next chapter.

A consequence of demand paging is that a set of contiguous pages in virtual memory can be mapped to page frames scattered all over physical memory. Neighboring cache lines in virtual memory may be quite far away from each other in physical address space if the cache lines cross a page boundary.

Exercise 4.4.1. Explain why all processes cannot use the same page tables for virtual addresses above `PAGE_OFFSET`.

Exercise 4.4.2. Explain why certain parts of the kernel should never be swapped out to hard disc.

Exercise 4.4.3. Is `%cr3` (see figure 4.11) the virtual or physical address of the base of the global page directory?

4.5   References

D.P. Bovet and M. Cesati. *Understanding the Linux Kernel.* O'Reilly, Sebastopol, California, 3rd edition, 2005.

V. Bubka and P. Tuma. Investigating cache parameters of x86 processors. In D. Kaeli and K. Sachs, editors, *SPEC Benchmark Workshop 2009*, LNCS 5419, pages 77–96. Springer-Verlag, New York, 2009.

M. Frigo, C.E. Leiserson, H. Prokop, and S. Ramachandran. Cache oblivious algorithms. *Foundations of Computer Science, 40th Annual Symposium*, pages 285–297, 1999.

S. Goto and R. A. van de Geijn. Anatomy of high performance matrix multiplication. *ACM TOMS*, 34:art:12, 2008.

J.L. Hennessy and D.A. Patterson. *Computer Architecture: A Quantitative Approach.* Morgan Kaufmann, San Francisco, 1st-5th edition, 1990-2011.

B. Jacob, S. Ng, and D. Wang. *Memory Systems: Cache, DRAM, Disk.* Morgan Kaufmann, San Francisco, 2008.

D. Molka, D. Hackenberg, R. Shöne, and M.S. Müller. Memory performance and cache coherency effects on an intel nehalem multiprocessor system. *18th International Conference on Parallel Architectures and Compilation Techniques*, pages 261–270, 2009.

Chapter 5

Threads and Shared Memory

Programming with threads is a paradigm of great range and utility that encompasses everything from cell phones to web servers to supercomputers. The processor cores of today are clocked at around the same rate as the processor cores of 2005. However, the number of processor cores on the same package continues to increase dramatically. In addition, multiple processor packages can be connected using a fast interconnect. All the processors in the interconnected processor packages share the same DRAM memory. Nodes with multiple processor cores are so powerful that problems with a billion grid points can be tackled on a single node. Multithreaded programming is set to remain a leading programming paradigm.

This chapter is organized into four sections. Section 5.1 is an introduction to OpenMP. OpenMP is an industry standard that enables programming with threads. It is implemented by `icpc`, `gcc`, `pgcc`, and other compilers. One only needs to add an option such as `-openmp` and `-fopenmp` during compilation and linking if OpenMP syntax is used. The syntax is so simple that the transition to threaded programming is easy and barely noticeable. All of OpenMP syntax used much of the time can be made to fit into half a page or less.

OpenMP programs are written as if they are sequential. To begin with, there is a single thread of execution. Whenever the program enters a parallel region, multiple threads come alive. Because memory is shared between threads, the different threads can split the work between them. They can either operate on the same locations in memory or split the memory between themselves.

Although the OpenMP syntax is simple, sharing memory between threads has many pitfalls that can trip up the novice as well as the experienced programmer. Suppose we define a variable `var` to be an `int`. If this is a shared variable and one of the threads does `var+=1`, it is natural to assume that the update in the value of `var` is seen by all the threads. That assumption can be wrong, however. The variable `var` may be stored in a register, and the update on one thread may *never* be propagated to the other threads.

The memory issues that arise in threaded programming are exceedingly intricate, subtle, and deceptive. Even the simplest OpenMP program that uses multiple threads to add a list of numbers relies on the OpenMP memory model in ways that are not always appreciated. In section 5.1, we explain OpenMP's memory model thoroughly.

Section 5.2 introduces techniques to optimize OpenMP programs. Most of these techniques are minor modifications of techniques for memory access already seen in the last chapter. There is only one substantially new point that arises. Although all processor cores on a computing node have access to all the memory (DRAM) on that node, some of the memory is closer to some processor cores and far away from others. As may be expected, accesses of near memory are faster. It is important to make sure that memory mainly accessed by a certain processor core is close to it.

The nonuniformity of access between near and far memory can be dealt with during memory initialization, as explained in section 5.2. However, it is a definite negative as far as program modularity is concerned. Program modularity is promoted by uniformity of access, where the cost of memory access is independent of which processor is accessing which region of memory. If memory access is uniform, the subdivision of a task between multiple processors can stay closer to logic intrinsic to the problem domain. Nonuniform memory access burdens memory initialization with an interpretation that is completely extrinsic to the problem domain and dependent only on the conveniences and constraints of hardware design.

The unwary are apt to assume that a computer with 12 cores is 12 times faster than a computer with one core. Bandwidth to memory does not increase linearly with the number of processor cores, and most significant programs are limited by bandwidth to memory, as explained in section 5.2.

Although OpenMP is of much utility in scientific computing, it is a limited framework. It applies mainly in those situations where the data layout is static and access patterns are regular. In these situations, one can think of a parallel program as a sequential program that splits naturally between threads every time a parallel region is entered. This model is totally inapplicable to web servers, for example, where every thread does its own thing, according to the demands placed on it by its client, and interacts with other threads in complex ways.

When scientific computing was dominated by classical physics, the types of problems that arose fit reasonably well into the OpenMP framework. However, newer and growing areas of scientific computing, such as genomics and data science, have some of the qualities of computer science applications. Problems in such areas may not be as complex and dynamic as web servers or Internet applications, but a trend in that direction is undeniable.

In section 5.3, we look at Pthreads, which are a far more fundamental way to program with threads than OpenMP. Pthreads can be used for everything from web servers to scientific applications. In fact, Pthreads help us understand OpenMP better.

The treatment of Pthreads in section 5.3 exhibits interactions between threads and computer architecture. Cache coherence is essential for threaded programming. However, if several threads share the same cache line, there can be considerable overhead in propagating writes from one cache to another. TLB flushes can incur overheads when threads of different applications share the same core. In addition, section 5.3 explores the overhead of thread creation and briefly introduces memory fences.

Much of the complexity of threaded programming is the complexity of sharing memory between concurrent threads. In section 5.4, we take a look at the organization of program memory into stacks and heaps. We explain how recursion works. Segmentation faults are the bane of C/C++ programming, and dealing with them occupies much of the programmer's time. In section 5.4, we make another excursion into the Linux kernel and explain exactly how these segmentation faults are triggered.

As in the previous chapters, we run programs on SSE2, AVX, and AVX2 platforms (see tables 3.1 and A.1). As far as what we say about program optimization is concerned, there is no great difference between any of these machines, or with AVX-512 machines that are set to appear in the future.

5.1   Introduction to OpenMP

Section 5.1.1 introduces OpenMP.[1] Nearly all the syntax that most programmers will ever need is brought out by parallelizing the summation of the Leibniz series in two different ways.

OpenMP programs look much like sequential programs, and the syntax is easy to learn. The simplicity is mostly illusory, however. Whenever concurrent programs share memory, as OpenMP programs do, the programming model inevitably becomes very subtle. OpenMP syntax conceals much of this subtlety behind a sophisticated memory model. Every OpenMP programmer would be well advised to understand this memory model. The correctness of even the simplest OpenMP program relies on it. The memory model is discussed in section 5.1.2.

Section 5.1.3 is about the overheads associated with OpenMP parallel regions and other constructs. When a task is divided between threads using OpenMP, the division itself will incur overhead. If this overhead is too great relative to the size of the task, the task may not be worth parallelizing. OpenMP parallelism works best at a coarse level and for outer regions of the program. One may think of a program as being essentially sequential and split certain tasks within that sequential flow between threads using OpenMP constructs. Where and whether such a split makes sense or not is entirely determined by OpenMP overheads.

In section 5.1.3, we describe the implementation of mutual exclusion on x86 machines. Mutual exclusion is so fundamental to threaded programming that the x86 instruction set has supported it for many decades. Much of the overhead of OpenMP constructs is incurred through instructions related to mutual exclusion.

5.1.1   OpenMP syntax

OpenMP syntax is beguilingly simple. A simple function for computing the nth partial sum of the Leibniz series follows:

```
double leibniz(long int n){
      long int i;
      double ans=4.0;
```

---

[1] The website *www.openmp.org* has a document titled "OpenMP Application Program Interface" describing the OpenMP standard. Chapman et al. (2008) is an easily paced introduction to OpenMP.

```
for(i=1; i < n; i=i+2){
      ans -= 4.0/(2.0*i+1);
      ans += 4.0/(2.0*i+3);
}
return ans;
}
```

As it is written, this function runs on a single processor core. We will rewrite it to run on multiple cores using OpenMP. By writing the OpenMP program in different ways, we expose much of the basic syntax of OpenMP. There is a lot more syntax to OpenMP than we will discuss here, but much of it is hardly ever needed. OpenMP constructs are embedded into C or C++ code. The GNU, Intel, and PGI compilers support OpenMP. With icpc, the option -openmp must be used during compilation and linking. For gcc/g++, the corresponding option is -fopenmp.

A single important OpenMP construct does not arise (explicitly) in the two ways of summing the Leibniz series we explore. This is the

```
#pragma omp barrier
```

construct. OpenMP allows the programmer to embed statements such as this in C or C++ programs. In such constructs, omp is an abbreviation of OpenMP and #pragma is a compiler directive.

If a running thread encounters a barrier, it must stop until all other threads in the same team have also arrived at the same barrier. The threads get in sync at a barrier construct. If the program is parallelized in phases, and each phase must wait for the preceding phase to complete before it begins, we must use barrier constructs in between phases. For example, if one phase of the program assembles a stiffness matrix in parallel and another phase solves the stiffness matrix, the two phases must be separated by a barrier construct in principle. In practice, however, there are implicit barriers in a number of OpenMP constructs such as parallel for and parallel, as we will see, and only rarely is the barrier construct needed.

omp parallel for

The simplest way to sum the Leibniz series in OpenMP is to use the parallel for directive.

```
1        double ans=0;
2  #pragma omp parallel for                        \
3        reduction(+:ans)
4        for(long int i=0; i < n; i = i+2)
5            {
6                    ans += 4.0/(2*i+1);
7                    ans -= 4.0/(2*i+3);
8            }
```

Except for lines 2 and 3, this could be a sequential program to sum the Leibniz series. Line 2 is the **parallel for** construct, which specifies that the for-block extending from lines 4 through 8 must be parallelized. When the program encounters this statement, it splits into multiple threads. Each thread will execute a chunk of the iterations of the for-loop.

The **reduction** clause on line 3 is of much importance. It states that **ans** is a reduction variable that is tagged +. The compiler understands that each thread should compute its own **ans**, and the result from all the threads should be reduced into a single **ans** using addition.

An attractive feature of OpenMP is that parallel programs can be written using syntax that is close to that of sequential programs. The programmer is asked to make only minimal adjustments to write parallel programs, although these adjustments can be quite subtle and their simplicity a major pitfall.

Not every for-loop can be parallelized using the OpenMP **parallel for** construct. The compiler has to be able to look at the for-loop and generate the code for the for-loop that is to be executed by each thread. The for-loops that can be parallelized are said to be in canonical form. The complete definition of for-loops in canonical form is too complicated to be useful for anyone except compiler writers. It is usually possible to tell whether a for-loop is in canonical form by looking.

Even when a for-loop is in canonical form, one has to make sure that there are no dependencies between successive iterations of the loop. If the later iterations depend on the execution of an earlier iteration, the loop cannot be parallelized correctly. An example of a for-loop with a dependency across iterations is the following:

```
factorial[0] = 1;
for(int i=1; i < n; i++)
    factorial[i] = i*factorial[i-1];
```

This loop is in canonical form. If the OpenMP `for` construct is used, the compiler will be able to break it up syntactically into a separate loop for every thread. However, the result will be incorrect. To respect the loop-carried RAW dependency, every iteration has to wait for the previous iteration to be complete. That does not happen when the for-loop is split and the threads start executing their share of the iterations in parallel. Applying the `parallel for` construct to this for-loop results in an incorrect program.

There is an implicit barrier at the end of the OpenMP `parallel for` construct. Due to the implicit barrier, we may think of the for-loop as part of a sequential program that is executed in parallel by multiple threads.

In much of OpenMP programming, one does not need to go beyond `parallel for`. However, the `parallel for` as shown makes a number of implicit assumptions. Those assumptions are made explicit below using less concise syntax:

```
1  double parallelfor(long int n, int nthreads){
2        assert(nthreads%2==0);
3        double ans=0;
4  #pragma omp parallel for                      \
5        num_threads(nthreads)                   \
6        schedule(static)                        \
7        default(none)                           \
8        shared(n)                               \
9        reduction(+:ans)
10       for(long int i=0; i < n; i = i+2)
11           {
12                   ans += 4.0/(2*i+1);
13                   ans -= 4.0/(2*i+3);
14           }
15       return ans;
16 }
```

The `parallel for` on line 4 and the `reduction` clause on line 9 are the same as before. The `parallel for` construct (or compiler directive) applies to the entire for-loop from lines 10 through 14.

The `num_threads()` clause on line 5 specifies the number of threads to be created. Here we have required `nthreads`, which is an argument to `parallelfor()`, to be even.

If the `num_threads` clause is omitted, by default, the number of threads is usually the number of processor cores. It may be set to some other value using the shell variable `OMP_NUM_THREADS`. Relying on the default behavior is simpler and better most of the time.

The `schedule()` clause on line 6 tells the compiler how to split the for-loop across threads. The scheduling option is given as `static`. Static scheduling, which we describe presently, is the most useful in practice and the default. Assuming n to be even, the loop variable i of the for-loop on line 10 steps through the list of values

$$0, 2, \ldots, n - 2.$$

Because the schedule is given as `static` on line 6, each thread will get a contiguous set of iterations of roughly the same size. For example, if there are N threads, each thread gets approximately n/N iterations, and the iterations of thread number t extend from $i \approx t \times n/N$ to $i \approx (t + 1) \times n/N$. Other schedules are possible. The iterations can be assigned in a round robin fashion or dynamically.

Variables declared within the parallel block are private to each thread. Therefore, the variable `i`, which is declared on line 10, is unique to each thread.

The question arises whether variable names such as `ans` and `n` that occur within the parallel block, but are declared and defined outside the block, are names for the same location in memory. Such variables may be shared or unused (or even private—but it is hard to think of a meaningful use of this feature) in the parallel block. One can make all the variables defined outside the parallel block into shared variables using the clause `default(shared)`. In this example, the clause `default(none)` on line 7 is used to say that the variables declared outside are not visible inside the parallel block by default. The clause on line 8 declares that the variable `n` is visible inside the block and shared by all the threads. The variable `ans` is not marked as shared because it is a reduction variable.

omp critical

The `omp critical` construct is similar to `omp barrier` in the following way. Both are rarely used constructs yet important to understand. The `barrier` construct is important to understand because it occurs implicitly at the end of parallel regions, enabling us to think of OpenMP programs as sequential programs with parallel regions. Critical regions are employed implicitly whenever reduction variables are used and the `critical` construct makes critical regions explicit.

The `ompfor()` function listed below introduces the eponymous `omp for` construct and the `omp parallel` directive in addition to `omp critical`.

```
1  double ompfor(long int n){
2        double ans=0;
3  #pragma omp parallel                                    \
4        default(none)                                     \
5        shared(n, ans)
6        {
7              double sum=0;
8  #pragma omp for
9              for(long int i=0; i < n; i = i+2)
10                 {
11                       sum += 4.0/(2*i+1);
12                       sum -= 4.0/(2*i+3);
13                 }
14 #pragma omp critical
15             ans += sum;
16        }
17        return ans;
18 }
```

The parallel directive on line 3 applies to the block (or region) that begins on line 6 and ends on line 16. This block will be executed in parallel by each of the threads.

The `default(none)` clause on line 4 states that no variable is shared by default. In this parallel region, both **n** and **ans** are declared as shared by the **shared()** clause on line 5. We have made all that explicit to give an example of syntax in which multiple variables are declared as shared.

The variable **sum** defined on line 7 is local to each thread. The `omp for` construct on line 8 splits the for-loop extending from lines 9 through 13 between the threads. The threads are already in a parallel region when the for-loop is encountered. Therefore, the `parallel for` construct must not be used. The `omp for` compiler directive on line 8, which splits the for-loop between threads without creating new threads, is appropriate here. Each thread adds its total into **sum**, which is local to itself.

The `critical` construct on line 14 applies to the block immediately following, which in this case is simply line 15, which is `ans += sum`. On this line, every thread adds its local `sum` to `ans`. Because `ans` is a shared variable, the threads may overwrite each other if they access it simultaneously. The `critical` construct ensures that the threads take turns in executing line 15. Whenever a reduction variable is used, critical regions are employed implicitly.

By definition, critical regions are mutually exclusive, and only one thread can occupy a critical region at any one time. This is true even if the critical regions encountered by the threads are not the same syntactically.[2]

There can be no doubt that the earlier `parallel for` syntax is simpler. Indeed, that should be the preferred syntax in most situations. However, the more complex `ompfor()` is twice as fast as `parallelfor()` on the 3.6 GHz AVX2 machine, although they are equally fast on the 2.2 GHz AVX machine (see table A.1). Here we are seeing the same point for the umpteenth time: although the hardware on newer machines is faster, the compilers are yet to catch up.

There is an implicit barrier at the end of each parallel region and at the end of an `omp for` block. Thus, in `ompfor()`, there are implicit barriers on lines 13 and 16. The parallel region comes to end on line 13, and beyond that point there is only one thread (the master thread). In summary, implicit barriers are found at the end of parallel regions and `omp for` constructs, but no implicit barrier occurs at the beginning of a parallel region or in a `critical` construct.

Some more syntax

The OpenMP library defines the function

```
int omp_get_thread_num();
```

which returns the thread number of the calling thread. The thread number is 0 for the master thread. If the number of threads is N, the threads are numbered $0, 1, \ldots, N-1$. The library also defines the function

```
int omp_get_num_threads();
```

---

[2]OpenMP allows finer control of mutual exclusion when the critical regions are named. The critical region that follows `#pragma omp critical` on line 14 is unnamed.

which returns the total number of threads in a parallel region when called by any thread. Calls of these functions are legal only inside parallel regions. They may not be called from functions that are called from parallel regions. However, the `critical` construct can be used even in functions called from parallel regions.

In addition to the two functions above, constructs such as `omp master`, `omp section`, and `omp ordered` are occasionally useful.

5.1.2 Shared variables and OpenMP's memory model

Let us look again at the `critical` construct.

```
#pragma omp critical
        ans += sum;
```

As stated earlier, the `critical` construct ensures that the statement `ans += sum` is executed by only one thread at a time. That might seem sufficient to ensure the correctness of the program because each thread will separately add its local sum to the final answer, but it is not.

The compiler may decide to store the variable `ans` in a register and add its local sum to a register when `ans += sum` executes. The code for copying the register to the memory location of `ans` may be inserted *after* the critical block. In that case, we are back to the situation where the threads interfere with each other.

Why is that not a problem? In answering this question, we arrive at the `flush` feature, which is a vital part of the OpenMP memory model. When a thread has a shared variable such as `ans`, it is allowed to keep a copy of that variable in a register. Indeed, when the compiler generates assembly instructions, it may keep multiple copies of the same variable in memory and in the register file for its convenience. When an OpenMP `flush` operation is executed, a thread must make all its writes visible to other threads even if the writes have only modified locally stored copies of a shared variable. The temporary view of all shared variables must be synced with the global view in shared memory.

The OpenMP standard requires that a thread should implicitly carry out a `flush` operation when it enters and leaves a critical or parallel construct, and at each barrier it encounters. Even the basic program for summing the Leibniz series relies on this rule for its correctness. Each thread syncs its local copy of `ans` with the global copy in shared memory when it enters the critical region, updates its local copy in the critical region, and syncs the updated value with the global copy of **ans** in shared memory before it exits the critical region.

A more complex example

The OpenMP memory model is in play every time threads use a shared variable to communicate directly or indirectly. For finding the partial sum of the Leibniz series, the threads communicate indirectly using a shared variable to which each thread adds its part of the sum. The correctness of almost every OpenMP program depends on **flush** operations that are implicitly carried out at the beginning and end of parallel and critical constructs and at every barrier.

In general, OpenMP allows the compiler to generate assembly for a parallel region or for chunks of a for-loop assigned to a thread, as if the code is sequential—except for implicit **flush** statements. Of course, the compiler must also handle reduction variables correctly.

The peculiar implications of the OpenMP memory model can be difficult to grasp with just a single example. Therefore, we give another more complex example here. The variable **x** is the only variable shared by the two threads created by the function **printstuff()**, whose listing follows.

```
1  void printstuff(){
2      int x;
3  #pragma omp parallel            \
4      num_threads(2)          \
5      default(none)           \
6      shared(x)
7      {
8          int tid = omp_get_thread_num();
9          if(tid==0){
10             x = 0;
11         }
12         else if(tid==1){
13             x = 1;
14             printf("x = %d\t", x);
15             printf("x = %d\n", x);
16         }
```

```
17            }
18  }
```

The parallel region extends from lines 7 to 17. The thread with `tid` (abbreviation of thread identifier) equal to 1 prints the shared variable `x` on lines 14 and 15.

The function `printstuff()` may print $x = 0$, $x = 0$ if thread 0 executes line 10 after thread 1 executes line 13 but before it prints on lines 14 and 15. If thread 1 executes line 13 after thread 0 executes line 10, the function prints $x = 1$, $x = 1$. A little thought will show that $x = 1$, $x = 0$ is another possibility.

A legal compilation of `printstuff()` may produce behavior that is different from picking one of these three possibilities, but that is illustrative of the implications of OpenMP's memory model.

The function may even print $x = 0$, $x = 1$. Because the compiler is allowed to treat the parallel region as if it were sequential, it may store x in a register R in addition to the memory location `x`. The assignment on line 13 may update both the register R and the memory location. The first print statement on line 14 may access x using the shared memory location `x`, and the print statement that follows may access x using the register R. It may seem idiosyncratic for the compiler to generate such code. But the point here is that generating such code is legal if the parallel region is treated as sequential code. If the compiler generates such code, the function may print $x = 0$, $x = 1$.

Alternatively, both the print statements may access x using the register R. If so, the function will always print $x = 1$, $x = 1$.

5.1.3   Overheads of OpenMP constructs

OpenMP constructs are embedded into C/C++ programs to create teams of threads that work in parallel. The parallel, barrier, and for constructs introduce overheads. Work may need to be assigned to threads, threads may need to be created and destroyed, or synchronization and serialization may need to be implemented using system calls to the operating system kernel. These activities consume cycles. If the parallelized task is too small, the benefits of parallelization will be overwhelmed by the overheads. Effective programming requires knowledge of the overheads of OpenMP constructs.

Table 5.1 reports the overhead of entering and exiting from a parallel region. The entries of the table are based on many invocations of the following program:

Computer	Number of Cores/Threads	min	median	max
3.6 GHz AVX2	2	1176	1332	3.4×10^6
2.6 GHz SSE2	12	4888	6188	3.2×10^6
2.2 GHz AVX	16	5025	6573	1.8×10^7

Table 5.1: Overhead (in cycles) of the parallel construct on three different computers. For the full names of the machines, see table A.1 of the appendix.

```
1  void parallelA(int nthreads, StatVector& stats){
2      TimeStamp clk;
3      clk.tic();
4  #pragma omp parallel                                    \
5      num_threads(nthreads)                               \
6      default(none)
7      {
8          dummy();
9      }
10     double cycles = clk.toc();
11     stats.insert(cycles);
12 }
```

Every call of parallelA() enters and exits from a parallel region. The master thread times the entire parallel region and inserts the cycle count into the stats object on line 11. The parallel regions consists of a single call to dummy() on line 8. As its name suggests, dummy() does nothing. Its definition

```
void dummy(){}
```

is stashed in a separate compilation unit to force the compiler to generate a function call in the parallel region. The statistics of entering and exiting the parallel region are accumulated in the stats object after a large number of calls to parallelA().

Several points emerge from table 5.1. The worst case is much worse than the median cost (or the mean cost—median and mean are approximately equal). The median or mean cost of a parallel region is in the thousands of cycles. The worst cost is of the order of millions of cycles. The worst case occurs at the first entry to parallel region and only occasionally later on, for reasons that will be explained later. It is

Number of Threads	Barrier	for	for with nowait
1	26	66	36
2	1178	1401	93
3	1250	1451	101
4	1671	1758	96
6	2427	2555	100
8	2710	2731	99
10	2346	2458	99
12	2516	2415	101
16 (2.2 GHz AVX)	3262	3743	371

Table 5.2: Overheads of OpenMP constructs reported as number of cycles. All the entries of this table are for a 2.6 GHz SSE2 machine, except the last, which is for a 2.2 GHz AVX machine (see table A.1 for the full names of the machines).

important not to change the number of threads between parallel regions. Doing so will trigger the worst-case cost. The reason for that will also become clear later.

Thus, assuming all parallel regions use the same number of threads, the cost we have to contend with is the median or mean cost, which is in the thousands of cycles. The median cost is much lower for the two-core machine than for the 12-core or the 16-core machines (see table 5.1). The two core machine has only one processor package for both cores. In the other two machines, the cores are split between two processor packages (as in figures 3.6 and 4.2b). More processor packages implies greater cost.

The typical cost of around 5,000 cycles for a parallel region is not prohibitive. Even a for-loop that iterates 10^5 or 10^6 times may be parallelized effectively. However, an inner loop that iterates only 100 or 1,000 times cannot be parallelized effectively. The overhead of entering and leaving the parallel region will overwhelm any benefit from parallelization. Thus, OpenMP parallelism is not as fine in scale as the parallelism involved in XMM/YMM/ZMM registers (see table 3.1) or the instruction pipeline.

Table 5.2 reports the overheads of the `barrier` and `for` constructs. The programs for calculating these overheads are similar to the one we just saw. Therefore, the programs are not listed.

The most striking inference from table 5.2 is that most of the cost of the `omp for` construct seems to be due to the implicit barrier at the end of the construct. To confirm that is indeed so, we modified the for construct slightly. In particular, the `nowait` clause was added to the `omp for` construct. The `nowait` clause removes the implicit barrier at the end of the for construct. The last column of table 5.2 shows that of the `omp for` construct with the `nowait` clause has an overhead of around 100 cycles and no more. The `omp for` construct is virtually cost free if the implicit barrier at the end of the construct is removed.

Comparing tables 5.1 and 5.2, it becomes clear that the cost of entering and leaving a parallel region too is due to a considerable extent to the implicit barrier at exit. The implicit memory `flush` occurs during entry/exit of parallel regions but does not apply to the `omp for` construct. Therefore, parallel regions are somewhat more expensive.

As far as understanding the cost of parallel regions and other OpenMP constructs is concerned, we are left with two questions. The first is regarding the high cost in millions of cycles that occurs during the first entry into a parallel region, or whether the number of threads in a parallel region is changed, and rarely otherwise. The other is regarding the cost of a barrier. We will address the first question later, when we study Pthreads. The cost of a barrier is due to the way mutual exclusion is enforced, and we turn to it right now.

Mutual exclusion on x86 computers

The x86 instruction set provides instructions to simplify the implementation of mutual exclusion and critical regions. One of these instructions is `XCHG`. The `XCHG` instruction swaps a register with a memory location and is guaranteed to be atomic. Suppose the memory location is a lock variable named `lockvar`. If the lock variable is 0, it means no process is in the critical region. If the lock variable is 1, it means some process is in the critical region. To enter the critical region, a process will set some register, say `EAX`, to 1. Next it exchanges `EAX` and `lockvar` using `XCHG`. If the value that is exchanged into `EAX` is 0, the process enters the critical region with the assurance that it set `lockvar` to be 1 and the critical region is now locked. In contrast, if the value that is exchanged into `EAX` is 1, it means some other process has locked the critical region. The recommended way (from Intel) to enter the critical region is as follows:

```
SpinLock:
      CMP $0, lockvar
      JE GetLock
```

```
        PAUSE
        JMP  SpinLock
     GetLock:
        MOV  $1 , EAX
        XCHG  lockvar , EAX
        CMP  $0 , EAX
        JNE  SpinLock
```

This code avoids executing XCHG too frequently and uses PAUSE inside the loop. The protocol for exiting the critical region is much simpler: MOV $0, lockvar. This solution works with any number of competing processes or threads.

This little segment of code gives insight into the cost of a barrier. A single access of lockvar will involve cost that is of the order of latency to memory. Thus, the cost of a barrier is equal to a multiple of the latency to memory. The multiple depends on how many threads need to be synchronized. One method of implementing a barrier would be for each thread to enter a critical region and increment a shared variable to notify others of its presence. A more efficient implementation may pair off the threads in a binary tree and synchronize by walking up to the root of the tree.

There are two distinct families of solutions to the mutual exclusion problem. One family uses busy waiting. The use of XCHG is of that type. Another family of solutions is wait-free. Classical semaphores and mutexes are of that type. In wait-free synchronization, a process or thread gives up the processor core and goes to sleep when it is waiting. It is woken up again when some condition flag has changed. Because wait-free synchronization involves putting processes or threads to sleep and then waking them up, it necessarily involves the scheduling function of the operating system kernel. Device drivers typically use wait-free synchronization to access shared resources. In contrast, interrupt handlers are not allowed to go to sleep and must use spinlocks if they need to synchronize or serialize.

Exercise 5.1.1. Write an OpenMP program in which threads print their identifiers in reverse order.

Exercise 5.1.2. Write an OpenMP program that reverses an array in place. How long should the array be before OpenMP parallelism proves advantageous?

Exercise 5.1.3. Write an OpenMP program that calls qsort() defined in the C library from each thread. The sections of the array that are sorted by each thread are merged to complete sorting the entire array. The easy way to do a merge is to leave it all to the master thread. A more sophisticated way is to merge pairwise while assigning the pairs to different threads. Time and compare the two sorting routines, with two different ways of doing a merge, with a single threaded sort.

If the merge is implemented pairwise, it could be important to ensure that the number of threads in the parallel regions remains the same, even if some threads remain inactive. Explain why that could be the case.

Exercise 5.1.4. An array, or equivalently a pointer to its first entry, is a shared variable. Array entries are modified independently by different threads using the same pointer. Is an OpenMP `flush` essential to make such changes made by one thread visible to the other threads?

Exercise 5.1.5. Write an OpenMP program to find the minimum entry of an array using the `parallel for` construct with an appropriate reduction clause.

5.2   Optimizing OpenMP programs

In OpenMP, program memory is often naturally split between threads. In an example such as matrix transpose, for instance, certain blocks of the matrix are mainly handled by certain threads. When multiple threads occupy processor cores across multiple packages, there is much to be gained by allocating memory for each thread in a memory channel that is close to it.

The way to do this is explained in section 5.2.1. At first one may suspect that memory is allocated during a call to `malloc()` or its equivalent. In fact, during `malloc()`, the memory that gets allocated is typically virtual and not physical. It is only during first access, and the resulting page fault, that a page of virtual memory is mapped to a page of physical memory. Therefore, the allocation of page frames in near memory depends on the initialization protocol. Briefly, each page in virtual memory must first be accessed by the thread most likely to use it.

It is certainly possible that a page of virtual memory is heavily used by a certain thread in a certain phase of the program and by another thread in another phase of the program. In such situations, the best option is to try to map the threads that use the same pages of memory to nearby cores. This technique is also explained in section 5.2.1.

It is commonly believed that a program running on 16 cores is 16 times faster than a program that runs on 1 core, ignoring communication costs. This belief is completely mistaken. Bandwidth to memory does not scale linearly with the number of cores. Although linear speedup is often claimed in scientific computing research, such claims are a consequence of the program not going out of cache, a surprisingly common occurrence. Algorithms that use memory in a nontrivial manner and achieve linear speedup are rare.

In section 5.2.2, we find that the bandwidth to memory increases by only a factor of 3 or 4, when we go from 1 thread to 12 threads on a 12-core machine. Similarly, the speedup is sublinear and between 4 and 8 on a 16-core machine.

In section 5.2.3, we find the improvement in the realized bandwidth in effecting a matrix transpose is a factor of four on a 12-core machine, and seven on a 16-core machine. The Fast Fourier Transform (FFT) is one of the more arithmetic-intensive algorithms. As explained earlier, the cost of memory accesses cannot be completely hidden in the FFT. In section 5.2.4, we find the speedups for the FFT to be nine and 12 on 12- and 16-core machines, respectively. The speedups are impressive but still sublinear. The only commonly used algorithms that would result in linear speedups, assuming nontrivial utilization of memory resources, seem to be dense matrix algorithms such as LU factorization and matrix multiplication.

5.2.1   Near memory and far memory

To explain the distinction between near and far memory, we turn to figure 5.1. That figure shows a 12-core machine, with the processors divided into packages. All memory references to far memory, which is those page frames that reside in a memory channel connected to the other processor package, have to go through an interconnect. This interconnect is similar to a fast network channel and its use makes references to far memory more expensive. For example, on a 2.6 GHz 12-core SSE2 machine, the latency to near memory is 180 cycles, whereas the latency to far memory is 300 cycles. On another machine (2.2 GHz 16-core AVX) with two processor packages, the latency to near memory is again around 180 cycles and the latency to far memory is again much greater, being more than 350 cycles.

Thus, it is advantageous if a page frame that is mostly used by a thread resides in near memory. If page frames are in far memory, the speed of the program can degrade by more than a factor of two.

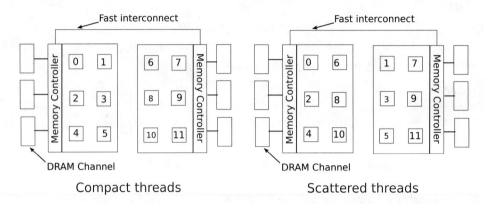

Figure 5.1: Assignment of threads numbered 0 through 11 to processor cores with compact and scatter affinities.

The assignment of pages to page frames can be enforced through some kind of an initialization routine. An example follows:

```
void init_manycore(double *list, long len, int nthreads){
#pragma omp parallel for               \
     num_threads(nthreads)                    \
     default(none)                      \
     shared(list, len, nthreads)
     for(long i=0; i < len; i++)
          list[i] = 0.0;
}
```

This initialization routine must be called soon after the array list[] is allocated and before any access of any entry of the array. The initialization may not be doing anything useful. The point is that the array is split between the threads, and each thread initializes the memory it is mostly likely to use.

The first time an entry of list[] that begins a page (the address at page beginning is 0 module the page size, which is typically 4096), there is a page fault. The page fault handler typically finds a page frame in memory that is near the thread that triggered the fault.[3]

---

[3]In principle, first-touch allocation depends on assumptions about C/C++ memory management. The key assumption is that the memory that is returned by malloc() exists in virtual memory

In this example, the allocation of page frames in near memory is accomplished using an explicit initialization routine and as a consequence of demand paging. In other programs, it may be more natural to make an invocation of the most intensive part of the program. For example, in a certain program, the most cycle-intensive segment may be computing the FFT using multiple threads. In such a program, the allocation of pages in near memory may be effected by making a dummy call of the FFT routines. The results of this dummy call will be useless. In fact, it is important not to initialize memory prior to the call. Its only purpose is to allocate page frames in near memory.

In a program with many phases, such as an FFT phase, a transpose phase, and a solver phase, it may be impossible to ensure that a page frame is in near memory during each phase. We can still pick one of the phases, perhaps the most cycle intensive among the phases, and ensure that page frames are in near memory during that phase.

Another useful technique is to control the assignment of threads to processor cores. In the `icpc` compiler, there are two ways of doing that. The assignment of threads to cores can be specified on the Linux command line as

```
export KMP_AFFINITY=scatter
```

or

```
export KMP_AFFINITY=compact
```

The default assignment is to scatter the threads. The `icpc` runtime library looks up the environment variable `KMP_AFFINITY` and uses Linux system calls to control the binding of threads to processor cores (for the distinction between `compact` and `scatter`, see figure 5.1). Another way to control thread binding to processor cores with `icc/icpc` is to use the `kmp_set_defaults()` function.

For programs that assign a thread to each processor core, `compact` is often better, although `scatter` is the default. It may be a better idea to keep nearby threads in nearby processor cores because threads with nearby identifiers are more likely to be correlated and access nearby pages. All our timings assume the `compact` thread affinity.

In general, one can try to fix the assignment of threads to processor cores completely. Although this sounds simple in principle, it is cumbersome to get it to work in nontrivial programs.

---

but has no associated page frames.

5.2.2   Bandwidth to DRAM memory

The sum_onecore() function listed below is the engine for measuring read bandwidth
to memory.

```
double sum_onecore(double *list, int n){
    double ans = 0;
#pragme vector always
    for(int i=0; i < n; i++)
        ans += list[i];
    return ans;
}
```

The icpc compiler generates excellent code for this function. It unrolls the loop
and generates packed double instructions so that the cost of adding is irrelevant.
The pragma directive gives a strong suggestion to icpc to use XMM/YMM/ZMM
registers and packed double instructions. Other compilers would ignore this directive.

The sum_onecore() function is called by each thread created by the function
sum_manycore(), whose listing follows.

```
double sum_manycore(double *list, long len,
                                    int nthreads){
    double ans = 0;
#pragma omp parallel                          \
    num_threads(nthreads)                     \
    default(none)                      \
    shared(ans, list, len, nthreads)
    {
        int tid = omp_get_thread_num();
        long first = len*tid/nthreads;
        long next = len*(tid+1)/nthreads;
        double s = sum_onecore(list+first,next-first);
#pragma omp critical
        ans += s;
    }
    return ans;
}
```

Computer	# of Threads/Cores	read	write	copy
2.6 GHz SSE2	12	15.0 (3.3)	9.51 (3.2)	9.48(2.5)
2.2 GHz AVX	16	36.7 (7.5)	34.7(16)	22.5 (4.4)

Table 5.3: Bandwidth to memory in bytes per cycle (for reading, writing, and copying) on two different computers. The parenthesized numbers are the speedups relative to bandwidth from a single core (for the full names of the computers, see table A.1).

This program splits the entries of list[] between the threads in a certain way. That is the same split as in init_manycore(), assuming nthreads to be the same. Therefore, we can send page frames to near memory by making either a call to init_manycore() or a dummy call to sum_manycore() *even before* list[] is initialized.

The following functions were called from each thread to determine the write and copy bandwidths:

```
void write_onecore(double *list, int n){
#pragma vector always nontemporal
    for(int i=0; i < n; i++)
        list[i] = i;
}

void copy_onecore(double *list, int n){
#pragma vector always nontemporal
    for(int i=0; i < n/2; i++)
        list[i] = list[n/2+i];
}
```

Here the **pragma** directive, specific to icpc and ignored by other compilers, asks for nontemporal writes. Nontemporal writes are streamed directly to DRAM, bypassing the write-back cache, using the movntpd instruction.

Table 5.3 lists the read, write, and copy bandwidths for two different computers. In neither case do we get anything close to linear speedup for reading and copying. The speedup for the write bandwidth on the AVX machine is linear as a consequence of nontemporal writes. However, the speedup is only slightly more than a quarter as much for copying despite the same **pragma** directive, suggesting that the magic of the nontemporal **pragma** may be limited to the occasional toy example. The bandwidth for copying remains the same even when the **pragma** is omitted.

The peak read bandwidth on the SSE2 machine is 40 GB/s. The peak read bandwidth on the AVX machine is nearly twice as great. The peak copy bandwidths are 25 GB/s and 50 GB/s, respectively.

5.2.3   Matrix transpose

The function `blocktransx()` defined below is similar to the one defined in chapter 4. This definition differs by allowing the matrix stored in the array `b[]` to have a leading dimension greater than the number of rows.

```
void blocktransx(double *restrict a, double *restrict b,
                 int ldb, int m, int n){
   assert((m%B==0)&&(n%B==0));
   for(int i=0; i < m; i+=B)
      for(int j=0; j < n; j+=B)
         for(int ii=0; ii < B; ii++)
            for(int jj=0; jj < B; jj++)
               b[j+jj+(i+ii)*ldb] = a[i+ii+(j+jj)*m];
}
```

The function listed below is a multithreaded implementation of the matrix transpose, which uses `blocktransx()`.

```
1  void blocktrans(double *restrict a, double *restrict b,
2               int m, int n, int nthreads){
3        assert(m%B==0);
4        assert(n%(nthreads*B)==0);
5  #pragma omp parallel                              \
6        num_threads(nthreads)                       \
7        default(none)                          \
8        shared(a, b, m, n, nthreads)
9        {
10             int tid = omp_get_thread_num();
11             int nn = n/nthreads;
12             int nfst = tid*nn;
```

Computer	# of Threads/Cores	B	bw
2.6 GHz SSE2	12	125	7.60 (4)
2.2 GHz AVX	16	75	16.2 (7)

Table 5.4: Bandwidth to memory (in bytes per cycle) realized in transposing a square matrix of dimension close to 40,000 on two different computers. The block size is $B \times B$. The parenthesized numbers are speedups relative to a single core (for the full names of the machines, see table A.1).

```
13              int ldb = n;
14              blocktransx(a+m*nfst, b+nfst, ldb, m, nn);
15         }
16 }
```

The function `blocktrans()` assumes that the array `a[]` stores an $m \times n$ matrix (with leading dimension m) and saves its transpose in `b[]`. The transposed $n \times m$ matrix is stored in `b[]` using leading dimension n. The threads split the columns of `a[]` equally between themselves on lines 11 and 12. The matrix transposed by each thread has dimension $m \times nn$, where `nn` is defined on line 11. The function call on line 14 shifts the first entry of `a[]` by `nfst` columns and the first entry of `b[]` by `nfst` to isolate the submatrix that the thread works on.

Table 5.4 shows that the bandwidth realized for varying number of threads and varying block sizes B. The matrix transposed was square with dimension as close to $40,000$ as possible subject to the divisibility conditions assumed on lines 3 and 4. On both the 12-core SSE2 machine and the 16-core AVX machine, the bandwidth realized in transposing is nearly 80% of the bandwidth for copying, as may be verified by comparing with table 5.4. Although we had complaints about the compiled code for a single processor with a single thread, such complaints may not be justified here. Getting to 80% of the best possible in a matrix transpose is quite good.

The following code was used to ensure that page frames reside in near memory:

```
double *a = new double[m*n];
double *b = new double[m*n];
blocktrans(a, b, m, n, nthreads);
```

The first call to `blocktrans()` is made even before the arrays are initialized. The memory accesses generated by `blocktrans()` induce a favorable mapping to page frames. The same page of memory in either a[] or b[] may be accessed by more than one thread. In that case, whichever thread races to the page first gets a page frame close to itself. If the two threads are on the same processor package, the page will be near both the threads.

5.2.4   Fast Fourier transform

For a purely arithmetic program, such as summing the Leibniz series, the speed of the program increases linearly with the number of cores, provided the number of terms summed is large enough to outweigh the overhead of entering and leaving an OpenMP parallel region. Other tasks, such as transposing a matrix, are limited by bandwidth to memory. The bandwidth to memory does not increase linearly with the number of cores employed. Many problems in scientific computing—finite differences or finite elements on a 3D mesh to give two examples—fall in the latter category.

Dense linear algebra problems, such as matrix multiplication, are limited by bandwidth to memory if implemented in a straightforward way. In chapter 3, we showed how to write a microkernel for matrix multiplication that takes advantage of parallelism in the instruction set. Chapter 4 showed how to cleverly hide the cost of accessing memory. A multithreaded matrix multiplication must account for cache memory slightly differently because the L3 cache is common to all the processor cores on the same package. Yet linear speedup with increasing processor cores can be achieved without drastic rethinking.

Hiding the cost of memory accesses and making efficient use of processor resources are essential for optimized FFT routines as well. The inverse Discrete Fourier Transform (DFT) of the sequence $a_0, \ldots, a_{N-1}$ is given by

$$b_j = \sum_{k=0}^{N-1} \omega^{jk} a_k$$

where $\omega = \exp(2\pi i/N)$ is a primitive Nth root of unity. This transformation is sometimes called the DFT, but we prefer to call it the inverse DFT to maintain an analogy with Fourier analysis. If the a_j are discrete Fourier coefficients, we may think of b_j as equispaced samples in the time domain. The FFT is a fast algorithm for computing the DFT or its inverse.

Computer	# of Threads/Cores	N	bw
2.6 GHz SSE2	12	64	0.35 (8)
		1024	0.29 (8)
		8192	0.33 (9)
2.2 GHz AVX	16	64	0.16 (7)
		1024	0.15 (12)
		8192	0.14 (13)

Table 5.5: Bandwidth (more precisely, the inverse bandwidth) given as the number of cycles consumed by an FFT of size N divided by $N \log_2 N$. The parenthesized numbers are speedups relative to a single core (for the full names of the machines, see table A.1).

In chapter 2, we discussed the FFTW and MKL libraries and their interfaces to the 1D inverse DFT. Here we return to that topic to make a few points about the FFT and its implementation.

Table 5.5 shows the number of cycles used by the FFT for various N as a function of the number of threads. The speedups are quite good and reach 75% of linear speedup for some of the values of N. The numbers in the table were obtained by lining up many blocks of N complex numbers (or $2N$ double-precision numbers) in 16 GB of memory. The number of blocks is approximately $10^9/N$, and the FFT of each block was computed. The blocks were split between threads using OpenMP. Each thread applied MKL's 1D FFT to its share of the blocks.

Notes on 1D versus 2D FFT

Let us suppose that $N = 2n$. The basic idea of the radix-2 FFT is as follows.[4] First rearrange the data $a_0, a_1, \ldots, a_{2n-1}$ as a $2 \times n$ matrix:

$$\begin{pmatrix} a_0 & a_2 & \cdots & a_{2n-2} \\ a_1 & a_3 & & a_{2n-1} \end{pmatrix}.$$

---

[4]For the FFT algorithm see, van Loan (1992) and Cormen et al. (2001). The Wikipedia pages on the FFT and related topics have a wealth of information.

The original vector is recovered by reading this matrix in column-major order. The first step is to take the n-dimensional FFT of each row to get

$$\begin{pmatrix} \tilde{a}_0 & \tilde{a}_2 & \cdots & \tilde{a}_{2n-2} \\ \tilde{a}_1 & \tilde{a}_3 & & \tilde{a}_{2n-1} \end{pmatrix}.$$

The next step is to multiply by the twiddle factors to get

$$\begin{pmatrix} \tilde{a}_0 & \tilde{a}_2 & \cdots & \tilde{a}_{2n-2} \\ \tilde{a}_1 & \omega\tilde{a}_3 & & \omega^{n-1}\tilde{a}_{2n-1} \end{pmatrix}.$$

Here $\omega = \exp(2\pi i/N)$. If this matrix is multiplied by

$$\begin{pmatrix} 1 & 1 \\ 1 & -1 \end{pmatrix},$$

which is the 1D transform matrix with $N = 2$, we will have the inverse DFT of the original matrix organized as a matrix in column-major format. The mathematical justification of this claim is omitted.

The $5N \log_2 N$ operation count of the FFT is obtained by recursive applications of the same idea, which is possible if N is a power of 2. An implementation that follows the resulting scheme will be quite inefficient, however. The scheme as it is presented will lead to a lot of cache conflicts.

The first decomposition, which we described in detail, thinks of a vector a_i, $0 \le i < N - 1$, as two vectors of length $N/2$. The two vectors are

$$a_i, a_{i+2}, a_{i+4}, a_{i+6}, \ldots$$

with $i = 0, 1$. These two vectors appeared as the rows of an $2 \times N/2$ matrix in the first step. If we assume N is a power of 2 and go to a depth of k in the recursion, we find that the FFT is breaking the given data into 2^k vectors of length $N/2^k$. These 2^k vectors are given by

$$a_i, a_{i+2^k}, a_{i+2.2^k}, a_{i+3.2^k}, a_{i+4.2^k}, \ldots$$

for $i = 0, 1, \ldots, 2^k - 1$. The successive entries of each of these vectors are separated by 2^k in the original sequence. As we found in chapter 4, locations separated by powers of 2 are likely to map to the same sets in L1 and L2 cache and create a lot of cache conflicts. This problem may be tackled using the bit-reversed permutation as explained in chapter 2.

Suppose the data is 2D and arranged in an $M \times N$ matrix:

$$\begin{pmatrix} a_{0,0} & a_{0,1} & a_{0,2} & \cdots \\ a_{1,0} & a_{1,1} & a_{1,2} & \cdots \\ a_{2,0} & a_{2,1} & a_{2,2} & \cdots \\ \vdots & \vdots & \vdots & \ddots \end{pmatrix}_{M \times N} .$$

The 2D FFT of this matrix is obtained by applying an FFT of size M to every column followed by an application of an FFT of size N to every row. The structure of the algorithm is similar to the recursive decomposition of a 1D FFT of size MN into FFTs of size M and N, but there are no twiddle factors this time. The 2D structure is imposed by the data not by the algorithm.

If the data is in column-major order, the application of 1D FFTs of size M to columns involves no new point. However, the rows are different. If M is a large power of 2, for example, the successive entries in a row are separated by a large power of 2 in memory, increasing the risk of cache conflicts. Thus, it is not a good idea to apply 1D FFTs row by row. It is far better to directly invoke library functions for 2D FFT.

Exercise 5.2.1. Suppose a large array needs to be reversed. What is the best way to split the array between threads, so that most of the entries that are accessed are in near memory? Explain why the `init_manycore()` function would not be suitable for initializing entries.

Exercise 5.2.2. Suppose a large array needs to be sorted. Would the `init_manycore()` function be a good way to initialize the array to allocate pages in near memory?

Exercise 5.2.3. Implement an in-place transpose of square matrices using OpenMP. Estimate the bandwidth to memory realized by your program.

Exercise 5.2.4. Implement an out-of-place FFT for multiple threads (using library functions). Determine the resulting speedup on a machine with multiple cores.

Exercise 5.2.5. Refer to table 5.5 and determine that the fraction of the peak bandwidth realized is 35% and 28%, respectively, for the 12-core 2.6 GHz SSE2 machine and the 16-core 2.2 GHz AVX machine (see table A.1 for information about these machines).

5.3   Introduction to Pthreads

So far our discussion of threads has been limited to OpenMP. OpenMP is a limited programming model. It applies mainly to those situations where the data is static and the access patterns are regular. Pthreads are a more powerful programming model.

The Pthread interface for creating and running threads is supported by the Linux kernel. In Linux, each thread is a separate process. Thread creation is the same as process creation. The distinguishing feature of a group of threads is that they all use the same page tables. The same virtual address generated by different threads in the same group maps to the same physical memory location. Thus, threads offer a seamless way for different processes to share memory.

Pthreads are a powerful programming model. The range of programs that can be written using Pthreads goes well beyond scientific computing. In this section, we introduce Pthreads, beginning with the elementary and progressing to more advanced topics.

In section 5.3.1, we introduce Pthreads using a simple program to print messages. The two main techniques for achieving mutual exclusion, mutexes and spinlocks, are introduced. Summing the familiar Leibniz series is another example.

Every thread needs a stack to save its state through a succession of function calls. The user mode stack (explained in the next section) can be used by only one thread (the master thread). In section 5.3.1, we explain how a stack is set up for each thread. Thread stacks are normally just a few MB and not large. Therefore, it is important not to abuse the stack in threaded programming.

In section 5.3.2, we determine that the overhead of thread creation is typically around 10^5 cycles and can be 10 or 100 times as large on occasion. This number explains the large overhead of the first parallel region an OpenMP program enters. Threads are created the first time an OpenMP program enters a parallel region, and thread creation overhead is a major cost. The cost can even go into the milliseconds.

Section 5.3.3 considers several advanced topics. The theme of that section is to implement OpenMP-type parallel regions using Pthreads. Several implementations are explored. If the number of threads in the parallel region remains constant, threads created for the first parallel region can be reused repeatedly. This explains the low cost of a typical OpenMP parallel region compared with the first parallel region.

Section 5.3.3 shows the central role played by memory fences and cache coherence in threaded programming. Although the role of cache coherence is invisible to the pro-

grammer, unless it is looked for, there can be no multithreaded programming without
cache coherence. Propagating writes from cache to cache, when the same cache line
is used by multiple threads, can be a considerable source of overhead. Section 5.3.3
also shows the way in which TLB flushes can impact threaded programming.

5.3.1   Pthreads

We begin our discussion of Pthreads with a function that could be in a simple sequential program. The function `print_message()` uses basic C syntax and has no Pthread
construct in it. Indeed, it is compiled into assembly instructions as if it were a single
threaded program—an important point that has already come up in our discussion
of OpenMP. Each Pthread will later take control by executing this program.

```
1  void *print_message(void *arg){
2        char *s = (char *)arg;
3        char ss[400];
4        int l = strlen(s);
5        for(int i=0; i < l; i++){
6             ss[2*i] = s[i];
7             ss[2*i+1] = (s[i]==' ')?' ':'_';
8        }
9        ss[2*l] ='\0';
10       printf("%s",s);
11       printf("\n");
12       printf("%s", ss);
13       printf("\n");
14       printf("ss = %p \n\n", (void *)ss);
15       return NULL;
16 }
```

The only sign that `print_message()` may have something to do with Pthreads occurs
in its first line. It is declared to be a function that takes a single argument of type
void * and returns a single value also of type **void** *. Whatever arguments we want
to send to a Pthread must be packed into a region of memory and sent to the Pthread
as a pointer of type **void** *. Any pointer can be cast to the type **void** *.

The argument to this function is a message or character string. On line 2, this message is recovered by casting it back to type char *.

The statements that extend from line 3 through line 9 define another string ss, and copy the characters in s into its even positions. The odd positions are filled with the underscore character except when the preceding even position has a blank character. Line 9 ensures that the string is properly terminated with '\0' following C convention.

The program prints the string s, the string ss, and the pointer ss on lines 10, 12, and 14, respectively.

Presently, we will introduce Pthreads. For the ensuing discussion, the key items are the definition of ss on line 3 and the address that is printed on line 14 of print_message().

Pthreads are created inside call_pthreads() whose definition follows.

```
1  #include <pthread.h>
2  void call_pthreads(){
3       pthread_t thread1, thread2, thread3;
4       char s[600];
5       sprintf(s, "Message for thread1");
6       sprintf(s+200, "Message for thread2");
7       sprintf(s+400, "Message for thread3");
8       pthread_create(&thread1, NULL, print_message,
9            (void *)s);
10      pthread_create(&thread2, NULL, print_message,
11               (void *)(s+200));
12      pthread_create(&thread3, NULL, print_message,
13               (void *)(s+400));
14      void *result;
15      pthread_join(thread1, &result);
16      pthread_join(thread2, &result);
17      pthread_join(thread3, &result);
18  }
```

The function call_pthreads() creates three threads and sends a character string as the argument to each of them. The three threads print the message in the character string and return. There are four threads in this program, including the master thread.

Each of the four threads will probably run on a different processor core on a processor with 4 or more cores.

On line 3, the program defines variables of the type `pthread_t`. The Pthread library will access administrative information about the threads using these variables.

The library function `pthread_create()` is used to create threads on lines 8, 10, and 12. The first argument is of type `pthread_t *`. During the call on lines 8 and 9, the pthread library will create a thread and make the variable `thread1` point to information about that thread. Later information about the created thread can be accessed using `thread1`.

The second argument to `pthread_create()` will always be `NULL` for us.

The third argument to `pthread_create()` is `print_message`, which is a function pointer. The third argument is the function that the thread will start executing as soon as it is scheduled to run. The third argument must be a pointer to a function that takes an argument of type `void *` and returns an argument of type `void *`. In this program, all three threads that are created will run the same function.

The fourth argument to `pthread_create()` must be of type `void *`. When the thread starts running, it will get this pointer as an argument. In this program, each of the threads gets a different character string as its argument.

The library function `pthread_join()` may be used to retrieve the pointer returned by a thread. In this program, the pointer returned by each thread is saved in `result`. The variable `result` is defined on line 14 to be of type `void *`. The threads do not return anything meaningful here. If they did, the pointer `result` could be used to access the data returned by the threads.

The Pthread library has a fairly transparent syntax. By going over the definition of `call_pthreads()`, it is easy to see where threads are being created and how.

C/C++ compilers Pthread header files by themselves without any prompting. The Pthread library may be linked using the `-lpthread` option.

Thread stacks

Each thread gets its own stack. This stack is used for storing the local variables defined by functions the thread executes. When a thread makes a function call, the return address is pushed onto its stack.

On line 14, the function `print_message()` prints the value of `ss`, which is a pointer to a location in the thread stack. The three threads print as follows:

```
ss = 0x4173bf90
ss = 0x4193cf90
ss = 0x41b9cf90
```

These do not look like stack addresses: they do not begin with 0x7fff, as in section 4.4.1. The addresses are in the region that belongs to dynamic memory. During thread creation, each thread is allocated a thread stack in dynamic memory.

The difference between values of the address ss printed by the three threads is about 2 MB, and the maximum thread stack size on the system we used is about 2 MB. That is typical.

Mutexes and spinlocks

The function print_message() prints to the terminal, which is shared by all the threads. The message may get garbled as in the following fragment:

```
Message for thread3Message for thread2
M_e_s_s_a_g_e_ f_o_r_ t_h_r_e_a_d_2_
```

Each thread must treat the block of print statements as a critical region.

Mutexes are one mechanism for implementing mutual exclusion in the Pthread library. The function below uses a single mutex to ensure that a block of print statements is executed by a single thread at a time.

```
pthread_mutex_t mutex=PTHREAD_MUTEX_INITIALIZER;
void *print_message_mutex(void *arg){
    char *s = (char *)arg;
    char ss[400];
    int l = strlen(s);
    for(int i=0; i < l; i++){
        ss[2*i] = s[i];
        ss[2*i+1] = (s[i]==' ')?' ':'_';
    }
    ss[2*l] ='\0';
    pthread_mutex_lock(&mutex);
    printf("%s",s);
    printf("\n");
```

```
        printf("%s", ss);
        printf("\n");
        printf("ss = %p \n\n", (void *)ss);
        pthread_mutex_unlock(&mutex);
        return NULL;
    }
```

The new syntax used in this function is quite simple and hardly requires an explanation. On the first line, a variable `mutex` is defined and initialized. The mutex is locked before entering the block of print statements and unlocked at exit.

Another mechanism for mutual exclusion is the spinlock. The spinlock version of the function for printing messages follows:

```
pthread_spinlock_t spinlock;
void *print_message_spinlock(void *arg){
    char *s = (char *)arg;
    char ss[400];
    int l = strlen(s);
    for(int i=0; i < l; i++){
        ss[2*i] = s[i];
        ss[2*i+1] = (s[i]==' ')?' ':'_';
    }
    ss[2*l] ='\0';
    pthread_spin_lock(&spinlock);
    printf("%s",s);
    printf("\n");
    printf("%s", ss);
    printf("\n");
    printf("ss = %p \n\n", (void *)ss);
    pthread_spin_unlock(&spinlock);
    return NULL;
}
```

The first line defines a spinlock but does not initialize the spinlock. The spinlock is locked before entering the block of print statements and unlocked after the printing is done. The spinlock is initialized by the master thread as follows:

```
pthread_spin_init(&spinlock, PTHREAD_PROCESS_PRIVATE);
```

Classical mutexes, which differ in behavior from Pthread mutexes, were introduced during the early days of computers, when most computers had a single processor. When a process attempts to lock a classical mutex but the mutex is already locked, the kernel will put the process to sleep and schedule some other process to run. The sleeping process will be reawakened and scheduled to run when the mutex is available to be locked.

Spinlocks may be a preferred way to enforce mutual exclusion if every thread may be assumed to have possession of a processor core. Spinlocks do not relinquish the processor but wait in a loop until the lock is available. Mutual exclusion is achieved by spinlocks using a shared locking variable accessed using atomic instructions.

In simple programs, the behavior of Pthread mutexes is closer to spinlocks than classical mutexes. In more complex programs, Pthread mutexes can behave like classical mutexes.

Partial sums of the Leibniz series

Our discussion of Pthreads has been confined to printing messages. We turn to the Leibniz series to illustrate how multiple arguments can be passed and how to retrieve the answer computed by a thread.

In the code fragment that follows, the number of threads, including the master thread, is fixed at four, with the assumption that the program is run on a quad-core machine. The number may be set equal to the number of cores, whatever that may be, as long as it is even.

```
const int NTHREADS = 4;
struct leib_stuff{
     int offset;
     int n;
     double sum;
};
```

Each thread is given a pointer to `struct leib_stuff`. The struct holds three items of information. The first item is the offset from which that particular thread must start summing the Leibniz series. The second item is how many terms of the Leibniz series must be summed. The third item is used by each thread to return its part of the partial sum of the Leibniz series. Each thread assumes all terms in its share of the partial sum to be of the same sign. Therefore, the number of threads must be even.

In the earlier examples, the master thread does not participate with the workers. There is some inherent asymmetry between the master thread and other threads. For example, the master thread makes use of the user mode stack, which none of the other threads can. Yet the ideal is to make all the threads, including the master thread, do exactly the same amount of work. In the present example, the master thread will sum its share of the terms of the Leibniz series. Therefore, only three threads are created explicitly.

Each of the three created threads gets control with the following function:

```
void *leibniz(void *arg){
    int offset = ((struct leib_stuff *)arg)->offset;
    int n = ((struct leib_stuff *)arg)->n;
    double sum = 0;
    for(int i=offset; i < n; i += NTHREADS)
        sum += 4.0/(2*i+1);
    ((struct leib_stuff *)arg)->sum = sum;
    return arg;
}
```

We can read this the way we read a function meant for single-threaded execution. Its peculiarity is in the roundabout way in which arguments are passed and the computed sum is returned. The thread finds out its **offset** and the number of terms in the partial sum **n** from two of the items in **struct leib_stuff** and stuffs its share of the sum into the third item. The argument passed and the value returned are both pointers to that struct.

The master thread computes its share of the Leibniz sum as well as accumulating the total from all the threads. It is defined below.

```
double leibsum(int nterms){
    pthread_t t[NTHREADS-1];
    struct leib_stuff linfo[NTHREADS-1];
    for(int i=1; i < NTHREADS; i++){
        linfo[i-1].offset = i;
        linfo[i-1].n = nterms;
```

```
            pthread_create(&(t[i-1]), NULL, leibniz,
                        (void *)(linfo+(i-1)));
    }
    double ans = 0;
    for(int i=0; i < nterms; i+=NTHREADS)
            ans += 4.0/(2*i+1);
    void *res;
    pthread_join(t[0], &res);
    ans -= ((struct leib_stuff *)res)->sum;
    for(int i=2; i < NTHREADS; i+=2){
            pthread_join(t[i-1], &res);
            ans += ((struct leib_stuff *)res)->sum;
            pthread_join(t[i], &res);
            ans -= ((struct leib_stuff *)res)->sum;
    }
    return ans;
}
```

The master thread here takes on the job of accumulating the final sum. This burden can be more equally distributed by making the threads join with each other in pairs. To implement such a strategy, the array t[] of type pthread_t must be defined globally and made visible to all the threads.

In this program, the master thread joins with the other threads to retrieve the results of their computations. Even if a thread returns nothing, the master thread or some other thread must join with each thread that terminates. Otherwise, the threads live on as zombies in the operating system kernel.

5.3.2   Overhead of thread creation

To find the cost of creating and destroying Pthreads, we use the following simple function, which each thread will execute:

```
void *addone(void *arg){
    long *p = (long *)(arg);
    *p += 1;
    return NULL;
```

```
    }
```

This function receives a pointer to `long` and adds 1 to the location its argument is pointing to. The function defined below is responsible for creating threads and asking each one of them to execute `addone()`.

```
void addone_list(long *list, int nthreads){
    pthread_t *plist = new pthread_t[nthreads-1];
    *list += 1;
    for(int i=0; i < nthreads-1; i++)
        pthread_create(plist+i, NULL, addone,
                            (void *)(list+i+1));
    for(int i=0; i < nthreads-1; i++){
        void *result;
        pthread_join(plist[i], &result);
    }
    delete[] plist;
}
```

This function was invoked many times with **nthreads** being three. On a 3.4 GHz AVX machine with four cores (see table A.1 in the appendix), there are three processes, two for the created threads and one for the master thread, each of which gets a core. The work that each thread does is trivial. During each invocation, most of the cycles are consumed by the creation and destruction of threads.

In 10^6 trials, the first five invocations of **addone_list()** used the following number of cycles:

```
364488
153068
102000
220218
290844
```

The worst five invocations of **addone_list()** were as follows:

```
1.48340e+07
1.28682e+07
7.52992e+06
```

```
5.57948e+06
5.06503e+06
```

The median number of cycles was $78,242$.

The typical cost of creating and destroying Pthreads appears to be somewhat less than 10^5 cycles. That number is not unreasonable given that each process descriptor used by the kernel is nearly 6 KB. The cost of creating threads will vary from system to system, but the numbers are qualitatively the same on many different systems. The 3.4 GHz AVX computer with four cores used here has a single processor package. The cost of creating a thread per core may be expected to be higher on computers with multiple processor packages.

However, the cost of creating three threads is much more likely to run into millions of cycles on the quad-core 3.4 GHz AVX computer than on a machine with a dozen or more cores, even if the processor cores are split into two packages. A thread is more likely to have to wait for the time quantum of some other process to expire on a quad-core computer than on a computer with 12 cores.

5.3.3   Parallel regions using Pthreads

This section begins with a simple OpenMP program. The OpenMP program alternates between two parallel regions. In the first parallel region, every thread runs a function called addone(). In the second parallel region, every thread runs a function called addtwo().

Later in the section, the parallel regions are implemented using Pthreads. The first implementation is plain C, except for creating and launching Pthreads. The second and third implementations use spinlocks and mutexes, respectively. The final implementation uses conditional variables.

The basic idea in all four implementations is as follows. If the number of threads is n, including the master thread, the master thread begins by creating $n-1$ workers. The worker threads do not exit when their job is done but keep waiting for the master to send them some more work. The threads exit only when the master tells them to.

Corresponding to the parallel regions of the OpenMP program, the master tells the workers to alternately execute addone() and addtwo(). The master thread itself alternately executes those two functions.

A glance at table 5.6 already throws up a number of questions. The spinlock and mutex implementations look quite similar. That is an artifact of the rather simple

nthreads	2	3	4	8
OpenMP (gcc/g++)	1,400	1,700	2,100	40,000
Plain C	720	975	1,200	8.1×10^7
Spinlocks (randomized)	760	2,000	4,200	*
Mutexes	900	2,200	6,500	9.2×10^7
Conditional variables	30,000	28,000	9,000	18,000

Table 5.6: The cost of entering and exiting a parallel region in cycles. All measurements were made on a 3.4 GHz quad-core AVX computer (see table A.1 for its full name).

setting of our experiment. If the threads were executing a complex function inside the parallel region, the two implementations would look quite different.

The plain C and the spinlock implementation do not yield the processor core voluntarily. In our setting, that is true for mutexes as well. As a result, all three implementations are highly wasteful when the number of threads is greater than the number of cores.

In the conditional variable implementation, the threads yield gracefully. As a result, it is the most efficient when the number of threads is greater than the number of cores.

Strangely, the conditional variable implementation is faster with four or eight threads on a quad-core machine than with two threads, which is faster than with one thread (see table 5.6). The explanation of this conundrum is important to understand, as it can happen in almost any threaded program. The explanation (TLB flushes) is given later.

The gcc/g++ implementation of OpenMP also creates threads only at the point of first entry into the parallel regions. Overall, it looks better than all our implementations. The first OpenMP parallel region that is entered is expensive because threads are created. If the number of threads changes from parallel region to parallel region, the parallel regions will be constantly hit by the same overhead.

The C implementation highlights the role of cache coherence, which is essential and fundamental to multithreaded programming. Propagating writes from cache to cache can cause significant overhead. The C implementation also introduces memory fences.

A simple OpenMP program

The two OpenMP parallel regions, in the program that will be listed shortly, alternately call the following two functions:

```
void addone(void *arg){
    long *p = (long *)(arg);
    *p += 1;
}

void addtwo(void *arg){
    long *p = (long *)(arg);
    *p += 2;
}
```

The functions receive a pointer to a long cast to void *, dereference it, and then add either 1 or 2 to the long location. It would of course be simpler to add 1 and 2 directly without having to call functions that work through pointers. The OpenMP parallel regions invoke these functions to preserve a close analogy to the Pthread implementations. The Pthread implementations also use these two functions.

Here is the OpenMP program with two parallel regions.

```
void ompmaster(long *list, int nthreads, int count){
    for(int i=0; i < count/2;i++){
#pragma omp parallel                                        \
    num_threads(nthreads)                                   \
    default(none)                                  \
    shared(list)
        {
                int j = omp_get_thread_num();
                addone((void *)(list+j));
        }
#pragma omp parallel                                        \
    num_threads(nthreads)                                   \
    default(none)                                  \
    shared(list)
        {
```

```
                  int j = omp_get_thread_num();
                  addtwo((void *)(list+j));
              }
          }
      }
```

This program has two parallel regions, one of which calls `addone()` to add 1 to an entry of `list[]`. Each thread adds to the entry whose index is the same as its thread id. The thread id is returned by `omp_get_thread_num()`. The other parallel region adds 2 to the same entry using `addtwo()`. Because the parallel regions are in a for-loop that is iterated `count/2` times, the effect of a single call to `ompmaster()` is to add `3*count/2` to as many entries of `list[]` as there are threads.

Parallel regions in plain C

The first implementation of parallel regions we consider makes minimal use of Pthreads. Most of it is in plain C.

The following global definitions are the basis of the C implementation of parallel regions:

```
    typedef void (*fnlist_t[nthreads])(void *);
    typedef void *arglist_t[nthreads];
    volatile fnlist_t fnlist;
    volatile arglist_t arglist;
    volatile long work_count[nthreads];
    volatile long done_count[nthreads];
```

This code segment defines two types, `fnlist_t` and `arglist_t`, and four variables. Here `nthreads`, whose definition is not shown, is a `const int` equal to the number of threads. For example, `nthreads` is 3 if the number of threads is 3.

The type `fnlist_t` is an array (of size `nthreads`) of pointers to functions with a single argument of type `void *` and returning `void`. The syntax for such complex types can be gotten right with a little trial and error. The type `arglist_t` is an array (of size `nthreads`) pointers to `void`.

All four of the variables `fnlist[]`, `arglist[]`, `work_count[]`, and `done_count[]` are defined to be `volatile`. The `volatile` qualifier is a message to the compiler that a variable may change unexpectedly, and the usual dependency analysis may not be valid. It prevents the compiler from saving variables in registers and carrying out other optimizations. In general, if a variable is declared `volatile`, the compiler assumes that the value of the variable can change unexpectedly because of some other thread, processor, or device.

These four `volatile` variables are used by the worker threads to communicate with the manager thread. The manager thread sets `fnlist[tid]` and `arglist[tid]` to tell the thread of identifier `tid` which function it should execute and what argument should be passed to it. For example, `fnlist[tid]` is set to `addone` to ask the worker thread with identifier `tid` to execute the `addone()` function defined earlier in this section.

The manager thread uses the array entry `work_count[tid]` to tell the worker thread of identifier `tid` how many units of work have been assigned to it from the beginning. The worker thread uses `done_count[tid]` to tell the manager how many units of work it has completed.

Making the four arrays used for communication between the manager thread and the workers `volatile` ensures that every single reference generates a load or store instruction. In particular, the compiler will not assign any of these items to a register, which would get in the way of communication between the manager and the workers.[5]

Every thread created using `pthread_create()` begins execution with a function that takes a pointer as an argument and returns a pointer. The worker threads begin execution with the following function:

```
1  void *worker(void *arg){
2      int tid = *((int *)arg);
3      while(1){
4          while(work_count[tid] == done_count[tid]);
5          if(work_count[tid]==done_count[tid]+1){
6              (*(fnlist[tid]))(arglist[tid]);
7              asm volatile("mfence");
8              done_count[tid] += 1;
9          }
10     }
```

[5]The `volatile` qualifier suppresses compiler optimizations. It does not ensure any kind of mutual exclusion. See `https://www.kernel.org/doc/Documentation/volatile-considered-harmful.txt`

11 }

On line 2, the pointer `arg` is cast to `int *` and dereferenced to recover `tid`. In the Pthread library, the responsibility of assigning `tid` rests with the programmer. Lines 3 to 10 form a while-loop, which always tests positive. On line 4, the worker loops as long as the work count is equal to the count of items it has already completed. The compiler generates load instructions for `work_count[tid]` and `done_count[tid]` because they are volatile locations. The manager signals work to be done by incrementing `work_count[tid]`. Thus, on line 5, the worker enters an if-block to do work that has been assigned to it.

Line 6 is where the worker thread does the work assigned to it. On line 6, `fnlist[tid]` is the function pointer assigned to this worker. The worker dereferences that pointer as in

```
(*(fnlist[tid]))
```

and applies it to `arglist[tid]`, which is the `void *` argument assigned to it by the manager thread.

On line 8, the worker thread signals that the unit of work assigned to it is complete by incrementing `done_count[tid]`. The memory fence instruction `MFENCE`, which occurs on line 7, is essential to the correctness of this program. On line 6, the worker thread launches the function it is told to execute, and this function leads to a potentially long instruction stream. After returning from the function, the worker increments `done_count[tid]`, but the processor may look ahead in the instruction stream and increment even before the function returns. Such a thing would be valid in a single-threaded program but would corrupt the communication with the manager thread here. The memory fence on line 7 ensures that all load and store instructions that occur before it are complete before any loads and stores after it occur. It is a serializing instruction for memory references. Here the memory fence makes sure that the processor does not jump ahead and signal completion of work too early.

The worker threads spin in place (on line 4), do work (line 6), and go back to spinning in place to wait for work to be assigned. How do the threads terminate? To terminate a worker, the manager sets the function pointer `fnlist[tid]` to the `exitfn`. The exit function is defined below.

```
void exitfn(void *arg){
    pthread_exit(NULL);
```

```
    }
```

To keep things simple, the worker threads do not return anything. They could return a pointer at the point of exit, which is `pthread_exit()` in this case. If some other thread joins to this one, it can pick up the returned pointer when it joins (as in the `leibsum()` example).

The manager creates threads, assigns work to worker threads, does its own share of the work, and shuts down the worker threads. It uses the following function to create threads:

```
1  void  spawn_workers(){
2         pthread_t  plist[nthreads-1];
3         static  int  tidlist[nthreads];
4         for(int  i=0;  i  <  nthreads;  i++){
5             work_count[i]  =  0;
6             done_count[i]  =  0;
7             tidlist[i]  =  i;
8             if(i>0){
9                 pthread_create(plist+i-1,  NULL,  worker,
10                                (void  *)(tidlist+i));
11                pthread_detach(plist[i-1]);
12            }
13         }
14  }
```

The manager thread uses the array `tidlist[]` defined on line 3 and initialized on line 6 to pass the thread identifier to the workers. Notice that threads are created only if `i>0` (lines 8 through 12) because the manager thread has identifier 0. The initialization on lines 5, 6, and 7 is complete before the thread is created on lines 9 and 10, as it must be.

There are two new elements in this function that merit comment. Why is `tidlist[]` defined on line 3 specified to be `static`? Variables defined to be `static` persist in memory even after the function exits (and may be reused when the function returns). The function `spawn_workers()` may exit before the worker threads start executing, in which case the storage allocated to `tidlist[]` may disappear before the threads access it. The `static` specifier ensures that the storage persists in memory.

The other new bit of syntax is `pthread_detach()` on line 11. When a thread is detached after creation, it is no longer joinable. The operating system kernel discards detached threads after they return. If a thread is not detached, the threads are kept alive until the manager or some other thread joins with them. If a thread that is not detached returns but no other thread joins with it, it becomes a zombie.

The manager thread executes the following function:

```
1  void manager(long *list, int count){
2       spawn_workers();
3       for(int i=0; i < count; i++){
4            for(int j=0; j < nthreads; j++){
5                 fnlist[j] = (i%2==0)?addone:addtwo;
6                 arglist[j] = (void *)(list+j);
7                 asm volatile("mfence");
8                 work_count[j] += 1;
9            }
10           (*(fnlist[0]))(arglist[0]);
11           done_count[0] += 1;
12           for(int j=0; j < nthreads; j++)
13                while(work_count[j]>done_count[j]);
14      }
15      shutdown_workers();
16 }
```

The function assigned to the worker thread (with tid equal to j) on line 5 is either `addone()` or `addtwo()`, as in the OpenMP example. The memory fence on line 7 separates the assignment of work to a thread (lines 5 and 6) from the statement that signals assignment of work (line 8).

The manager does its own share of work on line 11.

The while-loop on line 13 spins in place as long as thread j is busy. Each iteration of the for-loop from lines 3 to 14 counts as one parallel region.

For completeness, we list the function for shutting down workers.

```
void shutdown_workers(){
     for(int i=1; i < nthreads; i++){
          fnlist[i] = exitfn;
          asm volatile("mfence");
```

```
              work_count[i] += 1;
        }
    }
```

The manager does not join with any of the worker threads after it tells them to shut down. The worker threads were detached earlier. If the worker threads were not detached, the manager must join with the worker threads to prevent them from turning into zombies.

Cache coherence and the cost of propagating writes

Table 5.6 shows that the plain C implementation we have described takes only 720 cycles per parallel region on an average when the number of threads is two. Why does each parallel region take 720 cycles? In answering that question, we run into a vital part of the hardware infrastructure for supporting threaded programming, namely, the cache coherence protocols.

The worker threads and the manager are exchanging information using the arrays `work_count[]`, `done_count[]`, `fnlist[]`, and `arglist[]`. The locations of these arrays are specified to be volatile. So we may think of the array entries as residing in DRAM memory, but that is not really correct. In a simple program such as this, the array entries are certain to be in L1 cache of each thread. That brings to light a new issue. Suppose the manager increases the `work_count[]` of a worker thread. The increment will take place in its own L1 cache. But when the worker accesses the same entry, it will look up its own L1 cache. How do writes propagate from L1 cache to L1 cache?

The manner in which writes propagate from cache to cache is vital for the validity of threaded programs. Much of the time we must try to make each thread work on its own portion of the memory and keep the threads as independent as possible. But threads cannot synchronize without shared memory. Because memory is mirrored in caches, any method of synchronization using shared memory is dependent on the manner in which writes propagate from cache to cache.

Many computers, such as those listed in table A.1 of the appendix, handle writes to cache as follows. Suppose a processor wants to write to a shared cache line. Before the write is complete, the hardware sends a signal to other caches to invalidate their copy of the same cache line. If the other caches do not hold a copy of the same cache line, nothing needs to be done. Indeed, the hardware stores sharing information for each cache line. If a cache line is exclusive, the protocol for invalidating other copies of the cache line will be omitted. If other copies need to be invalidated, the write to cache is not complete until all duplicate copies have been invalidated. When another processor wants to read the same cache line, a cache-to-cache transfer is triggered.

It is possible that two or more processors may attempt to write to a cache line that is duplicated in L1 caches belonging to each of them. If so, the hardware resolves the race condition so that one of the processors wins. The hardware implementation of cache coherence protocols has been stated to be a "major complication." The degree of complication increases as the number of processors that share memory increases. Although the cache coherence protocols are complicated, they are indispensable for shared memory programming.

The L1 cache to L1 cache transfers are a significant cost in our implementation of parallel regions using plain C. On the 3.4 GHz quad-core AVX computer, the cost for three threads is 975 cycles and for four threads 1,200. The cost is so low thanks to excellent implementation of cache coherence by the hardware. When the number of threads is 8 on this quad-core computer, the cost jumps to more than 10^7 cycles, however (see table 5.6). This high cost is due to dependence on context switches triggered by timer interrupts and reflects the time quantum assigned to each process by the Linux kernel.

Parallel regions using spinlocks

Here we use spinlocks in the Pthread library to implement parallel regions in which threads alternately add 1 or 2 to entries of a list.

The following variable definitions are global:

```
void (*fnlist[nthreads-1])(void *);
void *arglist[nthreads-1];
int workflag[nthreads-1];
pthread_t pthrd[nthreads-1];
pthread_spinlock_t spin[nthreads-1];
```

As in the plain C implementation, `fnlist[]` and `arglist[]` are arrays used by the manager thread to tell the worker threads which functions they must execute on which argument. In the plain C implementation, the manager thread updated a count of units of work assigned to each thread, and each worker thread updated a count of the number of units of work it had completed. In this implementation, the manager and workers synchronize using the workflag[] array, each entry of which is 0 or 1. The manager sets workflag[tid] to tell thread tid that it has work to do, and the worker sets the same flag to 0 after it has completed the work.

The array pthrd[] is used for creating the worker threads. The manager thread must not assign work when a worker is busy. The spinlocks used to enforce mutual exclusion between the manager assigning work and the workers are in the array spin[].

None of the global variables is specified to be volatile.

The worker threads begin execution with the following function:

```
1  void *worker(void *arg){
2       int tid = *((int *) arg);
3       while(1){
4            pthread_spin_lock(spin+tid-1);
5            if(workflag[tid-1]==1){
6                 (*(fnlist[tid-1]))(arglist[tid-1]);
7                 workflag[tid-1] = 0;
8            }
9            pthread_spin_unlock(spin+tid-1);
10       }
11       return NULL;
12  }
```

The spinlock spin[tid-1] is used for mutual exclusion between the worker thread tid and the manager whose tid is 0. The worker repeatedly locks (line 4) and unlocks (line 9). Every access of workflag[tid-1] (lines 5 and 7) is protected inside the lock.

The exit function, whose pointer is passed by the manager to shut down a worker, has the following definition:

```
void exitfn(void *arg){
     int tid = *((int *) arg);
     pthread_spin_unlock(spin+tid-1);
     pthread_exit(NULL);
}
```

The exit function must unlock as it is invoked by the worker thread after gaining the lock.

The manager uses the following function to assign a single unit of work to worker thread `tid`:

```
1  void assignwork(int i, int tid, long *list){
2      int j = tid-1;
3      while(1){
4          pthread_spin_lock(spin+j);
5          if(workflag[j]==0){
6              fnlist[j] = (i%2==0)?addone:addtwo;
7              arglist[j] = (void *)(list+tid);
8              workflag[j]=1;
9              pthread_spin_unlock(spin+j);
10             return;
11         }
12         pthread_spin_unlock(spin+j);
13     }
14 }
```

Lines 5 through 11 are protected by a spinlock, and in this region the manager attempts to assign a single unit of work to the worker thread `tid`. If the worker is not busy (line 5), it assigns a single unit of work (lines 6, 7, and 8) and unlocks (line 9) before returning (line 10).

None of the global variables is specified to be volatile. So we may wonder whether the worker thread will see the values assigned to the entries `fnlist[j]`, `arglist[j]`, and `workflag[j]` by the manager thread. The processor may execute the assignments out of order, yet we have not included a memory fence to force a consistent view of memory. Is this a correct program? It is in fact correct because of the memory model of the Pthread library.

The POSIX specification of memory synchronization between threads is a little vague. But the standard does require memory sync during locking and unlocking. The Pthread library must insert a memory fence or another equivalent instruction during locking and unlocking. The user is freed from that responsibility. Memory fences alone are not sufficient. The compiler may decide to store some of the variables in registers.

In that case, the compiler must issue store instructions and write registers to memory before a memory sync.

For completeness, we give the definition of the function invoked by the manager thread to assign work to worker threads and do its own share of the work.

```
void manager(long *list, int count){
    spawn_workers();
    for(int i=0; i < count; i++){
        for(int tid=1; tid < nthreads; tid++)
            assignwork(i, tid, list);
        if(i%2==0)
            addone((void *)list);
        else
            addtwo((void *)list);
    }
    shutdown_workers();
}
```

The manager creates worker threads, assigns work, does its own share of the work, and finally shuts down the worker thread before exiting. The definitions of functions that spawn and shut down workers are omitted, as they involve no new point.

Fairness and the cost of spinlock implementation

What is the average cost of a parallel region in the spinlock implemenation on the 3.4 GHz quad-core AVX machine? To get the answer given in table 5.6, we have to dig deeper into spinlocks and modify our implementation.. The answer is much worse with our current implementation. On three different runs, we got the following three figures for the average cost in cycles:

```
1641
120361
1190550
```

Each average was computed over at least a million trials. The cost of a spinlock varies so unpredictably because the spinlocks are not guaranteed to be fair. If one thread gains a lock and another thread fails to gain it, it is fair to expect that the second thread must have priority after the first thread releases the lock. But spinlocks in the Pthread library do not guarantee such fairness,[6] and the highly erratic performance we see is an undesirable consequence.

When the manager thread wants to assign work, it repeatedly locks and unlocks until it can assign work. Once the master thread does its share of the work, it goes back to locking and unlocking repeatedly. The worker thread repeatedly locks and unlocks while performing work assigned to it. Yet the efficient performance of this implementation of parallel regions depends on alternation between the manager and the worker. If the spinlock is fair, we may expect them to alternate in a reasonable fashion, but that is not the case here. One of the processors may have faster access to the lock variable, for example, because it has a faster route to cache. In such a scenario, the spinlock will be unfair, and either the manager or the worker may monopolize the lock, resulting in the sort of erratic performance we are seeing.

We can insert a little random wait time to obtain an imperfect kind of fairness, which is still enough to show how significant it can be. The definition of `worker()` is modified as follows.

```
1  void *worker(void *arg){
2       int tid = *((int *) arg);
3       srand((tid+1)*28887);
4       while(1){
5             pthread_spin_lock(spin+tid-1);
6             if(workflag[tid-1]==1){
7                   (*(fnlist[tid-1]))(arglist[tid-1]);
8                   workflag[tid-1] = 0;
9             }
10            pthread_spin_unlock(spin+tid-1);
11            int rcount = rand()%TIEBREAK;
12            for(int i=0; i < rcount; i++)
13                  dummy();
14       }
15       return NULL;
16  }
```

---

[6]For a rigorous discussion of fairness in locking, see Herlihy and Shavit (2008).

This definition of `worker()` is a randomized version of the definition given earlier. The random number generator on each thread is seeded differently (line 3). A random integer between 0 and `TIEBREAK` is generated (line 11). TIEBREAK is a constant whose definition is not shown. On lines 12 and 13, the worker thread makes a random number of calls to `dummy()`, which is a function defined in another compilation unit that does nothing. The objective of inserting a random number of calls is to introduce a random wait time between unlocking and the next attempt to lock.

We do not show the modified version of `assignwork()` because the modifications are practically identical. Once again, the point is to insert a random wait between unlocking and the next attempt to lock to prevent one thread from monopolizing the lock.

In table 5.6, `TIEBREAK` was 10, 400, and 600 for 2, 3, and 4 threads, respectively. Spinlocking is less efficient than the plain C implementation, even after randomization. The performance is highly sensitive to the choice of `TIEBREAK`, which is one of the many imperfections in our attempt to ensure fairness.

Our implementation of parallel regions has highlighted the unfairness of spinlocks. Fairness is of so much consequence here because the same threads repeatedly lock and unlock the same locking variable. It must be noted, however, that fairness is not always essential or of so much consequence. For example, when an interrupt handler gains control, it typically uses a spinlock to do a little bit of work while ensuring access to shared data structures is protected by mutual exclusion. It releases the lock soon after, and the use of the same spinlock is only occasional.

When spinlocks are used, it is always a good idea to ensure that the thread is likely to be running and not waiting for a processor.

Parallel regions using mutexes

The implementation of parallel regions using mutexes is similar to that using spinlocks. There is a close parallel in the Pthread library between functions for handling mutexes and functions for handling spinlocks, as we have already seen.

The global variables in the mutex implementation of parallel regions are as follows.

```
void (*fnlist[nthreads-1])(void *);
void *arglist[nthreads-1];
int workflag[nthreads-1];
pthread_mutex_t mtx[nthreads-1];
```

```
pthread_t pthrd[nthreads-1];
```

The only difference here is that the array of locks `mtx[]` is of type `pthread_mutex_t` and not `pthread_spin_t`.

Below we list the definitions of `worker()` and `assignwork()` in the mutex implementation.

```
void *worker(void *arg){
    int tid = *((int *) arg);
    while(1){
        pthread_mutex_lock(mtx+tid-1);
        if(workflag[tid-1]==1){
            (*(fnlist[tid-1]))(arglist[tid-1]);
            workflag[tid-1] = 0;
        }
        pthread_mutex_unlock(mtx+tid-1);
    }
    return NULL;
}

void assignwork(int i, int tid, long *list){
    int j = tid-1;
    while(1){
        pthread_mutex_lock(mtx+j);
        if(workflag[j]==0){
            fnlist[j] = (i%2==0)?addone:addtwo;
            arglist[j] = (void *)(list+tid);
            workflag[j]=1;
            pthread_mutex_unlock(mtx+j);
            return;
        }
        pthread_mutex_unlock(mtx+j);
    }
}
```

The Pthread library functions

```
pthread_spin_lock()  and pthread_spin_unlock()
```

have been replaced by

```
pthread_mutex_lock() and pthread_mutex_unlock()
```

and that is all.

During locking and unlocking of mutexes, the local view of memory is serialized and made visible to other threads using a memory fence, and the compiler takes care to commit variables stored in registers to memory. None of the global variables needs to be specified as volatile.

We omit the definitions of **spawn_workers()** and **shutdown_workers()** as before.

Cost of mutex implementation

Table 5.6 shows that the average cost of a parallel region implemented using mutexes is 900 cycles with two threads, 2,200 cycles with three threads, and 6,500 cycles with four threads on the quad-core 3.4 GHz AVX computer. The cost is comparable to and slightly worse than the spinlock implementation. The plain C implementation is much faster.

If mutexes were implemented in the classical manner, a process that attempts to gain a mutex lock that is not available is put to sleep by the operating system. When the lock is released, one of the sleeping processes in the queue for that mutex lock is woken up. With classical mutexes, the average cost of a parallel region would be more.

Mutexes in the Pthread library on Linux are not implemented in the classical manner. They are implemented using futexes, which are supported by Linux system calls. Mutexes implemented using futexes do not enter the kernel at all if there is not much contention. In our setting, each thread that gains the lock releases it so quickly that the contending thread is rarely put to sleep. If a thread holds onto a lock for a long time, a Pthread mutex will put the contending thread to sleep.

Parallel regions using conditional variables

Using Pthread conditional variables, a more predictable alternation between the manager thread assigning work and the worker threads performing that work can be obtained. When conditional variables are used, the manager thread sends a signal to a worker when work has been assigned to it. A worker thread does not repeatedly lock and unlock a mutex when it is looking for work. Instead, it waits for a signal. Correspondingly, the worker thread sends a signal to the manager when it has completed that work, which means that the manager thread does not repeatedly lock and unlock to check whether a worker thread is free.

The global variables in the conditional variables implementation of parallel regions are the following:

```
void (*fnlist[nthreads])(void *);
void *arglist[nthreads];
int workflag[nthreads-1];
pthread_mutex_t wrklock[nthreads-1];
pthread_cond_t cv_work[nthreads-1];
pthread_cond_t cv_free[nthreads-1];
pthread_t pthrd[nthreads-1];
```

The variables `fnlist[]`, `arglist[]`, `workflag[]`, and `pthrd[]` have the same meaning as in the mutex implementation. As before, the manager sets `fnlist[tid]` and `arglist[tid]` to let worker thread `tid` know which function to execute on which argument. As in all implementations of parallel regions considered in this section, the workers are made to alternate between `addone()` and `addtwo()`. The exit function has the following definition:

```
void exitfn(void *arg){
    int tid = *((int *) arg);
    pthread_mutex_unlock(wrklock+tid-1);
    pthread_exit(NULL);
}
```

Because a worker thread executes `exitfn()`, as well as other functions it is told to execute, after locking the mutex `wrklock[tid]`, it must unlock before it exits. The conditional variables `cv_work[]` are used by the manager to tell the workers that there is work to do. The conditional variables `cv_free[]` are used by the workers to tell the manager that they have completed the work assigned to them. Conditional variables are always used in coordination with mutexes. The conditional variables `cv_work[]` and `cv_free[]` coordinate with the mutexes `wrklock[]`.

The worker threads gain control with the following function:

```
1   void *worker(void *arg){
2       int tid = *((int *)(arg));
3       while(1){
4           pthread_mutex_lock(wrklock+tid-1);
5           if(workflag[tid-1]==0)
6               pthread_cond_wait(cv_work+tid-1, wrklock+tid-1);
7           (*(fnlist[tid-1]))(arglist[tid-1]);
8           workflag[tid-1]=0;
9           pthread_cond_signal(cv_free+tid-1);
10          pthread_mutex_unlock(wrklock+tid-1);
11      }
12      return NULL;
13  }
```

The worker thread locks `wrklock[tid-1]`, the mutex corresponding to worker `tid`, on line 4. On line 5, it checks `workflag[tid-1]`, a region of shared memory accessed by both the worker and the manager, as soon as it gains the lock. If there is no work to be done, it waits on a conditional variable on line 6.

The library function `pthread_cond_wait()` takes a pointer to a conditional variable as well as a pointer to a mutex as an argument. It *unlocks* the mutex and puts the thread to sleep—atomically with respect to any attempt to access either the mutex or the conditional variable by some other thread. When the conditional variable is signaled by some other thread, the sleeping thread is ready to be woken up, but it must lock the mutex before waking up.

The unlocking of the mutex before putting the thread to sleep during

```
pthread_cond_wait()
```

implies that the worker thread does not contend for the lock when it is looking for work. This unlocking is the central element in the semantics of conditional variables.

On line 7, the worker thread performs the work assigned to it, and on line 8, it sets an entry of the `workflag[]` to indicate it is free. On line 9, a signal is sent indicating that the worker thread is free, and the mutex is freed on line 10. The Pthread memory model requires a memory sync at each of the library functions in the while block from lines 3 through 11. Thus, we may be sure that the work is indeed complete and the `workflag[]` entry is appropriately modified in memory before the `cv_free` signal and unlocking of the associated mutex.

The corresponding function executed by the manager thread is as defined below.

```
void manager(long *list, int count){
    for(int i=0; i < count;i++){
        for(int j=0; j < nthreads-1; j++){
            pthread_mutex_lock(wrklock+j);
            if(workflag[j]==1)
                pthread_cond_wait(cv_free+j, wrklock+j);
            fnlist[j] = (i%2==0)?addone:addtwo;
            arglist[j] = (void *)(list+j+1);
            workflag[j]=1;
            pthread_cond_signal(cv_work+j);
            pthread_mutex_unlock(wrklock+j);
        }
        if(i%2==0)
            addone((void *)list);
        else
            addtwo((void *)list);
    }
}
```

The manager does its own share of the work outside the locked region, but the signal cv_work indicating that the work has been assigned must be sent inside the locked region. If the signal is sent outside the locked region, it may arrive after the worker thread has gained the lock and verified workflag[tid-1] to be 0 and before it calls pthread_cond_wait() to wait on cv_work[tid-1]. If such a thing happens, the signal will be lost and the program will deadlock. The manager does its share of the work, invoking either addone() or addtwo() outside the parallel region.

A little more syntax is needed for using conditional variables. To exhibit that, we give a listing of the function used to create the worker threads.

```
void spawn_workers(){
    static  int tidlist[nthreads-1];
    for(int i=0; i < nthreads-1; i++){
        workflag[i] = 0;
        tidlist[i] = i+1;
        pthread_mutex_init(wrklock+i,NULL);
```

```
            pthread_cond_init(cv_work+i,  NULL);
            pthread_cond_init(cv_free+i,  NULL);
            pthread_create(pthrd+i,NULL,worker,  tidlist+i);
      }
  }
```

The reason for specifying the definition of tidlist[] as static has been explained
before. The only new syntactic element here is the function for creating and initializing
condition variables. The conditional variables, as well as the mutexes and the threads,
are created with the NULL or default attribute.

The listing of the function for destroying threads is given in full.

```
void  shutdown(){
      static int tidlist[nthreads-1];
      for(int i=0; i < nthreads-1; i++){
            pthread_mutex_lock(wrklock+i);
            if(workflag[i]==1)
                  pthread_cond_wait(cv_free+i, wrklock+i);
            tidlist[i]  =  i+1;
            fnlist[i]  =  exitfn;
            arglist[i]  =  tidlist+i;
            workflag[i]=1;
            pthread_cond_signal(cv_work+i);
            pthread_mutex_unlock(wrklock+i);
      }
      for(int i=0; i < nthreads-1; i++){
            pthread_join(pthrd[i],  NULL);
            pthread_mutex_destroy(wrklock+i);
            pthread_cond_destroy(cv_work+i);
            pthread_cond_destroy(cv_free+i);
      }
  }
```

The workers are terminated by asking them to execute exitfn(). The new syntax
here is the function for destroying a conditional variable. The manager thread must
join with a worker thread before destroying the conditional variables and the mutex
corresponding to that worker thread.

When parallel regions are implemented using conditional variables, the manager thread puts itself to sleep if it wants to assign work but the worker is busy. The worker threads put themselves to sleep if they are free to work but find that no work has been assigned. The spinlock-like behavior of mutexes does not occur here. There is regular and predictable alternation between assignment of work by the manager and its completion by the worker threads.

TLB flushes and cost of conditional variables implementation

Table 5.6 shows that the average cost of a parallel region implemented using conditional variables is 30,000 cycles with two threads. On a quad-core 3.4 GHz AVX machine (see table A.1 for its full name), the cost is much lower and only 9,000 cycles with four threads. Even with eight threads, the average cost per parallel region is 18,000 cycles and much lower than the cost for two threads.

The explanation of this conundrum appears to be as follows. With two, four, or eight threads, there will be context switches during the alternation between assignment of work and its completion by the worker threads. With two threads, the threads get switched around between the four cores of the 3.4 GHz AVX machine. When either the worker or manager thread is switched out, an editor, a web browser, or a kernel thread may get the processor. With eight threads, there are many more context switches per parallel region on an average, but nearly every context switch is between two threads in the same group of eight. Context switches between two threads in the same thread group are much less expensive. The kernel does not need to switch page tables or flush the TLB. The TLB flush is essential to preserve the integrity and correctness of the memory system when two processes with different virtual address spaces are switched. The greater expense of context switches and related factors appear to explain the reason the conditional variables implementation is so much more expensive with just two threads.

Exercise 5.3.1. Write a program to reverse a long array using Pthreads. Does your program need mutexes or spinlocks? Do you expect your program to be faster or slower than an OpenMP program for the same task? Explain.

Exercise 5.3.2. Explain why the `volatile` qualifier is used in the plain C implementation of parallel regions but not in the implementations using mutexes, spinlocks, or conditional variables.

5.4   Program memory

In the virtual memory setup described in section 4.4, every process has its own page tables to map virtual memory to physical memory, and every instruction with a memory reference invokes this map from virtual to physical memory. The virtual memory system allows many distinct processes to coexist on the same computer. Threads are a group of processes that share the same map from virtual to physical memory. In addition, each thread may define its own local variables in an area that is ordinarily invisible to other threads. Thus, the concept of threads is tied to the memory system, and understanding program memory facilitates understanding threads.

In this section, we limit ourselves to single-threaded programs but take a deeper look into the way program memory is set up and organized. Section 5.4.1 shows how to define a new system call in Linux. The operating system is a program, like any other program, and system calls are the set of functions used by user programs to invoke it. Thus, there are system calls to read and write files and so on. Writing one's own system call should almost never be done. Linux provides an extensive set of system calls,[7] so extensive that it is difficult to get a good grip on the many facilities it provides.

Despite this caveat, the system call defined in section 5.4.1 serves usual pedagogical purposes. Later, we will insert print statements into the Linux kernel to examine the memory system and thread creation. The system call is used to turn those print statements on or off.

The first lesson from implementing a system call is to simply understand that the operating system is just another program, although an exceedingly complicated one. Because the operating system manages distinct and simultaneous processes as well as multifarious devices, handling concurrency has always been an issue with operating systems. Many of the topics of threaded programming, such as mutual exclusion, came up long ago in the context of operating systems.

Programs rely on operating systems in many more ways than most programmers realize. When we try to understand program speed or some other characteristic in depth, we are inevitably led inside the operating system kernel. The little forays we make into the Linux kernel will help us understand segmentation faults, memory errors, and thread creation.

---

[7]For Linux system calls, see Kerrisk (2010).

Section 5.4.2 introduces stacks. The stack is one of the simplest and most important data structures. All programming models are based on function calls, and the stack is the data structure used to save program state at the point of call and to restore it at the point of return. Understanding how program state is saved and restored is useful for all kinds of programming. Another advantage is that it helps clarify programming abstractions that may look artificial in their abstract setting. In section 5.4.2, we explain how recursion works using stacks. Without knowledge of stacks, the idea of recursion can look vaguely abstract, although in fact it is quite straightforward.

Much of a C/C++ programmer's time is spent dealing with segmentation faults and memory errors. Section 5.4.3 explains how these errors arise and are caught. Segmentation faults are caught deep inside the operating system kernel, and memory errors can escape detection for a long while. The memory system is set up for speed and efficiency, not to make the C programmer's life easier. It is often true that memory errors are hard to detect and crash the program at a location far away from the bug, making memory errors difficult to deal with. Section 5.4.3 explains why this is so.

Many scientific programmers have the habit of allocating large amounts of space statically on the stack. This habit is a holdover from Fortran. Section 5.4.3 shows why this is a bad idea.

5.4.1   An easy system call

The operating system kernel offers its services to user programs through system calls. There are system calls for dealing with every single part of the computing system. There are system calls related to the file system, networks, memory management, and process creation and scheduling. Every `printf()` or `malloc()` begins life in the C library but finds its way into the operating system kernel through a system call.

System call definition and invocation

The system call defined in this section gives us a peek into the Linux kernel. The system call sets a global flag. The global flag is used to turn print statements on and off elsewhere in the kernel.

The definition of the system call is placed at the end of the file `kernel/sys.c` in the Linux source tree (Version 3.6).[8]

```
1  int dv_print_flag=0;
2  EXPORT_SYMBOL(dv_print_flag);
3
4  asmlinkage long sys_set_dvflag(int flag){
5       dv_print_flag = flag;
6       return 77;
7  }
```

Line 1 defines a global variable of type `int`. This global variable is used to control the level of printing in other parts of the kernel. For example, if the value of the variable is in the range $[100, 200)$, kernel functions related to thread/process creation will print messages. For some other range, functions related to file I/O will print messages. The purpose of these messages is to help us understand what is happening inside the kernel. Printing these messages requires modifications to other parts of the kernel.

Line 2 exports the global variable. The Linux kernel is built by linking thousands of compilation units, and `sys.c` is only one of them. Some parts of the kernel, such as device drivers, are loaded dynamically using `vmalloc()`. The global variable is exported to make it visible to the dynamically linked modules. Some of our print messages will be inside device drivers and other modules.

The `asmlinkage` qualifier on line 4 is a new element in the definition of this system call. It is the first hint here that a system call is not like any function. If an ordinary function has a single argument of type `int`, by convention that argument is passed using the `%edi` register in 64-bit Linux.[9] No such convention is in effect when a system call is made. All the arguments to a system call are passed on the kernel stack (kernel stacks are discussed in the next section). The `asmlinkage` qualifier is telling the compiler that the function will receive all its arguments on the stack.

Exiting a system call is special, just like entry. The `SYSEXIT` instruction is used to exit from system calls.

---

[8]See Love (2010).

[9]For function call conventions pertaining to registers on GNU/Linux, see the gcc manuals or part 5 of Agner Fog's optimization document posted on his web page: `http://www.agner.org/optimize/`.

To make the global variable `dv_print_flag` visible to all the compilation units, the declaration

```
extern int dv_print_flag;
```

is placed in `include/linux/printk.h` in the source tree. The kernel is not linked against the C libraries. So the kernel cannot call `printf()`. But the Linux kernel has `printk()`, which is similar.

Unlike ordinary functions, system calls are not called using their names. Instead there is a system call table. We need to make an entry in the table and make the declaration of the system call visible in a header file. The table entry goes into the file

```
arch/x86/syscalls/syscall_64.tbl
```

in Linux 3.6 and takes the form

```
313   common    set_dvflag         sys_set_dvflag
```

The system call number is 313. There are 312 system calls already. The name of the function is given at the end. Although system calls are called by number and not by name, it is conventional to wrap the call inside a function or macro. For this system call, the name of the wrapper function or macro would be `set_dvflag`. It is typical to derive the name by dropping the `sys` prefix.

The system call table is a table of function pointers prepared by the kernel and made available to the processors. The function that implements the system call must be declared in `include/linux/syscalls.h`. For system call number 313, the declaration is

```
asmlinkage long sys_set_dvflag(int flag);
```

The kernel is now in a position to set up the table of function pointers.

If the kernel is built and loaded,[10] we may invoke system call number 313 as follows:

```
#include <unistd.h>
#include <asm/unistd.h>
```

.

---

[10]For a guide to building and loading the Linux kernel, see `http://kernelnewbies.org/ KernelBuild`. The directions worked smoothly on Xubuntu Linux but not Fedora Linux.

.

```
long y=syscall(__NR_set_dvflag,100);
```

When the kernel is rebuilt, it uses the information we entered into `syscall_64.tbl` and defines `__NR_set_dvflag` as 313. So we don't need to remember the system call number explicitly. The system call is generated using `syscall()`. The first argument is the number of the system call. Later arguments are passed to the system call on the kernel stack. The system call is issued using the `SYSENTER` instruction. The `syscall()` shown here passes 100 as an argument. The global print flag gets set to 100. We may discard the returned value `y` or verify that it is 77 as it should be.

Cost of making a system call

By timing a large number of calls to `set_dvflag()`, we find that the average call takes approximately 190 cycles. In contrast, the cost of calling a function that does something similar is just 5.2 cycles. The timing was done on a 3.4 GHz AVX machine (see table A.1 of the appendix).

Why is it so much more expensive to call and return from a system call? Every time a system call is made, the processor automatically saves all the general-purpose registers[11] on the kernel stack and restores all the registers when the system call returns. Saving and restoring the registers must be a big part of the overhead of a system call.

The system call we have considered here is particularly simple. More complicated system calls will have an overhead greater than 190 cycles. A few system calls have lengthy argument lists, and it takes time to save the arguments on the kernel stack. The same is true for more complicated function calls.

Whenever a function or system call is timed inside a loop, there will be many fewer cache misses than will be the case in a more realistic scenario. The function pointer will be in cache, and so will be the instructions in the body of the function. When the function is called as part of a more complex activity, the function definition is much less likely to be in cache.

An overhead of around 200 cycles is not cheap but is not too bad. Kernel calls perhaps get a little too much blame for being expensive. Some kernel calls may be

---

[11]For a full list of registers saved during a system call, see Bovet and Cesati (2005).

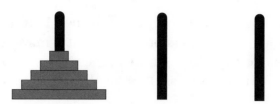

Figure 5.2: Towers of Hanoi. The discs must be moved from peg 0 to peg 1 without ever place a bigger disc on top of a smaller disc.

expensive because they invoke complex algorithms, but user space implementations of the same algorithms would incur the same expenses. If a single kernel call is made to transfer 10 MB of data over a network, the overhead of calling the kernel is negligible and immeasurably small. However, if a kernel call is made for every single byte that is written to a file of size 10 GB, the overhead may freeze the system.

5.4.2 Stacks

The stack is a collection of objects that supports two operations: push and pop. If an object is pushed on the stack, it lands right at the top. If another object is pushed, it goes on top above the last object that was pushed. The objects of a stack are ordered with the most recently pushed object on top. The pop operation removes the topmost object from the stack.

In terms of its representation in memory, the stack is a simple data structure. To represent a stack of `ints`, for example, we may simply use an array of type `int` and another variable to keep track of the size of the stack. Every pop operation decreases the size of the stack by 1, and every push operation increases the size of the stack by 1.

In terms of the way data is represented or accessed, there is nothing new to stacks. The novelty is in the abstract view of a collection of objects that constitute a stack. As with a stack of plates, we can insert and remove only at the top.

Towers of Hanoi

Stacks are useful for implementing recursion and function calls. The Towers of Hanoi, a classic example, illustrates the usefulness of stacks.

The problem is to move n disks from peg 0 to peg 1. In a single move, we may move the topmost disc of one peg to another peg, but a move is not allowed to place a bigger disc over a smaller disc. To begin with, the n discs on peg 0 are ordered with the biggest disc at the bottom of the smallest at the top—to form a tower (see figure 5.2).

The notation hanoi(A, B, n) stands for the problem of moving n discs from peg A to peg B. We begin by pushing hanoi($0, 1, n$) on top of the stack:

$$\text{hanoi}(0, 1, n).$$

If the problem instance on top of the stack is hanoi(A, B, n) and $n = 1$, the lone disc is moved from A to B and the problem instance is popped to reduce the size of the stack. If $n > 1$, the strategy is to move $n - 1$ discs from A to C, where C is the third peg, move the last disc from A to B, and then move $n - 1$ discs from C to A. The topmost problem instance is popped from the top of the stack and three other problem instances are pushed on the stack. If $n > 1$, we get:

$$\text{hanoi}(0, 2, n - 1)$$
$$\text{hanoi}(0, 1, 1)$$
$$\text{hanoi}(2, 1, n - 1)$$

If $n > 2$, the topmost problem instance is popped and hanoi($0, 2, n - 1$) is replaced by three other problem instances to get the following stack:

$$\text{hanoi}(0, 1, n - 2)$$
$$\text{hanoi}(0, 2, 1)$$
$$\text{hanoi}(1, 2, n - 2)$$
$$\text{hanoi}(0, 1, 1)$$
$$\text{hanoi}(2, 1, n - 1)$$

The process is repeated. The topmost problem instance is popped and either removed or replaced with three other problem instances until the stack is empty. If the number of discs is equal to 1 and the problem instance is hanoi($A, B, 1$), the message "move from A to B" is printed out when the problem instance is popped and removed.

If we write a recursive function in C/C++ for solving Towers of Hanoi, the function will make two recursive calls if $n > 1$ and print a message if $n = 1$. The stacking of problem instances occurs during nested recursive function calls. Alternatively, the problem may be solved by using a stack explicitly. The stack is the natural mechanism for nesting function calls with or without recursion.

The user mode stack

Stacks are useful for maintaining the state of running processes. This application is so important that the stack is hardwired into the x86 instruction set as well as most other instruction sets.

In a running process, certain variables are allocated using definitions such as `int x`. The state of a running process includes the values of all its variables, the values stored in all memory locations that may be referenced using those variables, and the next instruction the processor will execute, whose address is stored in `%rip`.

However, these three items of information are not enough to fully capture the state of a running process. The next instruction to be executed may be deeply nested inside function calls. Each of these functions must return to the instruction that immediately follows the point where the functions were called. The return address of each function in a nested series of calls is essential information for capturing the state of a running process. This is where stacks come in.

Conceptually, the local variables of the function that is currently running are topmost on the stack. The stack pointer (the pointer to the top of the stack) is stored in the `%rsp` register. During a function call, the return address is pushed on top of the stack by the `call` instruction. The newly called function may allocate other variables on the stack. Variables declared locally using declarations such as `int x` or `int y[100]` are allocated on the stack. If the newly called function makes another function call, it does so after pushing its return address on the stack and so on.

When a function returns, it first cleans up its stack by restoring the stack pointer `%rsp` to its original value. The stack pointer is restored by performing simple arithmetic or copying back its original value saved in some other register. After cleaning up its stack, the returning function executes the `RET` instruction, which pops the stack to find the return address.

This conceptual picture hits the main ideas, but the actual picture is more complicated. The complications arise because of the way registers are used to store certain variables, differing conventions with regard to different registers, and conventions for passing arguments to and returning values from functions.

The user mode stack grows every time the process makes a function call and shrinks every time a function returns. It is natural to ask what happens when a program makes a system call. A system call transfers control to a function defined in the operating system's kernel. The kernel functions use another stack called the kernel stack. Every process has a kernel stack in addition to its user space stack.

Kernel mode stack

In Linux, `PAGE_OFFSET` divides the virtual address space into two parts, as shown in figure 4.8. The lower part is for user processes and the upper part is for the kernel. The user area in virtual memory is occupied by the program, its global data, user mode stack, and dynamically allocated memory. The program is in a low region of the address space and the stack is in a high region, as we explained in an earlier chapter (see figure 4.8).

Nested function calls are stacked one above the other on the user mode stack. What happens if there is a system call? Every program requests services from the kernel directly or indirectly. Print statements, requests for dynamic memory, and reading and writing to a file end up as system calls. Unlike ordinary function calls, system calls and the kernel functions they call are not pushed onto the user mode stack.

In Linux, every process gets a kernel mode stack, in addition to its user mode stack. The user mode stack occupies a high region in the user area, and the kernel mode stack is in the kernel area of virtual memory.[12] The kernel mode stack is much smaller than the user mode stack. The maximum size of the user mode stack is configurable and is typically several megabytes (this number may be found using the GNU/Linux command `ulimit -a`). The kernel mode stack has a fixed size that is typically equal to two pages or 8,192 bytes. The two pages that constitute the kernel mode stack of a process are next to each other and are allocated in the linearly mapped region of kernel memory.

When a process is running in user mode, the `%rsp` register points to the top of the user mode stack. After a system call is made and the process switches to kernel mode, the `%rsp` register points to the top of the kernel mode stack. When the system call returns, the stack pointer reverts to the user mode stack. When the kernel mode stack is created, a pointer to the process descriptor is stored in the kernel stack of that process. The process descriptor is a kernel data structure that holds all kinds of

---

[12]The virtual address space immediately above `PAGE_OFFSET` is linearly mapped to page frames using `alloc_pages()` and `kmalloc()`. A part of the kernel's virtual address space is mapped non-linearly to page frames using `vmalloc()`. The kernel mode stack of each process is allocated in the linearly mapped region immediately above `PAGE_OFFSET`.

information about the process. The Linux kernel defines a macro called `current` that extracts the process descriptor from the kernel stack.

System calls, kernel functions that implement system calls, and page fault handlers execute in process context. Kernel functions that execute in process context may use `current` to obtain information about the process on whose behalf they are executing. Interrupt handlers, however, live on borrowed time and do not execute in process context.

5.4.3 Segmentation faults and memory errors

The use of pointers exposes the programmer to errors that corrupt memory. Memory errors can befuddle even expert programmers. An erroneous program with memory errors may work on some systems but crash on others. The point where the program crashes can be far away from the point where the error occurs. The program may work for some inputs but not for others. In multithreaded programs, memory errors may be triggered by race conditions that are hard to reproduce, making debugging difficult.

In this section, we take a detailed look at segmentation faults and memory errors. Throughout this section, we assume that the maximum size of the stack is at least 2^{23} bytes or 8.389 MB. The examples can be easily modified for smaller stacks. The size of the stack may be determined using the GNU/Linux command `ulimit -a`.

Most of the segmentation faults and memory errors are caught by the paging system. Suppose a user process issues an instruction such as `movq $80, (%rsi)` to load the number 80 into the 64-bit location to which the register `%rsi` is pointing. The processor first looks up the TLB to map the virtual address stored in `%rsi` to a physical address. If there is no TLB entry for that address, it uses the `%cr3` register to access the page tables. If there is no page table entry, there is a page fault and the page fault handler is invoked. Many memory errors are caught by the page fault handler.

The mere fact that the page fault handler has been invoked does not imply a memory error. The page might have been swapped out to disc. More likely, the memory may have been allocated dynamically using `malloc()` or statically on the stack using a definition such as `int x[1000]` but uninitialized. A page is mapped to a page frame only at the point of first use (demand paging).

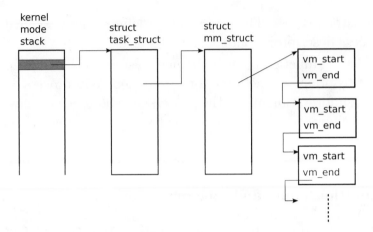

Figure 5.3: Illustration of how vm areas are accessed.

VM areas in the Linux kernel

VM (virtual memory) areas[13] are data structures maintained by the kernel for each process that specify which virtual addresses the program may legally generate.

The definition of sys_getpid(), which implements the getpid() system call, is found in kernel/timer.c in the source tree of Linux version 3.6. This system call is modified to access the vm area that contains the user mode stack. The following code is inserted into sys_getpid():

```
if((300<=dv_print_flag)&&(dv_print_flag<400)){
  struct vm_area_struct *dv_vmptr
    = find_vma(current->mm,current->mm->start_stack);
  printk(KERN_ALERT "vm_start = %lx \n",
      dv_vmptr->vm_start);
  printk(KERN_ALERT "vm_end = %lx \n",
      dv_vmptr->vm_end);
}
```

The print flag, which is set using the system call of section 5.4.1, is used to turn the print statements on or off.

---

[13]See Bovet and Cesati (2005).

Figure 5.3 is a schematic depiction of how vm areas are accessed. The vm areas are stored in a linked list. Each vm area specifies the beginning and end of a valid area of virtual memory.

For every process, the kernel creates a process descriptor, and the process descriptor contains a pointer to an `mm_struct` that contains a pointer to the list of vm areas that the program may legally access. There is a single vm area that corresponds to the stack of the process. There can be multiple vm areas corresponding to dynamically allocated memory.

If the generated address page faults but belongs to one of the vm areas, there is no memory error. The page fault handler will assign a page frame to the page (assuming one is available) that contains the address and update the page tables. There is a memory error (segmentation fault) only if the address does not belong to any of the vm areas of the process.

Functions `ff0()`, `f0()`, and `f1()`

We shall write a few simple functions to exercise the user mode stack and trigger segmentation faults in a controlled manner.

The function `sum_arr()` prints the sum of an array of `long`s. Its definition is listed for completeness.

```
void sum_arr(long *p,long len){
    long ans=0;
    for(long i=0; i < len; i++)
        ans += p[i];
    printf("sum = %ld\n",ans);
}
```

The heart of our attempts to exercise the user mode stack is the function `ff0()`. Its definition follows:

```
void ff0(long *a0, long *list, long n){
    for(int i=0; i < 1000; i++)
        a0[i] = 0;
    for(long i=0; i < n; i++)
        a0[list[i]] = list[i]*list[i];
    printf("in ff0: ");
```

```
            sum_arr(a0, 1000);
    }
```

The function ff0() is always called by f0(), and f0() defines a0 using long a0[1000]. To begin with, the entries of the array a0[] are set to zero. The pointer list is allocated dynamically, and the entries of list[] are not stored on the stack.

The usefulness of list[] lies in being able to generate controlled illegal accesses into a0[]. For example, if list[] is the sequence $0, -1, \ldots, -1000$, locations of lower addresses than a0 are accessed. If list[] is the sequence $-500, \ldots, -1000$, locations with addresses lower than a0 are accessed after skipping 500 locations. If list[] is the sequence $1000, \ldots, 1999$, then a thousand locations with addresses higher than a0, and just beyond the legal limit of the array a0[], are accessed.

The chief purpose of f0(), whose definition is given below, is to call ff0(), which it does at the end.

```
    void f0(long *list, long n){
        long a0[1000];
        printf("a0 (in f0)= %p\n", a0);
        printf("pid (in f0) = %ld\n", getpid());
        ff0(a0, list, n);
    }
```

The array a0[] is allocated on the stack and takes up 8,000 bytes. Because of the modifications made to the Linux kernel, getpid() will print the start and end of the vm area of the stack. The array list[0..n-1] specifies entries of a0[] that will be modified by the call to ff0().

The function f1() defined below calls f0(), which as we have seen calls ff0(). It defines an 8 MB array on the stack.

```
    void f1(long *list, long n){
        long a1[1000*1000];
        for(int i=0; i < 1000*1000; i++)
            a1[i] = 0;
        f0(list, n);
        printf("in f1: ");
        sum_arr(a1, 1000*1000);
    }
```

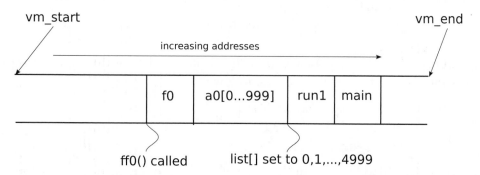

Figure 5.4: The stack resulting from an invocation of `run1()` from `main()`, just after call to `ff0()`. Notice that the stack grows leftward beginning with `main()`, the first function to be called and which calls `run1()`, which calls `f0()`.

This function defines the array `a1[]` and claims 8 MB on the stack.

The key thing to remember is that the arrays `a0[]` and `a1[]` are both allocated on the user mode stack—`a0[]` by the function `f0()` and `a1[]` by `f1()`. The arrays `a0[]` and `a1[]` are defined to have 10^3 and 10^6 entries, respectively.

Segmentation fault caused by illegal virtual address

We begin exercising the stack with the following function:

```
void run1(){
    long *list = new long[5000];
    for(int i=0; i < 5000; i++)
        list[i] = i;
    f0(list, 5000);
    delete[] list;
}
```

The stacking of function calls is shown in figure 5.4. Figure 5.4 shows a0 between `f0` and `run1`, with `f0` to its left, because the array `a0[]` is defined after `run1()` calls `f0()` but before `f0()` calls `ff0()`.

What is `run1()` doing? It is in effect forcing `ff0()` to generate accesses to entries numbered $0\ldots4999$ of the array `a0[]`. Of course, `a0[]` defined by `f0()` has only

10^3 entries (see figure 5.4). We will understand exactly how the segmentation fault occurs.

Just before f0() calls ff0(), which is the situation depicted in figure 5.4, the vm area corresponding to the stack looks as follows:

```
vm_end  =  0x7fffc64a5000
    a0  =  vm_end -  13312
vm_start  =  vm_end - 139264
```

Here the address vm_end is given in hex, but a0 and vm_start are given as offsets from vm_end in decimal for convenience. The pointer a0 is 13,312 bytes below vm_end even though the array a0[] has only 8,000 bytes. The system appears to use up around 5,000 bytes near the top of the stack. There is also a lot of padding between a0 and vm_start.

Because a0[] is an array of type long and $4,999 \times 8 > 13,312$, the locations accessed go well beyond vm_end. When the address generated crosses vm_end, there is a page fault. The page fault handler will find that there is no valid vm area containing the address and trigger a segmentation fault. With a little trouble, we can calculate exactly which iteration of the for-loop in ff0() triggers a segmentation fault. That iteration is $i = 13,312/8 = 1,664$.

Segmentation fault caused by overwriting return address

The second run we look at also seg faults, but in a quite different manner, as we will see.

```
void run2(){
    long *list = new long[2000];
    for(int i=0; i < 2000; i++)
        list[i] = i;
    f1(list, 2000);
    delete[] list;
}
```

Figure 5.5 shows the order in which pointers are pushed on the stack: main, run2, f1, and f0. Each of these is a pointer to the point of return. The array a1[] is defined by f1() to be large enough for 10^6 longs or 8 MB. The vm area of the stack and the value of a0 just before the call to ff0() inside f0() looks as follows:

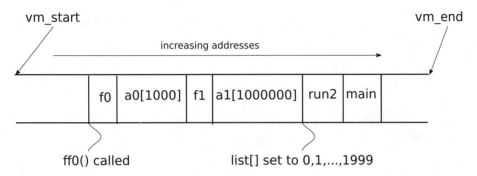

Figure 5.5: The stack resulting from an invocation of `run2()` from `main()`, just after call to `ff0()`. Notice that the stack grows leftward.

```
vm_end  =  0x7fff325e2000
    a0  =  vm_end  -  8019136
vm_start  =  vm_end  -  8028160
```

Notice that there is more than 8 MB of room in the stack above `a0`. Much of that is memory allocated for `a1[]` by the function `f1()`.

When control reaches `ff0()`, the initialization of `list[]` in `run2()` triggers the execution of the statement `a0[j]=j*j` for $j = 0, \ldots, 1,999$ in the for-loop on lines 4 and 5 in `ff0()`. There is so much room above `a0` in the vm area that includes the stack that none of the iterations of the loop will seg fault. Indeed, the print statement at the end of `ff0()` prints

```
in ff0:  sum  =  332833500
```

It may be verified that $\sum_{i=0}^{999} i^2 = 332,833,500$.

Despite the memory error, not only does `ff0()` complete its loop, it also prints the sum correctly. Why then is there a segmentation fault? To answer this question, we must go back to figure 5.5 and look at it closely. The pointer `a0` is pointing to a location between `f1` and `f0`. The gap between `f1` and `f0` on the stack is large enough for 1,000 `long` entries and is approximately 8,000 bytes—8 KB being the memory allocated to the array `a0[]`. When `ff0()` indexes into the array `a0[]` and goes from `a0[0]` to `a0[1999]`, it writes over the address `f1` that has been carefully saved to allow `f0()` to complete its return. That is where the problem arises.

So `ff0()` is able to complete successfully. During return, it finds the return address `f0` on the stack, and it is able to return to `f0()` correctly. However, when `f0()`

tries to return, its return address f1 has been overwritten by something. There is a segmentation fault when f0() tries to return to f1().

Memory error without segmentation fault

In fact, we can modify run2() slightly so that there is no segmentation fault, although the program is erroneous.

```
void run3(){
    long *list = new long[2000];
    for(int i=0; i < 2000; i++)
        list[i] = i+10000;
    f1(list, 2000);
    delete[] list;
}
```

The stacking of functions with run3() is identical to that with run2(). The difference is in the way the 2,000 entries of list[] have been set up. The for-loop on lines 4 and 5 of ff0() executes the statement a0[j]=j*j for $j = 10^4, \ldots, 10^4 + 1{,}999$. So it skips over the first 1,000 entries of a0[] as well as f1—the address that f0() must return to—and modifies certain entries of a1[]. The program prints the following:

```
in ff0: sum = 0
in f1: sum = 242644667000
```

We may verify that $\sum_{i=0}^{1999} \left(i + 10^4\right)^2 = 242{,}644{,}667{,}000$ to validate our explanation.

In run1(), run2(), and run3(), all the entries of list[] were ≥ 0. We may fill list[] with negative entries to examine scenarios that break the stack in the opposite direction, which is the direction the stack grows. If the entries of list[] are all negative and $\leq -1{,}000$, for example, the local variables of ff0() and the return addresses are not overwritten. The program will run to completion if the maximum limit on the size of the stack is not exceeded. In a more complex program, the point where the program fails can be far away from the error.

The kernel does not shrink the stack, even when a function that uses a lot of memory on the stack returns. Once the kernel adopts the policy that it will let the stack expand up to its maximum limit, whenever the process generates memory references in the stack area, there is no reasonable way for the kernel to shrink the stack. Functions return using the RET instruction. No kernel function is called during every function return—it would be a huge waste to do so. The kernel has no way of knowing when a process scales back its use of the stack.

Many computing clusters set the maximum stack size to be as large as 8 GB. Such a large limit on the stack size is not a good thing, although it might be helpful to inexperienced programmers. Memory acquired on the stack is never released and the performance of programs that abuse the stack may degrade.

Corruption of dynamically allocated memory

Dynamic memory allocation using `malloc()`, `_mm_malloc()`, or `new[]` can invoke algorithms of considerable complexity. Functions such as `malloc()` and `free()` invoked by user programs are defined in runtime libraries in user space.

Our discussion of dynamic memory errors is confined to the following simple function:

```
void mreg(long *a, long n){
    for(long i=0; i < 5; i++)
        a[i] = i;
    a[n] = n;
}
```

This function initializes the first five entries of the array `a[]`. Each entry is a `long`. Finally, `mreg()` stores n in the $n+1$st entry `a[n]`. We will attempt to cause memory corruption by passing invalid values of n and understand how the system responds.

The function `mreg()` is called by `run()`, whose definition follows:

```
void run(long n){
    long *a = (long *)malloc(5*sizeof(long));
    mreg(a, n);
    free(a);
}
```

It is evident that `run()` allocates `a[]` to point to 5 entries of type `long`. It then calls `mreg[]` to assign to `a[n]`.

The point to be noted is that the vm area where the array `a[]` is allocated typically has a lot of padding in either direction.

If we make the call `run(5)`, we may expect that there is no segmentation fault because the vm area is most probably larger than 5 entries of the type `long`. There is in fact no segmentation fault, but the runtime library detects an error when we try to free the pointer. How could that be? It turns out that the runtime library is storing a magic number in the location `a[5]`. When freeing the pointer, it checks whether that magic number has been overwritten. The runtime `glibc` library catches this error and produces a lengthy error report, which includes the memory map of the process—as if that were just the tonic to cheer up the programmer. In a more complex program, the point where the error is caught can be far away from where it occurs.

Let us try `run(6)` or `run(7)` or `run(10000)`. None of these function calls produces an error message. They all run smoothly. All of them access illegal locations, but it turns out the kernel has created a pretty large vm area expecting more memory to be allocated dynamically. The runtime `glibc` library fails to catch the error. The magic number is stuffed into the first entry past the legal boundary but not ones after that. Stuffing a magic number in the entries just after the legal boundaries is a low overhead way to catch memory corruption errors. Unfortunately, the point where the error is caught can be far away from the place where the error is committed, and in some cases, the error may not be caught.

There is one last point we make about dynamic memory. Freeing a pointer can be a high overhead activity. When a pointer is freed, the runtime library may decide to give up a vm area. When the vm area of a running process is deleted, the kernel must change the page tables. When the page tables are changed, the entire TLB must be flushed to prevent the process from accessing memory illegally.

After our discussion of stack and dynamic memory, the very idea of what is a legal memory access may seem fuzzy. In fact, the notion is fuzzy. There may be a notion of what is a legal memory reference with respect to program semantics. Neither the runtime library nor the Linux kernel enforce that notion too stringently. As a result, memory errors can be quite hard to catch, especially in multithreaded programs. The point where the program crashes can be quite far away from the point where the error is committed. The programmer's best defense is to know what is going on.

Dynamic memory is sometimes referred to as heap. For example, `malloc()` is said to allocate memory on the heap. In this usage, "heap" is a reference to the data structure that was used to keep track of dynamically allocated memory at some point in history. It may well be that `glibc` uses the heap. But Linux does not use the heap to organize vm areas. It uses linked lists and red-black trees.

Exercise 5.4.1. Look up `linux/syscalls.h` on your Linux system and find out the number of system calls available.

Exercise 5.4.2. In section 5.4.1, the cost of a system call is compared to the cost of a function call, both of which have short argument lists and an insignificant body. In addition, the function and system call definitions were in L1 instruction cache during timing. Redo the timing in such a way that the function and system call definitions are out of cache during each timing. Compare the out-of-cache timing figures to the in-cache figures.

Exercise 5.4.3. Explain why it is a good idea to have a separate kernel stack for every process to make system calls, which typically call other kernel functions, rather than use the user mode stack.

Exercise 5.4.4. If a large amount of memory is claimed on the stack, explain why the memory is not given back to the system until the program terminates.

Exercise 5.4.5. A program can commit memory errors in the following ways:

- By writing to a virtual address that is illegal.

- By incorrectly writing over a virtual address that may be legally accessed but indirectly triggers an illegal access later.

Give examples of programs that commit these errors for the two cases where the virtual address in question is either in the stack area or is dynamically allocated.

Exercise 5.4.6. Suppose you allocate n bytes using `malloc()`. The size of the vm area allocated will typically be larger than n. Write a program that determines the size of the vm area (without going into the kernel). You may supply your own signal handlers to prevent the program from crashing when it generates illegal memory accesses.

5.5   References

D.P. Bovet and M. Cesati. *Understanding the Linux Kernel.* O'Reilly, Sebastopol, California, 3rd edition, 2005.

B. Chapman, G. Jost, and R. van der Pas. *Using Open MP.* MIT Press, Cambridge, Massachusetts, 2008.

T.H. Cormen, C.E. Lieserson, and R.L. Rivest. *Introduction to Algorithms*. MIT Press, Cambridge, Massachusetts, 2nd edition, 2001.

M. Herlihy and N. Shavit. *The Art of Multiprocessor Programming*. Morgan Kaufmann, San Francisco, 2008.

M. Kerrisk. *The Linux Programming Interface*. No Starch Press, San Francisco, 2010.

R. Love. *Linux Kernel Development*. Addison-Wesley, Upper Saddle River, 3rd edition, 2010.

C. van Loan. *Computational Frameworks for the Fast Fourier Transform*. SIAM, Philadelphia, 1992.

Chapter 6

Special Topic: Networks and Message Passing

For many, computer networks are synonymous with the Internet. The Internet is a means for rapid communication, propagation of information and data, and delivery of services. Much of the activity is between clients and servers. Peer-to-peer activity is less common.

In scientific computing, networks of thousands of computers are deployed to solve large-scale problems. The coordination between the computers is much tighter than in the Internet. The subproblem tackled by each computer typically has dependencies on other subproblems, which often implies that interprocess communication must be deeply integrated into the computation. Accordingly, the architecture of high-performance computing networks features much tighter integration than the Internet.

The principal framework for programming high-performance networks is Message Passing Interface (MPI). MPI is a library that allows processes running concurrently on different nodes to communicate by sending and receiving messages. Each computing node will have a few dozen (this number is growing rapidly) or so processor cores and threads running on the same node share memory. However, threads on different nodes do not share memory but can use the MPI library to communicate by sending and receiving messages. Ideally, the sending and receiving of messages is done solely by the master thread on any given node.

Many MPI programs were written years ago when each node had just a single core. Even now, when nodes have dozens of processor cores, one may pretend that each processor core is a separate node and put a single MPI process on each core. Then the MPI processes on the same node ignore that they share memory and communicate using the MPI library. Although this practice is common, it is not a good one. It ignores the powerful market forces that are putting more and more processor cores on the same node. Message passing is an inefficient way to communicate when processors share memory.

Normally, we compile sources into object files, build an executable, and then just run it at the command line. The process of running an executable is a little different with MPI. The executable must be simultaneously launched on multiple computers, and the MPI processes on the different computers must become aware of each other before they can send and receive messages.

Because the manner in which MPI processes start running is a little different, section 6.1 begins by showing how to initialize and run MPI. In section 6.2, we describe the architecture of high-performance networks. The particular architecture we discuss is the one most common today, and other high-performance networks are built on similar ideas. The MPI standard and its wide adoption within scientific computing have provided powerful impetus to innovation in this area. For more than two decades, the biggest scientific computations have been performed using MPI.

Section 6.3 discusses a range of examples. Each of these is informed by the discussion of network architecture in the earlier section. In many examples, memory optimizations studied in previous chapters are of greater consequence than network optimizations. When optimizations such as overlapping processor activity with network activity do make a difference, they do so only after memory accesses have been carefully dealt with. Overlapping processor activity with network activity requires deep knowledge of the manner in which MPI library functions map to the network's architecture. One of the examples in section 6.3 is a discussion of bandwidth to disk from MPI programs.

It is likely that the largest scientific computations in the world will be performed using MPI for several years to come. The main competition to MPI is not from other networking libraries but from the increasing power of a single computing node. The sort of applications amenable to MPI are often ones that are also amenable to OpenMP. Programming such applications for a single node using OpenMP is far simpler. Already one can fit complex 3D computations with a billion grid points into a single node. That figure will grow rapidly as a consequence of market forces that are driving DRAM capacity and putting more and more processor cores on the same node. When problems of such size can be solved on a single node, the convenience of working on a single node makes MPI less attractive.

Although the sort of applications that are amenable to OpenMP and MPI tend to be the same, there is an important difference between the two programming models. In the OpenMP model, the program is written much like a sequential program. The parallel regions appear only in relatively inner parts of the program, although not the innermost. MPI parallelism intrudes on both outer (we have already noted that the act of launching the program must be specialized for MPI programs) and inner parts of the program. Although the basic MPI calls may appear as simple as OpenMP syntax, this makes MPI programming considerably more difficult. Even printing a simple variable can be a hassle, and on many supercomputing clusters, the program does not have ready access to a terminal.

The Internet is a different kind of a network from the high-performance clusters targeted by MPI. It is far wider in extent and far more decentralized. If some market forces may make MPI less attractive, the Internet by itself is one of the powerful market forces. The Internet's relevance to emerging areas of science is unquestionable. The huge volumes of investment that are and will flow into the Internet will imply that it is integrated more and more deeply into science and scientific computing. Conversely, one should not forget that the World Wide Web was invented by a physicist. Section 6.4 gives an overview of the TCP/IP protocol, which powers the Internet, as well as clients and servers. The connection between Internet bandwidth and congestion windows is explained using actual programs.

6.1 MPI: Getting started

Section 6.1.1 explains how to compile, link, and run an MPI program. MPICH, MVA-PICH2, and Open MPI are the three major MPI implementations. The details of compilation, linking, and running vary between these implementations as well as between different sites. However, the general picture is the same. The Open MPI-specific discussion in section 6.1.1 may be altered to other implementations in a straightforward manner.

It is typical to compile and link MPI programs using commands such as `mpiCC` or `mpicxx`. In such usage, MPI pretends to be an extension of C/C++. However, MPI is in fact a library, like many other libraries, although it influences program structure in a quite radical way. The compilation and linking syntax exhibited in section 6.1.1 does not use wrappers such as `mpiCC` or `mpicxx`. Instead, both compilation and linking use the C/C++ compiler. This is a minor point, but our preference is to make a library look like a library.

From the first MPI program in section 6.1.1, we run MPI with one process per node and not one process per core. The much more common one process per core MPI programs must be discouraged. Such usage is directly in opposition to powerful market forces that are increasing the number of cores on a single node. To make MPI processes on the same node communicate using messages is to completely ignore the shared memory architecture of each node. Because there is a single network card per node, the processes on the same node will contend for the network card when passing messages to other nodes. The penalty for such negligence is likely to increase. In our programs, the master thread on each node will use OpenMP to create a thread on each core. All the message passing is handled by the master thread.

Section 6.1.2 introduces `MPI_Send()` and `MPI_Recv()`. These two function calls, together with variants to be introduced later, are the backbone of the MPI library. Both function calls block. That means `MPI_Send()` does not return until the library verifies that whatever is sent has been received. Similarly, `MPI_Recv()` does not return until whatever is expected to be received is completely received.

The blocking semantics of `MPI_Send()` and `MPI_Recv()` is natural from the point of view of a user. Indeed, these calls are widely used. However, the way they map to network architecture creates inefficiencies. The use of blocking calls wastes network bandwidth as we will see later. In section 6.1.2, we write a program called `unsafe()` that shows how blocking send and receive can easily deadlock a program.

The `unsafe()` example of section 6.1.2 is well known. The common explanation that the program works for short messages and fails for longer messages because of the size limitation of a secret internal buffer is not entirely correct, however. MPI implementations use different protocols for short and long messages, and a buffer is employed only for short messages, for reasons explained in later sections.

6.1.1   Initializing MPI

MPI[1] is the most commonly used library for solving scientific problems on networked
computers. MPI calls itself a fully featured library—with some justice. It has a lot
of features. We will use only a thin sliver of MPI. As our goal is to write programs
informed by the underlying network architecture, many of MPI's features are of little
concern to us. The features we use are the ones that are best optimized by MPI
implementations.

When an MPI run is set up, each node will have a process on it. For example, if
the run is with 8 processes, each of the 8 nodes in figure 6.1 may have one process
on it. The processes communicate by sending and receiving messages. We begin by
looking at how the processes are set up and turn to message passing later.

Our first MPI program follows. This program assumes that the processor name is
shorter than 199 characters.[2]

```
 1  #include <mpi.h>
 2  int main(int argc, char **argv){
 3      MPI_Init(NULL, NULL);
 4      int numprocs, rank;
 5      MPI_Comm_size(MPI_COMM_WORLD, &numprocs);
 6      MPI_Comm_rank(MPI_COMM_WORLD, &rank);
 7      char procname[200];
 8      int procnamelen;
 9      MPI_Get_processor_name(procname, &procnamelen);
10      cout<<"proc name="<<procname<<" rank="<<rank<<endl;
11      MPI_Finalize();
12  }
```

On line 10, each process prints the name of the compute node it is running on. Thus,
the purpose of this program is to print the names of the nodes that the processes run
on. If the program is started up with 10 processes, there will be 10 names printed.

---

[1]The MPI standard is posted at http://www.mpi-forum.org/docs/docs.html. Also see Snir
et al. (1998) and Gropp et al. (1998).

[2]In general, it would be better to use MPI_MAX_PROCESSOR_NAME instead of guessing the maximum limit on the length of the processor's name. It is not employed here to prevent our first MPI
program from getting too complicated.

Calls to the MPI library occur on lines 3, 5, 6, 9, and 11. Each MPI function begins with the prefix MPI. The declarations of the MPI library functions are found in mpi.h, the header file included on line 1.

The MPI_Init() function on line 3 must be called before messages can be sent or received. Presumably, it initializes data structures essential to other MPI functions. Both its arguments are NULL.

On line 5, the function MPI_Comm_size() is used to determine the size of an MPI communicator. MPI communicators are one of many MPI features we do not get into. The only communicator that occurs in this chapter is MPI_COMM_WORLD. All the MPI processes are members of this communicator. If the MPI run is started up with 10 processes, line 5 will set the value of the int variable numprocs to 10.

Each of the processes has a rank, much as each OpenMP thread has a thread identifier. If the number of processes is 10, the process ranks will go from 0 through 9. On line 6, the int variable rank is set to be equal to the process rank by calling MPI_Comm_rank().

MPI functions such as MPI_Comm_size() and MPI_Comm_rank() may be made to return error codes. Our aim being to understand the dependence of program performance on computer architecture, we follow our usual custom and ignore error handling. Eliminating error handling saves considerable clutter in the program. By default, MPI implementations abort when an error occurs. Although the default behavior can be changed, it is just fine by us.

On line 9, the processor name is read into a character string. The function used on that line is self-explanatory.

MPI programs must call MPI_Finalize() at the end, as this program does on line 11.

The program is saved in the file procname.cpp and compiled using the following command in the implementation we employ:

```
icpc -c -O3 -prec-div -no-ftz -DNDEBUG \
'mpiCC -showme:compile' procname.cpp
```

The compilation command can be quite different between MPI implementations. We are using Open MPI. All the icpc options have been discussed in earlier chapters. The only new option here is

```
'mpiCC -showme:compile'
```

The effect of this syntax is to treat the back-quoted string as a shell command and splice in its output. The output of `mpiCC -showme:compile` is

```
-I/home1/00013/tg456871/openmpi-1.6.3/include -pthread
```

The `-I` option gives the directory where the header file `mpi.h` is found. A simpler command to compile this MPI program is

```
mpiCC -c procname.cpp
```

Here we have omitted options to the C++ compiler for simplicity. Depending on the flavor of MPI, the compilation command may be `mpicxx` or `mpic++` or `mpiCC` or `mpiicpc`. The simpler form is the one that is used almost universally. All that the simpler form does is pass suitable `-I` options to the compiler.

The linking command is

```
icpc 'mpiCC -showme:link' -o procname.exe procname.o
```

Like the compiling command, this linking command too is specific to the Open MPI implementation. This time the string that is spliced in is

```
-pthread -L/home1/00013/tg456871/openmpi-1.6.3/lib\
-lmpi_cxx -lmpi -ldl -lm -lnuma -Wl,--export-dynamic\
-lrt -lnsl -lutil
```

The first line here ends with the shell continuation character \ for convenient displaying. The libraries are linked dynamically. Therefore, the program must be able to find the libraries at runtime using `LD_LIBRARY_PATH` or some other mechanism. The simpler form of the linking command is

```
mpiCC -o procname.exe procname.o
```

All that the simpler form does is link a few libraries automatically.

The compilation and linking of MPI programs is no different from that of any sequential program. The declarations of the library functions must be visible at compile time, and the executable is linked against libraries. However, the manner in which the program is run is quite different. An MPI program must be started up simultaneously on several nodes. During startup, the processes on different nodes have to set up data structures to recognize each other across the network. A typical command[3] for running the program is as follows:

---

[3]The command for running an MPI program varies between installations. The command `mpiexec` recommended by the MPI standard is unavailable on any implementation this author has accessed.

```
mpirun -np 5 -bynode procname.exe
```

Like the `mpiCC` linking and compilation commands, this command too is installation-specific. The `-np` option indicates the number of processes, given here as 5. The `bynode` option says that every process must be on a different node. The command to run MPI can vary considerably from installation to installation.

A program run with the `-np 5` option produced the following output:

```
proc name = c341-111.ls4.tacc.utexas.edu rank = 3
proc name = c340-114.ls4.tacc.utexas.edu rank = 0
proc name = c341-105.ls4.tacc.utexas.edu rank = 2
proc name = c340-107.ls4.tacc.utexas.edu rank = 4
proc name = c341-313.ls4.tacc.utexas.edu rank = 1
```

The manner in which MPI jobs are submitted varies from cluster to cluster. The `ls` in the processor names probably stands for Lonestar, the name of the cluster we used. We have no control over the order in which the processes print, although we could use `MPI_Barrier()` to make them print in the order of their rank. The technique of making the processes print to standard output does not scale well with job size but is good enough for this simple program.

6.1.2 Unsafe communication in MPI

All MPI processes execute the same program. If the `-bynode` (or an equivalent) option is used, each process runs on a different node. The processes communicate by sending each other messages across the network. MPI syntax allows a process to use either blocking or nonblocking function calls to send and receive. A blocking send or receive waits until the operation is complete. Blocking communication is more vulnerable to deadlocks. Because two processes have to participate in message passing, the processes may get stuck waiting for each other. Even relatively simple programs can deadlock when blocking calls are used, as we show in this section.

At the beginning, each MPI process has to determine its rank and the total number of processes. The following function is called for doing so:

```
void mpi_initialize(int& rank, int& nprocs){
    MPI_Init(NULL, NULL);
    MPI_Comm_rank(MPI_COMM_WORLD, &rank);
```

```
            MPI_Comm_size(MPI_COMM_WORLD, &nprocs);
   }
```

Using `mpi_initialize()` saves us the trouble of remembering the syntax of three MPI library functions. Before making any calls to the MPI library, a program may execute the following code fragment:

```
      int rank;
      int nprocs;
      mpi_initialize(rank, nprocs);
```

After this fragment, each process knows its rank and the total number of processes. Before exiting, each process must call `MPI_Finalize()`. Each MPI process uses process rank to identify the process to which it sends a message or from which it receives a message.

Our first example of sending and receiving messages is the function **unsafe()** listed below.

```
1  void unsafe(int numOFdoubles, int rank, int nprocs,
2            double *sendbuf, double *recvbuf)
3  {
4        int tag = 0;
5        MPI_Status status;
6        MPI_Barrier(MPI_COMM_WORLD);
7        if(rank==0){
8            MPI_Send(sendbuf, numOFdoubles, MPI_DOUBLE,
9                    nprocs-1, tag, MPI_COMM_WORLD);
10           MPI_Recv(recvbuf, numOFdoubles, MPI_DOUBLE,
11                   nprocs-1, tag, MPI_COMM_WORLD,
12                   &status);
13       }
14       else if(rank==nprocs-1){
15           MPI_Send(sendbuf, numOFdoubles, MPI_DOUBLE,
16                   0, tag, MPI_COMM_WORLD);
17           MPI_Recv(recvbuf, numOFdoubles, MPI_DOUBLE,
18                   0, tag, MPI_COMM_WORLD, &status);
19       }
```

20 }

We will assume that the MPI program is started up with exactly two processes and that each process calls `unsafe()`. The two processes send a certain number of `doubles` to each other. The number of `doubles` transmitted is given by the first argument. It is assumed that `rank` and `nprocs` have been appropriately initialized by both processes after calling `mpi_initialize()`. These are passed to `unsafe()` as arguments on line 1. The buffers for sending and receiving appear as arguments `sendbuf` and `recvbuf` on line 2. These buffers are allocated by each process before the call to `unsafe()`.

The MPI syntax that appears in `unsafe()`, supplemented by variants of send and receive described in a later section, is nearly all the MPI syntax we need. Line 5 defines `status` to be of type `MPI_Status`. The `MPI_Recv()` function returns information in `status` on lines 12 and 18. Other MPI variants for message passing and message probing also return status information.

The `MPI_Barrier()` on line 6 stalls until all processes have entered the barrier. Its argument is a communicator, and the only MPI communicator we ever use, `MPI_COMM_WORLD`, includes all processes. The barrier plays no essential role in the function `unsafe()`. MPI processes get in sync while sending and receiving messages. The situation is quite different from shared memory where threads may conflict while reading and writing from the same location. Processes that communicate or coordinate using shared memory must use spinlocks, mutexes, critical regions, or barriers. Barriers are useful in MPI as well, but they are less frequently used. There is a degree of synchronization inherent in message passing.

The if-block of statements from lines 8 through 12 is executed only by the process with rank 0. The else-if block of statements from lines 15 through 18 is executed only by the process with rank `nprocs-1`. Because we are assuming exactly two processes, the else-if block is executed by the process with rank 1. This manner of using process rank to distinguish between processes is typical of MPI in the same way that the use of thread identifiers is typical of OpenMP.

The crucial bits of syntax in `unsafe()` are `MPI_Send()` and `MPI_Recv()`. On lines 8 and 9, the process with rank 0 sends a message to process with rank 1. The first argument to `MPI_Send()` is a pointer to the send buffer. This argument is declared to be of type `void *`. On line 8, the argument is of type `double *`, which is automatically cast to the right type. Any pointer may be type cast to `void *`. The second argument is the number of items in the buffer, and the third argument is the data type of each item. The data type is given as `MPI_DOUBLE`. MPI has elaborate constructions for data types. MPI data types are difficult to comprehend in full generality, and it is difficult to imagine how they could be useful. Most programs can get by with `MPI_CHAR`, `MPI_INT`, and `MPI_DOUBLE`. By giving the data type as `MPI_DOUBLE`, we are indicating that each item is a `double` and is 8 bytes wide as in C/C++ .

On line 9, the fourth argument to `MPI_Send()` is given as `nprocs-1`. This argument is the destination of the message and is indicated here to be the process with rank `nprocs-1` or 1. The fifth argument is the tag. The tags must agree when receives are matched with sends. The last argument must be a communicator.

`MPI_Recv()` has seven arguments, one more than `MPI_Send()`. The first three arguments given on line 11 are the receive buffer, the number of items to be received, and the data type of each item. The fourth argument, which is given on line 12, is the source of the message—the sender specifies the destination and the receiver specifies the source. The source is specified to be `nprocs-1` or the process with rank 1. The fifth argument is the tag and the sixth argument must be a communicator.

The MPI receive must match the corresponding MPI send. In the case of `unsafe()`, the send on line 8 matches the receive on line 17. The send on line 15 matches the receive on line 10. In MPI jargon, a receive and send must have the same message envelope to match. The message envelope consists of the source, destination, tag, and communicator.

In `unsafe()`, the number of items received is equal to the number of items sent. In general, the number of items may be less than or greater than the number of items sent. The last and seventh argument to `MPI_Recv()` is a pointer to `MPI_Status` (pointer to `status` on line 12). The status may be passed to `MPI_Get_count()` to discover the number of items received.

The tag argument in a receive may be given as `MPI_ANY_TAG`. The source argument may be given as `MPI_ANY_SOURCE`. The ability of a message to have an envelope that matches any tag and any source is not of the greatest use in scientific computing. When the same problem is being solved on multiple compute nodes, the processes must discriminate between messages depending on their source and possibly tag. However, an analogous facility supported by TCP/IP sockets is part of the basis of the Internet. In a typical transaction on the Internet, a client connects with a server to initiate a search, retrieve a document, or make a purchase. The client must know which server it wants to connect to, but the server has no way to know which client may want a connection. The server uses syntax similar to `MPI_ANY_SOURCE` to allow clients to make a connection to it.

The else-if block of statements from lines 15 through 18 mirrors the if-block. In the if-block, the process with rank 0 sends its send buffer to the process with rank `nprocs-1` or 1. In the else-if block, the process with rank 1 (we are assuming `nprocs` to be 2) receives that message into its receive buffer. Similarly, the send buffer of the process with rank 1 is copied to the receive buffer of the process with rank 0. As with the process of rank 0, the send on line 15 precedes the receive on line 17.

Both `MPI_Send()` and `MPI_Recv()` are blocking calls. They do not return until the transaction is complete. The deeper discussion of network architecture in the next section is essential to understanding what it means for a transaction to complete. The function `unsafe()` runs as expected if the number of `double` items in the messages is 1,500 or fewer. It deadlocks if the number of items is 1,600 or more. Both processes execute send before receive. But a send must match with receive before it can complete. The deadlock occurs when both the sends stall waiting for the corresponding receive. But then why do messages with fewer than 1,500 items not deadlock? Open MPI uses a different protocol for transmitting messages that are smaller than 12 KB for reasons related to network architecture. The absence of deadlocks is an unintended side effect of Open MPI's short message protocol, which is discussed later.

The use of blocking calls is unsafe unless the program is careful not to deadlock. In a later section, we find that blocking sends and receives waste network bandwidth. `MPI_Send()` and `MPI_Recv()`, although familiar to many users, must be avoided in favor of safer and more efficient variants.

Exercise 6.1.1. Write an MPI program that makes the processors print their names in the reverse order of their ranks.

Exercise 6.1.2. Suppose there are three processes $0, 1, 2$, and the ith process sends data to $i + 1 \bmod 3$ and receives data from $i - 1 \bmod 3$. Devise a communication protocol that uses blocking send and receive yet avoids deadlocks.

6.2 High-performance network architecture

A network connects many computers together. Each computer is an independent entity. Thus, every communication between two computers requires coordination. The coordination is much looser in the vast and decentralized Internet than it is in high-performance networks used in scientific computing.

Infiniband, which is an open standard, is a leading technology in high-performance networking. The technology has stabilized over the past decade or so, and almost all large and even small computing clusters use Infiniband or a proprietary variation. In this section, we review three principal features of Infiniband: network topology, kernel-free message passing, and one-sided communication. These aspects of the network have an influence on the way MPI programs are written, as shown in the next section.

Network topology is the graph used to connect computers together. On the Internet, the graph is not regular or structured, although it is far from being random (the Internet is a heavily designed network). In high-performance networks, the graphs are far more regular and structured.

Every time information is transferred over the Internet, the message passes through the operating system kernel at both the sender and the receiver. For example, when a send button is pressed on an email client, the email is first copied to kernel buffers. It is transferred to the network card at the client site before traveling to the server. The network card on the server again copies the email to kernel buffers before passing it along to some other server or the receiving client.

Kernel copies create considerable overhead and the Linux kernel goes to great lengths to avoid excessive copying. In Infiniband, kernel copies can be avoided altogether. Information is copied directly between the Infiniband network card and the DRAM memory owned by the client program.

Communication over the Internet is two sided, although that would be invisible to most users. When a web link is followed to download a page, the web server executes `send()` calls (these are defined inside the operating system kernel) to transmit the page and the browser executes matching `recv()` calls (these too are in the kernel) to receive it.

In a one-sided network such as Infiniband, the entire transaction may be carried out by making a single call at either the sender or the receiver. There is no reason to match sending with receiving.

To be clear, one-sided communication does not mean that all the network activity is at either the sender or receiver but not both. In any communication, there will be network activity involving the Infiniband adapters at both the sender and the receiver. One-sidedness means that a function call to initiate and complete the data transfer is made at either the sender or the receiver but not necessarily both.

In section 6.2.1, we describe the fat-tree network topology. In a large network, a typical user gets control of only a small fraction of the nodes. An advantage of the fat-tree is that the bandwidth realized is relatively independent of how MPI processes are mapped to nodes of the fat-tree. The fat-tree topology is common among high-performance networks, although actual networks are approximations and not perfect realizations of the fat-tree.

In section 6.2.2, we turn to a deeper study of the Infiniband network. The discussion of MPI in the next section is informed by the many architectural issues that arise in this study.

Like almost all modern networks, Infiniband is packetized. Data is broken up into packets before it travels over the network. Each packet has an envelope in addition to the data, and the layout of the envelope together with the data constitutes the packet format. Every packet needs an envelope for the same reason that every parcel mailed needs an envelope carrying the addresses of the sender and the receiver. The parcel would be undeliverable otherwise.

Packetization and the consequent change in data format means that copying to buffers is inevitable. In Infiniband transmission, the buffers exist on the Infiniband network card (the so-called host channel adapter), and packetization does not require kernel intervention. Error correction, flow control, and congestion control are also handled by the network card.

Read Direct Memory Access (RDMA) is the distinctive feature of Infiniband. RDMA allows either the sender or the receiver to make a single function call to transmit data. The function call is made from a user program. The kernel does not participate in any way in executing that function call. Data transfer is entirely the responsibility of the Infiniband adapters and network.

Section 6.2.2 includes two applications to actual programming, with many more to follow in the next section. The first application is a discussion of the latency of Infiniband networks. The second application is an explanation of what makes the program `unsafe()` of the previous section deadlock for long messages but not for short messages.

6.2.1   Fat-tree network

In many high-performance clusters, nodes are networked using fat-trees.[4] A defining property of fat-trees, shown in figure 6.1, is that the number of links between levels is

---

[4]Fat-trees were discovered and made popular by Leiserson (1985).

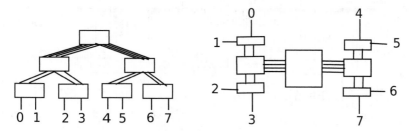

Figure 6.1: Fat-tree with 8 nodes. Switches are shown as rectangles. The ideal fat-tree is a perfect binary with the number of links between levels being approximately constant. The fat-tree is particularly easy to lay out on the plane, as shown on the right-hand side.

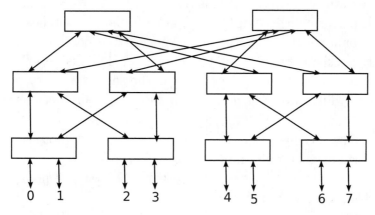

Figure 6.2: A fat-tree with 8 nodes implemented using switches, each with 4 ports.

roughly a constant. More links join switches at higher levels than at lower levels. With a suitable switching algorithm and assuming that any two nodes are equally likely to communicate, the load on each link is roughly the same. Of course, the switches at higher levels will use more hardware. Yet a fat-tree is particularly easy to lay out in the plane, as shown in the figure on the right.

An entire fat-tree can be implemented within a single box with external ports for connecting nodes. A fat-tree can also be built using switches. The fat-tree shown in figure 6.2 is built using 10 switches, each of which has 4 ports. Each of the four switches at the lowest level is connected to 2 computing nodes, and the remaining ports are connected to switches at the next higher level. The number of compute nodes in this fat-tree is 8. In figure 6.2, there are 8 links from the compute nodes to

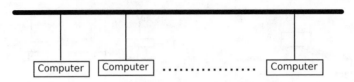

Figure 6.3: Multiple access network.

switches at the lowest level. There are 8 links between the four switches at the lowest level and the four switches at the intermediate level. The number of links from the intermediate level to the two switches at the topmost level is also 8.

The network we study in this chapter is Infiniband. Infiniband technology is widely deployed in high-performance computing. The Infiniband switches are designed to deliver the same bandwidth at every port. The fat-tree configuration ensures that there is no bottleneck at any level of the network.[5] Thanks to such a layout, the bandwidth between two nodes of the network is the same for every possible pairing. In theory, the bandwidth does not diminish if there is traffic between other pairs in the network.

The switches shown in figure 6.1 have only four ports. A more realistic count for the number of ports of an Infiniband switch is 36. If each computer and link in the figure is multiplied ninefold, we get a fat-tree with 72 compute nodes built using 10 Infiniband switches, each with 36 ports.

When large networks are built, it is typical to subsume the higher levels of the fat-tree within gigantic director switches. Indeed, the ability to do so is one of the advantages of the fat-tree. As shown in figure 6.1, the switches at higher levels can be neatly laid down on a plane. Director switches with as many as 648 ports are available on the market.

6.2.2   Infiniband network architecture

Figure 6.3 is a sketch of a multiple access network. The host computers connected to the shared cable can communicate directly with each other. In a switched network such as figure 6.2, the communication must pass through a switch. Ethernet Local Area Networks (LANs) are in part multiple access networks.

---

[5]The Infiniband network is oversubscribed in many installations, which may create bottlenecks.

In both kinds of networks, data must change format when it travels from one computer to another. To begin with, the transmitted data resides in a set of pages in the DRAM memory of the source computer. However, the physical link does not handle data the way the memory system does. In modern networks, data travels across the physical link in packets or frames.

Each packet is made up of headers with information about the source and destination in addition to the payload, which is the data to be transmitted. In packet switched networks, such as Infiniband or the Ethernet, data in DRAM memory is converted to a sequence of packets by the source. The packets are transmitted across the network. The packets are reassembled at the destination and stored once again in DRAM memory.

The change in data format is fundamental to packet switched networks. Although the amount of data to be transmitted can be several gigabytes, packets are typically a few kilobytes. Other aspects of network architecture are either related to the change in data format or follow as consequences. We highlight three features of network architecture: buffering, error correction, and flow/congestion control. Each of these features occurs at multiple levels of the network partly because the data format changes at each level.

Some amount of buffering is inevitable when the data format changes. When a long stream of data is transmitted as a sequence of packets, some of the packets may need to be resent if packets are dropped by the network. The packets must be buffered by the sender in some form. Similarly, the receiver must buffer the packets if it is to have the ability to assemble packets that arrive out of order. Additional buffering occurs at the level of the physical link.

A network without error control is like a leaky freight train. It is probably true that every modern network has some form of error control. In packet switched networks, every packet carries checksums and other error control information. The checksums may apply to the payload or parts of the header. When a long stream of data is broken up into packets, the header usually carries information about the sequence number of each packet. Using the sequence number, the receiver can reassemble the data even if the packets arrive out of order, and it can detect missing packets.

A computer that is sending data may need to slow down because the receiver is not able to consume packets fast enough. Or the sender may have room to speed up because the receiver can consume faster. In flow control, the sender and receiver exchange information to ensure that the receive buffers do not overflow repeatedly.

A typical mechanism is for the receiver to advertise the size of the unfilled part of its receive buffer to the sender. The sender adjusts its behavior based on that information. In Infiniband, as in many other networks, there is flow control at the level of packets as well as at the level of the physical link.

Congestion control is related to but distinct from flow control. The network is a resource shared by several hosts. Excessive traffic between two hosts can impede traffic between two other hosts. If the hosts are unmindful of the traffic in the network as a whole, a large network will become congested quickly because of overly aggressive usage by the hosts. It is the sender's job to monitor not only the available room in the receiver's buffer but also the level of traffic in the network as a whole. If the sender finds that the network is congested, it must adjust its behavior to reduce congestion. However, if the network is lightly loaded, the sender may be able to increase the rate of data transmission. Congestion control algorithms make the host computers into good citizens with respect to their network usage.

Flow control and error handling are typically hidden from user programs, and that is certainly true of MPI programs. However, user applications are not spared from having to buffer messages. Buffering can add significantly to the overhead of exchanging messages, especially over fast networks such as Infiniband. When a large matrix stored on several computers is transposed, for example, the program on each computer must decide what part of its data must be transmitted to another computer on the network. If the network expects the user program to hand it contiguous data, the sender has no option but to use buffers to pack data headed for each destination. The receiver will get chunks of its part of the transposed matrix from several senders. Receive buffers will be needed to gather incoming data before the transposed matrix is assembled.

When Internet protocols are implemented over the Ethernet, data is broken up into a sequence of packets and frames by software. A significant innovation in the Infiniband network architecture is that the host channel adapter is responsible for breaking up a message into packets. Intelligent use of MPI is aided greatly by knowledge of network architecture. At the end of this section, we explain why the function `unsafe()` defined in section 6.1.2 deadlocks if messages are more than 12 KB but not if messages are smaller than 12 KB. Discussion of MPI syntax and usage in later sections is closely tied to Infiniband network architecture.

Figure 6.4: Infiniband data packet format.

Infiniband data packet format

Telephone networks of yesteryears established point-to-point connections between communicating agents. The network bandwidth was shared using either time or frequency domain multiplexing. Modern computer networks, such as Infiniband, are packet switched. Packet switched networks are more flexible, are easier to configure, and make more efficient use of network resources.

The data packet is the fundamental unit of data transmission in a packet switched network. Figure 6.4 shows the layout of a typical Infiniband packet. Infiniband data packets serve many different purposes, and packets that serve different purposes have slightly different layouts.[6]

The local routing header (LRH) is 8 bytes. This field occurs right at the top of the packet. It is used by the switches to route the packet from source to destination. Within the header, 2 bytes are reserved for the source address and 2 bytes are reserved for destination address.

The base transport header (BTH), which occurs right after LRH, is 12 bytes. When a packet arrives at its destination, the host channel adapter at the destination uses information in the base transport header to handle the packet. For example, if a message must be assembled from a stream of packets, the information for message assembly is found in the base transport header. Every base transport header has a 24-bit field that gives the packet sequence number.

The payload is either the message or part of the message that must be delivered at the destination. How large can the payload be? The Linux command `ibv_devinfo`

---

[6]The Infiniband architecture is described in *Infiniband Architecture Specification*, vols. 1 and 2, Infiniband Trade Association, 2007. (Paul Grun, *Introduction to Infiniband for End Users*, Infiniband Trade Association, 2010) is another reference. (Ashok Raj, *Infiniband Host Channel Adapter Verb Implementer's Guide*, 2003) is helpful for understanding the verb layer. The verb interface is documented in (*RDMA Aware Networks Programming User Manual*, Mellanox Technologies, 2009). The verb interface is not part of the Infiniband standard but is implemented with the same interface by several vendors.

gives the Maximum Transmission Unit (MTU) as 2,048 bytes on our system. Each Infiniband packet must be 2 KB or smaller. When a large message is transmitted, the typical packet has a size that is nearly 2 KB.

The two fields of the Infiniband data packet that follow the payload are invariant Cyclic Redundancy Checksum (CRC) and variant CRC. CRC error detection/correction information is calculated using polynomial arithmetic. The invariant CRC is 32 bits and the variant CRC is 16 bits. Certain fields of the data packet may change when it travels from source to destination. The invariant CRC refers only to those fields that do not change. The variant CRC refers to the whole packet. The CRC fields are generated and verified at the link layer. If a packet has an error that cannot be fixed, it is silently dropped at the destination.

Infiniband packets may have additional fields. If a network is so large that it uses routers, in addition to switches, each packet includes a global route header (GRH) right after the local route header and before the transport header. Most high-performance computing networks (or maybe all) in use today are built without routers, and the global route header is absent from their Infiniband data packets.

Remote Direct Memory Access (RDMA) is a notable feature of Infiniband technology. RDMA may either write into or read from the memory of a remote computer on the network. RDMA read request packets, which initiate an RDMA read, and the very first RDMA write packet include an extended RDMA transport header (RETH). This header occurs right after the base transport header. It is 16 bytes long. It has three fields—a 64-bit virtual address, a 32-bit remote key, and a 32-bit field that gives the size in bytes of the remote DMA transfer.

Acknowledgment (ACK) packets include the 4-byte acknowledgment extended transport header (AETH). The same packet may carry both an ACK header and payload, and thus serves a double purpose. For example, during an RDMA read, the very first response packet carries an ACK header acknowledging the request and some of the remotely read data in its payload. The very last response packet too doubles up in the same manner. The first and last packets in a sequence are marked in the base transport header.

High-performance computing networks are built using switches and are currently not large enough to need routers. One consequence, we have already mentioned, is the absence of the global routing header from the data packets. Another consequence is that an Infiniband data packet always follows the same path through the switches from a given source to a given destination.

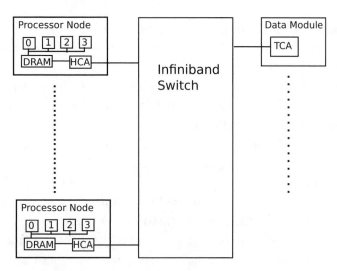

Figure 6.5: This depiction shows processor nodes, each with 4 processor cores, and data modules connected to a single Infiniband switch. In general, multiple switches can be connected to each other. HCA stands for Host Channel Adapter and TCA for Target Channel Adapter. TCAs do not support the Verb layer. The connection of processor cores to HCA via the PCIe bus is not shown here.

Protection domains and queue pairs

The Infiniband network has several unusual features. These unusual features cannot be detected solely from the data packet format. Some of the features particular to Infiniband become visible when we look inside host channel adapters. Host channel adapters are hardware devices used on host computers to interface to the Infiniband network.

Figure 6.5 shows an infiniband network with several processors and data modules connected to a big switch, which presumably implements some version of fat-tree internally. The processor is connected to the host channel adapter via the PCIe bus. The Infiniband host channel adapters take over most of the networking activity. Not much is left to the software layers.

Suppose a message is sent over the Internet from a source computer that is on an Ethernet LAN. Once a connection is established, the user program executes the send() function on a socket to send the message. The send function is a kernel system call. It is the first of a cascade of function calls within the kernel. The message is broken up into packets and frames by the kernel, and the kernel eventually invokes the network device driver. The device driver places the frames on the Ethernet cable connected to the source computer.

In Infiniband, the user program executes a single function call to initiate a message transfer. This function call goes *directly* to the host channel adapter. Information initiating the message transfer is directly written into the host channel adapter. At that point, the host channel adapter takes over, and there is nothing more for the processor to do to transmit the message.

The host channel adapter can use direct memory access to retrieve data in DRAM without intervention of the processor. In the Infiniband network architecture, the host channel adapter at the source can read data to be sent from source DRAM, and the host channel adapter at the destination can write that data to its DRAM without intervention of the processor. Thus, the entire transmission of the message can be completed without processor intervention.

Infiniband vendors provide a Verb library that is used by user programs to access Infiniband facilities. Some of the Infiniband Verbs are functions that call the kernel and the Infiniband driver. Other Verbs are entirely in user space. Important examples of Infiniband Verbs that are entirely in user space are `ib_post_send()` and `ib_post_recv()`. These are used by user programs to post send and receive requests directly to the host channel adapter.

The key concept that enables user programs to talk to the host channel adapter directly is that of protection domains. The host channel adapters have their own memory and their own buffers. A part of the memory on the host channel adapter may be mapped to the virtual memory of the user process to create a protection domain. A user process can use virtual addresses within a protection domain to write to the host channel adapter and read from it.

It is not such a simple matter for user processes to share a resource and access it without the intervention of the kernel. User processes can interfere with each other and render the system insecure. We have seen the elaborate and complicated paging system infrastructure that is set up to allow user process to share DRAM memory and access it directly. A similar infrastructure is implemented by the host channel adapter to enforce protection domains. The Verbs to create and release protection domains—`ib_allocate_pd()` and `ib_deallocate_pd()`—call the kernel (probably using the `ioctl()` system call).

It is unusual, but not unheard of, to map device memory into the virtual address space of a user process. An example where that is done is the X window system in Linux, which uses a client-server architecture. The server is a privileged user space program that maps video memory into its virtual address space. An unusual feature of Infiniband is that any user process, even an unprivileged one, can talk to the host channel adapter directly.

User processes use "queue pairs" to post send and receive requests. The queue pair is a data structure created within a protection domain using a Verb.

The queue pair is a C structure of type `struct ibv_qp`. It resides on the host channel adapter and not in DRAM memory. The queue pair has a send queue and a receive queue. A single user process can create thousands of queue pairs to communicate with other processes on the network. A single host channel adapter may hold tens of thousands of queue pairs corresponding to several user processes on the same computer.

Send requests are posted to queue pairs using the Verb `ibv_post_send()`. The request is posted to the send queue. The function `ibv_post_recv()` is used to post requests to the receive queue. Its declaration is similar. Neither function calls the kernel. Work requests go directly to the host channel adapter, and the kernel has no idea that data is being transferred over the network.

When a work request is completed, the host channel adapter places a completion work element on the completion queue. Like queue pairs, completion queues reside on the host channel adapter and are tied to protection domains. A user process finds out whether a work request has been completed by polling the completion queue.

The completion queue is polled using the Verb `ibv_poll_cq()`. This Verb also bypasses the kernel completely. Using these Verbs, processes can send messages to each other and check completion of their work requests with no help from the kernel once protection domains and other data structures have been set up.

Infiniband also provides a facility to trigger events when work requests are completed. However, interrupt-driven event handling scales poorly with network size and traffic. Even Ethernet drivers switch off interrupt mode and resort to polling when there is heavy traffic on the network card.

RDMA write and RDMA read

Much of the action in Infiniband networking is on the host channel adapters. We have seen that protection domains reside on the host channel adapters and that queue pairs and completion queues are tied to protection domains. Our purpose here is to explain RDMA reads and writes, but we will begin by making one more point about host channel adapters.

Infiniband host channel adapters maintain virtual memory tables. A little reflection will show that such a facility is essential. Work requests for sending and receiving messages are posted directly to queue pairs that reside on host channel adapters. The memory address for accessing data resides within the work request. Because the work request is created by a user process, the only kind of address that a work request can pass on to the host channel adapter is the virtual address.

If the host channel adapter is to access DRAM memory directly, it must be able to convert the virtual address it receives into physical addresses. The kernel maintains page tables to map virtual addresses to physical addresses, but the host channel adapter cannot and does not access the page tables. Indeed, the whole point of Infiniband design is to bypass the kernel and concentrate all the layers of networking within the host channel adapter. To enable the host channel adapter to map virtual addresses to physical addresses, Infiniband requires the user process to register memory before posting a work request.

The Verb that registers memory is `ibv_reg_mr()`. This Verb uses a system call to map a region of virtual memory, supplied to it via arguments, to physical addresses. The map is saved on the host channel adapter using a protection domain. All commands that transfer data across the network are required to register memory. A memory region is unregistered (or deregistered) using the verb `ibv_dereg_mr()`.

Protection domains, queue pairs, completion queues, and memory registration are the mechanisms that enable messages to be sent and received while completely bypassing the kernel. Having discussed all these mechanisms, we are at last ready to talk about how messages are sent and received across Infiniband networks.

Infiniband provides conventional channel semantics as well as RDMA read and write. We will first discuss conventional channel semantics. In conventional channel semantics, a queue pair at the sender is bound to a queue pair at the receiver to create a channel. A send work request is posted on the send queue of the queue pair at the sending side. A receive work request is posted on the receive queue of the receiver. The send work request must be matched with a receive work request to complete a data transfer across the channel.

Channel-based communication is not what Infiniband technology is about. Channels are unsuitable for large messages and have lower bandwidth for even small messages. Infiniband allows a user process on one computer to directly transfer data into the virtual memory region of a remote process using RDMA read or RDMA write. Such RDMA transfers have low latency and excellent bandwidth. RDMA data transfers are the heart of Infiniband technology. A queue pair at the source is bound to a queue pair at the destination in reliable RDMA communication as it is in reliable channel-based communication.

To understand RDMA, we must look a little more deeply into the memory registration facility. When memory is registered using `ibv_reg_mr()`, a local key and a remote key to the memory region are created. These keys are stored in separate fields of `struct ibv_mr`. If a process has a remote key to the memory region created on a remote computer on the network, it can use that key to initiate memory transfers between the remote host channel adapter and the remote memory region.

RDMA write works as follows. The requester obtains a remote address key from the responder. The Infiniband standard does not specify how remote address keys are sent from the responder to the requester. An implementation may use queue pairs and channel semantics to transmit this information or it may use datagrams. It may even use TCP/IP sockets. The requester prepares a work request using the remote address key and a local memory region. The work request asks that data in the local memory region must be written to the remote memory region. This work request is posted to the send queue of a queue pair on the requester using `ibv_post_send()`.

RDMA transfers are one sided. The requester posts an RDMA write to a send queue on its host channel adapter. But no user process posts a receive request at the responder. Send and receive requests are not matched. An RDMA write takes place as follows. The requester accesses its local memory and generates a sequence of Infiniband data packets. The RDMA extended transport header, which is present in the first packet, has a field to store a 32-bit remote key. When the sequence of packets arrives at the responder, the responder uses the remote key to write data in the packets it receives to one of its local memory regions. The responder generates an ACK when the data transfer is complete. The RDMA write is completely one sided because the responder, which is the receiver, transfers data from its host channel adapter to its DRAM memory without intervention of a processor or the operating system.

In an RDMA write, the requester is the sender and the responder is the receiver. In contrast, in an RDMA read, the requester is the receiver and the responder is the sender. An RDMA read begins with an RDMA request packet from the receiver to

RDMA write latency	1.83 μsecs
RDMA read latency	3.42 μsecs
RDMA write bandwidth	6.24 GB/s
RDMA read bandwidth	6.16 GB/s

Table 6.1: Latency and bandwidth of bidirectional data transfer between two hosts on a QDR Infiniband network.

the sender. When the sender receives the request packet, it responds by initiating the data transfer. Like RDMA write, RDMA read is completely one sided. Once the receiver acquires a remote address key, it posts a work request, but no work request is posted at the sender.[7] The responder, which in this case is the sender, transfers data from its DRAM memory to its host channel adapter without intervention of a processor or the operating system.

Infiniband latency and bandwidth

Linux Infiniband installation provides commands for measuring network latency and bandwidth. Measurements carried out using the commands

```
ib_write_lat , ib_read_lat , ib_write_bw , ib_read_bw
```

are reported in table 6.1. The measurements are between two nodes. The latencies depend on the distance between the two hosts on the Infiniband network.

Both RDMA read and write have excellent point-to-point bandwidth of 6.2 GB/s. The realized bandwidth is well in excess of the advertised maximum of 40 Gbps or 5 GB/s for QDR infiniband. Interestingly, bandwidths above 6 GB/s are realized between MPI processes as well.

The RDMA read latency is nearly twice the RDMA write latency. We will look more closely at RDMA write and RDMA read to attempt to explain this phenomenon. The microsecond latencies of table 6.1 are impressive. The overhead of a simple spin-lock can be a few microseconds. Infiniband network latencies are only about a factor of 10 greater than latencies to DRAM.

---

[7]RDMA read requests may be posted to the send queue using `ibv_post_send()`, just like RDMA write requests.

To measure RDMA write latency, one of the two hosts will do as follows. An RDMA write is posted using `ibv_post_send()`. The same host that posts the request immediately begins to poll the completion queue. The transfer is complete the moment a completion element is detected on the completion queue. RDMA write latency is the time elapsed from the moment before the request is posted to the moment after the completion is detected.

The RDMA write latency measurement comprises the following events:

1. The host channel adapter of the sender (or requester) initiates a DMA transfer. It prepares a single Infiniband data packet after the DMA transfer is complete. In addition to the local routing header and the base transport header, this data packet will have a 16-byte RDMA extended transport header. The RDMA header has a field for the remote key. Because this is a latency test, the amount of data transferred must be small enough to be the payload of a single packet.

2. This packet travels to the receiver (or responder). The receiver reads the headers. It uses the RDMA header and its own virtual memory table to figure out the physical address it must write to. It initiates a DMA transfer to write the payload into its local DRAM memory.

3. The host channel adapter of the receiver (or responder) generates an ACK or acknowledgment packet and sends it to the requester.

4. The host channel adapter of the sender (or requester) generates a completion element and places it on the completion queue as soon as it receives ACK.

RDMA write latency is approximately equal to the time taken by a round trip from source to destination and back.

RDMA read latency comprises the following events:

1. The receiver (or requester) generates an RDMA request packet.

2. The sender (or responder) initiates a DMA transfer using information in the RDMA request packet and its own virtual tables. As soon as the DMA transfer is complete, the sender prepares a single Infiniband packet with the appropriate payload and sends it to the receiver. This first response packet must include an ACK header as required by the Infiniband standard.

3. The host channel adapter of the receiver receives the first response packet and initiates a DMA transfer of its payload to local memory.

If the RDMA read is considered to be complete at this point, it too would comprise one round trip from the source to destination. Why then is the RDMA read latency nearly twice the RDMA write latency? Our best surmise is that the RDMA read cannot be considered to be complete at this point.

To implement a reliable connection, the sender has to wait for acknowledgment of receipt of packets from the receiver. If it does not receive an acknowledgment within a specified time frame, it must resend the packet. Resending of dropped packets is the basis of a reliable network.

In the case of RDMA read latency test over a *reliable* connection, the receiver cannot conclude that the transaction is complete as soon as it gets a data packet. The sender will repeatedly resend the same data packet if it does not receive a message that the transaction is over—such resending being the basis of reliable connections. Therefore, the receiver must generate another packet and send it to the sender to tell it not to resend. In addition, the receiver must wait to make sure that the message has reached the sender before shutting down the transaction and placing a completion element on the completion queue. Therefore, the RDMA read latency test must comprise two round trips, thus explaining why the RDMA read latency is nearly twice the RDMA write latency.

Generating ACK packets and resending data packets can get quite complicated at the level of the physical link. For example, an ACK packet itself may get lost. The agent that generated the ACK packet has to detect this loss based on repeated resends by the opposite agent. A second ACK packet must be generated and sent. At the other end, the network has to allow for the possibility that the first ACK packet was not really lost but only slow to arrive. Failure to handle such events correctly can leave the network in an inconsistent state.

A typical RDMA write or read transaction will not involve packet loss. However, the protocol used to send and receive packets must plan for all eventualities.

Infiniband technology is notable for low latency as well as excellent bandwidth. Bypassing the kernel is advantageous for both latency and bandwidth. With regard to latency, bypassing the kernel saves at least one system call and at least one copy to kernel buffers at each end. With regard to bandwidth, it is quite likely that the conversion of data in program memory to Infiniband data packets is pipelined on the host channel adapter.

MPI protocol for short messages

MPI libraries use RDMA to transmit large messages over Infiniband networks. The responder must send its remote key to the requester before an RDMA operation is initiated. There are other overheads that arise when MPI library calls are mapped to Infiniband Verbs. Latency measurements do not include these overheads. For large messages, the overheads are a small fraction of the transmission time and therefore not significant. However, the overhead of setting up RDMA transfers can prove to be too great for small messages.

The other alternative is to use channel semantics. When two communicating processes use a channel, the sender posts a send work request to the send queue of a queue pair, and the receiver posts a receive request to the receive queue of another queue pair that is bound to the sender's queue pair. When the sent message arrives at the receiver, it has no information about the region of memory to which its payload must be copied. The send must be matched with a receive to complete the data transfer. Having to match sends with receives implies that the MPI library has to implement flow control to the extent it uses channel semantics. The need for flow control, which brings with it the need to retry and resend messages, makes channel semantics unattractive.

For long messages, the overhead of arranging a rendezvous between the sender and receiver before initiating an RDMA transfer is not significant. For short messages, this overhead can be avoided if there are preassigned buffers to which the messages are copied.[8] Open MPI and other MPI implementations do just that. They use preassigned buffers and RDMA transfer for short messages. The buffers at the sender and the receiver are matched in advance. The sender will copy its short message to a send buffer as soon as a send function call is issued in the MPI library. The buffer is transmitted using RDMA write. The receiver polls the corresponding buffer on the receive side to check whether the receive is complete. A special flag is written into the receive buffer to indicate that the data transfer is complete.

---

[8]The transmission of short messages using preassigned buffers and RDMA is described by Liu et al. (2004).

Using preassigned buffers and RDMA transfers means that short messages must be copied to and from buffers. MPI implementations may use a combination of RDMA with preassigned buffers and channel semantics for short messages.

In this chapter, we attempt to tie discussion of the MPI library to Infiniband architecture as far as possible. An advantage is that some phenomena that otherwise look arbitrary will begin to look more reasonable. Knowledge of how the network actually works helps us make better use of the MPI library. An example is the connection of the short message protocol to the behavior of `unsafe()` defined in section 6.1.2. The function `unsafe()` deadlocks if the message is longer than 12 KB but not for shorter messages. What is special about messages smaller than 12 KB? The command `ompi_info` reveals that by default Open MPI treats messages as short if they are shorter than 12 KB. For short messages, `MPI_Send()` copies the message to a local buffer and returns immediately. The buffer will be transmitted using RDMA.

However, for longer messages, the MPI library registers the buffer in `MPI_Send()` and sends the remote key to the destination. The destination is expected to initiate an RDMA read when it comes across a matching `MPI_Recv()`. The `MPI_Send()` returns after the RDMA operation is complete. For longer messages, the processes of rank 0 and 1 each execute `MPI_Send()` in `unsafe()` and wait for an RDMA read operation to be initiated by the opposite party. They deadlock in that state because neither of them gets to execute the matching `MPI_Recv()` and initiate an RDMA read operation.

Exercise 6.2.1. Consider a perfect binary tree with 2^n leaves at level n. Assume that messages pass between each pair of leaves in either direction with equal probability. Calculate the expected number of messages passing between level k and level $k+1$ for $k = 0, \ldots, n-1$. The number of edges between levels k and $k+1$ is 2^{k+1}. By what factor does the number of messages per edge vary?

Exercise 6.2.2. Figure 6.1 shows how a fat-tree with 8 leaves may be laid out on a plane surface. Describe the layout for fat-trees with 16, 32, and 64 leaves.

Exercise 6.2.3. In the Infiniband architecture, what is the maximum number of bytes that can be broken up into a single train of packets?

Exercise 6.2.4. Find out the format of TCP/IP packets as well as Ethernet frames. Are the Infiniband packets more similar to TCP/IP packets or to Ethernet frames?

Exercise 6.2.5. Is it possible to create protection domains without kernel intervention? Is it possible to set up page tables without kernel intervention?

Exercise 6.2.6. To initiate an RDMA write, the initiating node or the requester needs to know the remote address into which the data should be written. Should this address be a virtual address or a physical address or can it be either?

Exercise 6.2.7. When an RDMA read or write function call is made, the requester needs to know the memory location at the responder that will be involved in the data transfer. Therefore, there must be a prior exchange of information between the requester and the responder before the RDMA transaction is initiated. This prior exchange involves an overhead. Explain why RDMA reads and writes can be efficient despite this overhead.

6.3   MPI examples

In this section, we get more deeply into MPI syntax. Our account of MPI syntax is not extensive. However, every bit of syntax introduced is related to computer architecture. MPI can make programming a lot more challenging. Yet users take the trouble to write MPI programs to make programs faster and solve bigger problems. MPI syntax can look a bit monochromatic, and by looking at MPI syntax (or semantics), one cannot gain any sense of how effective MPI facilities may be in speeding up programs. The discussion of Infiniband network architecture in the previous section will help us learn MPI with a double focus on syntax and its effectiveness.

We introduce standard optimizations such as load balancing and overlapping processor activity with network activity. At a conceptual level, these optimizations are no more than common sense. At a practical level, implementing such optimizations effectively can be quite challenging.

Section 6.3.1 is about sending and receiving of messages. Three versions of send and receive are discussed. In persistent send/receive, the sender and the receiver preallocate memory using the MPI library. All the sends and receives are from or to the same preallocated memory. In nonblocking send/receive, the send/receive function returns quickly, and it is up to the user to use functions such as `MPI_Wait()` and `MPI_Test()` to confirm that the sending and receiving has indeed completed. Persistent send/receives are nonblocking. We also discuss blocking send/receive and explain why they are slower than the nonblocking versions.

On Infiniband clusters, all MPI sends and receives map to RDMA transactions. MPI send and receive are not one sided. MPI requires that receives must be matched against sends. However, RDMA transactions are one sided. Typically, the effect of an

MPI send/receive is an exchange of message envelopes to enable RDMA transactions to be set up. The actual RDMA transaction is initiated later after the envelopes have been matched. MPI send/receive transactions can be mapped to either RDMA send or RDMA receive. For reasons explained in section 6.3.1, RDMA receive is slightly more natural, and Open MPI opts for it.

Our systems/architecture perspective brings out some other aspects of sending and receiving in MPI. Persistent MPI send/receive may seem the best because MPI is given advance notice of the memory that will be used in subsequent sends and receives. In fact, giving advance notice of memory to be used is not a good idea in Open MPI. When MPI receives advance notice of memory to be used, it allocates page frames for all the memory. That has the undesirable effect of making it impossible to use demand paging to allocate pages in near memory, when the MPI process is multithreaded.

Much of the time, the nonblocking `MPI_Isend()` and `MPI_Irecv()` variants are the best options. In modern networks such as Infiniband, the bandwidth of data transfer out of a single node can be around 10% to 20% of the peak bandwidth to DRAM memory from a single node. Such remarkably high bandwidths have raised the potential of network computing. A great range of scientific problems, from optimization and data mining to numerical PDE, are amenable to parallelization across high-performance networks.

In section 6.3.2, we turn to the Jacobi iteration, a standard example in the MPI world. There is a single MPI process on each computing node, which is true in all our examples, and each MPI process uses OpenMP threads to carry out its share of the Jacobi iteration. In the Jacobi example, the cost of MPI message passing is negligible. The optimizations that make a difference are the sort of memory optimizations we have already studied. This situation is not uncommon.

The matrix transpose example of section 6.3.3 gives a good picture of how MPI optimizations work. In this example, each process communicates with every other process. We use the matrix transpose example to illustrate both load balancing and the overlapping of processor activity with network activity.

In matrix transposition, the data format at the receiver differs from the data format at the sender. Having to cope with changes in data format comes up in all kinds of network programming. The change in data format implies a need for buffers and copying into and out of buffers. The challenge in matrix transposition is to hide the cost of copying into and out of buffers by overlapping with network activity.

Prior to that, one has to ensure that copying is done in an efficient manner. In section 6.3.3, we find that a more efficient and multithreaded copy improves the effective network bandwidth from less than 15% of the peak to about 50%.

Overlapping network activity with processor activity requires knowledge of exactly how RDMA calls are issued by the MPI library. MPI calls can be mapped to RDMA in several ways. In Open MPI, the RDMA calls are typically issued, not during send or receive, but when calls such as `MPI_Test()` are used to verify whether nonblocking send/receive have completed. Other implementations of MPI may differ in this respect. Once the processor activity is overlapped with network activity, the effective network bandwidth rises to between 75% and 90% of the peak capability of the network. Further optimizations may be possible as discussed in section 6.3.3.

In sending and receiving, an MPI call made by the receiver is typically matched against an MPI call made by the sender. In collective communication, all MPI processes participate. For example, in a minimizing reduction, all the process cooperate to find the minimum of data that is uniformly split between the processes. Section 6.3.4 is an introduction to collective communication in MPI.

Section 6.3.5 introduces complex MPI syntax for reading and writing files in parallel. The Lustre file system is also introduced. While the bandwidth to disk on a typical file system is of the order of 100 MB/s (see section 4.3), Lustre bandwidths can be a hundred times as much. The downside is the complexity of the interface.

Much of the MPI syntax in this section may look simple. Yet even simple MPI programs can become quite difficult to maintain. Data input and output to MPI programs can be cumbersome to manage. Because the data is laid out across multiple nodes, even basic tasks can require coordination between MPI processes. In general, MPI programs are difficult to interact with.

A programmer will do well to first ask whether the task at hand can be dealt with on a single node. OpenMP-type multithreaded programs are much easier to handle, and the range and size of problems that can be tackled on a single computer is growing rapidly.

6.3.1 Variants of MPI send and receive

Function calls that send and receive messages are the heart of the MPI library. An MPI user who masters sending and receive messages, but not much more, can get by quite well.

Figure 6.6: Data exchange between two nodes.

Although the syntax for sending and receiving messages is simple (relative to other MPI syntax), the MPI function calls do not map to RDMA directly. MPI send is issued by a process without explicitly accounting for the matching receive on the remote process. Indeed, the remote process may use multiple receives to match a single send. If MPI function calls are mapped directly to the network, the network will have to use channel semantics. Channel semantics implies the need for wasteful buffering and flow control inside the MPI library. RDMA calls completely bypass the kernel and do not require the MPI library to implement flow control. However, MPI send and receive do not map to RDMA function calls directly.

In this section, we describe several variants of send and receive in the MPI library. We begin with the variant that maps to RDMA in the best possible manner. The blocking variants are in wide use, but they waste nearly half the network bandwidth, as we will see.

Figure 6.6 shows the communication pattern we will implement in this section. We consider the situation with just two hosts. Each host has a send and a receive buffer. Each host sends its send buffer to the other host. The other host copies the received message to its receive buffer.

This type of exchange communication between two hosts is a good place to start. Even if the network has many active hosts, the communication between any two hosts is likely to fit this pattern. On the Internet, TCP/IP connections between a client and a server involves a pattern of communication similar to that shown in figure 6.6.

The network bandwidth is measured at each host as the number of bytes that are transferred into or out of that host in a single cycle. This manner of measuring network bandwidth is in line with the fat-tree architecture of the Infiniband network. The fat-tree is designed to realize good bidirectional bandwidth at each port of each switch.

Persistent exchange

In persistent communication as described here, user processes secure memory using the MPI library (or even a facility such as `malloc()` or `new[]`—but that is not recommended). Send and receive request objects are initialized using memory secured from the MPI library. Sends and receives are initiated using the same request objects. The termination of the data transfer is also verified using the request objects.

The `Exchg` C++ class, which will be described, is an interface for persistent exchange of data between two hosts. The usage of C++ confirms to earlier practice in this book. The C++ class is mainly a convenient interface that reduces burden on the programmer's memory. Class constructors and destructors are convenient for setting up and tearing down persistent communication between MPI processes.

The `Exchg` class is as follows:

```
1  class Exchg{
2  private:
3        double *sendbuf;
4        double *recvbuf;
5        int bufsize;
6        MPI_Request req1;
7        MPI_Request req2;
8        TimeStamp clk;
9  public:
10        Exchg(int rank, int nprocs, int bufsize);
11        ~Exchg();
12        void post();
13        double wait();
14        int getbufsize(){return bufsize;}
15        double *getsbuf(){return sendbuf;}
16        double *getrbuf(){return recvbuf;}
17  };
```

The class constructor (line 10) takes the MPI rank and the total number of MPI processes as its first two arguments. Its third and last argument is the buffer size (line 10). Each process gets an `Exchg` object of its own. If we have two processes, the send and receive buffers of lines 3 and 4 exchange data as shown in figure 6.6. The constructor uses the process rank and the total process count to set up persistent communication.

The MPI request objects, which are used to initialize and initiate message passing, are defined on lines 6 and 7. The message passing transactions are initiated by the member function post() (line 12). The member function wait() (line 13) returns when the transactions are complete. The clock defined on line 8 starts ticking when the transactions are posted. The member function wait() returns the time taken for the exchange transaction.

The member functions defined on lines 14, 15, and 16 access the buffer size, the send buffer, and the receive buffer, respectively.

The class constructor is defined as follows:

```
1  Exchg::Exchg(int rank, int nprocs, int bsize){
2       assrt(nprocs==2);
3       bufsize = bsize;
4       MPI_Alloc_mem(bufsize*8, MPI_INFO_NULL,
5                   (void *)(&sendbuf));
6       MPI_Alloc_mem(bufsize*8, MPI_INFO_NULL,
7                   (void *)(&recvbuf));
8       int tag = 0;
9       if(rank==0){
10          MPI_Send_init(sendbuf, bufsize, MPI_DOUBLE,
11                      nprocs-1, tag, MPI_COMM_WORLD, &req1);
12          MPI_Recv_init(recvbuf, bufsize, MPI_DOUBLE,
13                      nprocs-1, tag, MPI_COMM_WORLD, &req2);
14      }
15      else if(rank==nprocs-1){
16          MPI_Send_init(sendbuf, bufsize, MPI_DOUBLE,
17                      0, tag, MPI_COMM_WORLD, &req1);
18          MPI_Recv_init(recvbuf, bufsize, MPI_DOUBLE,
19                      0, tag, MPI_COMM_WORLD, &req2);
20      }
21  }
```

This constructor works correctly even if the total number of MPI processes is greater than 2. However, other member functions assume the number to be 2. Thus, the assertion that `nprocs` must be exactly 2 on line 2.

The constructor sets up persistent communication between processes of ranks 0 and 1 (or `nprocs-1`). The send and receive buffers (`senbuf` and `recvbuf`) are allocated on lines 4 and 6. The function `MPI_Alloc_mem()` takes three arguments. The first argument is the size of the buffer in bytes. The second argument has a null value as shown on lines 4 and 5. It is another of MPI's features we prefer to stay away from. The third argument is used to return the allocated memory. This function as well as most other MPI functions return error codes. The error codes are ignored by this constructor.

The library function `MPI_Alloc_mem()` will register memory. Memory allocation using `malloc()` or `new[]` will allocate a memory region in virtual address space. The actual mapping to physical pages is done by the page fault handler during first access of the allocated memory. Allocation using `MPI_Alloc_mem()` has a different effect. Not only are physical page frames allocated, but an Infiniband Verb is invoked and the mapping from virtual address space to physical pages is registered on the host channel adapter.

The syntax for setting up send and receive requests appears in the if-block on lines 9 through 14 as well as else-if block on lines 15 through 20. The first block is for the process of rank 0 and the latter block for the process of rank 1. The first three arguments to `MPI_Send_init()` are the buffer, buffer size, and the type of items in the buffer. The next three arguments are the destination rank, message tag, and the communicator. These six arguments have exactly the same order and meaning as the six arguments of `MPI_Send()` discussed in section 6.1.2. The seventh argument is new here, however. The seventh argument is a pointer to an MPI request object. The MPI library will allocate and initialize the request object.

The syntax of `MPI_Recv_init()` closely matches that of `MPI_Recv()` discussed in section 6.1.2. The first six arguments have the same order and meaning—buffer, buffer size, type of items in the buffer, message source, message tag, and communicator. The seventh argument differs, however. The seventh argument of `MPI_Recv_init()` is a pointer to a request object. The library allocates and initializes the request object.

The buffers used by `MPI_Send_init()` and `MPI_Recv_init()` may be allocated using `malloc()` or `new[]`. But doing so would imply no particular advantage in issuing Infiniband RDMA calls. When send and receive request objects are initialized, as in this constructor, usage of `MPI_Alloc_mem()` to register memory is recommended.

The destructor of the `Exchg` class is defined as follows:

```
1  Exchg::~Exchg(){
2        MPI_Free_mem(sendbuf);
3        MPI_Free_mem(recvbuf);
4        MPI_Request_free(&req1);
5        MPI_Request_free(&req2);
6  }
```

The library function `MPI_Free_mem()` is used to deallocate memory allocated using `MPI_Alloc_mem()`. Requests allocated when send and receive are initialized by `MPI_Send_init()` and `MPI_Recv_init()` are deallocated. A useful guideline is to confine memory allocation to class constructors and memory deallocation to destructors as far as possible. The definition of this destructor follows that guideline.

Posting the send and receive requests could not be easier:

```
void Exchg::post(){
     clk.tic();
     MPI_Start(&req1);
     MPI_Start(&req2);
}
```

All the message passing information gets tucked away in the request objects when the send and receive are initialized. So the syntax for issuing a request is quite simple. Notice that the argument to `MPI_Start()` is a pointer to `MPI_Request`. The library function `MPI_Start()` is nonblocking. It returns as soon as the request is issued. The clock starts ticking before the requests are initiated.

The definition of the member function that waits for the requests to complete follows.

```
double Exchg::wait(){
     MPI_Wait(&req1, MPI_STATUS_IGNORE);
     MPI_Wait(&req2, MPI_STATUS_IGNORE);
     double cycles = clk.toc();
     return cycles;
}
```

The library function `MPI_Wait()` takes a pointer to an `MPI_Request` as its first argument. It blocks until that request completes. The second argument is a pointer to `MPI_Status`. The number of items actually received may be fewer than the maximum number of items the receive buffer can hold. In that case, the status object can be passed to `MPI_Get_count()` to figure out the exact number of items received. Our exchange class uses the same buffer size on processes of ranks 0 and 1, and for receiving and sending. There is no need to query the status object. The status object that occurs as the second argument to `MPI_Wait()` also carries error handling information. The error handling information is ignored by the member function `wait()`. The member function `wait()` reads the clock after the requests complete and returns the number of cycles elapsed after the requests were initiated in `post()`.

In general, between posting a request and waiting for it to complete, a process can do useful computation. MPI provides another function called `MPI_Test()`. This function probes to find out whether the request is complete and returns immediately with the result of the probe. The probe function creates more sophisticated possibilities for overlapping communication across the network with computation within the processors.

To conclude our discussion of persistent message passing using the `Exchg` class, we give a code fragment that shows how the `Exchg` class may be used.

```
int rank;
int nprocs;
int bufsize = 100;
mpi_initialize(rank, nprocs);
Exchg exchg(rank, nprocs, bufsize);
double *sbuf = exchg.getsbuf();
double *rbuf = exchg.getrbuf();
for(int i=0; i < bufsize; i++)
    sbuf[i] = rank*100;
exchg.post();
exchg.wait();
for(int j=0; j < bufsize; j++)
    sbuf[j] = rbuf[j];
MPI_Finalize();
```

The function `mpi_initialize()` was defined in section 6.1.2. It is assumed that the MPI run is set up with two processes. The way to set up an MPI run was discussed in section 6.1.1.

We emphasize use of the `-bynode` option (or equivalent) when setting up an MPI

n	Persistent	Nonblocking (pinned)	Nonblocking (pipelined)	Blocking
10^2	0.11	0.11	0.13	0.05
10^3	0.43	0.42	0.53	0.27
10^4	1.43	1.27	0.79	0.73
10^5	1.90	1.88	1.40	0.98
10^6	1.76	1.72	1.22	0.96
10^7	1.74	1.71	1.21	0.96
10^8	1.73	1.71	1.24	0.96

Table 6.2: Bandwidth in bytes/cycle for exchanging data between two hosts over a QDR Infiniband network. All hosts are 3.33 GHz SSE2 machines (see table A.1). The data exchanged consists of n double-precision numbers. Each reported bandwidth is the median of several measurements.

run. Use of that option is crucial for the validity of the numbers reported in table 6.2. If that option is absent, the two MPI processes may run on two processor cores of the same computer. None of the message passing will be over the network. When processes run on the same compute node, the faster, easier, and more modular way for them to communicate is using shared memory.

The bandwidth for persistent exchange reported in table 6.2 is well in excess of the advertised bandwidths. The maximum reported bandwidth is $1.90 \times 3.33 = 6.33$ GB/s, which is well above the advertised maximum of 40 Gbps or 5 GB/s for QDR Infiniband. Such high bandwidths are a consequence of implementing MPI message passing using RDMA. The bandwidth reported is the number of bytes transferred into or out of the process with rank 0 in a single cycle.

If the number of double-precision numbers exchanged is $n = 10^2$ or $n = 10^3$, each message is shorter than 12 KB. Open MPI, the implementation we use, uses the short message protocol already described in the previous section. The manner in which longer messages are mapped to RDMA transfers remains to be explained.

To pass messages of size longer than 12 KB, the MPI implementation has to choose between RDMA read and RDMA write. Open MPI chooses RDMA read. RDMA read has a bandwidth that is slightly lower than that of RDMA write but is a better fit to MPI semantics. When sender posts a send request, the MPI library will package the key to the registered memory or the send buffer, along with other information about the message such as its tag and communicator. This little package of information can be immediately sent over to the receiving host. The manner in which the remote key is transmitted is not prescribed by the Infiniband standard. The MPI library is free to use channel semantics over Infiniband or even TCP/IP sockets to transfer this little package of information.

When a receive request is posted at a receiving host, the MPI library can go over all the information received from senders and quickly look for a fit. An RDMA read can be initiated as soon as a match is found.

RDMA read is a slightly better fit for MPI message passing for the following reasons. The remote key must be exchanged before an RDMA transaction is initiated. Sending the remote key suits the sender better. MPI semantics allows a receive to consume only part of the data in a sent message. Determining exactly how many items will be consumed from a sent message is easier to calculate at the receiving side.

Once the RDMA read is complete, the receiver can discover the completion by checking the completion queue. Because RDMA read is completely one sided, the sender has no way to discover the completion directly. The receiver has to send a message to the sender to notify completion of the transaction.

Table 6.2 shows a significant jump in bandwidth from $n = 10^3$ to $n = 10^4$. This jump corresponds to the transition from the short message protocol to RDMA read.

For $n \geq 10^4$, the bandwidth is maximum for $n = 10^5$ and then begins to fall slightly. The network appears to prefer message lengths of around 1 MB. It is possible, but not certain, that this preference for message lengths of around 1 MB is related to the size of buffers inside the host channel adapter.

Nonblocking exchange

Persistent send and receive, which we just discussed, is nonblocking. There is a more direct way to initiate nonblocking send and receive operations, which avoids the need to initialize request objects.

A function for exchanging data between two MPI processes using nonblocking calls follows:

```
1 double exchange_nonblocking(int rank, int nprocs,
2                             double* sendbuf,
```

```
3                     double* recvbuf,
4                     int bufsize){
5       TimeStamp clk;
6       int tag = 0;
7       double cycles=0;
8       MPI_Request req1, req2;
9       int other = (rank==0)?nprocs-1:0;
10      clk.tic();
11      MPI_Isend(sendbuf, bufsize, MPI_DOUBLE, other,
12                tag, MPI_COMM_WORLD, &req1);
13      MPI_Irecv(recvbuf, bufsize, MPI_DOUBLE, other,
14                tag, MPI_COMM_WORLD, &req2);
15      MPI_Wait(&req1, MPI_STATUS_IGNORE);
16      MPI_Wait(&req2, MPI_STATUS_IGNORE);
17      cycles = clk.toc();
18      return cycles;
19  }
```

The nonblocking `MPI_Isend()` occurs on lines 11 and 12. Its first six arguments are as before: buffer, buffer size or number of items in the buffer, type of each item, destination, tag, and communicator. The seventh and last argument is a pointer to a request object. The nonblocking `MPI_Irecv()` occurs on lines 13 and 14. Its fourth argument is `other`, which is the source of the message received. The seventh and last argument is a pointer to a request object as before.

This function uses `MPI_Wait()` on lines 15 and 16 to wait for the completion of the nonblocking send and receive. A program could do some useful computation after posting a nonblocking send or receive and before waiting for its completion. This function does not. The function returns the number of cycles used during the exchange.

How this function uses the Infiniband network depends on the way the send and receive buffers (`sendbuf` on line 2 and `recvbuf` on line 3) are allocated. If the buffers are allocated using `MPI_Alloc_mem()`, this function is no different from persistent exchange. It will map to RDMA read in exactly the same way. There is not much to choose between persistent and nonblocking communication in that case.

We will assume that both `sendbuf` and `recvbuf` are allocated using `new[]` or `malloc()`. Even with this assumption, it is preferable to use RDMA for large messages. But `new[]` and `malloc()` do not register memory, and difficulties arise when registering memory.

If the data in the send buffer of one process is to be transferred to the receive buffer of another process using RDMA, both the buffers must be registered. Registering the memory has the following effect. The host channel adapter will note down the map from virtual to physical memory, as already mentioned. But another element we have not mentioned so far becomes quite important here. This other element in registering memory is that physical memory page frames must be pinned. Otherwise the page frames may be assigned to different pages by the operating system kernel when the host channel adapter is moving data between DRAM and the network.

Although pinned memory[9] is essential if RDMA is to avoid the use of wasteful buffers, it is problematic for an Infiniband Verb to pin memory allocated outside MPI's control using `new[]` or `malloc()`. We will discuss three different ways this problem can be tackled.

The safest method is for MPI to register memory using an Infiniband Verb when a send/receive transaction is initiated and deregister the memory after the transaction is completed. The safe method is never used. It is too expensive and defeats the entire purpose of the Infiniband architecture. Pinning and unpinning memory require calling the operating system kernel. These calls are exposed to much of the complexity of the kernel's memory management system and are expensive. The Infiniband architecture sets up host channel adapters, protection domains, and queue pairs so that messages can be sent directly from user processes to the host channel adapter while bypassing the kernel. Thus, to register and deregister memory at each transaction would defeat one of the principal goals of Infiniband design, which is to bypass the kernel during send and receive. Another safe method is for the MPI library to use internal buffers that are registered and pinned in advance. This safe method is also expensive and defeats the other principal goal of Infiniband design—avoiding wasteful buffering and buffer copies.

The second method is fast but not perfectly safe. It is the method used by default by most MPI implementations. In this method, buffers are registered before commu-

---

[9]The limit on pinned memory can be quite low. On the author's desktop it is just 64 KB. However, on many high-performance clusters, this limit is set to infinity to enable RDMA communication. The limit may be found using the GNU/Linux command `ulimit -a`.

nication, if they are not already registered. But the buffers are not deregistered once the communication ends. The expectation is that the same buffers will be repeatedly used for communication. Later communication incurs no overhead because of registering and deregistering memory. The deregistration may be performed during `MPI_Finalize()`.

This method is unsafe for the following reason. The user process may deallocate memory without knowledge of the MPI library. If it does that, the virtual memory table inside the host channel adapter becomes invalid. The user process may later claim some more memory that is mapped to the same virtual addresses as the deallocated memory but to different page frames in DRAM. Dangerous memory errors will follow. Techniques such as replacing `malloc()` and `free()` with MPI versions at link time can render this method safe. It is unclear how completely these are implemented within MPI libraries and how effective the implementations are in preventing memory errors.

Table 6.2 shows that the combination of memory allocation using C/C++ libraries and nonblocking communication leads only to a small loss in bandwidth if the second method is used. This method corresponds to the column marked "pinned" in the table.

While the second method is the default method, Open MPI implements a third method. This third method is turned on by setting the Open MPI parameter

```
mpi_leave_pinned
```

to zero. This third method is called pipelined RDMA.[10] Table 6.2 shows that the third method leads to a loss of bandwidth but is still quite fast.

In pipelined RDMA, the long message is broken up into pieces. Some of the pieces are sent using channel semantics. When these pieces are in transit, the MPI library registers some of the other pieces, and it deregisters them as the transfer completes. Pipelined RDMA overlaps registration and deregistration of memory with communication over the network so that the bandwidth is not severely compromised. It is perfectly safe.

Pipelined RDMA uses RDMA write, not RDMA read. The activity of breaking the message into pieces and overlapping memory registration with network activity is best performed at the sender's end. Although RDMA write is one sided, like RDMA

---

[10]For pipelined RDMA, see Woodall et al. (2006).

read, it provides a facility to pack immediate data into the last packet. This immediate data causes the host channel adapter to recognize completion of the RDMA write and inform the responder or receiver. The information is passed up to the Verb layer by placing a completion element on the completion queue.

Of course, the pros and cons of the various methods for implementing nonblocking communication are rendered moot if the user process allocates buffers using `MPI_Alloc_mem()`. With such memory allocation, communication is safe but not necessarily fast.

It might seem that it is always better to allocate send and receive buffers with `MPI_Alloc_mem()`. The MPI library can be relieved of the hassle of registering and deregistering memory. Yet there are important situations where the programmer is better off using `new[]` or `malloc()`. One such situation occurs when we discuss the matrix transpose later in this chapter. In Open MPI, `MPI_Alloc_mem()` assigns page frames to the allocated virtual memory pages immediately. The page frames will not be allocated in memory that is nearest to the processor core that accesses it for the first time or most frequently. In multithreaded programs, the use of `MPI_Alloc_mem()` may imply additional overhead in copying to send buffers and copying out of receive buffers. Such is the speed of the Infiniband network that this additional overhead in filling and emptying buffers can be quite significant, as we find in a later section on the matrix transpose.

Blocking exchange

The syntax of the blocking calls `MPI_Send()` and `MPI_Recv()` were discussed in section 6.1.2, and there is not much to add. The function defined below reverses the order of send and receive on the process of rank 1 (or `nprocs-1`) to avoid deadlock.

```
double exchange_blocking(int rank, int nprocs,
            double* sendbuf, double* recvbuf,
            int bufsize){
    TimeStamp clk;
    int tag = 0;
    double cycles=0;
    if(rank==0){
        clk.tic();
        MPI_Send(sendbuf, bufsize, MPI_DOUBLE,
```

```
                         nprocs-1, tag, MPI_COMM_WORLD);
              MPI_Recv(recvbuf, bufsize, MPI_DOUBLE,
                         nprocs-1, tag, MPI_COMM_WORLD,
                                MPI_STATUS_IGNORE);
              cycles = clk.toc();
        }
        else if(rank==nprocs-1){
              MPI_Recv(recvbuf, bufsize, MPI_DOUBLE,
                0, tag, MPI_COMM_WORLD, MPI_STATUS_IGNORE);
              MPI_Send(sendbuf, bufsize, MPI_DOUBLE,
                      0, tag,MPI_COMM_WORLD);
        }
        return cycles;
    }
```

Table 6.2 shows that blocking communication nearly halves the network bandwidth. The Infiniband network is bidirectional, but blocking communication forces unidirectional communication. Blocking communication should not be used on modern networks such as Infiniband. It is much too inefficient and has a tendency to cause deadlocks.

Cyclic exchange

Using data exchange to learn MPI syntax, as we did, has a few advantages. Although the setting with only two processes communicating is quite limited, the syntax carries over with few changes to the setting where many processes are communicating with each other. Here we will look at cyclic data exchange.

Figure 6.7 illustrates cyclic exchange of data. The processes are arranged on a cycle, and each process communicates with the neighbor to its left as well as the neighbor to its right. The communication between pairs of neighboring processes is much like the data exchange we have studied in detail. Consequently, no new points of MPI syntax arise. Therefore, we give the interface to the Cycle class but omit its definition from the text.

The main purpose is to examine network bandwidth as the number of communicating agents increases. Network bandwidth depends on the pattern of communication between host computers. Two hosts exchanging data is one of the simplest patterns.

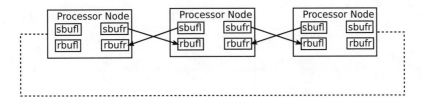

Figure 6.7: Cyclic data exchange.

The cyclic pattern is also a simple one, but it allows us to examine how well the network bandwidth holds up when there are many communicating agents on the network. We will find that it holds up quite well.

The `Cycle` class follows:

```
class Cycle{
private:
      double *sendbufl, *sendbufr;
      double *recvbufl, *recvbufr;
      int bufsize;
      MPI_Request sreq1, sreq2;
      MPI_Request rreq1, rreq2;
      TimeStamp clk;
public:
      Cycle(int rank, int nprocs, int bufsize);
      ~Cycle();
      void post();
      double wait();
      double *getsbufl(){return sendbufl;}
      double *getsbufr(){return sendbufr;}
      double *getrbufl(){return recvbufl;}
      double *getrbufr(){return recvbufr;}
};
```

This class has an interface similar to the `Exchg` class. The difference is that it has send and receive buffers to communicate with the process to its left as well as the process to its right.

To time cyclic exchange, the send and receive requests are posted using `post()`

n	nprocs = 2	nprocs = 10	nprocs = 20	nprocs = 50	nprocs = 100
10^3	0.66	0.627	0.64	0.43	0.50
10^5	1.92	1.58	1.49	1.63	1.62
10^8	1.71	1.56	1.59	1.69	1.59

Table 6.3: Bandwidths in bytes/cycle for cyclic data exchange on QDR Infiniband. All hosts are 3.33 GHz SSE2 machines (see table A.1). The number of double-precision numbers in each message is n.

on each MPI process. The `post()` is immediately followed by `wait()`, although in general a program may perform some computations before it waits for the posted requests to be complete.

Table 6.3 shows that the network bandwidth holds up quite well as the number of communicating agents increases from 2 to 100. The bandwidth is measured by each host as the number of bytes transferred into or out of it in a single cycle. The reported numbers are medians of a large number of trials and correspond to the process of rank 0. For this simple pattern of communication, the bandwidths realized are often in excess of the advertised QDR Infiniband port bandwidth of 5 GB/s, which corresponds to 1.5 bytes/cycle.

6.3.2   Jacobi iteration

The Jacobi iteration is a technique for solving linear systems that arise when certain partial differential equations are discretized. Jacobi is an iterative method. The method is started off with an initial guess for the solution. Successive iterations improve the guess with each iteration, reducing the error by a factor greater than 1. The iterations are stopped when the error is deemed to be low enough.

Poisson's equation $u_{xx} + u_{yy} = f$ is amenable to the Jacobi iteration once the equation is discretized using finite differences or finite elements. The Jacobi iteration by itself is not a particularly effective method for solving such differential equations. However, the Jacobi iteration can be supplemented by other ideas, such as multigrid, and turned into a powerful method.

The data in the Jacobi iteration is laid out as a matrix a_{ij}, $0 \le i < m$ and $0 \le j < n$. The matrix is split between MPI processes by column. Each MPI process gets a contiguous set of columns. The iteration is taken to be

$$b_{ij} \leftarrow \frac{a_{i-1,j} + a_{i+1,j} + a_{i,j-1} + a_{i,j+1}}{4}.$$

In this form, the iteration does not directly correspond to any partial differential equation. There is no right-hand side vector corresponding to the source term in the partial differential equation. We have simplified the Jacobi iteration to focus better on certain aspects of its implementation. Nevertheless, we do have to specify boundary conditions on the data a_{ij} at the boundary points $i = 0$ or $i = m - 1$ or $j = 0$ or $j = n - 1$. Our version of the Jacobi iteration generates indices that fall outside the domain for boundary points a_{ij}. For example, $a_{i-1,j}$ has a negative row index if $i = 0$. We interpret all row indices modulo m and all column indices module n. Thus, row indices of -1 and m are interpreted as $m - 1$ and 0, respectively, and column indices of -1 and n are interpreted as $n - 1$ and 0, respectively. In differential equations jargon, we are assuming periodic boundary conditions here.

This section illustrates how OpenMP constructs may be mixed with MPI message passing. There will be only one MPI process on each node of a 12-core 3.33 GHz SSE2 computer (see table A.1), but that MPI process will use OpenMP constructs to create multiple threads. The matrix a_{ij} is split across the compute nodes, and each compute node will do a further split to assign part of the Jacobi iteration to each of its threads. As far as program optimization is concerned, it will emerge that the MPI part is irrelevant. The program speed is determined by optimizing the Jacobi iteration within a single node.

The Jacobi class

If the matrix a_{ij} is $m \times n$ globally, each MPI process out of a total of P processes gets approximately n/P columns. The Jacobi iteration entails accessing entries in neighboring rows and columns. Thus, each process must exchange messages with the process to its left and the process to its right. The pattern of communication is cyclic.

The organization of data in the `Jacobi2D` class, whose definition follows, is guided by the pattern of communication.

```
1  class Jacobi2D{
2  private:
3        int nthreads;
```

```
4         int dim1;
5         int dim2;
6         double *a, *b;
7         int lrank;
8         int rrank;
9         MPI_Request reqlist[4];
10        void leftrightinit();
11        void initialize(int col1, int col2);
12        void update(int col1, int col2);
13        void copy(int col1, int col2);
14   public:
15        Jacobi2D(int rank, int nprocs, int d1, int d2,
16                                         int nth);
17        ~Jacobi2D();
18        void initializepp();
19        void postsendrecv();
20        void wait();
21        void updatepp();
22        void copypp();
23        double* geta(){return a+dim1;}
24   };
```

The dimension of the matrix stored on each processor node is $dim1 \times dim2$ (lines 4 and 5). The matrix is stored in the arrays a[] and b[] (line 6). In each step of Jacobi, the entries of b[] are computed using the entries of a[].

Figure 6.8 shows the data layout assumed by the Jacobi2D class. Although the matrix in each node is only $dim1 \times dim2$, the actual matrix stored is $dim1 \times (dim2+2)$. The leftmost column is a copy of a column to the left and the rightmost column a copy of the column to the right, as shown in the figure. Both the arrays a[] and b[] are of length $dim1 \times (dim2+2)$. Thus, during any single Jacobi iteration, a processor node can update all its $dim2$ columns using data stored on itself.

Assuming jacobi is an object of class Jacobi2D, any single iteration looks as follows:

```
jacobi.postsendrecv();
jacobi.wait();
```

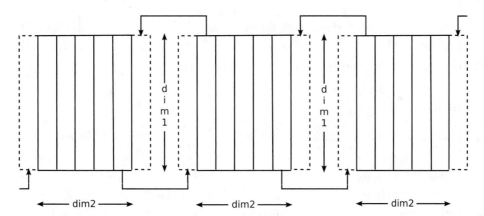

Figure 6.8: Sketch showing data layout of `Jacobi2D` class across three nodes. Each processor node holds a matrix of dimension $dim1 \times dim2$. In addition, there is an extra column on the right, which holds a copy of the rightmost column of the node to the right (see the arrows above) and an extra column to the left. The extra column to the left holds a copy of the leftmost column of the node to the left (see the arrows below).

```
jacobi.updatepp();
jacobi.copypp();
```

First, every node sends its leftmost and rightmost columns to its left and right neighbors, respectively, using the member function `postsendrecv()` (line 18). All the nodes wait for the sending and receiving to complete. The member function `updatepp()` (line 20) applies the Jacobi iteration to `a[]` and saves the result in `b[]`. The member function `copypp()` (line 21) copies `b[]` back to `a[]` to prepare for the next iteration. Notice that the first data member in the class `Jacobi2D` (line 3) is `nthreads`. Both copying and the Jacobi iteration are done in parallel using Open MP with a thread count of `nthreads`.

The data layout of this class is partly determined by the communication pattern that arises when MPI processes execute the Jacobi iteration in parallel. If we had tiled the matrix into rectangles while splitting columns as well as rows, the communication pattern would have changed. The data layout would change correspondingly. Similarly, for other discretized systems, such as finite differences in 3D or finite elements, the data structures must reflect the structure of the discretized systems. When discretized systems are solved in parallel, the additional data structures that arise must reflect the communication pattern, as we see here with the `Jacobi2D` class. The data members `lrank` (rank of node to the left, line 7), `rrank` (rank of node to the right, line 8), and `reqlist[]` (line 9) are used to set up sends and receives.

Implementation of the Jacobi class

The implementation of the `Jacobi2D` class includes member functions of two types. The class constructor, the destructor, and the member functions for sending and receiving messages fall under the first type. These member functions do not make use of OpenMP constructs at all. The member functions for default initialization and carrying out the Jacobi iteration fall under the second type. These functions use OpenMP constructs. MPI communication must be restricted to the master thread. Thread-level parallelism is used to carry out activities other than message passing. The division of member functions into two types is a natural consequence.

We first discuss member functions that do not use OpenMP constructs. This part of `Jacobi2D` is similar to the `Cycle` class, which is not surprising given that the pattern of communication is cyclic. Indeed, an alternative implementation may use a `Cycle` class object inside `Jacobi2D` to send and receive messages. The definition of the constructor of the `Jacobi2D` class follows:

```
Jacobi2D::Jacobi2D(int rank, int nprocs,
        int d1, int d2, int nth){
    nthreads = nth; assrt(nthreads%2 == 0);
    dim1 = d1; assrt(dim1%2 == 0);
    dim2 = d2; assrt(dim2%nthreads == 0);
    assrt(dim1%2 == 0);
    assrt(dim2%2 == 0);

    a = new double[dim1*(dim2+2)];
    b = new double[dim1*(dim2+2)];

    lrank = (rank==0)?nprocs-1:rank-1;
    rrank = (rank==nprocs-1)?0:rank+1;

    int tag = 0;
    double *left = a;
```

```
        double *al = a + dim1;
        double *ar = a + dim1*dim2;
        double *right = a + dim1*(dim2+1);
        MPI_Send_init(al, dim1, MPI_DOUBLE, lrank, tag,
                MPI_COMM_WORLD, reqlist+0);
        MPI_Send_init(ar, dim1, MPI_DOUBLE, rrank, tag,
                MPI_COMM_WORLD, reqlist+1);
        MPI_Recv_init(left, dim1, MPI_DOUBLE, lrank, tag,
                MPI_COMM_WORLD, reqlist+2);
        MPI_Recv_init(right, dim1, MPI_DOUBLE, rrank, tag,
                MPI_COMM_WORLD, reqlist+3);
}
```

This constructor uses the same tag for both left-going and right-going messages, unlike the constructor for the `Cycle` class. The `Jacobi2D` class must be used only when the number of MPI processes is greater than two. The dimensions $dim1$ and $dim2$ are assumed to be divisible by two and `nthreads`, respectively, to reduce clutter in the implementation. The number of threads is also assumed to be divisible by two.

The arrays `left[]` and `right[]` point to the leftmost and rightmost columns (dashed columns in figure 6.8). The arrays `al[]` and `ar[]` point to the leftmost and rightmost columns "owned" by the current node. The array `al[]` is sent to the node on the left of rank `lrank`, and the array `ar[]` is sent to the node on the right of rank `rrank`. Data from the left is received into `left` and data from the right into `right`. The pattern of communication is as shown in figure 6.8.

The definition of the destructor is included for completeness.

```
Jacobi2D::~Jacobi2D(){
    assrt(gl_mpi_onoff == MPION);
    MPI_Request_free(reqlist+0);
    MPI_Request_free(reqlist+1);
    MPI_Request_free(reqlist+2);
    MPI_Request_free(reqlist+3);
    delete[] a;
    delete[] b;
}
```

The constructor initializes sends and receives. The actual sending and receiving is left to the following member function:

```
void Jacobi2D::postsendrecv(){
    MPI_Startall(4, reqlist);
}
```

Once the sends and receives are posted, each node waits for them to complete.

```
void Jacobi2D::wait(){
    MPI_Waitall(4, reqlist, MPI_STATUSES_IGNORE);
}
```

We now turn to member functions of the Jacobi2D class that use OpenMP constructs: the member functions for default initialization, carrying out the Jacobi iteration, and copying back the updated data.

The public member function initializepp(), whose definition is given below, is invoked to initialize both a[] and b[].

```
void Jacobi2D::initializepp(){
#pragma omp parallel                           \
    num_threads(nthreads)                      \
    default(shared)
    {
        int tid = omp_get_thread_num();
        int col1 = tid*dim2/nthreads;
        int col2 = (tid+1)*dim2/nthreads;
        initialize(col1, col2);
    }
}
```

The helper member function initialize() ensures that a[] and b[] are initialized, the former to a checkerboard pattern of +1 and −1.

```
void Jacobi2D::initialize(int col1, int col2){
    for(int j=col1+1; j < col2+1; j++)
        for(int i=0; i < dim1; i++){
            a[i+j*dim1] = ((i+j-1)%2==0)?1:-1;
            b[i+j*dim1] = 0;
```

```
                          }
      }
```

Notice that col1 and col2 are shifted right by 1 to ensure that the leftmost and right-most columns are skipped. The assumption made in the class constructor, through assrt() statements, that *dim*1 and nthreads are even and *dim*2 is divisible by nthreads simplifies the checkerboard initialization of a[]. Thanks to that assumption, the MPI process is freed from checking the parity of its rank before initializing data into a checkerboard-like pattern.

The initialization of the Jacobi2D class serves two purposes. The first purpose is verification of the correctness of the implementation. If the global matrix is initialized into a chessboard-like pattern of ± 1, the pattern reverses with each Jacobi iteration. This reversal in the initialization pattern over a large number of iterations is a good test of the correctness of the implementation. It tests the correctness of communication with neighbors as well as the Jacobi update that is local to each MPI process.

The other purpose of the initialization functions is to enable allocation of page frames in near memory. If the problem size is large, the arrays a[] and b[] will hold many pages of data. For program speed, these pages must be mapped to page frames near to the thread that accesses the pages most frequently. The member functions for default initialization split the data between threads in exactly the same manner as the member functions that implement the Jacobi iteration. If the Jacobi2D object is initialized using the member functions immediately after it is created, the page frame for each thread is allocated during first touch, which occurs during initialization. Thus, the page frames will end up near threads that use them most frequently. The initialization of b[] to zero on line 5 is significant in this respect, although it is not necessary for program correctness.

The task of carrying out the Jacobi iteration on entries of a[] and storing the result in b[] is left to the following two member functions:

```
1  void Jacobi2D::update(int col1, int col2){
2       for(int j=col1+1; j < col2+1; j++)
3           for(int i=0; i < dim1; i++){
4               int iup = (i+dim1-1)%dim1;
5               int idown = (i+1)%dim1;
6               b[i+j*dim1] = 0.25*(a[iup+j*dim1]
```

```
 7                                        + a[idown+j*dim1]
 8                                        + a[i+(j-1)*dim1]
 9                                        + a[i+(j+1)*dim1]);
10               }
11  }
12
13  void Jacobi2D::updatepp(){
14  #pragma omp parallel                              \
15         num_threads(nthreads)                      \
16         default(shared)
17         {
18               int tid = omp_get_thread_num();
19               int col1 = tid*dim2/nthreads;
20               int col2 = (tid+1)*dim2/nthreads;
21               update(col1, col2);
22         }
23  }
```

Notice that updatepp() splits columns between threads in exactly the same way as the initialization routine. Almost all the time expended during a Jacobi step is inside update(). The (i, j)th entry of b[] is set equal to the average of the North, South, East, and West entries stored in a[] on lines 6 through 9. To access the West and East entries of a[], the program simply decrements and increments j on lines 8 and 9. That works because the first and last columns of b[] or a[] receive special treatment (see figure 6.8). Assignments to conditional expressions are used on lines 4 and 5 to generate indices to go North and South. Such conditional expressions prevent the compiler from generating good code for the loop, severely degrading performance of the Jacobi2D class.

The two member functions copy b[] to a[] at the end of every iteration:

```
void Jacobi2D::copy(int col1, int col2){
    for(int j=col1+1; j < col2+1; j++)
        for(int i=0; i < dim1; i++)
            a[i+j*dim1] = b[i+j*dim1];
}
```

```
void Jacobi2D::copypp(){
#pragma omp parallel                              \
       num_threads(nthreads)                      \
       default(shared)
       {
             int tid = omp_get_thread_num();
             int col1 = tid*dim2/nthreads;
             int col2 = (tid+1)*dim2/nthreads;
             this->copy(col1, col2);
       }
}
```

The structure of the member functions copypp() and copy() is similar to that of member functions used for default initialization and carrying out the Jacobi iteration. The division of work between threads is by columns and is done the same way while copying, initializing, or updating. Dividing data between columns the same way ensures that the threads access near memory most of the time, assuming the object is initialized using the member function initializepp() soon after it is created. If it is not initialized appropriately, the program will be much slower.

Iterating with the Jacobi class

The function for iterating and timing the Jacobi2D class looks as follows:

```
1  double time_jacobi(int rank, int nprocs,
2                     int dim1, int dim2,
3                     int nitns){
4      int nth = get_nthreads();
5      Jacobi2D jacobi(rank, nprocs, dim1, dim2, nth);
6      jacobi.initializepp();
7      TimeStamp clk;
8      clk.tic();
9      for(int i=0; i < nitns; i++){
10            jacobi.postsendrecv();
11            jacobi.wait();
12            jacobi.updatepp();
```

nprocs	dim1	dim2	cycles/entry/itn
4	10^5	12×10^3	8.3
20	10^5	12×10^3	7.2
100	10^5	12×10^3	7.7

Table 6.4: Performance of the `Jacobi2D` class on `nprocs` nodes, each a 12-core 3.33 GHz SSE2 machine (see table A.1).

```
13                      jacobi.copypp();
14          }
15        return clk.toc();
16  }
```

The OpenMP constructs are hidden away inside the implementation of the `Jacobi2D` class. There are no OpenMP constructs within the iteration loop.

The `wait()` on line 11 immediately follows `postsendrecv()` on line 12. The implementation waits for the message passing to be complete after initiating sends and receives. No attempt is made to overlap computation with communication because there is no need for it. Message passing takes up an insignificant amount of time in this program, and any effort to hide its cost by overlapping it with computation would be wasted. Indeed, an attempt at such an optimization may make the loop nests in the member functions `update()` and `copy()` more complicated, leading to a slightly slower program.

Timing the Jacobi class

The three trials reported in table 6.4 take $dim1 = 10^5$ and $dim2 = 12,000$ on each MPI process. The number of MPI processes, with one process per Xeon 5680 compute node, is varied from 4 to 100. The size of the matrix local to each MPI process or compute node is thus equal to $10^5 \times 12,002$. The performance figure reported is the number of cycles consumed per iteration divided by the number of entries local to each MPI process.

During each iteration, four arithmetic operations (three additions and a multiplication) are performed to update each entry. Corresponding to each update, two entries, one within the array `a[]` and one within `b[]`, are accessed. Thus, approximately 16 bytes of data are accessed for every set of four arithmetic operations, and the figure is 32 bytes if we include the cost of copying from b[] to a[]. The cost of this computation will be determined by memory accesses. The bandwidth to memory realized on a 3.33 GHz machine is between 12 and 14 GB/s.

The realized bandwidth to memory and the speed of this program can be improved considerably. In fact, the running time of this program can be nearly halved. This program spends much of its time within the nested for-loop on lines 2 through 10 in the member function update(). That loop nest, unfortunately, has too many inefficiencies in it. The body of the inner loop contains two conditional expressions, and the loop nest does not use blocking.

It is amusing that although the communication pattern and OpenMP thread level parallelism have such a big impact on the structure of this program, its speed is determined by a single nested and sequential for-loop. To improve the speed of this program, the conditional assignments must be removed from the body of the program. The for-loops must be rewritten to implement the Jacobi iteration in blocks to improve cache and TLB usage. Yet another optimization is to use restrict qualifiers.

All timing numbers were obtained on the Lonestar cluster at the Texas Advanced Computing Center. The recommended MPI on that cluster is MVAPICH2. The Jacobi2D class was slower by more than a factor of four using mpicxx, which is the compilation/linking command of MVAPICH2.[11] OpenMP constructs are recognized by mpicxx. So the C/C++ compiler it invokes must be generating suboptimal code for the member function update(). The tendency of MPI implementations to subsume compilation/linking within commands such as mpicxx, mpiCC, or mpiicpc is one we do not endorse. In many programs such as this one optimization of C/C++ compilation is of far greater consequence than MPI message passing. The user's access to the compiler should not be obscured by hiding the compiler beneath another layer. MPI is a library, and one should be able to include it and link to it like any library.

6.3.3 Matrix transpose

So far in this chapter, we have considered data exchange between two MPI processes and cyclic transfer of data between several MPI processes. Both of these are especially

---

[11] A similar slowdown by a factor of 4 was observed on the more recent Stampede cluster using the recommended MVAPICH2.

simple patterns of communication. In this section, we implement the transposition of large matrices stored on several host computers connected by QDR Infiniband network. The number of host computers ranges from 10 to 100 and the largest matrix handled has 5×10^4 rows and 5×10^5 columns. There is exactly one MPI process per host computer.

In the matrix transpose, as we implement it, there is communication between every pair of host computers. Such a setting, where every possible line of communication is active, exercises additional features of the Infiniband network and the MPI library implementation. The Infiniband architecture relies on the host channel adapter to convert data stored in page frames in DRAM memory to Infiniband data packets, each of which is 2 KB or less on the system we use. The MPI processes initiate RDMA read and write transactions by writing directly to queue pairs that reside on the host channel adapter. When many lines of communication are active, there will be a large number of queue pairs on each host channel adapter. The communication pattern tests the ability of the MPI library implementation as well as the host channel adapter to manage a large number of queue pairs.

In a cyclic pattern of communication, every MPI process communicates only with its neighbors to the left and right. It is likely that neighboring host computers are connected to the same switch at the leaf of the Infiniband fat-tree. If that is the case, most of the network traffic does not reach switches at higher levels of the fat-tree. The all-to-all pattern of communication that occurs in the matrix transpose is a better test of the capability of the Infiniband fat-tree network to sustain high bandwidth at each host channel adapter.

The matrix transpose brings out another important aspect of networking—namely, the overhead of copying into and out of buffers. During a matrix transpose, the data format changes in such a way that copying into and out of buffers is inevitable. The receiver's view of the data differs significantly from the sender's view of the data. We will find that the performance of the MPI program is determined largely by copying into and out of buffers.

The Jacobi iteration of the previous section does not require application-level buffering, whereas the matrix transpose of this section does. The data layout in a 2D Jacobi iteration is so simple that the sender's view of the data transmitted coincides with the receiver's view. Both the sender and receiver think of the transmitted data as a column of the global matrix and store it as such. If the program can be designed so that the sender and receiver have the same view of transmitted data, it is usually advantageous to adopt such a design. Data does not need to be copied into send buffers or copied out of receive buffers. Applications such as 2D or 3D finite differences on a regular rectangular grid are amenable to this type of design.

The more difficult scenario is when the data is irregular, or structured but changes format between the sender and the receiver, as in matrix transpose. In such scenarios, the MPI application has to copy into send buffers and out of receive buffers. The way buffering is handled becomes as important as it is in the TCP/IP protocol stack or in the hardware implementation of the Infiniband network architecture. The matrix transpose program uses buffering to handle the change in data layout between the matrix at the sending MPI process and the transposed matrix at the receiving process.

Balanced matrix partitions

If an $m \times n$ matrix is stored in column-major order, with a leading dimension equal to column size in the array a[], the (i,j)th entry of the matrix is a[i+j*m]. In row-major order, the (i,j)th entry is at a[j+i*n]. If the matrix is transposed and stored in column-major order, the (j,i)th entry of the transposed matrix would be at a[j+i*n]. On a single computer, transposing a matrix is equivalent to switching from column-major order to row-major order.

Figure 6.9 shows a matrix is partitioned along columns as well as rows. If the global matrix is $M \times N$, it is partitioned across P MPI processes by allocating approximately N/P columns to each process. Each process gets a contiguous set of columns. Matrix transposition is equivalent to switching the partitioning scheme from columnwise to rowwise, but with a twist. As shown in the figure, the set of columns of process P_i intersects the set of rows of process P_j in a block matrix. During matrix transposition, this block must be transmitted from process P_i to process P_j. Bidirectional data transfer occurs between every pair of processes.

The twist arises as follows. Every block that is transmitted must be transposed. The block that is transmitted is stored in column-major order with leading dimension equal to M, the column size of the global matrix. When it is transposed and stored, the lead dimension changes to N, the row size of the global matrix.

The function BlockDivide(), defined below, is used for columnwise as well as rowwise partitioning.

```
1  void BlockDivide(long n, int P, long *fst){
2       long  Q = n/P;
```

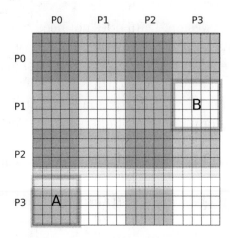

Figure 6.9: Columnwise and rowwise matrix partitions of a matrix between four processor nodes. When the columnwise partitioning is switched to rowwise partitioning, submatrix blocks must be transmitted between nodes. For example, the block labeled A must be sent from $P0$ to $P3$ and the block labeled B must be sent from $P3$ to $P1$.

```
3          long   R = n-Q*P;
4          fst[0] = 0;
5          for(int p=0; p < R; p++)
6               fst[p+1] = fst[p] + (Q+1);
7          for(int p=R; p < P; p++)
8               fst[p+1] = fst[p]+Q;
9   }
```

BlockDivide() partitions n items between P processes. The partitioning is stored in the array fst[]. The number of items that each process gets would be exactly equal to the quotient $Q = n/P$ (line 2) if the remainder $R = n - QP$ (line 3) were zero. If $0, 1, \ldots, n-1$ are the n items, the items i assigned to process p lie in the interval fst[p] $\leq i <$ fst[p+1]. Equivalently, the assignment to process p begins at fst[p]. The for-loop on lines 5 and 6 assigns $Q+1$ items to each of the first R processes. The remaining $P - R$ processes are assigned Q items by the for-loop on lines 7 and 8.

It must be noted that fst[] is an array with $P + 1$ entries, although there are only P processes. The entry fst[P] always gets sets to n.

The division of work between the processes is nearly evenly balanced. Some of the processes get at most one extra item. When the number of items (columns and rows in matrix transposition) is large, as it must be for parallelization to be meaningful, the slight imbalance by a single item will be inconsequential.

The general principles of algorithm design assume a highly simplified but still useful and pertinent model of the computer. General principles that have a direct bearing on parallel programming are few. Load balancing is one of them. Load balancing requires that work should be nearly evenly partitioned between processes that utilize equally powerful hardware. The speed of a parallel program is determined by the slowest process, which is the one with the highest load.

The principal of balancing the load is no more than common sense. Indeed, it barely requires knowledge of arithmetic. Yet it must not be taken lightly because the consequences of ignoring it can be severe. For example, a careless division of n items between P processes might assign $Q + R$ items to process P_0 and Q items to all others. If n is much larger than P^2, Q will be much larger than R, and the resulting imbalance will not be too great. However, if n is of the order of P^2, which is not unrealistic, process P_0 may end up with nearly twice the work of any other process.

The Transpose class

The `Transpose` class defined below does not hold any part of the matrix to be transposed nor does it store the transposed matrix. It holds send and receive buffers and a few other items. It provides public member functions for data transfers that arise during matrix transpose and to copy data from matrices to its own buffers.

```
1  class Transpose{
2  private:
3        int p; //process rank
4        int P; //number of processes
5        long  M;
6        long  N;
7        long *fstM;
8        long *fstN;
9        double *sendbuf, *recvbuf;
10       MPI_Request *sreqlist, *rreqlist;
11
12 public:
```

```
13          Transpose(int rank, int nprocs, long Mi, long Ni);
14          ~Transpose();
15          long ffstM(int rank){return fstM[rank];};
16          long ffstN(int rank){return fstN[rank];};
17          void copyTOsendbuf(double *localMN);
18          void postsend();
19          void postrecv();
20          void wait();
21          void copyFROMrecvbuf(double *localNM);
22          void transpose(double *localMN, double *localNM);
23 };
```

This class stores just enough data to implement the matrix transpose. It stores the
process rank (p on line 3), the total number of MPI processes (P on line 4), and
dimensions of the global matrix (M and N on lines 5 and 6). The arrays fstM[] (line 7)
and fstN[] (line 8) are used to partition the M rows and the N columns, respectively.
This partitioning is done identically on all the MPI processes, and each process has
its own copy of the arrays fstM[] and fstN[] on its own Transpose object. Each
MPI process relies on its knowledge of the partitioning of rows and columns across all
processes when sending and receiving data. Data is mapped from the locally stored
part of the $M \times N$ matrix to the send buffer (sendbuf on line 9) using fstM[]. Data
is mapped from the receive buffer (recvbuf on line 10) to the locally stored part of
the transposed $N \times M$ matrix using fstN[].

The public interface to the Transpose class consists of the constructor, the destructor, and functions to step through the matrix transpose. There is also a single
member function, namely, transpose() (line 21), for effecting the transposition. The
two arguments of this member function are localMN[], which stores the local part of
the $M \times N$ matrix, and localNM[], which stores the local part of the $N \times M$ matrix.

The class constructor is defined as follows:

```
1 Transpose::Transpose(int rank, int nprocs,
2                             long Mi, long Ni)
3        :p(rank), P(nprocs), M(Mi), N(Ni)
4 {
5        fstM = new long[P+1]; fstN = new long[P+1];
6        BlockDivide(M, P, fstM);
```

```
 7          BlockDivide(N, P, fstN);
 8          long ncols = fstN[p+1]-fstN[p];
 9          long nrows = fstM[p+1]-fstM[p];
10
11          assrt(ncols > 0);
12          sendbuf = new double[ncols*M];
13
14          assrt(nrows > 0);
15          recvbuf = new double[nrows*N];
16
17          sreqlist = new MPI_Request[P];
18          rreqlist = new MPI_Request[P];
19 }
```

The constructor uses `BlockDivide()` to calculate the entries of `fstM[]` (on line 6) and `fstN[]` (on line 7). The matrix is partitioned columnwise, and the columns held by process of rank p have indices

$$\text{fstN}[p] \leq j < \text{fstN}[p+1].$$

When the matrix as transposed, it is in effect partitioned rowwise (see figure 6.9), and the rows it will hold have indices

$$\text{fstM}[p] \leq i < \text{fstM}[p+1].$$

The number of columns `ncols` of the matrix and the number of rows `nrows` of the transposed matrix held on the current process of rank p is calculated on lines 8 and 9, respectively.

The send buffer is allocated on line 12. Each process sends out all the data it holds (we do not attempt to optimize for the diagonal blocks that remain on the same processor node). Thus, the size of the send buffer, which is `ncols*M` on line 12, accounts for every column and every entry of the matrix held by the process. For similar reasons, the size of the receive buffer allocated on line 15 is `nrows*N`, accounting for every entry of the transposed matrix held by the process.

After the discussion extolling the benefits of registering memory explicitly in section 6.3.1, it may seem a bit strange that the send and receive buffers are allocated using **new[]**, rather than **MPI_Alloc_mem()**. As mentioned earlier, there is a reason for allocating with **new[]**. **MPI_Alloc_mem()** would register memory explicitly, and pages in virtual memory would also be assigned to page frames immediately after allocation. With **new[]**, in contrast, demand paging remains in place. With demand paging, page frames are assigned in near memory during first access. Allocation of page frames in near memory speeds up the **Transpose** class significantly.

The class destructor is listed for the sake of completeness.

```
Transpose::~Transpose(){
      delete[] fstM;
      delete[] fstN;
      delete[] sreqlist;
      delete[] rreqlist;
      delete[] sendbuf;
      delete[] recvbuf;
   }
```

A matrix stored across P MPI process is transposed when each process makes a single call to the member function **transpose()**. The definition of that member function gives an overview of the **Transpose** class.

```
1  void Transpose::transpose(double *localMN,
2        double *localNM){
3        TimeStamp clk;
4        clk.tic();
5        copyTOsendbuf(localMN);
6        trans_timer.scopy += clk.toc();
7
8        clk.tic();
9        postsend();
10       postrecv();
11       wait();
12       trans_timer.mpi += clk.toc();
13
14       clk.tic();
15       copyFROMrecvbuf(localNM);
16       trans_timer.rcopy += clk.toc();
```

17 }

The part of the global $M \times N$ matrix held by the current MPI process is in `localMN[]` (line 1). The part of the transposed $N \times M$ matrix that will be held by the same MPI process goes to `localNM[]` (line 2).

To effect a matrix transpose, each process copies `localMN[]` to its send buffer (line 5), posts sends and receives (lines 9 and 10), waits for the sends and receives to complete (line 11), and finally copies its receive buffer to `localNM[]`. The `wait()` on line 11 immediately follows sending and receiving on lines 9 and 10. This class does not attempt to overlap communication across the network with copying to and from buffers. Overlapping network and processor activity is a sophisticated optimization that we will get to near the end of this section.

The definition of `transpose()` also displays some of the timing infrastructure of this class. The program variable `trans_timer` is an externally defined `struct`. Timing information will be omitted later.

Sending data

During matrix transpose, each process sends a block matrix to every process (see figure 6.9). The block matrix must be transposed. The block matrix may be transposed when it is either copied to the send buffer or copied out of the receive buffer. We transpose before sending.

The definition of a function for transposing follows.

```
void transposewlda(double *in, int lda,
                      long nrows, long ncols,
                   double *out){
    for(long i=0; i < nrows; i++)
        for(long j=0; j < ncols; j++)
            out[j+i*ncols] = in[i+j*lda];
}
```

The array `in[]` will typically have a leading dimension of M that is greater than the number of rows. However, the array `out[]`, which holds the transposed matrix and corresponds to a segment of the send buffer, is tightly packed with leading dimension equal to `ncols`. Notice the interchange of i and j in the body of the inner for-loop.

This is not the best program for transposing a matrix, and we will make it better later.

The member function `copyTOsendbuf()` copies `localMN[]` to the send buffer.

```
1  void Transpose::copyTOsendbuf(double *localMN){
2      long ncols = fstN[p+1] - fstN[p];
3      for(long q=0; q < P; q++){
4          long nrows = fstM[q+1] - fstM[q];
5          long sbufindex = ncols * fstM[q];
6          long localindex = fstM[q];
7          long lda = M;
8          transposewlda(localMN+localindex, lda,
9                  nrows, ncols,
10                 sendbuf+sbufindex);
11     }
12 }
```

On line 2, `ncols` is initialized to the number of columns of the $M \times N$ matrix stored locally. The local MPI process has rank `p`, whereas the for-loop variable `q` (line 3) loops over the ranks of all the P processes. The number of rows of the block matrix to be sent by the current process of rank `p` to the process of rank `q` is calculated on line 4 using `fstM[]`. The index into the send buffer is equal to the total number of entries to be sent to processes with rank less than `q` (line 5). The index into `localMN` is simply equal to the index of the first entry in its first column that gets sent to the process of rank `q`. The row number of that entry is equal to `fstM[q]` (line 7). The call to the transposing function (lines 9 through 11) extracts the submatrix to be sent from the current process of rank `p` to the process of rank `q` by adding `localindex` to `localMN` and setting `lda` equal to M.

The member function for posting send requests uses `fstM[]` and `fstN[]` in a similar manner.

```
void Transpose::postsend(){
    long ncols = fstN[p+1]-fstN[p];
    for(int q=0; q < P; q++){
        long nrows = fstM[q+1]-fstM[q];
        long sbufindex = ncols*fstM[q];
        int count = ncols*nrows; //MPI cant do long
```

```
            int tag = 0;
            MPI_Isend(sendbuf+sbufindex,count,MPI_DOUBLE,
                        q, tag, MPI_COMM_WORLD, sreqlist+q);
        }
    }
```

The number of columns (`ncols`) to be sent is equal to the number of columns owned by the current process of rank p. It is calculated using `fstN[]` outside the for-loop. The number of rows to be sent to the process of rank q is equal to the number of rows of the transposed matrix assigned to the process of rank q. It is calculated inside the loop body using `fstM[]`. The calculation of the index into the send buffer here matches that in the member function `copyTOsendbuf()`, as it must for correctness.

The send buffer `sendbuf` was allocated using `new[]`. The send buffer is registered using an Infiniband Verb by the Open MPI implementation during the first invocation of the member function `postsend()`. The memory gets deregistered only at the end of the program.

Receiving data

The member functions of the `Transpose` class for receiving data closely parallel the member functions for sending. The member function `postrecv()` parallels `postsend()`.

```
void Transpose::postrecv(){
    long ncols = fstM[p+1]-fstM[p];
    for(long q=0; q < P; q++){
        long nrows = fstN[q+1]-fstN[q];
        long rbufindex = ncols*fstN[q];
        int count = nrows*ncols;//MPI cant do long
        int tag = 0;
        MPI_Irecv(recvbuf+rbufindex,count,MPI_DOUBLE,
                    q, tag, MPI_COMM_WORLD, rreqlist+q);
    }
}
```

Once the receive requests have been posted, the program must wait for the requests to complete.

```
void Transpose::wait(){
```

```
    for(long  q=0;  q < P;  q++)
        MPI_Wait(sreqlist+q, MPI_STATUS_IGNORE);
    for(long  q=0;  q < P;  q++)
        MPI_Wait(rreqlist+q, MPI_STATUS_IGNORE);
}
```

In principle, we only need to wait for the receive requests to complete before copying out of the receive buffers. Waiting for the send requests to complete can be put off until the send buffer needs to be reused. Doing so brings no benefit and only makes the structure of the program more complicated.

Data is copied out of the receive buffers as follows:

```
void copywlda(double *in, int nrows, int ncols,
                    double *out, int lda){
    for(long j=0;  j < ncols;  j++)
        for(long i=0;  i < nrows;  i++)
            out[i+j*lda]  =  in[i+j*nrows];
}


void Transpose::copyFROMrecvbuf(double *localNM){
    long ncols = fstM[p+1]-fstM[p];
    for(long q=0;  q < P;  q++){
        long nrows = fstN[q+1]-fstN[q];
        long rbufindex = ncols*fstN[q];
        long localindx = fstN[q];
        long lda = N;
        copywlda(recvbuf+rbufindex, nrows, ncols,
            localNM+localindx, lda);
    }
}
```

The member function `copyFROMrecvbuf()` extracts the segment of the buffer received from the process with rank q as well as the submatrix of `localNM` it must be copied into. The copying is done by `copywlda()`. There is no transposing when copying out of the receive buffers. Notice that in the body of the inner for-loop of `copywlda()`, the indices i and j are not exchanged.

nprocs (or P)	M	N/P	b/w	send copy	MPI	recv copy
10	5×10^4	5×10^3	0.19	77.5%	15.5%	6.4%
20	5×10^4	5×10^3	0.20	70.4%	21.2%	8.5%
50	5×10^4	5×10^3	0.20	70.9%	20.5%	7.9%
100	5×10^4	5×10^3	0.25	64.6%	26.2%	10.2%

Table 6.5: Bandwidth in bytes transferred into or out of a single node per cycle on QDR Infiniband and 12-core 3.33 GHz SSE2 machines (see table A.1). The percentage of time spent in copying to the send buffer, MPI message passing, and copying out of the receive buffer are also reported.

Faster copying for improved network bandwidth

Table 6.5 shows that 75% of the running time of our implementation of the matrix transpose is spent copying into and out of buffers. As a result, the bandwidth realized is unimpressive. The bidirectional bandwidth at a host is about 0.7 GB/s, which is a small fraction of the advertised peak of 5 GB/s for QDR Infiniband. The data reported in the table are medians of 100 measurements.

A great proportion of the time is being spent copying in and out of buffers. The functions `copywlda()` and `transposewlda()` are inefficient. We know that a single core cannot reach high bandwidth to memory and a direct implementation of transpose results in too many cache and TLB misses. In particular, `transposewlda()` fails to utilize cache lines completely. The cure for these ills is to alter the implementation of transpose to use blocking and to use OpenMP thread-level parallelism during copying.

The definition of `transposewlda()` is altered as follows:

```
#define B 50
void transposewlda(double *in, int lda,
                   long nrows, long ncols,
                   double *out){
#pragma omp parallel for                        \
     num_threads(NTHREADS)                      \
     default(none)                              \
     shared(in, lda, nrows, ncols, out)
     for(int i=0; i < nrows; i+=B)
```

```
for(int j=0; j < ncols; j+=B){
    int iib = (nrows-i < B)?nrows-i:B;
    int jjb = (ncols-j < B)?ncols-j:B;
    for(int ii=0; ii < iib;ii++)
        for(int jj=0; jj < jjb;jj++)
        out[j+jj+(i+ii)*ncols]
            = in[i+ii+(j+jj)*lda];
}
}
```

This for-loop nest implements matrix transpose block by block. In a large problem, most blocks are $B \times B$, but the block sizes are adjusted using iib and jjb at the far edges of the matrix. The outermost loop is parallelized using OpenMP. Matrix transpose with blocking was discussed in chapters 4 and 5. The choice of $B = 50$ as the block size here is influenced by that earlier discussion.

The definition of copylda() is altered as follows:

```
void copywlda(double *in, int nrows, int ncols,
                double *out, int lda){
#pragma omp parallel for                        \
    num_threads(NTHREADS)                       \
    default(none)                               \
    shared(in, nrows, ncols, out, lda)
    for(long j=0; j < ncols; j++)
        for(long i=0; i < nrows; i++)
            out[i+j*lda] = in[i+j*nrows];
}
```

The modification here is simpler. The outer for-loop has been qualified using the OpenMP parallel-for construct.

Table 6.6 shows the considerable improvement in bandwidth from using faster programs to copy into and out of buffers. The bidirectional bandwidth realized at a host is greater than 2.5 GB/s in every case. Nearly 55% of the advertised bandwidth of QDR Infiniband is reached with 100 host computers on the network.

Yet there is much room for improvement. Table 6.6 shows that nearly 30% of the cycles are still being used when copying into and out of buffers. It is not possible to

nprocs (or P)	M	N/P	b/w	send copy	MPI	recv copy
10	5×10^4	5×10^3	0.93	16.9%	68.6%	14.5%
20	5×10^4	5×10^3	0.81	15.1%	71.1%	13.0%
50	5×10^4	5×10^3	0.76	13.7%	74.3%	12.0%
100	5×10^4	5×10^3	0.82	14.1%	72.3%	13.6%

Table 6.6: Improved bandwidth in bytes per cycle, following the use of OpenMP thread-level parallelism for copying into and out of buffers. The network was QDR Infiniband and the host computers were 3.33 GHz SSE2 machines (see table A.1).

nprocs (or P)	M	N/P	b/w	send copy	MPI	recv copy
10	5×10^4	5×10^3	1.39	27%	-	24%
20	5×10^4	5×10^3	1.14	23%	-	20%
50	5×10^4	5×10^3	1.22	23%	-	21%
100	5×10^4	5×10^3	1.11	19%	-	20%

Table 6.7: Bandwidth in bytes per cycle with network activity overlapped with processor activity as well as fast copies. Multiply by the clock frequency of 3.33 GHz to get bandwidth in GB/s. The network was QDR Infiniband and all host computers were 12-core 3.33 GHz SSE2 machines (see table A.1).

make the copying much better but we can try to overlap MPI message passing with copying.

Overlapping network and processor activity

Table 6.7 shows the improvement in bandwidth when network activity is overlapped with processor activity, in addition to using fast copies as discussed. The realized network bandwidth is 75% of the peak of 5 GB/s with 100 nodes. With 10 nodes the realized bandwidth is more than 90% of the peak.

The new class `FastTrans` shows how network activity may be overlapped with processor activity.

```
class FastTrans{
private:
    int p; //process rank
```

```
        int P; //number of processes
        long  M;
        long  N;
        long *fstM;
        long *fstN;
        double *sendbuf, *recvbuf;
        MPI_Request *sreqlist, *rreqlist;
        int *sendorder;
        int *rcvd_list;
   public:
        FastTrans(int rank, int nprocs, long Mi, long Ni);
        ~FastTrans();
        long ffstM(int rank){return fstM[rank];};
        long ffstN(int rank){return fstN[rank];};
        void copyTOsendbuf(int q, double *localMN);
        void postsend(int q);
        void postrecv(int q);
        void wait(); /* wait on all sends */
        void copyFROMrecvbuf(int q, double *localNM);
        void transpose(double *localMN, double *localNM);
   };
```

The class **FastTrans** is similar to **Transpose** in many ways, although there are some changes. In the private section, two new items appear: **sendorder** and **rcvd_list**. These are used by the member function **transpose()** to order sends and keep track of receives.

In the public section, the member functions **postsend()** and **postrecv()** take the argument **int q**. The send and receive requests are no longer initiated simultaneously. The member function **transpose()** orders sends and receives to overlap network activity with processor activity.

The array **sendorder[]** is initialized by the class constructor.

```
1  FastTrans::FastTrans(int rank, int nprocs, long Mi,
2        long Ni):p(rank), P(nprocs), M(Mi), N(Ni)
3  {
4        fstM = new long[P+1];
```

```
5        fstN = new long[P+1];
6        BlockDivide(M, P, fstM);
7        BlockDivide(N, P, fstN);
8        long ncols = fstN[p+1]-fstN[p];
9        long nrows = fstM[p+1]-fstM[p];
10
11       assrt(ncols > 0);
12       sendbuf = new double[ncols*M];
13
14       assrt(nrows > 0);
15       recvbuf = new double[nrows*N];
16
17       sreqlist = new MPI_Request[P];
18       rreqlist = new MPI_Request[P];
19
20       sendorder = new int[P];
21       rcvd_list = new int[P];
22
23       sendorder[0] = 0;
24       for(int i=1; i < P/2 + P%2; i++){
25            sendorder[2*(i-1)+1] = i;
26            sendorder[2*(i-1)+2] = P-i;
27       }
28       if(P%2 == 0)
29            sendorder[P-1] = P/2;
30
31       for(int i=0; i < P; i++)
32            sendorder[i] = (sendorder[i]+p)%P;
33 }
```

The initialization of the row and column partition indices `fstM[]` and `fstN[]` are as in the class `Transpose`. The send and receive buffers have exactly the same size as before. However, the sending and receiving will be done in quite a different manner. On lines 23 through 29, the array `sendorder[]` is initialized to be

$$0, 1, P - 1, 2, P - 2, 3, P - 3, \ldots$$

This send order is valid assuming the local rank is $p = 0$. To obtain the send order for the current process of rank p, the for-loop on lines 31 and 32 modifies entries of sendorder[] by adding the rank p module P, where P is the total number of MPI processes.

The order of sends assumes that a process of rank p is next to those of rank $(p-1) \bmod P$ and $(p+1) \bmod P$. In fact, the assignment of ranks to processor nodes can be almost random. No such assumption can be true. Even so, there appears to be some benefit in the reciprocity found between the send orders of processes of two different ranks.

The definition of the destructor is given for completeness.

```
FastTrans::~FastTrans(){
    delete[] fstM;
    delete[] fstN;
    delete[] sreqlist;
    delete[] rreqlist;
    delete[] sendbuf;
    delete[] recvbuf;
    delete[] sendorder;
    delete[] rcvd_list;
}
```

The definitions of copyTOsendbuf() and copyFROMrecvbuf() are the same as before, except they take an argument int q. They copy only that part of the matrix that is being sent to or received from the process of rank q.

```
void FastTrans::copyTOsendbuf(int q, double *localMN){
    long ncols = fstN[p+1] - fstN[p];
    long nrows = fstM[q+1] - fstM[q];
    long sbufindex = ncols * fstM[q];
    long localindex = fstM[q];
    long lda = M;
    transposewlda(localMN+localindex, lda,
                nrows, ncols,
                sendbuf+sbufindex);
}
```

```
void FastTrans::copyFROMrecvbuf(int q,double *localNM){
    long ncols = fstM[p+1]-fstM[p];
    long nrows = fstN[q+1]-fstN[q];
    long rbufindex = ncols*fstN[q];
    long localindx = fstN[q];
    long lda = N;
    copywlda(recvbuf+rbufindex, nrows, ncols,
            localNM+localindx, lda);
}
```

Unlike the corresponding member functions of the class Transpose, these member functions do not use a for-loop to communicate with every other MPI process. As a result, they are slightly more transparent. The functions transposewlda() and copywlda() are exactly the same as the fast versions given earlier and are omitted.

The member function postsend() and postrecv() communicate with a single other process of rank q.

```
void FastTrans::postsend(int q){
    long ncols = fstN[p+1]-fstN[p];
    long nrows = fstM[q+1]-fstM[q];
    long sbufindex = ncols*fstM[q];
    int count = ncols*nrows; //MPI can't handle long
    int tag = 0;
    MPI_Isend(sendbuf+sbufindex, count, MPI_DOUBLE,
            q, tag, MPI_COMM_WORLD, sreqlist+q);
}

void FastTrans::postrecv(int q){
    long ncols = fstM[p+1]-fstM[p];
    long nrows = fstN[q+1]-fstN[q];
    long rbufindex = ncols*fstN[q];
    int count = nrows*ncols;//MPI can't handle long
    int tag = 0;
    MPI_Irecv(recvbuf+rbufindex, count, MPI_DOUBLE,
            q, tag, MPI_COMM_WORLD, rreqlist+q);
}
```

As before, the absence of a for-loop makes these functions slightly more transparent. The member function wait() waits for sends to complete but not for receives.

```
void FastTrans::wait(){
        MPI_Waitall(P, sreqlist, MPI_STATUSES_IGNORE);
}
```

The MPI function MPI_Waitall() is used to wait for all the P send requests in sreqlist[]. We do not wait for receives to complete in the same manner. Waiting for receives is folded into the structure of transpose() and is part of the strategy for overlapping network activity with copying to and from buffers.

The member function transpose(), whose definition we now turn to, is the heart of the class FastTrans. It is much more complicated than the corresponding member function of the class Transpose. Before getting into it, we ask what we want it to do. Of course, at one level, the answer is simple: we want it to overlap network activity with copying to and from buffers. The other member functions have been defined to facilitate this overlap. The member functions copy to and from buffers one block at a time and not all at once. Similarly, the sending and receiving is done one process at a time and not all at once.

The true answer is a good deal more complicated. To overlap network activity with processor activity, we must understand exactly when RDMA read requests are issued by the Open MPI library. When an RDMA request is issued, the network activity becomes decoupled from processor activity.

To gain a sense of how RDMA requests are issued, we went back to the original Transpose class. We modified the version 1.6 of the Open MPI library by inserting print statements at many locations. The original class effects a matrix transpose by copying to send buffers, initiating a series of nonblocking sends and receives, waiting for them to complete, and finally copying from the receive buffers. The program was run with $P = 20$ (or nprocs=20). The following output was recorded from the process of rank 0:

```
DV MESG:: MPI_Isend() entry
DV MESG:: MPI_Isend() exit
[Isend message repeats total of 20 times]
...
DV MESG:: MPI_Irecv() entry
DV MESG:: MPI_Irecv() exit
```

```
[Irecv message repeats total of 20 times]
...
DV MESG:: MPI_Wait() entry
DV MESG:: MPI_Wait() exit
DV MESG:: MPI_Wait() entry
DV MESG:: issuing RDMA read
[RDMA read message repeats total of 19 times]
...
DV MESG:: MPI_Wait() exit
DV MESG:: MPI_Wait() entry
[Wait message repeats 38 times after RDMA]
...
```

No RDMA request is issued during the first 20 sends followed by the first 20 receives. No RDMA request is issued during the first `MPI_Wait()` either. The first wait on process of rank 0 waits for the send from rank 0 to itself to complete. That send involves no network activity. All the RDMA requests are issued during the second wait, which waits on the send to process of rank 1. The waits for the 38 other sends and receives follow. None of those results in an RDMA request. All 19 RDMA requests from the process of rank 0 during a single matrix transpose are generated after the second wait.

If we attempt to overlap network activity with copying to and from buffers while thinking that RDMA requests may be issued during sends or receives, we will not make much headway. As shown here, Open MPI is very reluctant to issue RDMA requests during sends or receives. It does so only very occasionally. However, when we were waiting on one particular send request, the Open MPI library issued RDMA requests corresponding to all other processor nodes, although most of them were not a subject of the request we were waiting on.

The library function `MPI_Wait()` is a blocking call and therefore unsuitable for overlapping network activity with processor activity. Other library functions, such as `MPI_Test()` and `MPI_Testany()`, serve the purpose. `MPI_Test()` returns immediately with information about whether the request supplied to it is complete or not. Analogously, `MPI_Testany()` takes an array of requests and returns immediately. If any one of the requests is completed, it indicates that using a flag. Fortunately, the

Open MPI library is willing to generate RDMA requests during `MPI_Testany()`.[12]

The definition of the member function `transpose()`, which is the heart of the class `FastTrans`, follows:

```
1  void FastTrans::transpose(double *localMN,
2                            double *localNM){
3      for(int q=0; q < P; q++)
4          postrecv(q);
5      int nrcvd = 0;
6      for(int i=0; i < P; i++){
7          int q = sendorder[i];
8          copyTOsendbuf(q, localMN);
9          postsend(q);
10         int flag;
11         MPI_Testany(P, rreqlist, &q, &flag,
12                 MPI_STATUS_IGNORE);
13         if(flag != 0){
14             rcvd_list[nrcvd] = q;
15             nrcvd++;
16         }
17     }
18
19     int ncpyd = 0;
20     while(nrcvd < P){
21         if(ncpyd < nrcvd){
22             int q = rcvd_list[ncpyd];
23             copyFROMrecvbuf(q, localNM);
24             ncpyd++;
25         }
26         int q;
27         int flag;
28         MPI_Testany(P, rreqlist, &q, &flag,
```

---

[12]In view of the considerable investment in Infiniband and Infiniband-like technologies, it is unfortunate that it is so difficult to find out when MPI send/receive result in RDMA transfers, with the answer being implementation dependent.

```
29                              MPI_STATUS_IGNORE);
30              if(flag != 0){
31                      rcvd_list[nrcvd] = q;
32                      nrcvd++;
33              }
34      }
35
36      assrt(nrcvd == P);
37
38      while(ncpyd < P){
39              int q = rcvd_list[ncpyd];
40              copyFROMrecvbuf(q, localNM);
41              ncpyd++;
42      }
43
44      wait(); /* verify sending is finished */
45 }
```

The member function `transpose()` begins by posting all the receives (lines 3 and 4). An RDMA read request can be issued when a receive is matched with a send from an external process. Because the receives are nonblocking, the program will run past the for-loop on lines 3 and 4 almost instantly.

Beginning on line 5, the program keeps track of the number of receives that are known to be complete in the variable `nrcvd`. On line 5, it is initialized to be zero.

The for-loop that runs from lines 6 through 17 overlaps copying to send buffer with network activity. It begins by picking the destination q, which is next in send order (line 7). On line 8, a member function is invoked to copy that part of `localMN[]`, the array that holds the part of the global $M \times N$ matrix assigned to the current processor node, which must be sent to q. A nonblocking send is issued by calling a member function on line 9.

To understand how network activity gets overlapped with processor activity, we must take a careful look at the call

```
MPI_Testany(P, rreqlist, &q, &flag,
            MPI_STATUS_IGNORE);
```

that occurs on lines 11 and 12. Here, `rreqlist[]` is the array of receive requests corresponding to the nonblocking receives issued in the for-loop on lines 2 and 3. There are in total P of them. The fourth argument is a pointer to an `int` equal to `&flag` above. When the function returns, `flag` is 0 if none of the requests in the list is complete. If any of the requests is complete, `flag` is 1. The third argument is also a pointer to an `int` and equal to `&q` above. If a request is complete, q will equal the corresponding index in the array `rreqlist[]`. The request object `rreqlist[q]` is set to `MPI_REQUEST_NULL`, which means that `rreqlist[q]` becomes inactive and is no longer considered pending.

Crucially, if the MPI library notices that it can issue an RDMA read corresponding to any pending read, it goes ahead and issues it during `MPI_Testany()`.[13]

The if-block on lines 13 through 16 records nonblocking receives that are complete.

When the for-loop exits on line 17, all the copying to send buffer is done. However, the receives may not all be complete. The while-loop from lines 20 through 34 overlaps copying from receive buffer to the array `localNM[]` with network activity. The invocation of `MPI_Testany()` on lines 28 and 29 has the same role as before. It records any receive that is newly completed and issues RDMA reads that can be issued. Thanks to its ability to issue RDMA reads, the copying from receive buffer in this while-loop is overlapped with network activity, which is managed by the host channel adapter.

When the while-loop exits on line 34, there may still be completed receives that have not been copied out of the receive buffer. The while-loop on lines 38 through 42 cleans those up. Finally, the member function `transpose()` ensures that all pending sends are complete by invoking the member function `wait()` on line 44 and exits.

By examining the trace of Open MPI (customized with print statements), we find that RDMA reads are sprinkled across calls to `MPI_Testany()`. Thus, our design is working, which is also confirmed by the improvement in network bandwidth seen in table 6.7.

Table 6.7 shows a degradation in bandwidth from 90% of the peak to 75% of the peaks as the number of communicating nodes increases from 10 to 100. It is likely that optimizations which mostly prevent that degradation exist. However, implementing such optimizations is not feasible on most high-performance clusters. On most clusters, the user has no control over which nodes in the network are assigned to a pro-

---

[13]This statement, of course, may apply only to the Open MPI implementation.

nprocs:	120	240	600	1200
bw:	0.70	0.60	0.53	0.27

Table 6.8: Network bandwidth (bw) in bytes/cycle when an MPI process is assigned to every core on QDR Infiniband network with 12-core 3.33 GHz SSE2 machines (see table A.1). Therefore, dividing `nprocs` by 12 gives the number of nodes.

gram. Even if that information is available, information about network topology and internals of the network are almost never available. So any attempt to sequence sends and receives cleverly by taking network internals into account is frustrated at the beginning. In addition, network activity initiated by other users has an unpredictable effect and makes refined optimizations difficult.

If we attempt to increase the number of nodes from 10^2 to 10^4, it is equally certain that more scaling issues will appear. The largest clusters in 2014 have about 10^4 nodes. In our design, `MPI_Testany()` looks at all pending receive requests. When the number of nodes is really large, it may pay to block the pending receive requests that are tested for completion.

One MPI process per core is a bad idea

Assigning one MPI process for each core remains quite popular. It saves users the trouble of learning about threads. Table 6.8 gives part of the reason it is a bad idea. To generate the numbers of this table, the same MPI program used for table 6.7 was used. The program was compiled with the same C/C++ compiler with the same flags and linked against the same Open MPI library. The difference was that `NTHREADS` (a `#define` macro variable) was set to 1 to turn off threading and an MPI process was assigned to every core.

Table 6.8 shows that the bandwidth of data transfer across the network at a node drops precipitously. With 10 nodes it is less than 50% of the peak, and with 100 nodes it is not even 20%.

Having a process on every core increases contention for the host channel adapter. Even if the loss in performance were not so severe, it is a bad idea. Assigning a process to every core ignores the modularity of hardware design. The processor node is a hardware module with multiple cores, and there is one network card on every node most of the time. There is modularity in hardware design from the register level up. There is a single memory system to manage all the cores. It is difficult to sustain good design practices if users at one level ignore the modularity of software or hardware they rely on.

6.3.4   Collective communication

The MPI programs we have written so far transfer data using versions of `MPI_Send()` and `MPI_Recv()`. Such function calls are made autonomously by individual processes, but their completion is subject to matching calls made by other processes. The MPI library provides several function calls for collective communication. A collective function call must be made by all processes in a group. The result of collective calls such as `Bcast`, `Scatter`, `Gather`, and `Alltoall` is data transfer involving all the processes.

The only collective call we have encountered so far is `MPI_Barrier()` in the function `unsafe()` on page 377. The barrier was inserted with the sole purpose of exhibiting MPI syntax. It had no effect on the function `unsafe()`.

In this section, we look at `MPI_Bcast()`, `MPI_Scatter()`, `MPI_Alltoall()`, and `MPI_Reduce()`. All these collective functions transfer data between participating processes and can, in principle, be implemented using send and receive operations between processes. For broadcast, the send/receive implementation is too slow.

The all-to-all transfer of data effected by `MPI_Alltoall()` can be implemented using send/receive. However, if we restrict ourselves to send/receive syntax introduced so far, the resulting implementation is not as fast as the library function. In deriving an effective send/receive implementation, we encounter an aspect of send/receive syntax of much value. Not surprisingly, this new syntax is of value because it could be related to a facility provided by the Infiniband hardware.

In typical MPI programs, the problem to be solved is split between several processes. Not infrequently, the solution involves reduction operations such as finding the minimum, maximum, or sum of data scattered across several computers and processes. The `MPI_Reduce()` function may be implemented using send/receive operations, but an effective send/receive implementation requires a tree-like or recursive pattern of communication. Just like matrix transpose, reduction provides opportunities for overlapping network activity with processor activity. In the case of the matrix transpose, the processor activity involves copying to and from buffers. In reduction, the processors must also minimize, maximize, or sum.

Thus, with regard to broadcast, all-to-all communication, and reduction, it is instructive to examine send/receive implementations. In each case, comparison with a send/receive implementation brings to light special features of Infiniband hardware.

Broadcast

In a broadcast operation, the root process sends out data to every other process. The following function was used to time `MPI_Bcast()`:

```
double bcast(int rank, int nprocs, double *buffer,
                int bufsize){
    TimeStamp clk;
    int root = 0;
    clk.tic();
    MPI_Bcast(buffer, bufsize, MPI_DOUBLE, root,
            MPI_COMM_WORLD);
    double cycles = clk.toc();
    return cycles;
}
```

This `bcast()` function must be called by each MPI process with exactly the same value for `bufsize`. The `bcast()` function calls `MPI_Bcast()`, which is a collective operation. In general, all processes in the communicator must make the call for a collective operation to take effect. In addition, the calls must match. More specifically, the number of bytes must be exactly equal in all the invocations of `MPI_Bcast()`. An MPI receive can match an MPI send although it consumes only part of the data in the send. The matching rules for collective functions are stricter and do not allow partial consumption of data. The effect of `MPI_Bcast()` is to copy the buffer of the root process to all the other processes. In this example, the root process has rank 0.

A broadcast operation can be implemented by having the root process send a message to every other process individually. But table 6.9 shows that such an implementation would be much worse than using `MPI_Bcast()`. The send/receive implementation realizes only a fraction of the bandwidth and gets worse rapidly as the number of host computers increases.

With $n = 1$ for the buffer size, table 6.9 shows that `MPI_Bcast()` returns in less than a few microseconds on a 3.33 GHz SSE2 machine. For $n = 10^5$ and $n = 10^6$,

		$n = 1$ (cycles)	$n = 10^5$ (bytes/cycle)	$n = 10^6$ (bytes/cycle)
$P = 10$	bcast	7,100	0.39	0.70
	send/recv	10,000	0.11	0.11
$P = 20$	bcast	8,800	0.78	0.46
	send/recv	23,000	0.05	0.05
$P = 50$	bcast	11,000	0.78	0.78
	send/recv	84,000	0.02	0.02

Table 6.9: The broadcast operation on P MPI processes, with one process per host computer and buffers of size equal to n double-precision numbers. The network was QDR Infiniband, and each computer was a 3.33 GHz SSE2 machine (see table A.1).

the bandwidth is reported as the number of bytes transferred out of the root per cycle. The maximum bidirectional bandwidth at a single port of the QDR Infiniband switch is advertised to 1.5 bytes/cycle. The broadcast operation uses the link in only one direction, and we find that that it reaches more than 0.75 bytes/cycle in some instances. The performance does not degrade as the number of host computers increases. On the contrary, it gets better.

Infiniband, like many other network architectures, supports broadcast in hardware. The MPI library function `MPI_Bcast()` uses the hardware-level architectural facility for broadcasting. The advantages of supporting broadcast in hardware are obvious. In the fat-tree, a single Infiniband switch may be connected to many other switches, which in turn may be connected to many host computers. The hardware can move the broadcast data to a switch just once and route it to all the host computers that may be reached from that switch. The send/receive implementation is forced to send data through the switch multiple times, once for each host computer that may be reached from that switch. The Internet supports a broadcast protocol for radio broadcasts, sporting events, and the like.

The MPI standard states that all collective function calls are blocking. Therefore, a broadcast initiated at the root must wait until every process has made a matching call to `MPI_Bcast()`. The overhead due to blocking will be of the order of several thousand cycles and is insignificant when the data being transferred is a megabyte or more, as shown by table 6.9.

All-to-all data transfer

`MPI_Scatter()` has the following prototype

```
int MPI_Scatter(void *, int, MPI_Datatype,
                void *, int, MPI_Datatype,
                int, MPI_Comm)
```

A call can be made as in

```
MPI_Scatter(sendbuf, n, MPI_DOUBLE, recvbuf, n,
                MPI_DOUBLE, root, MPI_COMM_WORLD)
```

In this call, the count following `sendbuf` and the count following `recvbuf` are both given as `n`. The meaning of the call is somewhat opaque partly because this is a collective call and partly because the syntax is not suggestive of the role played by `root`. Every process has to supply a `recvbuf`, but only the root needs to supply a valid `sendbuf`. The `sendbuf` supplied by the other processes is ignored.

The other complication in `MPI_Scatter()` is related to the send and receive counts (these are given as n in the call above) and their interpretations. The relation of receive count to receive buffer is easier to understand. On each process, including the root, `recvbuf[]` must be large enough to hold n items. The size of `sendbuf[]` on the root must be $n \times$ nprocs items (assuming the `WORLD` communicator) and not just n items. The effect of this collective call is to copy items $r * n$ through $(r + 1) * n - 1$ in the `sendbuf[]` of the root to the `recvbuf[]` of the process of rank r for every possible value of r.

The amount of data sent should be exactly equal to the amount of data received. Why then does the function ask for both a send count and a receive count? In principle, the data types could be different for different receiving processes, and the syntax allows for that. Although it is uncommon to use different data types at the sender and receiver, or to use anything other than `WORLD` as the communicator, MPI syntax burdens every single usage with its rules for data types and communicators. Like any library, MPI has its imperfections. These imperfections exist partly because MPI came into prominence in the early days of parallel computing and has been widely used ever since. As with the x86 architecture and its tortured instruction encoding, success comes with a cost.

The following function illustrates usage of `MPI_Scatter()`:

```
double scatter_all2all(int rank, int nprocs,
                double *sendbuf, double *recvbuf,
                int n){
    TimeStamp clk;
    clk.tic();
    for(int root=0; root < nprocs; root++)
        MPI_Scatter(sendbuf, n, MPI_DOUBLE,
        recvbuf+n*root,n,MPI_DOUBLE,
        root,MPI_COMM_WORLD);
    double cycles = clk.toc();
    return cycles;
}
```

This function must be called simultaneously by all the processes. Both sendbuf[] and recvbuf[] must be of length $n \times$ nprocs. In this function, each process takes its turn being the root. The data in sendbuf[] of all processes may be arranged in a matrix with one column per process:

$$
\begin{pmatrix}
a_{00} & a_{01} & \cdots & & \\
a_{10} & a_{11} & \cdots & & \\
\vdots & \vdots & \ddots & & \\
& & & a_{\text{nprocs-1,nprocs-1}} &
\end{pmatrix}.
$$

Here, the sendbuf[] of the process of rank r is lined up in column r. The entry a_{ir} represents

    sendbuf[i*n],...,sendbuf[(i+1)*n-1]

in the sendbuf[] array of the process of rank r. The effect of a collective invocation of the function is to copy the data in row i of the matrix to the recvbuf[] of the process of rank i. In particular, the entry a_{ir} is copied to

    recvbuf[r*n],...,recvbuf[(r+1)*n-1]

in the recvbuf[] array of the process of rank i.

The MPI library provides a single function call that effects this all-to-all transfer of data. Its usage is as shown below.

P	n	scatter	send/recv	alltoall
10	10^5	0.27	1.45	1.53
10	10^6	0.27	1.54	1.56
20	10^5	0.13	1.07	1.13
20	10^6	0.13	1.12	1.14
50	10^5	0.05	1.23	1.35
50	10^6	0.05	1.34	1.41
100	10^5	0.02	1.03	1.16
100	10^5	0.02	1.09	1.19

Table 6.10: Bandwidth in bytes/cycle for three implementations of all-to-all transfer on P MPI processes, one per host computer. Multiply by 3.33 GHZ to get bandwidth in GB/s. The network was QDR Infiniband, and each host computer was a 3.33 GHz SSE2 machine (see table A.1). Data consisting of n double-precision numbers is exchanged between every pair. The reported numbers are medians.

```
double mpi_all2all(int rank, int nprocs,
            double *sendbuf, double *recvbuf,
            int n){
    TimeStamp clk;
    clk.tic();
    MPI_Alltoall(sendbuf, n, MPI_DOUBLE, recvbuf, n,
            MPI_DOUBLE, MPI_COMM_WORLD);
    double cycles = clk.toc();
    return cycles;
}
```

Once again the number of items in the data transfer must be indicated as n for both `sendbuf[]` and `recvbuf[]` because MPI allows send and receive data types to be different in general, a facility we never use.

Table 6.10 shows that all-to-all transfer between MPI processes is much faster using `MPI_Alltoall()` than with repeated calls to `MPI_Scatter()`. Both collective functions are blocking calls, but the transfer of data in each scatter operation is from the root to other processes. The scatter operations do not utilize the bidirectional nature of the Infiniband network.

The network bandwidth is, as always, measured as the number of bytes transferred into or out of a single host computer (which is for convenience the MPI process of rank 0) in a single cycle. The all-to-all operations in MPI reach (and even exceed) the peak advertised bandwidth of the QDR Infiniband network. In contrast, the bandwidth realized by the scatter implementation falls rapidly as the number of processes increases (see table 6.10). In the scatter implementation, each process takes its turn to be the root, which serializes network traffic and fails to utilize much of the parallelism in the all-to-all operation.

As shown by the table, a send/receive implementation can perform nearly as well as MPI's all-to-all function. To do that well, the send/receive implementation must use `MPI_Startall()` to start all the sends and receives simultaneously. Doing so enables the MPI library to sequence sends and receives in a good order and perhaps to issue RDMA read requests expeditiously. Certain Infiniband vendors support technology that allows programs to initiate multiple sends and receives simultaneously on the host channel adapter.[14]

Because the plan is to initiate several send and receive operations simultaneously, `MPI_Isend()` and `MPI_IRecv()` are not appropriate. Instead, the send/receive implementation of all-to-all data transfer begins by initializing send and receive operations. The initiation of the operations is deferred to another function.

```
MPI_Request *all2all_init(int rank, int nprocs,
                double *sendbuf, double *recvbuf,
                int n){
    MPI_Request *reqlist = new MPI_Request[2*nprocs];
    for(int i=0; i < nprocs; i++) {
        int dest = i;
        int tag = rank;
        MPI_Send_init(sendbuf+dest*n, n, MPI_DOUBLE,
        dest, tag, MPI_COMM_WORLD, reqlist+i);
    }
    for(int i=0; i < nprocs; i++){
        int source = i;
        int tag = source;
```

---

[14]An example of such a technology is CORE-Direct available on ConnectX-2 hardware from Mellanox corporation.

```
            MPI_Recv_init(recvbuf+source*n,n,MPI_DOUBLE,
                source, tag, MPI_COMM_WORLD,
                reqlist+nprocs+i);
    }
    return reqlist;
}
```

This function returns an array of **2*nprocs** objects of type **MPI_Request**. A request object is created for sending to and receiving from each process. In this implementation, a process sends data to itself using MPI messages. The request objects are destroyed, when no longer needed, using the following function:

```
void all2all_finalize(MPI_Request *reqlist){
    delete[] reqlist;
}
```

The send/receive implementation of all-to-all transfer is completed by the following function definition:

```
double all2all(int rank, int nprocs, MPI_Request*
            reqlist){
    TimeStamp clk;
    clk.tic();
    MPI_Startall(2*nprocs, reqlist);
    MPI_Waitall(2*nprocs, reqlist, MPI_STATUS_IGNORE);
    double cycles = clk.toc();
    return cycles;
}
```

The MPI library function **MPI_Startall()** sends all the requests to the MPI library in one batch. At that point, it is up to the Open MPI library (or the network hardware) to sequence the requests intelligently and issue RDMA requests promptly.

Reduce

If $f(x_0, \ldots, x_{P-1})$ takes the minimum, maximum, or sum of its arguments, the reduce operation based on f gathers data x_r from each process of rank r, $0 \le r < P$,

P	n	allreduce	send/recv
10	1	3.4×10^4	4.2×10^4
10	10^6	3.7×10^7	8.7×10^7
20	1	4.6×10^4	5.6×10^4
20	10^6	3.8×10^7	1.0×10^8
50	1	7.1×10^4	7.7×10^4
50	10^6	4.1×10^7	1.2×10^8
100	1	8.9×10^4	9.6×10^4
100	10^6	5.1×10^7	1.5×10^8

Table 6.11: The number of cycles consumed by reduction on P MPI processes, one per host, on QDR Infiniband with each host a 3.33 GHz SSE2 machine (see table A.1). The data on each process is a `double` array of size n. The MPI function is compared with a send/receive implementation.

and deposits the result with either one or all the processes. The following function illustrates MPI's reduction capability:

```
double reducemin(int rank, int nprocs,
          double *sendbuf, double *recvbuf,
          int bufsize){
    TimeStamp clk;
    clk.tic();
    MPI_Allreduce(sendbuf, recvbuf, bufsize,
      MPI_DOUBLE, MPI_MIN, MPI_COMM_WORLD);
    double cycles = clk.toc();
    return cycles;
}
```

The array `sendbuf[]` stores the data to be reduced. The effect of calling the MPI library function `MPI_Allreduce()` is to gather the `sendbuf[]` array from all the processes, apply a reduction operation, and store the result in the array `recvbuf[]`. All processes must call `reducemin()` to initiate the reduction. Here, the reduction operation is given as `MPI_MIN`.

Table 6.11 shows that using `MPI_Allreduce()` is nearly three times faster than a send/receive implementation that does not overlap processor activity with network activity. Details of that tree-based implementation are omitted.

6.3.5   Parallel I/O in MPI

In parallel I/O, a number of MPI processes simultaneously write to or read from the same file. Typical file systems lock a file when it is being accessed by one process, which precludes other processes from accessing it. Parallel I/O is possible only if the file system allows it.

For parallel I/O to be meaningful, the file system must be capable of storing or *striping* a single file across multiple hard disks. If the entire file is stored on a single hard disk, accesses from multiple processes will have to be serialized, and parallel I/O from multiple processes will not bring any great advantage.

MPI syntax for parallel I/O is quite complicated. We step through the syntax once for writing and once for reading a file in parallel. For both writing and reading, we exhibit and exercise MPI functionality for parallel I/O in its simplest form. The function write_mpi() defined below is called simultaneously by MPI processes to write to a file in parallel. The data to be written is the array of bytes data[] of length len, data[] and len being the first two arguments to write_mpi(). The other two arguments to write_mpi() are fname, which is the name of the file, and disp. Because many processes may write to the same file, each process must specify its *view* of the file. A process's view of the file is the part of the file that is visible to it. The final argument disp specifies the beginning of the view as an absolute displacement (in bytes) from the beginning of the file. It must be noted that both len and disp are of type long and not int. An int can count up to $2^{31} - 1$, which is not enough for files that can go up to terabytes or petabytes.

```
 1  void write_mpi(void *data, long len,
 2               char *fname, long disp){
 3       MPI_File ofile;
 4       MPI_File_open(MPI_COMM_WORLD,
 5               fname,
 6               MPI_MODE_CREATE|MPI_MODE_WRONLY,
 7               MPI_INFO_NULL,
 8               &ofile);
 9       char datarep[200];
10       sprintf(datarep, "native");
```

```
11        MPI_File_set_view(ofile,
12                          disp,
13                          MPI_BYTE,
14                          MPI_BYTE,
15                          datarep,
16                          MPI_INFO_NULL);
17        long offset = 0;
18        int maxcount = 2000*1000*1000;
19        while(len > 0){
20              int count = (len<maxcount)?len:maxcount;
21              MPI_File_write_at(ofile,
22                          offset,
23                          data,
24                          count,
25                          MPI_BYTE,
26                          MPI_STATUS_IGNORE);
27            offset += count;
28            data = ((char *)data+count);
29            len -= count;
30        }
31        MPI_File_close(&ofile);
32 }
```

On line 3, ofile is defined to be of type MPI_File. MPI_File is defined as a pointer to a struct in mpi.h. The struct it points to will hold information about file attributes, file size, and file location.

The MPI_File_open() call, which spans lines 4 through 8, is a collective call. Accordingly, its first argument (on line 4) is the WORLD communicator. The second argument on line 5 is the file name. The third argument on line 6 says that the file should be created if it does not already exist and the file is opened for writing. In C/C++, a file that is opened for writing loses its previous data but not so in MPI. Line 6 is a null argument, and line 7 supplies the file pointer as the final argument.

The MPI_File_set_view() call, which spans lines 11 through 16, is also a collective call. Each process specifies the part of the file that is visible to itself. The first argument (line 11) is the file pointer, and the second argument (line 12) is disp, which marks the beginning of the file view of the calling process, as already explained. The third argument is the *elementary type,* and the fourth argument is the *file type* for accessing the file. The elementary and file types can be used to specify file views of mind-bending complexity. Lines 13 and 14 give both arguments as `MPI_BYTE`, thus specifying the process's view of the file as a sequence of bytes. Viewing the file as a sequence of bytes keeps things simple for the programmer, the MPI implementation, the file system, and the hardware. The fifth argument (of type `char *` and not `const char *`)is given as `datarep` (line 15). The variable `datarep` holds the character string "native" (lines 9 and 10). Presumably, a byte is a byte in the native representation. The final info argument is given as null on line 16.

The `MPI_File_write_at()` call spanning lines 21 through 26 gets down to the business of writing to the file. But there is a problem. The `count` (line 24) of the number of bytes to be written is an `int` and not a `long`. The process will not be able to write all the data in

```
data[0],...,data[len-1]
```

if `len`, which is of type `long`, is greater than $2^{31} - 1$. However, the offset relative to the beginning of the file view can be of type `long` (line 22). The variable `maxcount`, which is the maximum number of bytes the process will try to write with a single function call, is initialized to 2×10^9 (which is less than $2^{31} - 1$) on line 18. The while-loop spanning lines 19 through 30 writes to the file in stages. The variable `len` is the number of bytes yet to be written at the top of the loop, and line 20 calculates the `count` of bytes to be written in the current iteration. Once the data is written, the variable `offset`, which is the offset relative to the beginning of the file, and `data`, which points to the first entry in the array that is yet to be written, are both incremented by `count` (lines 27 and 28). The variable `len` is decremented by `count` (line 29) because the number of bytes yet to be written is fewer by `count`.

The library function `MPI_File_write_at()` is not collective, but MPI provides a collective version (obtained by appending `_all` to the function name). The collective version would deadlock if the while-loop spanning lines 11 through 30 did not have exactly the same iteration count on every MPI process. Therefore, we have used the noncollective version. The collective version can be slightly faster, however.

The `MPI_File_close()` call (line 31) is collective, like the calls for opening a file and setting its view. Calls to a collective MPI function made by different processes must match. As long as we restrict ourselves to the `MPI_BYTE` data type, the matching

requirements of functions for opening and closing files, or setting the process's view
of an open file, are satisfied.

The definition of read_mpi() closely parallels that of write_mpi().

```
1  void read_mpi(void *data, long len,
2           char *fname, long disp){
3      MPI_File ifile;
4      MPI_File_open(MPI_COMM_WORLD,
5               fname,
6               MPI_MODE_RDONLY,
7               MPI_INFO_NULL,
8               &ifile);
9      char datarep[200];
10     sprintf(datarep, "native");
11     MPI_File_set_view(ifile,
12              disp,
13              MPI_BYTE,
14              MPI_BYTE,
15              datarep,
16              MPI_INFO_NULL);
17     long offset = 0;
18     int maxcount = 2000*1000*1000;
19     while(len > 0){
20         int count = (len<maxcount)?len:maxcount;
21         MPI_File_read_at(ifile,
22                  offset,
23                  data,
24                  count,
25                  MPI_BYTE,
26                  MPI_STATUS_IGNORE);
27         offset += count;
28         data = ((char *)data+count);
29         len -= count;
30     }
31     MPI_File_close(&ifile);
```

32 }

The function `read_mpi()` differs from `write_mpi()` in opening the file for reading rather than writing (see line 6) and using the function to read on line 21 instead of the function to write.

The two functions `write_mpi()` and `read_mpi()` match line by line except at two points, and some programmers may argue that the function definitions should reflect this parallelism. The two functions may be collapsed into one, saving lines of code, by passing a flag to indicate whether the function should write or read. The usage of the flag at two points far away from each other breaks the flow of the code and makes it hard to read. The C++ language provides more structured facilities such as inheritance and templates to avoid code bloat in a fairly smooth way. There are surely many instances where such facilities are appropriate, although they fall outside the domain of this author. The parallelism between `write_mpi()` and `read_mpi()` is syntactic and not semantic. Writing to a file and reading from it are different operations. Keeping the function definitions apart has the advantage of prioritizing meaning over form.

Lustre file system

Figure 6.10 is a depiction of a Lustre file system[15] realized over Infiniband. It is similar to figure 6.3, with the difference that the file system components are shown in more detail. As in that figure, HCA and TCA are acronyms for Host/Target Channel Adapter. Unlike HCA, TCA do not support the Verb layer. The Metadata Server connected to the network makes information about file names and directories available to clients (or processor nodes). The metadata about file names and directories is stored in the Metadata Target. In general, several Metadata Servers can be connected to the same Metadata Target to guard against server failure. The Metadata Target is a storage module with redundancies built in to guard against disk failure.

Figure 6.10 shows two among possibly many Object Storage Servers connected to the network. Each Object Storage Server is connected to two Object Storage Targets. Object Storage Targets are the components that hold data. Like the Metadata Target, they too will have redundancies built in. As many as eight Object Storage Targets

---

[15]For the Lustre file system, see the operations manual at `http://wiki.lustre.org/index.php/Learn`.

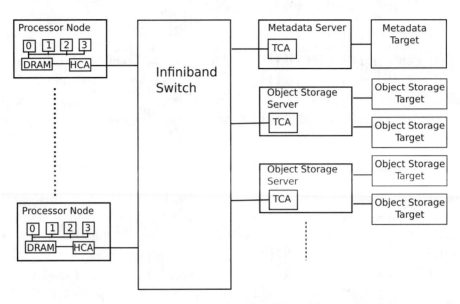

Figure 6.10: Lustre file system. The processor nodes (clients) as well as the metadata server and the object storage servers are connected to a single big Infiniband switch in this depiction. More generally, they may be connected to different switches, which are in turn connected to each other.

can be connected to the same server. The Object Storage Server is their interface to the network.

A typical configuration may have hundreds of processor nodes, tens of Object Storage Targets, and one Metadata Server. The Lonestar system at the Texas Advanced Computing Center has more than 1,000 processor nodes and 90 Object Storage Targets. The total capacity of its Lustre file system is 1 petabyte. There are Lustre file systems of 10 times that capacity.

The number of stripes of a Lustre file may be retrieved using the `lfs getstripe` command. For a 2 TB file, `lfs getstripe` produced the following output:

```
lmm_stripe_count:    50
lmm_stripe_size:     1048576
lmm_stripe_offset:   15
obdidx           objid           objid           group
    15           57347983        0x36b0f8f               0
```

9	56348442	0x35bcf1a	0
65	45034528	0x2af2c20	0
4	56025829	0x356e2e5	0

$$\cdots$$

This file has 50 stripes, which means that it is spread across 50 object storage targets. The stripe size is 2^{20} bytes or 1 MB, which is Lustre's default value for stripe size. The list of 50 object storage targets, beginning with `obdidx` 15, is only partially shown.

If the stripe size is 1 MB, the first 1 MB is stored on the first object storage target (here the one with `obdidx` of 15), the next 1 MB on the next target (here the one with `obdidx` of 9), and so on in a cyclic fashion. The `lfs setstripe` command may be used to set the stripe count and stripe size of a directory or newly created file.

The C++ class `LustreFile` given below is an easy interface for striping and using Lustre files from MPI.

```
class LustreFile{
private:
    char dir[200];
    char fname[200];
    int rank;
    int nprocs;
    long totalsize;
    long localsize;
public:
    LustreFile(int ranki, int nprocsi,
        const char *diri, const char *fnamei,
        long sizei);
    long getlocalsize() {return localsize;}
    void setstripe(int count, int stripesize=1);
    void printinfo();
    void write(double *v);
    void read(double *v);
};
```

This class is useful for writing and reading a sequence of `doubles`.

The class constructor has the following definition:

```
LustreFile::LustreFile(int ranki, int nprocsi,
                const char *diri, const char *fnamei,
                long sizei){
    rank = ranki;
    nprocs = nprocsi;
    strcpy(dir, diri);
    strcpy(fname, fnamei);
    totalsize = sizei;
    localsize = totalsize/nprocs;
    if(rank==(nprocs-1))
            localsize = totalsize - (nprocs-1)*localsize;
}
```

All the MPI processes must participate in the creation of an object of class `LustreFile`. If all the processes create a class object as in

```
Lustrefile lustre(rank, nprocs, dir, fname, totalsize)
```

there will of course be a separate `LustreFile` object on each process. To exercise the functionality of this class, the objects must match across all the processes. In particular, the directory, file name, and total size must be identical in all the MPI processes.

The total size is the number of `doubles` stored in the entire file. The class constructor calculates the number of `doubles` in the local view of each process. The local size is the same in all MPI processes except possibly the last (of rank `nprocs-1`). An alternative, and possibly more useful, interface to the class might be for each process to call the constructor with the local size of the file. The constructor can then compute the total size using a reduction operation.

This constructor does not create the file. The file is created when the member function `setstripe()` is invoked.

```
1  void LustreFile::setstripe(int count, int stripesize){
2      if(rank==0){
3          char cmd[200];
4          sprintf(cmd, "rm %s/%s", dir, fname);
5          system(cmd);
6          sprintf(cmd,
```

```
 7              "lfs setstripe --size %dM --count %d %s/%s",
 8              stripesize, count, dir, fname);
 9              system(cmd);
10        }
11        MPI_Barrier(MPI_COMM_WORLD);
12 }
```

The task of creating the file is left to the process of rank 0. The rank 0 process removes the file if it is already present. On line 4, the character string `cmd[]` is constructed. On line 5, the library function `system()` (it is declared in `stdlib.h`) invokes the shell and executes the command. The command for striping is composed as a string on lines 6, 7, and 8. If we want 50 stripes and a stripe size of 4,000 MB, the command is

```
lfs setstripe --size 4000 M --count 50 <filename>
```

Such a command is issued through the shell on line 9. It creates a new file.

Although the process of rank 0 is the only one to handle striping, all the processes must call the member function `setstripe()`. The barrier at the end (line 10) ensures that none of the processes returns before file creation is complete. The barrier is essential for ensuring that none of the processes attempts to access the file before it is created.

The member functions `write()` and `read()` invoke `write_mpi()` and `read_mpi()` as follows:

```
void LustreFile::write(double *v){
     long disp = 8*rank*(totalsize/nprocs);
     char fnamex[200];
     sprintf(fnamex, "%s/%s", dir, fname);
     write_mpi((void *)v, 8*localsize, fnamex, disp);
}

void LustreFile::read(double *v){
     long disp = 8l*rank*(totalsize/nprocs);
     char fnamex[200];
     sprintf(fnamex, "%s/%s", dir, fname);
     read_mpi((void *)v, 8l*localsize, fnamex, disp);
}
```

nprocs	stripes	write (lsize=8MB)	read (lsize=8MB)	write (lsize=20GB)	read (lsize=20GB)
1	1	0.5	0.3	0.2	0.5
10	10	0.3	1.3	1.6	2.3
20	20	0.6	2.3	3.3	4.1
50	50	1.3	3.2	6.9	6.2
100	50	2.6	6.3	6.6	7.6

Table 6.12: Bandwidth in GB/s on a 1 petabyte Lustre file system connected via QDR Infiniband. The reported numbers are maximums over five trials. The total size of the file divided by the number of processes (nprocs) is given as *lsize*.

The class definition is completed by the member function `printinfo()`.

```
void LustreFile::printinfo(){
    if(rank!=0)
        return;
    char cmd[200];
    sprintf(cmd, "ls -l %s", dir);
    system(cmd);
    sprintf(cmd , "lfs getstripe %s/%s", dir, fname);
    system(cmd);
}
```

Like `setstripe()`, `printinfo()` uses `system()` to issue commands through the shell.

Table 6.12 reports bandwidth measurements on file sizes that vary from 8 MB to 2 TB. Some of the measurements in the table, especially the ones with *lsize* of 8 MB, are probably influenced by caching. On the Lonestar cluster, the Lustre file system reaches a bandwidth of nearly 7 GB/s with 50 stripes. The cluster is used by a large number of scientists, and it is quite possible that the measurements are influenced by other jobs being run on the cluster. We do not think that is likely, however. Similar numbers were obtained during measurements made on different days at different times.

Like almost all file systems, the Lustre file system also goes through a page cache on each client (for page caches see, section 4.3). The maximum size of this page cache is recorded in the file

```
/proc/sys/lustre/max_dirty_mb.txt
```

as 12.6 GB. That is half the total memory on each 3.33 GHz SSE2 computer in this cluster. Even when each MPI process writes and then reads 20 GB of data to the same file, the page cache may still influence the measured bandwidth. It is not worth the trouble to completely eliminate the page cache effects. Eliminating cache effects will lead to contortions that are applicable to few real programs. Programs, which do not saturate available memory, will benefit from the page cache. The runs corresponding to the last two columns of table 6.12 hold a 20 GB array on each MPI process. More than 80% of the 24 GB of memory available on each Xeon 5680 host computer is used up and unavailable for page caching. Early versions of Lustre did not use caches on the Object Storage Servers, but newer versions can cache on the Object Storage Servers as well.[16]

If the number of stripes is fixed at 50, table 6.12 shows that nearly the same bandwidth is realized with either 50 or 100 processes. With 10 stripes, the read bandwidth is approximately 2.6 GB/s, and the write bandwidth is approximately 1.70 GB/s with 10, 20, or 50 clients running on as many Xeon 5680 host computers (see table A.1 for information about the machine). If the number of stripes is 10 and the file is accessed by a single client, the bandwidths are somewhat less than 1 GB/s. Lustre remains robust when the number of client processes is increased while fixing the number of stripes.

Exercise 6.3.1. Suppose 2^k MPI processes are assumed to correspond to the 2^k vertices of a k-dimensional hypercube. Implement a class that allows each process to exchange data with its k neighbors. Measure the bandwidth of data transfer with persistent, nonblocking, and blocking communication.

Exercise 6.3.2. Explain why `MPI_Isend()` and `MPI_IRecv()` must be normally preferred over the blocking and persistent versions for sending and receiving messages.

Exercise 6.3.3. Rerun the Jacobi example while initializing all the data from a single core. By how much does the program slow down? Why does it slow down?

Exercise 6.3.4. Much of the time in the Jacobi example is spent in `update()`. The loop nest in `update()` can be improved in two ways. First, it can be blocked. Second, it can

---

[16]Thanks to Oleg Drokin, Andrew Lundgren, and Cliff White for information about caching in Lustre, posted on an Internet forum in response to a question posed by Jordan Mendler.

be rewritten so that the modular arithmetic for computing `iup` and `idown` is replaced by something as simple as `i=i-1` or `i=i+1`, which holds for all except terminal values of `i`. The terminal values of `i` will need to be treated separately. Make these two changes and discuss the resulting speedup.

Exercise 6.3.5. Explain why blocking data is a good idea for `transposewlda()` but not for `copywlda()`.

Exercise 6.3.6. 3D data d_{ijk} with $0 \le i < L$, $0 \le j < M$, and $0 \le k < N$ can be stored in array of length LMN in six different ways. For example, if i is innermost and k is outermost, d_{ijk} will be in the location with global index $i + j \times L + k \times LM$. The other five storage formats correspond to the five other orderings of i, j, k. The array must be partitioned between P MPI processes, such that only the outermost index is split. Write an MPI program to convert from one storage format to another.

Exercise 6.3.7. Recursive doubling is a method of effecting a reduction where each process begins by representing its rank as a binary number $b_k \dots b_1 b_0$. At level i, it flips its ith bit from b_i to $1 - b_i$ to find the rank of its ith level peer. All the pairs of peers at level i exchange their data and take the minimum (or do whatever other reduction operation). The reduction is complete when all processes step through levels $i = 0$ to $i = k$. Implement this reduction algorithm.[17]

6.4   The Internet

The main function of the Internet, as it exists today, is to connect people. There is no doubt that the Internet is one of the most successful technologies. The Internet is not the result of a single act of invention. Even now its design is evolving to accommodate new uses and technologies.

Ever since the invention of the transistor, computing technology has been driven simultaneously by market forces and the possibility of technological innovation. The market forces driving the Internet today are among the most powerful. At the same time, a number of entities are well organized for innovation. The scope for new technologies in this area appears considerable. One may struggle to get bandwidth of even 1 MB/s between Michigan and Texas today, but that will surely change in the not too distant future.

---

[17]For a discussion of recursive doubling and other strategies for reduction, see Kandalla et al. (2012).

It would be folly for scientific programmers to ignore the Internet and think that MPI is the end of the world in networking as far as scientific applications are concerned. The volume of investment in the Internet is far, far greater, and so is the potential for technological innovation. The highly decentralized nature of the Internet gives it powerful advantages over centralized technologies such as MPI and Infiniband.

The Internet will intrude into scientific computing in more and more ways. The maintenance of databases is one area where that has already happened. In many scientific applications, moving data from one place to another is too expensive, leaving no choice but to coordinate data analysis over the Internet.

In this section, we give an overview of the Internet at the level of the TCP/IP protocol. The TCP/IP protocol is packetized. Indeed, it was one of the first packetized network protocols. In section 6.4.1, we outline the manner in which TCP/IP packets are formed. The TCP protocol adds application information, specifically the port numbers at the source and destination. The IP protocol adds address information so that the packet may be routed from source to destination.

Section 6.4.2 describes the way `send()` and `recv()` work. These functions, part of the TCP/IP/sockets API, are defined by the operating system kernel—in our case, the Linux kernel. A new wrinkle here is the manner in which a connection is terminated. Normally, `recv()` returns the number of bytes received. It returns zero if the sender has closed the connection. The sender may close the connection by closing a socket. Servers as well as receivers are implemented using `send()` and `recv()`.

Section 6.4.3 describes how a server is set up. To begin with, a socket is bound to a port. Well-known protocols such as `http` and `https` have port numbers known to all computers (80 and 443, respectively). For the client-server example in this section, we make up our own port number. After the socket is bound to a port, it is marked for listening using the function `listen()`.

The socket may then be used by the server to accept connections using the function `accept()`. Once a connection is accepted, the client and server can begin to communicate. Typical servers are multithreaded and can engage multiple clients simultaneously. The server in our simple example is single-threaded. So if it is communicating with a client, all the other clients will have to wait until the communication is fully over.

The client initiates a connection using `connect()`, which is the counterpart of `accept()`. If a matching server is running, a connection is made. A client program is described in section 6.4.4.

In all probability, the reader's computer can run either servers or clients. To run the example in this section in real time, it is enough to have an ssh connection to some remote site so that the client and server may be run at different locations.

Section 6.4.5 is a discussion of Internet latency, which we define as the round-trip time. The path that packets take from a destination back to the source can be different from the path they take from the source to the destination. A significant fraction of Internet latency can be due to the finite speed of light. During their journey between source and destination, TCP/IP packets spend time in buffers maintained by enormous routers. The buffers are typically linked lists and are therefore exposed to latency to DRAM memory. Buffering is another source of latency.

On a good day, the bandwidth between Michigan and Texas can be 2 MB/s. That figure is lower than the bandwidth to hard disk by a factor of 100. The bandwidth to hard disk can be lower than the bandwidth to DRAM by a factor of nearly a 1000. The gap between Internet bandwidth and the bandwidth to hard disk may narrow in the coming years. In section 6.4.6, we relate Internet bandwidth to congestion windows.

On the whole, the aim of this section is to give a view of the Internet from inside a computer program. The discussion is illustrated using programs throughout. Algorithms for flow control and congestion control internal to the Internet are not discussed.

Our discussion is based on functions in the sockets API, such as **getaddrinfo()**, **bind()**, **listen()**, **accept()**, **connect()**, **recv()**, and **send()**. The prototypes of these functions are in various header files.[18] Here we list all the header files to be included in our programs.

```
#include <unistd.h>
#include <sys/types.h>
#include <sys/socket.h>
#include <netinet/in.h>
#include <netinet/tcp.h>
#include <netdb.h>
```

---

[18]A readable introduction to the sockets API is given by Hall (2009). See http://beej.us/guide/bgnet/. Peterson and Davie (2010) and Tanenbaum and Wetherall (2010) are two well-known textbooks on computer networks.

```
#include <arpa/inet.h>
```

There are possibly a few redundancies here.

6.4.1 IP addresses

To the average person, the Internet is a place for news, commerce, and entertainment. To the programmer, the Internet is a software interface to produce and consume TCP/IP packets. The variety of information exchanged over the Internet eventually turns into TCP/IP packets. Thus, looking at TCP/IP packets is a good place to start.

TCP/IP packets

Suppose a server on the Internet wants to send data to a host computer connected to it. We may think of the data to be sent as a bit stream:

$$b_0, b_1, b_2, \ldots$$

The first step is to break down the bit stream into Transmission Control Protocol (TCP) packets of the following type:

$b_0, b_1, \ldots, b_k$ + source port + destination port + sequence number + more TCP info.

The number of bytes in a TCP packet can go up to 64 KB, but such large packets are unusual. Most packets are only 1.5 KB for reasons that will become evident presently. The source port identifies the application on the server that is sending the data, and the destination identifies the application on the client. When a TCP packet arrives, the operating system kernel looks at the destination port to route the packet to the correct application. The packets, which hold segments of the bit stream the sender is transmitting, may arrive out of order at the destination. The packets may take different routes from source to destination. The 32-bit sequence number is used by the operating system kernel to arrange the TCP segments in order. The application at the destination sees the same bit stream transmitted by the source.

The packet hops from router to router as it makes its way from source to destination. The routing is determined by Internet Protocol (IP) information. The IP packets look as follows:

TCP packet + source address + destination address + more IP info.

The routers do not look at the data inside the TCP portion of TCP/IP packets. Their job is to look at the destination address and send the packet to either the destination or some other router. If the server is `www.xsede.org`, for example, the text string `www.xsede.org` corresponds to an IP address. The client computer also has an IP address. Both these IP addresses show up in the IP header.

For the most part, the Internet may be identified with the TCP/IP protocol. The TCP/IP protocol is a software standard. It makes no assumption about the hardware transmitting packets between computers. When an IP packet is ready to be transmitted, the operating system kernel hands it over to a device driver. The hardware-dependent information is handled by the device drivers and falls out of the purview of the TCP/IP protocol.

This author's desktop is connected to the Internet via Ethernet. Ethernet is a multiple access network based on coaxial copper cables. In a multiple access network, many computers use the same cable to talk to each other (for security purposes, each computer's connection to Ethernet is via a switch). The device driver (the device driver in use is reported by the Linux command `lspci -v`) turns the TCP/IP packet into an Ethernet packet.

TCP/IP packet + MAC address + more Ethernet info.

The Media Access Control (MAC) address identifies the local computer or router to which the packets are forwarded via Ethernet. The TCP/IP packet includes the address of the destination, which could be many thousands of miles away. The MAC address identifies a router that is in the basement of the same building as the author's desktop. The Address Resolution Protocol (ARP) is used to figure out the MAC address from the IP address of the destination. The MAC address is easily predicted most of the time and is stored in an ARP cache.

Ethernet packets are limited to 1,500 bytes, which is the Maximum Transmission Unit (MTU) configured on the author's desktop (the MTU is reported by the Linux command `ifconfig`). The kernel ensures that TCP/IP packets fit into a single MTU.

Between two routers connected via optical fiber, or for a host computer connected to the Internet via a technology other than Ethernet, the MTU may be different from 1,500 bytes. Even an Ethernet connection may be configured to use an MTU other than 1,500 bytes. The dependence of MTU on network hardware and the hardware independence of TCP/IP mean that fragmentation of IP packets is inevitable. If an IP packet that arrives at a router is too large for its next hop, the router must fragment the IP packet, and the packet has to be reassembled by the receiver. The frequency of IP packet fragmentation in Internet traffic is unclear.

IP addresses

The IP address is crucial to the architecture of the Internet. Data leaves the source computer in the form of TCP/IP packets. The TCP/IP packets hop from router to router until they end up at the destination. During every hop, the destination address is inspected to determine the hardware link to be used to route the packet. The IP address is visible to both the application and the hardware link layer.

The function defined below takes a character string such as www.xsede.org as its only argument (inaddr) and returns the IP address in a form that is intelligible to various levels of the network stack.

```
1  struct addrinfo *saddrlist(const char *inaddr){
2      struct addrinfo hint;
3      memset(&hint, 0, sizeof(hint));
4      hint.ai_family = AF_UNSPEC;
5      hint.ai_socktype = SOCK_STREAM;
6      struct addrinfo *llist;
7      getaddrinfo(inaddr, NULL, &hint, &llist);
8      return llist;
9  }
```

On line 2, this function defines hint to be of type struct addrinfo. The function returns a pointer to struct addrinfo. The sockets API is not the best example of clean design in the UNIX world. However, struct addrinfo makes the API a little more pleasant to use. It has the following definition:

```
struct addrinfo {
    int             ai_flags;
    int             ai_family;
    int             ai_socktype;
    int             ai_protocol;
    socklen_t       ai_addrlen;
    struct sockaddr *ai_addr;
```

```
        char             *ai_canonname;
        struct addrinfo *ai_next;
    };
```

The last field `ai_next` is a pointer that links to another `struct addrinfo` object to form a linked list. We will explain other fields as they arise. On line 3 of `saddrlist()`, `memset()` sets all the fields of the object `hint` to be zero. Lines 4 and 5 give `ai_family` and `ai_socktype` as `AF_UNSPEC` and `SOCK_STREAM`, respectively. The address family can be either IPv4 or IPv6. By saying `AF_UNSPEC`, we are allowing it to be either. The socket type is `SOCK_STREAM` for TCP sockets. There are other types for datagrams and control messages. To an overwhelming extent, the Internet is powered by TCP sockets. The field `ai_protocol` is set to 0, meaning that all protocols are allowed. We can set it to specific values to restrict the `hint` to TCP, UDP, or multicast.

The actual call to `getaddrinfo()` is made on line 7 of `saddrlist()`. The function `getaddrinfo()` returns 0 on success and various error codes otherwise. Because our objective is to illustrate TCP/IP and no more, we omit all error handling. The first argument `inaddr` could be `www.xsede.org` or some other Internet address. The second argument is given as NULL, but specific values can be used to specify services such as http or ssh. The third argument is the pointer to `hint`. The final argument is the pointer to `llist`. On line 6 of `saddrlist()`, the variable `llist` is defined to be of type `struct addrinfo *`. On return, it is a pointer to a linked list of `struct addrinfo` objects, each of which holds information about a socket corresponding to the argument `inaddr` and confirming with the hint.

The function `printlist()` defined below walks through `llist` and prints some of the information contained in each node of the linked list.

```
    void printlist(struct addrinfo *llist){
        while(llist != NULL){
            printinfo(llist);
            llist = llist->ai_next;
        }
    }
```

The actual printing is done by the function `printinfo()`.

```
1   void printinfo(struct addrinfo *p){
2       char ipver[200];
```

```
3         void *addr;
4         if(p->ai_family==AF_INET){
5              struct sockaddr_in *ipv4 =
6                   (struct sockaddr_in *)p->ai_addr;
7         addr = &(ipv4->sin_addr);
8         strcpy(ipver, "IPv4");
9         }
10        else if(p->ai_family==AF_INET6){
11             struct sockaddr_in6 *ipv6 =
12                  (struct sockaddr_in6 *)p->ai_addr;
13             addr = &(ipv6->sin6_addr);
14             strcpy(ipver, "IPv6");
15        }
16        else
17             return;
18        char ipstr[INET6_ADDRSTRLEN];
19        inet_ntop(p->ai_family, addr, ipstr,
20        INET6_ADDRSTRLEN);
21        std::cout<<ipver<<" address : "<<ipstr<<endl;
22 }
```

This function is the only example of object-oriented programming in this book, and it is in plain C (except for line 21). The **struct addrinfo** object ***p** could be an IPv4 or IPv6 address. IPv4 addresses are handled in the if-block from lines 4 through 9 and IPv6 addresses in the else-if block from lines 10 through 15. The principal difference lies in the interpretation of **p->ai_addr** (lines 5/6 and 11/12). In either case, a pointer **addr**, which points to the IP address, is extracted (lines 7 and 13). The IP address is 32 bits for IPv4 and 64 bits for IPv6. The function call **inet_ntop()** on line 17 converts the IP address to a more presentable format (**ntop** stands for network to presentation).

For a complete understanding of **printinfo()**, we will look into **struct sockaddr**, **struct sockaddr_in**, and **struct sockaddr_in6**. We shall only mention that the first two are exactly 16 bytes, whereas **struct sockaddr_in6** has two extra bytes to accommodate longer IPv6 addresses. The first 2 bytes in each of the three **struct**s is a **short int** storing the address family. This field is called **sa_family**, **sin_family**,

and `sin6_family` in the three `struct`s, respectively, but has the same interpretation.
We define one more function to simplify printing IP addresses:

```
void print_ipaddr(const char* addr){
    std::cout<<"          IP addresses of "<<addr<<endl;
    struct addrinfo *llist;
    llist = saddrlist(addr);
    printlist(llist);
    cout<<endl;
    freeaddrinfo(llist);
}
```

The linked list that `llist` points to is allocated within `getaddrinfo()`, which is
called inside `saddrlist()`. The linked list is freed using `freeaddrinfo()`.

The function call `print_ipaddr("www.sagemath.org")` reports the following:

```
        IP addresses of www.sagemath.org
IPv4 address : 23.235.44.223
```

For `www.ft.com`, we get

```
        IP addresses of www.ft.com
IPv4 address : 23.67.60.67
IPv4 address : 23.67.60.96
```

in Michigan and

```
        IP addresses of www.ft.com
IPv4 address : 192.124.233.18
IPv4 address : 192.124.233.9
```

in Texas. Many commercial sites, such as the Financial Times, use content mirroring
services and locate servers at multiple points. A text string such as `www.ft.com`
resolves into different IP addresses at different geographic locations.

The use of IPv6 addresses is yet uncommon in the United States, but some Internet
search engines have IPv6 addresses. Here are a few examples:

```
IPv6 address : 2001:559:0:4f::6011:4dd0
IPv6 address : 2001:559:0:4f::6011:4d20
IPv6 address : 2607:f8b0:400f:801::1013
```

IPv4 addresses are only 32 bits and can take on 4 billion different values (although not all of these are valid addresses). There are so many points of connection to the Internet, via desktops, laptops, and mobile devices, that the address space has been expanded to 64 bits in IPv6.

6.4.2 Send and receive

Every network interface comes down to sending and receiving data. We use the following function for sending data:

```
1  int block_send(int sockfd, void *buf, int len){
2      int total_sent = 0;
3      int num_sends=0;
4      while(total_sent < len){
5          int ns = send(sockfd, buf, len-total_sent, 0);
6          buf = (char *)buf+ns;
7          total_sent += ns;
8          num_sends += 1;
9      }
10     return num_sends;
11 }
```

This function sends `len` bytes out of the buffer `buf[]`. Where the data gets sent to is determined by the socket file descriptor `sockfd` (line 1). To send data in the form of TCP/IP packets, the Linux kernel needs the IP address of the destination as well as the port numbers at the source and the destination. The sending and receiving applications cannot be identified without the port number. Although the socket file descriptor `sockfd` is a mere `int`, the Linux kernel can use it to look up the IP address of the destination as well as the port numbers at the source and the destination. The information is hidden from the application program, although there are ways to get hold of it. The manner in which the socket file descriptors are set up is described later.

The function `block_send()` uses the Linux system call `send()` (line 5). The first argument is the socket file descriptor, the second argument is the buffer, and the third argument is the number of bytes to be sent. The final argument is a flag, which is given as 0 on line 5. Other flag values such as `MSG_MORE` may be used to alter socket behavior. The send() may not transmit all the data. It returns the number of bytes transmitted and -1 on error. The while-loop (lines 4 through 9) repeatedly calls send() until all the data has been sent out.

The function for receiving is quite similar.

```
1  int block_recv(int sockfd, void *buf, int len){
2       int total_recv = 0;
3       int num_recv = 0;
4       while(total_recv < len){
5            int nr = recv(sockfd, buf, len-total_recv, 0);
6            if(nr==0){
7                 num_recv=0;
8                 break;
9            }
10           buf = (char *)buf+nr;
11           total_recv += nr;
12           num_recv += 1;
13      }
14      return num_recv;
15 }
```

There is only one thing to add. If recv() (line 5) returns 0, it is a signal that the opposite party has terminated the connection. Normally, this function executes recv() in a while-loop and returns the total number of receives (line 14). However, if the connection is terminated, it sets num_recv to zero (line 7), breaks out of the loop (line 8), and returns 0, so that the caller knows the connection has been terminated.

6.4.3   Server

The server described here receives a sequence of double-precision numbers from its client and sends back their partial sums. Before we get to partial sums, we must explain how the server listens for connections on a designated port. Special port numbers are designated for major applications. For example, http uses port 80 and https uses port 443. On Linux, the list of port numbers in use can be found in the file /etc/services. The port number for our series summing server is taken to be 28537.

```
    const char* PORTNUM="28537";
```

To begin with, the server opens a socket to this port and marks the socket for listening.

```
 1  int bind2port(const char* portnum){
 2      struct addrinfo hint;
 3      hint.ai_family = AF_UNSPEC;
 4      hint.ai_socktype = SOCK_STREAM;
 5      hint.ai_flags = AI_PASSIVE;
 6      struct addrinfo *llist;
 7      getaddrinfo(NULL, portnum, &hint, &llist);
 8      int sock2port = socket(llist->ai_family,
 9                             llist->ai_socktype,
10                             llist->ai_protocol);
11      bind(sock2port,llist->ai_addr,llist->ai_addrlen);
12      int backlog=10;
13      listen(sock2port, backlog);
14      int yes = 1;
15      setsockopt(sock2port, SOL_SOCKET, SO_REUSEADDR,
16                 &yes, sizeof(int));
17      return sock2port;
18  }
```

On line 5, the `ai_flags` field of `hint` is given as `AI_PASSIVE` to indicate that the socket will accept connections from any Internet address. The `getaddrinfo()` call on line 7 uses the hint to prepare another `struct addrinfo` object `llist`. The second argument to `getaddrinfo()` is the service. It can be a character string such as "http" or "ssh" or it can be a character string representing a port number as in "28537."

Various fields of `llist` are accessed when opening the socket (lines 8, 9, 10). Because of the way the hint was set up, we will get a TCP socket.

The socket is bound to a port on line 11. The type of the second argument to `bind()` is `const struct sockaddr *`. The port to which the socket is bound is obtained from the `struct` the second argument points to. The fact that this socket accepts connections from any Internet address is indicated within the same `struct`. It is possible to set up that `struct` explicitly and do away with the hint and `getaddrinfo()`, but the `getaddrinfo()` interface we have used is much cleaner. The `getaddrinfo()` interface works for both IPv4 and IPv6 addresses. Its other advantage is to hide the conversion of the port number from host to network format (most likely little endian to big endian format).

The system call `listen()` on line 13 marks the socket for listening with a backlog of 10. The socket `sock2port` will keep up to 10 clients waiting for a connection but no more. The system call `listen()` is nonblocking. It does not actually listen.

Lines 15 and 16 use `setsockopt()` to ensure that the port address can be safely reused immediately after the server is shut down. This function returns the socket file descriptor `sock2port` (line 17).

Many servers have firewalls that block incoming connections on all ports except a chosen few. For this program to work, the firewall must be modified to accept connections on port 28537.

Once the socket has been bound to a port and marked for listening, it is ready to accept connections.

```
int connect2client(int sock2port){
    int sock2client;
    sock2client = accept(sock2port, NULL, NULL);
    return sock2client;
}
```

The first argument to the system call `accept()` is a socket file descriptor. The second argument could be a pointer to the address of another socket. Here `sock2port` has already been bound to a local port and marked for listening. Therefore, the second argument must be given as `NULL`. The third argument, which is the size of the `struct` the second argument points to, must also be `NULL`. By default, the system call `accept()` blocks until a connection is made. It returns a socket called `sock2client` here. The operating system kernel can use this socket to find out the IP address of the client as well as the port numbers at the client and server for this connection. The port number 28537 was used by the server to listen for connections. Once a connection is made, the connection gets a different port number on the server as well as the client. Port numbers are generated dynamically by the Linux kernel. If the server is multithreaded, it may accept new connections even while it is servicing clients.

After connecting to a client, the server runs the following function:

```
1  void partialsum_server(int sock2client, int blocksize){
2      double *recvbuf = new double[blocksize];
3      double *sendbuf = new double[blocksize];
```

```
 4        double S=0;
 5        while(1){
 6             int nrecv=block_recv(sock2client, recvbuf,
 7                                     8*blocksize);
 8             if(nrecv==0)
 9                  break;
10             for(int i=0; i < blocksize; i++){
11                  S += recvbuf[i];
12                  sendbuf[i] = S;
13             }
14             block_send(sock2client, sendbuf, 8*blocksize);
15        }
16        close(sock2client);
17        delete[] recvbuf;
18        delete[] sendbuf;
19  }
```

This function uses the variable S defined on line 4 to keep track of partial sums. On line 6, it receives blocksize double-precision numbers in the buffer recvbuf[] (allocated on line 2). If the returned value nrecv is zero, the client has terminated the connection and the server breaks out of the while-loop on line 9. If it receives a block of numbers, it updates the partial sum and stores it in sendbuf[] (lines 11 and 12). The array of partial sums is sent back to the client (line 13).

The server is invoked using the following function:

```
void server(int blocksize){
    int sock2port= bind2port(PORTNUM);
    while(1){
         int sock2client = connect2client(sock2port);
         partialsum_server(sock2client, blocksize);
    }
}
```

This function binds to the port 28537 (which is the value of PORTNUM) and listens for connections. As soon as it makes a connection to a client, it calls partialsum_server().

6.4.4   Client

The client mirrors the server in some ways but differs in others. The client begins by establishing a connection with the server.

```
1  int connect2server(const char *server,
2                 const char *portnum){
3      struct addrinfo hint;
4      memset(&hint, 0, sizeof(hint));
5      hint.ai_family = AF_UNSPEC;
6      hint.ai_socktype = SOCK_STREAM;
7      struct addrinfo *llist;
8      getaddrinfo(server, portnum, &hint, &llist);
9      int sock2server = socket(llist->ai_family,
10                              llist->ai_socktype,
11                              llist->ai_protocol);
12     connect(sock2server, llist->ai_addr,
13                          llist->ai_addrlen);
14     freeaddrinfo(llist);
15     return sock2server;
16 }
```

The argument server (line 1) is the name of machine on which the server is running. It could be login.univ.edu, for example. The hint specifies a TCP connection (line 6) but not the address family (line 5). The call to getaddrinfo() on line 7 gives the name of the server (as in the program for printing IP addresses) but also specifies a port number. The specified port number is the second argument to this function. It should be the character string "28537" to agree with our earlier convention. It opens a TCP socket on lines 9, 10, and 11. The socket sock2server is connected to the server on lines 12 and 13 using the system call connect(). There is much subtlety in the way connections are established and terminated over the Internet that is not discussed here.

The system call connect() is the client-side counterpart of accept(). The second argument to connect() is of type const struct sockaddr *. The struct it points to (*llist) has information about the IP address of the server as well as the port number on which it is expected to be listening. That struct of course is constructed by `getaddrinfo()` (line 8). In general, `getaddrinfo()` returns a linked list of `structs`. In principle, for robustness, we must loop through entries of that linked list until a connection attempt succeeds with one of them. For reasons given earlier, no attempt is made to detect and handle error conditions.

To find the partial sums of a series, the client uses the following program:

```
void partialsum_client(int sock2server,
                       double *series, int n,
                       int blocksize,
                       double *psum,
                       StatVector& stat_ts,
                       StatVector& stat_tr){
    assert(n%blocksize==0);
    int count = n/blocksize;
    double cycles;
    TimeStamp clk;
    for(int i=0; i < count; i++){
        clk.tic();
        int nsend=block_send(sock2server, series,
                                8*blocksize);
        cycles = clk.toc();
        stat_ts.insert(cycles);
        clk.tic();
        int nrecv=block_recv(sock2server, psum,
                                8*blocksize);
        cycles = clk.toc();
        stat_tr.insert(cycles);
        series += blocksize;
        psum += blocksize;
    }
    close(sock2server);
}
```

There is not much new to say here. The client alternately calls `block_send()` to send a block of `series[]` and `block_recv()` to store the partial sums in `psum[]`. The calls to `block_send()` and `block_recv()` are timed. Statistics for the number of cycles consumed during send and receive are gathered using `StatVector` objects.

The listing of the client program is completed by the following function definition:

```
void client(const char* server, int blocksize){
    int n;
    if(blocksize < 1000)
        n = 1000*blocksize*10;
    else
        n=1000*1000*20;
    n = (n/blocksize)*blocksize;
    int sock2server = connect2server(server, PORTNUM);
    double *series= new double[n];
    for(int i=0; i < n; i++)
        series[i]=(i%2==0)?4.0/(2*i+1):-4.0/(2*i+1);
    double *psum=new double[n];
    int count = n/blocksize;
    StatVector stat_ts(count), stat_tr(count);
    TimeStamp clk;
    clk.tic();
    partialsum_client(sock2server, series, n,
                blocksize, psum, stat_ts, stat_tr);
    double cycles = clk.toc();
    /* output code omitted */
    std::cout<<"bandwidth = "
            <<16.0*n/cycles*1e9*CPUGHZ/1e3
            <<" kbps"<<endl;
    delete[] series;
    delete[] psum;
}
```

The first argument is the name of the server.[19] The second argument to `client()` is `blocksize`. This argument must have the same value it does on `server()` for this program to run correctly. Notice that the number of terms in the series is always an

---

[19]To run this program, one needs to know the name of the computer that is running the server either in the form `www.somewhere.org` or as an IP address. There are many web services you can use to find out the IP address of your computer.

integer multiple of the block size. The array `series[]` is initialized with the Leibniz series.

Most of the code for producing output is omitted. But we do show the bandwidth calculation, which includes bytes sent as well as bytes received. The constant `CPUGHZ` must be defined equal to the CPU clock speed in GHz.

The bandwidth calculated here is not the bidirectional bandwidth. The client first sends and then receives and resumes sending only after the receive is complete. To compute the bidirectional bandwidth, both the server and client should use separate threads to send and receive. The data transfers should be streamed and should not block. One advantage of the program in its current form is that it may be used to find the network latency, which is our next topic.

6.4.5   Internet latency

To find the network latency, we take the block size to be 100 double-precision numbers or 800 bytes. Such a block fits comfortably within a single TCP/IP packet smaller than 1.5 KB (Ethernet MTU). Thus, the client in effect sends a single TCP/IP packet and waits for the partial sums, which arrive in a single TCP/IP packet.

All measurements were performed by running the server at the Texas Advanced Computing Center (TACC) and the client at the University of Michigan (UM). The median time for send + recv was close to 55 milliseconds in several trials. Therefore, we may take the round trip latency between UM and TACC to be 55 milliseconds.

Understanding why the latency is 55 milliseconds is a fascinating problem. The distance from UM to TACC is more than 1,000 miles. Therefore, the velocity of light by itself seems to account for more than 10 milliseconds of the latency.

In fact, things are much more complicated. The Linux command `traceroute` shows that the packets take a different route from UM to TACC and the way back.[20] A packet sent from UM to TACC travels from the author's desktop to a router located 2.3 miles almost immediately south (after several hops). The router 2.3 miles south of the author's desktop is managed by Merit Networks. From that router, it jumps to a router in Lubbock, Texas, covering most of the distance from UM to TACC in a single hop. The router in Lubbock, Texas, is managed by LEARN. The packet travels from Lubbock, Texas, to a TACC router in several quick hops. Much of the latency

---

[20]Thanks to Barmar (email expert) for a July 2005 post on a Comcast forum explaining a few of the intricacies of `traceroute`.

in the journey from UM to TACC seems to be incurred at routers located 2.3 miles south of the author's UM desktop and at the router in Lubbock, Texas.

On the way back, from TACC to UM, the packets take an entirely different route. The TACC servers send the packet to a router in suburban Los Angeles. The routers in Los Angeles are managed by National LambdaRail. After several quick hops in Los Angeles, the packet makes a long trip to a router located 2.3 miles south of the author's desktop at UM. Although the postal address is the same, the IP address of this router is not the same as the one that sent packets to Lubbock, Texas. After several quick hops, the packet lands on the author's desktop. Much of the latency during the return trip (excluding latency due to finite speed of light in optical fibers) seems to be incurred at a router in Los Angeles and another router 2.3 miles south of the author's desktop. It is difficult to be certain without access to the routers.

For a lot of Internet traffic, the return route is not the same as the forward route. If a company that owns a router recognizes that a packet is destined for routers owned by some other company, it gets rid of the packet as quickly as possible.

The long round trip from UM to TACC to Los Angeles back to UM is almost 4,000 miles. Velocity of light might account for almost 20 milliseconds of the observed latency. That still leaves around 35 milliseconds of latency for us to explain.

The routers buffer a lot of IP packets using linked lists. One may imagine a router that picks up a packet and almost immediately routes it to the appropriate network interface. If routing were to behave in that manner, very little latency would accumulate at the routers. However, it is impossible for a router that executes flow control and congestion control algorithms—which are vital for the survival of the Internet—to route packets immediately. The router has to buffer packets.

It is helpful to consider a simpler situation than Internet routing to get some intuition for why buffering is essential. Suppose there is a pipeline, let us say a processor pipeline, with two stages labeled P1 and P2. If P1 and P2 take exactly 10 cycles for every operation, there is no need for a buffer between the two pipeline stages. The stages P1 and P2 can be synced so that P1 passes its result to P2 as soon as it is done. Suppose, however, that the average time for an operation in either stage is 10 cycles, but there is a variance of 5 cycles. In such a situation, buffering is essential to keep the pipeline flowing. If P1 performs an operation that takes only 2 cycles while P2 is working on an operation that takes 15 cycles, the result from P1 must be buffered. As the number of stages and variance in the number of cycles consumed by a pipeline stage increase, there is a corresponding need to increase the size of the

Block Size	1 May (Noon)	3 May (2 pm)	3 May (3 pm)
80 KB	0.8 MB/s	1.6 MB/s	0.8 MB/s
800 KB	0.9 MB/s	0.9 MB/s	0.9 MB/s
8000 KB	*	1.9 MB/s	2.5 MB/s

Table 6.13: Internet bandwidth between UM and TACC in 2014.

buffers.

Internet routers may be thought of as stages in pipelines between more than a billion Internet hosts that act as sources or destinations. The hosts operate at hugely varying rates. The loads on the routers can be utterly unpredictable. The Internet would collapse if the routers did not buffer. Flow control and congestion control are impossible without buffering.

Our surmise is that 35 milliseconds of latency that accrues on routers located 2.3 miles south of the author's desktop and on routers in Lubbock, Texas, and Los Angeles are mainly due to buffering. The IP packets at a router are maintained in a linked list. Traversing a single link in a linked list incurs overhead that is determined by the latency to DRAM memory. Although the routers may use sophisticated hashing and other data structures to minimize the number of links traversed, exposure to latency to DRAM cannot be avoided in the dynamic environment in which the routers exist. In addition, the routers likely run multiple threads on multiple processor cores. If so, spinlocks, which must be used when shared data structures are accessed from multiple threads, must be another significant source of overhead. Our surmise is that the big routing stations between UM, TACC, and back buffer at least 10^5 IP packets. It would not be surprising if the buffers were 100 times that estimate.

Internet latencies are worse than Infiniband latencies by more than a factor of 10^4. Of course, a big reason is geographical separation, and nothing much can be done about it. However, it may be possible to improve the latencies that accrue at the routers.

6.4.6 Internet bandwidth

Table 6.13 shows the bandwidth recorded between UM and TACC on three different occasions. In each of the trials reported, 160 MB of data was sent from the client to the server. The server sent back 160 MB of data. The client and server traded data in varying block sizes reported in the table. The bandwidths vary much more from trial to trial than latencies.

Host computers can inject packets into the network at great speed. If an application issues a `send()` system call, the data to be sent must fall through the TCP layer, the IP layer, the ARP layer, and the device driver before it reaches the network. The Linux TCP/IP stack is heavily optimized. One major optimization in Linux as well as many other implementations is to avoid repeated copies. In fact, the data is copied just once from the application's user space to kernel buffers. The kernel buffers for TCP/IP packets are of the type `struct sk_buff`. This `struct` is organized in such a way that the TCP header, IP header, and Ethernet header can be tacked on without copying the data.

The realized bandwidth is determined to a great extent by TCP's congestion control algorithm. TCP implements both flow control and congestion control. In flow control, the sender keeps track of the available room in the receiver's buffer. The sender slows down if there is too little room in the receiver's buffer. The sender continually adjusts its speed to avoid overwhelming (or starving) the receiver with packets.

The basic flow of packets in TCP is from the sender to the receiver. The receiver may have to reorder the packets, and some packets may be dropped by the routers. Just as in Infiniband, the receiver sends an ACK when it receives a packet. The sender has to retransmit packets if they have not been acknowledged for a long while. The ACK packets the sender receives have a field in which the receiver advertises the window available in its buffers. The ACK packets may carry data if the receiver has executed a `send()` system call after receiving. The receiver's advertised window is the basis for flow control.

For data transfer between UM and TACC, congestion control has a much greater bearing on realized bandwidth than flow control. In this setting, both endpoints can inject and remove packets quickly from the network, but the Internet would strain and buckle if all the hosts inject packets at a rapid rate. In TCP, senders keep track of dropped packets and maintain a congestion window. The size of the congestion window is abruptly reduced when packets are lost and gradually increased when packets are not getting lost. The sender tries to ensure that the number of packets in flight, which is the number sent but not yet acknowledged, is within the congestion window.

Figure 6.11 shows the variation of the congestion window with time in three trials.

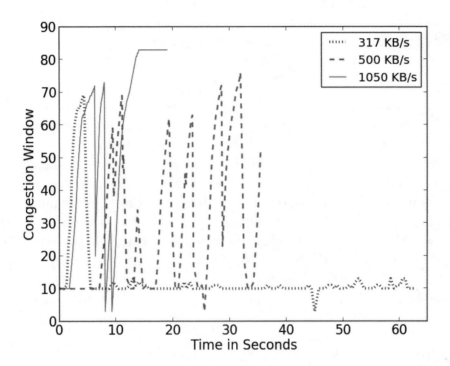

Figure 6.11: Congestion window as a function of time in three separate connections between University of Michigan and Texas Advanced Computing Center.

In each of the three trials, the client at UM sent 10 MB of data to the server at TACC and received 10 MB in return. Data was exchanged in 80 KB blocks. The congestion windows displayed in the figure were measured at UM.

Evidently, there is excellent correlation between the average congestion window and realized bandwidth. In the three trials, average congestion window sizes of 17, 40, and 65 are correlated with bandwidths of 317 KB/s, 500 KB/s, and 1050 KB/s, respectively.

The congestion window is extracted as follows:[21]

---

[21] The extraction of the congestion window is described by René Pfeiffer (Measuring TCP congestion windows, *Linux Gazette*, March 2007 (#136)). See `http://linuxgazette.net/136/pfeiffer.html`.)

```
struct tcp_info info;
int tisize = sizeof(struct tcp_info);
getsockopt(sockfd, SOL_TCP, TCP_INFO,
           &info, (socklen_t *)&tisize);
int cgwin = info.tcpi_snd_cwnd;
```

Here `info` is a `struct` of size `tisize` bytes. The crucial syntax here is the call to `getsockopt()`. Its first argument is a socket. It could be the socket used by the server to talk to the client or the socket used by the client to talk to the server. The second and third arguments `SOL_TCP` and `TCP_INFO` ask the function to fill `info` with the right kind of information. When `getsockopt()` returns, `info` has a variety of information about packets lost, packets acknowledged, packets retransmitted, and so on. In the code fragment, the congestion window is extracted and stored in `cgwin`.

The limit on the congestion window implies a connection between Internet latency and bandwidth. Figure 6.12 shows that the congestion window in a connection between two computers nearby. The congestion window ramps up quickly and then stays constant around 85. The upper limit on the congestion window appears to be about 85. Because the congestion window is the number of packets in flight, we have

$$\text{bandwidth} \leq \text{Max congestion window} \times \text{MTU}/(\text{half of round-trip time}).$$

For the connection between nearby computers in figure 6.12, the MTU is approximately 1.5 KB, and the round-trip time is 0.23 milliseconds. Therefore, 110 MB/s is an upper bound on the bandwidth. The network is operating at close to its advertised peak of 1 Gigabit per second.

Exercise 6.4.1. Implement a multithreaded version of the partial sum server using Pthreads. Verify that your server is capable of servicing multiple clients simultaneously.

Exercise 6.4.2. Write a TCP/IP program to synchronize with a central database. The central database is assumed to have a number of data items. For simplicity, you may forbid deletion of data items. Each client program will upload new data items from the client to update the central database and will then download the entire database, including items pushed by other clients.

Exercise 6.4.3. Write a decentralized TCP/IP program that has similar functionality to the program in the previous exercise. To decentralize, each client will have to run a server that accepts requests from other clients that query its database.

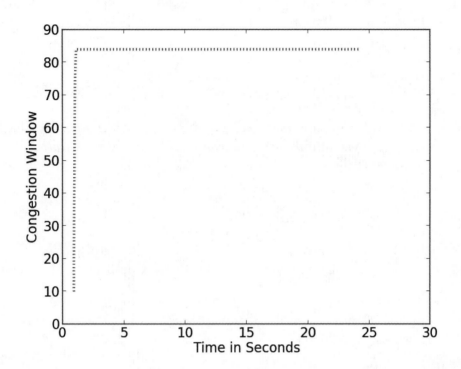

Figure 6.12: Congestion window measured between the author's third floor office at the University of Michigan and a computer in the basement of the same building. The recorded bandwidth reached more than 100 MB/s. The round-trip latency appeared to be 0.23 milliseconds.

6.5   References

W. Gropp, S. Huns-Lederman, A. Lumsdaine, E. Lusk, B. Nitzberg, W. Saphir, and M. Snir. *MPI—The Complete Reference The MPI Extensions*, volume 2. MIT Press, Cambridge, Massachusetts, 1998.

B.J. Hall. *Beej's Guide to Network Programming Using Internet Sockets*. Lulu Marketplace, 2009.

K. Kandalla, U. Yang, J. Keasler, T. Kolev, A. Moody, H. Subramoni, K. Tomko, J. Vienne, B.R. de Supinski, and D.K. Panda. Designing non-blocking allreduce with collective offload on Infiniband clusters: a case study with conjugate gradient solvers. *IEEE 26th International Parallel and Distributed Processing Symposium*, pages 1156–1167, 2012.

C.E. Leiserson. Fat-trees: Universal networks for hardware-efficient supercomputing. *IEEE Trans. on Computers*, 34:892–901, 1985.

J. Liu, J. Wu, S.P. Kini, P. Wyckoff, and D.K. Panda. High performance RDMA-based MPI implementation over infiniband. *International Journal of Parallel Programming*, 32:167–198, 2004.

L.L. Peterson and B. Davie. *Computer Networks: A Systems Approach*. Morgan Kaufmann, San Francisco, 5th edition, 2010.

M. Snir, S. Otto, S. Huss-Lederman, D. Walker, and J. Dongarra. *MPI—The Complete Reference: The MPI Core*, volume 1. MIT Press, Cambridge, Massachusetts, 2nd edition, 1998.

A.S. Tanenbaum and D.J. Wetherall. *Computer Networks*. Prentice Hall, Upper Saddle River, 5th edition, 2010.

T.S. Woodall, G.M. Shipman, G. Bosilca, and A.B. Maccabe. Recent Advances in Parallel Virtual Machine and Message Passing Interface. In *Lecture Notes in Computer Science*, volume 4192, pages 76–85. Springer, New York, 2006.

Chapter 7

Special Topic: The Xeon Phi Coprocessor

The Top 500 organization[1] has published a list of the top supercomputers every year since 1993. This list has been a huge contribution to scientific computing. The considerable profits in computer technology lie in entertainment, everyday convenience, creating new enthusiasms, reinforcing preexisting ones, and commerce. The profits from scientific computing are almost negligible. The wide publicity that Top 500 generates has ensured that scientific computing is not ignored by major corporations.

The Top 500 list ranks computers on the basis of flop (floating point operation) rate realized in solving large linear systems using pivoted LU factorization (the LIN-PACK benchmark). The computation must be in double-precision. The flop rate has increased from 60 GFlops/s (6×10^{10} flops/s) in 1993 to 34 PFlops/s (3.4×10^{16}) in 2015. A total of 500 computers are listed in the rankings.

The relationship between scientific computing and mainstream computing is symbiotic, although the latter is dominant. Many technologies pertaining to networks, visualization, and other topics have traveled from mainstream to scientific comput-

---

[1]See www.top500.org.

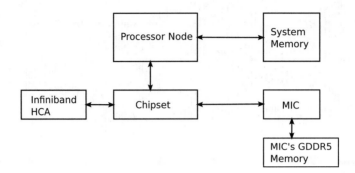

Figure 7.1: In this sketch, the Xeon Phi coprocessor is labeled MIC (Many Integrated Cores). The MIC and the Infiniband HCA (host channel adapter) are connected to the chipset on PCIe bus.

ing. Technologies such as wide register sets were first exploited in scientific computing, helping large computing clusters climb up the Top 500 list. Later these technologies have found applications in more mainstream areas such as image processing and data analysis.

Co-processors with peak ratings in excess of a tera-flop were first introduced to market by NVIDIA. Such coprocessors are particularly efficacious for dense matrix computations and, in particular, for the LINPACK benchmark used to rate the TOP 500 supercomputers. In 2015, as in some years before, the biggest supercomputers have no choice but to use these coprocessors to hold their place in the TOP 500 list. Because the TOP 500 list is widely publicized, so widely that the topmost positions are a source of national pride, the coprocessors have impressive marketing potential. Intel could not afford to ignore this marketing angle.

The Intel Many Integrated Cores (MIC) or Xeon Phi coprocessor supplements the processor nodes and increases floating point throughput. Figure 7.1 shows a typical setup.[2] The peak floating point rating of the coprocessor may be three times that of the processor node, going beyond 1 TFlop/s.[3]

Section 7.1 is an outline of the architecture of the Xeon Phi core. The Xeon Phi used in this chapter has 61 cores. The number of cores will increase in the future.

---

[2]Knight's Landing, the successor of Knight's Corner microarchitecture, moves the Xeon Phi away from the coprocessor model. Section 7.2, the middle third of this chapter, will cease to be relevant. The rest of the chapter will still apply with minor changes.

[3]In 2015.

Each core of the Xeon Phi implements the AVX-512 instruction set (see table 3.1), which is yet to make its way into mainline x86 computers. The AVX-512 instruction set is an enhancement of the AVX2 instruction set used in mainline x86 computers. The AVX-512 instruction set features 512-bit ZMM registers, twice the size of YMM registers in AVX/AVX2.

In addition, each core of the Xeon Phi has a hardware thread picker. During each cycle, the thread picker picks one of four or fewer threads mapped to any particular core. The thread picker prefers to schedule in round-robin fashion and never picks the same thread in two successive cycles. Therefore, the natural number of threads to use (on a 61-core Phi) in OpenMP programs is $4 \times 61 = 244$ and not 61, as we explain in section 7.1.

Section 7.1 also explains how to run programs on the Phi in native mode. In native mode, one can log onto the Phi device like any computer and run programs on it like we do on any computer. In the beginning days, the native mode is not very stable, but when it works it can be a great convenience. Many OpenMP programs can be made to run on the Phi with no changes beyond compiling with the `-mmic` flag.

Another way to run programs on the device is in the offload mode. This mode, which has been perfectly stable from the beginning, requires modifications to the C/C++ source. New syntax is used to send parts of the computations off to the Phi devices. The offload mode is the topic of section 7.2.

Section 7.3 discusses two main examples. The first example is the Fast Fourier Transfrom (FFT). For $n = 64$, the Phi can be twice as fast as its AVX host. However, already for $n = 8{,}192$, the Phi is no faster than its 2.7 GHz AVX host (see table A.1 for the full name of this machine). For $n = 2^{26}$, the AVX host is eight times faster, suggesting that the MKL library is not yet fully optimized for the Phi.

As discussed in chapter 3, the most important optimizations for scientific algorithms such as the FFT are instruction pipeline optimizations. The second example in section 7.3 is a discussion of instruction pipeline optimizations for matrix multiplication. We show how to write a program that gets to nearly 50% of the peak floating point capability of a Phi device. The discussion brings out some features of the AVX-512 instruction set that are not found in the SSE2 instruction set used in chapter 3. However, not all the techniques found in that chapter are repeated. The discussion only goes far enough to indicate that the application of those techniques would result in a matrix multiplication routine that reaches 85% of peak bandwidth like Intel's MKL library.

The peak floating point capability or bandwidth is relevant to only a small fraction of scientific programs. Even a computationally intensive algorithm such as the FFT reaches only 15% of the peak floating point bandwidth. The bandwidth to memory of the Phi device is less than twice that of its AVX host. Scientific programs that benefit from the coprocessor as much as matrix multiplication or the Top 500 headline numbers are few.

New technologies such as NVIDIA's GPUs and Intel's Xeon Phi have gained traction partly because of the Top 500 list. Such new technologies must be welcomed. Even if they do not endure, they point to new directions and encourage innovation in hardware design. Nevertheless, it must be pointed out that the marketing hype is not perfectly concordant with practical realities.

In earlier chapters, we have seen that the gap between capabilities of processors and the code generated by compilers is growing. That is especially true where instruction pipeline optimizations are involved. The gap can be a factor of 10 for AVX2 computers, as we saw in chapter 3. The gap is even wider for the coprocessor devices.

As this gap widens, an even greater gap has developed between the skill of a typical scientific programmer and what it takes to program modern computers efficiently. The mainline x86 computers featuring SSE2, AVX, AVX2, or AVX-512, the last of which is yet to be released to market, have a modular architecture at the hardware level. Processor cores and processor packages share memory.[4] Programs that respect that modularity may be written using OpenMP or Pthreads. The heterogeneous coprocessor model breaks this modularity.[5] On the same computer, we have disparate and dissimilar entities competing to do the same task in a rather ad-hoc manner. Programming such heterogeneous setups is much less tractable.

The modifications to C/C++ introduced for the Phi appear relatively straightforward at first sight. However, the lack of modularity at the hardware level makes it much harder to organize and maintain programs effectively. NVIDIA's CUDA model requires fine-grained parallelism within programs, which is quite a bit harder to handle, as we will see in the next chapter.

The majority, perhaps the vast majority, of programs that feature in scientific research and seminars do not go out of cache. It is unlikely that these programs are

---

[4]The allocation of pages in near memory through demand paging and the first-touch policy may be viewed as a violation of modularity with regard to the way memory is shared between processes.

[5]Knight's Landing, the successor to Xeon Phi from Intel, has been announced to move away from the coprocessor model.

well optimized in a meaningful way. The potential offered by coprocessors, although enticing, must be viewed in light of this sobering reality. Many scientific programs are written in Matlab or Python and for good reasons. But these interpreted languages are very slow. A good C program can be more than 1,000 times faster than Matlab or Python on a single core. On multicore processor packages, the speedup from C will be even greater. Yet there is a market for GPU computing in these interpreted languages. While the marketing potential of color coating an anodyne is undeniable, the logic of this exercise is a little difficult to discern.

7.1 Xeon Phi architecture

In this section, we give an overview of the Xeon Phi's architecture in three steps. The first step is to calculate the peak floating point bandwidth of the Phi in section 7.1.1 and compare it to that of its AVX host. The Phi turns out to be better by a factor of 3. This is perhaps the most favorable comparison one can make for the coprocessor. Applications in which that factor is approached are few.

The second step in section 7.1.2 is to introduce the thread picker. The thread picker is a hardware module on each Phi core. During every cycle, it picks one of four threads. Section 7.1.2 also introduces the ZMM registers in the context of the thread picker. Section 7.1.2 explains how to compile and run a Phi program in native mode.

Compiling and running a Phi program in native mode differs very little from what is usual on mainline computers. In fact, almost every OpenMP program of chapter 5 can be run on the Phi with little effort and almost no modifications. Thus, in section 7.1.3, we reuse the same programs to measure the Phi's latency and bandwidth to memory.

The Phi's bandwidth to memory is not even twice that of its AVX host. The copy bandwidth is better by a factor of 1.72. This improvement in bandwidth comes at the expense of a latency that is nearly four times as high, although on the positive side the Phi's memory system is uniform with no distinction between near and far memory. Coprocessors such as the Phi and NVIDIA's GPUs are worthless for programs that rely on dynamic data structures such as linked lists because such programs are exposed to latency to memory. However, they can yield a speedup in programs whose memory accesses are regular and predictable.

7.1.1   Peak floating point bandwidth

Figure 7.1 shows a typical setup for a Xeon Phi coprocessor. The host computer is a 2.7 GHz AVX machine (see table A.1 for its full name). It has 16 cores, each equipped with 256-bit YMM registers, wide enough for four double-precision numbers. Each core can issue a `vaddpd` and a `vmulpd` instruction simultaneously in each cycle. Therefore, the peak floating point bandwidth is:

$$16 \text{ cores} \times 8 \text{ flops/cycle/core} \times 2.7 \text{ billion cycles/sec} = 345.6 \text{ Gflops/sec.}$$

The host is quite powerful by itself.

The Xeon Phi coprocessor is attached to the chipset on the PCIe bus, like the Infiniband network card of the previous chapter.[6] The coprocessor has its own memory (8 GB on our system) and cannot access the processor node's memory. Any data sent from the processor node to the coprocessor has to flow through the chipset.

The Phi used here packages 61 cores. Each core implements the fused multiply add instruction (to be discussed later) on the ZMM registers, which are wide enough for eight double-precision numbers. Thus, each core can execute 16 double-precision operations in a single cycle. The coprocessor clock is 1.09 GHz. Its peak floating point throughput of

$$61 \text{ cores} \times 16 \text{ flops/cycle/core} \times 1.09 \text{ billion cycles/sec} = 1.064 \text{ Tflops/sec}$$

is slightly more than three times that of its AVX host.

This peak bandwidth is approached by dense matrix multiplication and LU factorization. However, the peak floating point bandwidth is an irrelevant theoretical number for almost every other application, and even the FFT realizes only 15% of the peak, as we will see later.

7.1.2   A simple Phi program

From here onward, we use Phi device and MIC device interchangeably. MIC is the acronym of Many Integrated Cores and includes the microarchitecture of Phi-like devices. We begin by explaining why the right number of threads on a MIC/Phi device is typically four times the number of cores.

---

[6]In fact, the Xeon Phi card can talk to the Infiniband HCA directly via the chipset without processor intervention. It is unclear whether the facility is really so useful.

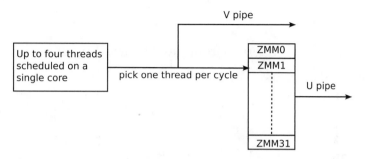

Figure 7.2: A preliminary view of the architecture of a Xeon Phi core.

Thread pickers and ZMM registers

Processor cores of mainline computers run one thread at a time.[7] The operating system must be invoked to switch from one thread to another at a cost of around 10^4 cycles.

In contrast, four threads can be scheduled to a single Phi core.[8] All four cores can remain active, and the thread picker, which is a hardware module, switches between them in a single cycle (see figure 7.2). During every cycle, one of the four threads is picked to run. The thread picker prefers round-robin scheduling, where it cycles between the four threads, and it never picks the same thread in two successive cycles. Therefore, one must create at least two threads for every core to prevent alternate cycles from being wasted. Much of the time it is best to create four threads for every core. On our Phi card, with 61 cores, the ideal number of threads is 244.

Each Phi core has 32 ZMM registers (see figure 7.2). In fact, the number of registers in hardware is really 32×4. Each of the four threads scheduled to a Phi core has its own register file so that the hardware can switch between threads in a single cycle. This replication of registers is another reason to set the number of threads to be four times the number of cores.

In a thread or program, the registers may be referred to as ZMM0 through ZMM31. The Phi does not support XMM or YMM registers. The ZMM registers must be used for floating point operations. Each ZMM register may be thought of as a vector of eight double-precision numbers.

---

[7]We are assuming that hyperthreading is turned off.

[8]Much of the information here is from *Intel Xeon Phi Co-processor System Software Developer's Guide*, June 2013.

Hello world

Our first Phi program is no different from any OpenMP program.

```
#include <stdio.h>
#include <omp.h>

int main(){
#pragma omp parallel
    printf("hello from thread: %d of %d\n",
        omp_get_thread_num(), omp_get_num_threads());
}
```

The parallel region here omits the **num_threads** clause. Instead, the environment variable

```
OMP_NUM_THREADS
```

is set to determine the number of threads in the parallel region. On a MIC device, it may be set as

```
export OMP_NUM_THREADS=244
```

if the MIC device has 61 cores and as

```
export OMP_NUM_THREADS=16
```

on its host if the host has 16 cores.

The program is compiled and linked as follows:

```
icpc -mmic  -openmp -c hello.cpp
icpc -mmic  -openmp -o hello.exe hello.o
```

To keep the compilation syntax simple, we have omitted all but the most essential flags. Flags such as -restrict and -O3 for optimization must certainly be used almost all the time. The -mkl flag must be used if the MKL library is being invoked. The new flag here is -mmic, which makes icpc generate an executable that runs on the MIC/Phi device.

The compilation is done on the host. Although the MIC device is powerful for certain scientific applications, it is not powerful enough to run a compiler. To run the program on a MIC device, one must first connect to it as follows:

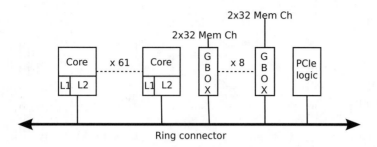

Figure 7.3: Phi cores and memory controllers connected using a bidirectional ring. The memory controllers are labeled GBOX.

```
ssh mic0
```

If the host file system is not mounted on the MIC device, the executable must be copied to it from the host as follows:

```
scp hello.exe mic0:hello.exe
```

After sshing to the MIC device, the environment variable `OMP_NUM_THREADS` must be set correctly. Another crucial environment variable is

```
LD_LIBRARY_PATH
```

It must be set to include the path to all the runtime libraries that may be needed.

To receive 244 greetings, we may now say `hello.exe`. The same program may be compiled and run on the host. The only change would be to drop the `-mmic` flag.

7.1.3 Xeon Phi memory system

The Phi has its own memory, which is accessed through a ring (see figure 7.3). Eight memory controllers are connected to the same ring. Each memory controller drives two 32-bit (or 4-byte) channels of GDDR5 memory. There are 16 channels in total. The Phi supports 4 KB as well as 2 MB pages. The timing in this chapter was done with 2 MB paging enabled. Latency and bandwidth to memory are measured by making slight changes to earlier programs.

n	AVX (near)	AVX (far)	MIC (near)	MIC (far)
4	28 ns	43 ns	241 ns	244 ns
20	30 ns	47 ns	260 ns	260 ns
50	72 ns	135 ns	291 ns	291 ns
100	73 ns	137 ns	307 ns	308 ns

Table 7.1: Latency to memory in nanoseconds for a 2.7 GHz AVX host (see table A.1 for its full name) and the Phi coprocessor. The measurements were carried out using n pages.

Latency to memory

Our strategy for measuring latency was as follows. Suppose a measurement is carried out with n pages, each of 4 KB. Because a cache line is 64 bytes or 512 bits, the number of cache lines in n pages is $64n$. These $64n$ cache lines are first flushed from cache and then accessed in random order. Latency is taken to be equal to the average time of access.

To measure latency to near and far memory, we used a program with two threads. The n pages used to measure latency were allocated close to one thread and far away from the other.

The measured latencies for the Phi as well as its 2.7 GHz AVX host are found in table 7.1. The memory access on the AVX host is definitely nonuniform. The Phi cores have uniform memory access. There is no distinction between near and far memory when coprocessor cores and memory controllers are connected to the same bidirectional ring. All memory accesses go through the same ring logic. The ring is also used for enforcing cache coherence.

Bandwidth to memory

The programs to measure read, write, and copy bandwidths to memory are the same as in chapter 5 for the most part. One modification was to adjust the length of the array as follows:

```
#ifndef __MIC__
    const long len = 21*1000*1000*1000;
#else
    const long len = 11*1000*1000*200;
```

	AVX	MIC
Read	90 GB/s	161 GB/s
Write	85 GB/s	130 GB/s
Copy	50 GB/s	86 GB/s

Table 7.2: Bandwidth to memory from 16 threads of the 2.7 GHz AVX host (see table A.1 for its full name) and 244 threads on the Phi (MIC).

```
#endif
```

The preprocessor variable `__MIC__` is defined when the code is targeted at a MIC device but not otherwise. Here it is used to ensure that the length of the array used to determine bandwidth to memory does not overflow on the Phi.

Table 7.2 reports bandwidths to memory for the AVX host and the Phi. The Phi realizes higher bandwidth by utilizing a wide interface to memory consisting of 16 channels. For estimating copying bandwidth, one byte copied is counted as two, a byte read and a byte written. The copy bandwidth appears to suffer on both the AVX host and the Xeon Phi possibly because of write-back caching. The read bandwidth on the Phi is far short of the theoretical peak.[9]

Bandwidth during matrix transpose

In many scientific programs, data is organized in regular 2D or 3D grids. An example is the problem of transposing a matrix. When data is arranged in 2D or 3D grids, it is advantageous to block data accesses. Blocking increases cache hits and reduces TLB misses. The program for transposing a matrix using $B \times B$ blocks on a single core is as follows:

```
void blocktransx(double *restrict a, double *restrict b,
          int ldb, int m, int n){
  assrt(m%B == 0 && n%B == 0);
  for(int i=0; i < m; i+=B)
```

---

[9]The theoretical peak is 352 GB/s. It may be approached by using prefetch instructions as described by E. Saule, K. Kaya, and U.V. Çatalyürek (Performance evaluation of sparse matrix multiplication kernels on Intel Xeon Phi, *arxiv:1302.1078v1*, 2013). These authors find that the Phi outperforms cutting-edge GPUs in sparse matrix multiplication.

```
      for(int j=0; j < n; j+=B)
        for(int ii=0; ii < B; ii++)
          for(int jj=0; jj < B; jj++)
            b[j+jj+(i+ii)*ldb] = a[i+ii+(j+jj)*m];
  }
```

The leading dimension of the $m \times n$ matrix stored in `a[]` is assumed to be m, while the leading dimension of the transposed $n \times m$ matrix in `b[]` is `ldb`, which may be n or greater.

When all 16 cores of the 2.7 GHz AVX host work together, bandwidth to memory realized during matrix transpose is 34 GB/s. For 244 threads on 61 cores of the Phi, the bandwidth is 59 GB/s. In either case, the bandwidth is nearly the same for block sizes $B = 25, 50, 100$.

Exercise 7.1.1. Explain how using a hardware thread picker that picks between four threads on every core of the Phi can help with bandwidth to memory.

Exercise 7.1.2. Estimate the Xeon Phi's bandwidth to memory when transposing a square matrix in place.

7.2   Offload

The offload mode[10] has been a stable way to program the Phi device since the beginning. The "hello" program has shown us that the syntax for writing Phi programs is virtually identical to the syntax for writing ordinary C/C++ programs. In offload mode, the master thread of the main program is assumed to be on the host. However, the program holds several segments that are meant to be outsourced to the Phi devices.

In section 7.2.1, we write a simple function called `mic_init()`. Much of the time, the only thing that needs to be changed when an OpenMP program is run on a Phi/MIC device is the number of threads. Typically, the Phi has more cores, and the number of threads on the Phi is four times the number of cores. The `mic_init()` function sets the number of threads correctly for the host as well as the Phi/MIC device once and for all.

---

[10]If the Xeon Phi architecture moves away from the coprocessor model, this section will cease to be relevant.

Section 7.2.2 introduces the `target(mic)` compiler directive. This directive, which is currently implemented only by the Intel compilers, may be applied to function definitions as well as to globally defined variables. Any function that is prefixed with `target(mic)` will be compiled to run on Phi/MIC devices as well as the host.

Section 7.2.3 uses the familiar Leibniz example to show how the Phi/MIC device can communicate with the host. The `offload` compiler directive is supported by clauses such as `in`, `out`, `nocopy`, and `inout` to enable communication between the coprocessor and the host. Variables are automatically copied into the Phi when an `offload` region is entered and are copied back when the region exits. Arrays are sent back and forth using clauses appended to the `offload` directive.

The `offload` extension supports addressing an array `v[]` on the host and its copy on the Phi/MIC device using identical syntax. If `v[i]` refers to an entry on the host, `v[i]` refers to its copy or mirror image on the Phi device. The `offload` extension supports partial views of an array. For example, we may offload `v[offset:len]` to copy the segment

$$v[offset], \quad v[offset+1], \quad \dots, v[offset+len-1]$$

to the Phi device. The entry `v[i]` on the Phi still corresponds to the entry `v[i]` on the host, but on the Phi, the legal range for the index is limited to offset $\leq i <$ offset+len. These elegant conventions simplify offloading to multiple Phi devices.

Section 7.2.4 shows that the bandwidth from host to Phi/MIC device is similar to the bandwidth at a single node of an Infiniband network. The bandwidths are good enough to enable nontrivial usage of coprocessor devices but are far from heart stopping. The bandwidths are less than a tenth of bandwidth to memory from the AVX host.

The discussion in this section may make offloading to Phi devices seem easy. It is indeed easy, even elegant, in simple programs. However, the basic setup where dissimilar coprocessor devices and the host compete to do the same work breaks modularity at the hardware level. In more complex programs, offloading will look far less felicitous than it does here.

7.2.1   Initializing to use the MIC device

The host computer can use the function `mic_init()` defined below to find out the number of MIC devices and set the default number of OpenMP threads. In all the offloading programs, it is assumed that `mic_init()` is called at the beginning.

```
1  #include <offload.h>
2  #include <omp.h>
3
4  int gl_host_nthreads = -1;
5  int gl_mic_nthreads = -1;
6
7  void mic_init(int &nmic){
8      char *s = getenv("OMP_NUM_THREADS");
9      assrt(s != NULL);
10     gl_host_nthreads = atoi(s);
11     omp_set_num_threads(gl_host_nthreads);
12
13     nmic = _Offload_number_of_devices();
14     s = getenv("MIC_OMP_NUM_THREADS");
15     assrt(s != NULL);
16     gl_mic_nthreads = atoi(s);
17     for(int i=0; i < nmic; i++)
18         omp_set_num_threads_target(TARGET_MIC, i,
19                                    gl_mic_nthreads);
20 }
```

On line 8, this program reads `OMP_NUM_THREADS`. On line 11, the default number of OpenMP threads on the host is set to the value of this environment variable. The default number of threads on the host is globally visible thanks to the definition on line 4.

The function used on line 13 to find out the number of MIC devices is declared in `offload.h` (which is included on line 1). The environment variable prefixed with MIC is read on line 14, and the for-loop on lines 17 to 19 sets the default number of OpenMP threads on every MIC device to the value of that environment variable.

Simply defining `OMP_NUM_THREADS` and the same environment variable with the prefix MIC is enough to set the default number of threads correctly. The function `mic_init()` makes that setting explicit within the structure of the program.

7.2.2 The `target(mic)` declaration specification

The `icpc` compiler has the ability to compile a function written in C/C++ to produce assembly for both the host computer and MIC device.

The function definition below is prefixed with `__declspec(target(mic))`. It is defined in the compilation unit `leibniz_init.cpp`.

```
__declspec(target(mic))
double hostmic_sum(double *v, long len){
    printf("sum:host/mic pointer v = %p \n", v);
    double sum = 0;

#pragma omp parallel for              \
    reduction(+:sum)
    for(long i=0; i < len; i++)
        sum += v[i];

    return sum;
}
```

This function simply sums the array `v[]`. When compiled (without the `-mmic` flag), two object files are produced from the same source. The object file `leibniz_init.o` has function definitions using the instruction set of the host computer. The object file `leibniz_initMIC.o` has function definitions using the instruction set of the MIC device.

Compiling with the `-S` flag and inspecting the assembly shows that the code for the MIC device uses ZMM registers and `vaddpd` instructions. On the AVX host, the assembly code uses XMM registers but not the wider YMM registers. That is either a sign that compiler technology is yet to catch up fully with AVX or an indication that the compiler has figured out that the use of YMM registers brings no benefit in this program, which is limited by bandwidth to memory.

The rest of `leibniz_init.cpp` has the following definition:

```
/*
 * gl_scl = 4.0^(1.0/3.0)
 */
__declspec(target(mic)) const double gl_scl
```

$$= 1.5874010519681994;$$

```
__declspec(target(mic))
void hostmic_scale(double *v, long len){
    printf("scale:host/mic pointer v = %p \n", v);

#pragma omp parallel for
    for(long i=0; i < len; i++)
        v[i] *= gl_scl;

#pragma omp parallel
#pragma omp master
    printf("num of threads = %d\n",
           omp_get_num_threads());
}

void leibniz_init(double *v, long len){
#pragma omp parallel for
    for(long i=0; i < len; i+=2){
        v[i] = 1.0/(2*i+1);
        v[i+1] = - 1.0/(2*i+3);
    }
}
```

The global variable `gl_scl` is initialized to $4^{1/3}$. Thanks to the `target(mic)` qualifier, it is defined on both the MIC device and the host. The function `hostmic_scale()` multiplies every entry of the array `v[]` by $4^{1/3}$. It, too, is compiled for both the host and MIC device. The last function `leibniz_init()` initializes the array `v[]` to terms of the Leibniz series $1 - 1/3 + 1/5 - \cdots$. This function is not qualified using `target(mic)`, and it is compiled only for the host.

Although compilation of `leibniz_init.cpp` using `icpc` generates an object file `leibniz_init.o` compiled for the host and the object file `leibniz_initMIC.o` compiled for the MIC device, only the first of these needs to be linked. The `icpc` linker appears to automatically look for and find the other object file.

7.2.3   Summing the Leibniz series

We will discuss four different programs to sum the Leibniz series to compute π. All four programs initialize the array `v[]` to terms of the series $1 - 1/3 + 1/5 - \cdots$ and then scale each term by $4^{1/3}$ three times before summing the series. Together the programs expose nearly all the offload syntax one needs to know. Work is offloaded using the `offload` directive. Communication between the host and the Phi device is controlled using `in`, `out`, `inout`, or `copy` clauses.

Each program works as follows. To begin with, the array `v[]` is initialized with entries of the series $1 - 1/3 + 1/5 - \cdots$ on the host using `leibniz_init()` defined above. Subsequently, three calls are made to `hostmic_scale()`, also defined above, and a single call to `hostmic_sum()`, which too was defined above.

The three calls to `hostmic_scale()` and the one call to `hostmic_sum()` may be on either the host or Phi device. Each call to `hostmic_scale()` multiplies the terms of the series by $4^{1/3}$, and the effect of three calls is to multiply by 4. The call to `hostmic_sum()` will therefore return an approximation to π.

In `leibniz1()`, the three calls to `hostmic_scale()` and the call to `hostmic_sum()` are all offloaded to the Phi device. The syntax in this case is the simplest.

The function `leibniz2()` is similar, except for one big difference. When the master thread encounters a typical offload region, such as the offload region in `leibniz1()`, it blocks until the Phi device exits the offload region. In `leibniz2()`, we show syntax that allows the master thread to offload without blocking and then wait for the offload region to complete. That type of syntax is essential to make the Phi coprocessor and the host work in parallel.

The function `leibniz3()` exhibits facilities for communication between the host and the Phi coprocessor in considerable detail. In this function, the first two scalings are done on the Phi device and the third scaling on the host. The sum is then computed on the Phi device.

Finally, the function `leibniz4()` shows how multiple Phi devices may be used in parallel. In `offload` directives, syntax such as `v:length(n)` is used to offload `v[0,...,len-1]` to the coprocessor. Parallelism between Phi devices is facilitated by the syntax `v[offset:len]`, which offloads

```
v[offset, offset+1,...,offset+len-1]
```

to the coprocessor.

Offloading from the processor to the Phi

The first of the four functions `leibniz1()` is the simplest.

```
 1  void leibniz1(){
 2      int nmic;
 3      mic_init(nmic);
 4      long n = 11*1000*1000*800;
 5      long nbytes = n*8;
 6      double* v = (double *)_mm_malloc(nbytes, 64);
 7      leibniz_init(v, n);
 8
 9      double sum;
10  #pragma offload target(mic:0)                              \
11      mandatory                                              \
12      in(v:length(n) align(64))
13      {
14          hostmic_scale(v, n);
15          hostmic_scale(v, n);
16          hostmic_scale(v, n);
17          sum = hostmic_sum(v, n);
18      }
19      printf("    leibniz1:  sum = %f\n", sum);
20
21      _mm_free(v);
22      mic_exit();
23  }
```

The number of MIC devices `nmic` is initialized on line 3. The initialization function `mic_init()` also sets the default number of threads for MIC as well as the host, as described. The 6.4 GB array `v[]` is initialized to entries of the Leibniz series $1 - 1/3 + 1/5 - \cdots$ on line 7.

The `#pragma offload` construct begins on line 10. The first clause, which is on line 10, is `target(mic:0)`. This clause says that the computation in the ensuing block (lines 13 through 18) must be offloaded to the MIC device numbered 0. If there are `nmic` MIC devices, the devices are numbered from 0 to `nmic-1`.

If there is in fact no MIC device on the system, the program by default ignores the offload directive and executes the ensuing block on the host itself. The `mandatory` clause on line 11 forces the program to abort if no MIC device is found.

The offload statement block (lines 13 through 18) refers to the array `v[]` and the variables `sum` and `n`. Before an offload region is entered, all the variables input to the offload region are automatically gathered and sent to the MIC device. During exit, the MIC device gathers all the variables to be output and sends them back to the host. Therefore, we do not need to do anything special to propagate the variables `sum` and `n` to the MIC device and back.

However, the 6.4 GB array `v[]` needs special handling. The `in` clause on line 12 tells the compiler that `v[]` is an input to the offload region. The modifier `length(n)` tells the compiler that this is an array of length `n`. By default, the compiler will allocate a 6.4 GB array on the MIC device also named `v[]`. An `in` clause always has the effect of copying the array `v[]` on the host to the corresponding array `v[]` on the MIC device. By default, the array `v[]` that resides on the MIC device is deallocated at exit from the offload region.

The `printf()` statement on line 19 runs on the host, but the sum it prints is computed on the MIC device.

The signal/wait facility

Next we use the function `leibniz2()` to illustrate the signal/wait facility of the offload construct.

```
void leibniz2(){

    ...

#pragma offload target(mic:0)                                 \
    in(v:length(n) align(64))                                 \
    signal(0)
    {
        hostmic_scale(v, n);
        hostmic_scale(v, n);
        hostmic_scale(v, n);
        sum = hostmic_sum(v, n);
    }
```

```
#pragma offload_wait target(mic:0)  wait(0)
    printf("    leibniz2:  sum = %f\n", sum);


        . . .

}
```

This function is exactly the same as `leibniz1()`, except that the `offload` construct
is modified and the following `printf` on line 19 is inside an `offload` region. The
`offload` construct here omits `mandatory` and adds the `signal` clause. If there is no
`signal` clause, the host processor will block until the offload completes execution.
With a `signal` clause, it will issue the `offload` and then charge ahead without
blocking. In general, using signals enables overlapping host processor activity with
MIC activity.

   If a `signal` clause is used, the target MIC device must be numbered. More specifically, the `target` clause can read `target(mic:0)` or `target(mic:1)`, but it cannot
read `target(mic)`. The signal can be given any `int` as a number. Here `signal(0)`
specifies the signal's number as 0.

   The matching `offload_wait` construct waits for a signal from MIC device 0
with signal number 0 before issuing the `printf` statement. Note that the `printf`
in `leibniz2()` is issued on the MIC device and not on the host as in `leibniz1()`.

More complex offload patterns

The function `leibniz3()` makes the offload syntax more explicit. Its opening fragment is similar to what we have already seen.

```
1   void leibniz3(){
2       int nmic;
3       mic_init(nmic);
4       assrt(nmic > 0);
5       long n = 11*1000*1000*800;
6       long nbytes = n*8;
7       printf("             nbytes = %ld\n",nbytes);
8       double* v = (double *)_mm_malloc(nbytes, 64);
9       leibniz_init(v, n);
10      printf("    host pointer v = %p \n", v);
```

The following offload construct allocates the 6.4 GB array `v[]` on the MIC device
and copies to it:

```
11  #pragma offload target(mic:0)                              \
12        in(v:length(n) align(64) alloc_if(1) free_if(0))
13        {}
```

The default conventions for allocating when entering an offload region and deallocat-
ing during exit can be a little confusing. Here the allocation and deallocation have
been made explicit. The modifier `alloc_if(1)` says that the array `v[]` should be
allocated on the MIC device at entry. The modifier `free_if(0)` says that the array
`v[]` should not be freed at exit. It can be reused by later offloads. Because this is
an `in` clause, the array `v[]` will always be copied from host to MIC at entry. Such
copying is the principal effect of this clause because the body of the construct (line
13) is empty.

The next offload construct has a nonempty body.

```
14  #pragma offload target(mic:0)                              \
15        nocopy(v:length(n) alloc_if(0) free_if(0))
16        hostmic_scale(v, n);
```

The `nocopy` clause (line 15) means that the array `v[]` is copied at neither entry nor
exit. The `alloc_if(0)` and `free_if(0)` modifiers imply that memory is not allocated
on the MIC device at entry nor is it deallocated at exit. The sole effect of this offload
construct is to offload the function call `hostmic_scale()` on line 16 to the MIC
device. Once that call is complete, the array `v[]` that resides on the MIC device will
be scaled by $4^{1/3}$, but the array `v[]` on the host is unchanged.

Further scaling is done as follows:

```
17  #pragma offload target(mic:0)                            \
18        out(v:length(n) align(64) alloc_if(0) free_if(0))
19        hostmic_scale(v, n);
20
21        hostmic_scale(v, n);
```

The offload load construct here has an `out` clause. The array `v[]` is not copied from
host to MIC at entry, but it is copied from MIC to host at exit. The array is neither
allocated nor freed on the MIC device. The offload region (line 19) is again a single

call to `host_mic()`. At exit from the offload construct, the array `v[]` is scaled by $4^{2/3}$ on both the host and MIC device.

The function call `hostmic_scale()` on line 21 occurs on the host. At the end of this call, the array `v[]` is scaled by 4 on the host and by $4^{2/3}$ on the MIC device.

The definition of `leibniz3()` is completed as follows:

```
22          double sum;
23  #pragma offload target(mic:0)                                    \
24          in(v:length(n) align(64) alloc_if(0) free_if(1))
25          sum = hostmic_sum(v, n);
26
27          printf("                    sum = %f\n", sum);
28          _mm_free(v);
29          mic_exit();
30  }
```

Notice that the `in` clause (line 24) copies `v[]` from host to MIC. The array `v[]` is scaled by 4 on the host but by only $4^{2/3}$ on the MIC device. Therefore, a copy is essential if we are to get the correct value of π. Here `v[]` is freed on the MIC device at exit. The sum is computed on the MIC device on line 25.

Host and MIC pointers

The function `leibniz3()` shows the close connection between the array `v[]` stored on the host and its counterpart on the MIC device. The function prints the pointer `v` on the host (line 10). There are three calls to `hostmic_scale()` (lines 16, 19, and 21), two of them from the MIC device and one from the host. Each of these calls prints the value of the pointer `v`. The following lines are printed:

```
          host pointer v = 0x2af1d0000040
scale:host/mic pointer v = 0x7fe5cd0f7040
scale:host/mic pointer v = 0x7fe5cd0f7040
scale:host/mic pointer v = 0x2af1d0000040
```

Evidently, the pointer has a different value on the host and the MIC, although it has the same name `v` in the program.

During entry to an offload region, the host needs to know the value of the pointer on the MIC device to set up function calls correctly and to implement clauses such as `in`. During exit from the offload region, the MIC device needs to know the value of the pointer on the host to complete `out` clauses and copy data back to the host.

The runtime environment on the host and the MIC device conceal all these details and provide a simple interface to the user.[11] If an array `v[]` is offloaded, we may use `v[i]` to refer to the ith entry of the offloaded array on the Phi device and to the ith entry of the original array on the host. The two arrays are like images of each other.

Offloading to multiple MIC devices

On systems with multiple MIC devices, the host may offload parts of the computation to each device and keep a portion to itself. The most natural way to do that is to split an array `v[]` and assign part of the array to each MIC device.

The offload syntax for splitting an array across several devices is uncomplicated. However, the way the correspondence is set up between host and MIC pointers is a little more subtle. The opening fragment of the function `leibniz4()` is as follows:

```
void leibniz4(){
    int nmic;
    mic_init(nmic);
    long n = 11*1000*1000*800;
    long nbytes = n*8;
    double* v = (double *)_mm_malloc(nbytes, 64);
    leibniz_init(v, n);

    double sum[nmic];
```

Here `sum[]` is an array with as many entries as the number of MIC devices. Each MIC device will leave its part of the sum in one of the entries of the array.

The new syntax for splitting an array across MIC devices appears below.

```
/*
 * alloc mem on mic devices
```

---

[11]Every `in`, `out`, `inout`, or `nocopy` clause will either set up or access a table mapping between host and MIC pointers. On the host this correspondence is presumably stored by the MIC's device driver and accessed by the host program using the runtime libraries. On the MIC device, the correspondence between pointers may be stored in the Manycore Program Software Stack (MPSS) and accessed by the offloaded program using runtime libraries.

```
    */
    for(int mc=0;  mc < nmic;  mc++){
        long shft = mc*n/nmic;
        long len = (mc+1)*n/nmic - mc*n/nmic;
#pragma offload_transfer target(mic:mc)                    \
    nocopy(v[shft:len]:align(64) alloc_if(1) free_if(0))
        {}
    }
```

In the body of the for-loop, the part of the array v[] allocated to the MIC device numbered mc begins with the entry v[shft] and ends with the entry v[shft+len-1]. The offload region here allocates corresponding memory on the MIC device. It has an empty body, and nothing is copied.

The crucial bit of syntax here is v[shft:len]. An array of len items is allocated on the MIC device. As before, the pointer v on the host corresponds to some other value of v on the MIC device inside the body of the offload region. Even in this setting, v[i] refers to the ith entry of v[] on the Phi as well as on the host, but the legal values of the index i must be in the range shft $\leq i <$ shft + len. The copy of v[] on the Phi is again an image of the array v[] on the host, but only a segment of the original array is represented in the image.

The rest of the definition of leibniz4() shows more instances of this offload syntax.

```
    /*
     * offload scaling and summing to mic devices
     */
    for(int mc=0;  mc < nmic;  mc++){
        long shft = mc*n/nmic;
        long len = (mc+1)*n/nmic - mc*n/nmic;
#pragma offload target(mic:mc)                             \
    in(v[shft:len]:alloc_if(0) free_if(0))                 \
    out(sum[mc:1])                                         \
    signal(1)
        {
            hostmic_scale(v+shft, len);
            hostmic_scale(v+shft, len);
```

```
                    hostmic_scale(v+shft, len);
                    sum[mc] = hostmic_sum(v+shft, len);
            }
    }

    printf("                        nmic = %d\n", nmic);

    /*
     * wait for mics to get back
     */
    for(int mc=0; mc < nmic; mc++){
#pragma offload_wait target(mic:mc)  wait(1)
    }

    /*
     * free mem on mic devices
     */
    for(int mc=0; mc < nmic; mc++){
        long shft = mc*n/nmic;
        long len = (mc+1)*n/nmic - mc*n/nmic;
#pragma offload_transfer target(mic:mc)                     \
 nocopy(v[shft:len]:align(64) alloc_if(0) free_if(1))
    }

    double ans = 0;
    for(int mc=0; mc < nmic; mc++)
        ans += sum[mc];
    printf("     leibniz4: sum = %e\n", ans);

    _mm_free(v);
    mic_exit();
}
```

Notice that the first argument to `hostmic_scale()` and to `hostmic_sum()` is `v+shft` and not just `v`. The offload region that scales and sums is preceded by the **signal** clause. It makes no sense to use blocking offloads if multiple MIC devices are in play.

7.2.4   Offload bandwidth

If the Phi/MIC devices are used in offload mode, there is a significant cost to the data transfer between the host and MIC devices. The PCIe bus, which connects the host with the MIC devices (via the chipset; see figure 7.1), has low bandwidth. Its bandwidth is more than an order of magnitude less than the bandwidth to memory of the MIC devices or even the host. Data transfer between the host and the Xeon Phi coprocessors imposes serious limits on the advantages as well as utility of the coprocessor model.

To time the transfers between the host and the MIC devices, we use functions such as the following:

```
void xfer_in(double *v, long n, int nmic){
    long fst[nmic+1];
    for(int i=0; i <= nmic; i++)
        fst[i] = i*n/nmic;

    for(int mc=0; mc < nmic; mc++){
        long shft = fst[mc];
        long len = fst[mc+1] - fst[mc];
#pragma offload target(mic:mc)                              \
        in(v[shft:len]:align(64) alloc_if(0) free_if(0))\
        signal(1)
            dummy(v+shft, len);

    }

    for(int mc=0; mc < nmic; mc++){
#pragma offload_wait target(mic:mc) wait(1)
    }
}
```

This function transfers data into **nmic** devices. Analogous functions transfer data out of the MIC devices or use the **inout** clause to transfer data both into the MIC devices

	Cycles/Byte (One MIC)	Bandwidth (One MIC)	Cycles/Byte (Two MICs)	Bandwidth (Two MICs)
IN	0.42	6.48 GB/s	0.40	6.75 GB/s
OUT	0.42	6.48 GB/s	0.40	6.75 GB/s
INOUT	0.81	3.24 GB/s	0.77	3.51 GB/s

Table 7.3: Offload bandwidths in transferring data to one MIC device or simultaneously to two MIC devices. In cycles/byte, the cycles are of the 2.7 GHz AVX host.

during entry to the offload region and out at exit.

Table 7.3 shows that data can be moved into or out of a single MIC device at the rate of nearly 7 GB/s. That rate is quite close to the peak rating of the PCIe express bus. The bandwidth is nearly halved if data is input to the MIC device during entry to the offload region and output from the MIC device at exit. With the `inout` clause, data flowing in and data flowing out cannot be overlapped.

With simultaneous transfer to two MIC devices, the bandwidths are almost unchanged. The bandwidth cannot be doubled because both devices are on the same bus. Latencies for data transfer are of the order of a millisecond.

Exercise 7.2.1. Write a program to find the sum of a long array that outsources parts of the work to each Phi device on the system. Do you expect the program to result in any speedup?

Exercise 7.2.2. Write a program that during a single iteration replaces each entry of a 2D array (with periodic boundaries) by the average of its north, south, east, and west entries. The program must outsource parts of the computation to each Phi device on the system. Do you expect a speedup if only a few iterations are to be performed? What if the number of iterations is large?

Exercise 7.2.3. Assume that a matrix, whose dimensions you may assume to be suitably large, is split between the host and Phi coprocessors. Write a program that transposes this matrix. Discuss the difficulties that arise because of the heterogeneity between the processor and the coprocessors.

7.3   Two examples: FFT and matrix multiplication

Section 7.3.1 looks at the Fast Fourier Transform (FFT) implemented inside the MKL
library. For small n, the FFT on the Phi/MIC device is nearly twice as fast as it is
on the AVX host. For large n such as $n = 2^{26}$, the FFT does not appear to be well
optimized yet and is slower on the Phi/MIC device by more than a factor of 8. The
fact that even the FFT reaches only 15% of the peak floating point bandwidth shows
how misleading that metric can be.

Section 7.3.2 is a look at the Phi instruction pipeline in the context of matrix multiplication. We write a microkernel in assembly that reaches 50% of the peak floating
point bandwidth. The discussion is carried far enough to show that the principles of
instruction pipeline optimization, explained in depth in chapter 3, apply to Phi/MIC
devices. Not all the techniques pertinent to matrix multiplication and developed in
earlier chapters are reviewed. To approach the peak bandwidth more closely, as the
MKL library does, would require an application of the full range of techniques.

7.3.1   FFT

The FFT is a good basis for comparing the Phi against its AVX host. It is one of the
most frequently employed scientific algorithms. Unlike in the LINPACK benchmark
employed to rate supercomputers, the cost of memory accesses cannot be completely
hidden.

The same class `FFT` was employed to time FFTs on the MIC device as well as the
host.

```
__declspec(target(mic))
class FFT{
private:
    DFTI_DESCRIPTOR_HANDLE handle;
public:
    FFT(int n, long count);
    ~FFT();
    void fwd(double *f){
        DftiComputeForward(handle, f);
    }
    void bwd(double *f){
```

n	AVX Cycles/$n \log_2 n$	AVX Cycles/Byte	MIC Cycles/$n \log_2 n$	MIC Cycles/Byte
64	0.19	0.07	0.11	0.04
1,024	0.17	0.11	0.09	0.06
8,192	0.16	0.13	0.15	0.12
8,192 × 8,192	2.16	4.26	17.55	28.52

Table 7.4: Number of cycles consumed by complex to complex FFT of size n. For both the 2.7 GHz AVX host (see table A.1 for the full name) and the Phi/MIC coprocessor, the reported numbers are host cycles.

```
        DftiComputeBackward(handle, f);
    }
};
```

This class, like similar classes discussed in chapter 2, uses the MKL library. As far as the definition of this class is concerned, no new points arise with respect to either MKL or Phi/MIC syntax. Therefore, it is omitted. The FFT class may be used on the host computer, offloaded to the MIC device, or used natively on a MIC device if compiled with the -mmic flag. Both forward and backward transforms are in place. The forward transform is suitably normalized.

Table 7.4 shows that the Phi is faster than its host for $n = 64$ and $n = 1,024$. The multiple levels of cache found on the host are useful, even for a regular and arithmetic-intensive computation such as the FFT. For $n = 8,192$, the Phi and its host are almost of the same speed. For $n = 8,192^2 = 2^{26}$, MKL's FFT is not optimized on either platform, but the host is much better.

If a large number of FFTs are to be computed, we may ask, does it make sense to offload from the AVX host to the MIC coprocessor? The answer is emphatically no. For $n = 8,192$, the AVX host takes just 0.13 cycles per byte of data (see table 7.4). Table 7.3 shows that sending a byte to the coprocessor and getting it back will take 0.81 cycles, swamping the cost of the FFT.

Table 7.4 shows that a complex-to-complex FFT of size $n = 1,024$ takes $0.09n \log_2 n$ host cycles (with the AVX host clocked at 2.7 GHz) on the Phi. As shown in chapter 2, the number of arithmetic operations in a single complex FFT of dimension n, with n a power of 2, may be assumed to be $5n \log_2 n$. Therefore, the floating point throughput is $5/.09 \times 2.7 = 150$ GFlops/sec. This floating point throughput is only 15% of the theoretical peak of the Phi.

7.3.2   Matrix multiplication

Algorithms that are capable of approaching the theoretical peak are not many. These algorithms must involve a great number of arithmetic operations relative to the data they access. In addition, their structure must permit hiding the cost of multiple accesses of the same data item. Dense numerical linear algebra is the main source of such algorithms.

The number of arithmetic operations in $C = C + AB$, where A, B, C are $n \times n$ matrices, is $2n^3$. The number of double-precision numbers accessed is only $3n^2$. For large n, a great number of arithmetic operations are carried out for every byte that is accessed. It is true that every entry of A, B, or C is involved in n operations, but we may hide the cost of memory accesses, as shown in chapter 4.

Even if the cost of memory accesses is ignored, writing a microkernel that achieves peak floating performance, with all the data items in L1 cache, can be a formidable challenge. It requires knowledge of the register set as well as the instruction pipeline. In this section, we look at a small part of the Xeon Phi's instruction set[12] and then write a microkernel that achieves 45% of the peak floating point throughput. Although this microkernel falls short of the best possible by a factor of 2, it still gives a good understanding of the Xeon Phi's architecture, why it can be so fast, and why it can be so hard to write programs that approach its top speed. Difficulty in approaching peak floating point throughput is characteristic of all modern architectures. Later we turn to Intel's MKL library, which achieves 85% of the peak floating point throughput.

Xeon Phi instructions

Before taking a closer look at the Phi architecture, we go back to figure 7.2 and summarize a few features of the Phi architecture. Up to four threads can be scheduled to run on every Phi/MIC core. The hardware switches between threads in a single cycle. It prefers round-robin scheduling, and it never executes the same thread in

---

[12]The Xeon Phi's instruction set is documented in *Intel Xeon Phi Co-processor Instruction Set Architecture Reference Manual*, September 2012.

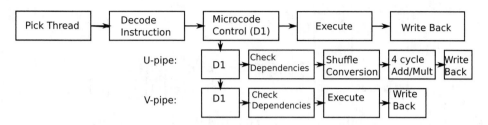

Figure 7.4: Xeon Phi pipeline.

consecutive cycles. Thus, to get to peak bandwidth, we need at least 2 threads per core, although we prefer to have 4.

There are 32 ZMM registers, each of them 64 bytes or 512 bits wide. The Phi supports all the general-purpose registers such as %rdi, %rdx, and %rax. The entire register file is replicated for each of the four threads on any coprocessor core.

Figure 7.4 is a more detailed depiction of the Xeon Phi pipeline.[13] The thread picker picks one of four threads every cycle. The next stage in the pipeline decodes instructions. Instructions that use general-purpose registers are sent to the usual x-86 pipeline. Vector instructions are sent to either the U- or V-pipe. Both these pipes are part of the Vector Processing Unit (VPU) extension of the coprocessor core. The U-pipe can execute all vector instructions. The V-pipe can execute only a few. Notice that the Add/Mult unit of the U-pipe has four cycle latency, which is the same as the number of threads. So if each thread issues an Add/Mult instruction during every cycle in round-robin scheduling, that unit can be kept completely busy. Because the V-pipe is separate from the U-pipe, the coprocessor core can issue two vector instructions in the same cycle.

We look at three vector instructions. The first of them is VMOVAPD. In usage such as

```
vmovapd (%rdi), %zmm0
```

the content of %rdi must be a 64-byte-aligned pointer. This instruction moves 64 bytes from the location %rdi points to the destination register %zmm0. In general, VMOVAPD can be used to move 64 bytes of data between ZMM registers or between

---

[13]The Xeon Phi pipeline is described in the document *Intel Xeon Phi Coprocessor Vector Microarchitecture*, September 2012.

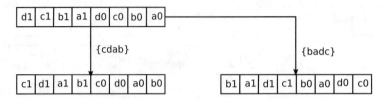

Figure 7.5: Two swizzle operations applied to a ZMM register. Each entry shown is a double-precision number.

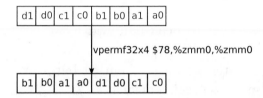

Figure 7.6: Effect of applying the `vpermf32x4` instruction to a ZMM register. Each entry shown is a double-precision number.

memory and a ZMM register. Of the three instructions we look at, this is the only one that can be scheduled on the V-pipe.

The next instruction we look at is **VFMADD231PD**. FMADD refers to fast multiply and add. As before, V and PD refer to "vector" and "packed double." The effect of

```
vfmadd231pd %zmm3, %zmm2, %zmm1
```

is equivalent to ZMM1 = ZMM1 + ZMM2 × ZMM3. Each ZMM register holds eight double-precision numbers. Each set of eight is subjected to the multiply-add operation. This single instruction is responsible for 16 flops.

The first source of the **VFMADD231PD** can be swizzled in two different ways.

```
vfmadd231pd %zmm3{cdab}, %zmm2, %zmm1
vfmadd231pd %zmm3{badc}, %zmm2, %zmm1
```

The effect of the swizzles is to permute the eight double-precision numbers stored in ZMM3 before subjecting it to the multiply-add operation. The permutations that the two swizzles {cdab} and {badc} correspond to are shown in figure 7.5. The 64-byte register is divided into halves, with each half holding four double-precision numbers, and both halves are subject to the same permutation.

The final instruction we consider is `vpermf32x4` shown in figure 7.6. The instruction

```
vpermf32x4 $78, %zmm0, %zmm0
```

treats the `ZMM0` register as divided into four blocks of 128 bits. In figure 7.6, these blocks are d0-d1, c0-c1, b0-b1, and a0-a1. The number 78 determines the permutation that is effected. In binary, 78 is $01|00|11|10$ or $4^3 \times 1 + 4^2 \times 0 + 4 \times 3 + 4^0 \times 2$. Therefore, in the permutation that takes effect, the block in second position moves to the zeroth position, the block in third position to the first position, and vice versa. Thus, we get the permutation shown in figure 7.6, which swaps the lower half of the ZMM register with the upper half. This instruction cannot be executed on the V-pipe.

A microkernel for matrix multiplication

The assembly code shown in figure 7.7 implements a function with the following declaration:

```
asm8x1x8(double *A, double *B, double *C);
```

All three pointers must be 64-byte aligned. An 8×1 column is stored in `A[]`, and a 1×8 row is stored in `B[]`. The function computes their outer product AB and adds it to the 8×8 matrix stored in `C[]`. To simplify implementation, the storage format of C is a little odd.

Figure 7.8 shows the eight diagonals of an 8×8 matrix. It is assumed that C is stored diagonal by diagonal, with the eight entries of diagonal 1 preceding those of diagonal 2 and so on. This is not an overly restrictive assumption. If each 8×8 submatrix of a large $8n \times 8n$ matrix is stored in this skewed manner, passing back and forth between the skewed and unskewed formats needs to be done only once and is much cheaper than the cost of multiplying such large matrices.

In figure 7.7, the function name `asm8x1x8()` is mangled according to C++/Linux conventions (lines 2 and 3). A C++ program (but not a C program) can call the function as simply `asm8x1x8()`. The first three arguments, which are pointers to the matrices A, B, and C, are passed in the three registers `%rdi`, `%rsi`, and `%rdx` (lines 4, 5, and 6), conforming with the GNU/Linux convention.

On lines 7 and 8, the matrices A and B are loaded into the registers `ZMM0` and `ZMM1`, respectively. On line 9, the first diagonal of C is loaded into `ZMM2`. On line 11, the first diagonal of C is updated using the `vfmadd231pd` instruction.

```
 1   .align      16,0x90
 2   .globl      _Z8asm8x1x8PdS_S_
 3   _Z8asm8x1x8PdS_S_:
 4   # parameter  1: %rdi  (a)
 5   # parameter  2: %rsi  (b)
 6   # parameter  3: %rdx  (c)
 7         vmovapd (%rdi), %zmm0
 8         vmovapd (%rsi), %zmm1
 9         vmovapd (%rdx), %zmm2
10
11         vfmadd231pd %zmm1, %zmm0, %zmm2
12         vmovapd 64(%rdx), %zmm3
13         vfmadd231pd %zmm1{cdab}, %zmm0, %zmm3
14
15         vmovapd 128(%rdx), %zmm4
16         vfmadd231pd %zmm1{badc}, %zmm0, %zmm4
17
18         vmovapd 192(%rdx), %zmm5
19         vmovapd %zmm1{badc}, %zmm1
20         vfmadd231pd %zmm1{cdab}, %zmm0, %zmm5
21
22         vpermf32x4 $78, %zmm1, %zmm1
23
24         vmovapd 256(%rdx), %zmm6
25         vfmadd231pd %zmm1, %zmm0, %zmm6
26
27         vmovapd 320(%rdx), %zmm7
28         vfmadd231pd %zmm1{cdab}, %zmm0, %zmm7
29
30         vmovapd 384(%rdx), %zmm8
31         vfmadd231pd %zmm1{badc}, %zmm0, %zmm8
32
33         vmovapd 448(%rdx), %zmm9
34         vmovapd %zmm1{badc}, %zmm1
35         vfmadd231pd %zmm1{cdab}, %zmm0, %zmm9
36
37         vmovapd %zmm2, (%rdx)
38         vmovapd %zmm3, 64(%rdx)
39         vmovapd %zmm4, 128(%rdx)
40         vmovapd %zmm5, 192(%rdx)
41         vmovapd %zmm6, 256(%rdx)
42         vmovapd %zmm7, 320(%rdx)
43         vmovapd %zmm8, 384(%rdx)
44         vmovapd %zmm9, 448(%rdx)
45
46         ret
```

Figure 7.7: Assembly code for $C = C + AB$, where A, B, C are 8×1, 1×8, and 8×8 matrices, respectively.

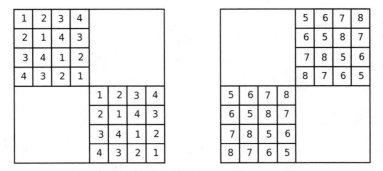

Figure 7.8: Eight diagonals of an 8×8 matrix.

On line 12, the second diagonal is loaded into the register ZMM3. When it is updated on line 13, notice that the ZMM1 register storing the matrix B is swizzled as {cdab}. The {badc} swizzle is used on line 16 to update the third diagonal. Both the swizzles are used (lines 19 and 20) to update the fourth diagonal.

On line 22, the upper and lower halves of the ZMM1 register, which stores the matrix B, are swapped. The other four diagonals are updated and then stored back in C (lines 37 through 44).

This program may be modified to compute the product of an $8 \times n$ matrix A, stored in column-major order, with an $n \times 8$ matrix B, stored in row-major order. The product of those two matrices may be computed as the sum of n outer products of 8×1 matrices (any of n columns of A) with 1×8 matrices (the corresponding row of B). Each product is added to the matrix C. To modify the program, one simply has to step through the columns of A and the rows of B while reproducing the logic of figure 7.7. The loading and storing of C needs to be done just once. The choice of n should be large enough to result in many arithmetic operations for every load/store instruction but not so large as to overflow the instruction cache.

With $n = 48$, this microkernel, running on 244 threads, reaches 473 GFlops/sec on a single Phi coprocessor. The theoretical peak is slightly more than twice as high. Even getting to 50% of peak bandwidth is not bad. We have seen that MKL's optimized FFT reaches only 15% of the peak. For matrix multiplication, the microkernel can get close to 100% of the peak bandwidth, but writing such a microkernel will require much greater attention to the instruction pipeline. We have paid little attention to the U- and V-pipes. In a nearly optimal microkernel, one has to arrange for almost all non fast-multiply-add instructions to go to the V-pipe. There are many bypasses between pipeline stages, which makes it less expensive to reuse recently computed destinations as sources. So one must take advantage of bypasses as well. These topics as well as instruction alignment are discussed in chapter 3.

Matrix multiplication using MKL

The function `mmult()`, whose definition follows, assumes all three matrices A, B, C to be square of dimension `dim` and to be stored in column-major order with leading dimension equal to `dim`. It makes a single call to the MKL library. The matrices are stored in the arrays `a[]`, `b[]`, and `c[]`, respectively.

```
__declspec(target(mic))
void mmult(double *a, double *b, double *c, int dim){
      char transa[3] = "N";
      char transb[3] = "N";

      double alpha = 1;
      dgemm(transa, transb, &dim, &dim, &dim, &alpha,
            a, &dim, b, &dim,
            &alpha,
            c, &dim);
}
```

This function `mmult()` may be called from the host, natively from a MIC device, or offloaded to a MIC device from the host. It may also be called from the host with automatic offload.

With automatic offload, the details of how the operation is offloaded to the MIC device are left to the MKL library. The syntax for automatic offload is shown below.

```
mkl_mic_enable();
mmult(a, b, c, dim);
mkl_mic_disable();
```

The MKL functions to enable and disable automatic offload must be called from the host.

On the 2.7 GHz AVX host (see table A.1 for its full name), the floating point throughput is 100% of the theoretical peak (see table 7.5). In fact, for $n = 8,000$,

n	AVX (host)	MIC (native)	MIC (offload)	MKL Auto
8,000	352 GF/s	837 GF/s	299 GF/s	731 GF/s
10,000	333 GF/s	845 GF/s	365 GF/s	926 GF/s
12,000	339 GF/s	859 GF/s	412 GF/s	1214 GF/s

Table 7.5: Floating point bandwidths in GFlops/sec.

the floating point throughput is slightly greater than the theoretical limit of 345.6 GFlops/s. The discrepancy is probably because the in-core "turbo" frequency of 3.5 GHz is greater than the input clock frequency of 2.7 GHz.

The MIC device reaches nearly 85% of its peak floating point throughput when run natively. Offloading the function mmult() to MKL does not do so well for unknown reasons. MKL appears to be set up for automatic offload. If part of the computation is to be offloaded to a MIC device, it is better to leave the offloading to MKL. With automatic offloading and $n = 12,000$, MKL manages to nearly sum the floating point throughputs of the MIC device and the AVX host to reach 1.2 TFlops/sec.[14]

Exercise 7.3.1. The name of the function asm8x1x8() is mangled according to C++ conventions. Unmangle the name and supply a header file to make the function callable from both C and C++.

Exercise 7.3.2. Write an LU factorization routine for the AVX-512 instruction set of the Xeon Phi. Compare with the speed of MKL library's implementation of the same function. By what factor do you expect your routine to fall short if it does not use any instruction-level optimizations?

---

[14]The 1 TFlops/sec barrier was crossed by a supercomputer for the first time in 1997.

Chapter 8

Special Topic: Graphics Coprocessor Programming Using CUDA

Graphics libraries such as DirectX and OpenGL are widely used in the computer gaming industry. The graphics libraries provide a number of functions for rendering, shading, texture manipulation, and similar tasks. Graphics devices accelerate the execution of such library functions. If a suitable graphics card and driver are installed, these functions are sent from the processor to the graphics card for faster execution.

The graphics cards are powerful processors in their own right. A high-end graphics card may have more than a billion transistors, same as a processor package. The instruction set and design of the graphics processor reflects its principal function. The graphics processor prefers to think in terms of pixels, and the instruction set architecture supports threading at a very fine level. If there is 1 GB of data to be handled, an OpenMP program may divide the data between a dozen threads. For a graphics processor program, it is natural to split the data between 10^4 or 10^5 or even more threads.

Despite the focus on pixels and images, the capabilities of graphics processors are fairly general. Such is the diversity and changeability of functions in DirectX and other libraries that it makes little sense for a graphics processor to attempt to hardwire the functions directly. Instead the instruction set architecture is built up using primitives, many of which are fairly general purpose. The graphics device is not flexible enough to run a web server or word processor effectively, but may be used as a coprocessor in many scientific applications.

As long as graphics devices and drivers are set up mainly to run graphics library functions, it is very hard to use them for scientific computing. In 2007, NVIDIA introduced the Compute Unified Device Architecture (CUDA) framework. CUDA added software layers to the device drivers and the GNU C/C++ compiler to greatly simplify the task of programming graphics coprocessors for scientific use.

The use of graphics coprocessors in scientific computation became an immediate sensation. Although there was some hype, it is undeniable that graphics coprocessors were significantly faster for many important applications. The innovative design of NVIDIA's Tesla, Fermi, and now Kepler and Maxwell devices gives a hint of what can be done with a billion transistors to go beyond the constraints of the x86 architecture and its reliance on backward binary compatibility. Systems with NVIDIA coprocessors began to appear near the top of the Top 500 list in 2010.

Intel, the foremost champion of the x86 architecture, has closed the gap considerably to the extent that the topmost supercomputer in 2015 uses Intel processors as well as coprocessors. One advantage enjoyed by the CUDA framework is its compilation model, which is the topic of section 8.2. Graphics devices attain backward compatibility using an intermediate assembly language that can be mapped to a variety of instruction sets. Removing the constraint of backward binary compatibility creates greater room for rapid innovation in the design of the graphics hardware. It may lower the cost of design as well.

A disadvantage is that programming graphics coprocessors is harder, much harder, than programming processors and likely to remain that way. In OpenMP, we may split the problem across threads or processes and write much of the program as if it were a sequential program. It is true that subtleties of parallel programming can never be eliminated entirely. Yet the difficulties of parallel programming may be localized to a considerable extent, which is true with Pthreads as well. Such a thing is not possible with CUDA's highly refined parallelism. A thread must always be conscious that it is part of a warp of 32 threads and that multiple warps compose a thread block. The arrangement of threads into blocks and grids affects the structure of even the

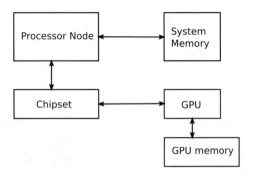

Figure 8.1: Graphics Processing Unit (GPU) is connected to the chipset via the PCIe bus. Both system memory and GPU memory are DRAM.

innermost loops. Writing a program to sum a sequence of numbers becomes quite a task, as we will see in section 8.2.

In the previous chapter, we pointed out the widening gap between programming skill and what it takes to program modern computers optimally. This is a particular concern with respect to CUDA, where even simple tasks can require complex programming. Gamers who pay for graphics devices surely make good use of them, and if Apple Computers is profitable, the people who pay for its products make heavy use of what they buy. In comparison, this author is not convinced that coprocessor deployment in the scientific world matches their utilization.

The organization of this chapter is similar to that of the previous chapter on the Xeon Phi. Section 8.1 introduces the architecture of NVIDIA's coprocessors, and section 8.2 is an introduction to programming those devices using CUDA. The examples in section 8.3 further illustrate how to program graphics coprocessors in relation to architectural considerations. The location of the Graphics Processing Unit (GPU) relative to the processor node and the chip set is similar to that of the Phi as shown in figure 8.1.

In the introduction to the previous chapter, we stated an opinion that coprocessors break modularity at the hardware level. This opinion is applicable to an even greater extent to GPU computing. As long as graphics devices are used to accelerate libraries such as DirectX, their usage is perfectly modular. In effect, the graphics device is a hardware library and fits nicely into the modular framework. Indeed, the traditional use of graphics devices is an excellent example of modularity at the hardware level. When graphics devices are used for general-purpose computing within the

CUDA framework, the situation is different. The CUDA model with its highly refined parallelism differs radically from ordinary C/C++. The heterogeneity that results is quite severe.

The basis of modular programming is to break up a task into subtasks and the subtasks into yet more subtasks in a hierarchical manner. Uniformity or near uniformity in subdivision promotes modularity. In GPU computing, GPU devices with pixel-level parallelism compete with processor packages. The programming models are quite different. It is difficult to sustain modularity when faced with discordance at such a fundamental level, and the resulting programs are likely to be difficult to maintain.

8.1   Graphics coprocessor architecture

The graphics device sits next to the processor node, as in figure 8.1. The K20 graphics device we use has 13 streaming multiprocessors. Each of these is roughly comparable to a processor core of the 16-core 2.7 GHz AVX host (for the full name of this computer, see table A.1).

Inside a streaming multiprocessor is different from a processor core. In section 8.1.1, we begin by examining the capability of the graphics device using a simple program. This program is run on the host and involves none of the complexity of CUDA programming. This program may be used to detect a number of available parameters, such as the major and minor revision number, clock rate, and available graphics memory.

Sections 8.1.2 and 8.1.3 introduce utilities that simplify programming. These utilities, too, run on the host. Section 8.1.2 presents a simple class for moving data to and back from the graphics device. The timing class in section 8.1.3 uses CUDA events but has a `tic()/toc()` interface similar to the `TimeStamp` class.

Section 8.1.4 is an overview of the K20's architecture. Basic knowledge of registers, warps, and thread blocks is essential for CUDA programming.

8.1.1   Graphics processor capability

NVIDIA graphics processors come in a great variety. The number of devices that are CUDA enabled and are of compute capability anywhere from 1.0 to 3.5 is more than

100. The first task is to find out exactly which graphics processor is available and what its capability is.

On a single computer system, several CUDA-enabled graphics processors may be available via the PCIe bus. With the following two lines, we can find out the number of CUDA-enabled graphics processors available:

```
int count;
cudaGetDeviceCount(&count);
```

CUDA programs look much like C programs. However, certain parts of the program run on the host, which is typically an x86 processor running either Linux or Windows, and certain other parts run on the device, which is the graphics processor. The `cudaGetDeviceCount()` function runs on the host. By invoking the operating system or some other means, it finds out the number of devices of capability 1.0 or higher. A program using this function call can be compiled using `nvcc`, which is NVIDIA's compiler driver. The compiler driver `nvcc` is a sophisticated wrapper around `gcc`, and in this case all that `nvcc` has to do is link the library in which `cudaGetDeviceCount()` is defined. No special option to `nvcc` is necessary. This and other similar functions are declared in `cuda_runtime.h`.[1]

Once we know the device count, we can find out about each device.

```
cudaDeviceProp prop;
cudaGetDeviceProperties(&prop, i);
```

Here `cudaDeviceProp` is a structure type with fields corresponding to various properties of the device. The structure is defined in the `cuda_runtime.h` header file. We do not have to bother to include the header file explicitly in our C++ program because `nvcc` will include the right header automatically. The `cudaGetDeviceProperties()` function may talk to the operating system to find out the properties of device number `i`, where `i` is the second argument in the function call. Alternatively, the information about device properties may be left in some location during the installation of the `nvcc` driver. In either case, no code is generated that must run on the graphics device.

The `prop` variable, which is set up in this way, has information about the graphics device. The line

---

[1] The three main sources of CUDA documentation are (*CUDA C Programming Guide*, August, 2014), (*CUDA Compiler Driver NVCC*, August, 2014), and (*CUDA Runtime API*, August, 2014). Functions like `cudaGetDeviceCount()` are documented in the last of these sources.

```
      cout<<"Device Name: "<<prop.name<<endl;
```

can be used to print the name of the device. Other fields of the structure **prop** are

```
clockRate
major
minor
totalGlobalMem
l2CacheSize
sharedMemPerBlock
regsPerBlock
maxThreadsPerMultiProcessor
warpSize
maxThreadsPerBlock
maxThreadsDim
maxGridSize
deviceOverlap
```

Part of the information returned on our machine was as follows.

```
            Device Count: 1
             Device Name: Tesla K20m
      Clock rate in GHz: 0.7055
  Major revision number: 3
  Minor revision number: 5
     Global memory in GB: 5.03271
```

The rest of the output will be given later. The machine we are using has only one graphics device, and it is Tesla K20m. The name of the device is slightly confusing. Tesla, Fermi, Kepler, and Maxwell are the names of successive generations of NVIDIA microarchitecture. The K20m's microarchitecture is Kepler. The Tesla in its name does not indicate its microarchitecture but appears to signify that it is targeted at the scientific computing market.

Its clock speed is only 705.5 MHz. Having a slow clock enables the K20m to be bigger and carry more transistors.

The major and minor revision numbers give the compute capability as 3.5. Graphics device functionality depends on the compute capability. For instance, only devices of capability 1.3 or higher support double-precision arithmetic.

The K20 device has 5.03 GB of memory. This DRAM memory is directly connected to the graphics device (see figure 8.1). For a large-scale computation, 5 GB of memory may prove to be too little.

8.1.2   Host and device memory

To set up any computation on the graphics device, data must be transferred from host to device memory. To retrieve the result of a computation on the graphics device, data must be transferred in the other direction from device to host memory. We use the following C++ class to transfer between host and device memory:

```
 1  template<class ttype > class dhstmem{
 2  private:
 3        ttype   *devicemem;
 4        ttype   *hostmem;
 5        int n;
 6        cudaError_t errcode;
 7  public:
 8        dhstmem(long int nin){
 9              . . .
10        }
11        ~dhstmem(){
12              . . .
13        }
14        ttype   *device(){return devicemem;}
15        ttype   *host(){return hostmem;}
16        void device2host(){
17              . . .
18        }
19        void host2device(){
20              . . .
21        }
22  };
```

This class is templated. It can be used for data of type double, int, or some other type. The private section of the class is given in full on lines 3 to 6, but the definitions of some of the public member functions are not shown. In the source, the definitions are included within the class itself but have been removed for better readability. They will be given later.

If we want memory equal to a million doubles, we can get that as follows:

```
dhstmem<double> dhmem(1000*1000);
```

The object `dhmem` will hold pointers to a million doubles in device memory and a million doubles in host memory. The private field `dhmem.n` will be set to a million. If we say

```
double *hmem = dhmem.host();
```

then `hmem` becomes a pointer to the million doubles allocated in host memory. This is evident from line 15 of the listing. We can initialize this memory in any way we want. If we say

```
double *dmem = dhmem.device();
```

then `dmem` becomes a pointer to device memory. Although `dmem` is declared and defined on the host, we are not allowed to use it in host code to touch device memory. Typically, `dmem` is passed by the host code as an argument to a function that will run on the graphics device. The function that runs on the graphics device is allowed to use `dmem` to access device memory. Despite its definition to be of type `double *`, `dmem` is not an ordinary pointer. In some way, it should encode information about memory set aside on the device. When a device function is called with this pointer as an argument, that information travels from the host to the device through a device driver.

Suppose we initialize host memory and want to copy it to device memory. The following call does that:

```
dhmem.host2device();
```

After this function call, the data in the host memory that `hmem` points to will be copied to device memory that `dmem` points to. A call such as this has to be routed through the device driver. Because the graphics processor is a peripheral device connected using the PCIe bus, the only way the host can access graphics memory is by talking to the graphics coprocessor using its device driver. Conversely,

```
dhmem.device2host();
```

copies from the device to host memory.

The class constructor and destructor are defined as follows:

```
1        dhstmem(long int nin){
2               n = nin;
3               errcode = cudaMalloc((void **)&devicemem,
4                            n*sizeof(ttype));
5               assrt(errorcode==cudaSuccess);
6               hostmem = new ttype[n];
7        }
8        ~dhstmem(){
9               delete[] hostmem;
10              cudaFree(devicemem);
11       }
```

The call to `cudaMalloc()` on line 3 looks somewhat like a call to `malloc()` to allocate memory. A notable difference is that whereas `malloc()` returns the pointer to allocated memory, `cudaMalloc()` returns an error code. The first argument of `cudaMalloc()` is an address, and the location that address points to is altered to correspond to the allocated memory. In the case of `malloc()` or `new[]` (line 6), the memory allocated is obtained from the operating system. In the case of `cudaMalloc()`, the memory allocated must be obtained from the graphics device. These definitions are inside the class, which is why the names of the constructor and the destructor are not qualified using `template<class ttype> dhstmem::`.

The public member functions used for transferring between host and device memory are defined as follows:

```
void device2host(){
     errcode = cudaMemcpy(hostmem, devicemem,
        n*sizeof(ttype),cudaMemcpyDeviceToHost);
}
void host2device(){
     errcode = cudaMemcpy(devicemem, hostmem,
        n*sizeof(ttype),cudaMemcpyHostToDevice);
}
```

Both member functions use `cudaMemcpy()` to effect the transfer (lines 2 and 9). The last argument is either of the flags

```
cudaMemcpyDeviceToHost OR cudaMemcpyHostToDevice
```

to indicate the direction of the transfer. The function `cudaMemcpy()` and the flags are declared and defined in header files and libraries that are automatically included and linked by the `nvcc` driver.

8.1.3   Timing CUDA kernels

The simplest programs have much to teach us as long as we time them carefully. Therefore, we begin by looking at mechanisms to time kernels that run on the graphics coprocessor.

We use the following class to time the graphics processor. The private data members of the class are shown in full. For the public member functions, the interface is shown, and the definitions will be given later.

```
class hstTimer{
private:
    cudaEvent_t start, stop;
public:
    hstTimer(){...};
    ~hstTimer(){...};
    void tic(){...};
    float toc(){...};
};
```

The private data members are two events named `start` and `stop`. The events will be "sent" to the graphics processor to record the time on the graphics processor and will be relayed back to the host.

To time a piece of code, we can use the class as follows:

```
hstTimer hclk;
hclk.tic();
[code]
float tms = hclk.toc();
```

The variable `tms` gets set to the time elapsed between `tic()` and `toc()` in milliseconds.

All member functions of `hstTimer` are defined within the scope of the class. Therefore, the names of the member functions are not qualified with `hstTimer::` in their definitions shown below. The constructor and the destructor are unremarkable.

```
hstTimer(){
        cudaEventCreate(&start);
        cudaEventCreate(&stop);
}
~hstTimer(){
        cudaEventDestroy(start);
        cudaEventDestroy(stop);
}
```

The events `start` and `stop` are probably opaque pointers.[2] Therefore, it is natural that their addresses are passed during event creation and the pointers themselves are passed during event destruction. It is good practice to check the error codes returned during event creation and destruction, although we have not done so here.

The member functions `tic()` and `toc()` are defined as follows:

```
1      void tic(){
2              cudaEventRecord(start, 0);
3      }
4      float toc(){
5              float time;
6              cudaEventRecord(stop, 0);
7              cudaEventSynchronize(start);
8              cudaEventSynchronize(stop);
9              cudaEventElapsedTime(&time, start, stop);
10             return time;//milliseconds
11     }
```

The call to `cudaEventRecord()` on line 2 has the effect of sending the event from the host to the graphics device in a streaming fashion. The second argument, which is

---

[2]Opaque pointers point to structures whose internal details are either hidden from us or we don't care about.

zero on line 2, merits discussion. The host can talk to the graphics device over several streams, and the second argument can be used to indicate the stream on which the event is recorded. But if the second argument is 0, the event is recorded after all preceding operations in the CUDA context have been completed.

The `stop` event is recorded by the member function `tic()` on line 6. When CUDA events are recorded using function calls, such as the ones on lines 2 and 6, the function call returns immediately after sending the event to the graphics device. It does not wait until the event is actually recorded. The function calls are nonblocking. The events `stop` and `start` are not available to be read on the host immediately after `cudaEventRecord()`. The calls to `cudaEventSynchronize()` (lines 7 and 8) block until the events are ready to be read. On line 9, the two events are read, and the time elapsed is calculated.

8.1.4   Warps and thread blocks

The K20's design is so different from that of conventional processors that to program it we need to understand a few things about its architecture. A sketch of its microarchitecture is shown in figure 8.2.

To get a better sense of the microarchitecture, we return to the `cudaDeviceProp` program of section 7.1 and show some more of its output.

```
      Total L2 cache (in bytes): 1310720
   Shared memory per MP (in bytes): 49152
      Number of registers per MP: 65536
      Max number of threads per MP: 2048
```

The heart of the microarchitecture is the streaming multiprocessor, and there are 13 of these in Kepler. The K20 has 1.3 MB of L2 cache on chip, a small figure compared to the 20 MB cache of its 2.7 GHz AVX host. The L2 cache is shared by the 13 multiprocessors.

Each multiprocessor has 64 KB of on-chip memory for itself. This memory is split between L1 cache and shared memory. The use of shared memory is under program control. On the K20, 48 KB is assigned to shared memory by default, and only 16 KB is left for the L1 cache. The split between L1 cache and shared memory can be changed by calling a function in the CUDA runtime library.

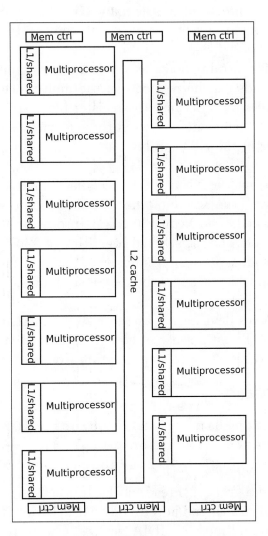

Figure 8.2: The Kepler microarchitecture consists of 13 streaming multiprocessors and 6 memory controllers.

The K20 coprocessor's 13 streaming multiprocessors are comparable with the AVX host's 16 processors. The K20 begins to look very different from its Sandy Bridge host if we note that each multiprocessor has as many as $64K = 65,536$ registers, each 32 bits wide. The AVX processor's register file of sixteen 256-bit YMM registers looks puny in comparison.

A large register file is central to how the K20 and other graphics coprocessors work. A large number of threads can be resident on the multiprocessor, and each thread gets its own subset of registers. Because the register file is split between threads, the streaming multiprocessor can switch between threads with zero overhead.

Each multiprocessor in the K20 can hold at most 2,048 threads. Therefore, each thread gets at least 64 registers.

When Intel brought out the Xeon Phi to reclaim ground in supercomputing, the large number of registers of the K20 and other graphics coprocessors was a key parameter the Xeon Phi matched. The Xeon Phi has 61 processor cores with four threads resident on each processor. The register file consisting of 32 512-bit ZMM registers is replicated for each thread. So the total number of registers on the Phi is equivalent to 125K 32-bit registers, which is approximately a sixth of the number of registers on the K20.

A thread on a graphics device such as the K20 is different from a thread on an x86 machine or the Phi. To get a sense of how threads work in the K20, we give the rest of the output of the `cudaDeviceProp` program from section 7.1.

```
        Number of threads per warp: 32
  Maximum number of threads per block: 1024
  Maximum of each dimension of block: 1024 x 1024 x 64
  Maximum of each dimension of grid: --->
                ---> 2147483647 x 65535 x 65535
```

Warps, thread blocks, and grids of thread blocks are the basis of GPU programming.

On the graphics device, a thread never really exists by itself. Threads are grouped into warps. On the K20 and most NVIDIA devices, a warp is 32 threads. The warp is fundamental to GPU programming. Instructions are executed by the entire warp and not by individual threads.

The threads in a warp must execute exactly the same instruction. If some threads in a warp diverge as a result of if-statements, for example, then the threads that do not enter the if-block idle and wait while other threads are still in the if-block. Thread

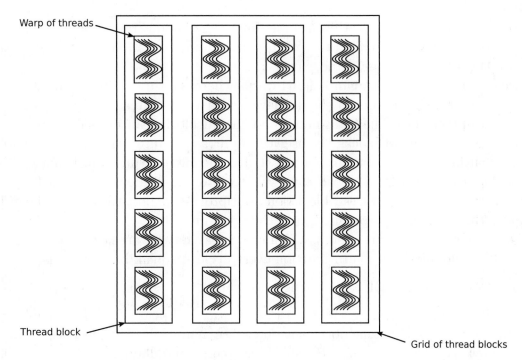

Warp of threads

Thread block

Grid of thread blocks

Figure 8.3: Warps, thread blocks, and grids.

divergence within a warp can incur heavy penalties. Because a K20 multiprocessor has a limit of 2,048 threads, at most 64 warps can be resident on a single multiprocessor.

In the Kepler microarchitecture, a multiprocessor selects up to four warps to execute during each cycle. Double-precision instructions use two 32-bit registers. Therefore, only two of the four warps can be executing double-precision instructions. Kepler has the ability to dispatch two instructions per warp during every cycle. Because the 755 MHz K20's cycles are so long, the ability to dispatch two instructions per cycle is probably essential.

If threads are grouped into warps, warps are in turn grouped into thread blocks, as shown in figure 8.3. On the K20, a thread block can have at most 1,024 threads or 32 warps. Threads are scheduled onto multiprocessors one thread block at a time. Switching between warps that are already resident on a multiprocessor has zero overhead. However, scheduling a new thread block will incur overhead.

In figure 8.3, the thread block shown is one dimensional. In general, the threads in a thread block can be two or even three dimensional and arranged along x, y, and z axes. For purposes of grouping threads in a multidimensional block into warps, the x axis takes precedence over y and y over z.

Because a multiprocessor can hold 64 warps whereas a thread block can hold only 32 on the K20, in general, one should have at least two thread blocks on each of the 13 multiprocessors. The total number of thread blocks can be many more than 26, however. The thread blocks themselves are arranged in a grid. The grid is one dimensional in figure 8.3, but in general it may be two or three dimensional. The number of thread blocks in a grid can even go into the millions. There will be an overhead to schedule new thread blocks on multiprocessors, but the overhead can be hidden if there is sufficient parallelism in the program.

The K20 has 13 multiprocessors, which can dispatch two warps executing a fused-add-multiply double-precision instruction every cycle. Its peak bandwidth is

$$13\,\text{MPs} \times 2\,\text{warps/cycle/MP} \times 32\,\text{instructions/warp} \times 2\,\text{flops/instruction} \times 0.706\,\text{GHz}$$

or 1.17 TFlops/sec, exceeding the Xeon Phi's theoretical peak of 1.064 TFlops/sec.

Kepler devices have six memory controllers (see figure 8.2). The interface to memory is 40 bytes or 320 bits wide. Thanks to prefetching and doubling of data rate, the effective memory clock is 5.2 GHz, although the actual clock will have much longer cycles. The theoretical peak bandwidth to memory is 208 GB/s.

In Kepler devices, the latency to memory is between 200 and 400 cycles. The latency to memory can be more than half a microsecond and is not far short of Infiniband network latencies. It takes a great deal of parallelism in the instruction stream to hide such a long latency. If there is sufficient parallelism, memory load/store instructions can be issued every cycle by all the executing warps and overlapped so that lots of memory instructions complete every cycle and effectively hide the long latency to memory.

Exercise 8.1.1. Print the `multiProcessorCount` field of the `prop` structure and find out the number of multiprocessors on your graphics device.

Exercise 8.1.2. Use the `dhstmem` class to determine the latency of transfers between host and device. Note that if a copy from host to device memory is less than 64 KB, the `cudaMemcpy()` function is nonblocking.

Exercise 8.1.3. Use the `dhstmem` class to determine the bandwidth of transfers between host and device memory.

Exercise 8.1.4. CUDA provides a facility to associate memory transfers with streams. Memory transfers associated with different streams may be overlapped. Modify the `dhstmem` class to use streams and replace `cudaMemcpy()` by `cudaMemcpyAsync()`, its nonblocking version. Use the new class to estimate bidirectional bandwidth, with transfers into device overlapped with transfers from device.

Exercise 8.1.5. Compare the `hstTimer` and `TimeStamp` classes and determine how closely they agree.

Exercise 8.1.6. Explain why a slower clock allows the K20 to pack more transistors.

Exercise 8.1.7. Each multiprocessor of the K20 has 192 single-precision "CUDA cores." Use this fact to explain why the peak single-precision floating point throughput is thrice, and not just twice, the double-precision throughput.

8.2   Introduction to CUDA

Section 8.2.1 uses the Leibniz example to introduce rudiments of CUDA programming. The first program to sum the Leibniz series relies on help from the x86 processor. The program introduces syntax for dealing with thread blocks and grids. Even for this simple program, one needs to ensure that sufficiently many thread blocks are created and that each thread block has the right dimensions.

The other program in section 8.2.1 also sums the Leibniz series but without taking help from the x86 processors. In this program, each thread computes part of the sum, and all the threads add their portion to the global result. For correctness, accesses of the global result by individual threads must be mutually exclusive. Mutual exclusion is enforced using an atomic exchange instruction supported in CUDA. The program shows how to handle warp divergence that arises during mutual exclusion.

The program for summing the Leibniz series is faster on the K20 than on the Phi by a factor of 2.5. The Phi is faster for some programs and the K20 for others. The factor of 2.5 must not be treated as a universal value. In the case of the Leibniz series, the K20's greater speed seems to be due to greater facility in handling divisions than x86 cores.

The first program for summing the Leibniz series is perhaps not so much harder to code than the corresponding OpenMP program, which runs on the Phi or any x86 machine. However, the second program, in which the entire sum is found on the K20, is easily 100 times harder to code. In addition, the enforcement of mutual exclusion implies that there is a cost associated with creating too many thread blocks. The ability to create many thread blocks makes CUDA programming more flexible. However, for summing the Leibniz series, it can slow the program down considerably.

Section 8.2.2 introduces the CUDA compilation model. Every CUDA program may be compiled into PTX, which is an intermediate language, or into machine instructions, or both. If the same program is run on a machine with a newer instruction set, the CUDA driver extracts the PTX from the executable and automatically generates code for the newer instruction set before running the executable.

8.2.1   Summing the Leibniz series

Threads are grouped into warps and warps into thread blocks. Thread blocks are arranged in a grid. The hierarchical grouping of threads can never be forgotten in writing CUDA programs. Thus, it is useful to have a utility header file `const.hh` that defines constants that other programs can reference.

```
const int NWARP = 32;
const int THinBLK = 1024;
const int BLKinMP = 2;
const int NMP = 13;

const int SQRTT = 32;
const int MAXTHMP = 2048;
const int GPUCLKMHZ = 706;
```

NWARP is the number of threads in a warp.[3] THinBLK is the maximum number of threads in a block. In our programs, the number of threads in a block is always set to this value. BLKinMP is the maximum number of blocks that can reside on a multiprocessor, assuming each thread block to have 1,024 threads. The number of multiprocessors is NMP. SQRTT is the square root of the number of threads in a block. It is useful when working with two-dimensional thread blocks. The other two consts are self-explanatory.

---

[3]Alternatively, the CUDA defined variable `warpSize` may be used to determine the number of threads in a warp.

The only parameter we vary when launching threads is the total number of blocks, which is denoted `NBLK` later. This is typically at least equal to `BLKinMP*NMP`, or 26, but can be much larger.

Summing with help from the CPU

Our first program for summing the Leibniz series

$$\pi = \frac{4}{1} - \frac{4}{3} + \frac{4}{5} - \frac{4}{7} + \cdots$$

on the K20 does not in fact sum the series entirely. It leaves part of the work to its AVX host. To begin with, we give the skeleton of the function that runs on the graphics device while omitting its body.[4]

```
1  __global__ void
2  __launch_bounds__(THinBLK, BLKinMP)
3  leibniz(long int n, double *result){
4      ...
5  }
```

Evidently, the definition of the `leibniz` function begins in a manner that is quite different from the C++ function definitions we are used to. It looks different because this function runs on the graphics device and not the x86 host.

The `__global__` keyword on line 1 is part of the C language extensions in the CUDA framework. The `__global__` qualifier indicates that the ensuing function definition is meant to run on the graphics device and something more. Not all functions that run on the graphics device are equal. Some of them can be called only from functions that run on the graphics device, and some can be called only from functions that run on the host processor. The `__global__` qualifier introduces a device function that can be called from the host. Such functions are called kernels. Device functions that can be called only by kernels or other device functions are introduced using `__device__`. We encounter such functions later.

Line 2 gives the launch parameters for this kernel. The launch parameters give the number of threads in a thread block and the number of thread blocks expected to be

---

[4]In addition to documentation from NVIDIA, CUDA programming is explained in Sanders and Kandrot (2010) and Kirk and Hwu (2010).

resident on a single multiprocessor.[5] The launch parameters are advisory in nature. They help the **nvcc** compiler determine how many registers to use in compiling the kernel.

The complete definition of the **leibniz()** kernel follows.

```
1  __global__ void
2  __launch_bounds__(THinBLK, BLKinMP)
3  leibniz(long int n, double *result){
4      int tid = threadIdx.x+blockIdx.x*blockDim.x;
5      double ans=0;
6      int step = blockDim.x*gridDim.x;
7      for(long int i=tid; i < n; i+=step)
8          ans = ans + 4.0/(2.0*i+1.0);
9      if(tid%2==1)
10         ans = -ans;
11     result[tid] = ans;
12 }
```

This program introduces four important CUDA defined variables on lines 4 and 6:

> **threadIdx.x, blockIdx.x, blockDim.x, gridDim.x**

These parameters determine the layout of threads (see figure 8.3) and the position of a particular thread within it.

CUDA kernels are never launched one thread at a time. Every time the kernel is launched, we must specify the number of threads in a block and the number of blocks in the grid. Because the Leibniz series is laid out in a line and for simplicity, we assume the thread block and grid to be one dimensional.

If we imagine a thread block as a single vertical column (similar to figure 8.3 but with the threads in a warp laid out vertically), **blockDim.x**, which is the number of threads in a block, is equal to the number of rows. The CUDA-defined variable **threadIdx.x** allows each thread to access its location along a thread block. It is then the same as the row index.

---

[5]Strictly speaking, the launch parameters are an upper bound on the number of threads in a block and a lower bound on the number of blocks resident on a multiprocessor. The bounds are merely advisory.

The number of thread blocks in the grid is equal to `gridDim.x`. In figure 8.3, it is the number of columns. The index of the thread block a particular thread block belongs to is `blockIdx.x`. In the figure, that would be the column index. We mention again that we are assuming the kernel to be launched with one-dimensional thread blocks and grid.

On line 4, each thread computes `tid`, its position in the grid as a whole. The index calculation is identical to the one that arises in locating the (i, j)th entry of an $m \times n$ matrix laid out in an array in column-major format. Its index in the array would be $i + j \times m$. Here, `tid` is set to

```
threadIdx.x+blockIdx.x*blockDim.x
```

in the same fashion.

On line 6, `step` is set equal to the total number of threads. In the loop on lines 7 and 8, each thread picks the term in the Leibniz series that corresponds to its position and skips terms in steps of `step`.

The threads do not attempt to combine their sums into a global sum. On line 11, each thread stores its sum in the location `result[tid]` in global memory. Here global memory refers to the DRAM memory of the graphics processor. The task of adding all the numbers in `result[]` to produce the nth partial sum of the Leibniz series is left to the host processor.

Variables `tid`, `ans`, `step`, and `i` defined on lines 4, 5, 6, and 7, respectively, are local to each thread. They are typically stored in registers.

The host code that invokes the kernel looks as follows:

```
1      /*fac assumed to be defined earlier*/
2      int NBLK = BLKinMP*NMP*fac;
3      int nthreads = THinBLK*NBLK;
4
5      double *dresult, *result;
6      dhstmem<double> dhmem(nthreads);
7      dresult = dhmem.device();
8      result = dhmem.host();
9
10     leibniz<<<NBLK, THinBLK>>>(n, dresult);
11
12     dhmem.device2host();
```

```
13          double ans = 0;
14          for(int i=0; i < nthreads; i++)
15               ans += result[i];
```

The number of thread blocks NBLK is calculated on line 2. On the K20, it is a multiple of 26 with the multiplier being fac. The total number of threads will be NBLK, the number of blocks, times THinBLK, the number of threads per block (1,024 in our program). Because each thread returns its sum in a separate entry of result[], the amount of memory to be allocated on the device is set equal to the number of threads (lines 3 and 6).

Lines 5 through 8 use the templated dhstmem class to allocate memory on the device, which is matched with the same amount of memory allocated on the host. The variable dresult (line 7) is a pointer to device memory and result (line 8) is a pointer to host memory.

The leibniz kernel is invoked on line 10. The parameters inside the angle brackets give the total number of thread blocks and the number of threads in each thread block. For the invocation on line 10, the thread block and grid are both one dimensional. Two- and three-dimensional thread blocks and grids use different syntax. Of course, the kernel has been written with the understanding that the thread blocks and grid used when it is invoked will be one dimensional.

Using triple angular brackets to specify the execution configuration of a kernel invocation, as on line 10, is a sensible choice. By themselves, < and > are relational operators and << and >> are overloaded for output and input in C++. In the kernel invocation

```
leibniz<<<NBLK, THinBLK>>>(n, dresult);
```

the execution configuration specifies the number of thread blocks and the number of threads per thread block.

The arguments of the leibniz() kernel call are n and dresult. The usual pass by value semantics of C and C++ holds. The way values are passed during a kernel call is quite complicated and must involve the device driver. These complications are expertly handled by the CUDA framework and need not concern the programmer. It must be noted that the second argument dresult is a pointer to device memory, not host memory.

If there are too many threads per thread block and the number of registers on an SM is insufficient to accommodate a thread block, the kernel will not launch. The following line may be used to catch errors:

```
printf("CUDA: %s\n",
             cudaGetErrorString(cudaGetLastError()));
```

This error does not occur in our program. As usual, error checking is omitted to improve readability of the code.

Each thread returns its part of the partial sum of the Leibniz series in a location in device memory. On line 12, the device locations are copied to the host, and the host goes on to generate the partial sum of the Leibniz series in the variable `ans`.

A later section will discuss compilation in greater depth. Here we note that if the entire program is in the source file `leibniz_all.cu`, it may be compiled as follows:

```
nvcc -arch=sm_35 -o leibniz_all.exe leibniz_all.cu
```

The 35 in `sm_35` is a reference to the compute capability of the K20 being 3.5.

Warp divergence

On the Phi or AVX host, the OpenMP program for summing the Leibniz series is almost identical to a sequential program. The program splits the work between threads, and after that point each thread runs a sequential program. At the end, the threads must perform a reduction operation to compute the total sum. The task of splitting the work is made automatic by the `parallel for` construct. The reduction can also be done in a number of simple ways.

There are many, many more threads in a CUDA program, and the arrangement of threads into blocks and grids can affect the structure of even the innermost loops. We see this already in the `leibniz()` kernel from the way in which `tid` and `offset` are calculated. This aspect of CUDA programs will become clearer when we try to make the graphics device compute the entire sum without help from the host.

In writing the `leibniz()` kernel, we paid no attention to the fact that threads are dispatched to the execution units in warps. Nor did we heed the fact that all threads in a warp execute the same instruction during the same cycle. This aspect of NVIDIA devices becomes important when making the graphics coprocessor compute the entire Leibniz sum on its own.

Let us consider the manner in which the following code fragment is executed by threads grouped into warps:

```
1        int x = threadIdx.x;
2        if(x%2==0)
3             x = x+1;
4        ans += x;
```

Because a warp is a group of 32 threads that execute the same instruction, the discussion will be more more precise if phrased using K20 instructions. However, the C statements in this code fragment map almost directly to instructions and will suffice just as well.

Let us suppose all 32 threads in some warp execute line 1. Once this warp instruction completes, all threads in the warp will check the condition on line 2. The condition evaluates to 1 (or true) for half the threads in the warp, and it evaluates to 0 for the other threads. The statement on line 3 will correspond to an entire instruction, and when a warp instruction is issued, only half the threads in the warp will be active. The inactive threads do nothing, but they stay in sync with the rest of the warp. Line 4 is executed by all the threads in the warp.

Branch instructions can split the threads in a warp so that only some threads are active in some regions of the code. The hardware has to use data structures to keep track of the execution sequence of the different threads so that it knows which threads are active and which ones are not. Warp divergence means that when a warp instruction is issued, the cores corresponding to the inactive threads must idle. In addition to wasting execution cycles, the manner in which warps diverge and converge has a bearing on program correctness, as we will now see.

Summing it all using atomic instructions

In the following kernel, `result` and `lock` are pointers to single `double` and `int` locations, respectively. The partial sum of the Leibniz series will be put in `*result`.

```
1 //result and lock must be initialized to zero.
2 __global__ void
3 __launch_bounds__(THinBLK, BLKinMP)
4 leibniztotal(long int n, double* result, int* lock){
5        int tid = threadIdx.x+blockIdx.x*blockDim.x;
```

```
 6        double ans=0;
 7        int step = blockDim.x*gridDim.x;
 8        for(long int i=tid; i < n; i+=step)
 9             ans = ans + 4.0/(2.0*i+1.0);
10        if(tid%2==1)
11             ans = -ans;
12        atomicAddDouble(ans, result, lock);
13 }
```

Two possibilities exist for warp divergence in this listing. In the for-loop on lines 8 and 9, n may be a multiple of neither `step` nor the warp size, which will cause exactly one warp to diverge near the end of the loop. All the warps will diverge when executing the conditional on lines 10 and 11.

These two instances of warp divergence have little impact on program efficiency and hide no subtlety related to program correctness. The warp divergence that occurs inside the device function `atomicAddDouble()` called on line 12 has a more subtle effect on program execution.

Each thread calls `atomicAddDouble()` to add its `ans` to the global `*result`. Of course, it is not correct to simply use the statement `*result += ans`. If the threads attempt to simultaneously use the global location `*result`, they will get in each other's way and `*result` will have an unpredictable and inconsistent value. The purpose of `atomicAddDouble()` is to ensure mutual exclusion between the threads and put `*result += ans` in a critical region that is executed by only one thread at a time. Crucially, the global locations `*result` and `*lock` must both be initialized to 0. The threads will use the location `*lock` to coordinate and decide which thread has the permission to enter its critical region.

Our first attempt at implementing `atomicAddDouble()` follows:

```
1 __device__ void atomicAddDouble(double ans,
2             volatile double *result, volatile int *lock){
3       int lockcopy=1;
4       while(lockcopy==1)
5             lockcopy = atomicExch((int *)lock, 1);
6       *result += ans;
7       atomicExch((int *)lock, 0);
8 }
```

This code has a fatal flaw. It will always deadlock.

Let us begin by understanding how this code is supposed to work. On line 1, the qualifier `__device__` is appended to the function definition. This qualifier is another C language extension of the CUDA framework. Functions defined using the `__device__` qualifier may be called by other device functions or kernels but not by host code.

On line 2, the pointers `result` and `lock` are declared with the `volatile` qualifier. The `volatile` qualifier is a hint to the compiler that several threads use these pointers. Therefore, the compiler knows that `*result` and `*lock` may change due to the action of some other thread. Thus, every time `*result` and `*lock` are used, the compiler will generate a reference to global memory and not get by with values cached in registers.

If we go back to the body of the function `atomicAddDouble()`, on line 5 we find the primitive `atomicExch()`. This primitive is provided by CUDA as an extension to the C language. When a thread executes `atomicExch(lock, 1)`, with `lock` a pointer to an `int`, `atomicExch(lock, 1)` will return the content of the location `*lock` and will move 1 to the location `*lock`. The two actions of reading `*lock` and then writing to `*lock` are guaranteed to be an atomic unit. Between the actions of reading `*lock` and then writing to that location, the hardware guarantees that no other thread is allowed to read or write that location.

Our first attempt at implementing `atomicAddDouble()` attempts to enclose line 6, which is `*result+=ans`, within a critical region. If a thread reads the content of `*lock` to be 0, it assumes that the lock is open and can enter the critical region. Before entering the critical region, it writes 1 to `*lock`, as a result of `atomicExch()`, so that no other thread can be in the critical region simultaneously. On line 5, the value of `*lock` is read into `lockcopy`, which is a local variable, and 1 is written to `*lock` using an atomic operation. If `*lock` is already 1, then its value won't change, and the lock remains shut.

On line 7, the thread exits from the critical region by writing 0 to `*lock` and opening the lock.

CUDA syntax for writing device and kernel code encourages us to think of each thread as an independent entity. However, the hardware executes instructions warp by warp and not thread by thread. If we think of how a warp of 32 threads may step through our first attempt at `addAtomicDouble()`, it immediately becomes clear that the code will deadlock.[6]

Suppose all 32 threads of a warp execute line 3 and set their local variables `lockcopy` to 1. All threads of the warp will check the while-loop condition on line 4 using the same warp instruction. The condition will be valid for the entire warp and all the threads will next execute the `atomicExch()` instruction on line 5. Several warps may be competing to read `*lock`. Let us suppose this warp is lucky and one of its threads reads `*lock` to be 0. Then all the other 31 threads in the warp must read `*lock` to be 1. At this point, we have warp divergence. The thread that read 0 exits from the loop and waits for the other threads in the warp to converge to it. The other 31 threads will go back to line 4 and check the while-loop condition and then do the atomic exchange on line 5 repeatedly. While the other 31 threads are in this spin-loop, the thread that read 0 from `*lock` and diverged from the warp is inactive. The thread that read 0 cannot enter the critical region and execute the statement on line 6 until the other 31 threads in the warp converge with its execution sequence. The other 31 threads cannot get out of the spin-loop until the thread that read 0 gets to line 7 and releases the lock, which means the program is in a deadlock.

The following implementation of `atomicAddDouble()` does not deadlock. Crucially, it is assumed that `*result` and `*lock` are global locations that are initialized to zero before the kernel is called.

```
1  __device__ void atomicAddDouble(double value,
2      volatile double *result, volatile int *lock){
3      for(int i=0; i < NWARP; i++){
4          if(threadIdx.x%NWARP==i){
5              int lockcopy=1;
6              while(lockcopy==1)
7                  lockcopy=atomicExch((int *)lock, 1);
8              *result += value;
9              atomicExch((int *)lock, 0);
10         }
11     }
12 }
```

---

[6]Thanks to a member of an NVIDIA forum for explaining this point to me.

$NBLKS$	Partial	Total	$NBLKS$	Partial	Total
3	0.65	0.65	26	0.11	0.12
7	0.28	0.28	260	0.11	0.18
13	0.15	0.15	2600	0.12	0.88

Table 8.1: Number of cycles per term to sum the Leibniz series on the K20 coprocessor. The cycles are cycles of the 2.7 GHz AVX host. Data is given for both the kernel in which each thread returns its own sum (partial) and the kernel in which the threads combine to do a reduction (total).

This implementation has an if-statement (lines 4 though 10) nested inside a for-loop (lines 3 through 11). The threads in a warp take turns, and an attempt to enter the critical region is made only inside the if-block. Therefore, there is no deadlock.

Timing the kernels

Because the K20 has 13 multiprocessors and two thread blocks of 1,024 threads can reside on each of them, anything less than 26 blocks leaves the hardware under-utilized. Table 8.1 shows that the Leibniz summing program does not reach its best speed with fewer than 26 thread blocks.

Lots of thread blocks do not slow down the `leibniz()` kernel, although the `leibniztotal()` kernel, which uses atomic instructions to return a single sum, is slowed down considerably (see table 8.1). This outcome is partly because the timing measurements were taken using $n = 10^{10}$ terms of the Leibniz series. Much of the overhead of syncing would disappear if n were larger. Even so, the numbers in the table have a message. Using lots of blocks is not a problem if the thread blocks are mostly independent of each other. If the blocks need to sync frequently, the overhead can be substantial.

Summing the Leibniz series on the K20 is nearly 2.5 times faster than on the Xeon Phi. The K20 is faster for some problems and the Xeon Phi for others. The main distinction is the programming model. Yet the speedup of 2.5 is a little surprising. The speedup is probably due to divisions being handled better on the K20 than on the Xeon Phi.

8.2.2 CUDA compilation

So far we have made only brief remarks about compiling CUDA programs. The graphics device compilation model is a little different from compiling for the host, and we will look at it in greater depth here.

To begin with, we shall suppose that the entire Leibniz program discussed in the previous section is in one file called `leibniz_all.cu`. The compilation command in full, with \ being the line continuation character, is as follows:

```
1  nvcc -O3 \
2  -prec-div=true -ftz=false -Drestrict="__restrict__"\
3  -arch=sm_35 \
4  -Xptxas=-v -dc leibniz_all.cu
```

Here `nvcc` (line 1) is the name of NVIDIA's compiler driver, which is a wrapper around GNU's gcc/g++. The `-O3` option (line 1) sets the optimization level.

The options on line 2 are more generic compiling options. Precise division is required, and the flush to zero optimization is turned off. The keyword `restrict` is defined as a macro that expands to `__restrict__`. Some of our utility programs that print tables and so on use the `restrict` keyword, which is part of the C99 standard and supported in C++ programs by Intel's `icpc` compiler. In GNU, a C++ program must use `__restrict__` in place of `restrict`.

The `-arch` option (line 3) specifies the compute capability as 3.5. To see what effect it has, we run the command

```
cuobjdump leibniz_all.o
```

on the object file. The output of this command, with some lines omitted, is

```
Fatbin elf code:
================
arch = sm_35
code version = [1,7]
...

Fatbin ptx code:
================
arch = sm_35
```

```
code version = [3,2]
...
```

The object file is a fatbin (in CUDA terminology), including both binary elf code
and ptx code. The binary code will only run on devices whose architecture exactly
matches sm_35, but the ptx code will run on any device of compute capability 3.5 or
higher.

The PTX is an assembly-like intermediate language. It is in text not in binary
format. The inner loop of the leibniz() kernel looks as follows in PTX:

```
BB2_3:
     .loc 1 13 1
     cvt.rn.f64.s64 %fd6, %rd10;
     fma.rn.f64      %fd7, %fd6, 0d4000000000000000,\
                               0d3FF0000000000000;
     mov.f64   %fd8, 0d4010000000000000;
     .loc 3 3614 3
     div.rn.f64      %fd9, %fd8, %fd7;
     .loc 1 13 94
     add.f64   %fd12, %fd12, %fd9;
     .loc 1 12 17
     add.s64   %rd10, %rd10, %rd3;
     .loc 1 12 1
     setp.lt.s64     %p2, %rd10, %rd6;
     @%p2 bra   BB2_3;
```

The PTX can be compiled into elf binary format of any device of compute capability
3.5 or higher.

If the leibniz_all.exe program is run on an sm_35 device, the binary elf will
run. If the device has a compute capability that is higher than 3.5, then the driver's
just-in-time compiler will generate the binary from the PTX that is embedded in the
.exe program. So the .exe will run on the K20 as well as later generation Maxwell
devices.

The nvcc compiler driver offers options for generating .ptx files with only the
PTX or .cubin files with only the elf binary or even .o files with the elf binary for
multiple compute capabilities as well as PTX.

Going back to the `nvcc` compilation command, line 4 has the setting `-Xptxas=-v`. So the `-v` verbose option is passed to the PTX assembly phase. Its effect is to print the register usage of every device function and kernel. If register usage is excessive, a kernel may fail to launch. There are further options to control register usage in the PTX phase.

Another important option on line 4 is `-dc`. Usually `-c` generates the object file without linking and may be read as "compile only." Similarly, `-dc` generates an object file that includes both host and device code but does not link. Because we are using the `-dc` option, we may call the source `leibniz_all.cpp` instead of `leibniz_all.cu` and nothing changes.

The command for generating the executable is as follows:

```
nvcc -arch=sm_35 -o leibniz_all.exe leibniz_all.o
```

No libraries are being linked here, but for other programs we can link libraries on the command line. The `-lcublas` option links the cuBLAS library. The executable may be run on any computer equipped with an NVIDIA graphics coprocessor of capability 3.5 or higher.

To make a point about backward compatibility, we may go back and compile with `-arch=sm_20` instead of `-arch=sm_35`. The resulting object file and executable have binary only for `sm_20` devices. The executable, however, still runs on the K20, which is not an `sm_20` device. The driver's just-in-time compiler generates the binary for the K20 from the PTX that is embedded inside the executable.

The improvements made by NVIDIA from Tesla to Fermi to Kepler instruction set architectures appear quite substantial. The freedom to make such substantial changes while still being able to run older executables on newer devices is a consequence of just-in-time compilation of PTX embedded in the executables.

As always, the organization of source files must reflect the structure of the program, and it is not a good idea to put everything in one source file (in fact, it is a terribly bad idea). In the case of the Leibniz program, the source files are

```
leibniz.cu, atomicAdd.cu, time_leibniz.cu
```

In addition, some utilities for timing and making tables discussed in earlier chapters are also linked. With regard to linking multiple object files as well as libraries to generate an executable, there is nothing new to add to what we learned in chapter 2.

Exercise 8.2.1. Write a CUDA program to evaluate the sum

$$\sum_{m=1}^{\infty} \sum_{n=1}^{\infty} \frac{1}{m^4 + n^4}.$$

Exercise 8.2.2. Write a CUDA kernel to find the maximum of an array of numbers.

Exercise 8.2.3. Explain why warp divergence is impossible to avoid when sorting an array of numbers or when merging two presorted arrays.

8.3   Two examples

In this section, we look at two more examples to better understand the CUDA programming model and the speed of the K20 graphics device.

Section 8.3.1 compares the K20's bandwidth to memory to that of the Phi and the AVX host. The K20's read bandwidth is lower than that of the Phi, but its copy bandwidth is higher. The AVX host has read/copy bandwidths that are between a third and a half of the K20. If the disparity in memory bandwidths is significant, so is the much more extensive caching found on the AVX host. On programs where the memory accesses are not regular and structured, caching can be a great advantage.

Section 8.3.2 shows two implementations of matrix multiplication. The first implementation is relatively easy. However, it reaches only around a 20th of the peak capability of the K20 device. The other implementation using shared memory, which functions as a user-managed cache, reaches an eighth of the peak capability. These programs are comparable to the `multIJK()` program of chapter 3 with regard to how efficiently they utilize the machine. For comparison, the `multIJK()` program too falls short of the peak capability on AVX2 by a similar factor, which is a tenth. However, the shared memory program in CUDA is perhaps 100 times harder to write than `multIJK()` or its OpenMP version.

To approach peak bandwidth, there is no choice but to optimize for the instruction pipeline. We do not consider such optimization here,[7] although the basic principles of optimizing for the instruction pipeline do not change drastically from what is described in chapter 3.

---

[7] For instruction pipeline optimizations pertinent to GPUs, see Volkov and Demmel (2008).

8.3.1   Bandwidth to memory

The following functions are used to measure the K20's bandwidth to memory:

```
__global__
__launch_bounds__(THinBLK, BLKinMP)
void add(double *list, int n, double *result){
        int tid = threadIdx.x + blockIdx.x*blockDim.x;
        int stride = blockDim.x*gridDim.x;
        double ans = 0;
        for(int i=tid; i < n; i = i + stride)
                ans += list[i];
        result[tid] = ans;
}


__global__
__launch_bounds__(THinBLK, BLKinMP)
void copy(double *list, int n, double *copy){
        int tid = threadIdx.x + blockIdx.x*blockDim.x;
        int stride = blockDim.x*gridDim.x;
        for(int i=tid; i < n; i = i + stride)
                copy[i] = list[i];
}
```

Notice that data accesses from the threads are interleaved as in

$$0, 1, 2, 3, \ldots, 0, 1, 2, 3, \ldots, 0, 1, 2, 3, \ldots$$

and not blocked as in

$$0, 0, 0, \ldots, 1, 1, 1, \ldots, 2, 2, 2, \ldots, 3, 3, 3, \ldots$$

Blocking memory accesses is the right thing to do on x86 processors. On the K20 and other graphics devices, blocking will lose more than 90% of the bandwidth. Partly because instructions are executed warp by warp, memory accesses must be interleaved.

Table 8.2 compares the bandwidth to memory of the AVX host, the Phi, and the K20.[8] The Xeon Phi wins the race in reading, and the K20 is the winner, by far, for copying.

---

[8]If 1 GB of data is copied, it counts as 2 GB for the purpose of calculating bandwidth.

	AVX	Phi	K20
Read b/w	91 GB/s	161 GB/s	137 GB/s
Copy b/w	50 Gb/s	86 GB/s	133 GB/s

Table 8.2: Read and copy bandwidths in GB/s. The K20 is compared to the Phi and its 2.7 GHz AVX host (for the full name of the machine, see table A.1).

8.3.2   Matrix multiplication

If A, B, and C are $N \times N$ matrices, then $C = C + AB$ requires $2N^3$ floating point operations (flops). Half the operations are additions and half are multiplications. The amount of memory involved in matrix multiplication is $\mathcal{O}(N^2)$, but the number of flops is $\mathcal{O}(N^3)$. If N is large, there is a possibility that the cost of memory accesses can be hidden almost completely, and the program's speed is determined by the peak floating point bandwidth. On the K20, the peak floating point bandwidth is 1.17 TFlops/s. Although the programs we describe do not approach that speed, we compare them against a cuBLAS program that does.

Global memory

The first program for multiplying square matrices is as follows:[9]

```
__global__
__launch_bounds__(THinBLK, BLKinMP)
void mmult_gmem(double *A, double *B, double * C,
          int N){
    int tidx = threadIdx.x;
    int tidy = threadIdx.y;
    int bidx = blockIdx.x;
    int bidy = blockIdx.y;
    int i = bidx*blockDim.x + tidx;
    int j = bidy*blockDim.y + tidy;
    for(int k = 0; k < N; k++)
          C[i+j*N]  += A[i+k*N]*B[k+j*N];
```

---

[9]This program is adapted from (*CUDA C Programming Guide*, August, 2014).

```
}
```

This kernel is assumed to be launched with two-dimensional thread blocks in a two-dimensional grid. The size of the thread block is assumed to be `SQRTT x SQRTT`. On the K20, we take `SQRTT` to be $32 = \sqrt{1,024}$ because 1,024 is the maximum number of threads in a block.

The matrix dimension `N` is assumed to be divisible by `SQRTT`. The grid is assumed to be `N/SQRTT x N/SQRTT`. The total number of threads is thus equal to N^2. There is a natural map from threads to each entry of the $N \times N$ matrix C. The `mmult_gmem()` kernel calculates the indices of (i, j) of the entry the thread maps to and then updates the corresponding entry of `C[]`. Thus, each entry of the matrix `C[]` is given to a different thread for updating.

The syntax for launching this kernel using two-dimensional thread blocks and grids is shown in the listing below. Multiple dimensions are specified using `dim3` objects.

```
double mmult(double *A, double *B, double *C, int N){
    assrt(SQRTT*SQRTT==THinBLK);
    assrt(N%SQRTT==0);

    dim3 grid(N/SQRTT, N/SQRTT);
    dim3 tblk(SQRTT, SQRTT);

    dhstmem<double> dhA(N*N);
    dhstmem<double> dhB(N*N);
    dhstmem<double> dhC(N*N);
    for(int i=0; i < N*N; i++){
        dhA.host()[i] = A[i];
        dhB.host()[i] = B[i];
        dhC.host()[i] = C[i];
    }
    dhA.host2device();
    dhB.host2device();
    dhC.host2device();

    mmult_gmem<<<grid, tblk>>>(dhA.device(),
            dhB.device(), dhC.device(), N);
```

```
        dhC.device2host();
        for(int i=0; i < N*N; i++)
                C[i] = dhC.host()[i];
    }
```

Copying data into and out of the device using the **dhstmem** class implies extra copying. That is an overhead we accept in the interest of a more modular program.

Shared memory

In the Kepler microarchitecture, each multiprocessor owns some on-chip memory that is split between L1 cache and shared memory (see figure 8.2). On the K20, by default, there is 48 KB of shared memory for each of its 13 multiprocessors. Accesses of shared memory are considerably faster than global memory accesses.

The following program assumes **SQRTT x SQRTT** thread blocks and **N/SQRTT x N/SQRTT** grid just as before. However, it uses shared memory and blocking.

```
1   __global__
2   __launch_bounds__(THinBLK, BLKinMP)
3   void mmult_smem(double *A,double *B,double * C,int N){
4        int tidx = threadIdx.x;
5        int tidy = threadIdx.y;
6        int bidx = blockIdx.x;
7        int bidy = blockIdx.y;
8
9        __shared__ double smem[3*THinBLK];
10       double *smemA = smem;
11       double *smemB = smem+THinBLK;
12       double *smemC = smem+2*THinBLK;
13       int i = tidx + bidx*blockDim.x;
14       int j = tidy + bidy*blockDim.y;
15
16       smemC[tidx + SQRTT*tidy] = C[i + N*j];
17       for(int k = 0; k < N; k += SQRTT){
18            smemA[tidx + SQRTT*tidy] = A[i + N*(k+tidy)];
```

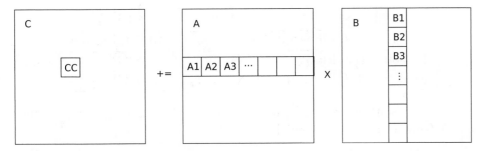

Figure 8.4: Depiction of $C = C + AB$, with A, B, and C being square matrices. Each submatrix shown is `SQRTT x SQRTT`, matching the dimensions of the thread block.

```
19                    smemB[tidx + SQRTT*tidy] = B[(k+tidx) + N*j];
20                    __syncthreads();
21                    for(int kk=0; kk < SQRTT; kk++){
22                            smemC[tidx+SQRTT*tidy] +=
23                        smemA[tidx+SQRTT*kk]*smemB[kk+SQRTT*tidy];
24                    }
25                    __syncthreads();
26            }
27        C[i + N*j] = smemC[tidx + SQRTT*tidy];
28 }
```

This is not the longest C/C++ listing in this book, but it may be the hardest to decipher.

To help decipher this program, we turn to figure 8.4. Each submatrix `CC` as well as the submatrices `A1`, `B1`, and so on are assumed to be `SQRTT x SQRTT` matching the dimensions of the thread block. Because the grid is of dimension `N/SQRTT x N/SQRTT`, we may assume that each submatrix `CC` belongs to a certain thread block. The entries of `CC` are further split between the threads in the thread block.

The kernel `mmult_smem()` thinks of the updating of `CC` in block terms:

$$CC+= A1 \times B1 + A2 \times B2 + \cdots + An \times Bn$$

where n = N/SQRTT.

On line 9, the program claims shared memory using the `__shared__` qualifier. The memory is split between a subblock of A (line 10), a subblock of B (line 11), and

N	gmem	smem	cuBLAS
8,000	47 GFlops/s	126 GFlops/s	1045 GFlops/s
10,000	47 GFlops/s	127 GFlops/s	1038 GFlops/s
12,000	48 GFlops/s	127 GFlops/s	1047 GFlops/s

Table 8.3: Comparison of floating throughput of the `mmult_gmem()` (gmem) and `mmult_smem()` (smem) kernels with cuBLAS.

the subblock CC (line 12). Each thread also computes the indices (i, j) of the entry of C it will update (lines 13 and 14).

The outer for-loop (line 16) steps through the blocks `Aj`, `Bj`. The index k is incremented in steps of `SQRTT`. So to get the jth block, we must take k=j*SQRTT. Each subblock `Aj` is split between the `SQRTT x SQRTT` threads in the thread block. On line 18, the subblock `Aj` is loaded into shared memory, with each thread loading exactly one entry. Similarly, on line 19, the subblock `Bj` is loaded into shared memory.

In the inner for-loop (line 21), each thread updates the entry of `CC` that corresponds to its position in the thread block. The inner for-loop accesses entries of A, B, and C that are already in shared memory.

The `__syncthreads()` function called on line 20, just before the inner for-loop, is one of the CUDA intrinsic functions. It is a barrier across all the threads in the same thread block. Another call to `__syncthreads()` is made after the inner for-loop. These barriers are essential to separate the copying to shared memory outside the inner for-loop from the accesses to the copied locations inside the body of the inner for-loop.

The `mmult_smem()` is an example of a program where the thread hierarchy affects the structure of the entire loop nest, making the code difficult to comprehend.

cuBLAS

Table 8.3 compares the global and shared memory implementations of matrix multiplication with cuBLAS. The use of shared memory speeds up the program by more than a factor of 2, but the sped-up program reaches only slightly more than 10% of peak floating point throughput. In contrast, cuBLAS gets close to the theoretical floating point peak of 1.17 TFlops/s.

On older Intel machines, a fairly straightforward matrix multiply goes beyond 25% of the peak floating point throughput. On the K20, even the quite complex `mmult_smem()` kernel gets just around 10%. That disparity is partly because the Intel compilers are more mature for older Intel machines. However, it is also true that fine-grained parallelism with threads arranged in a hierarchy makes it harder to write programs.

The implementation of cuBLAS is proprietary. Matrix blocking and good use of registers are key ideas.[10] The `CuMult` class is our interface to the matrix multiplication routine in cuBLAS.

```
#include <cublas_v2.h>

class CuMult{
private:
    int N;
    dhstmem<double> memA, memB, memC;
    cublasHandle_t h;
public:
    CuMult(int Ni);
    ~CuMult();
    /*
    * C = C + A*B, A[], B[], C[] are NxN matrices
    * returns time in millisecs
    */
    double mult(double *A, double *B, double *C);
};
```

The handle `h` is one of the private data members. It is used to access the cuBLAS facilities.

The class constructor is defined as follows:

```
CuMult::CuMult(int Ni)
    :N(Ni), memA(N*N), memB(N*N), memC(N*N){
    cublasStatus_t code;
```

---

[10]For an explanation of how to implement dense linear algebra routines, including matrix multiplication, efficiently in CUDA, see Volkov and Demmel (2008).

```
        code = cublasCreate(&h);
        assrt(code == CUBLAS_STATUS_SUCCESS);
    }
```

The main task of the constructor is to initialize the handle by calling cublasCreate().
It also initializes vhstmem objects memA/B/C used for sending and retrieving data from
the device. The destructor releases the handle.

```
CuMult::~CuMult(){
        cublasStatus_t code;

        code = cublasDestroy(h);
        assrt(code == CUBLAS_STATUS_SUCCESS);
    }
```

The definition of the member function mult() follows.

```
1  double CuMult::mult(double *A, double *B, double *C){
2          cublasStatus_t code;
3
4          for(int i=0; i < N*N; i++){
5                  memA.host()[i] = A[i];
6                  memB.host()[i] = B[i];
7                  memC.host()[i] = C[i];
8          }
9          memA.host2device();
10         memB.host2device();
11         memC.host2device();
12
13         double alpha = 1.0;
14         double beta = 1.0;
15
16
17         hstTimer hclk;
18         hclk.tic();
19         code = cublasDgemm(h,
```

```
20                          CUBLAS_OP_N , CUBLAS_OP_N ,
21                          N , N , N ,
22                          &alpha ,
23                          memA.device() , N ,
24                          memB.device() , N ,
25                          &beta ,
26                          memC.device() , N);
27        double tms = hclk.toc();
28        assrt(code == CUBLAS_STATUS_SUCCESS);
29
30        memC.device2host();
31        for(int i=0; i < N*N; i++)
32              C[i] = memC.host()[i];
33
34        return tms;
35 }
```

The matrices A[], B[], and C[] are copied into dhstmem objects (lines 4 through 8) and then copied to device memory (lines 9, 10, and 11). The cuBLAS function implements $C = \alpha AB + \beta C$. Both the parameters α and β are set to 1 (lines 13 and 14).

In the call to the library function cublasDgemm(), the first argument is the handle h initialized by the constructor (line 19). The arguments on line 20 specify that neither A nor B needs to be transposed. Line 21 specifies that all the matrices are $N \times N$. The leading dimensions of all three matrices are given as N (lines 23, 24, and 26).

Exercise 8.3.1. Write a CUDA kernel for transposing a matrix. Measure the bandwidth to memory of your kernel.

Exercise 8.3.2. Build a C++ class interfacing to the cuBLAS functions that solve linear systems. Determine the peak floating point throughput of cuBLAS linear solvers.

Exercise 8.3.3. On platforms with multiple GPU devices, the cuBLAS functions can be sent to a chosen device or tiled between the GPU devices. Modify the CuMult class and endow it with such functionality.

8.4   References

D.B. Kirk and W.W. Hwu. *Programming Massively Parallel Processors.* Morgan Kaufmann, San Francisco, 2010.

J. Sanders and E. Kandrot. *CUDA by Example.* Addison-Wesley, Upper Saddle River, 2010.

V. Volkov and J.W. Demmel. Benchmarking GPUs to tune dense linear algebra. *Proceedings of the 2008 ACM/IEEE Conference on Supercomputing*, pages 1–11, 2008.

Appendix A

Machines Used, Plotting, Python, GIT, Cscope, and gcc

In this appendix, we give a list of machines used in this book as well as several pointers for downloading and using the program code.

The command line is not used as much anymore. However, the command line, supplemented by a good `.bashrc` file, encourages a logical view of the computer. A good `.bashrc` file must alter the prompt to display the current directory at the command prompt. Although this appears to be a minor point, it is essential for maintaining a logical view of the file system. The prompt can also be altered to display the GIT branch within a GIT repository.[1]

The two principal editors among Linux programmers are `vi` and `emacs`. Purists tend to prefer `vi/vim` for its greater simplicity and much cleaner design. `Emacs` can be more powerful, although it can seem a little arbitrary, especially without a good `.emacs` file.[2] Both `vi/vim` and `emacs` can be launched from the command line.[3]

---

[1]The author's `.bashrc` file is found under `sys/` in the GIT repo of this book.

[2]The author's `.emacs` file is found under `sys/` in the GIT repo of this book.

[3]On MacOSX, the default `emacs` does not work so well. A better `emacs` can be downloaded from the Internet.

Computer	Instn	Registers	Microarchitecture	Year	Moniker
Xeon 5650 (12 core)	SSE2	XMM	Nehalem/Westmere	2001/2010	2.6 GHz SSE2
Xeon 5680 (12 core)	SSE2	XMM	Nehalem/Westmere	2001/2010	3.33 GHz SSE2
E5-2660 (16 core)	AVX	YMM	Sandy Bridge	2011/2012	2.2 GHz AVX
E5-2680 (16 core)	AVX	YMM	Sandy Bridge	2011/2012	2.7 GHz AVX
Core i7-3770 (4 core)	AVX	YMM	Sandy Bridge	2011/2012	3.4 GHz AVX
Core i3-4350 (2 core)	AVX2	YMM	Haswell	2013/2014	3.6 GHz AVX2
Xeon Phi SE10P	AVX-512	ZMM	Phi/MIC	2013/2013	Phi/MIC

Table A.1: Machines used to run and time programs. The Xeon Phi, which is a coprocessor, uses a 1.09 GHz clock. The second column gives the highest level of instruction set pertinent to this book. For the interpretation and meaning of the instruction set, see table 3.1 and the associated discussion. The second to last column gives the year of the instruction set as well as the computer. The last column gives the name with which the machine is referenced in the text. Much of the information in this table may be verified at `ark.intel.com`.

A.1   Machines used

For cache parameters of the machines in table A.1, see section 3.1.4.

A.2   Plotting in C/C++ and other preliminaries

In this section, we describe C++ classes for plotting, gathering statistics, and making tables. These classes are used throughout the book. However, in almost every instance, the code showing how these facilities are invoked is suppressed.

Plotting in C/C++ programs

Plots and pictures that show output and display program data can make programs less cryptic and clarify what is going on. A picture can be worth a thousand lines of code.

Plotting libraries are not part of the C/C++ languages for a good reason. Although plotting is very helpful, it is too high level of an activity and far removed from the view of the machine that the C language offers. There are many libraries, external to the language, that may be used to generate plots. Some of these libraries offer precise control and many graphics capabilities. No single plotting library appears to be dominant. Some of the libraries are extensive enough to overwhelm those who are not dedicated to computer graphics. In such a situation, it is difficult for the programmer to decide whether any of the libraries is worth learning.

One solution is to use a simple C++ class that outsources all the plotting to Python. Such a class can be slow, but the programmer who is willing to wait a few hundred milliseconds is spared the trouble of learning how to use a C/C++ graphics library. The public interface to the PyPlot class follows.

```cpp
class PyPlot{
public:
    /*
     * name must be less than 25 chars
     */
    PyPlot(const char *namei);
    ~PyPlot();
    /*
     * functions for drawing lines
     */
    void plot(double *x, double *y, int n);
    void plot(double *y, int n);
    void semilogx(double *x, double *y, int n);
    void linestyle(const char* s);
    void linewidth(const char* s);
    void markersize(const char* s);
    /*
     * functions for specifying axes, properties
     */
    void axis(); //"tight"
    void axis(double x0, double x1,
              double y0, double y1);
    void title(const char* s);
    void xticks(double *ticks, int n);
    void yticks(double *ticks, int n);
    void ticksize(const char *s);
```

```
    /*
     * writes python command to pipe
     */
    void pycmd(const char *s);
    /*
     * functions for showing/output
     */
    void show();
    /*
     * eps output
     */
    void output();
    /*
     * save python script in FIGS/
     */
    void savescript();
};
```

The name supplied through the constructor is used for naming intermediate data files as well as the output. This class can show the plot, save an **eps** file, or save a Python script for generating the plot.

The Linux operating system provides a system call to open pipes to shell commands. For example,

```
FILE *pypipe = popen("python", "w");
```

opens a writable pipe to Python. We can treat this pipe as a file and write commands to be executed by Python to it as if we were writing to a file. For example, the following program fragment plots the sine function:

```
fprintf(pypipe,"import numpy as np\n");
fprintf(pypipe,"from matplotlib import pyplot as plt\n");
fprintf(pypipe, "x = np.linspace(-5.0, 5.0, 500)\n");
fprintf(pypipe, "plt.plot(x, np.sin(x))\n");
fprintf(pypipe, "plt.show()\n");
```

When the pipe is no longer needed, it may be closed using `pclose()`. The `PyPlot` class is implemented using pipes.

Within the C/C++ framework, we can use pipes and rely on Python for plotting as we just showed. Conversely, it is easy to integrate C/C++ programs into Python. The `ctypes` library in Python virtually erases the distinction between C and Python. Numpy supports the `ctypes` interface through the `ndpointer` facility, and the pointer corresponding to an array `x` can be accessed using the syntax `x.ctypes.data`.[4] Using Python's `ctypes` library, the whole C standard library can be loaded in a single easy line and the `printf` routine of the C standard library used to print messages in the next line—the `ctypes` library is quite remarkable.

The StatVector class

If we want to find out the number of cycles required to multiply two square matrices of dimension 1000, it is never enough to time just once. The computer system is so complicated with so many heavily designed parts that the first run is likely to be atypical. One must time the same program several times and look at the mean or median. System activities can make the occasional timing figure to be far in excess of the typical. Therefore, if our intention is to get an idea of whether the program is well optimized, it is often better to look at medians.

The public interface to the `StatVector` class, which is used to gather data and calculate means and medians, is as follows:

```
class StatVector{
public:
        StatVector(int n);
        ~StatVector();
        void insert(double x);
        double median();
        double mean();
        double max();
        double min();
        void flush();
```

[4]Passing an array to C using Numpy's `ndpointer` facility, although safer and more convenient, can be slow. The cost is more than 10^4 cycles per array. A C function call from Python using the `x.ctypes.data` syntax takes around one or two thousand cycles. Although far more expensive than a typical function call in C, which may consume just a few cycles, an overhead of around a thousand cycles is often manageable.

```
        void print(const char* banner = "");
    };
```

The class interface is self-explanatory for the most part. The argument to the constructor specifies the maximum size of the dataset. The member function `flush()` may be used to discard all the data items inserted and start over again.

The Table class

When programs such as the FFT are timed, it is natural to lay out the timing figures in a table. The rows may be indexed by the dimension of the FFT and the columns by the implementation. The following class is used to generate tables:

```
    class Table{
    public:
        Table();
        void dim(int nrows, int ncols);
        void rows(const char* rowsi[]);
        void cols(const char* colsi[]);
        void data(double *datai);
        void print(const char *banner="");
    };
```

This class interface too is almost self-explanatory. The member functions `dim()`, `rows()`, `cols()`, and `data()` must be called in that order. The class prints the data in a well-formatted table.

A.3   C/C++ versus Python versus MATLAB

How much faster C/C++ can be relative to interpreted languages such as Python and MATLAB is often not understood. That point is worth going into because it provides necessary motivation for the considerable effort of mastering C/C++ as well as techniques of program optimization.

The following is a simple Python program for identifying prime numbers less than n:

```
    import numpy as np
```

```
def primes(n):
    assert n >= 3
    p = np.zeros((n+1), dtype = bool)
    p[0] = False
    p[1] = False
    p[2] = True
    ksqrt = 1
    for k in range(3,n+1):
        if ksqrt*ksqrt < k:
            ksqrt += 1
        p[k] = True
        for j in range(2, ksqrt+1):
            if p[j] and k%j == 0:
                p[k] = False
                break
    return p
```

With $n = 10^7$, this program consumes 4.9×10^{11} cycles on a 3.6 GHz AVX2 machine (see table A.1). The same program in MATLAB consumes 4.7×10^{11} cycles. In C/C++, the program consumes 1.1×10^{10} cycles, which is less than 2.5% of the time taken by Python or MATLAB.

In fact, a C/C++ speedup of around 40 is at the low end. Much of the overhead in interpreted languages is due to symbol-table lookup. In a simple program such as this, the symbol-table lookup will be less expensive than in more complicated programs. In addition, the C/C++ compiler has no room to optimize this program for the instruction set architecture. So none of the vast range of optimizations possible in C/C++ can kick in.

However, if one limits oneself to a narrow idiom, relying mostly on BLAS/LAPACK routines and not much more, Python and MATLAB can be as fast as C/C++. However, such a thing is too constraining and not possible to sustain in more complex programs. For even moderately complex programs, C/C++ can be faster than MATLAB by more than a factor of 1,000.[5]

---

[5]For an example of a fairly simple program that is several hundred times faster in C/C++ than in MATLAB, see (B. Sadiq and D. Viswanath, Finite difference weights, spectral differentiation,

As a program becomes more complex, it becomes harder to write in C/C++ because one is forced to think about its memory layout precisely. In Python or MAT-LAB, one can think at a higher level and create objects in memory with much less care. That makes the interpreted languages easier to program in, but it also makes them much slower.

On multicore machines, one should expect an even greater speedup from using C/C++. The advantage, as well as the difficulty, of C/C++ lies in giving the programmer a relatively faithful picture of the machine. As the hardware platform becomes more complex, the speedup from C/C++ should be expected to increase.

It would be folly to say that the choice between C/C++ and Python or Matlab comes down solely to the matter of speed. A Python program can be written in a small fraction of the time that it takes to write a C/C++ program. Sometimes that is all that matters.

Another important point is how well a program can be structured. In C/C++, source files are organized in a source tree, and the program is built using the `make` utility or some equivalent tool. Python's facilities for structuring programs are far superior. These include consistent and uniform control of name spaces, modules, and packages, with special significance attached to `__init__.py` and `__main__.py` files. In addition, as mentioned on page 581, the `ctypes` library in Python virtually erases the distinction between Python and C. With judicious use of the `ctypes` library, one may attempt to approach the speed of C/C++ within the greater convenience and superior structure of Python.

A.4 GIT

The source code for this book may be obtained in its entirety using the command

```
git clone https://github.com/divakarvi/BOOK-SPCA
```

The `git` utility is a tool for managing sources.[6]

---

and superconvergence, *Mathematics of Computation*, 83 (2014), pp. 2403-2427). For an example of a more complex program that is 10^4 times faster, see (D. Viswanath, Spectral integration of linear boundary value problems, *Journal of Computational and Applied Mathematics*, 290 (2015), pp. 159-173).

[6]For GIT documentation and more, see https://git-scm.com/.

GIT is a cleanly designed and well-thought-out program. Although there are many facilities in GIT, GIT can be grasped easily by paying attention to its internal design. With that in mind, we mention a few points about GIT internals:

- GIT thinks of a file as an atom. If there is a slightest change to a file, it becomes a new object as far as GIT is concerned.

- As the source tree evolves, every file is stored in `.git/`, including older versions. The name and location of a file are obtained using its 160-bit SHA2 hash. Alternatively, GIT may compress several files into a single pack file.

- A commit is a tree-like hierarchy of files, with the working directory corresponding to one particular commit. Commit objects are also stored in `.git/`.

- GIT thinks of commits as being organized in a directed acyclic graph. Those vertices of the directed acyclic graph, whose files may be modified to produce new commits and grow the graph, are labeled using branch names.

- When a GIT repository is cloned, it is cloned in full, including all the ancestors of a branch.

A.5   Cscope

The `cscope` utility is invaluable for browsing source code. Using `cscope`, one can easily find the definition of a function, all the places where it is called, and search for patterns inside the entire source tree. It is a search utility that predates the era of Internet search by a few decades.

Suppose the source for this book is saved in the GIT repository `BOOK-SPCA`. To prepare `cscope` database files, we may run the command

```
cscope.py BOOK-SPCA
```

in the parent directory of `BOOK-SPCA`; `cscope.py` is the following Python script, which must be on the user's path:

```
#!/usr/bin/env python
import os, sys
```

```
if __name__ == '__main__':
    if len(sys.argv) != 2:
        print('Usage: cscope.py dirname')
        sys.exit(0)

    ddir = sys.argv[1]
    assert os.path.isdir(ddir)
    cmd = 'rm -rf cscope.*'
    print(cmd)
    os.system(cmd)

    cmd = 'find ' + ddir \
          + ' -name *.h' + ' -o -name *.hh'\
          + ' -o -name *.c' +' -o -name *.cpp' \
          + ' > cscope.files'
    print(cmd)
    os.system(cmd)

    cmd = 'cscope -b -q'
    print(cmd)
    os.system(cmd)
```

Once the database files are generated, one only has to say `cscope -d` to obtain access to the search facilities of `cscope`.

A.6 Compiling with gcc/g++

The Makefiles in the GIT repository `BOOK-SPCA` use Intel compilers for the most part. The switch to `gcc/g++` is not too complicated. The following points must be kept in mind:

- To enable the `restrict` qualifier, use the option `-Drestrict="__restrict__"`.

- To generate code for a specific instruction set such as AVX2, use an option such as `-mavx2`.

- `-openmp` becomes `-fopenmp`.

Index

Scientific and Engineering Computation

William Gropp and Ewing Lusk, editors; Janusz Kowalik, founding editor

Data-Parallel Programming on MIMD Computers, Philip J. Hatcher and Michael J. Quinn, 1991

Enterprise Integration Modeling: Proceedings of the First International Conference, edited by Charles J. Petrie, Jr., 1992

The High Performance Fortran Handbook, Charles H. Koelbel, David B. Loveman, Robert S. Schreiber, Guy L. Steele Jr., and Mary E. Zosel, 1994

PVM: A User's Guide and Tutorial for Network Parallel Computing, Al Geist, Adam Beguelin, Jack Dongarra, Weicheng Jiang, Robert Manchek, and Vaidyalingham S. Sunderam, 1994

Practical Parallel Programming, Gregory V. Wilson, 1995

Enabling Technologies for Petaflops Computing, Thomas Sterling, Paul Messina, and Paul H. Smith, 1995

An Introduction to High-Performance Scientific Computing, Lloyd D. Fosdick, Elizabeth R. Jessup, Carolyn J. C. Schauble, and Gitta Domik, 1995

Parallel Programming Using C++, edited by Gregory V. Wilson and Paul Lu, 1996

Using PLAPACK: Parallel Linear Algebra Package, Robert A. van de Geijn, 1997

Fortran 95 Handbook, Jeanne C. Adams, Walter S. Brainerd, Jeanne T. Martin, Brian T. Smith, and Jerrold L. Wagener, 1997

MPI—The Complete Reference: Volume 1, The MPI Core, Marc Snir, Steve Otto, Steven Huss-Lederman, David Walker, and Jack Dongarra, 1998

MPI—The Complete Reference: Volume 2, The MPI-2 Extensions, William Gropp, Steven Huss-Lederman, Andrew Lumsdaine, Ewing Lusk, Bill Nitzberg, William Saphir, and Marc Snir, 1998

A Programmer's Guide to ZPL, Lawrence Snyder, 1999

How to Build a Beowulf, Thomas L. Sterling, John Salmon, Donald J. Becker, and Daniel F. Savarese, 1999

Using MPI-2: Advanced Features of the Message-Passing Interface, William Gropp, Ewing Lusk, and Rajeev Thakur, 1999

Beowulf Cluster Computing with Windows, edited by Thomas Sterling, William Gropp, and Ewing Lusk, 2001

Beowulf Cluster Computing with Linux, second edition, edited by Thomas Sterling, William Gropp, and Ewing Lusk, 2003

Scalable Input/Output: Achieving System Balance, edited by Daniel A. Reed, 2003

Using OpenMP: Portable Shared Memory Parallel Programming, Barbara Chapman, Gabriele Jost, and Ruud van der Pas, 2008

Quantum Computing without Magic: Devices, Zdzislaw Meglicki, 2008

Quantum Computing: A Gentle Introduction, Eleanor G. Rieffel and Wolfgang H. Polak, 2011

Using MPI: Portable Parallel Programming with the Message-Passing Interface, third edition, William Gropp, Ewing Lusk, and Anthony Skjellum, 2015

Using Advanced MPI: Beyond the Basics, Pavan Balaji, William Gropp, Torsten Hoefler, Rajeev Thakur, and Ewing Lusk, 2015

Scientific Programming and Computer Architecture, Divakar Viswanath, 2017